Microsoft® Office
Access 2003:
The Complete Reference

D1361869

About the Author

Virginia Andersen became a writer and consultant after retiring from her defense contracting career. Since then, she has written over 35 books about personal-computer-based applications, including database management, word processing, and spreadsheet analysis. Virginia spent nearly 15 years teaching computer science, mathematics and systems analysis at the graduate and undergraduate levels at several southern California universities. During her years as a programmer/systems analyst, Virginia used computers for many diverse projects, including lunar mapping for the Apollo astronauts' landing, reliability engineering, undersea surveillance, weapon system simulation, and naval communications. She has also recently published her memoirs, "Digital Recall: Computers Aren't the Only Ones with Memory" describing many of these hands-on experiences.

Microsoft® Office Access 2003: The Complete Reference

Virginia Andersen

McGraw-Hill/Osborne

New York Chicago San Francisco
Lisbon London Madrid Mexico City
Milan New Delhi San Juan
Seoul Singapore Sydney Toronto

The McGraw·Hill Companies

McGraw-Hill/Osborne
2100 Powell Street, 10th Floor
Emeryville, California 94608
U.S.A.

To arrange bulk purchase discounts for sales promotions, premiums, or fund-raisers, please contact **McGraw-Hill/Osborne** at the above address. For information on translations or book distributors outside the U.S.A., please see the International Contact Information page immediately following the index of this book.

Microsoft® Office Access 2003: The Complete Reference

1234567890 DOC DOC 019876543

Book p/n 0-07-222918-7 and CD p/n 0-07-222919-5
parts of
ISBN 0-07-222917-9

Publisher	**Copy Editor**
Brandon A. Nordin	Marcia Baker
Vice President & Associate Publisher	**Proofreaders**
Scott Rogers	Marian Selig, Susan Carlson Greene
Acquisitions Editor	**Indexer**
Megg Morin	Jack Lewis
Project Editor	**Composition**
Elizabeth Seymour	Carie Abrew, Tara A. Davis, Lucie Ericksen
Acquisitions Coordinators	**Illustrators**
Tana Allen, Athena Honore	Kathleen Fay Edwards, Melinda Moore Lytle, Lyssa Wald
Technical Editor	
Margaret Levine Young	**Series Design**
	Peter F. Hancik, Lyssa Wald

This book was composed with Corel VENTURA™ Publisher.

Contents at a Glance

Contents

Part II Retrieving and Presenting Information

Acknowledgments

Revising this book for the third edition was a pleasure, due especially to working with the talented and highly professional Osborne editorial and production staff. Megg Morin, my Acquisitions Editor, is not only an efficient and professional member of Osborne's staff—I also consider her a good friend. I would also like to thank Tana Allen and Athena Honore for their efforts on behalf of this complex book. I appreciate Elizabeth Seymour for seeing this project through as my project editor. Margaret Levine Young, as the technical editor, applied her keen eye and clear understanding of the subject matter.

I would also like to express my appreciation to the production staff.

Thanks go, too, to the Coronado Police Department for sharing its Access database with me and my readers, as well as to my friends and neighbors who posed good-naturedly for the badge photos you can see in one of the databases. They tell me it's a good thing I'm a writer, not a photographer.

I also owe a big debt of gratitude to my literary agent of many years, Matt Wagner of Waterside Productions, for his continuing support and encouragement.

Finally, my husband, Jack, and all the cats must get a lot of credit for being so patient with me throughout this long, involved process. The cats don't really mind because, when I am working, I have a lap.

Introduction

A successful database is efficient, quick, accurate, and easy to use. This book shows you how to create just such a database with Microsoft Office Access 2003. The clearly written explanations of the database processes present exactly what you need to create an Access object or present information. The step-by-step exercises that follow the explanations further enhance your understanding by illustrating exactly how to complete the process successfully. The many tips, notes, and cautions help guide you to faster and better database management.

Whom Is This Book For?

This book is the ideal resource for anyone currently using Microsoft Office Access 2003 or who wants to learn how to use it. In planning this book, I envisioned it in the form of a large triangle, with the base scaled from the beginning user at the left end to advanced user at the right end. This book has enough material to get even the newest user of Access started with relational database management and has enough at the other end to help advanced users wade into the depths of customizing the Access workplace and designing special user interactive tools.

The bulk of the material lies between the two extremes under the peak of the triangle and that is of the utmost interest to the readers who fall in between. This book is extremely rich in the art of designing and creating efficient relational databases with all the appropriate queries, forms, and reports. Many different approaches are taken with respect to extracting and summarizing information in useful arrangements, including charts and graphs. After all, what good is data stored in a database if you can't get it out and turn it into useful and easy to interpret information?

This book is also intended for the users of the other Office applications, such as Word and Excel, who need to know how to interface with Access. With the boundaries between the programs rapidly vanishing, use of Access isn't limited to database managers. All the Office members can now interact with each other smoothly and with little translation.

What's in This Book?

This book is organized so you can progress at your own pace beginning with basic database and Access principles, and followed by increasingly advanced topics. The book is divided into four parts, each focusing on a specific aspect of Access database management.

Part I: Getting Started

Part I takes a quick tour of Microsoft Office Access 2003 and examines the concept of relational databases. Many tips are included to help you design an efficient database that is easy to maintain and can ensure data integrity. In Part I, the reader creates and relates tables, and then enters data into them. Several methods of validating new data are investigated and means of presenting data for editing are also addressed.

Part II: Retrieving and Presenting Information

Part II is concerned with retrieving information with filters and queries, as well as presenting that information in forms and reports. This important set of chapters includes how to create expressions to extract exactly the information you want. Five chapters are devoted to creating form and report designs (including synchronized data entry forms), creating reports that summarize grouped information, and even printing mailing labels in conjunction with Word 2003. The final chapter in this part describes how to create charts and graphs to include in forms and reports.

Part III: Improving the Workplace

Part III is a little more advanced and discusses customizing the workplace with special toolbars, menus, and dialog boxes for the more interactive applications. Several important means of optimizing Access performance are included in this part. Part III also introduces programming techniques with chapters about using macros, as well as understanding events and when events occur.

Part IV: Exchanging Data with Others

Part IV discusses the important topic of exchanging information with other users of Access and with other applications. Importing and exporting information in many forms, including text, is an integral part of developing a complete user application. This part also covers using Access in a multiple-user environment and investigates measures to ensure information security.

In Every Chapter

Every chapter is constructed to include basic learning tools, such as the following:

- Complete explanations of all processes involved in the creation and management of effective relational databases

- Numbered, step-by-step exercises with illustrations and explanations of each step

- Many tips, notes, and cautions that add shortcuts for many of the activities and pinpoint potential pitfalls

- A summary at the end of each chapter that reviews the material covered and highlights the more important topics discussed in that chapter

Quick Reference

In addition to the chapter material, this book includes a Quick Reference section on the accompanying CD. The Quick Reference contains complete lists and descriptions of elements of Microsoft Office Access 2003 database design and maintenance. This reference serves as an immediate resource for any details in question. It can save time when you need a specific piece of information by presenting concise lists and tables you can jump directly to without having to browse through the more descriptive chapter material in the book itself.

What's on the Companion CD?

Appendix B presents a thorough explanation of the contents of the CD that accompanies this book. This appendix explains how to install the Access databases on your computer and how to look up specific information in the Quick Reference.

The CD includes the following:

- The Quick Reference lookup resource

- The complete Home Tech Repair database

- A set of tables to use as the basis for creating the Home Tech Repair database

- The complete Police database

- A set of tables to use as the basis for creating the Police database

- Scanned image files required by the two databases

Conventions Used in This Book

To help make this book more useful and interesting, we included a few conventions and margin art that will attract your attention to important pieces of information. Following are descriptions of these conventions:

NOTE   *This is a note. Notes further define terms used in the text or point you in the direction of more information about the subject under discussion.*

TIP   *This is a tip. Tips often provide shortcuts to the process under discussion or offer useful pieces of advice about how to make better use of Access 2003.*

CAUTION   *This is a caution. Cautions warn you to be careful when you're about to make crucial decisions or take risky steps. Access tries hard not to put you in harm's way, but this does happens now and then. I post a caution for you when this does happen.*

 This is an example of the margin icons that often accompany a step in the numbered exercises in this book. The margin icons illustrate the toolbar button you need to click to accomplish the activity under way.

Sidebars

This is a sidebar. Sidebars are set somewhat apart from the normal text and include information related to the current subject, but that doesn't necessarily fit in the flow of information. Rather than interrupt the flow, I set the sidebars aside where you can return later to read this tangential information in detail.

What's New in Microsoft Office Access 2003?

This book attempts to show you the new look and feel that comes with Microsoft Office Access 2003. There are the many time-saving and user-friendly features that make Microsoft Office Access 2003 a total database management system.

Some of the new features in Microsoft Office Access 2003 apply to database design; others apply to creating database objects or to customizing the workplace itself. Here are some of the more significant improvements covered in this book:

- The new and improved task panes that include Getting Started, Help, Search Results, and Research give Access 2003 a new, more flexible and interactive look.

- An automatic error checking system helps you detect and fix common errors in forms and reports. When you enable error-checking, you can see the reason for the error and some suggestions for correcting it.

- You now have more control over the Name AutoCorrect feature so you can undo the automatic corrections, if necessary.

- When you modify a field property that is inherited by a control in a form or report, Access displays an option to update the property of all or only a few of the controls that are bound to that field.

- You can view the interdependencies among Access objects. You can ask to see what objects depend on the object you selected or see what objects your selected object relies on.

These are just a few of the new features you will see when you get to work on your database with Microsoft Office Access 2003.

Got Comments?

During my years spent teaching at the University of Southern California, I discovered, to my dismay, that I often learned as much from my students as I hoped they would learn from me. With this philosophy in mind, I invite you to share with me any new tricks or clever shortcuts you've devised. Please e-mail them to me at **vandersenz@aol.com**. In fact, I would enjoy hearing any comments, good and bad, you might have about the book or the databases I have developed as examples. Only by tapping fresh minds can I hope to make these books better and better.

I've been delighted to hear from readers all over the world about the last two editions of The Complete Reference. Some readers are from far away places as South Africa, Scotland, and Japan. I have certainly benefited from the correspondence and I hope I could resolve some of the readers' problems as well.

Quick Tour of Microsoft Office Access 2003

In this, the Information Age, we are surrounded by mountains of data. To use this data effectively, the information must be stored so it can be retrieved and interpreted with flexibility and efficiency. Microsoft Office Access 2003 is a top-notch database management system that you can use for all your information management needs—from a simple address list to a complex inventory management system. It provides tools not only for storing and retrieving data, but also for creating useful forms, reports, and interactive web data pages. All you need is a basic acquaintance with Microsoft Windows and a sense of exploration to build the database you need.

This chapter shows you how to start Microsoft Office Access 2003 and gives you a tour of the Access workplace. If you're already an experienced user, you might want to scan the material in this chapter quickly and move on to Chapter 2 for insight into the power of the tool called a relational database.

Starting Access and Opening a Database

You can start most software built for the Windows environment in the same way: by clicking the Start button and pointing to Programs in the Start menu. Depending on how you installed Access 2003, the name might appear as a separate item in the Programs (or All Programs, if you're using Windows XP) list or as one of the programs in the Microsoft Office menu. If you don't see Microsoft Access in the Programs list, choose Microsoft Office, and then click Microsoft Access 2003.

When first opened, the Access main window displays a Getting Started task pane, offering you a choice of accessing Microsoft Office Online, opening one of the existing database files, or creating a new file, as shown in Figure 1-1. The Open panel contains the names of recently opened databases (your list will be different). The Access opening window is where your session with Access begins.

The Getting Started task pane shown in Figure 1-1 appears automatically wh en Access first starts or when you choose File | New. Several other task panes are available to help with other activities. For now, click the Close button (the × in the upper-right corner) to close the task pane and leave the Access window empty for a tour of the window.

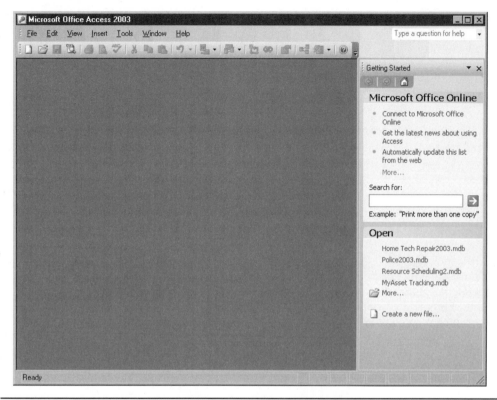

FIGURE 1-1   The Access opening window with the Getting Started task pane

Touring the Access Window

The Access window shows a title bar, a menu bar, and a toolbar common to Windows programs. In addition to displaying the program name—Microsoft Access—the title bar contains buttons you can use to manipulate the window:

- The *Close* button closes the program.
- The *Maximize* button appears only when the window is less than maximum size and enlarges the window to fill the screen.
- The *Restore* button replaces the Maximize button when the window is maximized and returns the window to its previous reduced size.
- The *Minimize* button reduces the window to an icon on the Windows taskbar.
- The *Control Menu icon* at the far-left end of the title bar opens a menu with the commands that accomplish the same things as the other buttons. Click the Control Menu icon to open the menu.

When the window is less than maximum size, you can move it to a new position on the desktop by dragging its title bar. You can also change its height and width by dragging either its borders or the resize handle in the lower-right corner, where you see the three diagonal lines.

Most of the menu commands are dimmed and unavailable in the empty Database window. The *File* menu offers options to create a new database, to open an existing one, or to search for a specific file. Other options, such as the *Toolbars* option in the View menu, let you tailor the database workplace. All the Help menu options are available.

The buttons on the toolbar offer shortcuts to many of the commonly used menu commands. Even if a button is dimmed, you can still rest the mouse pointer on the button and see its name displayed below the button in a *ScreenTip* (called a *ToolTip* in earlier versions of Access). The toolbar, as well as the menu bar, presents different options, depending on the current activity.

The status bar, located at the bottom of the Access window, provides a running commentary about the ongoing task and the Access working environment. The right side of the status bar also shows boxes that indicate the presence of a filter and the status of various toggle keys such as INSERT, CAPS LOCK, SCROLL LOCK, and NUM LOCK. You'll see some of these when you start working with a database.

Opening a Database

If the database you want to open is listed in the Getting Started task pane that appears when Access starts, you can open it by simply clicking the filename. If the one you want isn't on the list, click More. The Open dialog box appears, as shown in Figure 1-2. (Your list of folders and files will be different.) The same dialog box appears if Access is already running when you choose File | Open or click the Open toolbar button.

TIP   *If Access is already running, you can open a recently opened file by choosing File on the menu bar and selecting the filename from the list.*

FIGURE 1-2   The Open dialog box

The Groups pane at the left contains five buttons, which you can click to open other folders or to return to the Windows desktop.

- The top button, My Recent Documents, opens the new Recent folder that contains the name, size, type, and date of the last modification for each recently accessed database. When you click the My Recent Documents button, the Recent folder name appears in the Look in box.

- The Desktop button displays a list of the desktop components on your computer that you can move to, including such items as My Computer, My Documents, Network Neighborhood, and Online Services.

- The My Documents button (or the name of your personal default folder) shows the contents of that folder. This is the default display in the Open dialog box.

- The My Computer button displays the list of available hard disks, floppy disk drives, CD drives, and other data storage systems.

- In Windows 2000, the My Network Places button displays the folders and objects you saved in web folders. In Windows XP, you see the network drives on your LAN, as well as the names of any web folders you've set up.

The trick is to know where you stored your database. If you have used other applications, such as Word or Excel, you know how to find the file you want with the Open dialog box.

You use the Look in box to zero in on the folder that contains the database, double-click the folder name or icon to open it, and then simply select the one you want from the list that appears in the dialog box.

The Open dialog box contains several buttons that help you find the file you want to open. You can see the name of each button by resting the mouse pointer on the button in the command bar.

The Views drop-down list includes the following options:

- **Large Icons**   Displays the names of the files and subfolders located in the folder specified by the Look in box in rows accompanied by large type icons.

- **Small Icons**   Displays the file and subfolder names in rows with small type icons.

- **List**   Displays the file and subfolder names in a columnar list.

- **Details**   Displays the size, type, and date last modified for each file in the list.

- **Properties**   Displays the properties of the currently selected file, such as title, author, and application.

- **Preview**   Shows a preview of the file, if one is available, without opening it.

- **Thumbnails**   Creates thumbnail graphics of files in the selected folder if their file formats permit.

- **WebView**   Shows the web view of files in the selected folder, if available.

The Tools drop-down list includes the following options:

- **Search**   Opens the File Search dialog box that you can use to locate a database by means other than its name.

- **Delete**   Deletes the currently selected item. You're always asked to confirm the deletion before Access removes the file. Same as Delete command bar button.

- **Rename**   Enables you to change the name of the item.

- **Add to "My Places"**   Adds a shortcut to the Groups pane. The item appears in the dialog box list when you click the My Network Places button or the Web Folders button, depending on which version of Windows you're using.

- **Map Network Drive**   Enables you to indicate the drive and path to a network connection.

- **Properties**   Opens the Properties dialog box for the currently selected database.

To choose a different file type to open, click the down arrow next to the Files of type box and choose from the list of 18 types or All Files. The default file type for Access 2003 is Microsoft Access, which includes all Access databases and any other Office documents that have been linked to an Access database, such as an Excel spreadsheet or a Word document. Choose Microsoft

Access Databases to see only the database files in the current folder or Microsoft Access Projects to see only the list of projects.

Once you locate the database you want to open, double-click the name or select it and click Open.

NOTE *The Open button offers other ways to open the database, such as read-only, exclusive, or both. More about these options in later chapters.*

To start working with a database in Access 2003, let's open the Northwind sample database that comes with Microsoft Office. The Northwind database is an order-processing application that demonstrates the power and usefulness of a relational database. Even though the purpose of the database seems straightforward enough—taking and filling orders from customers for the company products—a lot of data still must be manipulated. The database is introduced in this chapter and discussed further in Chapter 2.

To open the Northwind sample database:

1. Start Access and click More in the opening Getting Started task panel. If Access is running and you closed the Getting Started task pane, click the Open button. The Open dialog box appears.

2. Click the Look in arrow at the top of the dialog box and click C: to revert to the root directory of your hard drive. (If Access is installed on another drive, choose that one instead.)

3. In the list of folders and files in the C: directory, double-click Program Files. Program Files now appears in the Look in text box. A list of the subfolders and files in that folder shows in the window.

4. Continue to open the folders for the Program Files\Microsoft Office\Office\ Samples path. If Office 2003 is installed in a different directory, use that pathname.

5. Select Northwind and click Open. If the Northwind Traders welcoming screen appears, click OK to close the screen.

6. If you're greeted by the Main Switchboard, click the Display Database Window button to open the Database window (see Figure 1-3).

TIP *If you don't have the Northwind database installed, you might need to reinstall Access and add the sample database. Also, if you don't want to be greeted by the Northwind welcoming screen every time you open the database, check the Don't show this screen again check box.*

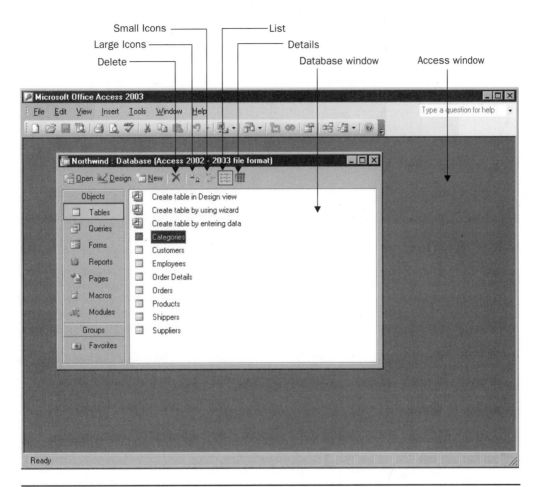

FIGURE 1-3   Viewing the Northwind database in the Database window

NOTE   *In the next section, a distinction is made between the Access window with the menu bar and toolbars, and the Database window that contains lists of all the objects in the database and has a separate command bar.*

Touring the Database Window

The Database window represents the database itself. When you close the window, you also close the database. You can see all the components of the database in the Database window. The left pane of the Database window shows a set of buttons grouped under the Objects title button. The buttons are labeled with the names of the Access database objects: Tables, Queries, Forms, Reports, Pages, Macros, and Modules.

Another title button named Groups includes buttons that open other folders, such as the Favorites folder. Groups can be quite useful if your database is used by more than one department, such as personnel and marketing. Each department can have a group of database objects they can use, such as favorite reports or data entry forms.

In Access 2003, you can define and name your own custom groups similar to the Favorites group. A user-defined group can contain any type of Access object, as well as objects from other Office applications, just like the Favorites group. When you click Groups, the Objects list collapses and the list of your custom groups appears in its place.

Before opening one of the tables in the Northwind database, let's examine the Database window more closely. More menu commands are now available, all of which are relevant to the open database. Many more toolbar buttons are also available now that a database is open.

The Database window is made up of several pages, each represented by a button in the left pane under Objects. Clicking an object button opens the page, which displays the names of any existing objects of that type. For example, if you want to see the names of all the forms you created for the database, click the Forms button in the left pane of Database window. Each object page also includes two or three "new object" shortcuts you can use to quick-start a new object design with or without the help of a wizard.

NOTE *Not only can you resize the Database window by dragging its borders, you can also change the width of the left pane by dragging the divider between it and the object pages.*

The toolbar at the top of the Database window includes buttons to open an existing object for viewing or modification, to create a new object, or to delete an existing object. In addition, you can change how the objects are listed in the Database window.

You can list the objects using large or small icons in alphabetical order by name or another arrangement. In addition, you can show details with the object name. Each of these options is available by clicking a button on the Database window toolbar or by selecting from the View menu.

Table 1-1 describes the object list viewing options.

Figure 1-4 shows the Northwind queries displayed with the Large Icons option. The object icons in the left pane also appear larger when you choose Large Icons.

Option	Description
Large Icons	Displays a large icon above each object name, arranged alphabetically across rows.
Small Icons	Displays a small icon before each object name, arranged alphabetically across rows.
List	Displays a small icon before each object name, arranged alphabetically in one column. If the number of objects exceeds the table height, the list moves to a second column, and so on.
Details	Displays a small icon before each object name, arranged alphabetically in a list with a description, date last modified, date created, type, and, often, the owner.

TABLE 1-1   Access Object Viewing Options

FIGURE 1-4   Viewing queries with Large Icons

TIP   *Notice the icon indicates the type of query. For example, the Customers and Suppliers by City query is a Union query, as specified by the joined rings icon, while the spreadsheet icon above the Quarterly Orders By Product query indicates a Crosstab query. See Chapters 8 and 9 for more information about creating and running queries.*

The list of tables when displayed with the Details option shows the same object properties you can view when using the Windows Explorer. The columns can be widened to see more of the detail or narrowed to hide some of the information. To resize a column, move the mouse pointer to the column divider in the header and, when it changes to a plus (+) sign with a double-pointed horizontal arrow, click-and-drag the boundary.

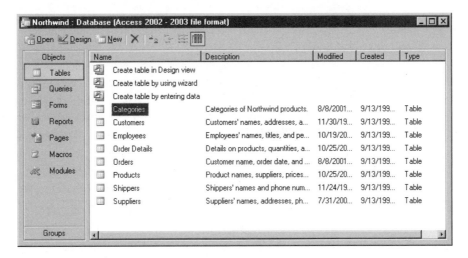

You can also rearrange the objects to list them in a different order. Choose View | Arrange Icons and you have a choice of arranging in alphabetical order by name (the default), by type of object, by date of creation, or by the date the object was last modified. All the arrangements are in ascending order, as you can tell from the arrows in the icons.

Each object page also has a toolbar with a set of buttons appropriate to that object type. All the object pages include the Design and New buttons. The first button depends on the object:

- The *Tables, Queries, Forms,* and *Pages* pages show the Open button, which opens the selected object for data entering or editing.
- The *Reports* page shows the Preview button that displays the report as it will be printed.
- The *Macros* page shows the Run button that executes the selected macro.
- The first button is dimmed on the Modules page.

NOTE   *If you maximize the Database window, the command bar appears immediately below the Database toolbar in the Access window.*

In addition to the objects in the list, each object page—except the Macros and Modules pages—includes two or three shortcut items that start the process of creating a new object. For example, the Tables page, as shown earlier in Figure 1-3, has the following three items in the list:

- Create table in Design view
- Create table by using wizard
- Create table by entering data

More about using these features in Chapter 4.

Looking at Menu Options and Toolbar Buttons

The standard Database menu bar and toolbar appear in the Access window. Not all the options are available to all the database objects and, some, such as the Save button, aren't available until a table or other object is opened. The Paste button is dimmed until you copy something to the clipboard. Table 1-2 describes the Database toolbar buttons and their equivalent menu commands and keyboard shortcuts, if any.

TIP   *If you don't see the toolbar, right-click in the menu bar and check Database in the list of available toolbars.*

Button	Button Name	Menu Equivalent	Shortcut	Description
	New	File | New...	CTRL-N	Opens the New File task pane with options for creating databases using wizard templates or a blank database.
	Open	File | Open...	CTRL-O	Opens the Open dialog box where you can locate and open the desired database file.
	Save	File | Save	CTRL-S	Saves the current object. If not already named, prompts for a name.
	File Search	File | File Search	(none)	Opens the Basic File Search side pane, where you can specify search criteria.
	Print	File | Print	CTRL-P	Prints the current object. The button sends the document directly to the default printer. File | Print and CTRL-P open the Print dialog box.
	Print Preview	File | Print Preview	(none)	Opens the current document in the Print Preview window.
	Spelling	Tools | Spelling	F7	Checks the spelling of all text and memo fields in the current document. If no document is open, the currently selected object is opened and the spelling is checked.
	Cut	Edit | Cut	CTRL-X	Removes selected text or object and places it on the clipboard.
	Copy	Edit | Copy	CTRL-C	Copies selected text or object to the clipboard.
	Paste	Edit | Paste	CTRL-V	Copies contents of the clipboard to the active object or window.
	Undo/Can't Undo	Edit | Undo/ Can't Undo	CTRL-Z	Reverses previous editing action. Not available if no reversible action has been taken.
	OfficeLinks	Tools | Office Links	(none)	Opens a submenu with options for linking with MS Word or MS Excel.

TABLE 1-2   Database Toolbar Buttons and Corresponding Menu Options

Button	Button Name	Menu Equivalent	Shortcut	Description
	Analyze	Tools | Analyze	(none)	Opens a submenu with choices of Analyzer tools.
	Code	View | Code or Tools | Macro | Visual Basic Editor	ALT-F11	Opens the Visual Basic Editor window showing code for the selected object.
	Microsoft Script Editor	Tools | Macro | Microsoft Script Editor	ALT-SHIFT-F11	Opens the Microsoft Script Editor window where you can add or view data access page script.
	Properties	View | Properties	ALT-ENTER	Opens the General property dialog box for selected object.
	Relationships	Tools | Relationships	(none)	Opens the Relationships window.
	New Object: AutoForm	Insert | AutoForm	(none)	Creates a new object of the type selected in the drop-down list.
	Microsoft Access Help	Help | Microsoft Access Help	F1	Starts the MS Office Assistant.

TABLE 1-2   Database Toolbar Buttons and Corresponding Menu Options *(continued)*

CAUTION   *The Undo button works with many actions, but not with all of them, so be careful. Some actions cannot be undone. When you're about to perform an action that's irreversible, Access displays a warning message. Take the time to read the message carefully and make sure you want to proceed.*

You can move the menu bar and toolbar to different locations in the window, docked at another edge or free-floating. To move either one, click the move handle located at the far-left edge of the bar (it looks like a stack of dots). Then, drag the bar away from the top of the window to another edge or leave it in the center of the window. Dragging the bar borders resizes the floating toolbar. To restore the menu bar to the top of the screen, click-and-drag the move handle. To restore the floating toolbar, drag it by its title bar to the top of the window.

Using Shortcut Menus

Shortcut menus are context-sensitive menus that appear when you click the right mouse button. The commands in the menu depend on where the mouse pointer is and what's happening when you click the button. Click anywhere outside the menu to close it. Pressing ENTER, ESC, or ALT also closes the shortcut menu. Only the most commonly used commands are included in the shortcut menu, but they might also include commands from several different menus on the menu bar.

FIGURE 1-5
Choosing from
the Database
shortcut menu

To choose a command from a shortcut menu, click the command or type the letter underlined in the name of the command. If the command shows a right arrow, such as View in Figure 1-5, it's a submenu. Rest the pointer on the item to open the list of commands, and then choose from the list. If the command shows an ellipsis (…) such as Import, a dialog box opens when you click it.

See Chapter 20 for information on how to customize menu bars, toolbars, and shortcut menus.

Opening a Table

To open one of the tables in the current database, double-click its name in the Tables page or select the name and click Open. The table appears with the data in rows and columns, much like a spreadsheet. This view of table data is called *Datasheet view.* Figure 1-6 shows the open Northwind Orders table in Datasheet view. Each row contains a single record with information for one order. Each column contains values for one field. Each field has a unique name and contains a specific item of data, such as the customer or employee name. The column headings show the field names. When you enter data in the table, you're putting actual values in the cells at the intersections of rows with columns.

TIP   *Another way to open a table is to click the right mouse button on the table name in the Tables page, and then choose Open from the shortcut menu. Other commands on this menu will be useful later.*

The status bar at the bottom of the Access window displays the description of the current field included in the table definition. For example, if the cursor is in the first field—Order ID—the status bar displays "Unique order number."

Scroll box

	Order ID	Customer	Employee	Order Date	Required Date	Shipped Date
⊞	10481	Ricardo Adocicados	Callahan, Laura	20-Mar-1997	17-Apr-1997	25-Mar-1997
⊞	10482	Lazy K Kountry Store	Davolio, Nancy	21-Mar-1997	18-Apr-1997	10-Apr-1997
⊞	10483	White Clover Markets	King, Robert	24-Mar-1997	21-Apr-1997	25-Apr-1997
⊞	10484	AB's Beverages	Leverling, Janet	24-Mar-1997	21-Apr-1997	01-Apr-1997
⊞	10485	LINO-Delicateses	Peacock, Margaret	25-Mar-1997	08-Apr-1997	31-Mar-1997
⊞	10486	HILARIÓN-Abastos	Davolio, Nancy	26-Mar-1997	23-Apr-1997	02-Apr-1997
⊞	10487	Queen Cozinha	Fuller, Andrew	26-Mar-1997	23-Apr-1997	28-Mar-1997
⊞	10488	Frankenversand	Callahan, Laura	27-Mar-1997	24-Apr-1997	02-Apr-1997
⊞	10489	Piccolo und mehr	Suyama, Michael	28-Mar-1997	25-Apr-1997	09-Apr-1997
⊞	10490	HILARIÓN-Abastos	King, Robert	31-Mar-1997	28-Apr-1997	03-Apr-1997
⊞	10491	Furia Bacalhau e Frutos do Mar	Callahan, Laura	31-Mar-1997	28-Apr-1997	08-Apr-1997
⊞	10492	Bottom-Dollar Markets	Leverling, Janet	01-Apr-1997	29-Apr-1997	11-Apr-1997
⊞	10493	La maison d'Asie	Peacock, Margaret	02-Apr-1997	30-Apr-1997	10-Apr-1997
⊞	10494	Comércio Mineiro	Peacock, Margaret	02-Apr-1997	30-Apr-1997	09-Apr-1997
⊞	10495	Laughing Bacchus Wine Cellars	Leverling, Janet	03-Apr-1997	01-May-1997	11-Apr-1997
⊞	10496	Tradição Hipermercados	King, Robert	04-Apr-1997	02-May-1997	07-Apr-1997
⊞	10497	Lehmanns Marktstand	King, Robert	04-Apr-1997	02-May-1997	07-Apr-1997

Record: ⏮ ◀ 50 ▶ ⏭ ⏮ of 830

Scroll bar   Scroll arrow

FIGURE 1-6   The Northwind Orders table in Datasheet view

Touring the Datasheet View

You might have noticed some changes that occur in the window when you open a table. For example, the title bar of the Database window now shows the name of the open table.

NOTE   *If the Database window is maximized, the name appears in the Access window title bar.*

The menu bar includes two new options—Format and Records—that are relevant to the open table. More of the toolbar buttons are also available.

The datasheet window shows scroll bars at the right side and in the right side at the bottom. To the left of the bottom (horizontal) scroll bar is a set of navigation tools you can use to move through the records in the table. The following paragraphs give you more detail about the toolbar buttons and the scroll bars.

Looking at the Table Datasheet Toolbar

The Database toolbar has been replaced by the Table Datasheet toolbar, which has many new buttons.

TIP   *If you right-click anywhere on the toolbar, you can see the Table Datasheet option is checked in the shortcut menu. This is a sure way to tell which toolbar is visible on the screen. You can also choose additional toolbars from the list to show in addition to, or instead of, the default toolbar.*

Several buttons on the Table Datasheet toolbar relate to activities involving table data, such as sorting, filtering, and locating.

Among the new buttons on the Table Datasheet toolbar, the only buttons with keyboard shortcuts are Find (CTRL-F), New Record (CTRL-++), and Database Window (F11).

TIP   *If you want to reach a specific record quickly, click on the scroll box and drag it down the scroll bar. You can see the record numbers as the scroll box moves.*

	10578	B's Beverages	Peacock, Margaret	24-Jun-1997	22-Jul-1997	
	10579	Let's Stop N Shop	Davolio, Nancy	25-Jun-1997	23-Jul-1997	
	10580	Ottilies Käseladen	Peacock, Margaret	26-Jun-1997	24-Jul-1997	
	10581	Familia Arquibaldo	Leverling, Janet	26-Jun-1997	24-Jul-1997	Record: 326 of 830
	10582	Blauer See Delikatessen	Leverling, Janet	27-Jun-1997	25-Jul-1997	
	10583	Wartian Herkku	Fuller, Andrew	30-Jun-1997	28-Jul-1997	
	10584	Blondel père et fils	Peacock, Margaret	30-Jun-1997	28-Jul-1997	

Navigating Among Records and Fields

You can move the cursor around the records and fields in your table in several ways, including simply clicking the desired location if it's visible. You should try them all and settle on the one that suits you best. The other methods are the following:

- Selecting from the Go To submenu on the Edit menu.
- Clicking the record navigation buttons at the bottom of the datasheet.
- Using keystrokes such as TAB and the arrow keys.

The Go To submenu on the Edit menu enables you to move to the first, last, next, previous, or to an empty new record.

Go To	▶		◀▮	First
			▮▶	Last
			▶	Next
			◀	Previous
			▶*	New Record Ctrl++

The record navigation buttons at the bottom of the datasheet window give you the same options as the Edit | Go To submenu. You can also enter a specific record number (if you know the number of the record you want to see) in the text box between the navigation buttons, and then press ENTER. This area also tells you what record the cursor is in and the total number of records in the table.

NOTE *If this is a filtered subset of the table, then the word "(Filtered)" appears after the total number of records, which is the number of records remaining after the filter has been applied.*

Pressing a key or combination of keys can be a faster way to move around the datasheet once you get used to the correlation between the keys and the resulting cursor movement. Here are some examples of what happens when you press various keys and key combinations.

- UP or DOWN ARROW moves to the same field in the previous or next record.
- RIGHT ARROW or TAB moves right one field in the same record. If you're in the last field in the record, the cursor moves to the first field in the next record.
- LEFT ARROW or SHIFT-TAB moves left one field in the same record. If in the first field in the record, the cursor moves to the last field in the previous record.
- PGUP or PGDN moves up or down one screen of records.
- HOME or END moves to the first or last field in the same record.
- CTRL-HOME or CTRL-END moves to the first field of the first record or the last field of the last record.

TIP *You can change the behavior of the ENTER and arrow keys. For example, you can prevent the cursor from moving to another record after you fill in the last field in one record. See Chapter 16 for information about customizing your workplace by setting options.*

Looking at a Subdatasheet

In a relational database, it's important to be able to view information related to the current data on the screen when you want to. This has always been possible with forms and subforms in which the main form contains data from one record in one table, while the subform contains data from one or more records in a related table.

When viewing data in Datasheet view, the related data is contained in a *subdatasheet,* which can easily be displayed. If the records shown in Datasheet view display a plus sign at the left end of the row, additional information in another table in the database is related to that record. To see this data, expand the subdatasheet by clicking the plus sign. The plus sign changes to a minus (-) sign when the subdatasheet expands. To collapse the subdatasheet, click the minus sign.

You can have as many subdatasheets expanded as you want in a single Datasheet view. Each subdatasheet corresponds to one record in the datasheet. You can expand them individually or set a table property that automatically expands all the subdatasheets when the table opens in Datasheet view. See Chapter 4 for information about setting table and other properties.

Figure 1-7 shows the Northwind Orders table with two subdatasheets expanded to show the products from the Order Details table, which were included in two of the orders in the Orders table. Notice the plus and minus signs indicating the current state of the subdatasheet.

Order ID	Customer	Employee	Order Date	Required Date	Shipped Dat
10248	Wilman Kala	Buchanan, Steven	04-Jul-1996	01-Aug-1996	16-Jul-19
10249	Tradição Hipermercados	Suyama, Michael	05-Jul-1996	16-Aug-1996	10-Jul-19
10250	Hanari Carnes	Peacock, Margaret	08-Jul-1996	05-Aug-1996	12-Jul-19
10251	Victuailles en stock	Leverling, Janet	08-Jul-1996	05-Aug-1996	15-Jul-19

Product	Unit Price	Quantity	Discount
Gustaf's Knäckebröd	$16.80	6	5%
Ravioli Angelo	$15.60	15	5%
Louisiana Fiery Hot Pepper Sauce	$16.80	20	0%
*	$0.00	1	0%

Order ID	Customer	Employee	Order Date	Required Date	Shipped Dat
10252	Suprêmes délices	Peacock, Margaret	09-Jul-1996	06-Aug-1996	11-Jul-19
10253	Hanari Carnes	Leverling, Janet	10-Jul-1996	24-Jul-1996	16-Jul-19
10254	Chop-suey Chinese	Buchanan, Steven	11-Jul-1996	08-Aug-1996	23-Jul-19

Product	Unit Price	Quantity	Discount
Guaraná Fantástica	$3.60	15	15%
Pâté chinois	$19.20	21	15%
Longlife Tofu	$8.00	21	0%
*	$0.00	1	0%

Order ID	Customer	Employee	Order Date	Required Date	Shipped Dat
10255	Richter Supermarkt	Dodsworth, Anne	12-Jul-1996	09-Aug-1996	15-Jul-19
10256	Wellington Importadora	Leverling, Janet	15-Jul-1996	12-Aug-1996	17-Jul-19
10257	HILARIÓN-Abastos	Peacock, Margaret	16-Jul-1996	13-Aug-1996	22-Jul-19
10258	Ernst Handel	Davolio, Nancy	17-Jul-1996	14-Aug-1996	23-Jul-19

Record: 1 of 830

FIGURE 1-7   Viewing subdatasheets in the Orders table in Datasheet view

NOTE   *If fields haven't been specified with which to link records in the subdatasheet with records in the datasheet, when you expand the subdatasheet, you'll see all the records in the related table. See Chapter 3 for more information about relating tables and what that can do.*

Looking at Data in a Form

So far, you've viewed the Northwind Products table data only in Datasheet view. This view is fine for reviewing the data in small tables, but the full datasheet is often too wide to fit all the fields on a single screen. A much more convenient way to see the data is in a form with only one record on the screen at once. Then you can usually see all the fields and move freely among them without having to use the scroll bars. Forms are dual-purpose objects: You can use a form to look up data or to enter and edit data.

Creating the Form

To create an AutoForm for a table, you needn't open the table first. Simply select the table's name in the Database window and click the arrow next to the New Object button. The list of new objects you can create includes AutoForm and AutoReport. Notice you can use this button to begin creating any of the Access database objects.

NOTE   *If you simply click the New Object toolbar button without choosing from the list, you automatically create an AutoForm because it's first on the list and, therefore, the default option. To create one of the other objects, click the down arrow and choose from the list.*

The *AutoForm* feature is a special wizard that doesn't ask you for any input about how you want the form to look or what data you want it to show: it falls back on a default form layout and style. The form includes every field in the table, arranged in a single column with the field names to the left, so you can identify the fields. The name of the table appears in the title bar of the form window. Figure 1-8 shows the Northwind Orders table in Form view after creating the AutoForm.

The Orders table has a related table—Order Details—which was available as a subdatasheet (refer to Figure 1-7). When Access creates an AutoForm, it automatically creates a subform containing data from the related table, which corresponds to the current record in the main form.

NOTE   *If more fields exist than can fit on a single screen, you can use the vertical scroll bar to see the rest.*

To use the form to add a new record to the Orders table, click the New Record navigation button to display an empty form. Use the TAB key to move from field to field as you enter data. To add a new record in the subform, enter the data in the blank row at the bottom of the subform datasheet.

FIGURE 1-8   Creating an AutoForm from the Orders table

When you finish with the form, you can give it a name and save it as a new database object or you can close the form without saving it. You can also choose to enter the form Design window and make changes to the AutoForm, and then save it as a custom form. You learn more about form design in Chapter 10.

Navigating in Form View

Moving about the table when it's in Form view isn't very different from moving around in Datasheet view. You still have the navigation buttons at the bottom of the window, which you can use to move to other records (and the Go To options in the Edit menu). The subform also has a navigation bar referring to the records in the subform. Moving from one field to another is a little different, however. Of course, you can simply click in the field you want to work with, but you might find using keystrokes easier. Experiment with the keystrokes to see where they take you in the form.

If the form contains a subform, pressing TAB cycles the cursor through all the fields of the main form, and then through the fields and records of the related subform. After leaving the last field of the last record in the subform, the cursor moves to the first field in the next record in the main form. The path is reversed when you press CTRL-TAB.

To switch back to Datasheet view, click the down arrow on the right side of the View button, and then choose Datasheet view from the list. You can also choose View | Datasheet View. The Form View option remains on the View drop-down list until you close the table without saving the new form.

Looking at the Wizards

If you used earlier versions of Access, you've already met some of the *wizards*, the experts that guide you through complicated processes in a few simple steps. Wizards can help create new databases, tables, and queries, as well as customize forms, reports, and data access pages with special features. A wizard presents each step as a dialog box in which you choose what you want to do and how you want the results to look. As you make choices, the wizard works in the background to create the Visual Basic code that can accomplish your goals.

Access 2003 has improved many of the old wizards and has added new ones, so you can get help with virtually anything you want to create. Some of the wizards are installed when you choose Typical Wizards during Setup. Additional wizards, such as the Security Wizard, Subform/Subreport Wizard, Input Mask Wizard, and many of the database utilities are installed when you select Additional Wizards from the feature tree during Setup. See "Changing the Access Environment" in the Quick Reference on the CD for a complete list of the wizards, builders, and add-ins, as well as how to reach them.

Getting Help

No matter how easy Access makes database management, you can't possibly remember how to do every task. That's where the Access Help feature comes in. You can get help with what you're doing in two ways:

- Use the Ask a Question box
- Use the Microsoft Access Help task pane

The Ask a Question box is always available in the upper-right corner of the menu bar so you can always get help, no matter where you are or what you're doing in Access. The box shows the Type a question for help message.

The Help menu is always on the menu bar as well. The Help button is also available on all built-in toolbars.

Asking a Question

You can use the Ask a Question box to get help quickly. Simply type a key word or phrase in the box, press ENTER, and then the Search Result task pane displays a list of relevant topics (see Figure 1-9).

Scroll down the list and click on the one that matches your question. The Help window opens and displays the text of the topic you chose. The topic often includes expandable items, such as Predefined calculations that use aggregate functions, as shown in Figure 1-10. To see the whole subtopic, click the expand arrow at the left of the selection.

If you want to see all the subtopics expanded, click the Show All link at the top right of the window. In addition to the list of subtopics, you might see many terms showing in a different color, which indicates they're expandable to show definitions and other short explanations. These are also expanded when you click Show All. You can also expand them individually by clicking the colored term. To collapse a single item, click it again. To collapse

FIGURE 1-9   Looking at the Search Results task pane

Auto Tile ——
Back ——
Forward ——
Print ——

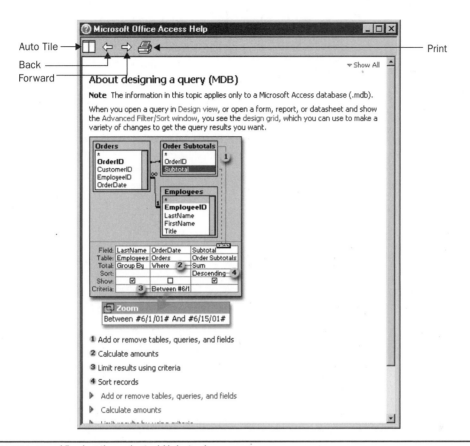

FIGURE 1-10   Viewing the selected Help topic

all the items, click the Hide All button. All items automatically collapse when you move to another topic.

The four buttons in the Help page do the following:

- The *Auto Tile* button tiles the Help window vertically with the Search Result task pane, so you can select another topic without closing the Help window.

- The *Back* and *Forward* buttons move among recently accessed Help topics.

- The *Print* button opens the Print dialog box, so you can print the current Help topic.

NOTE   *If you're working in a different language, the Ask a Question feature might not be supported.*

Using the Microsoft Access Help Task Pane

You have four ways to open the Microsoft Access Help task pane (see Figure 1-11):

- Press F1

- Choose Help | Microsoft Access Help

FIGURE 1-11   Opening the Microsoft Access Help task pane

- Click the Help toolbar button
- If you already see a task pane, click anywhere in the task pane title bar and choose Help from the list of available task panes

NOTE   *If you selected an object or other item before pressing F1, you might see a brief definition of the selected item rather than the Help task pane.*

You can use the Help task pane to search for a topic. Type specific words or phrases in the Search box and click the right-pointing arrow button.

If you want to browse through the Help file table of contents, click the Table of Contents hyperlink. The TOC displays a list of topics marked with the closed book icon. Click these to expand the topics into individual Help articles (see Figure 1-12).

If you're currently connected to the Internet, you also have access to all the current Help topics. Additional online help includes assistance, training courses, the latest product updates, click art and media, and a research library.

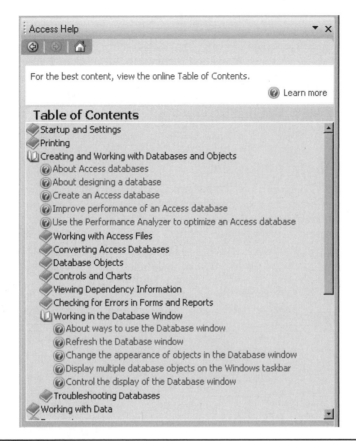

FIGURE 1-12   Viewing the Help Table of Contents

Asking the Office Assistant

If you want a little variety, you can activate the Office Assistant by choosing Microsoft Access Help | Show Office Assistant. When the assistant appears, click on the character to open a balloon asking What would you like to do? Type your question in the balloon and click Search. This functions much like typing your question in the Ask a Question box. You'll see a list of relevant topics in the same Search Results task pane as before and you can choose one to open the Help window.

NOTE   *If you haven't installed the Office Assistant, you'll see a dialog box asking whether you want to install it now. Click Yes and you'll be prompted to insert the Microsoft Office CD*

To remove the Office Assistant from the screen, choose Help | Hide Office Assistant or right-click the character and choose Hide from the shortcut menu. If you get tired of the paperclip, you can choose from six other characters. See Chapter 16 for information about customizing the Office Assistant and other features of the Access workplace.

Asking What's This?

Most of the Access dialog boxes include the What's This? tool. This gives you brief information about a specific element or choice in the box. Activating the What's This? help feature is a two-step process. First, click the **?** button in the dialog box title bar. The mouse changes to an arrow accompanied by a question mark. Then, click the element you want to know more about.

To return the mouse printer to its normal state without opening the What's This? help, press ESC.

Getting Help with What You're Doing

Without opening the Help window, Access gives you many hints and clues while you're working. The status bar offers information about the current activity or the position of the cursor. Many design windows include hint boxes that tell you about aspects of the design. Other windows and dialog boxes include samples or previews of the selections made.

For example, when you're working in the table Design window status bar information tells you how to move around the Design view and get help. The hint box on the right describes what should appear in the Field Name column.

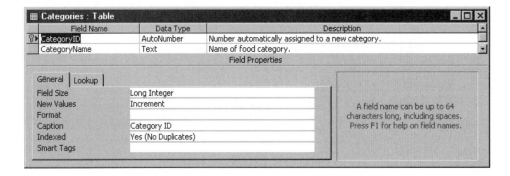

Summary

This chapter has shown you ways to start Access 2003 and get around in the Access window. You had a chance to try out the viewing options, menu bar commands, and toolbar buttons. Using the Access 2003 Northwind sample database, you were given a tour of the Database window and a glimpse of the power behind the Access design capabilities, including the many available wizards.

The final section covered the ways to get help while you're working with Access: by typing a question in the Ask a Question box, by using the Microsoft Access Help task pane, and with guidance from the Office Assistant.

Armed with this familiarity with the Access database management system, the next chapter introduces you to the concepts behind the relational database model and examines the types of relationships you can define between tables. That chapter also looks at the structure and components of a sample database, and how the data is related for efficiency.

Subsequent chapters present details about designing and creating a database, as well as populating it with tables and other Access objects.

CHAPTER 2

The World of Relational Databases

E very day, we're surrounded by databases, ranging in complexity from the weekend gardening list to what resides in the archives at the Internal Revenue Service. Our ability to succeed in this information age is directly related to the ability to manage information. Managing information means storing it efficiently and retrieving it quickly—in such a form as can be instantly useful. The relational database model has been developed to meet those requirements.

What Is a Relational Database?

A *database* is an organized collection of related information used for a specific purpose, such as keeping track of ongoing work order activities or maintaining a library. If you gathered data about the climate in East Africa and about the mineral deposits in southern Utah, you wouldn't call this a database because the data wouldn't normally be used together for a specific purpose. If you collected information about your company's work orders, the customers who contracted for the work, and your employees who would carry out the work, however, this would constitute a database.

NOTE *The terms "data" and "information" aren't interchangeable. Bits of data are combined in a logical way to impart specific information. For example, the numbers 999090009 constitute an item of data, but they don't constitute information until modified with special characters: 999-09-0009. Then the numbers become information in the form of a Social Security number.*

When you use a computerized database management system such as Access, the database is called *relational*. The principle behind a relational database is this: The information is divided into separate stacks of logically related data, each of which is stored in a separate table in the file. *Tables* are the fundamental objects at the heart of a relational database. They form the active basis for the information storage and retrieval system.

Once the information is arranged in separate tables, you can view, edit, add, and delete information with online forms; search for and retrieve some of or all the information with queries; and print information as customized reports.

In Access, the term *database* is more precisely used to define the collection of objects that store, manipulate, and retrieve data. These components include tables, queries, forms, reports, pages, macros, and modules.

Purpose of Relationships

Many advantages exist to distributing data among individual tables, rather than storing it all in one large two-dimensional table, called a *flat file*, such as you might find in a Word document or an Excel spreadsheet. Topping the list of advantages of using a relational database structure is the reduction of data redundancy, which not only reduces the required disk storage space, but also speeds processing. Other important advantages gained by implementing a relational database are the following:

- **Flexibility**   If your data changes, you need to update the value in only one place. All the queries, forms, and reports look in that place for the current values.

- **Simplicity**   The flat-file model used as the basis for a relational system dictates a simple, nonredundant method of data storage. Each table in the relational design is a single object containing data pertinent to a particular aspect of the database, such as an employee, a product, or an order.

- **Power**   Storing the data in separate related tables allows grouping, searching, and retrieving the information in almost unlimited ways.

- **Ease of management**   With smaller, less-complicated tables, the information is much easier to locate and manage.

For example, if you're tracking customer work orders, you could put all the data in a single table, creating a flat-file database. A separate record would exist for every work order under contract. Storing all the customer data with the work order information would mean repeating the same information. In addition, if the customer's phone number changed, every record containing that customer's information would have to be updated. Employee information in the work order table would also be repeated.

How much more efficient to have one table for work order information and separate tables for the customer and employee information. A short field containing a customer identifier could be added to the customer and work order tables to form a connection between the tables, called a *relationship*. Similarly, an employee identifier can link the work orders to the employee who is acting as the job supervisor.

Figure 2-1 shows how to implement the work order database as a relational database. The information is split into an efficient relational database containing three tables, with special fields added to provide the relationships.

The relationship line drawn between the CustomerID field in the Customers table and the CustomerID field in the Workorders table links the two tables. This relationship enables you to look up all the work order information for one customer, as well as the customer's name and phone number for a specific work order.

FIGURE 2-1   An example of a relational database

Similarly, the three relationship lines from the Employees table to the Supervisor, Principal Worker, and Helper fields in the Workorders table link the two tables in three ways. For example, you can ask Access for the name and pager number of the supervisor on a specific job.

When you're building a database, one of the main tasks is to decide how to distribute the data. Three clues guide you while designing a relational database. The first clue is the data that can be divided by user, such as by the personnel office or the production manager.

The second clue is the data redundancy. For example, in a customer-related service company, one customer might contract for several services. Storing all the customer data with the work order information would mean repeating the customer information in every work order record. This would result in many copies of the same information (if your business were successful enough to encourage repeat business).

The third clue is how many records you'll have in each category. For example, if you have 500 employees and 1,500 work orders, you can see that employees and work orders belong in separate tables.

The fourth clue is the dimension of time. If you have information you seldom use, such as an archive of completed work orders, storing this separately—and out of the way—and bringing it out only as needed is better.

Types of Relationships

Tables can be related in three different ways: one-to-many, one-to-one, and many-to-many. The type you define depends on how many records in each table are likely to have the same value.

To relate tables, one of them must have a field that contains a unique value in every record. This can be a primary key field or a field with a unique index that allows no duplicate values. A primary key or a unique index can also be a combination of two or more fields whose combined value is unique for all records. For example, the Employee ID can be a unique number that identifies an employee. If you want to use names in a key or index, you'd probably need to include both the first and last names to ensure unique values.

The most commonly used type of relationship is the *one-to-many relationship*, in which one record in one table can have one or many matching records in another table, or maybe none at all. The table on "one" side is often called the *parent* table and the other is called the *child* table. For example, the Customers table would have one record for each customer. The Workorders table might have more than one work order for the same customer. Both tables would include a field with a value representing that specific customer. In the parent table—Customers—the field must be the *primary key* or a field with an index that contains a unique value. In the child table, the field is called the *foreign key* and needn't be unique.

TIP   *You can speed processing, however, if the child table is indexed on the foreign key. See Chapter 4 for information on defining table structures including specifying indexes.*

In the previous Figure 2-1, both relationships are one-to-many, as denoted by the symbols at the ends of the relationship lines. The 1 appears at the end of the line attached to the table on the "one" side and the infinity symbol appears at the table on the "many" side of the relationship. Primary key fields are indicated by the field name appearing in boldface in the field lists. As you can see in the figure, all three tables in the database have primary keys. The foreign keys are identified by the relationship line pointing to the field name in the child table field list.

The *one-to-one relationship* is sometimes used as a form of lookup, in which each record in one of the tables has a matching record in the other table. Neither table is designated as the parent. The key fields in both tables are the primary keys. One use for this type of relationship is to store additional, seldom-accessed information about an item in the first table, such as an abstract of a book or the details of a work order.

The *many-to-many relationship* isn't permitted as such in a relational database. Many records in one table have the same values in the key field as many records in the second table. To implement this in Access, you must create a third table, called a *junction table*, to place between the first two, converting the many-to-many to two one-to-many relationships.

Figure 2-2 shows how the three types of relationships differ. Chapter 5 contains more information about defining and modifying relationships.

Referential Integrity

Referential integrity is an optional system of rules that guarantees the relationships are valid and the database will remain intact as data is entered, edited, or deleted.

The basic rule of referential integrity is this: For every record in a child table (the "many" side), one and only one matching record must be in the parent table (the "one" side). For example, in the relationship between the Customers table (parent) and the Workorders table (child), every current work order must have a reference to a customer. You cannot have a work order without a customer. The referential integrity rules also prevent you from deleting a customer record if work orders are still in progress.

To summarize the referential integrity rules that Access can enforce

- You cannot enter a child record for which no parent exists (start a work order without a customer).

A one-to-one relationship links the Bid Data table to the Workorders table:

BID DATA TABLE

Bid Number	Bid Date	Award Date	Workorder Number
105	03/03/03	04/01/03	003
106	03/15/03		
107	03/20/03	04/10/03	004

WORKORDERS TABLE

Workorder Number	Start Date	Completion Date
003	04/20/03	04/25/03
004	04/15/03	04/20/03
005	05/10/03	05/15/03

A one-to-many relationship links the Employees table to the Workorders table:

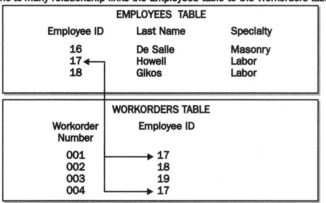

EMPLOYEES TABLE

Employee ID	Last Name	Specialty
16	De Salle	Masonry
17	Howell	Labor
18	Gikos	Labor

WORKORDERS TABLE

Workorder Number	Employee ID
001	17
002	18
003	19
004	17

A many-to-many relationship links the Workorders table to the Suppliers table:

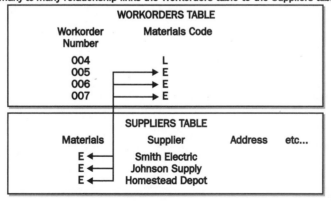

WORKORDERS TABLE

Workorder Number	Materials Code
004	L
005	E
006	E
007	E

SUPPLIERS TABLE

Materials	Supplier	Address	etc...
E	Smith Electric		
E	Johnson Supply		
E	Homestead Depot		

FIGURE 2-2   Three types of database relationships

- You cannot delete a parent record if related child records still exist (remove a customer before the job is completed).

- You cannot change a child record so its foreign key doesn't have a match in the parent table (change the customer field in a work order record to a nonexistent customer).

- You cannot change the primary key value in a parent table as long as related records are in the child table (change a customer link before the work order is finished).

These rules help to maintain an accurate and complete database with no loose ends. Before you can set referential integrity, you must make sure you meet the following conditions:

- The matching field in the parent table is the primary key or at least has a unique value, such as an AutoNumber field.

- Related fields are the same data type.

- Both tables are in the same Access database. You can set referential integrity between linked tables, providing they are both in Access format and you open the database that contains the linked tables.

The same rules can apply to a one-to-one relationship. Enforcing the referential integrity rules in such a relationship guarantees that every record in one table has one and only one matching record in the other table.

Defining Database Objects

Before going any further, let's take a closer look at the objects that make up a database. Access is an object-oriented database management system (DBMS), which means the entire database is composed of objects with certain characteristics or attributes called *properties* that determine their structure, appearance, and behavior. For example, table properties include a description of the table, the subject of the table, and the arrangement of records in the table, such as in alphabetic or chronological order, based on one or more fields.

In turn, each of the major Access objects is a container for other objects, which also have properties. For example, tables are made up of fields that are considered objects with properties of their own, such as name, size, format, data type, and so on. Reports and forms contain design objects, such as data fields, titles and labels, command buttons, page numbers, graphics, and so on. Each of these has a list of properties you can set to achieve the effect you want.

As you see in the Database window, the major database objects are tables, queries, forms, reports, pages, macros, and modules. The *tables* are the containers for all the data in your database. In a relational database system, the data is distributed among several related tables, instead of being placed in one large table.

A *query* is a question you ask of your database. You usually use a query to extract a specified set of records from one or more tables. For example, you might ask the database to show you a list of delicatessen customers who are vegetarians or who have a preference for exotic pasta products. Access answers your question by displaying the requested data. Because a query is a stored question instead of a stored answer, when you ask the question again, the results include the latest information. You not only can view the results, you can also use them in reports and forms.

Forms are often more convenient than a tabular datasheet for entering and editing table data, especially if a table includes more data than can fit across the screen and you have to scroll right to see the rest. A form can display a single record at a time, so all the data is visible at once and the fields can be arranged any way you want in a form design. You can also include data from more than one table or query as the basis for a single form. Forms are especially useful for creating a comfortable visual environment for data management. For example, you can create a form that resembles the paper form used to collect data in the workplace.

When you want to print the data, you usually create a *report*. The report can be a quick and easy dump of the table data—useful for checking specific data items—or it can be a glossy presentation of the data in a custom format suitable for the stockholders or a business manager. The report can also include totals and other summaries of values in a particular field, such as gross sales and monthly profitability. Adding charts and graphs to a report makes the report even more visually informative.

Access provides a special type of report you can use for printing mailing labels or envelopes. If you keep a mailing list in a database table, this type of special report can come in handy. You can also create form letters and merge them with the address list to print a personalized copy for each recipient.

The *data access page* object, which was new to Access 2000, is a special document containing data from an Access database designed to be viewed on a web site. The data access pages are designed specifically for Internet Explorer 5 or later and make use of dynamic Hypertext Markup Language (HTML) and Extended Markup Language (XML).

The final two types of objects are macros and modules. *Macros* contain a sequence of commands that perform a certain task and are useful for defining the actions that respond to button clicks or other events. *Modules* are programs written in Visual Basic for Applications, the programming language used by Access 2003. Procedures contained in the modules are the cornerstone of advanced Access applications.

Inspecting the Sample Database

The Northwind sample database introduced in Chapter 1 is an order-processing application. If it weren't for the use of the Access relational-database management features, the process could be both cumbersome and time-consuming. The following sections examine the sample database in more detail.

Looking at the Data Distribution

As mentioned earlier, a relational database consists of several tables, each of which contains data focused on an aspect of the database. After distributing the data among the tables, the tables are related to one another by means of identifying the matching fields.

The Northwind data is distributed among eight tables as shown in Figure 2-3. The principal tables are Products, Orders, and Customers. The other tables support the order-processing by providing additional data, such as the name of the employee who took the order, the category of product, product suppliers, and shipping methods. Each of these tables is a good example of grouping data items used for the same purpose.

The Orders table contains all the order information, such as order number; customer identifier; employee identifier; order date, date required, and date shipped; shipping method; and the complete name and address of destination.

FIGURE 2-3   Northwind data distributed among eight tables

The Customers table contains the customer identifier, as well as the complete address and phone number. If this weren't in a separate table, the information would be repeated in every order placed by the customer.

The Products table contains the current state of the inventory of each product. The fields include the product identifier, name, supplier identifier, category, quantity per unit, unit price, units in stock and on order, the reorder level, and a field that indicates whether the product has been discontinued.

The other tables contain peripheral information for the purpose of reducing data redundancy. The Employees table contains the employee identifier, birth date and hire date, name and address, telephone, a photo, the name of the employee's supervisor, and a memo field for notes. The Suppliers table includes the supplier identifier, name and address, and a point of contact. The Shippers table contains the company name and phone number, as well as the shipper identifier. The Categories table lists the categories of products with an identifier for each.

The last table—Order Details—is a junction table that links Products and Orders. This table is required to establish the many-to-many relationship between the Products and Orders tables. (An order could contain several products and a product might appear in several orders.)

Viewing Table Relationships

Most of the tables in the Northwind database are related in some way. To see the relationship scheme, click the Relationships button in the Database toolbar or choose Tools | Relationships. The Relationships window (see Figure 2-4) shows the eight tables with their relationship lines.

Each of the eight tables is related to at least one other table, thereby creating a relational database. All the relationships are one-to-many and specify the following:

- The *Suppliers table* is related to the Products table using the SupplierID as the linking field. The linking fields needn't have the same name, but it should be the same data type. More about creating relationships in Chapter 5.

- The *Categories table* is related to the Products table by the CategoryID field in both tables.

- The *Products table* is related to the Order Details table by the ProductID field in both tables.

- The *Orders table* is related to the Order Details table by the OrderID field in both tables.

- The *Employees table* is related to the Orders table by the EmployeeID field in both tables.

- The *Customers table* is related to the Orders table by the CustomerID field in both tables.

- The *Shippers table* is related to the Orders table by the ShipperID field in the Shippers table and the ShipVia field in the Orders table.

Identifying Primary Keys and Linking Fields

As you can tell from the symbols at the end of the relationship lines, all these relationships are one-to-many, the most common type. The parent table must be linked to the child table by its primary key. The primary key field appears in bold in the table field list. Notice all the primary keys are short identifiers for the subject of the table: customer, employee, order, category, supplier, and shipper. The primary key field in the Order Details junction table consists of two fields: OrderID and ProductID. This combination guarantees the primary key will have a unique value.

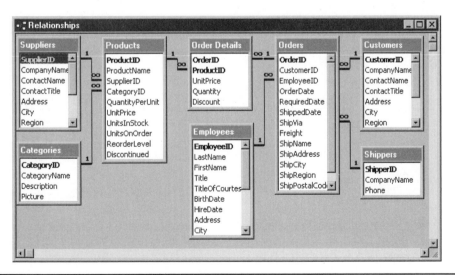

FIGURE 2-4   The Northwind database relationships

Looking at Relationship Properties

In addition to the relationship type, you can find out more about a relationship, such as whether referential integrity is enforced, the specific names of the linking fields, and the type of join implemented. The Edit Relationships dialog box opens when you right-click the middle of a relationship line and choose Edit Relationship from the shortcut menu, or when you choose Relationships | Edit Relationship. This dialog box specifies which are the linking fields in each table, the enforcement of referential integrity, and the type of relationship.

NOTE   *If you click the Join Type button, a second dialog box opens in which you can choose the join property you want to use for the relationship. See Chapter 5 for more information on join types and how they affect the data displayed.*

The Payoff

In addition to the efficiency of data storage, a relational database system offers large benefits when it comes to data retrieval. Forms can be designed for entry or display of data from related tables. As you enter data in the form, it's dispersed to and updates the proper table. As you view data in a multiple-table form, the data is synchronized automatically.

A Custom Form

The Northwind sample database includes several custom forms. To view the Orders form (shown in Figure 2-5), do the following:

1. In the Access window, choose File | Open and locate the Northwind database in the Open dialog box. Select the database name and click Open.

2. Click the Forms object button in the Database window to show the Forms page.

3. Double-click the Orders form name or select it, and then click Open.

The form is used to enter new orders or to view existing orders. Each order includes data from the related Customers, Employees, Products, and Shippers tables. While this form looks complicated, you'll see in Chapter 12 that such forms are easy to construct with Access 2003.

The Bill To: field has a down arrow button that controls the display of a list of customers derived from the Customers table. When the name is selected from the list, the address is automatically filled out in both the billing and shipping areas of the form. The user can enter a different shipping address, if necessary, as you can see from the white background in that area. The billing information is not editable from within the form, as indicated by the background shading in that area.

The Salesperson is also filled in from a list of employees. When the user checks the shipping method in the Ship Via group, the shipper information is automatically copied to the invoice, which is then printed by clicking the Print Invoice button.

The Order ID is a special type of field that's automatically incremented by Access, thereby guaranteeing a unique value for each record. The Order Date has a default value set to the current date, while the other dates must be entered.

The Product information is contained in a subform and the name is selected from a drop-down list. The Unit Price is copied from the Products table, while the quantity and discount fields are entered by the user. The Extended Price, Subtotal, Freight, and Total fields are calculated based on the entered information.

The Orders form has several *class* modules, such as the OnClick event procedure that executes when the Print Invoice button is clicked. A *class module* is a block of VBA code that belongs to, and is stored with, the form or report object. Figure 2-6 shows the printed invoice for the order in Figure 2-5.

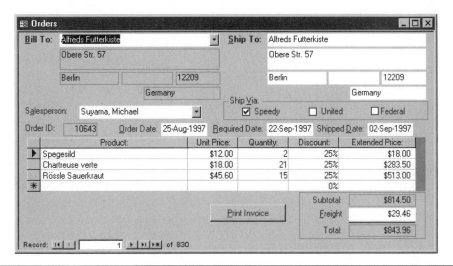

FIGURE 2-5   The Northwind Orders form

INVOICE

One Portals Way, Twin Points WA 98156
Phone: 1-206-555-1417 Fax: 1-206-555-5938

Date: 24-Oct-2003

Ship To: Alfreds Futterkiste
Obere Str. 57
Berlin 12209
Germany

Bill To: Alfreds Futterkiste
Obere Str. 57
Berlin 12209
Germany

Order ID:	Customer ID:	Salesperson:	Order Date:	Required Date:	Shipped Date:	Ship Via:
10643	ALFKI	Michael Suyama	25-Aug-97	22-Sep-97	02-Sep-97	Speedy Express

Product ID:	Product Name:	Quantity:	Unit Price:	Discount:	Extended Price:
28	Rössle Sauerkraut	15	$45.60	25%	$513.00
39	Chartreuse verte	21	$18.00	25%	$283.50
46	Spegesild	2	$12.00	25%	$18.00

Subtotal:	$814.50
Freight:	$29.46
Total:	$843.96

FIGURE 2-6   A printed Northwind invoice

A Custom Report

To preview the Products by Category report in the Northwind database, click the Reports button in the Database window. Then double-click the report name or select it and click Preview. Figure 2-7 shows a preview of the Products by Category report.

The Products by Category report is an example of a report containing information from more than one table. The report is based on a select query that gathers information from the Products and Categories tables. The query also excludes discontinued products.

The products are grouped in this report by category with a count of the number of products in each category.

FIGURE 2-7   The Products by Category report

Summary

This chapter contains some insight into the theory of relational database systems and how they can be used for efficient information storage and retrieval. The major building blocks of an Access database—tables, queries, forms, reports, pages, macros, and modules—were briefly discussed and samples shown. The relationships among the tables in the Northwind sample database were examined.

The next chapter discusses in-depth the process of designing a relational database and how to distribute data among tables. You see how to create a new database with the Database Wizard and how to create a blank database without the help of the Database Wizard.

3 CHAPTER

Creating a Database

The information in a relational database system is distributed among related tables to optimize information storage and retrieval. Common fields relate the tables so information can be extracted and presented in useful ways. A *database* can be an essential tool in managing personal or business information if it's properly designed and constructed. A poorly designed database is of less than no value. The more time spent on task and data analysis, the better the results. Once the design is completed and reviewed, building the database with Access is easy, with or without the Database Wizard.

Designing the Database

The design process begins with an analysis of the tasks to be required of the database. First, you find out what the system is intended to do for the prospective users. Interview all the users and get thorough descriptions of their expectations. What's essential to remember is the design process is also an iterative one: as the users get used to a new system, they can think of more features they can use, such as an additional data entry form, a special query, or a calculated field.

On the other hand, freezing the design at some point is critical, so you can proceed with the development. Then you can accumulate the user's later requirements and desires for the upgraded version.

Also important is to acquaint the user with the comprehensive form and report capability of Access 2003 by demonstrating some data entry forms and showing examples of printed reports.

The database design process can be broken down into seven steps, each with specific goals and products:

1. Determine what the users want from the database and what data is needed to provide the output.

2. Decide what tables to include in the database.

3. Identify the fields for each table.

4. Assign a unique field or combination of fields for each table that ensures no two records are the same.

5. Determine how the tables are related to one another.

6. Review design and step through procedures with users.

7. Create tables and enter data.

While numbering steps in a process implies one step is completed before the next begins, in reality, the design process is more fluid—each step overflowing into the next. You can return to a previous step anywhere along the line.

This chapter covers only the design and creation of the database itself. Chapter 4 discusses creating tables with and without the Table Wizard, Chapter 5 describes how to relate the tables, and Chapter 6 contains more information on entering and editing data in the database.

Introducing Home Tech Repair

The example used in the first chapters of this book is the Home Tech Repair database. *Home Tech Repair* is a small company specializing in maintenance and improvement of home structures. Its specialties are electrical, plumbing, structural, painting, and heating and air conditioning systems in the home. It doesn't undertake large construction or remodeling jobs.

The main purpose of the database is to keep track of work orders and to print invoices. Figure 3-1 shows an example of the manual record-keeping system in use before the development of the Access database.

Determining Goals of the Database

Step 1. Determine the Purpose of the Database   What do the users want to get from the database? What kind of reports do they want, and how do they want the information arranged and summarized? If adequate data collection forms already exist, use them as patterns for the Access forms. Look at other databases that address similar information management situations. Once the tasks are defined, a list of the required data items can be developed.

The main purpose of the Home Tech Repair database is to maintain up-to-date information about current work orders. To do this, the information must include forms for data entry and viewing of all table data, and it must relate the individual work orders to specific customers or employees.

In addition to the work-order tracking, the owner wants to conduct financial analyses, for example, to determine how much revenue has been generated by each employee or to review the total sales on a monthly basis. These analyses can include summary reports with charts and graphs depicting trends, as well as proportional distributions of types of jobs over a period of time. Such studies are helpful when planning for future work.

Distributing the Data

Step 2. Determine How the Information Should Be Divided Among Tables   This isn't as easy as it sounds, but you can follow these guidelines:

- A table shouldn't contain duplicate information among its records. With only one copy of each data item, you need to update it in only one place.

- The information in a table should be limited to a single subject. This enables you to maintain data about each subject independently of the others.

In the Home Tech Repair case, employee and customer information is repeated on several work order sheets. To reduce the redundancy, pull out both sets of information and put them in separate tables. Keeping payments in a separate table would add flexibility, especially if the work is paid for in installments, such as a deposit at the start of the contract and the remainder during the work.

If specific parts are routinely used, such as plumbing fixtures or electrical devices, the list should be kept in a separate table. The data in the parts table can be accessed by the form or report that brings the work order expenses together.

Other peripheral data can be included in separate small tables, such as shipping or payment methods. The Home Tech Repair company information can also be kept separately in one place, accessible to the report that prints the invoice. This table can include the company address, phone and fax numbers, e-mail and web addresses, and any short, standard message to include in correspondence.

FIGURE 3-1   The Home Tech Repair manual work order record

Step 3. Determine the Fields to Contain the Individual Facts About Each Subject All the fields should relate directly to the subject and not include any information that can be derived from other fields. Include all the information you need, but nothing extra. Break up the information into small logical parts, such as First Name and Last Name fields, rather than a single field. Name the fields, so you can locate specific records and sort by individual field values. You can always combine the fields later for finding and searching, if necessary.

CAUTION *The word "Name" is also a reserved word in Access. Name is one of the properties of Access objects and controls, as discussed in later chapters. Using a word that has a special meaning to Access as a field name isn't a good idea because this can cause unpredictable problems.*

Access offers ten data types that cover all the types of data you're going to include in your database. For example, text, memo, date/time, currency, AutoNumber, Yes, No, OLE Object, Hyperlink, and the most useful Lookup Wizard. You meet all these in later chapters. Meanwhile, try to categorize the data into specific data types.

Table 3-1 lists the fields in each of the Home Tech Repair tables and shows the data type and size, as well as a brief description of the data to be stored in the field.

Field	Data Type	Field Size	Description
Workorders Table			
Workorder Number	Number	Integer	Uniquely identifies work order
Customer ID	Text	50	Customer name
Bid Number	Text	5	Original bid number that contained text and well as numbers
Start Date	Date	N/A	Scheduled start date
Completion Date	Date	N/A	Expected completion date
Supervisor	Text	20	Name of employee in charge
Principal Worker	Text	20	Name of employee who is second in charge
Helper	Text	20	Name of helper
Material Cost	Currency	2 decimals	Cost of materials
Labor Cost	Currency	2 decimals	Cost of labor
Description	Memo	N/A	Description of work order
Drawing	Hyperlink	N/A	File of drawing, as required

TABLE 3-1 Distributing Data Among Home Tech Repair Tables

Field	Data Type	Field Size	Description
Employees Table			
Employee ID	Number	Integer	Uniquely identifies employee
First Name	Text	20	Employee's first name
Last Name	Text	25	Employee's last name
SSN	Text	10	Social Security number
Specialty	Text	25	Special labor skills
Address	Text	50	Employee's home address
City	Text	50	City
State	Text	2	State
ZIP	Text	9	ZIP code
Work Phone	Text	12	Office phone or pager
Pager	Text	12	Home phone
Hourly Rate	Currency	2 decimals	Salary hourly rate
Billing Rate	Currency	2 decimals	Customer's billing rate
Comments	Memo	N/A	Additional information
Badge Picture	OLE Object	N/A	Employee picture
Customers Table			
Customer ID	Number	Integer	Uniquely identifies customer
First Name	Text	20	Customer's first name
Last Name	Text	25	Customer's last name
Billing Address	Text	50	Address to send bill to
City	Text	50	City
State	Text	2	State
ZIP	Text	9	ZIP code
Phone Number	Text	12	Customer's phone
FAX Number	Text	12	Customer's FAX number
Notes	Memo	N/A	Additional customer information

TABLE 3-2   Distributing Data Among Home Tech Repair Tables *(continued)*

NOTE   *The AutoNumber data type would be better for the fields you intend to use as the primary key fields, such as Employee ID, Customer ID, Bid Number, and so on. Access creates the AutoNumber values to ensure they're unique within a table. The Home Tech Repair business already had a system of identifying the employees, work orders, and so on and, sometimes, it's easier to accommodate the users with codes they're familiar with. You can set those field properties so the value is always unique.*

After arranging the data in the tables, review the distribution carefully for further normalization. Remove any redundancies and make sure all fields in each table apply directly to that subject. For example, the overhead and the total work order costs are calculated fields, and so aren't included in the Workorders table.

Specifying Key Fields and Relationships

Step 4. Be Sure Each Table Has a Field That Will Contain a Unique Value   If no field exists, plan on asking Access to assign a special field to act as the primary key, so you can be sure each record in the table is unique.

Each of the three main tables of the Home Tech Repair database has a field that uniquely identifies a record: Workorder Number, Employee ID, and Customer ID. The values in these fields can be entered by the user or assigned by Access in the form of an incremental AutoNumber. If the number has no other significance, such as identifying the general location of the job, let Access enter the number, and then you can be sure no duplicates occur.

Step 5. Determine How the Tables Will Relate to One Another   Identify the common fields and the type of relationship.

The Workorders table has a field named Customer ID. Instead of using the customer's name, use the Customer ID, which is the primary key in the Customers table and can be used as the linking field between the two tables. Similarly, use the Employee ID in the Supervisor, Principal Worker, and Helper fields in the Workorders table, instead of the employee names. The Employee ID is the primary key field in the Employees table, which links it to three foreign keys in the Workorders table.

The relationship between the Customers and Workorders table is one-to-many because a customer might contract for more than one job. The relationship between the Employees table and the Workorders table is also one-to-many because an employee can work on more than one job at a time and in one of three slots in a single job.

Figure 3-2 shows the Home Tech Repair tables in the Access Relationships window. The field lists have been lengthened to display all the fields. The figure also shows a fourth table, Bid Data, which we'll add later.

Three instances of the Employees table are in the Relationships window because it's linked to three separate fields in the Workorders table. The table isn't really replicated, it's only displayed in the Relationship window, so the three separate relationships can be illustrated. Chapter 5 contains information about working in the Relationships window and defining or editing relationships.

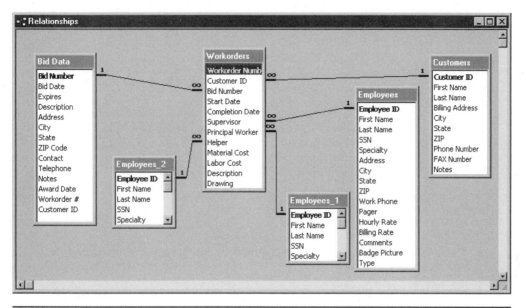

FIGURE 3-2   The Home Tech Repair tables

Completing the Database

Step 6. Thoroughly Review the Design, Complete with Sketches of Planned Reports and Prototype User Interfaces   Now it's time to consult with the users for additional comments and suggestions. Step through the operations you plan to carry out with the information.

Step 7. Create the Table Structures in Accordance with the Design and Enter Data   You might want to limit the data to only enough to test the application, and then complete the tables later. Create the forms, reports, and queries. If the database is for inexperienced users, you can add a switchboard and other custom tools to make their jobs easier. A *switchboard* is the user's main interface with the database and displays a list of actions the user could take. Clicking an item in the list opens a data entry form, previews a report, or offers the chance to change items on the switchboard. Carefully test the entire system. Time spent refining and verifying the design can save time revising the database later, after it's been populated with data.

After the design is established, Access gives you three ways to create a new database:

- Starting with the Database Wizard
- Starting from scratch with a blank database

If you start a new database with help from the wizard, you have a choice of ten different types of commonly used database templates, such as Contact Management or Order Entry. When you choose one, the wizard creates a complete version of the database, with all the relevant tables, forms, reports, and queries. You can even ask for sample data in the new database to try out the database and see how it looks with your own data.

When you build a new database from scratch, the Database window opens as before, but all the pages are blank because the database contains no objects as yet.

NOTE   *A third method is via the Windows Start menu by choosing New Office Document. There you again have a choice between a blank document and one of the wizard's templates. When you make your selection, Access launches and you proceed as usual.*

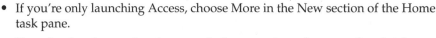

Using the Database Wizard

If you need a database for a common personal or business purpose, the Database Wizard can get you started. Once you build the database with the help of the wizard, you can add your own data and make modifications to the forms and reports that came with the turnkey application.

To start the Database Wizard, do either of the following:

- If you're only launching Access, choose More in the New section of the Home task pane.
- If you're already running Access, whether or not you have another database active, choose File | New, or click the New toolbar button.

Both steps open the New File task pane where you choose On My Computer in the Other Templates section to open the Templates dialog box. If you've used any of the templates recently, their names will also appear in the Other Templates section.

The Templates dialog box has two tabs: General and Databases. The General tab originally contains the Blank Database option, a Blank Data Access Page template, and two blank project templates: one for an existing database and one for a new database. The Databases tab (see Figure 3-3) contains ten database templates for prefabricated applications, ranging from a list of categorized expenses to a complex event-management system. If you're currently online, you can click the Templates on Microsoft.Com button to browse for templates on the Microsoft.Com web site.

NOTE   *The three buttons above the Preview pane change the way the templates are listed: Large icons, List, or Details.*

You can scroll through the sample templates on the Databases tab to find one close to the system you want. Looking through the icons, the Service Call Management database seems to match the Home Tech Repair requirements most closely.

Previewing the Database Templates

The Service Call Management database used as an example in this chapter uses nine related tables to contain all the relevant data. As you highlight each icon, the Preview pane shows an image reflecting the template style.

To get an idea of what information each database contains, you can start the Database Wizard. After defining the location where you want to store the database, the next window describes the information the database tables will contain. After reviewing the contents of the database template, you can proceed with the wizard or click Cancel and start over.

FIGURE 3-3   The Databases tab shows predefined database templates.

To start the Database Wizard, double-click the icon in the Templates dialog box, or select it and choose OK. The File New Database dialog box opens where you specify the location for the database file and give it a name or accept the suggested name. Then, click Create to continue with the wizard.

A blank Database window appears briefly while the wizard is looking for the database elements in the template, and then a window appears listing the contents of the tables to be in the design. Figure 3-4 shows the opening Database Wizard screen for the Service Call Management database.

NOTE   *If you want to see the details of any other template, click Cancel and go back to the Templates window. Then repeat the previous steps.*

Stepping Through the Wizard

Once you select the basis for your database—asset management, membership maintenance, order control, or whatever—the wizard leads you through a series of design steps. The steps include the following:

- Adding optional fields from a list of suggested fields for each table.
- Selecting your preferred screen display appearance.
- Selecting a report style for printed output.
- Entering a title for the new database.
- Including a picture to appear in forms and reports, such as a company logo.

FIGURE 3-4   This is the information the database will include.

You have a chance to customize your database to a limited degree during the process. After the wizard is through, you have much more flexibility with the design.

To continue creating the Home Tech Repair database with the Service Management template as the basis, choose Next to accept the template.

Selecting Tables and Fields

The second wizard dialog box displays the list of tables to appear in the Home Tech Repair database. You have no choice about the table list, but you can add more fields than the wizard has planned. As you highlight each table name, a list of fields appears in the right box. The field names that appear in regular font are required fields and are already checked. Optional fields appear in italic and aren't checked. Checking an optional field adds it to the table. Figure 3-5 shows the CCAuthoriz. # field as an optional field that can be added to the Payment information table. Click Next to move to the third dialog box.

REMEMBER   *If you change your mind or forget to select a particular option, you can always return to previous dialog boxes by clicking Back.*

Choosing Form and Report Styles

The next two dialog boxes give you a choice of ten different screen displays and six report styles. As you select an option, a sample appears in the preview pane on the left. Select an option and view the appearance in the sample pane. When you're satisfied, click Next.

FIGURE 3-5   Adding an optional field to a table

TIP   *The screen display and report style formats are also available when you click the AutoFormat button on the Form or Report Design toolbar. When you open the AutoFormat dialog box, you also have a chance to customize the format and put it back on the list, either as an updated format or as a new format. The customized formats are then available to the Database Wizard.*

Naming the Database

In the last wizard dialog box (see Figure 3-6), you can give the database a special name to appear in the switchboards and the title bar. You can also include a picture. The picture you

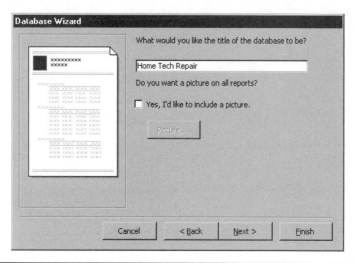

FIGURE 3-6   Enter a name for the database.

specify in this dialog box automatically appears in the header of all the reports generated by the wizard. If you don't select the picture in this dialog box, you have to add it individually to each report later.

To add a picture, check the Yes, I'd like to include a picture option and click the Picture button. The Insert Picture dialog box opens, in which you can browse for the folder that contains the picture you want. As you select images from the list, a preview appears in the right pane. Click OK to add the selected image and return to the previous dialog box. Choose Next, and then accept the Yes, start the database option in the last dialog box to start the database and click Finish.

While the wizard is constructing the database, you can see the process in the background behind the Database Wizard odometers. After a while, a message appears asking for your company name, address, and related information. Click OK and fill in the dialog box. When you close the form, the main switchboard for the new database appears on the screen (see Figure 3-7). This is the main user interface for working with the database.

NOTE   *The minimized Service Call Management Database window appears in the lower-left corner of the screen. Click the Database toolbar button or press F11 to restore the Database window at any time. You can also click the Control button in the minimized title bar and choose Restore.*

When the wizard is finished, you have a complete database application, with all the relevant reports, forms, and queries. All you need to do is input your data.

Figure 3-8 shows the structure of the application the Database Wizard created with the Service Call Management template. The Main Switchboard leads to several forms for entering and viewing table data, many of which include data from more than one table. The application also includes five reports that present and summarize current information.

FIGURE 3-7   The Home Tech Repair main switchboard

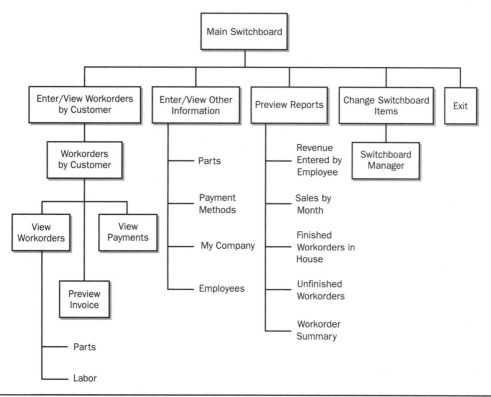

FIGURE 3-8   The application structure

Running the New Application

The Home Tech Repair application automatically displays the main switchboard at startup. The first option opens the main form for the application—Workorders by Customer—where you can enter new work orders or edit existing records.

NOTE *Depending on the choices you made in the Wizard dialog boxes, your form background and fonts might look different.*

To see individual work order information, select the work order in the subform and click the Workorders command button. The Workorders form contains specifics about a single work order, including the employees who work on the job, their billing rate, and the hours spent. The costs are calculated and displayed with payments credited to the work order and the remaining balance computed. To return to the previous form, close this form.

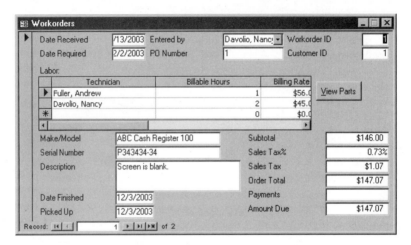

To see the payment history of a specific work order, select the work order and click the Payments command button. To preview an invoice for the work order, click the Preview Invoice command button. When you display the Print Invoice dialog box, you have the opportunity of rewording the default message that accompanies the invoice. The message is part of the company information table.

The third option in the main switchboard opens another switchboard listing the other data entry forms you can use. Figure 3-9 shows the list of reports designed and included in the Home Tech Repair application. Most of them require some user entry, such as a time interval, to create the report.

FIGURE 3-9   Choosing a report from the Reports switchboard

Many changes are required to have the wizard's database conform to the needs of the Home Tech Repair Company. Some fields are unnecessary and should be removed; others should be renamed. Additional forms and reports that depend on different queries, filters, or sort orders might be necessary. All these changes can be made to the Home Tech Repair database built from the Service Call Maintenance template. Changes to the table design are discussed in the next chapter. Queries are covered in Chapter 8, and form and report designs are discussed in Chapter 10 and later chapters.

Starting with a Blank Database

To create a new blank database, do the following:

1. Click the New toolbar button or choose File | New to open the New File task pane. Then select Blank Database in the New File task pane.

2. The File New Database dialog box opens as before, where you can enter a name for the new database and specify the folder in which you want to store it. Access opens the most recently opened folder or, if you are just launching Access, the My Documents folder. Then it gives a unique name to the new database: db1, db2, db3, and so on.

3. After entering a custom name for the new database and opening the folder where you want to store the database, click Create.

An empty Database window opens (see Figure 3-10) showing the Tables page. The first thing to do when starting a new blank database is to create one or more tables. To start a new table, do one of the following:

- Click New on the Database window toolbar.

FIGURE 3-10   Opening the new Database window

- Double-click Create table in Design view.
- Double-click Create table by using wizard.
- Double-click Create table by entering data.

More information about creating and modifying tables is available in Chapter 4.

Summary

In this chapter, the seven-step database design process was described and put into practice in the design of the Home Tech Repair database. You saw how to distribute the data among the tables, and then how to determine the key fields and specify the relationships between the tables. After completing the design, the wizard was invoked to create a database similar to the one the Home Tech Repair Company requires. This chapter also addressed starting a new application from a blank database, rather than a prefabricated template. In the next chapter, you learn how to create new and modify existing table structures. The many field properties that determine the appearance and behavior of the data are also discussed. You also learn how to improve the value of the information in a database by adding validation rules, default field values, and other features.

Creating and
Modifying Tables

Tables form the essential foundation of a relational database and the development of a database begins with building the tables to store the distributed data. Carefully designed table structures can make the difference between a smooth-running, error-free information system and a total disaster.

Access provides many useful tools for creating and customizing tables that help ensure accurate data entry, and facilitate information selection and retrieval. This chapter covers not only how to create a new table structure, but also how to customize the design for your specific data requirements.

NOTE   *In the New Table dialog box, the Table Wizard is only one option. You can also start from Design View or Datasheet View, import a table from an external source, or link with an external table. This chapter first discusses starting with the Table Wizard, and then looks at using Design View and Datasheet View. Tapping external sources is covered in Chapters 22 and 23.*

Creating a New Table Structure with the Table Wizard

In Access, a wizard is only a click away, no matter where you want help. Creating a new table is no different. The quickest way to start the Table Wizard is to double-click the Create Table by Using Wizard item in the Tables page of the Database window.

You can also begin a new table structure with the Table Wizard by choosing from the New Table dialog box.

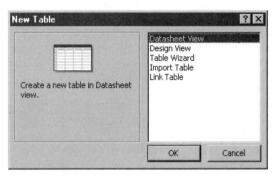

To start the Table Wizard, do the following:

1. Open the New Table dialog box with one of the following actions:

    • Click the New button in the Tables page of the Database window.

 • Click the arrow on the New Object button on the Database toolbar and choose Table from the list.

    • Choose Insert | Table.

2. Double-click Table Wizard in the New Table dialog box or select the option and click OK.

3. The first Table Wizard dialog box (see Figure 4-1) contains two lists of sample tables: one with the names of 25 common business tables and the other with 20 tables for storing data with more personal applications. Each sample table in the list contains a list of appropriate sample fields. You use this dialog box to build the basis for your new table by selecting the fields you want in the table.

4. Choose the category of table and the fields you want by clicking the Business or Personal radio button, and then scroll down the list of sample tables until you see the one that most closely matches your requirements. When you select a table in the list, the sample fields available for that table appear in the middle box.

The next step is to select the fields you want in the new table from the list of sample fields in the sample table.

Adding Fields

You can add all the fields from the sample table or only selected ones using the following methods:

• To include all the fields, click the double right arrow button.

• To remove all the fields from the new table list and start over, click the double left arrow button.

FIGURE 4-1   Selecting a table from the Table Wizard

- To add one field at a time, select the field name and click the single right arrow button.
- To remove a field from the new table list, select the field name and click the single left arrow button.

TIP   *You aren't limited to the fields in the sample table you chose. Fields from other tables can be added to the new table list. Simply select another sample table and choose fields from that. If you later discover you added unnecessary fields, they're easy to remove from the table structure.*

The fields appear in the table design in the order in which you select them from the list, so planning ahead pays. If you placed them in the wrong order, you can remove one or more and reinsert them, or you can rearrange them later in Design View. A field is inserted above the currently selected field in the new field list.

You also have the opportunity to rename the fields while you're creating the table design. Select the field in the Fields in My New Table list and choose Rename Field. Edit the name or enter a new one and click OK. Figure 4-2 shows the Table Wizard dialog box where a new Customer table is under construction and the default ContactFirstName field is being renamed to First Name.

After you select the names you want to appear in the table, click Next to move to the next Table Wizard dialog box.

Setting the Primary Key

The second Table Wizard dialog box lets you name the new table and offers to set a primary key for you. You can accept the default sample table name or enter your own. If you choose the first option, Yes, set a primary key for me, Access assigns consecutive numbers to the AutoNumber CustomerID field. If you want to set your own primary key, choose the

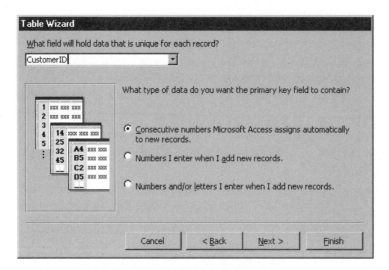

FIGURE 4-2 Renaming a field for the new Customers table

second option, No, I'll set the primary key, and then choose Next. If you chose to set your own key, the next dialog box asks you to name the field you want to use as the primary key (see Figure 4-3). If you let Access set the primary key, this box is skipped.

In the dialog box shown in Figure 4-3, you also specify what type of data the primary field will contain:

- The first option, Consecutive Numbers Microsoft Access Assigns Automatically to New Records, requires Access to make sure the field contains unique values.

FIGURE 4-3 Specifying the primary key for the new table

- The second option, Numbers I Enter When I Add New Records, relies on the user to assign a unique numeric value in each record.
- The third option, Numbers and/or Letters I Enter When I Add New Records, allows a unique combination of numbers and letters in the key value.

Relating to Existing Tables

In the next dialog box (see Figure 4-4), the wizard inquires about the relationship of the new table to the other tables in your database. To define a new relationship, select the appropriate Not Related To statement and click the Relationships button.

The Relationships dialog box opens (see Figure 4-5), where you can choose the type of relationship you want between the tables. Notice Access is quite specific about the one-to-many relationship because it knows the Customers table has the Customer ID field as the primary key, so it must be the parent table. The Bid Data table also has a field named Customer ID, but it isn't the primary key, so this table must be the child table.

If there's an obvious similarity between fields in the new table and those in an existing table, Access might assume a relationship exists and the previous dialog box says Related To instead of Not Related To. If this happens, you can accept the link or delete the relationship by selecting the statement and clicking Relationships. In the Relationships dialog box, choose The Tables Aren't Related and click OK. Access removes the relationship and the Table Wizard dialog box now shows the tables aren't related. You can also reverse the roles of the tables by choosing the third option in the Relationships dialog box.

NOTE   *If you specify a relationship between two tables that don't have a field name in common, Access copies the primary key field name to the child table to use as the foreign key, and then creates the relationship.*

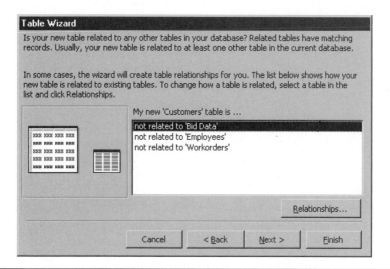

FIGURE 4-4   Examining existing relationships

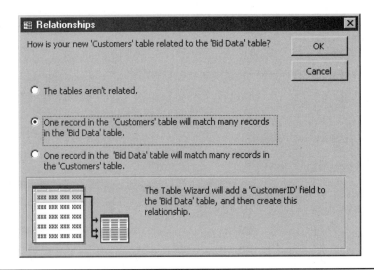

FIGURE 4-5 Setting a one-to-many table relationship

After clicking OK in the Relationships dialog box, you return to the Table Wizard where you can relate the new table to other tables, as necessary.

In the final dialog box, you can choose to go directly to the table Design View to make changes, open the table in Datasheet View to enter data, or have the wizard create a form for data entry. After making the final choice, click Finish. Here's a default form for entering data in the new Customers table.

NOTE *This form is the same as the AutoForm created by clicking the New Object:AutoForm button. You can begin entering data in the form now or name and save the form design for later data entry.*

Creating a New Table from Scratch

The easiest way to start a new table from a blank table design is to double-click the Create Table in Design View item in the Tables page of the Database window. You can also open the New Table dialog box as before and double-click Design View, or select Design View and click OK. An empty table appears in the table Design window, ready to add fields as shown in Figure 4-6.

Touring the Table Design View

The table Design window is divided horizontally into two panes. The upper pane is the field entry area where you enter the field name, data type, and an optional description. You also specify the field to serve as the primary key for the table in the upper pane. The lower pane is devoted to specifying the individual field properties that correspond to the field selected in the upper pane, such as size, display appearance, validity rules, and many more. The list of properties depends on the type of field you're entering. To the right of the Field Properties pane is a description of the currently active area of the screen. Once you start adding fields to the design, you can jump from one pane to the other, simply clicking where you want to be or pressing F6 with the cursor in an active row.

Some new buttons on the Table Design toolbar relate to the task of creating and modifying a table definition:

NOTE   *Several of these buttons have menu command equivalents on the View, Edit, or Insert menu. The Properties button is the only one with a shortcut key combination (Alt-Enter).*

Adding Fields

To begin adding fields to the table structure, do the following:

1. Click the first row of the field entry area and type the first field name. Field names can have up to 64 characters, including letters, numbers, and spaces. Don't begin a field name with a space, however. You also cannot use any of the characters Access attaches special meanings to, such as a period, exclamation mark, and brackets. Using a mixture of uppercase and lowercase letters can help explain the field to the user, but Access doesn't differentiate between cases in field names.

2. Choose an appropriate data type from the Data Type drop-down list.

3. Enter an optional description that can provide additional information about the field. The description appears in the status bar when the field is selected in a datasheet or form.

4. Move to the Field Properties panel and set any desired properties for each new field, such as a default value, a custom format, or a validation rule.

Caution   *Although including spaces in field names makes them easier to read, if there's a possibility you might want to export the table or the complete database to another database program, use a mixture of uppercase and lowercase instead. Access accepts spaces, but other applications might not.*

Because the most commonly used field type is Text, Access automatically specifies a new field as a Text field by default. To change it to another type, select from the drop-down list in the Data Type box.

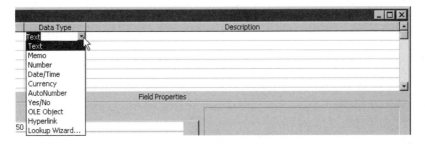

Tip   *Once you get used to the names of the available data types, you can simply type the first letter of the type name and Access then fills in the name.*

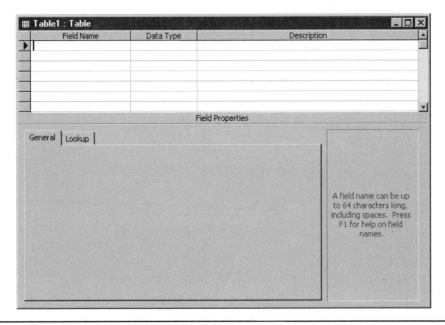

Figure 4-6   An empty table design window

Specifying Field Data Types

Several factors come into play as you decide what data types to use, including the following:

- The kind of values you plan to allow in the field and how you plan to use them.

- The availability of storage space. With some data types, the field size can be reduced for efficiency.

- The types of operations you can execute with the data. You can count the number of records containing a specific value of most data types in a field, but you can add up values only from Number and Currency fields.

- The way you want to sort or index records. You can sort or index on any field type except OLE Objects.

- The way you want to group records for a report or query. You can group on any field type except Memo, Hyperlink, and OLE Object fields.

TIP *You can use the Access Field Builder to help add new fields to your table. Simply click an empty row in the table design, and then click the Build toolbar button (the one that looks like a magic wand). The Field Builder contains the same sample table and field lists as the Table Wizard. The predefined fields are complete with names, data types, and other common properties.*

The following paragraphs briefly describe each of the ten data types and how they're used. If you're interested in the amount of disk space each type of field requires, refer to the Quick Reference section "Table Fields" on the CD that accompanies this book.

Text   The Text data type is the most common data type and can contain any combination of up to 255 characters and/or numbers. You would use the Text type for storing values that contain combinations of numbers and letters, such as addresses and job descriptions. Even when you think the field will contain only numbers, but you aren't expecting to perform any calculations with the values in the field, using the Text type is better. For example, ZIP codes might seem like numbers, but they often contain a dash, which isn't considered a number or a leading 0 that would be truncated. In addition, you won't be computing the sum or average of all ZIP codes, so using a Text type is more efficient.

Tɪᴘ   *If you're planning to sort records on a field that will contain only numbers, but won't perform any calculations, you're better off using the Number type rather than the Text type. When Access sorts numbers in a Text field, it reads the numbers from left to right, instead of right to left. For example, the numbers 9, 46, and 175 in a Text field would be sorted (ascending) in the reverse of their numerical order: 175, 46, and 9 because Access reads the first digits and sorts accordingly. If the first digits are the same, it reads the second, and so on.*

Access gives Text fields a default size of 50 characters, but you can reduce the size to 1 or increase it up to a maximum of 255 characters. If you expect the field to contain more characters than 255, you should consider using the Memo field type instead, which can contain much more data.

Memo   Use a Memo field to store long, but variable-length, text possibly relating to the other field data. For example, you could add comments to your employee records about their efficiency on the job or their skills when dealing with customers. You don't expect every record to include memo data, but when one does, the text can vary in size from a few words to up to 65,535 characters.

Nᴏᴛᴇ   *The handy Spelling Checker can be used to catch misspelled words in both Text and Memo fields. See Chapter 6 for more information about this useful tool.*

Number   Select the Number data type when you plan to sort on the values or use them in calculations, such as adding up the labor hours for a plumbing job or the hours worked by a certain employee during the fall season. If you're working with dollar sales figures, it's better to use a Currency type because you can choose from several monetary display formats. Currency values also maintain higher precision during calculations.

Currency   Use the Currency type when you want to store monetary values, such as the cost and bid price of contracted jobs. Currency fields can be used in arithmetic calculations, just like the Number fields. You have many more ways to specify the display appearance of Currency fields than Number fields, including how to indicate negative values. Currency values are accurate to 15 digits to the left of the decimal point and 4 digits to the right. Using Currency instead of the Number data type prevents inaccuracies caused by rounding off the results of calculations to two decimal points.

Cᴀᴜᴛɪᴏɴ   *Number and Currency fields are automatically assigned 0 as the default value. This can cause a problem if you plan to use the field to store lookup values. This also becomes a problem if you want to count records that contain a value in the field. Zero is considered a value and the record is then falsely included in the count. To prevent this complication, remove the setting in the Default Value property. See Chapter 6 for more information about lookup lists.*

AutoNumber   When you specify an AutoNumber field, Access guarantees each record in the table has a unique value in the field, thereby creating a field you can use as a primary key. Access generates a unique value for the field as you enter each new record. You have a choice of two types of AutoNumbers: Long Integers and Replication ID numbers. If you choose Long Integer, you have a choice of how Access generates new values: Increment or

Random. The most commonly used are incremental numbers, which start with 1 and simply count the records as you add them.

Date/Time   The Date/Time type is most useful when you want to sort records chronologically by the value in the field. You can also use a Date/Time field in calculations to determine elapsed time. With the Date/Time data type, you have a variety of ways to display the data as well. Formatting Date/Time and other data types is discussed in the section "Date/Time Fields."

Yes/No   The Yes/No field is useful when you want the equivalent of a check mark in your records. For example, suppose you want to know if a transaction has been posted or a job has been completed. By default, a Yes/No field appears as a check box in a datasheet, as well as in forms and reports. You can choose to display Yes or No, On or Off, or True or False. You can also create your own custom display for Yes/No fields.

NOTE   *The Yes/No data type is also called "Boolean" because of its binary logic.*

OLE Object   When you want to embed or link an object from another source in your table, you use an OLE Object type field. With this type of field, you can acquire data from such objects as an Excel spreadsheet, a Word document, graphics, sound, or other binary data.

Hyperlink   When you want the field to jump to another location, or to connect to the Internet or an intranet, store the hyperlink address in a hyperlink field. A *hyperlink field* can contain up to four parts, separated by the pound sign (#):

- **DisplayText**   Optional text that's displayed instead of the full hyperlink address (commonly referred to as a "friendly" link).
- **Address**   A Universal Resource Locator (URL) or a Universal Naming Convention (UNC) path.
- **SubAddress**   A page within the web address or a location within the file.
- **ScreenTip**   Text that displays when the mouse pointer rests on the hyperlink. You see these when you rest the mouse pointer on a toolbar button.

Only the address is required unless the subaddress points to an object in the current Access database. The other parts are optional.

Lookup Wizard   The *Lookup Wizard* creates a field limited to a list of valid values. When you select this data type, a wizard helps you create the list and attaches it to your table. You can type in the values you want to use or have the Lookup Wizard consult another table for the set of valid values. Then, as you enter table data, you can choose the value you want from a drop-down list. The field inherits the same data type as the primary key field in the lookup list, which is the value stored in the lookup field.

TIP   *Field descriptions are helpful. For example, if the field name itself isn't informative enough or you want to remind yourself the field is a link to another table, add a description. The text you enter in the Description column appears in the status bar when the field is highlighted in Datasheet View or in a form.*

Setting Field Properties

Field properties determine how the values in the field are stored and displayed. Each type of field has a particular set of properties. For example, you might want certain currency values displayed with two decimal places, a dollar sign, and a comma as the thousands separator. Or, you could specify the currency values be rounded off to the nearest whole dollar.

To specify a property setting, first select the field in the field entry pane (the upper portion of the window) in Design View, and then click the desired property in the Field Properties pane. Many of the properties show a down arrow when they're selected. Clicking the arrow displays a list of property options from which to choose. In most cases, you can also type in the setting you want.

A useful field property is the *Caption,* which is the text that appears in the column header in Datasheet View and as the label attached to a field in a form or report. The Caption property can display a more descriptive name for the values than the field name itself.

Access attaches default properties to every field. You can accept or change the settings to customize your fields. Because Text fields are the most common and most of the field properties apply to the Text data type, let's look at their properties first. Table 4-1 describes the properties of a Text field, most of which are also available to other types of fields, although they have different default settings for different data types.

Property	Effect
Field Size	Specifies the maximum number of characters allowed in the field. Default is 50 characters. The maximum is 255 characters.
Format	Determines the display appearance, such as forcing uppercase or lowercase characters. In a text field, a default format isn't specified.
Input Mask	Provides a template for data conforming to a pattern, such as telephone numbers or Social Security numbers, and adds literal characters to the field, if desired. Default is none.
Caption	Displays a name other than the field name in datasheets, forms, and reports. Default is none.
Default Value	Automatically enters the specified value in the field. Default is none.
Validation Rule	Specifies an expression that checks for invalid data. Default is none. (Unless the validation rule specifies that the field can be left blank, it can also have the same effect as setting the Required property to Yes.)
Validation Text	Displays this message if the entered data fails the validity rule. Default is none.
Required	Indicates this field cannot be left blank. Default is No.
Allow Zero Length	Differentiates between a blank field and a field containing an empty string of text (""). Helpful when a value is known not to exist (such as a fax number). Default is Yes.
Indexed	Indicates the table is indexed on this field. Default is No.
Unicode Compression	Allows string data that is now stored in Unicode format to be compressed to save storage space. Default is Yes.

TABLE 4-1   Describing the Text Field Properties

Property	Effect
IME Mode	Sets the IME mode for a field when focus is moved to it. *IME* is a program that enters East Asian text into programs by converting keystrokes into complex East Asian characters. Default is No Control.
IME Sentence Mode	Sets the type of IME sentence. Default is None.
Smart Tags	Recognizes and labels the field as a particular type. Default is none.

TABLE 4-1   Describing the Text Field Properties *(continued)*

The Text, Number, and AutoNumber field types are the only ones for which you can specify a field size. Access automatically sets fixed field sizes for the other types. Number and Currency fields have a property that lets you specify the number of decimal places to display as well. The AutoNumber data type also has the New Values property, which determines the method of assigning a unique number to the new record.

Other properties, such as Input Mask and Validation Rule, include a Build button that shows as a button displaying three dots (...) to the right of the property text box, which you can click to get help with the property. For example, if you click the button next to the Validation Rule property, the Expression Builder dialog box opens where you can get help with creating a valid expression. If you don't need help building an expression, you can simply type it in the property box. If the expression is invalid, Access lets you know. You learn more about validation rules in the section "Ensuring Data Validity."

Choosing a Field Size

A text field, such as a postal code or a job number that contains only a few characters, needn't take up the default 50 characters of disk space. You can change the size of the field by entering a different number. Another reason to specify the field size is to prevent data entry errors by limiting the number of characters that can be entered.

Number fields are sized a little differently, specifying the name of the number layout, rather than the number of characters. The options are as follows:

- **Byte**   Used to store positive integers (whole numbers) between 1 and 255. Uses 1 byte of storage.

TIP   *Save space with Number field sizing. If you know the field will contain only small integers, choose the Byte field size property to save disk space. This might not sound like much of a savings, but with extremely large tables, the results are significant.*

- **Integer**   Used to store larger integers and negative integers, between –32,768 and +32,768. Uses 2 bytes of storage.
- **Long Integer**   Default Number field size, which is used to store even larger integers between roughly –2 billion and +2 billion. Uses 4 bytes.

- **Single**   Stores single-precision floating-point numbers in IEEE format. Floating point numbers are expressed in exponential terms, for example .35 × E05. Uses 8 bytes.

- **Double**   Stores double-precision floating-point numbers in IEEE format. Uses 16 bytes.

- **Replication ID**   Used to store a globally unique identifier (GUID).

- **Decimal**   Makes the Precision and Scale properties available to control number entries.

AutoNumber fields are limited to Long Integer and Replication ID field sizes.

Changing the size of a Number field only changes the way it's stored, not the appearance of the numbers. To change their appearance, you need to change the Format property.

Formatting Field Data

The Format property is used to specify the appearance of the value when displayed. This has no effect on the way the value is stored and it doesn't check for invalid entries. A format makes sure all the field values look alike, no matter how you entered the data. For example, you can force all names to be displayed in uppercase characters or all dates to include four-digit year values. Access provides predefined formats for most data types, but you can also create custom formats for all data types except OLE Object.

Tip   *You can go through the Windows Control Panel to change the Country setting on the General Tab of the Regional Options dialog box to apply foreign currency and other formats to field values. For example, changing English (United States) to English (United Kingdom) changes the currency symbol from dollars ($) to pounds (£).*

When you set a field's Format property in Design View, Access applies that format to the values in Datasheet View. Any new controls on forms and reports also inherit the new formatting. Controls added to the form or report design prior to setting the custom formats are unaffected.

You can use the following custom formatting symbols with any data type:

- **!**   Enters characters from left-to-right instead of right-to-left, forcing left alignment.

- **(space)**   Enters a space as a literal character when the SPACEBAR is pressed.

- **"xyz"**   Displays the characters or symbols within the quotation marks.

- *****   Fills available space with the character that follows.

- ****   Indicates the character that follows is to be treated as a literal character. Often used with reserved symbols and characters.

- **[color]**   Displays the field data in the color contained within the brackets. You can use black, blue, green, cyan, red, magenta, yellow, or white.

Other custom formatting symbols are valid only for specific data types, as described in the following paragraphs.

Text and Memo Fields   Text and Memo fields use the same format settings, some of which are character placeholders that apply to individual characters and other settings affecting the entire entry. You can use the following symbols with Text and Memo field format settings:

- @   Indicates a character or a space is required.
- &   Indicates a character or a space is optional.
- <   Converts all characters to lowercase.
- >   Converts all characters to uppercase.

Custom Text and Memo format settings can have two sections, separated by a semicolon. The first section applies to fields containing text and the second applies to fields containing zero-length strings or null values.

Here are some examples of using the Text and Memo Format settings:

Format Setting	Entered As	Displays
@@@@-@@-@@@@	123456789	123-45-6789
>	jimmy	JIMMY
<	JIMMY	jimmy
@\!	Hello	Hello!
@;"No Data"	Horse	Horse
@;"No Data"	(blank)	No Data

Number and Currency Fields   You can format your Number and Currency data with one of Access's predefined formats or create your own using the special formatting symbols. The Format property of a Currency field is automatically set to Currency, but you can change it to any of the other settings. The Format property of a Number or Currency field displays a list of the predefined formats as described in Table 4-2.

Setting	Effect
General Number	Displays number as entered.
Currency	Displays number with currency symbol and thousands separator. Negative values appear in parentheses. Default is two decimal places. Default setting for Currency fields.
Euro	Displays number with Euro currency symbol and thousands separator. Negative values appear in parentheses. Default is two decimal places.
Fixed	Displays at least one digit. Default is two decimal places.
Standard	Displays thousands separator. Default is two decimal places.

TABLE 4-2   Number, AutoNumber, and Currency Predefined Format Settings

Setting	Effect
Percent	Displays value multiplied by 100 with added percent sign (%). Default is two decimal places.
Scientific	Uses standard scientific notation with exponents. For example, 243 displays as 2.43E+02.

TABLE 4-2   Number, AutoNumber, and Currency Predefined Format Settings *(continued)*

TIP   *When you specify the Percent format for a number field, you must change the Field Size property from the default Long Integer to Single. Otherwise, the field displays only the integer portion of the number you enter and leaves off the fraction. For example, it you enter 1, the field displays 100.00%, but if you enter 1.25, the field still displays 100.00%.*

Date/Time Fields   Date/Time fields include seven predefined format settings, in addition to some symbols you can use to create your own custom formats. Here are the formats Access provides.

Setting	Description
General Date	(Default) Combination of Short Date and Long Time settings. If no time, only date is displayed, if no date, only time. Examples: 5/21/04 3:30:00 PM (US) 21/5/04 15:30:00 (UK)
Long Date	Uses Long Date Regional setting. Examples: Friday, May 21, 2004 (US) Friday, 21 May, 2004 (UK)
Medium Date	21-May-04
Short Date	Uses Short Date Regional setting. Examples: 5/21/04 (US) 21/5/04 (UK)
Long Time	3:30:00 PM
Medium Time	3:30
Short Time	15:30

Date and Time format settings are specified according to the setting in the Regional Options dialog box in the Windows Control Panel.

NOTE   *In Access, Date/Time field data is always stored with four-digit year values. However, the user could have entered only two digits to represent the year. The Short Date setting assumes any dates between 1/1/00 and 12/31/29 are in the twenty-first century, that is, between January 1, 2000 and December 31, 2029. Dates between 1/1/30 and 12/31/99 are assumed to be in the twentieth century, between January 1, 1930 and December 31, 1999.*

Using special characters to represent the hour, minute, and second in a time format and the day, week, month, and year in a date format, you can create almost any display format you choose. The letter *d,* for example, can display the day of the month as one or two digits or as the full name, depending on how many times you use the letter *d* in the string. The letter *m* can also be used to represent the month from one or two digits to the full name The character *n* is used as the minute format symbol to avoid confusion with the month symbol, *m.*

See the Quick Reference section, "Custom Formatting Symbols," on the CD that accompanies this book for a complete list of the custom formatting symbols available for Date/Time values.

To include literal characters other than the date and time separators with the Date/Time values, enclose them in quotation marks. Some examples of using these special formatting symbols are the following:

Setting	Displays
ddd", "mmm d", "yy	Thurs, Jan 15, 04
dddd", "mmmm d", "yyyy	Thursday, January 15, 2004
h:n:s AM/PM	9:15:35 AM

In addition, you can add other characters to the display format by enclosing them in quotation marks. For example, entering the value 5/21/04 in a field with the format setting

"Today is " dddd " in week number " ww "."

displays

Today is Friday in week number 21.

Notice the spaces within the quotation marks that separate the characters in the string from the date values and the period added to the end of the expression.

NOTE   *If you specify a custom Date/Time format that's inconsistent with the settings in the Regional Options dialog box, the custom format is ignored.*

Yes/No Fields   Access automatically displays a default check box control when you specify a Yes/No data type. Any format settings you make are ignored with this choice. To display values in any other format, first change the Display Control setting on the Lookup tab to a text box or a combo box, and then you can have some fun formatting Yes/No field values. Access provides three predefined formats for displaying Yes/No, On/Off, or True/False, but you can also create a custom format that displays other text for the two values.

To change a Yes/No field Display Control property, open the table in Design View and do the following:

1. Select the Yes/No field.
2. Click the Lookup tab in the Field Properties pane.
3. Select Text Box from the Display Control list.
4. Return to the General tab to choose the desired display format.

The Yes/No custom format contains up to three sections, separated by semicolons. The first section isn't used, but you still need to enter the semicolon before entering another section. The second and third sections specify what to display when the value is Yes and No, respectively. For example, the following format:

;"Yes, indeed!"[Green];"No, never!"[Red]

displays

Yes, indeed!

in green when the value is Yes, and

No, never!

in red if the value is No.

If you choose Combo Box as the Display Control property instead of Text Box, more properties appear on the Lookup page where you can set the appearance and values of the list the combo box will display. More about using combo boxes and lookup lists in Chapter 6.

Setting the Number of Decimal Places

The Field Size, Precision, Scale, Format, and Decimal Places properties of Number and Currency fields are all related. The Field Size property determines whether the number is stored as an integer or with fractional values, and also specifies the degree of mathematical precision.

The Precision property applies only to Number fields with the Field Size set to Decimal. This property is used to limit the total number of significant digits that can be entered on both sides of the decimal point in a Number field. Leading and trailing zeros aren't counted; they're truncated. Enter a positive integer between 0 and 28 in the Precision property of the Number field. The default setting is 18.

The Scale property also applies only to Number fields with Decimal Field Size property. Scale limits the number of significant digits that can be entered to the right of the decimal point, not counting any trailing zeros. Enter a positive integer between 0 and 28 in the Scale property. The default setting is 0.

The Format property adds display features, such as dollar or percent signs, and commas as thousands separators.

The Decimal Places property determines how many digits to display to the right of the decimal point in a Number or Currency field. The Decimal Places setting has no effect on the precision of the stored number; that's specified by the Field Size or the Precision property. If the value is stored as an integer (Byte, Integer, or Long Integer data type), a number of zeros appear to the right of the decimal point equal to the setting in the Decimal Places property.

The default Decimal Places setting for Number and Currency fields is Auto, which displays two decimal places for fields with Format property settings of Currency, Fixed, Standard, Percent, and Scientific. You can choose any number from 0 to 15. However, the Decimal Places property has no effect unless you already specified the appropriate Format property for the field.

To change the number of Decimal Places in the display, click the arrow in the Decimal Places property box and choose a number from the list or simply enter the desired number.

If the field retains the default Long Integer property, the values are then rounded to the nearest integer, no matter how many decimal places you specify for the display.

TIP   *You can also set the Decimal Places property in a query, report, or form design and override the setting you specified in the table design.*

To change the number of decimal places stored in the field, change the Field Size property to one of the settings for real numbers, such as Single, Double, or Decimal, which aren't limited to integers.

Including a Caption

If someone else is going to use the database and you think the field names aren't descriptive enough, you can use the Caption property to change the column heading in the Datasheet View. A caption can contain up to 2,048 characters, in any combination of letters, numbers, special characters, and spaces. Be aware, however, that the space where the caption will be displayed might be limited.

The new caption also appears in queries and replaces the text in the field labels attached to controls in report and form designs. The field names remain the same; only the labels show the new caption text.

CAUTION   *If you rename the field later in Datasheet View, the Caption property is deleted. To prevent this, rename fields only in Table Design View.*

Choosing a Primary Key

In a relational database system, being able to gather and retrieve related information from separate tables in the database is important. To do so, each record in one table must be unique in some way. The field or fields that contain the unique value is the *primary key.* Access neither permits duplicate values in the primary key nor does it permit null values. A valid unique value must be in the primary key field or field combination throughout the table.

Setting a Single-Field Key

If your table has a field you're sure won't contain any duplicate values, you can use that field as the primary key. In the table Design View, click the field row you want to use as the primary key, and then you have three ways to designate the field as the primary key:

- Click the Primary Key toolbar button.
- Choose Edit | Primary Key.
- Right-click the field row in the upper pane and choose Primary Key from the shortcut menu.

To remove the primary key designation, repeat any one of the previous steps.

NOTE   *If you choose the field as the primary key after you enter data and duplicate values occur or one of the records has a blank value in that field, Access won't set the key. However, you can run a Find Duplicates query to locate and correct any duplicate entries. More about queries in Chapters 8 and 9. You can also solve the problem by choosing a different field as the primary key, adding another field to the key, or adding an AutoNumber field to use as the key.*

Setting a Multiple-Field Primary Key

If you can't guarantee the values in a single field will be unique throughout the table, you can combine two or more fields as the primary key. For example, in a list of customers, you might have several with the same last name, so that field couldn't be used as a primary key. You could combine first and last names to create unique values, though, or, if that still doesn't work, combine first, last, and middle initial or ZIP code. But, better yet, use an AutoNumber field instead.

TIP   *The multiple-field primary key field is left over from the days before Microsoft invented the AutoNumber data type. Rather than create a multiple-field primary key, adding an AutoNumber field to do the job is much simpler and safer. Access makes sure every record is unique. The main use for a multiple-field primary key is in a junction table, which is used to bridge two tables that are related with a many-to-many relationship, as described in Chapter 5.*

To set a primary key that combines two or more fields, hold down CTRL while you select each field. If the fields are contiguous in the list, select the top field row and hold down SHIFT while you select the last row you want to include. After you select all the fields you want in the key, use the Primary Key button or a menu option as before. Key icons appear in each row included in the multiple-field primary key. The following table has a three-field primary key that includes the first and last names with the ZIP code. Note the key icons in the field selectors at the left of the field names.

TIP   *The multiple-field primary key is constructed in the same order as the fields in the table structure. If a different field order is important, you can rearrange the fields in the Indexes window. More about the Indexes window in section "Creating a Multiple-Field Index."*

Letting Access Set the Key

The *AutoNumber field type* is an Access tool that can guarantee unique records in a table. Designating an AutoNumber field as the primary key for a table is probably the simplest way to set the key. You needn't worry about inadvertently entering duplicate values because Access uses unique numbers to identify each record. Once the number is generated, it can't be changed or deleted.

You can choose to have incremental numbers, random numbers, or Replication ID numbers, also called GUIDs. With incremental values, Access adds 1 to the value for each record you add. When you choose random numbers for the AutoNumber field format, Access uses a random number generator to create the value. Replication ID numbers are used to identify and synchronize database replicas uniquely.

When you finish a table design using the Table Wizard without having designated a primary key, Access asks if you want it to create one for you. If you answer Yes, Access either applies the primary key to an AutoNumber field—if one exists—or creates an AutoNumber field, which it then designates as the primary key. You can respond No and leave the table without a key for the time being.

Creating Other Indexes

Indexes help Access find and sort records faster, just as an index helps you find topics in a reference book. An *index* contains a pointer to the location of the data, rather than the data itself. The primary key in a table is automatically indexed, so I'm talking about secondary indexes created with other fields. An index can include a single field or multiple fields. You can index any field except an OLE Object field.

When deciding which fields to use as indexes, look at the fields you expect to search frequently for particular values or those by which you want to sort. Also, if you expect to use a field to create a relationship with another table, you might want to create an index on the field to improve performance. A field that could have many records containing the same value isn't a good candidate for an index because an index on such a field won't speed things up much.

Adding a Single-Field Index

To set a single-field index, simply change its Indexed property to Yes and decide whether to permit duplicate values.

To view the indexes specified for a table, click the Indexes toolbar button or choose View | Indexes. The Customers table includes two currently defined indexes. The primary key, Customer ID, is listed with the key icon as the first index and a single-field index based on the customer's last name as the second. Notice the primary key properties, shown in the Index Properties pane, specify the index as Primary with Unique values and not to ignore null values in the field.

Indexes: Customers			
Index Name	**Field Name**	**Sort Order**	
PrimaryKey	CustomerID	Ascending	
Last Name	Last Name	Ascending	

Index Properties

Primary	Yes	
Unique	Yes	The name for this index. Each index can use up to 10 fields.
Ignore Nulls	No	

Creating a Multiple-Field Index

In many cases, you might want to search or sort records based on more than one field at once. Creating a multiple-field index enables you to do just that. When you sort records using a multiple-field index, the records are sorted initially by the first field in the index. If Access finds duplicate values in the first field, it sorts by the next field and so on. For example, you want to see records for customers in particular areas of the city. To do this, you can create an index using both the City and ZIP code fields.

To create a multiple-field index, follow these steps:

1. With the Customers table open in Design View, click the Indexes toolbar button.

2. Click in the first empty row in the Indexes window.

3. Enter a name for the new index, such as **City Region**, and then press TAB to move to the Field Name column.

4. Click the down arrow and select City from the list of available fields.

5. Accept Ascending as the sort order for the City field and click the Field Name in the next row (leaving the Index Name blank because both fields are used in the same index).

6. Choose ZIP from the field list and change the sort order, if necessary.

7. If the index is intended to be the primary key, set the Primary property to Yes. (You must click the first row of the index, which contains the index name, to display the Index Properties pane.) If you want the index to contain unique values for each record, change the Unique property to Yes. If you want the index to ignore null values, change the Ignore Null property to Yes.

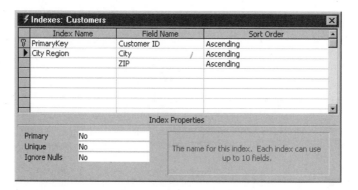

8. Close the Indexes dialog box, and then save the changes to the table.

You can specify up to ten fields in one index with a mixture of ascending and descending orders for the fields.

Saving the Table Design

The table design needn't be complete before you save it. In fact, a good idea is to save the design now, and then save it again during the design process to guard against catastrophes.

Access requires you to save the design before you can switch to Datasheet View to enter data. To save the table design, click the Save button or choose File | Save. The first time you save a new table, Access prompts you for a name.

The table name can have up to 64 characters in any combination of letters, numbers, and spaces, but it cannot begin with a space. You can also include special characters, except for those that have a special meaning to Access, such as a period (.), an exclamation point (!), an accent grave (`), or brackets ([]). You also cannot use any control character with an ASCII value between 0 and 31.

TIP   *If you want to undo the changes you just made to the table design, close the table design and respond No when Access asks if you want to save the changes.*

Modifying the Table Design

Even though you tried to include all the necessary features and properties in your table design, you'll undoubtedly find things that need changing. You might want to change Text fields to Memo fields so you can enter more information, add default values, or validation rules. Or, you might want to add a new field or delete one that isn't needed, after all. Maybe some of the field properties aren't quite what were expected or you want to change the field size or type.

You can make any of these changes to an empty table with no problems, but after you enter data, you risk losing data with some of the changes. Adding fields, increasing a field size, and rearranging the field order won't cause any data loss. But, if you decide to delete a field or reduce a field size in a table that already contains data, Access displays a warning if data loss could occur. Problems can also occur when changing a field type. Making a backup of the data before you make any changes to the table design is always a good idea.

TIP   *The quickest way to make a backup copy of a table is to right-click the table name in the database window and choose Copy from the shortcut menu. Then right-click in a blank area in the Database window and Paste from the shortcut menu. Accept the default name, Copy of ..., and click OK. You can use this method to copy other database objects as well.*

Switching Table Views

If you enter data in Datasheet View and you decide some changes need to be made in the table structure, you can quickly return to the Design View in one of the following ways:

- Click the View (Design) button.
- Choose View | Design View.
- If the window isn't maximized, right-click the Table window title bar and choose Table Design from the shortcut menu.
- If the window is maximized, right-click any empty area in the Table window outside the datasheet and choose Table Design from the shortcut menu.

Use the same methods to switch back to Datasheet View.

NOTE   *If you're viewing data in the AutoForm, switching to Design View takes you to the form Design View, not the table Design View. To switch to table Design View, you must first switch to Datasheet View, and then click the Design button.*

Adding/Deleting Fields

A new field can be added to the bottom of the list of fields or inserted anywhere among the existing fields. To add one to the bottom, click the first blank field and enter the field definition. To insert a field among existing fields, click the row below where the new one is to appear, and then do one of the following:

- Click the Insert Rows toolbar button.
- Choose Insert | Rows.
- Right-click the row and choose Insert Rows from the shortcut menu.

Whichever method you choose, the new blank field row is inserted above the row that contains the cursor and all the fields below are moved down one row. The insertion point is in the new row ready to enter the field definition.

NOTE   *If you select the existing row instead of clicking it, the new row is selected on insertion. You must click in the row to deselect it before you can begin entering the new field definition.*

For example, add a new field to the Workorders table that will contain a hyperlink to a drawing used for that job, such as a schematic for installing a bay window. To add the new field, do the following:

1. Right-click the Workorders table on the Tables page of the Database window, and then choose Design from the shortcut menu.
2. Click in the first empty row in the Field Name column and enter **Drawing**.

3. Click the Data Type arrow and choose Hyperlink from the list.
4. Add a description, such as Layouts of project, and then click Save.

TIP   *Another way to add a new field, one that inherits the same properties as one already in your table, is to copy the existing field to the clipboard, and then paste it in an empty row. Of course, you must change the new field's name before you can save the table because no two fields can have the same name. Only the field definition is copied; no previously entered data is copied.*

If you want to add several new rows at once, select the number of contiguous rows in the table design equal to the number of new fields you want to insert, and then use one of the previous methods. The same number of new blank rows appears above the top row in the selected group. Then click one of the new rows and begin entering the field definitions.

When you delete a field from the table design, you aren't only deleting the field name, but any data entered in the field. Before deleting a field that contains data, Access warns you'll permanently lose the data and asks if you really want to delete the field.

To delete a field, in Design View, click the row selector for the field (the gray button to the left of the field name) and do one of the following:

- Press the DEL key.
- Choose Edit | Delete Rows.
- Click the Delete Rows toolbar button.
- Right-click in the row and choose Delete Rows from the shortcut menu.

To delete several rows at once, select them all and delete them as a group.

NOTE *Using the DEL key works only if the row is selected. The other three methods delete the row that contains the insertion point, even if it isn't selected.*

CAUTION *You can cause a problem by deleting a field you've used in a query, form, or report. Be sure you remove any references to the field you're about to delete from the other objects before you try to delete it. Access won't let you delete a field that's a link in a relationship to another table without deleting the relationship first.*

Changing the Field Order

To change the order of fields in both the stored table and in the Datasheet View, rearrange them in Design View. To move a field to a new position in the table design, click the row selector to select the row, and then drag the row selector to move the field to its new position.

You can move several contiguous fields at once by selecting them all, and then dragging them as a group. To select more than one, use one of the following methods:

- Click the top field row selector and drag through the row selectors until all are selected.
- Click the top field row selector and hold down SHIFT while you click the field row at the end of the group.

NOTE *While you can select noncontiguous field rows by holding down CTRL as you select the rows, you cannot drag the group to a new position.*

If you want to keep the field order in the stored table, but would like to view them in a different order in the datasheet, you can rearrange the datasheet columns. See Chapter 6 for information about changing the appearance of a datasheet.

Changing a Field Name or Type

You saw earlier how to change the name that appears in the column heading in Datasheet View by changing the field Caption property. You can also change the actual field name in the design. Changing the field name has no effect on the data already entered into the field. However, any references to the field in other objects, such as queries, forms, and reports or in an expression, must be changed as well, unless you have checked the Name AutoCorrect option.

To change a field name in Design View, simply type the new name. After changing the name, you must save the table again.

NOTE *The Name AutoCorrect feature automatically corrects most side effects that occur when you rename a field, such as changing the name of a bound control in a form or report. This is one of the options you can turn on or off by choosing Tools | Options and clicking the General tab. A welcome new feature with Access 2003 is more complete error-checking for forms and reports. If you have an unassociated label, a circular reference or invalid sorting and grouping options, the errors are automatically identified and flagged in the design. When you click the flag, you see an explanation of the error and can choose from a list of options that will correct it. If you don't have the Name AutoCorrect feature turned on, the new feature catches name changes. See Chapter 10 for more information about creating form designs.*

Changing a field type is a little more complicated if the table already includes data. If no data is in the table, you can safely change any field data type. Some types convert easily to another type, but other conversions could result in loss of data. If data is going to be lost, Access displays a message showing the number of values to be affected before it makes any changes. If you used the field in an expression, you might also need to change the expression.

To change a field type, do the following:

1. Click the Data Type column.

2. Click the arrow and select the new data type.

3. Save the table design. If Access displays a warning message, respond No to cancel the changes or Yes to go ahead and make the changes. If no data is in the table, Access doesn't display any warnings.

You won't encounter any difficulties converting other data types to Text. Number fields convert to text with a General Number format, while Date/Time fields convert to text with the General Date format. Currency fields convert accurately to Text, but without the currency symbols.

Table 4-3 describes the relevant considerations when converting between data types.

From	To	Results	Comments
Text	Number, Currency, Date/Time	Converts to appropriate values	Values must fit new data type. Others are deleted. Date/Time and Currency formats follow Regional Settings
Text	Yes/No	Converts to appropriate values	Yes, True, and On convert to Yes. No, False, and Off convert to No
Number	Yes/No	Converts to appropriate values	Zero or null values convert to No and non-zero values to Yes
Memo	Text	Direct conversion	Memo data longer than field size is truncated
Number	Text	Converts values to text	Numbers appear in General Number format

TABLE 4-3 Converting Between Data Types

From	To	Results	Comments
Currency	Text	Direct conversion	No currency symbols are included
Date/Time	Text	Direct conversion	Values appear in General Date format
Yes/No	Text	Direct conversion	None
AutoNumber	Text	Direct conversion	Values might be truncated depending on field size
Currency	Number	Direct conversion	Values might be truncated depending on field size
AutoNumber	Number	Direct conversion	Values might be truncated depending on field size

TABLE 4-3   Converting Between Data Types *(continued)*

CAUTION   *If the field you're converting is a primary key field or a unique index and the conversion would result in duplicate values, Access deletes the entire record. Access warns you first, so you can prevent the deletion.*

TIP   *Once a table contains data, you cannot change any type of field to AutoNumber, even if you know the field contains unique values. If you need an AutoNumber field, add a new field and select the AutoNumber data type. Access assigns each existing record a sequential number.*

Changing a Field Size

Changing the Field Size property has no effect on the data if you're increasing the size. Obviously, if you want to reduce the field size, especially for a Number field, you should make sure no values are larger than permitted by the new field size. If the values are too large to fit the new field size, they're replaced with null values. If the new field size doesn't permit the number of decimal places currently specified, the values are rounded off.

Modifying or Deleting the Primary Key

You might find the primary key doesn't always have a unique value after all and decide to use a different field or create a primary key with two or more fields.

To change the primary key, select the row you want as the primary key and click the Primary Key button. The key icon is removed from the old key field and appears in the new one.

To add another field to the existing primary key, select both the old and new key fields, and then click the Primary Key button. The key icon appears in the row selector of both rows.

At times, you might want to disable the primary key temporarily—for example, if you're importing records from another table, some of which might contain values that duplicate your original table. You must remove any duplicates in the new data before restoring the primary key. This has no effect on the data stored in the field designated as the key: it removes the key field feature temporarily.

To remove the primary key designation, select the primary key field and click the Primary Key button. If the key is used in a relationship, you must delete the relationship before you can remove the key.

Modifying or Deleting an Index

To delete a single-field index, change the field's Indexed property to No. This removes only the index; it has no effect on the field itself or the underlying data.

In the Indexes dialog box, you can add or delete fields from a multiple-field index, change the sort order for any field in the index, or change the index properties. You can also change the field order in the index.

- To remove a field from a multiple-field index, display the Indexes dialog box, select the field row, and then press the DEL key.

- To remove the entire index, display the Indexes dialog box, select all the rows in the index, and then press the DEL key.

- To insert an additional field into the index, display the Indexes dialog box, select the field below where you want the new field to appear, press INSERT, and then enter the new field name.

- To change the field order in a multiple-field index, select and drag the field selector to the desired position in the index definition.

- To change the sort order for any of the fields in the index, choose from the Sort Order list.

After making changes to the table's indexes, be sure to save the table. Access reminds you to do so if you try to close the table or if you return to Datasheet View without saving.

Ensuring Data Validity

You've seen a few of the ways Access helps you ensure the values entered in your database are valid. The data type you choose for the field can limit the values to, for example, date and time values. You can also limit the number of characters in a Text field and prevent duplicate values. A direct way to ensure valid data is to set some rules the values must obey.

You can specify two kinds of data validation rules: field validation and record validation. A *field validation* rule can limit the value to a few specific values or to a range of values. The rule is checked when you try to move to another field in the same or another record. For example, a rule could limit a numeric value to a range between 1 and 100 or insist a date value fall in 2004.

A *record validation* rule is handy for comparing the values in two fields in the same record. The rule is checked when you move out of a record and Access attempts to save the record. Access won't save a record with a conflict between fields. For example, a record validation rule could prevent saving a record in which the Job Cost is greater than the Bid Price. Another record validation rule could ensure the elapsed time between dates in two separate fields doesn't exceed a specific value.

When either type of rule is broken, Access displays a message in a warning box that explains the violation and doesn't leave the field or record. The message you want to display is the Validation Text property in the table or field property. If you don't enter message text, Access creates a standard default message, such as the one shown here.

Defining Field Validation Rules

To define a field validation rule, follow these steps:

1. Select the field name in the upper pane of the Design window, and then click Validation Rule in the Field Properties pane.

2. Type the expression you want in the Validation Rule property box. For example, if the value must not exceed 100, enter **<100<** (less than or equal to 100).

3. Then move to the Validation Text property box and enter the message you want to display when the rule is broken.

NOTE   *The Validation Rule property has a Build button you can use to open the Expression Builder if you need help with the expression. See Chapter 8 for information about using the Expression Builder.*

You can also type wildcards in the expression. These are the same placeholders used in search strings: ? stands for a single character and * stands for any number of characters. When you enter an expression with a wildcard, Access converts it to an expression using the Like operator and adds quotation marks. For example, if you type **C*** in the property text box, it turns into Like "C*" when you move out of the property box. This expression means all values entered in the field must begin with the letter *C* or *c*. The expression is not case-sensitive.

A validation rule defined for a Date/Time field also includes special symbols when translated by Access. To enter a rule that says the date entered must be earlier than January 1, 2004, you type **<01/01/04** and Access converts it to <#01/01/04# to make sure it isn't confused with a Number value.

Validation rules can include more than one criterion for the same field by combining them using the AND or OR operators. Table 4-4 describes some examples of validation rules, the corresponding Access expression, and an appropriate Validation Text message.

Rule	Access Version	Typical Message
<>0	<>0	Value must not be 0, but it can be negative
100 Or 200	100 Or 200	Value must be either 100 or 200
C*	Like "C*"	Value must begin with *C*
C* Or D*	Like "C*" Or Like "D*"	Value must begin with either *C* or *D*
C??t	Like "C??t"	Value must be four characters long, begin with *C*, and end with *t*.

TABLE 4-4   Examples of Validation Rules and Text

Rule	Access Version	Typical Message
>=01/01/03 And <01/01/04	>=#1/1/03# And <#1/1/04#	Value must fall within the year 2003
Not CA	Not "CA"	Field can contain any value but CA

TABLE 4-4   Examples of Validation Rules and Text *(continued)*

NOTE   *You will see a lot more about creating expressions for queries in Chapter 8.*

Figure 4-7 shows the Bid Data table structure with a validation rule added to the State field. The rule specifies the State value must be one of CA, AZ, or NV and, if the rule is violated, the message Bid contracts only in California, Arizona, or Nevada displays in an information box.

If you enter a state value other than those specified, you'll see an error message when you try to move to the next record.

Invalid entry

NOTE   *The previous State validation rule causes a violation if the field is left blank because it insists on one of three values. If you want to leave the field blank, add Null to the list of valid values. You can also create a more complex record validation rule that insists on a value only if a no value is in the corresponding City field to allow for customers who deal solely over the Internet instead of by mail.*

As you add validation rules to a table, you can test them against existing data to see if any of the field values violate the new rule. To do this, choose Edit | Test Validation Rules or, if the Design window isn't maximized, right-click the Design window title bar and choose Test Validation Rules from the shortcut menu.

Access warns you the process also checks the Required and Allow Zero Length properties, could take a long time, and asks if you want to do it anyway. If you respond Yes, you're told you must save the design before testing the rules. Choose Yes to save the design and continue testing. If Access finds no violations, it displays a message saying all the data was valid for all the rules you defined. If a violation is found, Access stops checking and displays a message indicating which rule was violated and asks if you want to continue with the rule testing.

Field validation rules are enforced whenever you enter or edit data whether it's in the datasheet, in a form, or by means of an append or update query. These rules are also

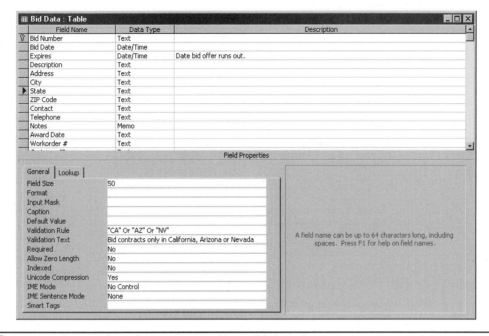

FIGURE 4-7 The new State field properties with a validation rule

enforced on data entered by Visual Basic for Applications (VBA) code or imported from another table.

Defining a Record Validation Rule

A record validation rule is a table property rather than a field property. You can define only one record validation rule for a table, but if you want to apply more than one criterion, you can combine them in an expression using the AND or OR operators.

The record validation rule is applied whenever you enter or edit table data. When you leave a record, Access checks the new record against the rule you defined. As with field validation rules, if you define a record validation rule for a table that contains data, Access asks if you want the rule applied to the existing data when you save the table.

To add a record validation rule to a table, open the Table Properties dialog box by one of the following methods:

- Click the Properties toolbar button.
- Choose View | Properties.
- Right-click the field entry area or the table Design window title bar (if the window isn't maximized) and choose Properties from the shortcut menu.
- Press ALT-ENTER.

Enter a description of the table in the Description property for later reference, the validation rule expression, and the text to display when the rule is violated. For example, the Expires date for a bid in the Bid Data table must be later than the Bid Date.

Table Properties	□×
General	
Description	Contains contract bid information
Default View	Datasheet
Validation Rule	[Bid Date]<[Expires]
Validation Text	Bid Date must be prior to the Exp
Filter	
Order By	
Subdatasheet Name	[Auto]
Link Child Fields	
Link Master Fields	
Subdatasheet Height	2"
Subdatasheet Expanded	No
Orientation	Left-to-Right

Requiring an Entry and Preventing Duplicates

One of the field properties is Required, which is set to Yes or No. The default value is No, but you can change it to Yes if the field should never be left blank. For example, every employee record must have a Social Security number, so you would change the field's Required property to Yes.

TIP   *All field and index properties that have only Yes and No settings can be toggled back and forth by double-clicking the property box.*

The Indexed property helps prevent duplicate values. A single-field primary key field always requires unique values, but you can have only one such field in a table. You might want to prevent duplication in other fields without assigning them as the primary key. To add this restriction, change the field's Indexed property to Yes (No Duplicates). If you open the Indexes window, you see the new single-field index with its Unique property set to Yes.

You can prevent duplicate values in a group of fields by creating a multiple-field index on the combination of fields. Once the index is created, change the Unique property in the lower pane of the Indexes window to Yes. Then no two combinations of the values in these fields can be the same.

Handling Blank Fields

You might leave a field blank because you don't know the value or because no value exists for that field in that record. Access distinguishes between those two kinds of blank values with null values and zero-length strings.

A *null value* indicates a missing or unknown value for the field. You would leave a field blank if you don't know the value or it isn't relevant to the current record. Access recognizes this and stores the value as a null value. Pressing ENTER without entering anything stores a null value.

A *zero-length string* is a string that contains no characters. If you know no value exists for this field (not that you simply don't know what the value is), you enter a zero-length string by pressing SPACEBAR or by typing a pair of double quotation marks ("") with no space between. The marks disappear when you move to the next field, but Access stores a zero-length string.

A good demonstration of the difference between null values and a zero-length string is the Pager field in the Customers table. If you don't know if the customer has a pager or, if she does, but you don't know the number, leave it blank. If you know the customer doesn't have a pager, enter a zero-length string.

Two special field properties control how blank fields are handled. The Required property determines whether a blank field is acceptable or the field must contain a value. The Allow Zero Length property, when set to Yes, permits zero-length strings. This property is available only to Text, Memo, and Hyperlink fields.

These two properties work together as follows:

- If you want to leave the field blank and don't care why it's blank, set both the Required and Allow Zero Length properties to No.

- If you never want to leave a field blank, set Required to Yes and Allow Zero Length to No. You cannot leave the field without entering a value, even if it's only "Don't know" or "None."

- If you want to tell why the field is blank, set Required to No and Allow Zero Length to Yes. Then you would leave the field blank if the information isn't known or enter quotation marks ("") to indicate the field doesn't apply to the current record (no pager exists).

- If you want to leave the field blank only if you know the field isn't relevant to a record, set both properties to Yes. Then the only way for you to leave the field blank is to enter a zero-length string either by typing "" or pressing the SPACEBAR.

NOTE   *When you allow blank fields, you can still use the Find and Replace options from the Edit menu to locate fields with null values or zero-length strings. To find records with blank values, place the insertion point in the field and choose Edit | Find or click the Find toolbar button. Type **null** in the Find What box to find the null values or type "" to find fields with zero-length strings. In the Match box, be sure to ask Access to match the whole field or you'll find a lot of fields with blanks between words. Also be sure to clear the Search Fields As Formatted check box. See Chapter 6 for more information about locating specific records.*

Assigning a Default Value

If one of your fields usually has the same value—for example, the State field in a list of local customers—use the Default Value property to have that value automatically entered when you add a new record. You can still change it to a different value when you enter data, but a default value can save time during data entry, especially if it's a long value like California or Pennsylvania. A newly assigned default value doesn't affect values already entered in the table; only new entries are affected.

A default value can be assigned to any type of field except an AutoNumber or an OLE Object. To assign one, enter the value in the Default Value property for the field. The type of value you enter depends on the data type. The value must also conform to the property settings and data type requirements. Some examples of default values are

Field	Data Type	Value
State	Text	CA
City	Text	"Los Padres" (If the value contains punctuation or spaces, it must be enclosed in quotation marks)
Hours	Number	8
Deposit	Currency	500
Entry Date	Date/Time	Date() (Automatically enters current system date)

TIP   *If you assign or change a default field value after entering record data, you can change the existing values to the new value by pressing* CTRL-ALT-SPACEBAR *with the insertion point in the field.*

NOTE   *If you want to assign a Yes/No field default value for use in a foreign country, enter an equal sign before the choice (=Yes) and the equivalent word from the local language of the computer will be displayed. For example, a Yes value would be displayed as Oui in France.*

You needn't be in Design View to create a new table; you can do it right in Datasheet View by entering data directly into a blank datasheet. Access automatically analyzes the data you enter and assigns the appropriate Data Type and Format to the field. If any ambiguity occurs, the field is considered to be a Text field.

To begin a new table in Datasheet View, do the following:

1. Start a new datasheet by one of the following methods:
   - Double-click the Create Table by Entering Data item in the Database window.
   - Open the New Table dialog box, choose Datasheet View, and then click OK.

2. A blank datasheet opens displaying 10 columns and 21 rows. The columns are named Field1, Field2, and so on.

3. Enter the field names in each column by double-clicking the column header and replacing the default Field*n* caption. If you enter the fields in the wrong order, you can always change the order later in Design View.

4. Enter the field data for each record, and then click Design View.

TIP   *To copy the field value from the previous record, use the ditto key combination,* CTRL-' *(apostrophe).*

---

5. Switch to Design View and save the table with the desired name. Access offers to assign a primary key when it saves the new table or you can designate one in Design View.

Figure 4-8 shows the design of a table created in Datasheet View.

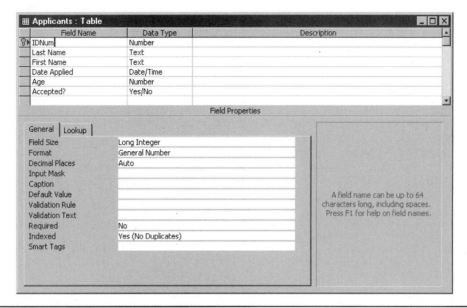

FIGURE 4-8   The table design created in Datasheet View

NOTE   *Access has automatically assigned data types to the fields depending on the data you entered. The unused fields are also eliminated from the design.*

Copying an Existing Table Structure

If you already have a table with a structure similar to what you need now, you can save time by copying the structure to a new table without the data. Then change the field names and properties as necessary. To copy the table structure, follow these steps:

1. Select the existing table name in the Database window.

2. Click Copy on the toolbar or choose Edit | Copy.

3. If you want to copy the structure to a different database, close the current one and open the target database; otherwise, keep the Database window open.

4. Click Paste or choose Edit | Paste to open the Paste Table As dialog box.

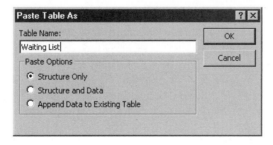

5. Enter a name for the new table, choose Structure Only, and then click OK.

The new table inherits the field properties from the original table.

Setting Table Properties

Two types of table properties are available in an Access database: table object properties and table definition properties. *Table object properties* include name, owner, dates of creation and last revision, and attributes, such as Hidden or Replicable. You can view these properties by one of the following methods:

- Right-click the table name in the Database window and choose Properties from the shortcut menu.

- Select the table name and choose View | Properties.
- Select the table name and click the Properties button.

Table definition properties related to the table structure itself are available when the table is open in Design View. To open the table property sheet, do one of the following:

- Choose View | Properties.

- Click the Properties toolbar button.
- Right-click the field entry area and choose Properties from the shortcut menu.

To see a description of a property, select the property and read the description in the status bar.

How to Change the Default Table Design Properties

You learned earlier that the default field size for a Text field is 50 characters. This is one of the default table design properties you can change. To modify this and other default properties, choose Tools | Options, and then click the Tables/Queries tab (see Figure 4-9). The options include

- **Text Field Size (default 50)**   To change the default Text field size, enter the desired number.
- **Number Field Size (default Long Integer)**   To change the Number field, choose from the drop-down list of Number field sizes.
- **Default Field Type (default Text)**   To change the default field type, choose from the drop-down list of field types. Notice the list doesn't include Lookup Wizard as a field type.
- **AutoIndex on Import/Create**   This option gives you the opportunity to specify text often used at the beginning or ending of a field name as the basis for indexes when importing or creating tables. For example, typing **"ID";"num";"code"** automatically creates indexes for all fields containing those characters either at the start or the end of the field name. For example, with this setting, an imported table would be indexed on fields named Customer ID, JobNum, and ZIP code.

FIGURE 4-9   Setting the table design default properties

Summary

This chapter contained a great deal of information about constructing and modifying new Access tables, beginning with the Table Wizard. A table was also created by entering field specifications directly into a blank table design. It included choosing the best data type depending on what value you intend to store in the field and the operations with which you intend to use it. Other field properties were discussed as were primary key fields and creating indexes on one or more fields.

Modifying a table structure can be troublesome in some cases, such as changing the data type or shortening the field size. Ensuring data validity is one of the most important features Access offers. We discussed several means, including requiring specific fields, adding validity rules, and assigning default values.

In the next chapter, you learn how to relate tables by linking the common field. The chapter also covers specifying the type of relationship and modifying an existing relationship. It also discusses the types of joins that control the way data is retrieved by queries.

Relating Tables

The advantages of relating tables in a database are many. For example, information retrieval routines operate much faster with matched fields and errors are less likely to get into the database during data entry. Tables related at the table level in the Relationships window are ready for use in queries, forms reports, and data access pages. When tables are related, you can add a subform or subreport that includes corresponding information from the related table. Relating tables also helps maintain data integrity and cohesiveness.

You can define relationships between tables at any time, but the best time is when the tables are new and contain little or no data. When you design the database, one of the important steps is to decide on the relationships between the tables and which fields they have in common. As you create new tables, the Table Wizard can help you define relationships or you can wait until you have all the table structures built, and then define all the relationships at once.

Defining a Relationship

To define a relationship between two tables, all you need to do is specify which fields the tables have in common. In a one-to-many relationship, the field in the parent table is called the *primary key* and must be either the table's primary key or a unique index. The field in the child table is called the *foreign key* and it needn't have a unique value. Data retrieval is faster, however, if the child table is indexed on the foreign key.

In a one-to-one relationship, both fields are primary keys or unique indexes in their tables. A many-to-many relationship is really two one-to-many relationships in which a third table is created. The primary key of this third table is a combination of the common fields from the other two tables. The junction table becomes the "one" side for relationships to both the original tables. See the "How to Create a Many-to-Many Relationship" sidebar later in this chapter for details.

TIP *Defining table relationships at the table level keeps the relationships active and makes the database easier to use. You can link two tables temporarily in a query when you want to draw information from more than one table, but the permanent relationship is preferred. You can always break it later, if necessary.*

Ready-Made Relationships

If you used the Table Wizard to create a new table, you might already have some defined relationships with the other tables in your database. As you saw in Chapter 4, when you add a new table to your database with the help of the Table Wizard, one of the dialog boxes asks you to specify how the new table is to relate to the existing tables in the database, if at all.

The first database illustrated in this chapter was created by adding tables to a blank database with the Table Wizard. Here are the relationships created by the Table Wizard that link the existing Employees and Customers tables to the newly created Time Billed table. The Employees and Customers tables weren't linked until the Time Billed table was added to the database.

TIP *The sequence in which you add tables to the database determines which relationships the wizard automatically builds. If you added the Time Billed table before the Employees table, Access wouldn't relate the Employees table to the Time Billed table.*

NOTE *The lack of symbols at the ends of the relationship lines indicates that referential integrity rules aren't enforced. When the Table Wizard creates a relationship, it doesn't automatically set referential integrity. To add this, you must modify the relationship in the Relationships window. You can still tell which is the "one" side of a one-to-many relationship by the primary key, which appears in bold. Because it must have a unique value, only one record in that table can match the field in the other table.*

Using the Relationships Window

Access provides a powerful, graphical tool to help you define and modify relationships. The Relationships window has all the tools you need to add a table or query to the relationship, relate the tables and queries, specify the type of relationship, set up the referential integrity rules, and choose the join type. To open the Relationships window, choose Tools | Relationships, or click the Relationships button on the Database toolbar. If no relationships are defined in the current database, the Show Table dialog box appears in a blank Relationships window. The dialog box displays a list of all the tables and queries in the current database. This database was created by using the Table Wizard to add the first three tables to a blank database. Then the Invoices table was created from the table Design window without the help of the Table Wizard.

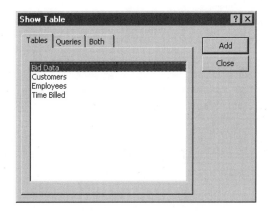

Relationships are usually drawn between tables, but you can also include queries. Queries can give you access to data from several tables at once without having to add all the tables referenced in the query.

NOTE   If any relationships already exist between tables in the database, Access goes directly to the Relationships window without displaying the Show Table dialog box. To add a table to the Relationships window, click the Show Table button on the toolbar or choose Relationships | Show Table to open the Show Table dialog box.

To add the tables you want to relate from the list, do one of the following:

- Double-click the table's name or select the table and click the Add button.

- To select multiple adjacent tables, select the first table to be included, hold down SHIFT as you select the last table in the list to be included, and then click the Add button. If the table names aren't adjacent in the list, hold down CTRL while you select the names.

- Click the Queries tab to add a query to the Relationships window.

- Click the Both tab to have access to a combined list of tables and queries.

After you add all the tables and queries you want to work with in the Relationships window, click Close.

Touring the Relationships Window

The Relationships window shows the field lists of the tables you chose. The lists display the primary key field, if any, in boldface. Use the scroll bars to see all the fields, or resize a field list box by dragging the bottom border to see more names or the right border to see complete field names. You can also drag the field list boxes around in the window for better viewing.

This particular Relationships window shows all four tables, three created by the Table Wizard, and the Invoices table created from scratch. Relationships exist only among the first three.

NOTE *If you use the Table Wizard to create all four of the tables, they would all show relationships.*

Before going on to join the tables, look at the new toolbar buttons on the Relationships toolbar and menu options in the Relationships window.

Toolbar Button	Description
Show Table	Opens the Show Table dialog box with lists of all tables and queries in the current database.
Show Direct Relationships	Displays the relationships for the selected table.
Show All Relationships	Displays all relationships in the current database.
Clear Layout	Removes all tables and relationships from the Relationships window. This doesn't alter the relationships themselves.

Three shortcut menus are available in the Relationships window by right-clicking a field list box, an empty area in the Relationships window, or on the center part of a relationship line:

- The Field List shortcut menu includes—in addition to Show Direct—the Table Design (or Query Design) option, which opens the Design view for the selected table or query, and the Hide Table option, which temporarily removes the table or query from the display, not the layout. Hide Table is also available from the Relationships menu.

- The Relationships window shortcut menu includes—in addition to Show Table and Show All—the Save Layout option, which saves the current arrangement of field list boxes in the Relationships window.

- The Relationship line shortcut menu includes Edit Relationship, which opens the Edit Relationships dialog box, and Delete, which removes the relationship you right-clicked. Edit Relationship is also available from the Relationships menu.

Drawing the Relationship Line

It couldn't be easier to relate two tables. You simply drag a field (usually the primary key) from one table and drop it on the corresponding field (the foreign key) in the other table. The field names needn't be the same, but they usually need to be the same data type and contain the same kind of information. If you intend to enforce referential integrity, the fields must be the same data type. If the fields are Number fields, they must also have the same Field Size property.

Two exceptions occur to the requirement to match data types in the related fields.

- An AutoNumber field with the New Values property set to Increment can be linked to a Long Integer Number field. AutoNumber values are stored as four-byte numbers. For the foreign key to have a matching value, it must contain a number of the same size: a Long Integer.

- An AutoNumber can be linked to a Number field if both fields have the Field Size property set to Replication ID.

TIP   *Dragging the foreign key field from the related table to the primary key field in the primary table creates the same relationship.*

To relate the Customer table to the Invoices table by CustomerID, do the following:

1. Click the CustomerID field in the Customers field list and drag it to the CustomerID field in the Invoices field list.

2. Drop the linking field into the child table. The Edit Relationships dialog box opens.

TIP   *Notice that Access recognizes this relationship as a one-to-many because one of the fields is a primary key and the other isn't. If both fields were primary keys, Access would recognize the relationship as one-to-one. If neither field is a primary key nor has a unique value, Access calls the relationship Indeterminate.*

---

3. Verify the field names that relate the tables, and then do one of the following:

   - If you want to change the field at either side of the relationship, you can select a different field from the drop-down field list under the table name.

   - If you want to add another relationship between the same tables that relates two different fields, move to an empty row in the grid, click the down button, and choose from the list for each table.

   - If you chose the wrong foreign key, choose Cancel in the Edit Relationships dialog box and start over in the Relationships window.

   - If you type the first few letters of the field name in the Edit Relationships dialog box grid, Access will fill in the rest for you.

   - To complete the relationship, choose Create and you return to the Relationships window. Figure 5-1 shows the Relationships window with the new link drawn between the tables.

   - To complete the relationships in the window, repeat the previous procedure to draw the relationship line from the EmployeeID field in the Employees field list to the EmployeeID field in the Invoices field list.

Relating to Two or More Foreign Keys

If you need to create relationships from a primary table to two or more foreign keys in the same table, Access creates additional instances of the table in the Relationships window.

FIGURE 5-1   A new relationship line is drawn between two tables.

You don't have two copies of the table in the database, only in the Relationships layout. Figure 5-2 shows a Relationships window with three copies of the Employees table with the EmployeeID primary key field relating to the Supervisor, Principal Worker, and Helper foreign keys in the Workorders table.

Note that the relationships all have referential integrity enforced, as you can tell by the symbols at the ends of the relationship lines. Referential integrity is discussed in the next section.

Enforcing Referential Integrity

As discussed in Chapter 2, *referential integrity* is a set of rules that attempts to keep a database complete and without loose ends. No related records can exist without a parent. When you want Access to enforce the referential integrity rules on the relationship you're defining, check Enforce Referential Integrity in the Edit Relationships dialog box. If, for some reason, the tables already violate one of the rules, such as the related fields not being of the same data type, Access displays a message explaining the violation and doesn't apply the enforcement.

NOTE   *Referential integrity isn't enforced on queries included in a relationship.*

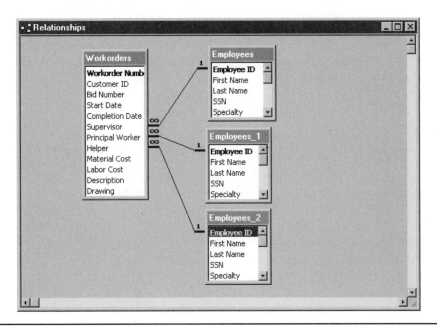

FIGURE 5-2   Relating one table to three fields in another table

When you check the Enforce Referential Integrity option, two options become available that let you override some restrictions.

With these options checked, if you delete a record from the parent table or change one of the primary key values, Access automatically makes changes to the child table to preserve referential integrity. Without checking one of these options, Access displays a warning message if you try to delete a parent record that still has child records.

The Cascade Update Related Fields option lets you change the value in the primary key field in the parent table and Access automatically changes the foreign key value in the child table to match. For example, if you change the CustomerID value in the Customers table, all records for that customer in any related table are automatically updated to the new value. This option preserves the relationship. Access doesn't display a message that the update operation is taking place. If the primary key in a table serves as a link to more than one table, you must set the Cascade Update Related Fields property for each of the relationships. If not, Access displays a message that referential integrity rules would be violated by the cascading operation and refuses to delete or update the record.

NOTE   *Setting the Cascade Update option has no effect if the primary key is an AutoNumber field because you can't change the value of an AutoNumber field.*

The Cascade Delete Related Records option enables you to delete a parent record, and then Access automatically deletes all the related child records. When you try to delete a record from the parent table of a relationship with this option selected, Access warns you this record and the ones in related tables will be deleted. For example, if you delete an Employee record, Access automatically deletes all the records for that employee in the related tables.

CAUTION   *Setting the Cascade Delete Related Fields property can be dangerous. If you delete records using a Delete query, Access automatically deletes the related records without issuing a warning.*

Creating a One-to-One Relationship

At times, you might want to store information about a particular subject—such as an item of merchandise or an employee—separate from the main pieces of information. For example, you might have data about an employee, such as name, address, and Social Security number

How to Create a Many-to-Many Relationship

In a many-to-many relationship, a record in one table (call it Table A) can have several matching records in another table (Table B) and vice versa. Neither table is considered the parent table because the linking field isn't the primary key in either table. The only way you can create such a relationship is by creating a third table, called a junction table. This new table has a primary key that's a combination of at least the primary keys from Tables A and B. The *junction table* acts as a bridge between the two tables when you build two one-to-many relationships between them. You can add other fields to the junction table like any other table.

Because several products could be included in a single order and several orders could include the same product, this represents a many-to-many relationship. To define the relationship in Access, the junction table Order Details was created with a primary key that combines the foreign keys from the Products table (ProductID) and from the Orders table (OrderID). Both field names appear in boldface in the Order Details table, indicating that, together, they constitute the primary key. Two one-to-many relationships then link the Products and Orders tables to the Order Details table.

in one table where they're readily available, but keep other data, such as the resume and employment history, in another table. These two tables are then related using a one-to-one relationship because only one record in each table matches one record in the other table. Both tables include a primary key field, such as the employee identification number.

To relate two tables with a one-to-one relationship, do the following:

1. Choose Tools | Relationships or click the Relationships toolbar button in the Database window.
2. If the tables you want to relate don't appear in the Relationships window, click the Show Table button.
3. Select the tables in the Show Table dialog box, and then click Close.
4. Drag the primary key field from one table and drop it on the key field on the other table. The direction you go doesn't matter; the same one-to-one relationship is created.

Specifying the Join Type

One of the most powerful Access tools is the query that extracts and brings together data from more than one source. Many queries also carry out an action with the data. For example,

---

Understanding Joins

You can specify three types of joins through the Join Properties dialog box:

- Option 1 includes only records where both parent and child have the same values in the linking fields (no orphans and no childless parents). This is called an *inner join* or an *equijoin* and it's the default join type.

- Option 2 includes all the records from the table on the left, even if no corresponding values are in the other table and only the matching records from the table on the right. This is called *a left outer join* (all parents, including the childless, but no orphans).

- Option 3 is the opposite of Option 2 and includes all the records from the table on the right and only matching records from the left table. Called a *right outer join* (all children, but no childless parents). If Referential Integrity is enforced, there will be no children without a parent.

If you have trouble deciding which table is the "left" in the relationship, look at how we read a sentence: from left to right. Read a relationship from primary table (left) to related table (right). Physical positioning in the layout doesn't matter.

If you select an outer join, an arrow at one end of the relation line points to the table whose value must match to be included in the query results. In a one-to-many relationship, the *one* side is considered the left table and the *many* side is the right table.

Note, you can also create a fourth type of join: a *self join*, which includes records from two instances of the same table. For example, you can add a self join to a query design to display the Supervisor's name instead of the Supervisor ID when extracting records from the Employees table. The Supervisor's name is in the Name field in the Employee record with the Supervisor ID value in the EmployeeID field.

you might want to see how much time each employee spent working on service for each current customer. To do so, you need information from the Time Billed, Employees, and Customers tables. Once the data is extracted, the query adds up the hours for records with matching employees and customers. See Chapter 8 for a full description of the power of queries.

For a query to know how to associate records from the three tables, the tables must be related. When you define each relationship, you can also specify the type of join you want for the tables. The join type specifies which records to display in a query based on related tables when they don't correspond exactly. For example, do you want the parent record to appear only if corresponding child records exist or do you want to see all parent records even if there are no related child records?

NOTE *The join type doesn't affect the relationship, it simply tells Access which records to include in a query.*

To modify the relationship between the Employees and Time Billed tables, and to set the join type, do the following:

1. In the Relationships window, right-click in the middle of the relationships line joining the Employees table with the Time Billed table and choose Edit Relationship from the shortcut menu. The Edit Relationships dialog box opens.

2. Click the Join Type button to open the Join Properties dialog box.

3. Select Option 2 as the type of join for this relationship because you want to see all the Employee records even if they have no related records in the Time Billed table. Notice the explanatory text is specific with respect to the tables you related.

4. Click OK in the Join Properties dialog box.

5. Click OK in the Edit Relationships dialog box.

Figure 5-3 shows the completed layout for four tables in a database that tracks customer billing and prepares invoices. The relationships that include referential integrity show a 1 on the "one" side and an infinity sign (∞) on the "many" side. Relationships with no referential integrity enforced appear as lines with small dots at each end. Relationship lines with no arrows represent inner joins. An arrow on a relationship line means the join is an outer join and the arrow points to the table whose values must match to be included in the query results. The relationship between Employees and Time Billed tables is a left outer join with referential integrity enforced.

No referential integrity enforced

Left outer join with referential integrity enforced

Inner join with referential integrity enforced

FIGURE 5-3   This layout contains four related tables.

Saving the Relationships Layout

All relationships are saved when you create them. You can also save the *layout,* the arrangement of the field lists in the Relationships window. Saving the layout has no effect on the tables in the database.

To save the layout, do one of the following:

- Right-click anywhere in the Relationships window (except on a field list) and choose Save Layout from the Relationships shortcut menu.

- Choose File | Save.

- Press CTRL-S.

If you made changes in the layout and try to close the Relationships window without saving the layout, Access prompts you to save it. If you want to discard the changes, choose No. When you open the Relationships window again, the previously saved layout is displayed.

TIP   *While you're defining relationships, you can always call for help. You can type a specific question in the Type a question for Help box, and then press* ENTER.

Viewing and Editing Relationships

To look at the relationships you defined for a database, open the Relationships window. If you plan on making any changes, be sure to close all open tables first.

Viewing Existing Relationships

You have a choice of viewing all the relationships you set in your database or only those involving a specific table. In the database window, click the Relationships toolbar button or choose Tools | Relationships.

TIP   *You can quickly switch to the database window by pressing* F11.

In the Relationships window, do one of the following:

- To view all the relationships in the current database, click the Show All Relationships toolbar button or choose Relationships | Show All.

- To see only the relationships for the table selected in the database window, click the Show Direct Relationships or choose Relationships | Show Direct.

If all the relationships already appear in the Relationships window, perform the following steps to see only one table's relationships:

1. Clear the layout by clicking the Clear Layout toolbar button. Click Yes to confirm the action.

2. Click the Show Table button, double-click the table name in the Show Table dialog box, and then choose Close. This adds the table back to the Relationships window.

3. In the Relationships window, click the Show Direct Relationships button. All the tables related to the first are added to the layout and the relationship lines are drawn.

Hiding or Deleting a Table

If the Relationships window becomes too crowded, you can hide a table or delete it from the layout. To delete the table from the layout, select the table and press DEL, or choose Delete from the Edit menu. This affects only the display of the layout and doesn't remove the relationship or the table from the database.

If you want to remove the table temporarily to make room for manipulating the relationships, hide the table instead. To hide the table, choose Relationships | Hide Table, or right-click the table and choose Hide Table from the shortcut menu. The next time you view the Relationships window, all the tables will reappear, unless you save the layout with the changes.

Restoring All Relationships

To restore the relationships layout to its previous arrangement, close the window without saving the changes. When you reopen the window, the old layout returns. If you want to keep the window open, right-click in the Relationships window and choose Show All from the shortcut menu, click the Show All Relationships toolbar button, or choose Relationships | Show All Relationships.

Modifying or Deleting a Relationship

Relationships aren't cast in concrete. You use the same Relationships window to edit a relationship that you used to create one.

TIP   *You can even open a Table Design window from the Relationships window and modify the table structure, as you see in the next section. This comes in handy if you need to make sure the related fields are the same data type or if you want to create an index to speed processing.*

Editing a Relationship

To edit an existing relationship, do the following:

1. Open the Relationships window as before.

2. If you don't see the relationship you want to change, choose Show Table from the Relationships menu, double-click the missing table, and choose Close.

3. When you see the join line that represents the relationship you want to change, do one of the following to open the Edit Relationships dialog box:

    - Double-click the line.

    - Right-click the line and choose Edit Relationship from the shortcut menu.

4. Make the changes you want, and then click OK.

Deleting a Relationship

To delete a relationship, click the join line to select it and do one of the following:

- Press DEL.

- Choose Delete from the Edit menu.

- Right-click the line and choose Delete from the shortcut menu.

Access asks for confirmation before permanently deleting the relationship, no matter which method you use. Be careful not to delete a relationship used by a query.

NOTE   *Pressing DEL with a table selected only removes the table from the layout, while pressing DEL with a relationship line selected permanently removes the relationship between the tables.*

Changing a Table Design from the Relationships Window

You might need to make a change in a table design to create the relationship you want. For example, the primary key might be a Text field, while the foreign key is a Number field. This is all right unless you want to enforce referential integrity, which requires the same data type in both fields. You can open the child table design and change the field type to Text. If you already set a relationship between the tables, you must delete the relationship before you can change the table design. You might also want to add a secondary index on the foreign key in the child table to speed processing.

To switch to the Table Design view from the Relationships window, right-click anywhere in the table's field list box and choose Table Design from the shortcut menu. When you finish changing the table design, save the changes and close the window. You then return automatically to the Relationships window.

Printing the Relationships

Documentation is always helpful, especially if you work with several databases or develop applications for others. Once you define all the relationships for the database, graphically documenting the structure is easy.

To print the table relationships diagram, do the following:

1. In the Relationships window, right-click in an empty area and choose Show All.

2. When all tables appear in the layout, choose File | Print Relationships. Figure 5-4 shows the printed layout of the Home Tech Repair database relationships.

Although the primary key fields don't appear in bold in the printed diagram, you can use the join line symbols as a guide to the linking fields.

TIP   *You might need to run Page Setup, and then reduce the left and right margins or change to Landscape orientation to print the entire diagram on one page.*

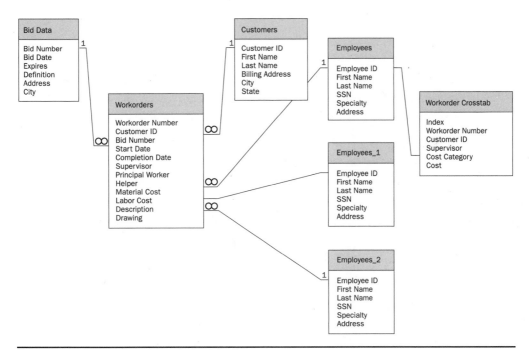

FIGURE 5-4   Printed database relationship diagram

If you want more precise information about the relationships you established in the database—including the attributes such as referential integrity and the relationship type—you can use the Documenter, one of the Access analytical tools.

1. Choose Tools | Analyze | Documenter. The Documenter dialog box opens showing eight tabs applying to the database objects and the database itself. If you see a message saying the Documenter isn't installed, you can have it installed now.

2. When the Documenter dialog box opens, click the Current Database tab, and then click the Relationships check box.

3. Click OK to print the relationships in table form. A preview of the Relationships document appears after a few moments. Figure 5-5 shows the printed first page of the documented relationships that exist in the sample Northwind database that comes with Access 2003.

Summary

In these first chapters, you learned the importance of creating relationships among tables in a database. The tables and their relationships form the structure on which the other database objects are based. Queries can extract related information from multiple sources. Forms and reports can include data from many tables.

You saw how to create and modify tables and, in this chapter, you learned how to create and modify relationships between the tables and set other properties, such as referential integrity and join type. Referential integrity matches data from different tables and helps to ensure data validity. The join type determines which records are to be extracted by a query.

Now you're ready to move on to entering and editing the table data you'll use in later chapters. The next chapter goes into detail about entering and editing data in tables, including creating lookup lists and customizing data entry. You also see how to use the versatile Spelling tool and the AutoCorrect feature that corrects your spelling as you type.

After the information is stored in your database, the world is yours. You can retrieve some or all of the information, display it in forms, and print it in reports. You can even export it to other applications or publish it on the Internet.

Relationships

EmployeesWorkorders

| Attributes: | Enforced |
| RelationshipType: | One-To-Many |

EmployeesWorkorder Crosstab

| Attributes: | Not Enforced |
| RelationshipType: | One-To-Many |

Bid DataWorkorders

| Attributes: | Enforced, Cascade Updates |
| RelationshipType: | One-To-Many |

CustomersWorkorders

| Attributes: | Enforced, Cascade Updates |
| RelationshipType: | One-To-Many |

EmployeesWorkorders

| Attributes: | Enforced |
| RelationshipType: | One-To-Many |

FIGURE 5-5   Printing the database relationships

Entering and Editing Data

D ata errors have a way of burrowing deep into the database where they're difficult to detect and remove. Trying to prevent errors from getting into the database in the first place makes sense. Access provides many helpful tools to ensure data validity, including specifying the data type, format, field size, and validation rules discussed in Chapter 4.

This chapter discusses more tools that improve the chances for achieving data validity, as well as speeding the data entry process. Techniques such as copying quantities of data from other sources, selecting values from lookup lists, and using shortcut keys all help ease the chore of data entry. Other Microsoft Office tools, such as the spelling checker and AutoCorrect features, also help to keep the database accurate and complete.

Entering New Data

When you open a new table, it appears in Datasheet view, ready for data entry. To add a new record, do one of the following:

- Click the New Record toolbar button.
- Click the New Record navigation button.
- Choose Edit | Go To | New Record.
- Choose Insert | New Record.

TIP   *You could also simply scroll down to the blank records at the end of the table and start typing.*

To navigate among records, use the vertical scroll bar, the navigation buttons at the bottom of the Datasheet view window, keyboard shortcuts, or the Go To command in the Edit menu. To move among fields or columns, use the horizontal scroll bar, the TAB or ENTER keys, or keyboard shortcuts. See Chapter 1 for details about moving about in Datasheet view.

When the insertion point moves to an empty field, type in the data. If you specified a custom format, the entered value adapts to that format when you move to the next column. If you created an input mask for that field, the mask appears when you enter the field and before you begin to type the data. See a later section in this chapter for details about input masks and how they compare with display format settings.

Date/time data can be entered in any valid format and Access converts it to the format you specified in the field property. Don't expect to enter decimal fractions in number fields that are defined as integers.

NOTE   *Choosing Records | Data Entry opens a blank datasheet for the current table where you can enter new records without having to view the existing records. This is called the Data Entry or Add mode and can be applied to forms, as well as to datasheets. After entering the new data and closing the additive datasheet, the new records are added to the underlying table.*

When the table contains many fields, some of them might not always be visible. Instead of scrolling right and left to enter data in long records, you can use the Go To Field box on the Formatting (Datasheet) toolbar.

The Go To Field box is leftmost on the toolbar and contains a list of all the fields in the current datasheet. Click the arrow next to the box to display the list of fields in the current table. When you click a field name in the list, the insertion point moves to that field in the current record.

NOTE   *The Formatting (Datasheet) toolbar might already be showing when you're in Datasheet view but, if you don't see it, you can display it easily. Right-click the menu bar or another toolbar and click Formatting (Datasheet) in the list. You can also choose View | Toolbars and select Formatting (Datasheet) from the list.*

NOTE   *Entering a large amount of text in a Memo field can be difficult in Datasheet view. One way to see all the text in the field is to use the Zoom box while you're entering the data. Press SHIFT-F2 to open the Zoom box and press ENTER to close it after entering the text. If you want to start a new paragraph or enter a blank line in the memo text in the Zoom box, press CTRL-ENTER. The Zoom box isn't limited to Memo fields. It can be used anywhere text is entered to give you a larger entry area.*

Copying and Moving Data

Access provides some shortcuts for entering repetitive data by copying or moving existing data. You can copy or move all the data or only individual field values from one record to another. Copying creates exact duplicates of the data in the new location. Moving cuts the data from one location and places it in another, leaving only one copy of the data.

When you collect items by copying or cutting them from their source, they're placed on the Office clipboard, which is shared by all Office programs. The clipboard is a task pane that can hold up to 24 items with previews of the text or pictures that have been copied (see Figure 6-1). You can paste them singly or as a group to a new location. When you reach the 25th item on the clipboard, the first item is deleted.

If you don't see the task pane, right-click in a blank area in the toolbar and choose Task Pane. If you've copied any items (not just from Access or even another Office program) during the current session, it will appear in the Clipboard task pane.

To paste an item from the clipboard, place the insertion point where you want to paste it and click the item in the clipboard. To delete an item from the clipboard, click the down arrow to the right of the item and choose Delete from the menu. To close the clipboard side

FIGURE 6-1   Copying items to the Clipboard

pane, click the Close button in the upper-right corner. To display it later, choose Edit |
Office Clipboard or click the icon on the Windows taskbar. If you see a different task pane,
click the Other Task Panes down arrow and select Clipboard from the list.

NOTE   *You can modify the behavior of the clipboard by clicking the Options button at the bottom of
the pane. The options include Show Office Clipboard Automatically, Show Office Clipboard When
CTRL-C Pressed Twice, Collect Without Showing Office Clipboard, Show Office Clipboard Icon
on Taskbar, and Show Status Near Taskbar When Copying. All but the second and third options
are usually selected by default.*

You can cut or copy items using the Edit menu or the toolbar buttons. You can also
display the Clipboard side pane and use it to copy-and-paste items.

- Click Copy to add the selected item to the clipboard.
- Select one item in the clipboard and click Paste.
- Click Paste All to paste all the items to the same document.

The items you've collected on the clipboard remain there until you close all the Office
programs you have running on your computer. If a number of items are still on the clipboard
when you close Access, Access might ask if you want to keep them there for use by another
Office program.

Copying and Moving Within the Same Table

To copy a record within the same table, first select the record you want to copy by clicking
the record selector—the small gray button to the left of the record. Then click the Copy
toolbar button or choose Edit | Copy. This copies the data to the clipboard. Click the record
selector in the record you want to replace, and then click Paste. The new record contains an
exact copy of the original record. If you want to add the copy as a new record rather than
replace an existing one, select the empty record at the bottom of the datasheet, and then click
Paste. To remove the data, once the record is selected, use the Cut option instead of Copy.

TIP   *Some neat key combination shortcuts: CTRL-C (Copy), CTRL-X (Cut), and CTRL-V (Paste)*

Access tries to save the copied record when you move out of it. If the table has a
primary key or a unique index, Access won't let you leave the new record until you replace
the duplicate value with a unique one.

TIP   *If the primary key field is an AutoNumber data type, Access automatically increments the
number rather than copying the original number—just another reason to use an AutoNumber
field as the primary key.*

To copy or move more than one record, select all the records before choosing Copy or
Cut. When replacing records, select the same number of existing records as you placed on
the clipboard, and then click Paste. If you want to append the new records to the table instead
of replacing existing ones, do one of the following:

- Select the new empty row at the bottom of the datasheet and click Paste.
- Choose Edit | Paste Append.

In either case, Access asks for confirmation when you try to paste multiple records.

If the table has a primary key or a unique index that isn't an AutoNumber, you can't paste multiple records without removing the key or index first. Unlike pasting a single record, Access would have to save all but one of the records and this would create duplicate values in the field. If you try, Access displays an information message.

If you need to paste the value in a single field to the next record while you're entering data, you can quickly copy the value from the corresponding field in the previous record to the new record by pressing CTRL-' (apostrophe).

Copying and Moving from Another Table

To copy or move records from another table, select the records in the source table and choose Copy or Cut. If you choose Cut, you're asked to confirm you want to delete the record(s) from the source table. Then switch to the destination datasheet and select the blank row at the bottom of the datasheet. When you click Paste, the new records are added to the destination datasheet.

CAUTION   *The fields in the copied records are pasted in the same order as they appeared in the original datasheet, regardless of the field names. You might need to rearrange the columns in the destination datasheet before pasting, so they correspond with the incoming fields. Inconsistent data types or sizes between the incoming records and the destination can result in problems.*

If you want to replace certain records in the destination datasheet with records from another table, select the records you want to replace before clicking Paste.

To append records from another table to the existing datasheet, choose Edit | Paste Append. If the source table has more fields than the destination table, the excess fields aren't pasted.

> **TIP**   *If you're pasting records from another application, be sure to check the arrangement of the data before attempting to copy or move it into an Access datasheet. It should be arranged in a spreadsheet, a word-processor table, or as text separated by tab characters before you select it. See Chapter 23 for more information on exchanging data with other applications.*

Fixing Paste Problems

You've heard this warning before, but here it is again—always save a backup copy of your data before attempting anything new. This applies to many of the copying and moving operations, which aren't vulnerable to Undo. If Access asks for confirmation before executing the operation, it most likely can't be undone once you say Yes.

When errors occur during a paste operation, Access creates a Paste Errors table and displays a message advising you of the errors as each is added to the table. To view the Paste Errors table, double-click the table name in the Tables page of the Database window.

Some of the problems you might encounter when trying to paste data into a datasheet include the following:

- You might try to paste values of incompatible data types, such as pasting a value that contains letters and numbers into a Currency field.

- The value you try to paste might be too long for the destination field. Compare the Field Size properties of both fields.

- You might have tried to paste a value into a hidden field. Return to the datasheet and choose Unhide from the Format menu to reveal the hidden columns.

- A value you're trying to paste might violate one of the property settings, such as the Input Mask, Validation Rule, Required, or Allow Zero Length setting.

When you open the Paste Errors table, you might be able to paste the data in the destination table field by field.

Inserting Pictures

The Home Tech Repair Employees table has a field reserved for the employee's badge picture. The Badge Picture field is an OLE Object data type and stores a file containing the digitized photograph.

An Object Linking and Embedding (OLE) object is created by an application outside Access and can be inserted into an Access table. Objects can be images, sounds, charts, video clips, or nearly any product of another application. Source applications can include Word, Excel, sound or video recorders, or an image scanner.

The object can either be linked to the Access table or embedded in it. *Linking* is the process by which the object remains in its source application and Access reaches it by means of a link or pointer to the object's location. If the linked object changes in the source application, the Access version also changes. Linking also helps keep database files from getting huge because picture files can be quite large. The disadvantage is that if you move the database, you have to restore the linkage. *Embedding* an object stores a static copy of the object in the Access table, form, or report. Changes in the original don't reach the Access copy automatically.

Two other definitions are called for here: bound and unbound objects. A *bound object* is one stored directly in an Access table as part of the stored data. An *unbound object* is one added as an element to a form or report design, and isn't directly related to the table data.

The Badge Picture photos are OLE objects created by a scanner and are contained in image files, such as .tif, .gif, or .pcx. Because the photos aren't expected to change, they're embedded in the table. In addition, they represent the value stored in the Badge Picture field, which means they're bound objects.

To insert an image in the Badge Picture field:

1. Place the insertion point in the Badge Picture field and choose Insert | Object, or right-click the field and choose Insert Object from the shortcut menu.

2. In the Insert Object dialog box, choose Create from File.

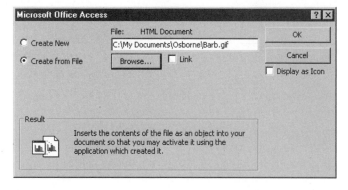

3. Type the path and filename of the image file in the File box, or click Browse and look for the object.

4. After entering the filename, choose OK to embed the picture in the field.

When you return to Datasheet view, the field now contains the name of the source of the OLE object.Other entries indicate other types of objects. To see the image, create a form by clicking New Object: AutoForm. Figure 6-2 shows one of the Employee records with the Badge Picture embedded. If you see the filename instead of the picture, double-click the filename.

Other options in the Insert Object dialog box include the following:

- Link, which creates a link to the OLE Object, rather than embedding it.

- Display As Icon, which displays only an icon representing the source object, instead of the object itself.

FIGURE 6-2   Viewing a picture inserted into a record

NOTE   *Chapter 10 contains more information about using OLE and other objects when creating form and report designs.*

Inserting Hyperlinks

A *hyperlink* is a connection to an object in the same or another Access database, to a document created in another Office program, or to a document on the Internet or your local intranet. You can link to any OLE or ActiveX application on your computer or local area network (LAN). The *hyperlink field* contains the address of the target object and, when you click the hyperlink, you jump to it. If the object is the product of another application, that application is automatically started.

In the Home Tech Repair database, the Workorders table contains a hyperlink field that contains the engineering drawings for that work order. The scanned drawings are saved as .gif files in the same folder as the database itself.

Defining the Hyperlink Address

A hyperlink address can contain up to four parts, separated by the pound sign (#)

displaytext#address#subaddress#screentip

of which only the address or, in some cases, the subaddress is required.

- The *displaytext* is optional text to display in the field in place of the actual address. If you don't include display text, the hyperlink address or subaddress appears instead.

- The *address* is either a Uniform Resource Locator (URL), such as a Web address, or a Universal Naming Convention (UNC) path to the document. An *absolute path* starts with \ \ and describes the exact location on the system or LAN. A *relative path* is related to the current path or the base path specified in the database properties. An address is required, unless you added a subaddress that points to an object in the current database.

- The *subaddress* contains a named location within the target object, such as a bookmark in a Word document, a particular slide in a PowerPoint presentation, or a cell range in an Excel spreadsheet.

- The *screentip* is the text that appears when you rest the mouse pointer on the hyperlink. If you don't specify a ScreenTip, the address is displayed.

Here are some examples of hyperlinks and their targets:

- *Presentation#c:\Demos\HomeTech.ppt#Click to preview Home Tech slide* jumps to the first slide in the PowerPoint presentation named HomeTech. Displays Presentation in place of the address and shows a ScreenTip.

- *Rhythm&Blues#c:\Favorites\Old Tunes.doc#RandB#Click to see a list of old tunes* jumps to the RandB Bookmark in the Word document named Old Tunes in the Favorites folder. Displays Rhythm&Blues in place of the address and shows a ScreenTip.

- *Summer Schedule#http://www.va.com/summer/schedule.html#Route* jumps to the location named Route within the HTML file on VA's web site named schedule.html. Displays Summer Schedule in place of the address and shows a ScreenTip.

Entering the Hyperlink Address

You have several ways to enter a hyperlink address that's unique for each record in a form or datasheet, depending on the intended target of the hyperlink:

- Type the hyperlink address directly in the field.
- Use the Insert Hyperlink toolbar button or choose Insert | Hyperlink.
- Copy-and-paste a hyperlink or hyperlink address from another source.
- Copy-and-paste text from another Office document.
- Drag-and-drop an Internet shortcut.

TIP *If you type the address, you must include the pound signs (#). If you use the Insert Hyperlink feature, Access adds them to the address for you when it assembles the address parts.*

The scanned drawings for the Workorders Drawing field are stored in the folder with the database. To use Insert Hyperlink to enter the hyperlink address, do the following:

1. Place the insertion point in the Drawing field in the Workorders datasheet.

2. Click Insert Hyperlink or choose Insert | Hyperlink. The Insert Hyperlink
   dialog box opens.

3. Click the Existing File or Web Page button under Link to, if not already chosen.
   Then do one of the following:

   - Type the path to the drawing file in the Address box. For example,
     c:\My Documents\Osborne\fireplace.gif.

   - If you've accessed the target of this hyperlink before, you can select it from
     the list of Recent Files or Browsed Pages.

   - Click the Browse For File button (the open folder) and locate the file in the
     Link to File dialog box. Then click OK.

4. Back in the Insert Hyperlink dialog box, enter the text you want to show in the
   field in place of the address in the Text To Display box. For example, you could
   enter **Fireplace**.

5. If you want to show a ScreenTip, click the ScreenTip button and enter the text in
   the Set Hyperlink ScreenTip dialog box. Then click OK.

6. Click OK to finish inserting the hyperlink and return to the Workorders datasheet where the hyperlink appears in the Drawing field. When you rest the mouse pointer on the hyperlink, you see the ScreenTip.

Workorders : Table			
Material Cost	Labor Cost	Description	Drawing
$1,182.43	$631.18	New Fireplace	Fireplace
$1,212.75	$882.00	Install 3 Attic V	
$893.03	$132.30	Inst 100g Heate	
$121.28	$330.75	Repl Countertop	
$275.63	$264.60	Move Washer &	
$787.50	$840.00	Ceiling Fans	
$2,625.00	$7,560.00	Finish Basemer	
$420.00	$787.50	Garden Window	Bay Window
$1,100.00	$450.00	SPA Heater	Heater
$183.75	$105.00	Repl Toilet	
$315.00	$1,365.00	Rpr Driveway	Fireplace
$294.00	$504.00	Erect Tool Shed	
$420.00	$1,155.00	Bay Window	Bay Window
$78.75	$315.00	Soaker System	
$441.00	$105.00	Install Dishwasl	

Click to show engineering drawing

7. Click the hyperlink to test it and Microsoft Picture Library opens, displaying the scanned fireplace drawing, as shown in Figure 6-3.

The other Link to buttons in the Insert Hyperlink dialog box help you:

- Link to objects in the current database.
- Create and link to a new document.
- Link to an e-mail address.

You can also click the Bookmark button and indicate a specific location in the target document.

Editing and Deleting Hyperlinks

Editing a hyperlink address is a little different than editing normal text because, if you click on the address, you jump to the target. You have two ways to edit the address:

- Open the Edit Hyperlink dialog box, which is similar to the Insert Hyperlink dialog box, and edit the address directly.
- Move to the field and switch to Edit mode.

To open the Edit Hyperlink dialog box, right-click the hyperlink, point to Hyperlink in the shortcut menu, and click Edit Hyperlink in the submenu.

Make the changes to the address in the Address box. You can also edit the display text and ScreenTip in the Edit Hyperlink dialog box the same way you specified them.

To edit the complete address in the datasheet, use the keyboard to move to the field. (Don't click in the field or you'll jump to the target.) Then press F2 to enter Edit mode and make changes in the address. If you can't read the whole address, press SHIFT-F2 to open the address in the Zoom box. You can change all parts of the address this way. The two consecutive

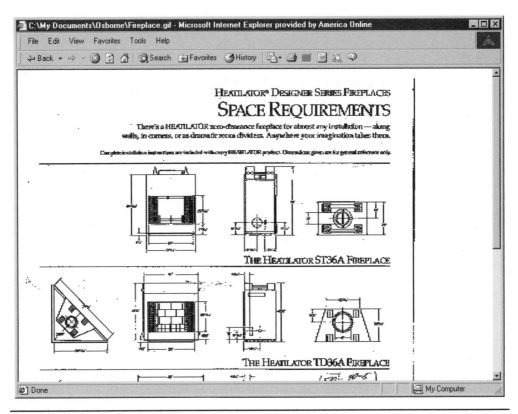

FIGURE 6-3 Viewing the target of the Fireplace hyperlink

pound signs between the address and the ScreenTip indicate no subaddress exists, but its relative position is preserved.

To delete a hyperlink address from a field, right-click the hyperlink and choose Cut from the shortcut menu or simply move to the hyperlink and press Delete. You can also point to Hyperlink in the shortcut menu and click Remove Hyperlink.

TIP   *Although Access removes the hyperlink address without asking for confirmation, you can easily restore it by clicking Undo or choosing Edit | Undo Delete.*

If you want to delete all the hyperlink addresses you inserted in a field, delete the field from the table design.

Customizing Data Entry

Data entry is, by nature, a time-consuming task. Access offers many tools to help improve its efficiency, some of which minimize the data entry process, while others assist in navigation in a datasheet or give you access to special symbols. The basic rule is "The more help you can provide, the better."

Adding Custom Input Masks

An *input mask* is a field property similar to the Format property, but with a different purpose. An input mask displays a fill-in blank for data entry, while a format is used to display field data with a consistent appearance. Setting the Format property affects how data is displayed after it's entered and offers no control over or guidance for the data being entered. Input masks can be used with Text, Number, Date/Time, and Currency fields.

To decide between a Format property and an Input Mask property, use the following guidelines:

- If you want to make sure the field values look the same when displayed, use the Format property to specify the desired appearance.
- If you want to have some control over data entry, use an input mask to guide data entry and make sure it's entered properly.

An input mask appears when the insertion point reaches the field, before any data is entered. The mask displays fill-in blanks with literal characters separating them. When you use an input mask, you can be sure the data fits the specifications you set by limiting the number of fill-in spaces. Depending on the characters you use in the mask, you can leave some fill-in spaces blank, but you cannot add more characters than spaces.

An input mask also can specify what kind of values you can enter in each space. Telephone numbers offer a good example to show the difference between Format and Input Mask properties.

- The format (@@@) @@@-@@@@ displays nothing on the screen before data is entered and displays (619) 555-8867 after you enter the phone number.
- The input mask (000) 000-0000 displays (___) ___-____ before data is entered and displays the same (619) 555-8867 after the number is entered.

The previous format displays the literal characters and the characters you enter or it leaves the spaces blank if no character is entered, but only after the record has been saved.

The input mask contains zeros, which require that all entries contain the right number of digits (and only digits) to represent a United States telephone number.

CAUTION   *If you set both a display format and an input mask, Access uses the input mask for entering and editing data, and the format setting for displaying entered data. If your results don't look quite right, you might have specified conflicting settings.*

You can create an input mask for Text and Date/Time fields with the Input Mask Wizard. If you want an input mask for a Number or Currency field, you must create it manually.

To create an input mask with the Input Mask Wizard, move the insertion point to the field in table Design view and click in the Input Mask property. Then do the following:

1. Click the Build button (...) at the right of the field's Input Mask property. The first Input Mask Wizard dialog box opens (see Figure 6-4) where you can select from a list of ten predesigned input masks appropriate for commonly used fields. The Try-It box shows how the mask works when displayed in Datasheet or Form view. Access might prompt you to save the table design before opening the first dialog box.

2. After selecting the mask similar to the one you need, click Next to move to the second dialog box. In this dialog box, you can make any necessary changes to the mask, such as changing the placeholder that displays as the fill-in blanks (the default is an underline character), and then click Next.

3. Choose to store the literal characters with the data, if desired. This uses more disk space, but the symbols are available when you want to use the value in a form or report, rather than having to specify them in the field format in the form or report design.

4. Click Finish to close the wizard.

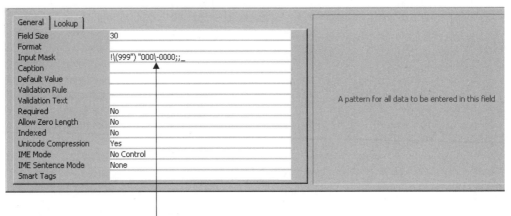

Input mask for Telephone field

If you have a customized field that isn't part of the Input Mask Wizard's repertoire, you can easily create your own mask manually with special symbols. The special symbols are placeholders that specify which entries are required and define what type of characters can

FIGURE 6-4   Choosing from predesigned input masks

be entered at each position in the mask. You can even add a custom mask to the wizard's list of predefined input masks. You cannot create an input mask for a Memo, AutoNumber, Yes/No, OLE Object, or Hyperlink field.

To build an input mask manually, enter the desired characters directly in the Input Mask property in Design view. Table 6-1 describes the symbols you can use in an input mask and whether they require an entry in that position.

In addition to the symbols in the previous table, you can add any of the characters that represent date and time separators, a decimal point, or a thousands separator. When you add these characters to the input mask, they appear in the fill-in field for data entry. Here are some examples of the effects of using input masks:

Input Mask	Description	Sample Valid Value
00000-9999	Zeros represent required entries, the 9s are optional.	92118-2450 or 92118-
(999) AAA-AAAA	Allows letters or digits. Area code is optional.	(301) 555-CALL
!>L0L 0L0	Converts all letters to uppercase. Fills left to right.	N0C 1H0
>L<??????????	Converts required initial letter to uppercase. Other characters are optional and converted to lowercase.	Henrietta
>LL0000-000	Two required letters converted to uppercase and seven required digits.	BT5430-115

To make a change in one of the wizard's masks, select the mask first in the Input Mask Wizard dialog box, and then click Edit List and proceed as in the previous table to make the desired changes.

Symbol	Entry	Entry Required?
0	Digit (0 through 9) with no + or − sign. Blanks display as zeros	Yes
9	Digit with no + or − sign. Blanks display as spaces	No
#	Same as 9, but allows +/− signs.	No
L	Letter (A through Z)	Yes
?	Letter	No
A	Letter or digit	Yes
a	Letter or digit	No
&	Any character or space	Yes
C	Any character or space	No
<	Converts letters to lowercase	N/A
>	Converts letters to uppercase	N/A
!	Characters typed into the mask fill it from left to right. Can appear anywhere in the mask	N/A
\	Next character is treated as a literal	N/A

TABLE 6-1   Input Mask Symbols

Three sections separated by semicolons are available in an input mask definition, as you saw in the Telephone input mask created earlier by the wizard:

!\(999") "000\-0000;;_

- The first section contains the mask itself, which has some interesting features. The exclamation mark tells Access to enter the characters from left to right. The opening parenthesis is preceded by a backslash telling Access the character that follows is a literal character. The closing parenthesis and the space that follows it are enclosed in quotation marks to indicate they're also literals. The dash separating parts of the phone number is also preceded by a backslash indicating a literal.

- The second section determines whether to store the literal characters with the data. Enter **0** in this section to store the characters; enter **1** or leave it blank to store only the characters entered in the fill-in blanks in the mask. In this example, the second section is blank.

- The third section specifies the character to use as the blank fill-in spaces in the displayed mask. For example, type a plus sign to use + in place of the default underline character. If you want to leave the fill-in spaces blank, type " " (space between the double quotation marks).

NOTE *Input masks defined in table Design view are automatically applied to the queries based on the table. They're also inherited by bound controls in forms and reports based on the table, if the form or report was designed after the mask was defined. Input masks for unbound controls must be manually set in form or report Design view. If you want to override the table-defined mask for a query or form (or report) design, change the Input Mask property for the control in the design. Clicking the Build button in the control's property sheet opens the Input Mask Wizard dialog box where you can make the changes. See Chapter 10 for more information on setting control properties in form and report designs.*

Creating Lookup Fields

A *lookup field* is an Access tool that makes entering data quicker and more accurate. A lookup field displays a list of values from which to choose. The most common type of lookup field, called a *lookup list*, gets its values from an existing table or query. The advantage of this type of lookup field is that the tables are related and, as the source list changes, the current values are available to the lookup field. The lookup table becomes the parent table and its primary key links it to the lookup field, which is the foreign key in the main data table.

Creating a Custom Input Mask

If you have a field that commonly appears in your tables or forms, such as the Canadian postal code, you can create a new input mask and save it in the Input Mask Wizard's list of predefined masks.

In table Design view, click the Input Mask property for the field, and then click the Build button to open the Input Mask Wizard dialog box.

1. Click Edit List. The Customize Input Mask Wizard dialog box displays the Phone Number input mask.

2. Click the New Record navigation button at the bottom of the dialog box to show a blank form.

3. Enter a description of the new mask, the mask itself, the symbol you want to use as the placeholder, and a sample of the data you intend to enter into the field.

> 4. Then select the Mask Type: Text/Unbound or Date-Time as the field data type to complete the definition for the Canadian postal code input mask.
>
>
> 5. Click Close. The new definition appears in the list of predefined masks.

The second type of lookup field gets its values from a list you type in when you create the field. This type is called a *value list* and is best used when the list is limited to a few values that don't change often, such as a short list of product categories or employee status. Once you add the list to a field, the list stays with it when you add the field to a data entry form.

You can add either type of lookup field in either Design or Datasheet view. If the field already exists in the table design and you want to change it to a lookup field, you must change the data type in Design view. To add a new lookup field to a table, do one of the following:

- In Design view, add a new field row and select Lookup Wizard from the Data Type list.
- In Datasheet view, click in the column to the right of where you want the new lookup field, and then choose Insert | Lookup Column. You might have to expand the menu list to see Lookup Column.

Either method starts the Lookup Wizard that displays a series of dialog boxes in which you specify the details of the lookup field. In the first dialog box (see Figure 6-5), you decide which type of lookup field to create: a lookup list that relates to a table or query, or a value list you type in.

If you choose to type in your list of values, the wizard displays a dialog box where you specify the number of columns you want in the list and enter the values. If you choose to get the values from another table, the wizard displays several more dialog boxes in which you do the following:

- Select the source table or query from the current database.
- Select the fields from the table you want to include.

FIGURE 6-5   Starting the Lookup Wizard

- Specify how you want the columns to look and whether to hide the primary key in the lookup table.
- Specify which field in the table is the key field.
- Enter a name for the lookup field.

Specifying a Lookup Column

As an example of defining a lookup field that gets its values from another table, insert a new field in the Workorders table of the Home Tech Repair database. The Workorders information can be easier to enter and read if a lookup field is used for the Supervisor, Principal Worker, and Helper fields. The list can display the last name of all the employees at Home Tech Repair. Then, rather than requiring the users to remember each employee's ID code, they can select the last name from a lookup column and have Access store the corresponding Employee ID value in the field. The Last Name is displayed, but the Employee ID will be stored. If two employees have the same last name, you can include the first name as well.

To add a lookup field to the Workorders table, follow these steps:

1. Open the Workorders table in Design view and insert a field named Supervisor between Completion Date and Principal Worker, choosing the Lookup Wizard data type.

2. In the first Lookup Wizard dialog box, choose the first option, I Want The Lookup Column To Look Up The Values In A Table Or Query. Then click Next.

3. Select Employees from the list of tables and click Next. You can also select a query as the source of the values.

4. In the next dialog box, double-click the Employee ID and Last Name fields in the list of available fields in the Employees table (see Figure 6-6). Then click Next.

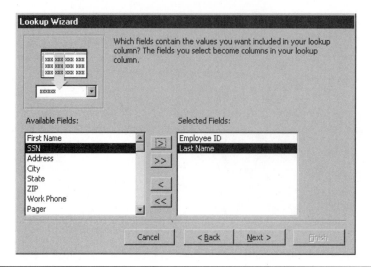

FIGURE 6-6   Selecting the fields for the lookup field

5. In the next dialog box, you can specify the sort order for fields in the lookup list. For example, by Employee ID, and then click Next.

6. The next dialog box (see Figure 6-7) shows you how the field values will look in the lookup column. If the column width is insufficient or unnecessarily wide, drag the right edge of the column header to change the width. (If no data exists in the lookup table, you won't see any values here, but the relationship is still created.) In addition,

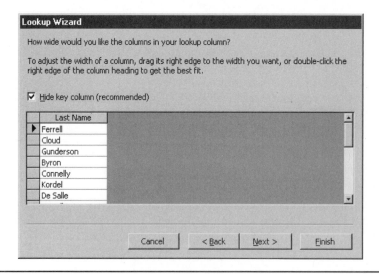

FIGURE 6-7   Changing the lookup column appearance

check the Hide Key Column (Recommended) option if not already checked, so you needn't view the Employee ID key value, only the last name. Click Next.

7. Accept the name Supervisor for the lookup column and click Finish. Access prompts you to save the table so the relationships can be completed. Choose Yes and you return to the table Design view.

The Lookup Wizard has set the properties for the new field based on your selections in the dialog boxes. You can view them on the Lookup tab of the Field Properties pane.

The *Lookup properties* specify the appearance and behavior of the lookup field when it appears in a datasheet or a form.

- The *Display Control property* determines the type of control implemented. The wizard chose a Combo Box. Other options are Text Box and List Box. See Chapter 10 for information about different types of controls.

- The *Row Source Type* indicates where the values come from that are displayed in the lookup column. Here the source is Table/Query. Other Row Source Types are Value List and Field List.

- The *Row Source property* specifies exactly the table and fields that comprise the list. To see the entire entry, right-click in the property text and choose Zoom from the shortcut menu. You can edit the statement in the Zoom box, if necessary, or change the font properties. Click OK to close the Zoom box.

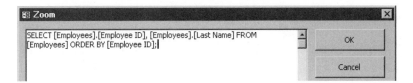

NOTE   *The SELECT statement in the Row Source property is a SQL statement created by the Lookup Wizard. See Chapter 9 for more information about creating and using SQL statements.*

- The *Bound Column* indicates which column in the list contains the linking field. The columns are numbered in the order they were selected in the wizard's dialog box. The Employee ID field—selected first—is the primary key in the Employees table, and so is assigned as the bound column for the lookup column.

- The *Column Count* specifies two columns from the related table are involved. One, the Employee ID, is stored in the Workorders table and the other, Last Name, is displayed in the lookup column.

- The No setting for Column Heads prevents the captions from the Employees table from displaying in the lookup list.

- The first Column Width setting is 0″, which keeps the first column, the Employee ID field, from being displayed. This selection was made when you checked the Hide Key Column option. The Last Name column is set to the width adjusted in the Lookup Wizard dialog box.

- *List Rows* tells Access how many rows to display at once, which indicates the height of the drop-down list.

- *List Width* specifies the overall width of the displayed list. If the text to be displayed in the list exceeds the column width in the datasheet or form, you can increase this value.

- The *Limit to List property* prevents the user from entering a value that isn't on the list. This is required in this case because the displayed value must be in the source table for the primary key value (Employee ID) to be retrieved and stored in the foreign key field in the Workorders table.

TIP   *With Limit to List set to Yes, you might still be permitted to leave the field blank. The combo box accepts null values unless the Required property of the Supervisor field is set to Yes.*

Switch to Datasheet view and click the down arrow in the Supervisor field to see the new lookup field used to locate employee names in the Employee table. The lookup field links the Employee table to the Workorders table by the Employee ID field. Although the employee's last name is displayed, the foreign key—Employee ID—is stored in the field, but isn't displayed.

Workorder Num	Customer ID	Bid Number	Start Date	Completion Date	Supervisor	Principal Worker	He
001	1032	98-101	2/25/2003	3/10/2003	Ferrell	Howell	
002	1033	98-103	3/15/2003	3/18/2003	Ferrell	Gikas	
003	1034	98-105	3/10/2003	3/5/2003	Cloud	Dobbins	
004	1035	98-107	4/15/2003	4/20/2003	Gunderson	Howell	
005	1036	98-108	5/10/2003	5/15/2003	Byron	Dobbins	
006	1037	98-111	5/12/2003	5/25/2003	Connelly		
007	1038	98-113	1/15/2003	9/15/2003	Kordel	Kordel	
008	1033	98-116	6/15/2003	7/1/2003	De Salle	Gikas	
009	1039	98-117	6/25/2003	6/26/2003	Howell	Howell	De Sal

Workorders : Table

Specifying a Lookup List

A static value list can be helpful when entering data in the Employees table. Because only a few valid values are in the Type field, this is a good candidate for streamlining. In the first Lookup Wizard dialog box, choose the second option, I Will Type In The Values I Want, and move to the next dialog box where you enter the values for the list.

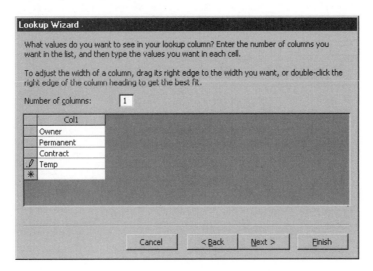

Field properties are inherited by forms and reports, including the lookup fields created in the table design. Figure 6-8 shows the new Type value list in the Employees AutoForm.

TIP   *When you use the value list in a form, you can set the control properties to allow the user to add values to the list during data entry. Be aware, though, if you change a value list definition after adding it to a form design, you must modify the control's Row Source property in the form's Design view to include the correct list. See Chapter 12 for more information about customizing form controls.*

Changing the Datasheet Appearance

Datasheet properties include the layout of the fields and records—the order in which the fields appear, the dimension of the rows and columns, and the column headings. Other properties are the font size and style, the colors of the text and the background, and special cell effects, such as raised or sunken.

You also have the option of hiding some fields from view if the data needn't be visible to all users of the database. Finally, if you have too many fields to view on the screen at once, you can keep one or more of the key fields on the left of the screen as you scroll right, so you can identify the current record.

Saving the modified datasheet appearance with the table preserves the appearance, so the next time you open the table in Datasheet view, it will look the same.

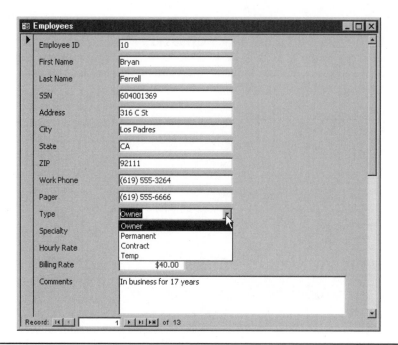

FIGURE 6-8   The lookup field property is inherited by the AutoForm.

Some datasheet properties, such as column width, can be changed directly in the Datasheet view. Others are accomplished with menu commands or dialog box options. Most of the formatting can be done easily by clicking buttons on the Formatting (Datasheet) toolbar.

Displaying Subdatasheets

After you open a table or query in Datasheet view, you can display a subdatasheet related to a row by clicking the expand indicator (+) to the left of the row. The indicator turns into a minus sign (–). To remove the subdatasheet from view, click the collapse indicator.

If the subdatasheet has a subdatasheet of its own, expand and collapse it using the same method. You can nest up to eight levels of subdatasheets. Each datasheet or subdatasheet can have only one nested subdatasheet. Figure 6-9 shows the Bid Data datasheet with three nested subdatasheets expanded: linked to the workorder, the supervisor, and other workorders supervised by the same employee.

NOTE   *Hiding and showing the columns in a datasheet or subdatasheet changes only the display and has no effect on the source object of the relationship.*

You can expand the subdatasheets for as many rows as you want. To display all the subdatasheets in the datasheet, choose Format | Subdatasheet | Expand All. To collapse them, choose Format | Subdatasheet | Collapse All.

By default, Access doesn't display the foreign key or matching field in the subdatasheet. The column is hidden from view. If you want to display the field, choose Format |

FIGURE 6-9   Expanding nested subdatasheets

Unhide Columns. Then, in the Unhide Columns dialog box, check the column you want to include and click Close. Displaying the column is only temporary. The next time you open the datasheet containing the subdatasheet, the column is hidden again.

NOTE   *Notice the navigation buttons at the bottom of the Datasheet window refer to the active subdatasheet.*

Moving and Resizing Columns and Rows

Access displays the data fields in columns in the same order as the fields appear in the table design, unless you change the column order. The columns, by default, are all the same width, so you might be unable to see the whole field value or the entire text of some of the field names. Other columns might be wider than necessary and waste screen space. The rows are also a standard height. You can change any of these datasheet properties:

Rearranging the Columns

You might always want some fields in your table to be visible in Datasheet view. If they're far down in the list of fields in the table design, they might be off the screen to the right. One solution is to change the order of the fields in the design, but it's easier to change the column order on the screen. You can move them to the left, so you won't have to scroll to see them.

To move a column, click the field selector and release the button. Then, move the mouse pointer to the field selector. When the mouse pointer changes shape to an arrow with a small rectangle, click-and-drag the column to the desired position. When you begin to move the column, a dark vertical line moves with it, showing you where the left boundary of the moving column is at that moment. The column itself doesn't move until you release the mouse button.

Changing the relative position of a column in the datasheet has no effect on the way the fields appear in the design or the way they're stored on the disk.

Changing the Column Width

Obviously, if all the columns are the same width, but your data and field names are all different widths, some adjustments might make the datasheet look better and make more efficient use of the screen area.

You can change a column width in three ways:

- By dragging the sizing line at the right border of the field selector button
- By double-clicking the column sizing line
- By setting the width in a dialog box

Dragging to a new width with the mouse is the easiest way to change a column width, but it isn't precise. To change the width with the mouse, move the mouse pointer to the column's right boundary line in the field selector. When the pointer reaches the right place, it changes shape to a plus (+) sign with right- and left-pointing arrows. Then click-and-drag the boundary to the right to increase or to the left to decrease its width.

TIP   *If you drag the right boundary all the way to the left until it reaches the left boundary, the column disappears. This is one way to hide a column. More about hiding columns in the section "Freezing and Hiding Columns."*

If you want the column just wide enough to fit the contents, double-click the right edge of the column heading.

If you need to be more precise about a column width, you can set the exact width in a dialog box. You can reach the Column Width dialog box in two ways after selecting one or more columns:

- By choosing Format | Column Width
- By right-clicking the field selector and choosing Column Width from the shortcut menu

The Column Width dialog box shown here displays the current column width, measured in characters, in the text box.

To change the width, type a new value in the Column Width text box, click to place a check mark in the Standard Width box to return to the default column width, or click Best Fit. The *Best Fit option* resizes the selected column or columns to fit the longest data in the field or the text in the column heading, whichever is longer.

NOTE *The only disadvantage to setting the column width to Best Fit is you might later enter some new data that's longer than anything before and, unless you return to the Column Width dialog box and recheck Best Fit, it won't be fully displayed in the new column width.*

If you want to change several or all column widths at once, so they fit the data and captions, you can select the columns before choosing Best Fit in the Column Width dialog box. Selecting Best Fit adjusts all the selected columns according to their contents.

NOTE *You cannot undo the changes you made in the column width by choosing Edit | Undo or by clicking the Undo toolbar button. If you want the columns restored to their original width, close the datasheet without saving the changes to the layout.*

Changing the Row Height

You can change column widths individually, but rows are different: they're all the same height and when you change the height of one, you change them all. For example, suppose you have a Memo field that usually contains two or three lines of text and you want to read them in Datasheet view. If you increase the row height to double or triple, you can fit the text in the space allowed. You might be able to combine adjusting the column width with increasing the row height to achieve the proper balance of dimensions.

The row height is modified the same way as the column width: by dragging a sizing line with the mouse or by entering the new height in a dialog box. To change the row height with the mouse, move the mouse pointer to any one of the row sizing lines in the record selector area. The mouse pointer changes shape to a plus sign again but, this time, with the arrows pointing up and down. Click-and-drag the line until the rows reach the desired height, and then release the button. All rows will be the same height.

To set a more exact row height, choose Format | Row Height to open the Row Height dialog box. The insertion point can be anywhere in the datasheet when you choose Format | Row Height. To use the shortcut menu, you must right-click in a selected row or any row selector, and then choose Row Height. The Row Height dialog box is similar to the Column Width dialog box, except there's no Best Fit option. The height is measured in points and the default height depends on the default font size.

Freezing and Hiding Columns

Two other properties of a datasheet deal with the display of the data. *Freezing* a column causes the data in it to remain on the screen as you scroll right to see fields in a long record.

Hiding a column prevents the data from displaying in the datasheet. Neither of these properties changes the way the data is stored, only the way it's displayed.

Freezing and Unfreezing Columns

If your datasheet has more columns than can fit across the screen, some of the information moves off the screen as you scroll right to see the rest of the data. One or two of these fields might contain information, such as the product number or a customer name that identifies the record. When you're editing the table data, keeping this data on the screen is helpful, so you can be sure you're editing the right records. When you freeze a column on the screen, the column and its contents are automatically moved to the left of the datasheet and kept on the screen, even when you scroll right.

To freeze a column, place the insertion point anywhere in the column you want to freeze, and then choose Format | Freeze Columns, or right-click in the column header and choose Freeze Columns from the shortcut menu. To freeze several adjacent columns, select them all before choosing Freeze Columns. If you want to freeze nonadjacent columns, freeze them one at a time in the order you want them to appear at the left of the screen. Access then moves them, one by one, to the left side of the datasheet.

To unfreeze the columns, choose Unfreeze All Columns from the Format menu.

TIP   Unfortunately, Access doesn't return the thawed column to the position it was in before freezing and moving it to the left. You have to move the thawed column back yourself after unfreezing it or close the table without saving the changes in the layout to restore the original arrangement.

Hiding and Unhiding a Column

If your table contains irrelevant information to the current activity, you might not want it to take up space on the screen. In this case, you can hide one or more columns from view. Again, this changes only the appearance of the datasheet, not the data stored in the table.

You saw earlier that you can hide a column by reducing its width to nothing. Another way to hide a column is to place the insertion point anywhere in the column and choose Format | Hide Columns. You can also right-click in a selected column or in the field selector and choose Hide Columns from the shortcut menu. The column immediately disappears from the screen. If you want to hide several adjacent columns, select them all first. If you want to hide nonadjacent columns, reposition them so they're adjacent, and then hide them as a group or hide them one at a time.

NOTE   If you try to copy or move records to a datasheet that currently has hidden columns, the data won't be entered and you'll get paste errors. Be sure to unhide all the hidden columns before attempting to copy or move records.

To return the hidden columns to the datasheet display, choose Format | Unhide Columns. The Unhide Columns dialog box appears with a list of all the fields in the datasheet. Check marks next to the field names indicate the fields currently in view. If a field doesn't show a check mark, it's currently hidden. To return a field to the datasheet display, check the box next to its name. You can see the data being restored to the screen behind the dialog box when you click the check boxes. Choose Close after you return all the desired fields to the display.

TIP   You can also use the Unhide Columns dialog box to hide columns at the same time by removing the check marks.

Changing the Font

Access uses 10-point Arial as the default font for datasheets. The font setting applies to all the characters in the datasheet—data and captions alike. You might want to reduce the font size to get more data on the screen. Or, you might want to enlarge the font size to make it more visible if a group is going to view the screen from a distance. You can also change to any font your computer system supports. The row height and column widths are automatically adjusted to accommodate the font changes.

To change the datasheet font, choose Font from the Format or the shortcut menu to open the Font dialog box (see Figure 6-10). Select the font, size, and effects you want, and then click OK.

You can also use the Formatting (Datasheet) toolbar buttons to change the font properties. Any changes you make affect the entire datasheet.

Changing Grid Lines and Cell Appearance

Now comes the fun part—making some dramatic changes to the appearance of the datasheet with colors and special effects. The *grid lines*—the horizontal and vertical lines that separate the datasheet into rows and columns—are displayed by default, but you can remove either the horizontal or vertical lines, or both. The *cells* are the boxes at the intersection of the rows and columns. In addition to changing the appearance of the grid lines, you can apply special effects to the cells to make them appear raised or sunken.

To change the datasheet properties, choose Format | Datasheet. The Datasheet Formatting dialog box opens, as shown in Figure 6-11.

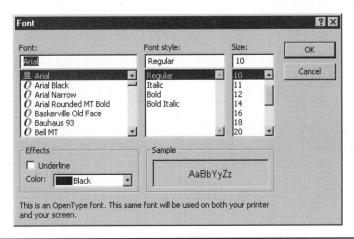

FIGURE 6-10   Customizing the datasheet font style

FIGURE 6-11   Setting cell and gridline formats

In the Datasheet Formatting dialog box, you can make the following changes:

- Set a special cell effect, such as Raised or Sunken.
- Show or hide either or both the horizontal and vertical gridlines.
- Change the color of the gridlines and the cell background.
- Change the style of the borders and gridlines to weights ranging from transparent to double-solid.
- Change the column display direction from left-to-right (the first field appears in the first column, the second in the column to the right, and so on) to right-to-left (the first field appears in the right-most column, the second in the column to the left, and so on).

As you make changes in the dialog box, the combined effects are shown in the Sample panel.

You can also use buttons on the Formatting toolbar to change the appearance of the datasheet gridlines and cells.

Clicking either *color* button displays a palette of colors from which to choose. Clicking the *Gridlines* button opens a palette with options for displaying both the horizontal and vertical gridlines, either, or none. Clicking the *Special Effects* button shows a palette with the three types of effects: Flat, Raised, and Sunken.

Setting Datasheet Default Options

To save the new datasheet appearance, save the layout with the table. To create a custom datasheet layout for use with all the tables in the database, change some of the default datasheet options. Choose Tools | Options to open the Options dialog box and click the Datasheet tab, as shown in Figure 6-12.

The available options are

- **Default colors**   Lists 16 colors you can use for the font, background, and gridlines.
- **Default font**   Specifies the font, weight, size, and style. The text appears in the color set in the Default Colors box.
- **Default gridlines showing**   Displays or hides horizontal and vertical gridlines. Gridlines displayed appear in the color set in the Default Colors box.
- **Default column width**   Sets the standard width for all the columns in the datasheet.
- **Default cell effect**   Specifies one of three cell effects: Flat, Raised, or Sunken.

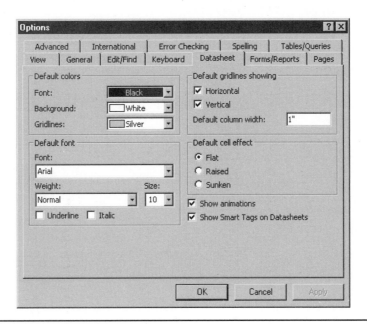

FIGURE 6-12   Setting datasheet default options

- **Show animations**   When checked, turns on the animations features, such as showing the columns sliding over to make room when you insert a new column.
- **Show Smart Tags on Datasheets**   When checked, displays a purple dotted line under text to indicate a smart tag.

Changing Table Definition in Datasheet View

Although the best place to modify the table definition is in Design view, you can make some limited changes in Datasheet view.

Inserting a Subdatasheet

If the Subdatasheet Name property for the table on the "one" side of a one-to-many relationship is set to Auto, Access automatically creates a subdatasheet with records from the table on the "many" side. The datasheet and subdatasheet are related by matching the primary key and foreign key fields. To see the table properties, open the table in Design view and click the Properties toolbar button.

You can add a subdatasheet to any table or query by specifying the source name in the Subdatasheet Name property and setting the linking fields. You can also use the Insert menu to add a subdatasheet to a table. Open the table or query in Datasheet view, and then do the following:

1. Choose Insert | Subdatasheet. The Insert Subdatasheet dialog box opens showing three tabs: Tables, Queries, and Both.
2. Click the tab that contains the datasheet you want to use for the subdatasheet.
3. Select the table or query name in the list.
4. Choose the foreign key field for the subdatasheet table or query in the Link Child Fields box.
5. Choose the primary key or matching field for the open datasheet in the Link Master Fields box (see Figure 6-13).
6. You can add other subdatasheets to the active table datasheet using the Insert subdatasheet dialog box and, when you finish, click OK.

NOTE   *If you want to link by more than one field, separate the field names with semicolons. Both field lists must contain the same number of field names and be in the same order.*

To remove a subdatasheet from a table or query, open the table or query in Datasheet view and choose Format | Subdatasheet | Remove. The subdatasheet is only removed from the display. The data isn't affected and the relationship remains intact.

TIP   *If your subdatasheet shows the same data for all the rows in the datasheet, you might not have specified the linking fields.*

FIGURE 6-13   Inserting a subdatasheet

Inserting/Deleting a Column

As you saw in Chapter 4, you can create a new table in Datasheet view by entering data directly in a blank datasheet. Access defines the data type to agree with the values you enter. The same principle applies to adding a new field in a table in Datasheet view. Insert a new column, change the caption to the name you want for the field, and then type in the data.

To insert a column, place the insertion point in the column to the right of where you want the new one and choose Insert | Column. A new blank column appears and the columns to the right move over. Double-click the field selector—usually labeled Field1—and rename the column with the appropriate field name.

NOTE   *If you want to change the data type Access assumes for the field, define a validation rule, or change other properties, you must switch to Design view.*

As discussed earlier in this chapter, the Insert menu offers two special columns: Lookup and Hyperlink. If you choose Lookup Column, the Lookup Wizard starts. Choosing Hyperlink Column inserts a new blank column, but the field is automatically specified as the Hyperlink data type.

To delete a column in Datasheet view, click anywhere in the field, and then choose Edit | Delete Column. Access warns you the deletion will be permanent. This is one of those cases where Undo doesn't work. Choose Yes to go ahead with the deletion or No to cancel. You can delete only one column at a time.

NOTE   *You cannot delete a field that's part of a relationship without first deleting the relationship. Either open the Relationships window to delete the relationship if you want to or accept Access's offer to delete it for you.*

Changing Field Names

You already learned how to create a name for a field in Design view. You also saw how to give a field a new name when you created a table from a blank datasheet. In Datasheet view, you have three ways to rename an existing column:

- Double-click the text in the field selector and type the new name.
- Select the column and choose Format | Rename Column.
- Right-click the field selector and choose Rename Column from the shortcut menu.

All three methods place the insertion point in the field name text where you can replace or edit the existing name. In addition, any existing field Caption properties are deleted.

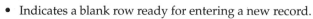

Editing Record Data

The standard methods of moving around a datasheet or form to edit record data haven't changed with Access 2003. You use the Edit | Go To menu or the navigation buttons at the bottom of the datasheet or form to move to another record: Next, Previous, First, Last, or New. The TAB key and the RIGHT ARROW and LEFT ARROW keys move to another field.

To change the entire value in a field, select the field and enter the new value. To edit only part of the value, change to Edit mode by clicking in the field or pressing F2. Once in Edit mode, the RIGHT ARROW and LEFT ARROW keys move the insertion point through the characters, instead of among the fields.

The icons that appear in the record selector at the far left of the datasheet row are the record indicators that show the status of the current record.

- Indicates the current record, not in the process of editing.
- Indicates changes are underway in the current record. Access saves the record when you move to another record.
- Indicates a blank row ready for entering a new record.

NOTE   *A fourth record indicator, a circle with a diagonal line through it—the international symbol meaning Don't—shows the record is undergoing changes and is locked by another user. If this appears, you must wait to make your changes to the record.*

The behavior of the ENTER, TAB, and the arrow keys can be customized, as described fully in Chapter 16. For example, by default, when you press ENTER to move to the next field, the field is selected. You can change this so the insertion point arrives at the first or last character in the value instead of selecting the field.

Selecting Records and Fields

The mouse is a convenient tool for selecting characters, fields, and records in Datasheet view. Table 6-2 describes the mouse techniques for selecting data.

To Select	Mouse Action
Characters in a field	Click at the start and drag across the data.
Entire field	Click the left edge of the field when the mouse pointer changes to a hollow plus sign.
Adjacent fields	Click the left edge of the first field and drag to extend the selection.
Column	Click the field selector.
Adjacent columns	Select the first column and, without releasing the mouse button, drag over the adjacent columns.
Record	Click the record selector.
Adjacent records	Select the first record and drag over the adjacent records.

TABLE 6-2   Using the Mouse to Select Fields and Records

You can also use many keyboard shortcuts to select data. The results of pressing certain keys and key combinations depend on the current mode in Datasheet view. When viewing a table in Datasheet view, you have a choice between Navigation or Edit mode. In *Navigation* mode, the insertion point isn't visible and you can move between fields and records using the arrow keys. If you're in *Edit* mode, the insertion point appears in a field and the arrow keys move it among the characters in the field.

To switch between Edit and Navigation modes, press F2 or click in the current field. While in Navigation mode, you can switch between selecting the first field of the current record or the entire record by pressing SHIFT-SPACEBAR.

Refer to Help topics for details of the many shortcut key combinations you can use to select table data. You can also see the shortcut key combinations with menu commands and as screentips with toolbar buttons, if those options are selected. See Chapter 20 for information about menus and toolbars.

If you often need to extend a selection, you can switch to Extend mode by pressing F8 one or more times. Each time you press F8, the extension applies progressively to the word, to the field, to the entire record, and, finally, to all the records. While in Extend mode, the right and left arrow keys extend the selection across the characters in the current field. If the entire column is selected, the arrow keys extend the selection to the adjacent columns in the datasheet. The UP ARROW and DOWN ARROW keys extend the selection to adjacent rows. If you change your mind, cancel the extension by pressing SHIFT-F8. To cancel Extend mode, press ESC.

TIP   *You can tell you're in Extend mode by the letters EXT appearing in the Datasheet view status bar.*

Locating Records

If a table doesn't contain a lot of records, you can probably find the record you want by scrolling down through the records in the datasheet or form, especially if the records are sorted by the field you're searching. If your table contains hundreds of records, however, that method is rather time-consuming. In the unlikely event that you know the number of the record you want to locate, you can find it using Edit | Go To or the navigation button.

Another way to locate a specific record is by the value in a specific field. Access has provided you with the Find feature, available as a toolbar button, as well as a menu option. Just tell Access what you want to find, and where and how to search for the value. The search can apply to the complete value in the field or only to certain characters within the field.

NOTE   *If you're looking for values in a datasheet with a subdatasheet or a form with a subform, Access searches only the object that contains the insertion point.*

Finding an Exact Match

 To find a record with a specific value in one of the fields, place the insertion point anywhere in the column and click the Find toolbar button, choose Edit | Find, or press CTRL-F. The Find and Replace dialog box opens, and you specify the search you want to conduct.

For example, place the insertion point in the Specialty field in the Employees table of the Home Tech Repair database and click Find. In the Find and Replace dialog box (see Figure 6-14), enter **Labor** as the value to look for in the Find What box, and then click Find Next. The insertion point moves to the next record with that value.

Clicking Find Next again finds subsequent records with the same value in the field. After Access has found the last record that matches the value, choosing Find Next displays

	State	ZIP	Work Phone	Pager	Type	Specialty	Hourly Rate	
+	CA	92111	(619) 555-3264	(619) 555-6666	Owner	Engineering	$30.00	
+	CA	92111	(619) 555-8912	(619) 555-8444	Contract	Engineering	$30.00	
+	CA	92111	(619) 555-7243	(619) 555-8456	Contract	Carpentry	$45.00	
+	CA	92111	(619) 555-1281	(619) 555-8478	Permanent	Finishing	$15.00	
+	CA	92111	(619) 555-5932	(619) 555-4533	Permanent	Plumbing	$40.00	
+	CA	92111	(619) 555-6193	(619) 555-4538	Permanent	Electrical	$40.00	
+	CA	92111	(619) 555-8346	(619) 555-4689	Contract	Masonry	$40.00	
+	CA	92111	(619) 555-2666	(619) 555-6890	Contract	Labor	$7.00	

Employees : Table

Find and Replace

Find | Replace

Find What: Labor

Find Next   Cancel

Look In: Specialty

Match: Whole Field

Search: All

☐ Match Case   ☑ Search Fields As Formatted

Record: 8 of 13

FIGURE 6-14   Finding records with a specific value in a field an information dialog box indicating no more records exist with that value. The Find in Field dialog box remains on the screen until you click the Close command button.

TIP *If you placed the insertion point in the middle of the table, Access searches to the last record, and then begins at the first record until all records have been examined.*

Limiting or Expanding the Search

By default, Access searches only the specified field in all the records. In the Look In box, you have a choice between the field that contains the insertion point or the entire table. You can expand the search by choosing the whole table—for example, Employees:Table— in the Look In box. Access searches for the value in all the Text and Memo fields in the table. This is slower than limiting the search to a single field, but it comes in handy for finding specific values in all fields, especially when you want to replace one value with another globally.

TIP *One way to speed up the search process is to index a field if you expect to search it often with Find and Replace.*

Two of the options can be used to limit or expand the search. If you're interested in finding only one occurrence of the value rather than all of them, you can limit the search to a subset of the records. The Search option drop-down list includes the following:

- **All (the default setting)** Begins at the current record, searches to the end of the table, and then begins again at the first record.
- **Up** Searches from the current record toward the first record.
- **Down** Searches from the current record through the remaining records.

TIP *You can close the Find and Replace dialog box anytime—you needn't find all the occurrences of the value before you can go on to something else.*

The *Match Case* option, when checked, treats uppercase and lowercase letters as different characters. For example, if you enter the value "labor" in the Find What box and check Match Case, Access won't find "Labor." If you check Match Case, Search Fields As Formatted is dimmed.

The *Search Fields As Formatted* option lets you look for the field based on the display format, rather than the stored value. For example, suppose you have a date field displayed in the format 15-May-04, but it's stored as the value 05/15/04. If you want to look for it as 15-May-04, check the Search Fields As Formatted option. This type of search is slower than looking for the stored value.

Finding an Inexact Match

Access offers two ways to find an inexact match in a Text or Memo field: by setting the Match option to limit the search to only part of the field or by using wildcards in the search string.

The Match options specify whether to require a complete and exact match or to accept a match with only part of the field. The Match options include the following:

- **Whole Field (default)**   Finds only records containing values that exactly match the search string.

- **Any Part of Field**   Finds records whose field contains the search string anywhere in the field. For example, if you want to find all work orders with the word "heater" somewhere in the description, you would ask Access to find a match anywhere in the field.

- **Start of Field**   Specifies the first one or more characters to match with the field values. For example, if you want to locate records for all customers whose last name begins with the letter *A*, you would use the Start of Field Match option.

Several wildcard characters can be used in the search string to represent one or more characters. For example, if you know only part of the value you want to find or if you want to find records that match a specific pattern, wildcards can be used in the search string.

Wildcards can be mixed and matched to create the string combination you need. Most of them can also be used in queries and expressions, as you see in Chapters 8 and 9. Table 6-3 describes the wildcard characters and gives examples of how each can be used.

TIP   *While wildcards are intended for use in search strings that locate values in Text and Memo fields, they can sometimes be used with dates and other data types. If you changed the Regional Settings properties for the other data types, the wildcards probably won't work.*

Wildcards can appear anywhere in the search string in the Find What box. For example, you can enter the string **12##[BC]*** to find all addresses in the 1200 block of any street that begins with *B* or *C*.

Wildcard	Matches	Example
*	Any number of characters	**b*** finds "bird," "belt," and "blueberry"
?	Any single character	**b??l** finds "ball," "beal," "bell," "bowl," but not "bali" or "bal"
[]	Any character within the brackets	**b[aeo]ll** finds "ball," "bell," and "boll," but not "bill" or "bull"
!	Any character not in the brackets	**b[!ae]ll** finds "bill," "boll," and "bull," but not "ball" or "bell"
- (hyphen)	Any character in the specified range of characters. The range must be in ascending order	**B[a-d]t** finds "bat," "bbt," "bct," and "bdt"
#	Any single numeric character	**10#** finds "100," "101," "102," and so on, but not "10A"

TABLE 6-3   Wildcard Characters

Looking for Wildcard Characters

The field value you're looking for could include one of the characters Access recognizes as a wildcard, such as an asterisk (*), a question mark (?), a number sign (#), an opening bracket ([), or a hyphen (-). If you use the character directly in a search string, Access treats it like a wildcard.

When you use wildcards in a string to look for one of these characters, you must enclose the item you're looking for in brackets. For example, to find a value that begins with ?B, you would use the string **[?]B***.

But, if you're looking for a hyphen along with another wildcard character, you need to treat it a little differently. Access interprets a hyphen (-) or a tilde (~) as an indication of a sequence of acceptable characters. You must put it before or after all the other characters inside the brackets, not between them. If you placed an exclamation point (!) inside the brackets to indicate a match excluding the characters within the brackets, place the hyphen right after the exclamation point.

If you're searching for an exclamation point or a closing bracket, you needn't use the brackets at all. Just place the characters in the string with the rest.

TIP   *If you included A inside the square brackets, Access would also find addresses on streets with Avenue as part of the street name.*

Finding Blank Fields

As mentioned in Chapter 4 in the discussion of zero-length strings and null values, you can use Find to locate records with blank fields. This is useful when you enter incomplete record data because all the information wasn't yet available. Then, when more data arrives, you can quickly look for the records that need to be filled in.

To find blank fields, enter **Null** or **Is Null** in the Find What text box. When Access finds a record with a blank in the field, the record selector moves to the record, but the field isn't highlighted. When you close the Find and Replace dialog box, the insertion point appears in the blank field, ready for you to enter data.

If you created a custom format for a Text or Memo field, which specifies a certain display if the field contains a null value, and a different display if it contains a zero-length string, you need to watch how you apply the Search Fields As Formatted option.

In addition, be sure to select Whole Field in the Match box when you're looking for either a null value or a zero-length string.

Finding and Replacing Data

A variation of the Find feature is the *Replace* tool, which lets you specify a value you want in the field in place of the one already there. The search options are the same. The only difference between the Find tab and the Replace tab is the addition of the Replace With box in which you type the replacement value.

To replace a certain value in a field with another value, click the Find button and open the Replace tab or choose Edit | Replace.

For example, suppose you want to replace all occurrences of the word "Lost" in the Award Date field of the Bid Data with the words "Not awarded." Follow these steps:

1. Place the insertion point in the Award Date column.

2. If you already had the Find dialog box open, click the Replace tab. Otherwise, choose Edit | Replace to open the Replace tab of the Find and Replace dialog box.

3. Enter **Lost** in the Find What box and **Not Awarded** in the Replace With box. Notice you have the same search options as with finding records.

4. Click Find Next, and then do one of the following:

   - Choose Replace to replace this instance of Lost. Access moves automatically to the next occurrence.

   - Choose Find Next to skip replacing this occurrence and move to the next.

   - Choose Replace All to replace all the values without reviewing them.

5. Access displays a message when it finishes searching the records. Click Cancel to close the dialog box.

If you have a large amount of data to replace, you can do that faster by using an update query. The only disadvantage is the update query replaces all the values without your confirmation of individual replacements. If you want to find and replace values in more than one field, the update query isn't as convenient as Find and Replace.

NOTE   *As with searching for a value, if the datasheet contains a subdatasheet or the form contains a subform, the replacement occurs only in the object containing the insertion point.*

Setting Edit/Find Options

Many of the Edit and Find options you choose in the Find and Replace dialog box have default settings that can be changed in the Edit/Find tab of the Options dialog box (see Figure 6-15). Choose Tools | Options to open the Options dialog box. The Default Find/Replace Behavior options present combinations of the Search and Match settings in the Find and Replace dialog box as follows:

   - **Fast search**   Searches the current field and matches the whole field.

   - **General search**   Searches all fields and matches any part of the field.

   - **Start of field search**   Searches the current field and matches the beginning characters in the field.

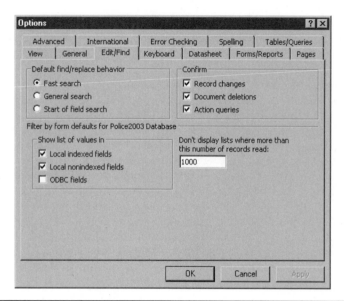

FIGURE 6-15   Setting Find/Replace default options

CAUTION   *The Confirm options specify when Access is to display a confirmation message: before changing records, deleting a document, or running action queries. A good idea is to leave these options all enabled because these actions cannot be reversed by Undo.*

The Filter By Form default settings are discussed in Chapter 7.

Deleting Data

To delete individual characters, place the insertion point in the field and press DEL to remove the next character or press BACKSPACE to remove the previous character. To delete all the data in the field, select the field and press DEL or BACKSPACE. Characters deleted from a field can be restored by choosing Edit | Undo Delete.

To delete an entire record, select the record and press DEL or choose Edit | Delete. Deleting a record cannot be reversed, so Access warns you before deleting the record. To delete several records, select them all, and then proceed as previously described. To delete a record without selecting it, place the insertion point anywhere in the record and click Delete Record.

TIP   *If you need to delete many records, you might be able to use a Delete query. See Chapter 9 for more information.*

Using the Spelling Checker and AutoCorrect

Among the most helpful editing tools is the spelling checker, which can check spelling as you type and offer suggestions for replacing misspelled words. The AutoCorrect feature can automatically correct commonly misspelled words. Access makes full use of these Office grammar and editing tools.

After you enter data in a Text or Memo field, select the records, columns, or fields you want to check, and then click the Spelling button, choose Tools | Spelling, or press F7. To check all the Text and Memo fields in the table, select the table name in the Database window and start the spelling checker.

If the spelling checker encounters a word that isn't in the dictionary, whether it's misspelled or simply not recognized, it displays a Spelling dialog box. If the word resembles one in the dictionary, a list of suggestions from which to choose is presented. You can accept one of the suggestions, enter a new word, add the word to your dictionary, or ignore it altogether.

You can specify some of the spelling options, such as what suggestions to make, what types of errors to ignore, and which language dictionary to use as a reference.

If you want Access to correct misspelled words and ones you habitually mistype as you enter text, activate the AutoCorrect feature. This feature can also be used to replace abbreviations with longer words. For example, you could speed data entry by having Access convert "Jr" to "Junior." When you type **Jr** and press SPACEBAR, TAB, ENTER, or a punctuation mark, Access automatically replaces it with "Junior."

To start automatic correction, choose Tools | AutoCorrect Options. The AutoCorrect dialog box opens with five options, plus a list of corrections and other replacements it's prepared to make. The options include the following:

- Correct TWo INitial CApitals
- Capitalize first letter of sentences
- Capitalize names of days
- Correct accidental use of cAPS LOCK key
- Replace text as you type

The fifth previous option contains a list of replacements for many typical spelling errors. You can add more replacements to the list. The AutoCorrect feature is used by all the Microsoft Office programs. Any entries you make in other programs are applicable to misspellings in Access.

You can also specify exceptions to the AutoCorrect rules by clicking Exceptions in the AutoCorrect dialog box. The First Letter tab contains a list of common abbreviations, all ending with a period. Normally, Access assumes a period signals the end of a sentence and capitalizes the first letter of the next word. To add to the list of exceptions, type the entry (with the period) in the Don't Capitalize After box and click Add. To remove one from the list, select the entry and click Delete. The INitial CAps tab is empty until you type text in the Don't Change box and click Add.

CAUTION   *Because these tools are shared by all programs in Microsoft Office, any changes you make will affect other users.*

Printing Table Data

The quickest way to print table data is to click the Print button with the table open or with the table name selected in the Database window. This sends the data directly to the default printer. You can also right-click the table name in the Database window and choose Print from the shortcut menu. This also sends the data directly to the printer.

NOTE *If you want to print the subdatasheet data, expand the subdatasheet before printing.*

If you want to choose other print options, such as printing multiple copies or printing only the selected records, you need to open the Print dialog box. Click the Print Preview toolbar button or choose File | Print Preview. To see how the printed data looks before you print it, open the Print Preview window. This is useful when you think the data might not fit across the page with the current page layout. If you want to adjust the page margins, paper size, or the page layout, open the Page Setup dialog box.

See Chapter 14 for complete information about previewing and printing reports, including changing print options and running Page Setup.

Summary

Access 2003 includes many tools that make your data entry and editing quicker and easier. Many of the table field properties can be set to ensure valid and complete data in all the tables in your database.

One of the most versatile of the Access data entry tools is the Lookup Wizard, which helps you create a list from which to choose the proper value for a field. The list can retrieve values from another table or merely specify a set of fixed values. Specifying a default value for a commonly occurring field value can save time during data entry, while adding a field or record validation rule can guard against incorrect data entry.

Access provides many ways to customize the appearance of your Datasheet view, including changing the column width and order, hiding and freezing columns, adjusting the row height, changing the font and cell appearance, and changing the field names.

The next chapter begins the discussion of manipulating table data by sorting and filtering the information.

PART

II

Retrieving and Presenting Information

Sorting, Filtering, and Printing Records

Once you've stored all the information in the related tables of your database, you need to retrieve specific data and arrange it in meaningful ways. The Access Sort and Filter features help you do just that. *Sorting* arranges the records in a specified order, while *filtering* hides records you don't want to see. Combining these two tools gives you the power to display only the records you want in the order you want.

Sorting Records

Access automatically sorts records by the value in the primary key field. During data retrieval and presentation, times will occur when you'll want the records arranged in a different order. For example, you might want to look up all the work orders sorted by the employee who's acting as the supervisor, so you can keep tabs on the workload.

To see records with this information grouped together in Datasheet or Form view, you can sort the records based on the value in a specific field. In Datasheet view, you can sort up to 255 characters in one or more fields to achieve a sort within a sort. The ascending sort order arranges text values in alphabetical order (*A* to *Z*), date/time values from earliest to latest, and number/currency values from lowest to highest. In ascending order, Yes/No fields sort by Yeses first, and then Nos. Use descending to reverse the order. You can sort on Memo fields using the first 255 characters. Access sorts Hyperlink fields by the Text to Display (if any) or the address. You cannot sort on OLE Object fields.

Sorting on a Single Field

To sort by a single field in a datasheet or form, click within the field you want to sort by, and then do one of the following:

 • Click Sort Ascending.

 • Click Sort Descending.

- Choose Records | Sort | Sort Ascending.
- Choose Records | Sort | Sort Descending.
- Right-click in the field and choose Sort Ascending from the shortcut menu.
- Right-click in the field and choose Sort Descending from the shortcut menu.

To restore the records to their original order, choose Records | Remove Filter/Sort or right-click in the datasheet or form, and then choose Remove Filter/Sort from the shortcut menu.

To sort records in a subdatasheet, display the subdatasheet by clicking the expand indicator (the plus (+) sign in the left margin), and then proceed as with a datasheet. When you specify a sort order for one subdatasheet in Datasheet view, all the subdatasheets of that level are also sorted accordingly.

When several records have the same value in one of the fields you want to sort by, you can sort on two or more fields at the same time in Datasheet view. In Form view, records can be sorted by only one field with the Sort feature.

TIP   *Later, you see the Order By form property that you can set to sort by more than one field in the form.*

NOTE   *If you're building a database for a different language, you can set the sort order accordingly. Choose Tools | Options and click the General tab. The New database sort order list (see Figure 7-1) offers a variety of language settings. Before you change the sort order to another language, be sure your operating system (OS) supports that language. Just to be safe, always back up your database before making such drastic changes.*

FIGURE 7-1
Changing the sort order to a different language

Sorting by Two or More Fields

To sort by more than one field, the fields must be adjacent in the datasheet. In addition, Access uses a sort precedence from left to right, so the records are sorted first by the values in the left column. If duplicate values appear in that column, a secondary sort is performed on those records by the values in the next column to the right. If the columns involved in the sort aren't adjacent or are in the wrong relative position in the datasheet or subdatasheet, move the columns before sorting the records. When all are in position, select the columns you want to sort on and click one of the Sort buttons as before, or choose from the Records or the shortcut menu.

The Employees Last Name and First Name columns are repositioned and selected, ready to sort by values in those fields. The records are sorted first by Last Name, and then, where these names are the same, by First Name.

	Employee ID	Last Name	First Name	SSN	Address	City	State	
⊞	10	Ferrell	Bryan	604001369	316 C St	Los Padres	CA	92111
⊞	11	Cloud	Ben J.	603-00-1423	2015 3rd St	Los Padres	CA	92111
⊞	12	Gunderson	Selma	613-00-1743	825 F St	Los Padres	CA	92111
⊞	13	Byron	David L	614-00-1663	1529 G St	Los Padres	CA	92111
⊞	14	Connelly	Fred C	629-00-1543	2001 5th St	Los Padres	CA	92111
⊞	15	Kordel	John C	627-00-1437	3560 H St.	Los Padres	CA	92111
⊞	16	De Salle	Don	629-00-1827	1519 8th St	Los Padres	CA	92111
⊞	17	Howell	Richard	720-00-2040	6122 L St.	Los Padres	CA	92111
⊞	18	Gikas	Calvin	720-00-2150	860 4th St	Los Padres	CA	92111
⊞	19	Dobbins	David	729-00-2150	3291 3rd St	Los Padres	CA	92111
⊞	20	James	Mary R	618-00-4666	1500 8th St	Los Padres	CA	92111
⊞	21	James	George	738005944	1500 8th St	Los Padres	CA	92111
⊞	22	Byron	Paul B	585003782	1529 G St	Los Padres	CA	92111

Employees : Table

Sorting Tips

If you stored numbers in a Text field, they're sorted as a character string instead of by numeric value. However, you can get around this by filling out the values with leading zeros, so the strings are all the same length. For example, the result of sorting the values 5, 15, 33, 242 in a Text field would be 15, 242, 33, 5. But, if you store them as 015, 005, 033 and 242, they're sorted properly in numeric order. Better yet, convert the field to Number if you're sure it won't ever contain letters or other characters.

When you sort records by two or more fields, Access performs a "simple" sort, in which the values in the fields are all sorted in the same order, ascending or descending. It won't mix ascending and descending orders. To mix sort orders, you must use the Advanced Filter/Sort operation described in the section "Filtering with Advanced Filter/Sort," later in this chapter.

Saving the Sort Order

If you close the table after sorting the records, Access asks if you want to save the changes to the design (this includes the sort order). Responding No saves the table in the original, primary key order. Responding Yes saves the sort order with the table and, the next time you open the table, the records appear in that order. In addition, any new forms or reports you create based on the table inherit the sort order and apply it to the new object.

Filtering Records

When you want to see only certain records in your datasheet, subdatasheet, or form, you can filter out the ones you don't want to see. The *filter* process screens the records and lets through only those that meet your criteria. The *criteria* is a set of conditions you specify to limit the display to a certain subset of records.

This can save time by focusing your attention on only the records that are important at the moment. Filtering doesn't remove the records from the table, it only removes them from your view of the table. A *filter* consists of conditions you specify, which can be as simple as "all the records for work orders in October 2003" or as complex as "all bids submitted during June or July that exceeded $500 and were awarded within 30 days of the bid offer."

The difference between finding records and filtering records is this: when Access finds a record, the cursor moves to the record and leaves all the rest on the screen. With a filter, the nonqualifying records are removed from the screen, leaving only the records you want to see. They all remain in the table, however.

In Access, you have five ways to filter records, depending on the conditions you want to set and whether you want the records sorted in a particular order:

- *Filter By Form* screens records with the criteria you enter into a table skeleton.
- *Filter By Selection* leaves only the records with the same value as the one you select in one of the records.
- *Filter Excluding Selection* leaves only the records that don't include the same value as the one you select in one of the records.
- *Advanced Filter/Sort* gives you, in addition to filtering, the capability to specify a complex sort. With a *complex sort,* you can sort the records by two or more fields using different orders—ascending or descending.
- *Filter For* displays a box in the shortcut menu where you enter the filter criteria directly.

When the records you see on the screen are the result of a filter, Access reminds you in three ways that you aren't viewing the entire table. The status bar shows FLTR, indicating a filter is in effect, and the navigation bar gives you the number of records qualified by the word (Filtered). In addition, the Apply Filter toolbar button appears pressed and the ScreenTip has changed to Remove Filter. Click the Remove Filter button to see all the records again.

When you apply a filter to a datasheet, the same filter is applied to any subdatasheets within it. When you create a filter on a subdatasheet, the filter is also available when you open the table in Datasheet view.

Filtering By Selection

Filtering By Selection is the most commonly used and the easiest filtering method. Simply select the value you want to use as the match for the records and click a button. When you apply the Filter By Selection, the records that remain on the screen are only those that contain the selected value. You can Filter By Selection on a value in any type of field, even hyperlink fields, except OLE Object fields.

Specifying the Filter Value

To set the filter value, find one occurrence of the value in the datasheet or subdatasheet, and select all or only part of it. You can also place the insertion point in the field that contains

---

Picking a Filter Type

To decide what type of filter you should use, look at what you want it to do:

- If you want to search for records that meet more than one criterion at the same time (combined with AND), you can use any of the five types of filters. Using Filter By Selection, you must specify and apply the criteria one at a time.

- If you want to combine criteria with the OR operator or enter expressions as criteria, you must use Filter By Form, Filter For, or Advanced Filter/Sort.

- If you also want the records sorted as part of the filter process, you must use the Advanced Filter/Sort. You can, however, sort the results of the other types of filters after applying the filter by clicking one of the Sort buttons on the toolbar.

the value for which you want to filter. Once you've defined the value, apply the filter in one of the following ways:

- Choose Records | Filter | Filter By Selection.
- Click Filter By Selection on the toolbar.
- Right-click the desired value and choose Filter By Selection from the shortcut menu.

The way you select the value determines what records pass the filter. Table 7-1 describes the various ways of selecting values for filtering and equates them to match settings in the Find dialog box, as discussed in Chapter 6.

Let's try out a few filters on the Home Tech Repair tables. First, filter the Employees table to show records for electrical specialists only.

1. With the Employees table open in Datasheet view, place the insertion point in a Specialty field with the value Electrical.

2. Click Filter By Selection. Only two records remain on the screen, both with Electrical in the Specialty field.

		State	ZIP	Work Phone	Pager	Type	Specialty	Hourly Rate	Bi
▶	⊞	CA	92111	(619) 555-6193	(619) 555-4538	Permanent	Electrical	$40.00	
	⊞	CA	92111	(619) 555-1281	(619) 555-9845	Permanent	Electrical	$17.00	

Record: 14 ◀ 1 ▶ ▶I ▶* of 2 (Filtered)

3. Click Remove Filter. All the records return to the datasheet or subdatasheet.

***

TIP *After you remove the filter and restore all the records to the display, you can reapply the most recently used filter by clicking the Apply Filter toolbar button or choosing Records |*
Apply Filter/Sort.

As an example of filtering to a partial value, filter the Bid Data table so you see only records that contain the word "heater" in the Description field.

Selection	Returns Records Where	Find Match Equivalent
Entire value or place insertion point in the field without selecting any characters.	Whole field matches selected value.	Whole Field Match option.
Part of value, including first character.	Field starts with selected characters.	Start of Field Match option.
Part of value, not including first character.	Field with matching value anywhere in field.	Any part of Field Match option.

TABLE 7-1 Value Selections for Filtering

1. In the Bid Data datasheet, select the "heater" part of Replace Waterheater in the Description field of the Bid Number 98-102 record.

2. Choose Records | Filter | Filter By Selection. Two records remain, both with the word "heater" at the end of the Description field.

	Bid Number	Bid Date	Expires	Description	Address	City	State
▶	⊞ 98-102	1/15/2003	3/1/2003	Replace Waterheater	176 3rd St	Los Padres	CA
	⊞ 98-117	5/18/2003	8/18/2003	SPA Heater	952 C St	Los Padres	CA
*							

Record: ◄◄ ◄ 1 ► ►I ►* of 2 (Filtered)

3. Click Remove Filter. All records return to the datasheet.

Filter By Selection applies only one filter condition at a time. If you need to filter based on a combination of two or more values, you can apply the second Filter By Selection criterion to the records that remain after the first filter is applied. This is equivalent to combining the filter criteria with an AND operator. For example, you might want to see records for work orders for heater jobs supervised by Ferrell. Apply a filter that limits the records to heater jobs, and then apply a second filter to the results of the first. The second filter further limits the result to records with both values. The order of applying the filters doesn't make any difference; the result is the same either way. When you click Remove Filter, the entire filter is removed, not only the last one you applied.

TIP *If you press TAB to reach the Drawing field (don't click it or you'll jump to the hyperlink target), and then click Filter By Selection, you can see all the records that refer to the same drawing. For example, the Bay Window drawing is used for two work orders.*

Using an Exclusion Filter

Instead of telling Access which records you want to see, sometimes it's easier to specify which ones you don't want to see. In this case, you can use the Filter Excluding Selection option, which screens out the records with the value you select, instead of including them. Filter Excluding Selection works much like Filter By Selection because you select the value or partial value in the datasheet or form.

For example, suppose you want to see the records for all work orders except those supervised by Ferrell. You select the value as before, and then choose Records | Filter | Filter Excluding Selection, or right-click the selection and choose Filter Excluding Selection from the shortcut menu. Filter Excluding Selection is also available from the Records | Filter menu.

Filtering By Form

Filter By Form isn't much different from Filter By Selection. Instead of selecting a value from the datasheet or subdatasheet as a filter criterion, you enter the value in a filter grid.

The *grid* is a table skeleton that resembles a blank record showing all the filterable fields in the table with space to enter filter values. One advantage of using Filter By Form is you can combine filter criteria. You can specify two or more conditions, so a record must meet any one or all of them to survive the filter. The multiple criteria can apply to a single field or to more than one field.

If you want to filter the records in a subdatasheet, click the expand indicator to display the subdatasheet records, and then proceed as with a datasheet filter.

Entering Filter Criteria

When you choose Filter By Form, the table grid appears on the screen as shown in the following illustration. The most recent filter saved with the table shows in the filter grid. If you've created a filter since you opened the table, this filter shows up in the grid. Notice Access has created an expression from your Filter By Selection criterion. The expression *Like "*heater"* means to show all records that have a value in the Description field ending with heater.

⊞ Bid Data: Filter by Form							_□×
Bid Number	Bid Date	Expires	Description	Address	City	State	
			Like "*heater" ▼				

Look for ⟨ Or ⟩

TIP *The asterisk in front of "heater" in the filter indicates the characters you selected appeared at the end of the value. The filter shows all other records that end with "heater." If you want records with the value anywhere in the field, add another asterisk, so the filter becomes Like "*heater*".*

The Filter/Sort toolbar has three handy buttons. The *Clear Grid* button removes the filter that appears in the skeleton, so you needn't delete every entry individually. The other button is the familiar Apply Filter button. The *Close* button lets you return to the datasheet without applying any filter.

To create a new filter, clear the grid of any existing filter and move to the field where you want to specify a value. When you move the insertion point to a field in the grid, an arrow appears in the field. Clicking this arrow displays a list of unique values that currently exist in the field, sorted in ascending order, for example, the list of values in the Completion Date field of the Workorders table. To filter on one of these values, select the value, and then click Apply Filter. This is equivalent to using Filter By Selection.

NOTE *If the table has many unique values in a field, Access might not build the list of values. Instead, you see only two choices: Is Null and Is Not Null. You can set the maximum number you want to show in the list by choosing Tools | Options and clicking the Edit/Find tab. More about customizing your workplace in Chapter 16.*

NOTE   *If you display a value list in one of the employee-related fields (Supervisor, Principal Worker, or Helper), you see the values in the lookup table you created in the last chapter. The values in the list are only for display. Access stores the value from the primary key field of the lookup list in the Workorders table. This creates a bit of a problem, as you can see in the section "Filtering with Advanced Filter/Sort."*

TIP   *If you don't see the value list in the table skeleton, the option could be turned off. To restore the option, choose Options from the Tools menu, and then click the Edit/Find tab. One group of the options on this page is Show list of values in, which offers the choices of Local indexed fields, Local nonindexed fields, and ODBC fields. Check the first two options to display the value list for all fields in the skeleton. More about customizing the workplace in Chapter 16.*

To filter Workorders records to show only those whose scheduled completion date is before July 1, 2003, follow these steps:

1. In the Workorders datasheet, click Filter By Form on the toolbar. The filter grid appears.

2. If entries are in the grid, click Clear Grid to remove them.

3. Place the insertion point in the Completion Date field and select 7/1/03 from the value list. Access automatically adds the date/time delimiter symbols (#) to the date you select from the list.

Filtering Memo, OLE Object, and Hyperlink Fields

When you apply Filter By Selection to a Memo, OLE Object, or Hyperlink field, you can see all the records with the same values in the field. But, with the other three filter operations, you can only filter based on whether the field has a value or is empty. When you click the drop-down list in one of these fields, the only available values are Is Null and Is Not Null. This filter option is also available for calculated fields in queries.

4. Place the insertion point at the beginning of the date and enter < (less than). You can also press F2 to switch to Edit mode, press HOME, and then enter <.

 5. Click Apply Filter. Only the eight records of Workorders scheduled to be completed before July 1, 2003 remain on the screen.

	Workorder Num	Customer ID	Bid Number	Start Date	Completion Date	Supervisor	Principal Worke
⊞	001	1032	98-101	2/25/2003	3/10/2003	Ferrell	Howell
⊞	002	1033	98-103	3/15/2003	3/18/2003	Gunderson	Gikas
⊞	003	1034	98-105	3/10/2003	3/5/2003	Byron	Dobbins
⊞	004	1035	98-107	4/15/2003	4/20/2003	Gunderson	Howell
⊞	005	1036	98-108	5/10/2003	5/15/2003	Ferrell	Dobbins
⊞	006	1037	98-111	5/12/2003	5/25/2003	Byron	
⊞	009	1039	98-117	6/25/2003	6/26/2003	Ferrell	Howell
⊞	010	1032	98-119	6/26/2003	6/26/2003	Ferrell	

Record: ⏮ ◀ 1 ▶ ⏭ ▶* of 8 (Filtered)

 6. Click Remove Filter or choose Records | Remove Filter/Sort to restore all the records. Remove Filter/Sort is also available from the Datasheet shortcut menu, which displays when you right-click anywhere in the datasheet.

Using Wildcards and Expressions in a Filter

You can use wildcards in filter criteria for Text and Memo fields the same way as in the Find criteria. They apply only to character strings. Refer to Chapter 6 for examples of using wildcards.

You can also enter an expression as the filter criterion, such as the earlier example of < 7/1/03 entered in the Completion Date field in the Filter by Form grid. To use an expression as a criterion, enter it directly in the filter grid. Here are some examples of expressions you can use as filter criteria.

Address	Like "*3ʳᵈ*"	Displays records with addresses on 3ʳᵈ Street.
Completion Date	Between #5/1/03# And #7/31/03#	Displays Workorders records for all jobs scheduled to be completed during May, June, and July 2003.
Last Name	>="P*"	Displays records for Customers whose last name starts with letters P through Z.
Bid Date	Year([Bid Date])=2003	Uses the Year() function to display Bid Data records with Bid Dates in 2003.
Workorder #	Is Null	Displays Bid Data records with empty Workorder # fields.

You need to obey a few rules when entering expressions in a filter condition, whether you're using the Filter By Form, Filter For, or Advanced Filter/Sort method.

- If a Text field value contains a space, any punctuation, or an operator character, the value must be enclosed in quotation marks. For example, **George** is OK, but **George Bart** must be entered as **"George Bart"**. If the entry is one of the values in the list, Access adds the quotation marks for you after you leave the criteria grid.

- To filter a Memo field, use the asterisk (*) wildcards to filter on embedded text.

- For Number, Currency, and AutoNumber fields, don't include characters, such as the currency symbol or the thousands separator. If you do, you'll see a data type mismatch error message. Decimal points and minus signs are okay.

- For Date/Time field values, abide by the options set on the Date tab of the Regional Settings Properties dialog box of the Windows Control Panel. These settings control the sequence of the month, day, and year values within the field. Access encloses the date or time value in pound signs (#).

- For Yes/No fields, you can enter Yes, -1, On, or True to filter for Yes values, or you can enter No, 0, Off, or False for No values.

Combining Filter Criteria with AND

You can use complex criteria that combine two or more filter conditions in the Filter By Form window. If you combine two conditions with the AND operator, you're limiting the records to those that meet both conditions. For example, you could ask Access to limit the Workorders records to only those with a Material Cost less than $1,000 and a Labor Cost greater than $500. This would give you a list of labor-intensive contracts.

To combine two filter conditions with AND:

1. In the Workorders datasheet, click Filter By Form on the toolbar.

2. Click Clear Grid to remove the previous filter conditions and click in the Material Cost field. Click the down arrow to display the stored values in the Material Cost fields without the dollar signs, which are part of the display format, not stored with the values.

3. Type **<=1000** and press TAB to move to the Labor Cost field, and type **>=500**, and then press ENTER.

4. Click Apply Filter. Four records meet the combined filter conditions that show the labor-intensive contracts.

5. Click Remove Filter to restore all the records in the datasheet.

NOTE *The previous example combined filter conditions in different fields with the implied AND operator. You can also combine filter conditions in the same field with AND by typing AND between the expressions. For example, if you enter the filter condition >=500 AND <=1000 in the Material Cost field, you would see only the records for work orders requiring between $500 and $1,000 worth of materials, inclusive. Another way to express the same criterion is to use the BETWEEN...AND...operator: BETWEEN 500 AND 1000.*

Combining Filter Conditions with OR

Using the AND operator to combine filter conditions reduces the resulting record set by demanding both criteria be met in each record. The OR operator, on the other hand, expands the resulting record set by including records that meet either of the conditions, but not necessarily both.

When you use Filter By Selection, you can combine conditions only with the implied AND operator by imposing a second filter on the set of records already filtered by the first criteria. With Filter By Form, you can apply as many filters as you want in one operation, using both AND and OR operators.

The Filter By Form window contains two tabs at the bottom of the window: Look for and Or. You enter the first filter condition, and any others you want to combine with it, using AND on the Look for page. If you want to add an OR filter condition, click the Or tab and enter the condition on the second page. If you change your mind and want to delete the Or tab, select it and choose Edit | Delete Tab.

NOTE *Another Or tab appears when you begin to add a filter to the first Or page.*

The OR combination comes in handy when you want to find records with any one of several values in a field. For example, suppose you want to see all the Workorders records for jobs on B or H Streets. You would enter *** B*** in the Address field in the filter grid on the Look for page, and then enter *** H*** in the Address field on the Or page.

TIP   *If you don't include a space before the* H *in the filter criterion, you'll see all records with the letter* H *anywhere in the Address field. For example, addresses on any street with "th," such as 5th or 6th. The leading space demands the letter* H *is the first letter of the word.*

To combine two filter conditions with OR:

1. In the Bid Data datasheet, choose Records | Filter | Filter By Form. The Filter window opens with the last filter condition in the grid.

2. Click Clear Grid, enter *** B*** (with a space before the *B*) in the Address field on the Look for page, and then press ENTER. Access translates the expression to *Like "* B*"*.

3. Click the Or tab at the bottom of the window. The Or page opens with the same empty grid as the Look for page. Notice a third tab, labeled Or, now shows at the bottom of the window.

4. Place the insertion point in the Address field, enter *** H***, and then press ENTER. The expression is changed to *Like "* H*"*.

5. Click Apply Filter on the toolbar. The datasheet now shows the five jobs with addresses on B or H Streets.

	Bid Number	Bid Date	Expires	Description	Address	City	State
⊞	98-104	2/25/2003	3/25/2003	New Garage Doors	560 B St	Los Padres	CA
⊞	98-106	3/15/2003	5/15/2003	Repair Driveway	1510 H St	Los Padres	CA
⊞	98-118	5/18/2003	6/18/2003	DSS Install	560 B St	Los Padres	CA
⊞	98-120	5/26/2003	6/26/2003	Repair Driveway	1510 H St	Los Padres	CA
⊞	98-123	6/5/2003	7/5/2003	Porch Roof	560 B St	Los Padres	CA

Record: 14 4 | 1 | ▶ ▶I ▶* of 5 (Filtered)

6. Click Remove Filter to restore all the records.

AND and OR Can Get Confusing

The logic can get a little confusing when you begin combining filter conditions with both AND and OR. For example, you might want to see all Bid Data records for jobs on B and H Streets that were lost. If the job was lost, Lost appears in the Award Date field. Obviously, B and H Streets are combined with the OR operator, but where does the Award Date (Lost) condition go?

The answer is to combine the Award Date filter with both the B and H Street filters using the AND operator in each case. On the Look for page, enter **"Lost"** in the Award Date field in the grid with * B* in the Address field. On the Or page, again enter **"Lost"** in the Award Date field with * H* in the Address field. If you didn't repeat the Lost value in both conditions, you would see all the bids for jobs on B Street that were lost, together with all the jobs bid on H Street, regardless of the outcome.

TIP   *If your filter doesn't return any records, you might have set conflicting criteria that were impossible to meet. For example, you might have asked for bids that were for jobs on both B and H Streets, when clearly a job cannot be in two places at once.*

Optimizing Filter By Form

In the *Filter By Form* grid, when you move to a field, you can display the list of unique values stored in that field by clicking the down arrow. To display the list, Access reads all the records and picks out the unique values.

In an extremely large table, the value lists can be quite lengthy and take a long time to display. To improve performance, you can display lists only for indexed fields in the current table and let the user enter the values to look for in the nonindexed fields, instead of choosing from a value list. You can also reduce the number of records to display in the list to less than the default 1,000 records.

To make changes in the Filter By Form default settings, choose Tools | Options and click the Edit/Find tab (see Figure 7-2). The *Show list of values in* group of options includes the following:

- *Local indexed fields* displays value lists for all the indexed fields in the current table.

- *Local nonindexed fields* displays value lists for other fields in the current table.

- *ODBC fields* displays value lists for linked tables in an external file.

Check only the Local indexed fields box to speed up the value list display. If this still takes too long, also clear that option.

The other option that affects Filter By Form is the *Don't display lists where more than this number of records read:* option. This represents the maximum number of records Access has to

FIGURE 7-2
Setting the Edit/
Find default
options for the
current database

read to come up with the list of unique values. If the number of records exceeds the number in this box, Access stops reading the records and no value list is displayed.

If you checked one or more of the *Show list of values in* options and you still don't see a value list for one or more fields, you might need to increase the number in the *Don't display lists…* box.

If you use the same nonindexed field in several filters, you might save time and improve performance by indexing it.

NOTE   *Be aware that these option settings apply to the entire database, not only to the current table.*

Filtering For

The *Filter For* option lets you filter records by entering the condition right in the open Datasheet or Form view. You use the same conditions and expressions you would use in the Filter By Form grid. To apply the filter, right-click in the field whose values you want to filter and type the value or expression in the Filter For box. For example, you might want to see only records in the Bid Data table with expiration dates before July 1, 2003.

After entering the value or expression, press ENTER to close the shortcut menu and apply the filter. If you want to apply the filter and keep the shortcut menu open to specify additional criteria, press TAB instead. Then return to the Filter For box and enter another criteria. You can add as many criteria as you need to refine the filter to only the records you want to see. This is equivalent to applying successive filters with Filter By Selection or combining conditions with AND in Filter By Form. The conditions are cumulative.

To filter more than one value in the same field, enter an expression that combines the criteria with an OR operator. You cannot combine criteria in different fields with an OR operator using Filter For.

To remove the filter, click the Remove Filter button, or choose Remove Filter/Sort from the Records menu or the shortcut menu.

Like the other filters, when you save the table, the filter is saved with it if you respond Yes to saving the table design. You can reactivate the filter when you reopen the table, if desired, by clicking Apply Filter.

Filtering with Advanced Filter/Sort

The Advanced Filter/Sort feature is the most flexible and comprehensive of the Access filtering tools. Not only does this feature include all the features of Filter By Form, it also enables you to specify mixed sort orders for different fields in the table. You enter all the filtering and sorting specifications in a single window.

The Advanced Filter/Sort window is divided horizontally into two parts. The upper part contains a box with a list of the fields in the table. The lower part is the design grid where you specify which fields you want to filter, the values to use as filters, and how you want the records sorted in the resulting record set. If you applied a filter recently, the criteria appears in the Criteria row of the grid. Click Clear Grid to remove it.

The process of creating an Advanced Filter/Sort is nearly identical to creating a query. See Chapter 8 for the details for creating queries that can be used to create Advanced Filter/Sorts, including the following:

- Selecting fields to filter and sort
- Specifying filter criteria
- Setting sort orders

Applying and Removing the Advanced Filter

Anytime during the design of an advanced filter, you can apply it to see if you're getting the data you want. Access gives you the same three ways to apply the advanced filter:

- Click Apply Filter on the toolbar.
- Choose Filter | Apply Filter/Sort.
- Right-click anywhere in the upper section of the Design window and choose Apply Filter/Sort from the shortcut menu.

When viewing the resulting record set, notice the toolbar and the navigation key area both warn you this is a filtered record set. If you want to abandon the filter design without applying it, click Close on the toolbar.

		Bid Number	Bid Date	Expires	Award Date	Description	Address	City
▶	+	98-103	2/3/2003	6/1/2003	3/1/03	Install 3 Attic Vents	329 5th St	Los Padres
	+	98-105	3/3/2003	7/2/2003	4/1/03	Install A/C	2478 9th St	Los Padres
	+	98-107	3/20/2003	7/19/2003	4/10/03	Replace Countertops	319 4th St	Los Padres
	+	98-108	3/28/2003	7/27/2003	5/1/03	Move Washer & Dryer	2111 J St	Los Padres
	+	98-109	3/28/2003	5/28/2003	Lost	Garden Window	156 8th St	Los Padres
	+	98-106	3/15/2003	5/15/2003	Lost	Repair Driveway	1510 H St	Los Padres
	+	98-104	2/25/2003	3/25/2003	Lost	New Garage Doors	560 B St	Los Padres
*								

Record: ◄◄ ◄ 1 ► ►► ►* of 7 (Filtered)

To remove the filter, do one of the following:

- Click the Remove Filter button.
- Choose Records | Remove Filter/Sort.
- Right-click and choose Remove Filter/Sort from the shortcut menu.

NOTE *You can base a new form or report on a filtered set of records if you create it while the filtered record set is displayed in Datasheet view or if you saved the filter with the table. While the filter and sort properties are inherited by the form or report, you can still override the settings in the form or report property sheets. See Chapter 10 for more information about creating forms and reports, and changing their properties.*

Filtering by Lookup Fields with Advanced Filter/Sort

Filtering on a field that gets its value from a lookup list with Advanced Filter/Sort can present a slight problem. When you choose to filter records by values in a Lookup field in Filter By Form, you pick from the value list that contains all the values in the lookup list created by the Lookup Wizard. What you don't see in the list are the values actually stored in the field. The value in the primary key field of the lookup list is stored instead of the more informative displayed value.

When you use Advanced Filter/Sort, you don't choose from the lookup list because only one table is in the Filter window. This means you must enter the stored value in the Criteria row to filter on a Lookup field. For example, to filter on Ferrell in the Supervisor field of the Workorders table with Filter By Form, you can select Ferrell from the list or type **Ferrell** in the grid. To do the same in Advanced Filter/Sort, you must enter **10**, Ferrell's Employee ID number, in the Criteria row.

Modifying a Filter

You use the same techniques to modify a filter that you used to create it. You can add more criteria or change existing ones in any type of filter. You can even switch between Filter windows to see how the filter is progressing or apply the filter during the process to see how the records are selected.

NOTE *When you filter a table, the records you see are limited to those that pass the criteria you set. You still see all the fields in every record. To limit the fields, as well as the records in the resulting set, you need to use a query. Chapter 8 discusses the difference between filters and queries, and tells how to decide which to use.*

Saving a Filter

The most recent filter is saved with the table—not as a separate object—if you respond Yes to save the table changes. When you reopen the table, the filter is no longer in effect, but you can reapply it by any of the methods discussed earlier. If you create a new filter, but want to keep the previous one available with the table, respond No when asked if you want to save the changes. Of course, if you've made other changes you do want to keep, you'll save the filter with them.

If you want to have more than one filter available to a table or want to save a filter permanently, you must save it as a query. Queries are stored as separate Access database objects. When you want to use the filter again, you can bring it back from the query to the Filter window or simply run it as a query.

To save an advanced filter as a query and load it again in the Filter window:

1. With the Filter window displayed, click the Save As Query button. You can also choose Save As Query from the shortcut menu or the File menu. Access asks for a name for the new query in the Save As Query dialog box.

2. Name the query and choose OK.

3. To restore the specifications to the Filter window, open a blank Advanced Filter/Sort window and click the Load From Query button. You could also choose Load from Query from the shortcut menu or the File menu.

4. The Applicable Filter dialog box shows a list of queries based on the Bid Data table.

5. Choose the query you want and click OK. All the filter parameters are returned to the grid, where you can choose to apply the filter or make changes.

NOTE   *If all you want to do is filter the records, simply run the query you saved from the filter. If you want to use the query as the basis for a new filter, load the filter from the query and make the changes.*

Removing and Deleting Filters

A difference exists between removing and deleting a filter. Removing a filter simply returns all the records to the datasheet or form. You can reapply the filter later. Deleting the filter erases the filter criteria and the filter cannot be reapplied without reconstructing it.

To remove a filter from a datasheet or form, do one of the following:

- Click Remove Filter.
- Choose Records | Remove Filter/Sort.
- Right-click anywhere in the datasheet and choose Remove Filter/Sort from the shortcut menu.

NOTE   *When you remove a filter from a datasheet, any filter you applied to a subdatasheet within it is also removed.*

To delete a filter entirely, you need to clear the filter grid and apply the empty filter to the datasheet by the following method:

1. Switch to the Advanced Filter/Sort window. It doesn't matter how you created the filter; you can still see it in the filter grid.

2. Click Clear Grid or choose Clear Grid from the Edit or the shortcut menu.

3. Click Apply Filter.

4. Click Close to close the datasheet and respond Yes to save the changes.

When you open the table again, the Apply Filter button is dimmed, indicating the filter has been removed. If you want to use the filter again, you have to reconstruct it.

Printing Table Data

You needn't create a fancy report to print your table data. You can print the datasheet as it appears in the Datasheet view or print in the default report format, called the *AutoReport*. To print a single copy of the datasheet, click the Print button. If you want to adjust the margin settings, the paper size, or the page layout, use the Page Setup dialog box. If you want to choose other print options—such as multiple copies or selected pages—you need to open the Print dialog box.

To see how the printed report looks before you print it, you can click the Print Preview toolbar button. This is useful when you think the datasheet might not fit across the page with the current page layout, in which case you can change the page setup before printing the data. For example, Figure 7-3 shows the Bid Data datasheet previewed in three pages.

TIP   *The Bid Data datasheet requires three page widths to print all the fields. If the page orientation were changed to landscape in the Page Setup dialog box, the data would fit on two pages.*

See Chapter 13 for more information about printing data and running the Print Preview and Page Setup features.

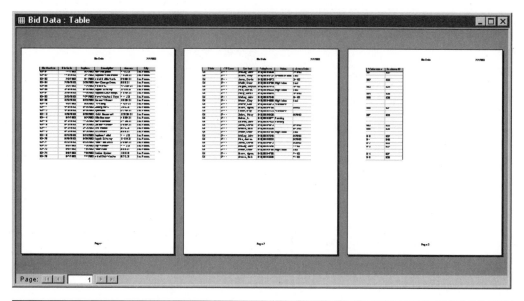

FIGURE 7-3   Previewing the Bid Data datasheet printout

Summary

You've now seen how to store information in related database tables and how to retrieve data using different type of filters. Filtering records has some limitations:

- You can limit only the records, not the fields. You can see all the fields of the resulting recordset.
- You can save only one filter or sort order with a table.
- Filtering is limited to records in a single table.

Queries provide an alternative to filters with distinct advantages, such as choosing specific fields from related tables and being stored as separate database objects. The next chapter introduces you to the subject of queries and their applications.

Extracting Information with Queries

When you work with information in an Access datasheet, you can filter and sort the records in many ways, but you can have even more flexibility with queries. You can not only limit the records to a specific subset, but you can also specify which fields you want to see in the result.

Query is a general term synonymous with question, inquiry, or quiz. In Access, to query a database is to ask a question about the information in the database. A query can be about the data in a single table or multiple related tables.

Access provides several types of queries, ranging from the popular select query that extracts specific data to the more exotic action queries that can insert, update, and delete records. This chapter discusses select queries and a few special purpose queries, while the next chapter covers the more advanced types.

How Do Queries Work?

Several types of queries do quite different things but, in general, an *Access query* is a set of explicit specifications that tell Access exactly what information you want to see and how you want it arranged or manipulated in the results. In the query, you specify the fields you want to include, add selection criteria that limit the records in the resulting record set, select the desired order for them to appear, and define any summary fields.

With Access queries you can do the following:

- View data from multiple tables sorted in a specific order.
- Perform many types of calculations on selected groups of records.
- Find and display duplicate or unmatched records.
- Update data, delete records, or append new records to a table.
- Create a new table with records from one or more tables.

NOTE   *The result of running an ordinary query is called a dynaset, which is short for dynamic subset. This is called "dynamic" because if you make a change to the data in the dynaset, Access makes the same changes in the data in the tables that provided the basic information. Other types of queries result in a static recordset that cannot be edited and this result is called a snapshot.*

Access Query Categories

Access queries fall into four general categories: select, special purpose, action, and SQL-specific. A *select query* is the most common category and is used for extracting specific information from one or more tables in a database. The results of a select query are displayed in a datasheet for viewing or editing, or are used as the basis for a form or report. With a select query, you can also group records and perform calculations on field values in the groups, such as sum, count, average, minimum and maximum, and other totals. Other types of queries can locate duplicate records in a table or unmatched records in a relationship, or they can automatically fill in field data or prompt for criteria.

An example of a *special purpose query* is the *crosstab* (meaning cross-tabulation) query that displays summarized values from one field in the table, grouped in two ways. Other special queries automatically fill in data or prompt for criteria.

Action queries are used to perform global data management operations on tables, such as updating or deleting groups of records, making a new table from an existing one, and appending new records to an existing table.

SQL-specific queries are accessible only through structured query language (SQL) statements. All queries have SQL statements in the background, but SQL-specific queries are constructed with the programming language, instead of a design grid like other types of queries.

Access has some new Query Wizards to help create many of these queries. You learn about the select queries and the special purpose queries you can create with a wizard for now, but you learn about the more advanced queries in Chapter 9.

When to Use a Filter and When to Use a Query

It might seem like filters and queries do the same thing, but some differences occur in the results. Filters and select queries both retrieve a subset of records from a table or another query. As a rule of thumb, use a filter to view or edit some records temporarily in a datasheet

---

Specific Types of Access Queries

The Access select queries include the following:

- *Simple Select queries* display data from one or more tables sorted in a specific order. You can also perform many types of predefined or custom calculations on values in all records or within groups of records.

- *Find Duplicate queries* display all records with duplicate values in one or more specified fields. For example, you can query to find customers who have more than one workorder. You can include any other fields you want.

- *Find Unmatched queries* display records in one table that have no related records in another table. For example, you can query to find customers who have no current workorders.

Special purpose queries include the following:

- *Parameter queries,* when run, display a dialog box where you enter the criteria for retrieving data or a value to insert into a field. You can apply parameters to other types of queries as well.
- *AutoLookup queries* are a special kind of select queries that automatically fill in certain field values in a new record in one or more tables.
- *Crosstab queries* calculate a sum or count and group the results in a spreadsheet format that correlates the data with two types of information, for example, total sales by product and quarter or district.

Action queries include the following:

- *Update queries* make global changes to a group of records in one or more tables, for example, raise all labor rates by 15 percent.
- *Append queries* add a group of records from one or more tables to the end of one or more other tables.
- *Delete queries* remove a specific group of records from one or more tables, for example, remove all records from the Bid Data table with "Lost" in the Award Date field.
- *Make-table queries* create a new table out of data from one or more tables.

SQL-specific queries include the following:

- *Union queries* combine fields from one or more tables into one field in the result.
- *Pass-Through queries* send instructions directly to ODBC databases using commands specific to the server.
- *Data-Definition queries* create or change database objects in an Access, SQL server, or other server database.
- *Subqueries* are SQL SELECT or other server statements that form a SELECT query within another query.

or form. If you want to return to the subset of records at a later time, you should use a query. Queries are separate database objects that appear in the Database window, while a single filter is saved with a table.

If you use a query, you needn't open the table first because a query is an object in its own right. With a filter, you must open the table first before you can view the results of the filter or design a new filter.

Use a query if you want to extract data from multiple tables, control which fields to display, or perform calculations on field values. None of these operations are permitted with filters.

The results of both filters and queries can be used as the source of data for forms and reports. You can also sort the results of both and save the sort order for use in a later work session. Both methods let you edit the data displayed in the results, if editing is otherwise permitted. If you need to extract data from more than one table, select only specific fields to include, or store as a separate object in the database, then you need to use a query. Queries are also required if you want to see the results without opening the underlying table, query, or form, or if you want to include calculated values in the result.

Even if you decide you need to have a query, you can use the easy Filter By Form or Filter By Selection tools to create a filter, and then save it as a query. Access translates your filter design into a proper query.

Creating Select Queries

As usual, Access gives you a choice of ways to begin a new query design:

- Click the New command button on the Queries page in the Database window.
- Click the New Object toolbar button and select New Query.
- Choose Insert | Query.

All three approaches open the New Query dialog box. As you can see, you can call on wizards for help with several types of queries.

If you want to create a select query, you can either start from scratch by selecting Design View in the New Query dialog box or choose one of the wizards to help you. Choosing Design View takes you directly to the Query Design window, which looks a lot like the Advanced Filter/Sort Design window. To create a select query with the wizard, choose Simple Query Wizard, which guides you through choices about the basic design of the select query. You can then go to the Design window to customize the query design, if necessary.

Using the Simple Query Wizard

To start the wizard, double-click Create query by using wizard in the Queries pane of the Database window. If you opened the New Query dialog box, double-click the Simple Query

Wizard or select it and click OK. The Simple Query Wizard displays a series of dialog boxes in which you specify the fields and records you want to include in the query and enter a name for the saved query. You can include fields from any of the tables or other queries in your database. Figure 8-1 shows the first Simple Query Wizard dialog box.

To add all the fields from a table, click the double right arrow (>>). To add a field to the Selected Fields list, double-click the field name or select the field in the Available Fields list and click the right arrow (>). If you change your mind about including a field, double-click it in the Selected Fields list or select it and click the left arrow (<). To add fields from another table, select the table (or query) from the Tables/Queries list box, and then select fields from the new list.

Tip   *Double-clicking the field name switches it from one list to the other. The fields appear in the query result in the order you selected them in the first dialog box. You can change the order later in Query Design view.*

To select more than one field at once, do one of the following:

- If the field names are contiguous, hold down SHIFT while you click the first and last names in the group.

- If the field names aren't contiguous, hold down CTRL while you click each name, one by one.

After selecting the fields, click the single right arrow. After you add all the fields you want in the query, click the Next button. The second Simple Query Wizard dialog box gives you two options.

- Create a detail query with all the record data.

FIGURE 8-1
Choosing which fields to include in the query

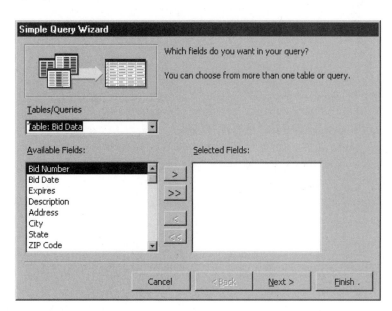

PART II

- Create a summary query that calculates totals based on the field values. When you choose to summarize field values, you need to specify the summary options in another dialog box, which is discussed in the section "Summarizing with the Wizard."

TIP   *If you haven't selected any Number or Currency type fields, no fields appear to summarize. The wizard then skips this dialog box and takes you directly to the third and last dialog box.*

In the final wizard dialog box, you enter a name for the query. You also choose whether to view the information immediately or go to the Query Design window to make modifications to the query.

Let's try out the Simple Query Wizard by building a list of current workorders and include information from both the Workorders and Bid Data tables.

To create a Current Workorders query:

1. In the Database window, click Queries, and then click New.
2. Select Simple Query Wizard from the New Query dialog box.
3. Select Table:Workorders from the Tables/Queries list box and use one of the methods previously discussed to move the Workorder Number, Supervisor, Material Cost, Labor Cost, and Description fields to the Selected Fields list.
4. Select Table:Bid Data from the Tables/Queries list box and add the Address, Bid Number, and Contact fields to the Selected Fields list.
5. Click Next and accept the Detail option, which shows every field of every record, and then click Next.
6. Enter Current Workorders as the name for the new query and accept the default option to open the query to view information.
7. Click Finish. The query results appear in a datasheet showing only the eight fields you selected, but all the records (see Figure 8-2). The column widths are adjusted in the figure to show all the information.

The wizard has helped you with the basic query definition. Now it's up to you to add the final touches, such as adding selection criteria to limit the records, changing the query and field properties, adding another table, specifying a sort order, or adding calculated fields.

Touring the Query Design Window

Like most Access objects, a query can be displayed in more than one view. Tables, for example, can be viewed as a datasheet in which you're looking at the data in the table. You can also look at the table in Design view to see the table structure and all the information about the fields, indexes, formats, and so on.

A query, like a table, can be viewed as a datasheet or a design. The *Datasheet view* shows you the data that results when you run the query (refer to Figure 8-2). The *Design view* is where you can look at the query structure and make changes to the query design or even create a new one. The third query view is the *SQL view,* which shows the SQL statements Access creates behind the scenes to implement the query. The SQL view has no counterpart with table objects.

FIGURE 8-2   Viewing the results of the new select query

To switch to Design view, click the View toolbar button and choose Design View from the drop-down list, or choose View | Design View.

The Query Design window looks a lot like the Advanced Filter/Sort window with two sections:

- The upper pane is the table pane, which displays the field lists for all the tables in the query.

- The lower pane is the Query By Example (QBE) design grid, which shows the elements of the query design.

The table pane for the Current Workorders query shows the two tables from which you selected fields: Bid Data and Workorders. Access has accepted the one-to-many relationship between the tables joining the Bid Number fields.

The design grid shows the field names you selected in the wizard dialog box, including the name of the table (or query) from which they came. The Sort, Criteria, and Or rows are the same as in a filter grid. The check marks in the Show row indicate all the fields are to appear in the result. Clearing the check mark hides the field from the query result. This is helpful when you want to filter or sort the results based on a field that you don't want to appear in the query results.

NOTE *Drag the dividing line between the two panes up or down to change their relative heights. You can also drag the edges of field list boxes in the table pane to enlarge them and see more of the field names. Similarly, you can drag the grid column dividers to change the column width.*

The Query Design toolbar has some new buttons and the menu bar also includes new options. The shortcut menu is specified by where you right-click to display it: in the table pane or the design grid.

The menu bar and shortcut menu have a few additional choices as follows:

- View | Table Names shows or hides the Table row in the design grid. The design grid shortcut menu also shows the Table Names option.

- With the insertion point in the Criteria row or an Or row, the design grid shortcut menu has the Zoom option that opens a window where you can enter and view long expressions. You can also open the Zoom window by pressing SHIFT-F2.

- When a relationship line is selected in the table pane, View | Join Properties opens the Join Properties dialog box. Right-clicking the join line and choosing Properties from the shortcut menu also opens the dialog box. Double-clicking the join line opens the Join Properties dialog box without using a shortcut menu. You can change the join properties to get different results with the query. Refer to Chapter 5 for a description of the types of joins.

- Edit | Clear Grid removes all entries in the design grid. The field lists remain in the table pane.

CAUTION   *Clear Grid is one of those actions that cannot be reversed by choosing Edit | Undo.*

- Query | Parameters opens the Query Parameters dialog box where you define the parameters to prompt for when running a parameter query. The table pane shortcut menu also includes the Parameters option. See Chapter 9 for more details about creating a parameter query.

Without the Wizard

Six basic steps create a query without the help of a wizard:

1. Select one or more tables and queries that contain the information you want to retrieve, and then add them to the table pane of the new query design.
2. Choose the fields from the field lists in the table pane and add them to the design grid.
3. Specify the sort orders for the field values, if any.
4. Add selection criteria that limits the records in the query results.
5. Add calculated fields that display the results of functions or expressions, if any.
6. Add summarizing expressions, if any.

When you finish with these steps, run the query.

TIP   *You can run the query to test the results while you're creating it by switching to Datasheet view or clicking the Run toolbar button. The query isn't saved until you close it.*

Each of these steps has many features, as you can see in this and subsequent sections.

To bypass the wizard and create your query from scratch, double-click Create query in Design view in the Queries pane of the Database window or select Design View from the New Query dialog box. The Show Table dialog box opens, in which you select the tables or queries you want to query.

As an example of creating a new query without the wizard, Home Tech Repair needs a list of workorders showing the following fields from the Bid Data and Workorders tables arranged in the following order:

- Bid Number (Bid Data)
- Supervisor (Workorders)
- Job Address (Bid Data)
- Description (Workorders)
- Award Date (Bid Data)
- Start Date and Completion Date (Workorders)

Later, you add the customer's Last Name and Phone Number from the Customers table. In addition, you add the cost data and compute the total cost. Then add criteria based on start date, total cost, and other factors to limit the records in the result.

To create the new query, do the following:

1. Choose New in the Queries tab of the Database window.

2. Select Design View and click OK. The Show Table dialog box opens with three tabs that display a list of Tables, Queries, or Both in the current database. (Your lists of tables and queries will be different).

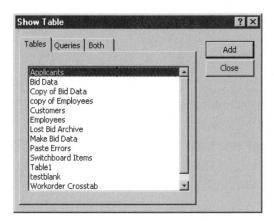

3. Select Bid Data (if it's not already selected) and choose Add. You can see the field list added to the query table pane behind the dialog box.

4. Double-click Workorders in the Show Table list, and then choose Close. Figure 8-3 shows the query design with the two tables. (Field lists have been expanded in the figure, so you can see the linking fields.)

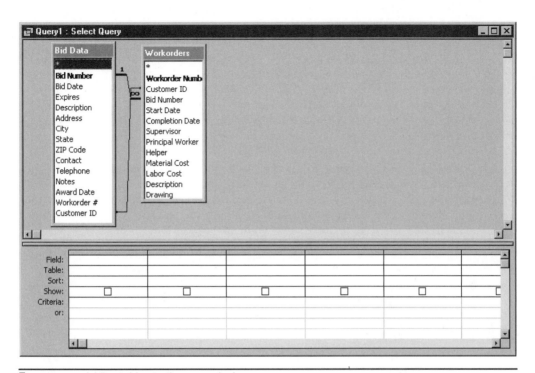

FIGURE 8-3   Adding tables to the query design

5. Keep the Query window open for adding fields to the design grid.

The next task is to choose the fields you want to appear in the query result and arrange them in the desired order. But, first, look at the relationships Access shows for the two Home Tech Repair tables, and then add a third table to the design.

Relating Multiple Tables in a Query

You begin to see the power of a relational database system when you build a query using more than one table. As you add tables, the query has access to more and more information.

To add a table to an existing query, click Show Table, choose Query | Show Table or choose Show Table from the shortcut menu. If the tables are already related at the table level, Access automatically displays the join lines when you add the table to the query design. You can tell by the appearance of the line if referential integrity is enforced and which table is the "one" side and which is the "many" side.

If the tables aren't related before adding them to the query, Access often assumes a relationship between them based on fields with the same name and data type, especially if one of them is a primary key. When Access joins the tables, referential integrity isn't enforced.

CAUTION   *If the tables aren't related at the table level and Access cannot join them, you must join them in the query or you'll get what is called a* Cartesian product: *each of the* n *rows in one table is matched with every one of the* m *rows in the second table, resulting in a recordset with n×m records.*

In the Home Tech Repair database, the relationship between the Bid Data and the Workorders table was defined as one-to-many, linked by Bid Number and with referential integrity enforced. The Workorders table is related to the Bid Data table by Customer ID, but referential integrity isn't enforced. You can see these relationships in the query table pane.

Add the Customers table to the new query and include the Last Name and Phone Number in the results, so you won't have to look them up to reach the customer.

To add the Customers table, do the following:

1. Click Show Table to open the Show Table dialog box.

2. Double-click the Customers table and click Close. The Customers table is added to the query design and the join lines show the relationships with the Bid Data and Workorders tables (see Figure 8-4). Referential integrity is enforced on the relationship with the Workorders table, but not on the relation with the Bid Data table. The tables are rearranged slightly in the figure to show the relationships more clearly.

If you added a table and decide you don't need it after all, click the field list in the table pane and press DEL, or right-click the field list and choose Remove Table from the shortcut menu. The table is removed from the query design, but it remains untouched in the database. Any fields you already placed in the design grid are also removed.

NOTE *You can also add a second copy of the same table and create a self-join.*

FIGURE 8-4 Adding a third table to the query design

Adding/Removing Fields

Adding fields to a query grid is much the same as adding them to an Advanced Filter/Sort grid. You can add all the fields at once, a selected group of fields, or one field at a time.

To add all the fields in a table to the grid at once, do one of the following:

- Double-click the asterisk (*) at the top of the field list. This method places the table or query name in the Field row of the column followed by a period and an asterisk—for example, Customers.*.

- Drag the asterisk from the field list to an empty column in the grid. This method does the same as the previous one.

- Double-click the field list title bar to select all the fields, and then drag the group to the grid. Access places each field in a separate column across the grid in the order in which they appeared in the field list.

TIP   *Using the asterisk method of adding all the fields to query is both an advantage and a disadvantage. The advantage is this: If fields are added or deleted from the underlying table or query, this query automatically makes corresponding changes to the design. The only disadvantage is if you want to sort or filter using one of the fields, it must be added separately to the grid.*

To add a group of fields to the grid at once, select them and drag them as a group. The standard use of SHIFT and CTRL to select adjacent and nonadjacent field names works here the same as with filters. When you drag the block of selected field names to the grid, Access spreads them to empty columns, beginning where you drop the group. If fields are already in the grid, the ones to the right of where you drop the group move over to make room.

To add fields to the grid one at a time, do any of the following:

- Double-click the field name to place it in the first empty column.

- Drag the field to an empty column or insert it between filled columns.

- Select the field name from the Field row drop-down list. The list in a blank column contains all the fields in all the tables in the table pane, as well as the table names with a period and asterisk.

Field:	Description	Award Date	Start Date	Completion Date	
Table:	Bid Data	Bid Data	Workorders	Workorders	Bid Data.*
Sort:					Bid Data.Bid Numbe
Show:	☑	☑	☑	☑	Bid Data.Bid Date
Criteria:					Bid Data.Expires
or:					Bid Data.Description
					Bid Data.Address
					Bid Data.City
					Bid Data.State

NOTE   *Fields added to a query inherit the properties from the underlying table or query. You can override some of these field properties in the new query design. More about this in the section "Changing Field Properties."*

To delete a field from the grid, click the column selector and press DEL, or choose Edit | Delete Columns. If you remove the check mark from the Show cell in a column with no Sort or Criteria entries, the field is automatically removed from the grid the next time you open the query.

You can adjust the column widths and drag a column to a new position, just as in a datasheet or advanced filter. Changing the column width has no effect on the query results datasheet unless you reduce it to zero and the adjustments aren't saved with the query.

NOTE   *You can ask Access to adjust a column width to fit its longest visible entry in the design grid, which might be the field name or one of the selection criteria. Move the mouse pointer to the right edge of the column selector and double-click when the pointer changes to a two-way arrow. This sets a fixed column width and, if you enter a longer value in the column later, you'll need to readjust the width to see it all.*

Figure 8-5 shows the new query, still unnamed, with all the required fields in place. The columns have been resized to fit their contents and some are off the screen out of sight.

Running and Saving the Query

As you progress with the query design, a good idea is to run the query to see if you're getting the information the way you want it. You have three ways to run the query:

- Click Datasheet view.
- Click Run.
- Choose Query | Run.

FIGURE 8-5   Adding fields to the query design grid

You needn't save the query design before looking at the results. Figure 8-6 shows the unfinished query in Datasheet view. The column widths and row heights have been adjusted, so all data appears onscreen.

You can query results in two other arrangements: PivotTable and PivotChart. These provide a shortcut to analyzing the data produced by the query.

When you try to close the query either from the Design view or from one of the query result views, Access prompts you to save the design.

Save the new query design before adding the sort order and filter criteria.

1. Return to the Query Design view and click Save.

2. Enter **Workorder Cost Sheet** in the Save As dialog box, and then choose OK.

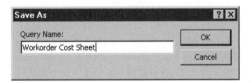

TIP   *You can usually cancel a query when it's running by pressing* CTRL-BREAK, *but extremely long queries might not comply.*

Bid Number	Supervisor	Address	Description	Award Date	Start Date	Completion Date	Last Name
98-105	Byron	2478 9th St	Install A/C	4/1/2003	3/10/2003	3/5/2003	Rogers
98-101	Ferrell	2115 J St	New Fireplace	2/15/2003	2/25/2003	3/10/2003	McCoy
98-103	Gunderson	329 5th St	Install 3 Attic Vents	3/1/2003	3/15/2003	3/18/2003	Jones
98-107	Gunderson	319 4th St	Replace Countertops	4/10/2003	4/15/2003	4/20/2003	Perry
98-108	Ferrell	2111 J St	Move Washer & Dryer	5/1/2003	5/10/2003	5/15/2003	Brown
98-111	Byron	186 G St	Ceiling Fans	5/5/2003	5/12/2003	5/25/2003	Selms
98-119	Ferrell	2111 J St	Replace Toilet	6/25/2003	6/26/2003	6/26/2003	McCoy
98-117	Ferrell	952 C St	SPA Heater	6/18/2003	6/25/2003	6/26/2003	Anders
98-116	Gunderson	329 5th St	Garden Window	6/10/2003	6/15/2003	7/1/2003	Jones
98-125	Gunderson	952 C St·	Install Dish Washer	7/1/2003	7/15/2003	7/15/2003	Anders
98-124	Gunderson	186 G St	Soaker System	7/1/2003	7/12/2003	7/15/2003	Selms
98-120	Kordel	1510 H St	Repair Driveway	6/25/2003	6/30/2003	7/15/2003	Norr

Record: 14 ◀ | 1 ▶ ▶I ▶* of 15

FIGURE 8-6   Viewing query results in Datasheet view

> **Optimizing Query Performance**
>
> If you created an important query, but it seems to take a long time to run, ways to streamline it might exist.
>
> - Make sure all the foreign keys in the related tables are indexed. If a field cannot be indexed, try not to sort on it.
> - Include in the design grid only those fields necessary in the results. Extra fields take more time to display.
> - Make sure you aren't using exorbitantly large data sizes. Unnecessarily large fields waste disk space and slow processing.

Hiding/Showing Fields

You might want to use one or more fields in filtering or sorting the query results, but you don't want the information to appear in the results. The check box in the Show cell of the design grid determines whether the field values will be displayed. Clear the check mark to hide the field; check it to show the field.

TIP   When you reopen the design of a query in which you hid some of the fields, you might think those fields were removed. Instead, Access moved the hidden fields to the rightmost columns in the design grid when you saved the query and they could be off the screen. However, if no Criteria or Show entries existed, the field is, indeed, removed from the design.

Specifying the Record Order

One of the features of Access is you can sort the results of a query in the Datasheet view by clicking one of the Sort buttons without having to set the sort order in the design. This gives you flexibility, but if you want to specify a sort order saved with the query, you should set it in the query design.

Setting a sort order in a query design is the same as setting it in an advanced filter. You choose from the Sort cell list box in the column containing the field you want to sort by. If you want to sort on more than one field, make sure you have the fields arranged in the proper order from left to right. They needn't be adjacent.

A sort order is saved with the query if you specify it in the design. Any new form or report based on the query then inherits the sort order. It needn't be applied, but it's an inherited property of the form or report.

Sorting on a lookup field can have confusing results. For example, Figure 8-7 shows the results of sorting the Workorder Cost Sheet records first by Supervisor, and then by Completion date. The lower window shows the underlying query grid with both fields sorted in ascending order.

The Completion Dates are in the correct order within the set of records for a given Supervisor. The Supervisor fields, however, don't appear to be in alphabetic order, either ascending or descending. When you specify a sort in the query grid, Access sorts on the

FIGURE 8-7   Sorting records on a lookup field

stored value, which in this case is the Employee ID number, not the employee name. If you want the records sorted by the displayed value, you need to sort in the Datasheet view, which has access to the related lookup list values.

NOTE   *The same is true when you try to filter records based on a value in a lookup field. You must enter the stored value in the Criteria cell in the query grid only with filtering on a lookup field with Advanced Filter/Sort, as discussed in the previous chapter.*

Like a sort order, you can apply a filter to the query results, instead of making it part of the query design. This has the same effect as adding the criteria to the design, but the filter won't be saved with the query.

Showing Highest or Lowest Values

Limiting the results to the few highest or lowest values in a field can be handy for isolating the more labor-intensive jobs or finding the employees who could use a raise. For example, you can ask Access to display only the records with the 15 highest or lowest values in a field, or the records with the highest or lowest 15 percent of values.

You use the Top Values box on the toolbar to specify how many or what percentage of the records to include in the results. The Top Values list includes 5, 25, and 100 records, and

5 percent and 25 percent of the values to choose from, as well as All. You can also type any percentage or number of values you want directly in the box.

Access selects the records starting from the top of the list, so before you select the Top Values setting, you must sort (descending) on the field you want to display the highest values. If you want the lowest values, sort in ascending order. If you specified a sort on any other field in the query, make sure the sorted field is to the right of the top values field, so the values will be subordinate to the Top Value list.

TIP *If you specify the number of top values you want to see, all values that match the last value in the list are also included, so you might see more than you expected. If you don't want to see the duplicate records, change the UniqueValues query property to Yes. You can also use the TopValues query property to limit the records to the top or bottom values. More about query properties in the section "Setting Query Properties" later in this chapter.*

Adding Selection Criteria

The last chapter introduced you to the concept of adding selection criteria when filtering records with Advanced Filter/Sort. The selection criteria in queries are also expressions defining a condition that must be met for the record to be included in the subset. An *expression* is a combination of symbols, values, identifiers, and operators used for many purposes, many of which you've already seen, and others you learn about in later chapters, including the following:

- Establishing field and record validation rules.
- Setting default field values.
- Defining filter criteria.
- Computing calculated field values.
- Specifying conditions under which a macro runs.
- Using as arguments in Visual Basic functions and procedures.

Symbols used in expressions include quotation marks, colons, asterisks, and other special characters. *Values* can be expressed as literal values, constants, the result of a function, or an identifier. *Identifiers* refer to the value of a field, a control in a form or report, or a property. An *operator* is a symbol or word that indicates an operation to be performed on one or more elements in the expression.

Using Wildcards and Operators

If you want to set a criterion for a text field and you want to match only part of the field, you can use the same wildcards you used in filters: **?** to represent a single character and ***** to represent any number of characters. For example, to find all Bid Data records for jobs on J Street, enter the expression

J St

in the Criteria cell in the Address column and press ENTER or TAB. Access examines the expression and completes the syntax by adding special characters:

Like "*J St*"

Operators are the key to more flexible expressions. Access has several classes of operators: arithmetic, comparison, concatenation, and logical. Table 8-1 lists the operators you can use in query criteria expressions and gives examples of each.

Operator	Description	Example	Limits Records to
Arithmetic Operators			
+	Addition	=Cost+50	Values equal to 50 more than the value in the Cost field
−	Subtraction	=Cost-50	Values equal to 50 less than the value in the Cost field
*	Multiplication	=Cost*2	Values twice the amount in the Cost field
/	Division	=Cost/2	Values half the amount in the Cost field
\	Integer division	=Cost\2	The integer portion of values that results from dividing the Cost field value by 2
Mod	Modulo division	=Cost Mod 2	The remainder of dividing the Cost value by 2
Comparison Operators			
=	Equals	=Books *or* ="Books"	Text value Books
>	Greater than	>7/15/03 *or* >#7/15/03#	Dates later than July 15, 2003
<	Less than	<1500	Values less than 1500
>=	Greater than or equal to	>=15	Values greater than or equal to 15

TABLE 8-1   Operators Used in Expressions

Operator	Description	Example	Limits Records to
<=	Less than or equal to	<=1/1/04 *or* <=#1/1/04#	Dates on or before January 1, 2004
<>	Not equal to	<>NY	Values other than NY
Between...And	Between two values, inclusive	Between 100 And 500	Numbers from 100 and 500, inclusive
In	Included in a set of values	In("Germany", "France")	Either Germany or France
Is Null	Field is empty	Is Null	Records with no value in the field
Is Not Null	Field is not empty	Is Not Null	Records with a value in the field
" "	Field contains zero-length string	=""	Records with zero-length string in the field
Like	With wildcards, matches a pattern	Like C*	Any text values that begin with C
Logical Operators			
And	Both conditions are True	>=10 And <=100	Values between 10 and 100, inclusive
Or	Either condition is True	Books Or Videos	Either Books or Videos
Not	Not True	Not Like AB*	All values except those beginning with AB

TABLE 8-1   Operators Used in Expressions *(continued)*

NOTE   *You can also enclose text values in expressions in quotation marks with the wildcards. For example, Not Like "AB*".*

When filtering on a Date field, you can use one of the date functions in the criteria expression. Table 8-2 shows examples of the date functions included in expressions used as criteria to limit the records in the Workorders table by values in the Completion Date field.

Function	Example	Result
Date()	<Date()+45	Displays workorders with Completion Date less than 45 days from today.
DateAdd()	>DateAdd("m",6,Date())	Displays workorders with Completion Date more than six months from today. The *m* isolates the month value.

TABLE 8-2   Using Date Functions in Expressions

Function	Example	Result
Year()	Year([Completion Date])=2003	Displays workorders whose Completion Date falls in 2003.
DatePart()	DatePart("q",[Completion Date])=2	Displays workorders whose Completion Date is in the second calendar quarter. The *q* isolates the calendar quarter.
Month()	Year([Completion Date])=Year(Now) And Month([Completion Date])=Month(Now)	Displays workorders with Completion Dates in the current year and month.

TABLE 8-2   Using Date Functions in Expressions *(continued)*

NOTE   *If the field name contains a space, a colon (:), or any Access special character, the name must be enclosed in brackets ([]) when used in an expression.*

Using a Single Criterion

You add a single selection criterion to a Criteria cell in the query design grid, exactly the same as in an advanced filter. For example, if you want to see information from the Workorder Cost Sheet for only those jobs supervised by Gunderson, do the following:

1. Open the Workorder Cost Sheet query in Design view and enter **12** (the Employee ID number for Gunderson) in the Criteria cell of the Supervisor column, and then press ENTER. Access adds quotation marks around 12 because the field is a text data type.

Field:	Bid Number	Supervisor	Address	Description	Award Date	Start Date
Table:	Bid Data	Workorders	Bid Data	Bid Data	Bid Data	Workorders
Sort:						
Show:	☑	☑	☑	☑	☑	☑
Criteria:		"12"				
or:						

2. Switch to Datasheet view to display the five records for Gunderson's jobs.

3. Now you want to see the records for all jobs started before July 1, 2003, without regard to the supervisor. Return to Design view and delete the Supervisor criteria by selecting the expression and pressing DEL.

4. Enter **<7/1/2003** in the Start Date Criteria cell and press ENTER. Access adds the date delimiters (#).

Field:	Supervisor	Start Date	Address	Description
Table:	Workorders	Workorders	Bid Data	Bid Data
Sort:	Ascending			
Show:	☑	☑	☑	☑
Criteria:		<#7/1/2003#		
or:				

5. Run the query to see the 11 records for jobs started before July 1, 2003.

When you move out of the Criteria cell after entering the expression, Access automatically parses the expression and inserts characters to complete the syntax:

- Brackets ([]) around field names
- Number signs (#) around dates
- Double quotation marks ("") around text
- Equal sign (=) before a calculated field expression

Using Multiple Criteria

To apply more than one selection criterion, you combine them with the And or Or operators, using the same logic as with filters:

- Use And to require both criteria be met to include the record in the query result.
- Use Or to return records that satisfy either expression.

NOTE *If you want to select records based on field values, the field must be in the design grid, even if you don't show it in the results.*

Where you enter the expressions in the design grid depends on how you want them applied:

- In one field using Or, enter one expression in the Criteria row and the second in the Or row.

Field:	Bid Number	Supervisor	Start Date	Address
Table:	Bid Data	Workorders	Workorders	Bid Data
Sort:				
Show:	☑	☑	☑	☑
Criteria:		"12"		
or:		"10"		

- In one field using And, enter both expressions in the Criteria row combined with the And operator. This combination is seldom used because a field usually can't have two different values at once, but it can be used to find a combination of text strings in a memo field.

TIP *If the expression is wider than the input area, press SHIFT-F2 with the insertion point in the cell where you enter the expression. This opens the Zoom box where you can enter and edit the expression. Even though the text wraps to multiple lines in the Zoom box, the expression is only one line.*

- In two fields using Or, enter one expression in the Criteria row of one column and the other expression in the Or row of the other column. It doesn't matter which is which.

Field:	Bid Number	Supervisor	Start Date	Address
Table:	Bid Data	Workorders	Workorders	Bid Data
Sort:				
Show:	☑	☑	☑	☑
Criteria:		"12"		
or:			<#7/1/2003#	

- In two fields using And, enter both expressions in the Criteria row.

Field:	Bid Number	Supervisor	Start Date	Address
Table:	Bid Data	Workorders	Workorders	Bid Data
Sort:				
Show:	☑	☑	☑	☑
Criteria:		"12"	<#7/1/2003#	
or:				

- In three fields using both And and Or, enter one pair of And expressions in the Criteria row and the other pair in the Or row.

Field:	Bid Number	Supervisor	Start Date	Address	Description
Table:	Bid Data	Workorders	Workorders	Bid Data	Bid Data
Sort:		Ascending			
Show:	☑	☑	☑	☑	☑
Criteria:		"12"	<#7/1/2003#		
or:			>#6/1/2003#	Like "*J St*"	

The results of this query are sorted by Supervisor (actually, by Supervisor ID).

Workorder Cost Sheet : Select Query

Bid Number	Supervisor	Start Date	Address	Description	Award Date	Completion Date	Last Name
98-119	Ferrell	6/26/2003	2111 J St	Replace Toilet	6/25/2003	6/26/2003	McCoy
98-103	Gunderson	3/15/2003	329 5th St	Install 3 Attic Vent	3/1/2003	3/18/2003	Jones
98-107	Gunderson	4/15/2003	319 4th St	Replace Counterto	4/10/2003	4/20/2003	Perry
98-116	Gunderson	6/15/2003	329 5th St	Garden Window	6/10/2003	7/1/2003	Jones
98-122	Connelly	7/10/2003	2111 J St	Bay Window	7/1/2003	7/20/2003	McCoy

Record: 1 of 5

The Advanced Filter/Sort saved as a query in the last chapter provides an example of a slightly different arrangement of multiple selection criteria in the design grid.

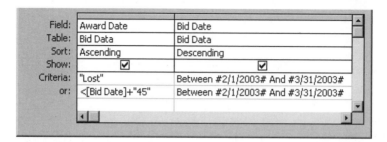

Field:	Award Date	Bid Date
Table:	Bid Data	Bid Data
Sort:	Ascending	Descending
Show:	☑	☑
Criteria:	"Lost"	Between #2/1/2003# And #3/31/2003#
or:	<[Bid Date]+"45"	Between #2/1/2003# And #3/31/2003#

The criteria specified in the Look for tab appear in the Criteria row of the design grid and the expressions entered in the Or tab appear in the Or row. The Bid Date column has been widened to show the entire expression. Another way to view the complete expression is to right-click the cell and choose Zoom from the shortcut menu to open the Zoom box.

TIP   *When working with expressions, you can use the Cut, Copy, and Paste buttons as shortcuts to enter criteria.*

Getting Help from the Expression Builder

When you need to enter a complicated expression in a query design as a selection criterion or you want to construct a calculated field, you can call on the Expression Builder for help. To open the Expression Builder, click in the cell where you want to place the expression, and then click Build in the Query Design view. You can also right-click in the cell where the expression will go and choose Build from the shortcut menu. If the cell already contains an expression, this is copied to the Expression Builder. For example, the Builder shows the expression with an Award Date criterion left over from an earlier query.

Notice the Workorder Cost Sheet folder is open and a list of fields is displayed in the center of the lower section.

The upper pane of the Expression Builder is where you enter the expression. The lower pane consists of expression elements divided into three levels. The leftmost panel contains all the groupings in the current session. When you open a folder in this panel, the contents of the selected item are listed in the middle panel. Selecting an item in the center panel opens a list of individual elements in the right panel. You can add one of these to the expression by double-clicking the name, or by selecting it and clicking Paste.

For example, suppose you want to use the Month() function to define a selection criterion on the Start Date field in the Workorder Cost Sheet query to display only records for jobs started in June. To accomplish this, do the following:

1. In the Query Design view, right-click in the Criteria cell of the Start Date column and choose Expression Builder from the shortcut menu. Delete any expression already in the upper pane.

2. Double-click the Functions folder to open two subfolders: Built-In Functions and Home Tech Repair.

3. Open the Built-In Functions folder. A list of function categories appears in the center panel.

4. Choose Date/Time. The right panel shows a list of all the date- or time-related built-in functions.

5. Scroll down the list and select Month, and then choose Paste. The Month() function is copied to the upper pane with the correct syntax.

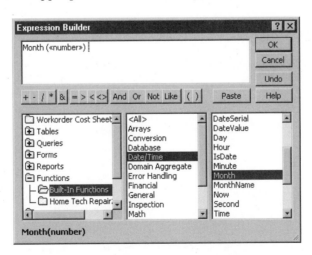

6. The Month() function requires an argument—a number—to tell Access which month you want to specify in the expression. Click to highlight <<number>> in the parentheses and enter **6** (for June).

7. Click OK. You return to the Query Design window where Month(6) now shows in the Criteria cell of the Start Date column.

Handling Blank Fields

Fields containing null values and zero-length strings can affect the query results. Consider these aspects when you work with potentially empty fields:

- If the field has been left empty because of incomplete data, it's easy to display those records in a datasheet where you can add the missing data. Use Is Null as the criteria to find null values and "" to find zero-length strings.

- Query results that include data from related tables display only those records in which neither matching field has a null value.

- When you use a field in an aggregate calculation, such as sum or count, Access doesn't include records with null values in that field. If you want to include records with a null value when you count the number of records, use Count with the * wildcard.

- If one of the fields in an expression that uses an arithmetic operator (+, −, *, /, \, ^) has a null value, the entire expression returns a null value.

- You can convert null values to zero-length strings with the Nz() function. If you want to display records with zero-length string values, but no null values, use Like "*" as the selection criterion.

Setting Query Properties

Like all other database objects, a query has a set of properties that controls its appearance and behavior. To open the Query Properties dialog box, place the insertion point in the table pane, and then do one of the following:

- Click Properties.
- Choose View | Properties.
- Right-click anywhere in the design window outside the field lists, and then choose Properties from the shortcut menu.
- Click in the table pane and press ALT-ENTER.

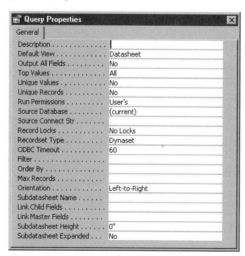

To see an explanation of a query property, click in the property box and read the description in the status bar. You can also press F1 to open the corresponding Help topic.

Modifying a Query

To open a query for modifying the design, select the query in the Queries page of the Database window and click Design. If you want to view the results of the query first, click Open, and then switch to Design view. You can also right-click the query name and choose Open or Design from the shortcut menu.

You use the Query Design window to make changes to the query, just the same as if you were creating it. You can add or delete a field, rearrange the columns, show or hide any of the fields, change the resulting records sort order, and add one or more selection criteria.

Inserting a Field and Changing the Field Order

If you want to add another field to the grid, drag the field name to the Field row of the column where you want the field. The field is inserted and the other columns move to make room.

TIP   *If you double-click the field name, Access puts it at the end of the line in the first empty column.*

Moving a field in the design grid works the same as in a datasheet. Select the field by clicking the column selector (the mouse pointer changes to a down arrow). Release the mouse button and click again when it changes to a left upward arrow. Then drag the column to a new position. When you see the dark vertical line where you want the column's left margin to appear, release the mouse button. The column moves and the other columns slide over to oblige.

Changing Field Properties

The fields that appear in the query results inherit the properties from the table design. You might want the field to look different or show a different name in the query results, however, especially if you're going to use them as the basis for a custom form or report. You cannot change all a field's properties, only those that appear in the field's property sheet in the query design.

TIP   *When you make changes to field properties in the table design, any new or existing queries usually inherit those changes. The exception to this rule is this: If you already changed field properties in the query design, any changes in the table design aren't carried over to override the query customization.*

You might want a field to show a more descriptive name. For example, Access assigns default names to calculated fields, such as Expr1 or CountOfAddress, which aren't very informative. When you change the name in the query design, the new name appears in the datasheet and in any new forms or reports based on the query. The new name doesn't affect the underlying table or any existing forms or reports.

To rename a field in the query design, do the following:

1. Place the insertion point to the left of the first letter of the name in the grid.

2. Type the new name followed by a colon (:). If you're replacing Expr1 or another Access-assigned name, replace only the name, not the expression following the colon.

3. Press ENTER.

TIP   *If you want to keep the name in the grid, but show a different name in the datasheet, change the field's Caption property in the property sheet.*

To change other field properties, click in the field on the grid and click Properties or press ALT-ENTER. You can also choose View | Properties or right-click the field and choose Properties from the shortcut menu. Entries in the field property sheets are blank; they don't contain the settings defined in the table design. Any entries you make in the Query Design window override the preset properties.

When you finish with the property sheet, click Close. Changing field properties in a query design has no effect on the underlying table design.

The field property sheet has two tabs: General and Lookup. The General tab shows four properties you can change in the query design, as follows:

- The *Description* is the text displayed in the status bar when you click the field in the Datasheet view. Any text entered here replaces the Description entered in the table definition. You can enter up to 255 characters.

- *Format* shows a list of applicable formats for the field. A Text field has no list, but you can enter a custom format.

- An *Input Mask* creates a data entry skeleton. You can either type the mask in the box or click Build to start the Input Mask Wizard.

- The *Caption* property specifies the column header for a datasheet, form, or report in place of the field name.

- The *Smart Tags* property specifies which available tags are attached to the field.

- If the field is a Number field, the *Decimal Places* property also appears in the property sheet.

TIP   If you want to change several field properties or even a query property, keep the property sheet open and the options will change when you click another object in the query design.

If the field is a lookup field, the Lookup tab has one option where you can change the Display Control to a Text Box, a List Box, or a Combo Box. The other properties on the Lookup tab are the same as those in the table design. If the field isn't a lookup field, this tab is blank.

TIP   Calculated fields don't inherit any properties from the table because they didn't exist in the table. The properties must be set in the query design. For example, if the calculated field contains currency data, set the field's Format property to Currency.

Performing Calculations in a Query

You can perform many types of calculations in a query that are recomputed each time the query is run, so you always have current data. The results of the calculations aren't stored in the table. In a query, two types of calculations exist: aggregate calculations and custom calculated fields.

The *aggregate calculations* are predefined operations performed on groups of records and provide totals, counts, averages, and other information about field values in all records or in groups of records. Think of these calculations as vertical computations. For example, add up the number of jobs on J Street or calculate the average labor cost for all jobs.

The *calculated fields* create new fields in a record by combining the values in other fields in the same record, producing a horizontal computation. You can create new numeric, date, or text fields for each record using custom calculations. For example, use the expression

```
[Completion Date]-[Start Date]
```

to create a new field named Job Time. After creating a calculated field, you can use it to analyze the data further. For example, after finding the Job Time for each job, you can compute the average time. Or, you can even add a selection criterion to limit the records to jobs in a specific area or supervised by a specific employee.

Adding a Calculated Field

To add a new field that displays the results of a calculation based on other fields in the grid, click the Field row of an empty column and enter an expression. The field names must be enclosed in brackets, so Access recognizes them as fields.

For example, add a calculated field to a query of the Home Tech Repair Workorders table that shows the total cost of each current job:

1. In the Query Design view, drag the fields you want to see in the result to the grid, including Material Cost and Labor Cost.

2. Click in the Field cell on the first empty column and enter the expression: **[Material Cost]+[Labor Cost]**, and then press ENTER. Access adds a default field name to the new field, Expr1. You can change the default field name to one that's more descriptive.

3. Move the insertion point to the left in the Field cell and replace Expr1 with **Total Cost**, keeping the colon.

4. Click Datasheet view. Figure 8-8 shows the results of the new calculated field.

If you want to see the total cost of each job, including a 15 percent markup for overhead expenses, add another calculated field using the expression: [Total Cost]*1.15.

TIP   *When you run the query, if you misspell a field name in an expression, Access assumes it's a parameter needed by the query and asks you to enter the value. Click Cancel to close the Enter Parameter Value dialog box and to return to the grid to correct the field name. See Chapter 9 for more information about query parameters.*

You aren't limited to Number and Currency fields in calculated fields. Text fields are easily combined with the concatenation operator (&). For example, if you want to create a new field showing employees' complete names in one field, use the following expression:

```
[First Name]&" "&[Last Name]
```

The quotation marks between the field names add a space.

Material Cost	Labor Cost	Description	Address	City	State	Contact	Total Cost
$1,072.50	$572.50	New Fireplace	2115 J St	Los Padres	CA	McCoy, John	$1,645.00
$1,155.00	$840.00	Install 3 Attic Vents	329 5th St	Los Padres	CA	Jones, David	$1,995.00
$850.50	$126.00	Install A/C	2478 9th St	Los Padres	CA	Rogers, Ohykki	$976.50
$115.50	$315.00	Replace Countertops	319 4th St	Los Padres	CA	Perry, Oliver	$430.50
$262.50	$252.00	Move Washer & Dryer	2111 J St	Los Padres	CA	McCoy, John	$514.50
$750.00	$800.00	Ceiling Fans	186 G St	Los Padres	CA	Brown, Agnes	$1,550.00
$2,500.00	$7,200.00	Finish Basement	1520 8th St	Los Padres	CA	Selms, Harry	$9,700.00
$400.00	$750.00	Garden Window	329 5th St	Los Padres	CA	Jones, David	$1,150.00
$1,100.00	$450.00	SPA Heater	952 C St	Los Padres	CA	Anders, Bob	$1,550.00
$175.00	$100.00	Replace Toilet	2111 J St	Los Padres	CA	McCoy, John	$275.00
$300.00	$1,300.00	Repair Driveway	1510 H St	Los Padres	CA	Norr, James	$1,600.00
$280.00	$480.00	Erect Tool Shed	329 5th St	Los Padres	CA	Jones, David	$760.00
$400.00	$1,100.00	Bay Window	2111 J St	Los Padres	CA	McCoy, John	$1,500.00
$75.00	$300.00	Soaker System	186 G St	Los Padres	CA	Brown, Agnes	$375.00
$420.00	$100.00	Install Dish Washer	952 C St	Los Padres	CA	Anders, Bob	$520.00

Record: 1 of 15

FIGURE 8-8   Displaying the new Total Cost field

If you want to include the employee's full name and add some text to the display, use an expression such as the following:

Field:	Full Name: [First Name] & " " & [Last Name]	SSN	Address	City
Table:		Employees	Employees	Employees
Sort:				
Show:	☑	☑	☑	☑
Criteria:				
or:				

The result of this calculated field looks like this:

Full Name	SSN	Address	City	State	ZIP
Bryan Ferrell	604-00-1369	316 C St	Los Padres	CA	92111
Ben J. Cloud	603-00-1423	2015 3rd St	Los Padres	CA	92111
Selma Gunderson	613-00-1743	825 F St	Los Padres	CA	92111
David L Byron	614-00-1663	1529 G St	Los Padres	CA	92111
Fred C Connelly	629-00-1543	2001 5th St	Los Padres	CA	92111
John C Kordel	627-00-1437	3560 H St.	Los Padres	CA	92111
Don De Salle	629-00-1827	1519 8th St	Los Padres	CA	92111

Record: 1 of 13

NOTE *If two tables in the query have a field with the same name, you must use the table name, as well as the field name in the expression, separated by an exclamation mark (!)—for example, [Bid Date]![Start Date] or [Employees]![Employee ID].*

Once you add the calculated field to the design grid, you can change its properties like any other field in the query. You can also summarize on a calculated field, as well as on a basic table field, as described in the next section. By using more complex functions in expressions, you can create a wide variety of calculated fields using many data types.

NOTE *You cannot edit a calculated field in the datasheet view of the query. If you want a different value, change one of the fields in the expression.*

Summarizing with the Wizard

As mentioned earlier in this chapter, if the query you're creating with the Simple Query Wizard contains any number, currency, or date/time fields, you're given the opportunity to create summary fields.

The second wizard dialog box offers two choices: Detail, in which all records are shown, or Summary. If you choose Summary and click the Summary Options button, the Summary Options dialog box opens where you can specify the types of summarization you want.

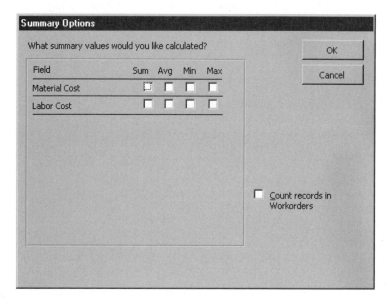

The two currency fields are listed with check boxes where you can choose the type of summary for each field. In addition, you have the option of counting the number of records in each group. After making your choices in this dialog box, click OK and return to the wizard. If any date/time fields are in the query, you have an opportunity to group on those values as well, by month, quarter, year, and so on.

Here are the results of choosing to calculate the total and average of both cost fields, as well as to count the number of work orders for each supervisor. When you add summaries to the query design, you can be much more creative.

Supervisor	Sum Of Material Cost	Avg Of Material Cost	Sum Of Labor Cost	Avg Of Labor Cost	Count Of Workorders
Ferrell	$2,890.00	$578.00	$1,854.50	$370.90	5
Gunderson	$2,165.50	$433.10	$2,305.00	$461.00	5
Byron	$2,000.50	$666.83	$2,026.00	$675.33	3
Connelly	$2,500.00	$2,500.00	$7,200.00	$7,200.00	1
Kordel	$300.00	$300.00	$1,300.00	$1,300.00	1

Summarizing with Aggregate Functions

If you want to know the material cost of all the current jobs or the average billing rate for all employees, you can add a summary calculation. The summaries work with values in a field from multiple records. You can summarize all the records in the result or group the records based on a specific field value—such as Supervisor—and calculate the summary value for each group separately.

Summarizing All Records

To summarize field values in a query, start with a select query, add the field you want to summarize, and then specify the way you want the fields summarized. For example, to find the total and average Material Cost for current workorders, do the following:

1. Start a new select query of the Workorders table and drag the Material Cost field to the grid.

2. Click Totals to add the Total row to the grid. You can also choose View | Totals or right-click in the grid and choose Totals from the shortcut menu.

3. Click the Total cell in the Material Cost column and choose Sum from the drop-down option list.

4. To summarize on the same field in two ways, you need another copy of the field in the grid. Drag another copy of the Material Cost field to the next empty column and choose Avg from the Total list.

5. Switch to Datasheet view to see the results.

This example is summarized over all the records in the table. You can also base a summary on a subset of records by using the Group By option in the Total cell for the fields that make up the group. For example, you could count the number of jobs assigned to each supervisor.

You have a choice of twelve options in the Total drop-down list, seven of which perform mathematical calculations, two return specific records, and the other three indicate other uses for the field. You can use all the mathematical and selection options with Number,

Date/Time, Currency and AutoNumber fields. If the field is a Text data type, you can use only the Min, Max, Count, First, and Last options.

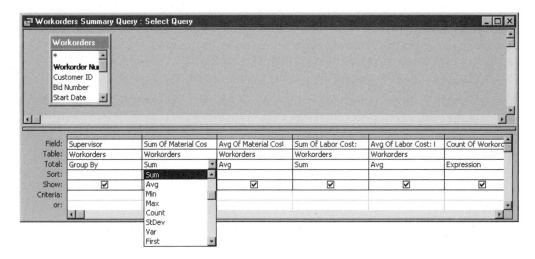

The other three options are

- *Group By*, which defines the groups you want the calculations to apply to—for example, show the average material costs for work orders grouped by supervisor.

- *Expression*, which creates a calculated field with an aggregate function in the expression.

- *Where*, which specifies selection criteria in a field not used in grouping. With this option, the Show check box is cleared by default.

NOTE   *Summaries usually don't include blanks, except in the case of Count. If you want to include records with null values, use Count with the asterisk (*) wildcard character: Count*.*

Summarizing by Group

When you add fields to the grid with the Total row visible, the default entry is Group By. To group records with the same value in that field, leave the Group By option in the Total cell. For example, to count the number of workorders under control of each supervisor, do the following:

1. Start a new select query with the Workorders table and drag the Supervisor, Workorder Number, and Labor Cost fields to the grid.

2. Enter the expression **Avg([Labor Cost]+[Material Cost])** and press ENTER.

3. The Total cell still holds the Group By option. Change this to Expression and press ENTER.

4. Change the default Expr1 name to **Average Total**.

Field:	Supervisor	Workorder Number	Labor Cost	Average Total: Avg([Labor Cost]+[Material Cost])	
Table:	Workorders	Workorders	Workorders		
Total:	Group By	Count	Avg	Expression	
Sort:					
Show:	☑	☑	☑	☑	
Criteria:					
or:					

5. Click Run.

Query1 : Select Query

Supervisor	CountOfWorkorder Number	AvgOfLabor Cost	Average Total
Ferrell	4	$343.63	$996.13
Gunderson	5	$461.00	$894.10
Byron	2	$463.00	$1,263.25
Connelly	1	$1,100.00	$1,500.00
Kordel	1	$1,300.00	$1,600.00
Howell	1	$480.00	$760.00
Dobbins	1	$7,200.00	$9,700.00

Record: 1 of 7

You can also sort the groups by the values computed in the summaries. For example, you could reorder the previous records in descending order of the average total cost of the workorders assigned to each supervisor.

Adding Criteria

You can add selection criteria to summary queries to limit the result in three ways:

- To limit the records before they're included in the group and before the group calculations are performed, add the field whose records you want to limit, and then enter the criterion. For example, in the Supervisor's group, you could include only those workorders whose labor costs exceed $500. If you're calculating any totals in the same query, change the Total cell to Where.

- To limit the groupings after the records are included in the group, but before the group calculations are performed, enter the criterion in the Group By field. For example, you could include a summary for specific Supervisors.

- To limit the results of the group summaries, enter the criterion in the field that contains the calculation. For example, you could display results only for Supervisor groups whose average total cost exceeds $1,000.

Adding Customized Expressions

To create your own customized expressions in a summary query, you can use any of the built-in Access functions in the query grid. The most useful functions for summarizing data in a query come in three basic groups:

- *Aggregate Functions,* such as you already saw that calculate statistical values from field data—for example, Avg, Sum, Count, and so on.

- *Domain Aggregate Functions* that compute the same statistical values, but use all the values in the table or query. Domain Aggregate Functions override any grouping restrictions. Examples are DAvg, DSum, DCount, and so on.

- *Formatting Functions* that extract and display parts of the data and combine or format the results in many ways. Examples are Format, Left, Mid, and Right.

Tip   *If you use an Aggregate or Domain Aggregate Function that computes the standard deviation or variance with a group containing only two records, the result is a null value.*

Creating Special Queries with the Query Wizard

As you saw in the New Query dialog box, more Query Wizards exist than the Simple Select Wizard. The list includes wizards that create crosstabs, queries that find duplicate records, and queries that find unmatched records in related tables.

Creating a Find Duplicates Query

A Find Duplicates query locates and displays records in which the specified field has the same values. For example, you could use a Find Duplicates query to display all the work orders supervised by a specific employee or all the bids made on jobs at a particular address. The Find Duplicates Wizard can create the query for you using the following steps:

1. Click New in the Queries page of the Database window and double-click Find Duplicates Query Wizard in the New Query dialog box. The first dialog box asks you to select the table or query you want to search.

2. Choose Bid Data and click Next.

3. In the next dialog box (see Figure 8-9), double-click Address in the Available Fields list to add it to the Duplicate-value fields list, and then click Next.

4. Next, select all the fields you want to display in addition to the field in which duplicates might occur—for example, Bid Number, Bid Date, Description, and Principal. Then click Next.

5. In the last dialog box, enter Duplicate Addresses as the name for the query and click Finish.

The resulting datasheet lists only those records that have duplicate Address fields. For example, there are two Bid Data records applying to 1510 H St. and three records for 2111 J St.

If you want to sort the results or modify the query in another way, choose to modify the query in the last wizard dialog box, instead of to view the results.

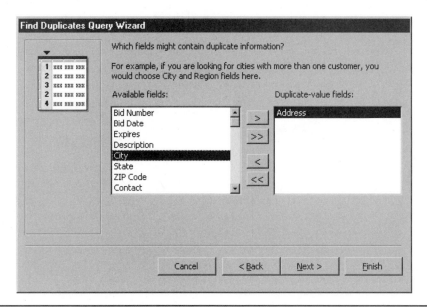

FIGURE 8-9   Choosing the Duplicate-value field

Creating a Find Unmatched Query

With the Find Unmatched Query Wizard, you can locate and display records in one table that have no match in a related table. For example, you can find customers who have no workorders, so you can send a letter to remind them of your services.

To create a Find Unmatched query, do the following:

1. Start a new query with the Find Unmatched Query Wizard.

2. In the first dialog box, choose Customers as the table whose records you want to display and click Next.

3. In the next dialog box, choose Workorders as the table you want to match with the Customers table. If there are any customers with no corresponding workorders, the Customer record is included in the result. Click Next.

4. In the next dialog box, specify the matching fields by choosing the field in each list and clicking the <=> button. If the fields have the same name, Access predetermines the relationship (see Figure 8-10). Click Next.

5. Then select the fields you want to see in the result, such as name, address, and phone number.

6. Accept the query name as Customers Without Matching Workorders, and then click Finish. You can see the three customers that have no workorders in progress.

FIGURE 8-10   Specifying the matching fields

If you switch to the query design, you see the wizard has created a left inner join for the two tables, which returns the records from the parent table (the one-side) only if no matching records are in the child table (the many-side).

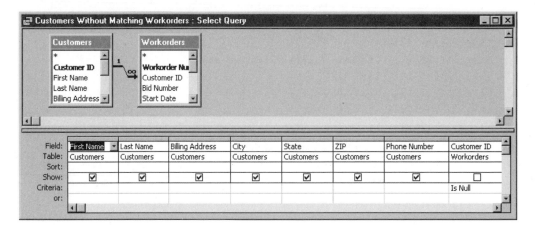

Creating a Crosstab Query

A *crosstab query* is a special type of summary query that correlates summary values between two or more sets of field values, such as sales of types of products within certain sales regions or categories of workorder costs correlated with the active supervisor. One set of facts is listed as row headings at the left of the crosstab and the other is listed as column headings across the top. The summarized values, sums, averages, or counts are contained in the body of the crosstab.

To create a crosstab, you need at least three output fields: row headings, column headings, and values. You can create a crosstab query from scratch or with the help of the Crosstab Query Wizard. The result of running a crosstab query is a snapshot and none of the data in the results is editable.

As an example of creating a crosstab query, use the table named Workorder Crosstab, which has all the costs in one field, with an additional field that indicates the category of the cost: labor or material. To use the Crosstab Query Wizard to create a crosstab that correlates the category of cost with the job supervisor, follow these steps:

1. Click New on the Queries page of the Database window and choose Crosstab Query Wizard from the New Query dialog box, and then click OK.

2. In the first dialog box (see Figure 8-11) choose the Workorder Crosstab table as the basis for the query, and then click Next. (The table used for a crosstab is a regular table and doesn't need to include the name Crosstab.)

3. In the next dialog box (see Figure 8-12), double-click Supervisor as the field to use as the row heading and click Next.

4. In the next dialog box, choose Cost Category as the column heading, and then click Next.

5. In the next dialog box, select Cost as the value field and Sum in the Function list. Clear the check mark next to Yes, include row sums if you don't want to see a Total

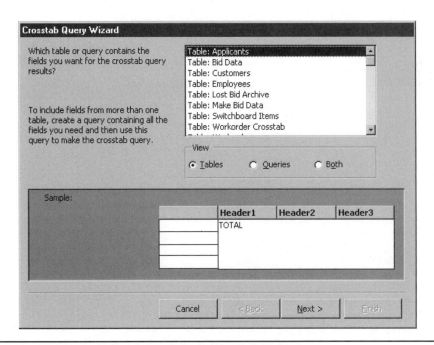

FIGURE 8-11   Working in the first Crosstab Query Wizard dialog box

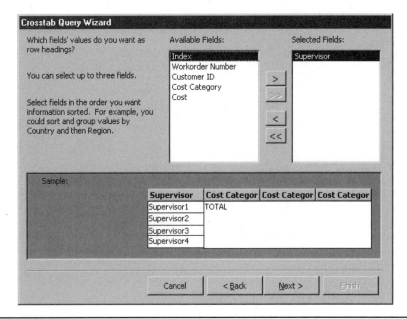

FIGURE 8-12 Choosing the row heading

of Costs column (see Figure 8-13). The sample pane shows how the fields will be arranged in the crosstab. Click Back to return to a previous dialog box to make changes or click Next to finish the query.

6. Enter the query name, Workorder Costs by Category and Supervisor in the final dialog box, and then click Finish.

Supervisor	Total Of Cost	Labor	Material
Ferrell	$3,950.00	$2,000.00	$1,950.00
Gunderson	$4,355.00	$2,250.00	$2,105.00
Byron	$9,700.00	$7,200.00	$2,500.00
Connelly	$1,420.00	$360.00	$1,060.00
Kordel	$1,600.00	$1,300.00	$300.00
Howell	$1,550.00	$800.00	$750.00
Dobbins	$1,035.00	$580.00	$455.00

You can make changes to the query design after the wizard is finished with it. For example, you can limit the records included in the crosstab by adding the field you want to set the limit on and setting the Total cell to Where. Then leave the Crosstab cell blank and enter the expression in the Criteria cell.

If you want to change the column headings in the crosstab, return to the query design and open the query property sheet. Enter the titles you want for the columns in the Column Headings property, in the order they are to appear in the result. Separate the headings with semicolons (;) or new line breaks (CTRL-ENTER). You can also type the list of column headings enclosed in double quotation marks separated with commas.

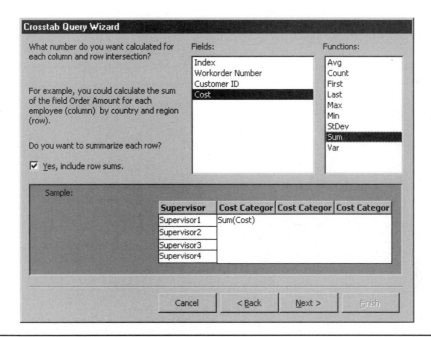

FIGURE 8-13   Choosing the values for the crosstab

You can have up to three row heading fields. The additional row headings effectively become subgroupings of the data. Each additional row heading multiplies the number of records in the result: two row headings doubles the records in the result; three headings triple the result.

You can also create a crosstab query from the Design view by starting a new query based on the same table. Then click Query Type and choose Crosstab Query. The crosstab row is added to the design grid. Here is the design of the query created by the Crosstab Query Wizard.

TIP   If you choose a Date/time field for a row or column heading, the wizard asks By which interval do you want to group your Date/Time column information? You can choose Year, Quarter, Month, Date, or Date/Time. So, you can do a crosstab by month or year, without having to create a calculated field for it.

Printing the Query Results

After you finish the query design and run the query, you can print the results in the datasheet the same way you print a table datasheet. To send the datasheet directly to the printer, click Print. If you want to select some of the printer options, such as multiple copies or specific pages, choose Print from the File menu, and then select options from the Print dialog box.

To preview the datasheet before printing, click Print Preview. You can use all the viewing and zoom capabilities you used with datasheets.

Deleting a Query

To delete a query, select the query in the Database window and choose Edit | Delete. You can also right-click the query name and choose Delete from the shortcut menu. Access then asks for confirmation before it deletes the query. Remember, the query will be deleted permanently and you won't be able to get it back once you delete it. But deleting the query doesn't delete any data from the underlying tables—it only deletes the query design.

Summary

You have almost limitless options when you want to extract and arrange data from one or more tables. This chapter introduced you to the basics of query design and construction with select queries and some special purpose queries.

Query Wizards can create queries that can at least get you started with the design you need. Then you can use the Query Design view to modify the query to include additional features, such as selection criteria and calculated fields.

The next chapter continues with query development and delves into some of the more advanced queries, such as the Parameter query that prompts for criteria from the user, and several types of action queries that update, append, or delete records in one or more tables.

Creating Advanced Queries

Queries are the primary means of retrieving information stored in an Access database. In addition to the popular select query discussed in the previous chapter, Access offers more flexible ways to retrieve data. Queries also can perform data management operations, such as adding, updating, or deleting data. You can even use an Access query to run a procedure stored in an external database.

In this chapter, you see how versatile Access queries can be. After examining two special purpose queries, the chapter discusses action queries, including update, append, make-table, and delete queries.

Creating Special Purpose Queries

Data retrieval queries needn't be static, always extracting the same information. They can be tailored at run time by the user entering the search criteria in a special dialog box. When you want to specify which group of data you want, use a parameter query. A *parameter query* is much the same as a common select query except Access prompts for one or more of the selection criteria before running the query. You can use parameters in other types of queries, as well, to get last-minute selection criteria.

Another special purpose query is the *AutoLookup query* that automatically fills in certain field values in related tables. The *AutoLookup field* can save data entry time by looking up the value you enter in the matching field and entering corresponding information into fields in the related tables.

Parameter Queries

Parameter queries are especially useful for looking up such information as activities during a specific time period, for example, sales during the holiday season or work orders started during the month of June. When you enter the starting and ending dates, Access retrieves all records whose values in that field fall between the two dates. You can have as many parameters in the query as you need. Access prompts separately for each one.

Parameters can be set in almost all types of queries, including select and action queries. You can use a parameter in any field in which you can type text in the Criteria row.

NOTE   *You can create parameter queries from the design grid, with SQL statements, or in the Record Source property of a form or report.*

To create a parameter query, start with a normal select query and, instead of entering the criteria in the Criteria cell, enter the text for the prompt enclosed in brackets ([ ]). The text you enter becomes the prompt in the dialog box, so be sure it's informative enough for the user to know how to respond. You cannot use the field name itself as the prompt, but you can include it in the prompt text.

For example, Home Tech Repair would like a list of a specific customer's current work orders. To allow the user to specify which customer, create a parameter query as follows:

1. Click New in the query page of the Database window, choose Design View in the New Query dialog box, and then click OK.

2. Hold down CTRL and choose the Workorders, Bid Data, and Customers tables from the Show Tables dialog box. Then click Add and Close.

3. Drag the Supervisor, Description, Start Date, and Address fields from the field lists to the grid. Then add the customer's Last Name field, which is the parameter the user enters.

4. Type **[Enter customer's last name]** in the Criteria row of the Last Name column. This displays as the prompt in the Enter Parameter Value dialog box when you run the query.

Field:	Supervisor	Description	Start Date	Address	Last Name	
Table:	Workorders	Workorders	Workorders	Bid Data	Customers	
Sort:						
Show:	☑	☑	☑	☑	☑	
Criteria:					[Enter customer's last name]	
or:						

5. Click Run and the Enter Parameter Value dialog box appears. Enter the desired Last Name (**McCoy**, in this example) and click OK.

6. When this query is run, the result shows four current work orders for McCoy.

Query1 : Select Query

Supervisor	Description	Start Date	Address	Last Name
Ferrell	New Fireplace	2/25/2003	2115 J St	McCoy
Ferrell	Repl Toilet	6/26/2003	2111 J St	McCoy
Connelly	Bay Window	7/10/2003	2111 J St	McCoy

You can also use a parameter query to find records that have a range of values, such as a time period. For example, you can show all the work orders started in the month of June. To do this, include parameters in the Between…And expression in the Criteria row. Access prompts for each parameter in a separate dialog box.

After entering 6/1/03 in the first prompt box and 7/1/03 in the second, Access runs the query and displays records for the four work orders begun during June.

By default, the data type of a parameter is Text. You can specify a different data type, however, by opening the Query Parameters dialog box while in the Query Design view using one of the following methods:

- Choose Query | Parameters.
- Right-click in the table pane and choose Parameters from the shortcut menu.

In the Query Parameters dialog box, enter the parameter exactly as it appears in the Criteria row (without the brackets), and then choose the data type from the Data Type drop-down list. Repeat this for each parameter for which you want to specify a data type, and then click OK.

NOTE *In most cases, Access can tell the data type of the parameter, but you must specifically define the data type for parameters if the field is a Yes/No data type or if it's used in a crosstab query. You must also set the Column Headings property for a crosstab query that prompts for a parameter.*

If you want to display the entered parameter value itself in the query result, add a calculated field with the parameter's name. For example, if you want to see the beginning date in the result of the previous query, enter the following expression in the Field row of an empty column: **Job Start:[Enter beginning date]**. The value will be the same in all the records in the result.

TIP *You can use the Format function to customize the parameter display. For example, use the expression* **Job Start:Format([Enter beginning date],"d mmm yyyy")** *to display the date as 1 Jun 2003 in the query result, such as a query, form, or report.*

Parameter queries are an excellent basis for reports. For example, you can print monthly reports simply by entering the month of interest and let Access do the rest.

TIP *Sometimes Access prompts for a parameter in a field you haven't designated as a parameter. This can be caused by misspelling the field name or changing the name in the table, but not changing it in other database objects. It also happens if you delete a field from a table, but forget to delete it from the query. If you checked the Name AutoCorrect option, field name changes are projected to all objects that include that field.*

In Chapter 12, you see how to create custom dialog boxes that prompt the user for input used in the form.

TIP   *If you created a parameter query that extracts fields from a specific set of records, you can also use the same query design to return all the records. Just add a criterion in the Or cell for the field used as the parameter and enter the same parameter prompt followed by Is Null.*

AutoLookup Queries

The AutoLookup query was invented to save time during data entry. The query does so by being used as the basis for a data entry form that contains data from more than one table. When you enter a valid Customer ID, for example, the query fills in all the rest of the information in the datasheet or form. An AutoLookup query uses two tables with a one-to-many relationship in which the matching field on the "one" side is either the primary key or a unique index. Referential integrity needn't be enforced.

NOTE   *An AutoLookup query is different from a lookup field because the query automatically fills in the data for you, while the lookup field merely displays a list from which to choose.*

To create an AutoLookup query, add the two related tables to the query design, and then drag the join field from the table on the "many" side to the grid. This type of query looks for the related record in the parent table—the "one" side—and retrieves values from other fields in the matching record. The field on the "one" side must be the primary key or have a unique index. But the field on the "many" side can neither be the primary key nor can it be a unique index.

Add any other fields from either table that you want in the form, but don't include the primary key field from the parent table.

Notice the Customer ID field in the design grid is from the Workorders table, the "many" side of the relationship.

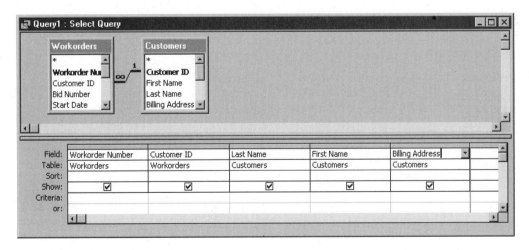

In the query result datasheet, when you add a new record or change the value of the join field on the "many" side, Access automatically looks up and displays the associated values from the table on the "one" side. When you enter a new record such as the Customer ID value—1033—and press the TAB key, the remaining three fields are filled in by Access.

	010	1032	McCoy	John, C	2115 J St
	011	1040	Norr	James	1510 H St
	012	1033	Jones	David	329 Fifth
	013	1032	McCoy	John, C	2115 J St
	014	1037	Selms	Harry	1520 8th St
	015	1039	Anders	Bob	952 C St
⏸	016	1033	Jones	David	329 Fifth
＊					

Record: ⏮ ◀   16   ▶ ▶▌ ▶＊ of 16

CAUTION   *Be sure the value entered in the join field on the "many" side exists in the table on the "one" side. If not, Access displays an error message when you try to leave the record. In addition, be sure to include all the required fields and those with validation rules in the query design grid and make sure their Show boxes are checked.*

You can always update the value of the join field from the "many" side and Access looks up and displays the associated values from the "one" side. If you want to update the value of the join field from the "one" side, you must have referential integrity enforced with the cascading updates option enabled for the relationship.

NOTE   *Whenever you update the data, Access recalculates any summary totals and expressions using that data.*

Once you design and save an AutoLookup query, it can be used as the basis for a data entry form, a report, or a data access page.

Designing Action Queries

Action queries are used to perform global data management operations on one or more tables at once. The four types of action queries reflect the most common database activities: updating field values, adding new records, deleting records, and creating new tables.

NOTE   *The results of action queries cannot be used as a record source for forms or reports. And you can't create an AutoForm or AutoReport from the result of an action query. However, if you save the result as a table first, you can use the table as a record source.*

Before undertaking any kind of action query, make a backup copy of the tables that will be involved. If you plan to change several tables, back up the entire database. To create a copy of a table, right-click the table name in the Tables tab of the Database window and choose Copy. Then right-click in an empty area and choose Paste. Enter a name for the copy in the Paste Table As dialog box and choose OK. Adding Copy to the original table name helps keep track of the tables as your database grows. If you plan to make several copies of the table design, you can add the current date to the table name.

Types of Action Queries

- An *update query* makes global changes to fields in a group of records. For example, you can run an update query to raise all the labor costs for jobs in a certain area of the city.

- An *append query* adds a group of records from one or more tables to the end of other tables. For example, when you consolidate another contractor's business with your own, add his customer list to your own.

- A *delete query* deletes a group of records from one or more tables. For example, you can use a delete query to delete records for completed workorders. This type of action query is less popular than the others, so the option appears in the expanded Query and Query Type menus. Click or rest the mouse pointer on the arrows at the bottom of the menu to see the expanded menu.

- A *make-table query* creates a new table from data in one or more existing tables. For example, you can archive outdated information into a new table or make a backup copy of an important table.

TIP   *An additional safety precaution you can practice while designing an action query is to switch to Datasheet view to check your progress, instead of running the query. Showing the results in Datasheet view doesn't actually run the query and carry out the intended action, so no data is changed.*

CAUTION   *The Edit/Find tab of the Options dialog box (choose Tools | Options) contains three Confirm options, one of which is Action Query. By default, this option is checked, so Access always asks for confirmation before carrying out an action query. You can clear this option to prevent the display of the confirmation box, but this is risky. Double-clicking a query name in the database window and running a query, even an action query, is so easy. If you cleared the Confirm option, you won't even be warned an action query is about to run.*

Update Query

Update queries are used to change one or more field values in many records at once. You can add criteria that screen the records to be changed, as well as update records in more than one table. Update queries can use most types of expressions to specify the update. Table 9-1 shows some examples.

For example, in the Home Tech Repair database, several bids have expired, but can be renewed. To renew the bids, the costs must be increased slightly to reflect inflation and a new expiration date set. This involves finding records in the Bid Data table whose Expires date is before August 15, 2003, for example, and then making changes to the related Workorders table to increase the Material Cost and Labor Cost values. If no corresponding Workorder record exists, the Update query doesn't change the Expires value because the relationship is defined as an inner join. Be sure to include one of the identifying fields in the query, so you can tell which records are going to be updated.

Field Type	Expression	Result
Currency	[Material Cost]*1.05	Increases Material Cost value by 5 percent.
Currency	[Workorders].[Material Cost]+[Workorders].[Labor Cost]	Updates the field with the sum of the costs from the Workorders table.
Date	#8/25/03#	Changes the value to August 25, 2003.
Text	"Completed"	Changes the value to Completed.
Text	"WO"&[Design]	Adds characters WO to the beginning of the value in the Design field.
Yes/No	Yes	Used with criteria, changes specific values to Yes.

TABLE 9-1   Sample Update Expressions

To create this update query, start with a new query design with the Bid Data and Workorders tables, and then do the following:

1. Click Query Type and choose Update Query from the list. You can also choose Query | Update Query or right-click the table area and choose Query Type | Update Query from the shortcut menu. A new row, Update To, appears in the grid.

2. Drag the Bid Number, Expires, Material Cost, and Labor Cost fields to the grid.

3. Enter the expression **<8/15/03** in the Criteria cell in the Expires column to limit the records. Access adds the pound sign (#) date delimiters.

4. Enter the following update expressions in the Update To cells:

   • Bid Number in the Bid Number column. Access adds quotation marks.

   • **[Material Cost]*1.05** in the Material Cost column.

   • **[Labor Cost]*1.05** in the Labor Cost column.

   • **[Expires]+90** in the Expires column.

5. Click Datasheet view to see which records will be affected by the update query. If the selection isn't correct, return to the Design view and make changes.

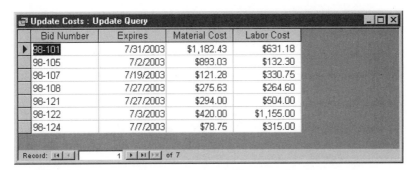

6. Click Design view to return to the Query Design window and save the query as Update Costs, if you haven't already, and then click Run or choose Query | Run. Access displays a message warning that the update is irreversible.

7. Choose Yes to update the records or No to abandon the process.

To see if the changes were correctly made, open both the copy of the original tables and the updated version, and then compare the results. Figure 9-1 shows a comparison of the updated Bid Data records with the backup copy. The seven records that appeared in the Datasheet view of the update query now show the Expires date updated in the left-hand datasheet.

As you can see in Figure 9-1, some of the records in the Bid Data table (for example, numbers 98–102 and 98–104) still have an Expires date prior to August 15, 2003. This might seem confusing or an error but, as mentioned earlier, they aren't updated because no matching record is in the Workorders record. The join is an inner join, which includes in the result only those records with matching values in the join field.

NOTE *If you enforced referential integrity between related tables in the database and checked the Cascade Update Related Records option on the "one" side, Access applies the updates to the matching fields on the "many" side, even if they aren't included in the query.*

When you name and save the query, it appears in the Queries tab with a warning icon. All the action queries appear with an exclamation point attached to the icon, which warns

FIGURE 9-1   Comparing updated and backup tables

you that double-clicking this query runs some sort of action. Access displays a confirmation message, however, before running the query, unless you turned off that option.

Tɪᴘ   *If you start a new query and you decide you want to create a different type, you needn't scrap the one you're working on. You can change the query type and proceed. To change the query type while in Design view, choose the type you want from the Query menu or right-click in the table area of the Query window, point to Query Type, and choose the type from the shortcut menu.*

Append Query

When you want to add records from one or more source tables to other tables, you first decide which fields you want to append, and then locate the target table and determine which fields in the target table correspond to the fields from the source. The field values are only copied—they aren't moved—to the target table.

Nᴏᴛᴇ   *To be matched, fields needn't have the same names, but they do need to be of the same data type. The target table also needn't have exactly the same structure as the source table.*

You can append records to a table in the current database or another Access database; establish a path to a FoxPro, Paradox, or dBASE database, or you can even enter a connection string to a SQL database.

For example, the Home Tech Repair Bid Data table gets large and cumbersome if none of the records are removed. The bids that have been lost are no longer needed in the current table, but they might be useful in an archive history of past bidding. Before you can archive the records, you need to create a new table with the same design as the Bid Data table to hold the records with the following steps:

1. Right-click the Bid Data table name in the database window and choose Copy.

2. Right-click in the Tables page and choose Paste.

3. In the Paste Table As dialog box, name the new table Lost Bid Archive, choose Structure Only, and then click OK.

The new table name appears in the Tables page of the Database window. Now you're ready to create the append query that will copy the records with Lost in the Award Date field to the Lost Bid Archive table. If the target table has the same field names as in this case, Access automatically fills in the field names in the query grid. If they aren't the same, you must enter the target field names.

To create the append query, do the following:

1. Start a new query, adding only the Bid Data table from the Show Tables dialog box, and then click Query Type, and choose Append Query. The Append dialog box appears.

2. Enter the table name, **Lost Bid Archive**, in the Table Name box, choose Current Database, and then click OK.

3. Because you want all the field data in the selected records to be archived, drag the asterisk (*) from the Bid Data field list to the grid. If you don't want all the fields appended, drag the fields individually to the grid.

4. To add the Lost criteria, drag the Award Date field to the grid and enter **"Lost"** in the Criteria cell.

5. Remove the field name from the Append To cell, so you won't append two copies of the Award Date field.

6. Switch to Datasheet view and check for Lost in the Award Date field to make sure the right records will be appended, and then switch back to Design view and save the query as Add to Archive.

7. Click Run. Access displays a message asking for confirmation to append six records.

8. Choose Yes to complete the addition or choose No to cancel the operation.

Once you copy the Lost Bid data records to the archive, the next step is to remove them from the original table.

Delete Query

The *delete query* might be the most dangerous action query of all. No action queries can be reversed, but deletion seems the most drastic—all the more reason to make a backup copy of all the tables before you begin a delete query.

A delete query removes entire records from the table, not only the specified fields. You can remove records from a single table, multiple tables related one-to-one, or multiple tables related one-to-many.

Deleting from a Single Table

Deleting records from a single table or several one-to-one tables is straightforward. Add the tables to the query design and specify the criteria for deleting the record, for example, the account is paid in full, the work order is completed, or the house has been sold.

To delete records from a single table:

1. Start a new query with the table from which you want to delete records, such as a copy of the Bid Data table.

2. Click Query Type and choose Delete Query or choose Query | Delete Query. The Delete Query command is on the expanded menu in both cases. The Delete row is added to the grid. The only choices in the Delete row are Where and From.

3. Drag the asterisk from the field list to the grid. The Delete row now shows From.

4. Drag the field containing the value that indicates the record should be deleted (for example, the value Lost in the Award Date field) and enter the criteria expression in the Criteria row.

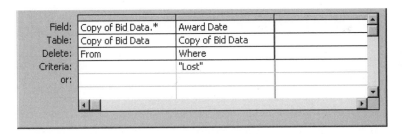

Field:	Copy of Bid Data.*	Award Date	
Table:	Copy of Bid Data	Copy of Bid Data	
Delete:	From	Where	
Criteria:		"Lost"	
or:			

5. Switch to Datasheet view to preview the records to be deleted and make any necessary changes in the query design.

6. Return to Design view and run the query. Respond Yes to proceed or No to cancel the operation.

Deleting from Related Tables

Deleting records from a table or multiple tables that are related with a one-to-many relationship can get complicated, especially if you're enforcing referential integrity and have selected Cascade Delete Related Records for the relationship.

If you have Cascade Delete Related Records enabled for the relationship, all matching records on the "many" side are deleted with the records on the "one" side. If the option isn't selected, you must run two delete queries to accomplish the job. First, delete the records from the tables on the "many" side, and then go after the records on the "one" side.

> **Warning About Cascade Delete**
>
> Checking the Cascade Delete Related Records option when enforcing referential integrity can be even more disastrous than the Cascade Update option. With *Cascade Delete* checked, Access automatically deletes all matching records whether or not the table is included in the query. For example, if you delete a customer, records for all the bids and work orders for that customer would also be deleted.
>
> Before you use a delete query, examine the relationships you've established between the table and others in the database. Of course, if referential integrity is enforced on a relationship without the cascade options, you might not be permitted to delete the records on the "one" side if this would leave orphans on the "many" side.

To delete records from multiple related tables, start a new query with all the involved tables, and then do the following:

1. Click Query Type and choose Delete Query.

2. Drag the field to use for criteria to the grid.

3. Drag the asterisk (*) from all the field lists of the tables on the "many" side of the relationships to the grid. Don't drag the "one" table to the grid yet.

4. Click Datasheet view to preview the records that will be deleted.

5. Return to Design view and click Run.

6. Remove the "many" side tables from the Query window.

7. Drag the asterisk (*) from the "one" table to the grid and run the query again to delete the records from that table.

Tip *You can combine an append query with a delete query using the same query design to create the two-step archive operation that adds the selected records to the history table and deletes the same records from the source table. After making sure you selected the right records to archive, run the append query to add the records to the target table. Then, in the Query Design view, click Query Type and change the query to a delete query. When you run the query again, it deletes the same records from the source table.*

Make-Table Query

The *make-table query* does exactly what it advertises: it makes a new table out of records from one or more tables or queries. Make-table queries are useful in many circumstances. Here are a few:

- To export records to another database, for example, to create a table of completed workorders to send to the billing department, which uses another system.

- To export consolidated information from related tables to a nonrelational application, such as Excel or Word.

- To control the information that's exported, such as screening out confidential or irrelevant data.

- To use as a record source for a report of events that occurred during a specific period of time. For example, a report of bids offered during June and July, and the results, including workorder information.

- To start the archive table by adding the first set of records, and then using an append query to add more later.

- To replace records in an existing table with a new set.

NOTE   *Make-table queries copy the data to the target table. The source tables and queries are unaffected. Use a delete query if you want to remove the records from the original table after you copy them.*

To build a make-table query, start a new query with the tables and queries you want records from, and then do the following:

1. Click Query Type and choose Make-Table Query. Access displays the Make Table dialog box requesting a name for the table, either a new table or an existing one.

2. Do one of the following:

   - If the target table is in the same database, enter the table name and click OK.

   - If the target table is an existing table, choose the table name from the drop-down list. Be aware that the query will replace the records in the existing table.

   - If you want the new table in a different database, select Another Database, type in the full path and filename of the database, enter the table name, and click OK. If the target isn't an Access database, follow the database name with the name of the application, such as "Paradox." You can also click Browse and look for the other database.

3. Drag the fields from the field lists to the design grid and include record selection criteria, the same as you do with a select query.

4. Click Datasheet view to preview the records to be included in the new table. Return to the Design window and click Run.

5. If you're replacing records in an existing table, Access asks for confirmation before proceeding:

- Respond Yes to continue.

- Respond No to abandon the operation.

- Click No and change the name of the target table by clicking Query Type and choosing Make-Table Query again. Then choose another table or enter a new table name.

6. Respond Yes or No to the final confirmation box that completes the make-table query.

Although you cannot undo an action query—including the make-table query—if the table isn't what you want, you can delete it and start over.

NOTE   *The only field properties inherited by the table created with a make-table query are the field size and data type. All other properties—including the primary key, format, default values, and input masks—aren't inherited and must be reset in the new table or in the form or report that uses the new table as a record source.*

Make-table queries create snapshots of the data as it was at the time it was run and, as such, aren't updateable manually. If the data in the source tables changes, run the query again to update the values.

TIP   *If you don't get the results you want with an action query, Access might be able to point you to a solution. The Help topic, Troubleshoot Queries, contains solutions to many of the problems you could encounter, such as appending the wrong records or dealing with key violations.*

Introducing Structured Query Language

Structured query language (SQL) is the language Access uses behind the scenes to program query operations. SQL is comprised of statements, each complying with specific language syntax and conventions. To view or edit SQL statements while working on a query, switch from Design view to SQL view by choosing View | SQL View.

You can enter a SQL statement in most places where you would enter a table, query, or field name, such as the record source for a form or report. If you use a wizard to create a form or report, the record source is a SQL statement created by Access.

TIP   *Using SQL statements instead of saved queries as record sources simplifies the database by having fewer objects to store and maintain.*

Looking at SQL Statements

Before going too far into the details of the language, look at some simple examples of SQL statements. The SELECT statement is the most common—and the most important—statement in SQL. All select queries start with the SELECT statement. For example, if you create a query that retrieves all the fields in records from the Bid Data table with "Lost" in the Award Date field, the SQL version would look like this:

```
SELECT *
FROM [Bid Data]
WHERE [Award Date]="Lost";
```

- The SELECT * command means to include all the fields, as does SELECT ALL.

- The FROM clause names the table(s) that contains the records to retrieve.

- The WHERE clause specifies the selection criteria. This is the same value you entered in the Criteria row of the Award Date column. Add the WHERE clause only if you included the FROM clause.

- SQL statements always end with a semicolon (;).

TIP   *If you create the query in the design grid, and then switch to SQL view, you see a lot of extra parentheses Access adds to keep things straight. You can enter the SQL statement as it's shown here and it'll work fine.*

If you don't want to retrieve all the fields, use the SELECT command with a list of field names. The following query displays the Bid Number and Expires fields for Bid Data records in which the Award Date field contains "Lost" or the Expires value is prior to June 1, 2003:

```
SELECT [Bid Number], Expires
FROM [Bid Data]
WHERE [Award Date]="Lost" OR Expires<#6/1/2003#;
```

TIP   *A field name that contains a space, such as Bid Number, must be enclosed in brackets. If no space is in the field name, you needn't add brackets, but Access usually does to be safe.*

All queries result in SQL statements that can be viewed by switching to SQL view. Choose SQL view from either the View button or the View menu.

Figure 9-2 shows the SQL views of a few queries in the Home Tech Repair database, including the action queries from the previous section.

Before going into the conventions and syntax of the SQL language, look at the Customers Without Matching Workorders (shown in the upper-left corner in Figure 9-2). This query was created to locate records in the Customers table that had no matching records in the Workorders table. The entire SQL statement is shown here:

```
SELECT DISTINCTROW Customers.[First Name], Customers.[Last Name],
Customers.[Billing Address], Customers.City, Customers.State,
Customers.ZIP, Customers.[Phone Number]
FROM Customers LEFT JOIN Workorders ON Customers.[Customer ID] =
Workorders.[Customer ID]
WHERE (((Workorders.[Customer ID]) Is Null));
```

This statement has two clauses in addition to the SELECT command: FROM and WHERE.

- The SELECT command determines which fields are included in the query result. Because two tables are involved in the query, field names must be qualified with the table name separated by a period (.).

FIGURE 9-2   SQL views of existing queries

- The FROM clause shows the table name and also specifies the join type that relates the Customers table with the Workorders table as a left outer join, using the Customer ID as the matching field.

- The WHERE clause sets the criteria that limits the result to Customer records with no matching records in the Workorders table. That is, the Customer ID field has a null value because no matching record exists.

Each clause begins on a separate line for readability; the entire statement is treated as a single line by Access.

SQL Conventions and Syntax

Like all programming languages, SQL has strict conventions and grammatical syntax. The more sophisticated the language, the more complex the rules and procedures. For the complete details of the SQL language, refer to the many Help topics Access provides.

The most significant elements in SQL are the statements, clauses, predicates, and declarations. Each statement has a precisely defined syntax that must be followed. The syntax is expressed using typical programming-language conventions.

Reading SQL Conventions

When you look up a SQL command or other element in the Help file, the syntax is expressed using certain conventions:

- All SQL keywords are in uppercase—for example, SELECT, WHERE, and FROM.

- Optional items are in italics and enclosed in brackets ([])—for example, SELECT [*predicate*].

- Choices are enclosed in curly braces ({}) and separated by vertical bars (|)—for example, {* | *table*.* | [*table*.]*field1*[,[*table*.]*field2*[,...]]}, which gives you the choice among including all records in a single table query (*), including all records in a named table (*table*.*), or specifying the fields one at a time, separated by commas.

- The ellipsis in the previous example indicate a repeating sequence.

Understanding SQL Syntax

The main elements in SQL are the statements and clauses that accompany the statements. You've already seen examples of the SQL statements (refer to Figure 9-2):

- SELECT retrieves all or specific records from one or more tables or queries.

- SELECT…INTO creates a new table from fields in existing tables (the make-table query).

- INSERT…INTO adds one or more records to a table (the append query).

- UPDATE changes specific values based on specified criteria (the update query).

- DELETE removes records from one or more tables (the delete query).

- TRANSFORM calculates values for a crosstab query.

The following shows the syntax of the SELECT statement. The other statements are similar in structure, using many of the same clauses and options.

```
SELECT [predicate]{*|[table.*|[table.]field1
[AS alias1][,table.]field2[AS alias2][,…]]}
FROM tableexpression [,…][IN externaldatabase]
[WHERE…]
[GROUP BY…]
[HAVING…]
[ORDER BY…]
[WITH OWNERACCESS OPTION]
```

Table 9-2 explains the parts of the SELECT statement.

NOTE   *Using the DISTINCT or DISTINCTROW predicate in the SELECT statement is equivalent to setting the query's Unique Values or Unique Records property to Yes.*

The SELECT statement has several clauses, most of which are optional. The only required one is the FROM clause, which specifies one or more tables or queries containing

Part	Explanation
Predicate	One of the four standard optional predicates: ALL to include all records, DISTINCT to omit records with duplicate data in selected fields, DISTINCTROW to omit data based on entire duplicate records, or TOPn [PERCENT] to limit the records to a certain number or percentage of records.
*	Includes all fields from the specified table or tables.
Table	Names the table containing the fields that determine which records to select.
field1, field2	Names the fields containing the data to retrieve.
alias1, alias2	Specifies text to use as column headers instead of the field names.
tableexpression	Names the table or tables containing the data to retrieve.
externaldatabase	Name of database containing the tables, if not in the current database.

TABLE 9-2   Parts of the SELECT Statement

the fields listed in the SELECT statement. The FROM clause can include the IN clause to retrieve data from an external database.

The other clauses in the SELECT statements are

- *WHERE* contains a criteria expression that specifies which records to retrieve from the tables in the FROM clause.

- *GROUP BY* combines records with identical values in the specified field. You can specify up to ten groupings. The order of the field names in the list determines the grouping levels from the highest to the lowest.

- *HAVING* specifies which grouped records to display. After the records are grouped in accordance with the GROUP BY clause, HAVING applies a criteria expression to the group.

- *ORDER BY* sorts the resulting records in ascending or descending order based on the value in one or more specified fields. ORDER BY is usually the last clause in a SELECT statement.

- *WITH OWNERACCESS OPTION* gives the user running the query the same permissions as the query's owner in a declaration.

You can use any valid expression in a SQL SELECT statement or in WHERE, ORDER BY, GROUP BY, or HAVING clauses. The same rules apply to expressions used in query statements as apply elsewhere.

When included, the INNER JOIN, LEFT JOIN, and RIGHT JOIN commands follow the FROM clause and specify the type of join to be used in the query. The update query created earlier resulted in the SQL statement shown in Figure 9-2 (second window on the right side). This query includes the command:

```
UPDATE [Bid Data] INNER JOIN Workorders ON ([Bid Data].[Bid Number] =
Workorders.[Bid Number]) AND ([Bid Data].[Bid Number] = Workorders.[Bid Number])
SET [Bid Data].Expires = [Expires]+90, Workorders.[Material Cost] = [Material
Cost]*1.05, Workorders.[Labor Cost] = [Labor Cost]*1.05
WHERE ((([Bid Data].Expires)<#6/15/2003#));The NNER JN operation establishes the id
Number as the joining fields in the two tables. The ET operation contains the
expressions entered in the update To rows used to update the three fields.
```

The WHERE clause contains the criteria expression that specified which records to update.

Refer to Chapter 5 for a review of the join types and how they can affect query results.

CAUTION   *If you query two or more tables, you must include a WHERE or JOIN clause or you get the Cartesian product of the number of records in the tables. For example, if one table has 50 records and the other 100, the query result will be 5000 records.*

Creating a Subquery

Subqueries are select queries within other select or action queries. You can use a subquery to specify a criterion for selecting records from the main query or to define a new field to include in the main query. Using subqueries is like layering filters to close in on the data you need, except the subquery runs first and results in a single criterion value, which is used in the main query.

Defining a Criterion

To define a criterion, enter the SELECT statement directly in the Criteria cell in the query design grid or in a SQL statement in place of an expression in a WHERE or HAVING clause.

For example, suppose you want to see fields from the Workorders table for all the jobs run by supervisors who have at least one job incurring more than $1,000 in material costs. Start a new query and add the Workorders table, and then place the Workorder Number, the Bid Number, Supervisor, and Material Cost fields in the grid.

To place this subquery in the query grid, type **IN (SELECT Supervisor FROM Workorders WHERE [Material Cost]>1000)** into the Supervisor field Criteria cell. Be sure to enclose the SQL statement in parentheses. If you switch to SQL view, you can see both the main query and the subquery created from the criteria:

```
SELECT Workorders.[Workorder Number], Workorders.[Bid Number],
Workorders.Supervisor, Workorders.[Material Cost]
FROM Workorders
WHERE (((Workorders.Supervisor) IN (SELECT Supervisor FROM Workorders WHERE
[Material Cost]>1000)));
```

When you run the query, you see that Supervisor Ferrell has four jobs listed, two of which have Material Cost over $1,000. Gunderson has five jobs, only one of which has Material

Cost over $1,000, and Dobbins has only one job listed. You can compare the results of this query/subquery to the full Workorders table to see how it works.

Workorder Num	Bid Number	Supervisor	Material Cost
001	98-101	Ferrell	$1,182.43
002	98-103	Gunderson	$1,212.75
004	98-107	Gunderson	$121.28
005	98-108	Ferrell	$275.63
007	98-113	Dobbins	$2,625.00
008	98-116	Gunderson	$420.00
009	98-117	Ferrell	$1,100.00
010	98-119	Ferrell	$183.75
014	98-124	Gunderson	$78.75
015	98-125	Gunderson	$441.00

Other predicates you can use with subqueries include the following:

- *ANY* or *SOME* which are synonymous and retrieve records in the main query that satisfy the comparison with any of the records retrieved by the subquery.
- *ALL* is more restrictive and retrieves only those records in the main query that satisfy the comparison with all the records retrieved by the subquery. For example, all the supervisor's jobs would need to have over $1,000 in material costs for the records to be retrieved by the main query.
- *IN* retrieves records in the main query for which some record in the subquery meets the comparison.
- *NOT IN* is the opposite of IN and retrieves records in the main query for which no record in the subquery meets the comparison.
- *EXISTS* is used in true/false comparisons to determine whether the subquery returns any records at all.

Defining a New Field

To use a subquery to define a new field, type the statement in the Field cell of an empty column. For example, the following subquery adds the field Address from the Bid Data table to the grid.

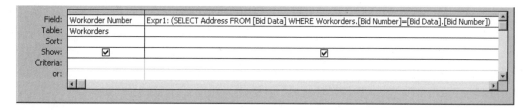

You can return to the Field cell and change the Expr1: default field name to a more informative one, but be sure to keep the colon (:)

Workorder Num	Expr1
001	2115 J St
002	329 5th St
003	2478 9th St
004	319 4th St
005	2111 J St
006	186 G St
007	1520 8th St
008	329 5th St
009	952 C St
010	2111 J St
011	1510 H St
012	329 5th St
013	2111 J St
014	186 G St
015	952 C St

New Field Sub : Select Query

Record: 1 of 15

Although this is a simple example, you can see that using subqueries to define fields based on values found in other tables can reduce the number of tables you need in a query. In this case, you didn't have to add the related Bid Data table to the query design to include the job address.

NOTE   *You cannot calculate totals with, or group records by, fields defined with subqueries.*

Summary

In the first chapters of this book, you learned how to construct tables and databases, and store information efficiently. Now, you've seen how to create a wide variety of queries that help you retrieve the information. Many queries selectively retrieve information based on carefully specified criteria, while others perform data management operations on records in one or more tables.

Queries have been the mainstays of data retrieval in the past and continue to provide valuable service. One of the principal uses for queries has been as the basis for form and report designs. With the development of the new form and report design capabilities, you might find you needn't create a query first, that you can do it right in the object design. The Form and Report Wizards also help select the proper data by filtering records and adding calculated controls.

The next five chapters discuss designing standard and custom forms and reports, including user-interactive data entry forms, special reports used for printing envelopes and mailing labels, and charts and graphs that visually represent trends and other data.

Creating Form and Report Designs

Now that you've seen how to store data efficiently in a relational database and how to retrieve the information you want in exactly the arrangement that will be most helpful, it's time to look at how you can present the information to the world. Information can be displayed on the screen in forms suitable for viewing or editing. These forms can contain data from more than one table, and they have a custom appearance that enhances the understanding of the information and improves the chances for accurate data entry.

If you need to print the information, such as for an annual report or form letter, or simply to transport the information to the outside world, Access offers you a variety of reporting features. You can even create a report that prints on preprinted forms, such as those required by the Internal Revenue Service.

This chapter begins the series that covers form and report development. With Access 2003, designs of the two objects contain mostly the same ingredients, so these common features are discussed in this chapter. Subsequent chapters delve more into features and capabilities that are limited to one object or another.

Deciding Which Database Object

Access 2003 offers four ways to arrange information for display or distribution. The choice of database object type depends on the specific purpose of the object and how you plan to distribute the information.

- Forms are commonly used for data entry and editing, as well as viewing. You can also print data from a form or save the form as a report for more customizing and printing.

- Reports are used primarily for distributing printed information to recipients within or outside the organization.

- Report snapshots are high-fidelity versions of a report that preserve the two-dimensional layout, graphics, and other embedded objects of the report. A snapshot is stored in a separate file that can be distributed via e-mail.

This chapter focuses on the design elements common to forms and reports. See Chapter 13 for a discussion on report snapshots, including how they're distributed and viewed.

Describing the Common Design Elements

Forms are used mostly for data entry and viewing. They can include user-interactive elements for acquiring additional information and executing user choices. *Reports* are mainly for presenting information in a static format, often printing the report for distribution to other members of the organization.

The design elements common to forms and reports include the record source that contains the data and the graphic objects added to the design. Many of the properties set to control the appearance and behavior of the form or report are also common to both.

Choosing a Record Source

The source of the data you want in the form or report can be table or query containing fields from one or more tables, or a SQL statement. For example, if you want to display a list of the Home Tech Repair customers, you would choose the Customers table as the record source for the form. If you want to print cost information for the current work orders, you would base the report on the Workorder Cost Sheet query that relates three tables and retrieves data from all three. A SQL statement can also be used in place of a query.

When you create a new form or report with the Form or Report Wizard, the first question asks what the record source is. Similarly, when you create a new object from scratch in the Design window, the first thing you do is choose the record source from the tables or queries in the current database. The individual fields in the underlying tables and queries become controls in the design.

Any sort orders and filters you saved with the table or query are inherited by the form or report. They aren't applied by default, but they are inherited, so you can easily apply them to sort or filter the information in the form or report.

The record source is one of the properties of every form and report. The only exceptions are special-purpose forms used for user input, such as pop-up forms, or switchboard forms that present alternative courses of action and don't involve data fields. Forms and reports that don't have a record source are called *unbound* objects.

Understanding Controls

The form or report design is made up of elements called controls. All the information shown on a form or report is represented by controls. A *control* is a graphical object you place on a form or report to display data, perform an action, or enhance the appearance of the form or report. Examples of controls are boxes that show field values, field labels, lines and rectangles, and command buttons.

Controls come in three basic types, depending on their relationship to values in the tables:

- A *bound control* gets its value from a field in the table and, as the data changes, the value of the bound control changes with it. The data fields you add to a form design are examples of bound controls.

- An *unbound control* has no tie to the underlying table data and retains the value you enter. Examples of unbound controls are lines, rectangles, labels, and images.

- A *calculated control* gets its value from values in the table and is an expression containing functions and operators, in addition to fields, that produces a result. The value shown in a calculated control changes as the values in the underlying fields change, but you cannot directly edit a calculated control.

Table 10-1 shows a list of the most common controls used in form and report designs. Most of them can be used in both, but a few are unique to one or another type of design. Although the user-interactive controls, such as command buttons and combo boxes, appear on the report toolbox, they aren't usually used in report designs.

Here's a form with many of the typical controls you can add to your form and report designs. The option group contains a set of option buttons but, in this case, they could also be check boxes or toggle buttons. The combo box is shown expanded to display the value list. Controls are all accessible from the toolbox, which you can display in the Design window.

NOTE *In Chapter 12, you learn about more special controls you can add to forms, including hyperlinks.*

Form and Report Design Properties

You saw in earlier chapters that databases, tables, queries, and fields have properties you can set to customize their appearance and behavior. Forms and reports, as well as all their controls, also have properties. This chapter discusses properties that apply primarily to forms and reports, as well as the controls they contain. Forms and reports have some of the same properties, such as record source, caption, width, and filter, but each has a few unique properties that you learn about in Chapter 10. For example, forms have properties that apply to user interfaces and events that occur when a user edits data, clicks a button, or presses TAB. Reports, on the other hand, have properties such as page header/footer text and record grouping for summary reports.

Control	Description
Bound object frame	A container that displays an OLE object stored in the record source.
Check box	A control that displays a Yes/No value from the record source. Can be used to represent one of a set of mutually exclusive options in an Option Group control.
Combo box	A control that combines a drop-down list of values with a text box for data entry.
Command button	A button that initiates an action, such as opening a linked form, running a macro, or calling a VBA procedure. Often shown with an image instead of text.
Image	An unbound picture, such as a company logo.
Label	Descriptive text, such as titles, captions, or instructions.
Line	A straight line used to divide parts of the design.
List box	A control that displays a list of choices, such as values for a field or search criteria.
Option button	A standalone control that displays a Yes/No value. Can be used to represent one of a set of mutually exclusive options in an Option Group control.
Option group	A frame with a limited set of alternatives in the form of check boxes, option buttons, or toggle buttons that relate to the same action or type of field value.
Page break	A control that creates a form with more than one page or causes a report to move to the next printed page.
Rectangle	A box that can be drawn for visually grouping fields or other text.
Subform/Subreport	A form or report contained within another form or report that shows data from related tables.
Tab	A control that shows a multiple-page form with tabs at the top of each page.
Text box	A control that displays field data from tables, queries, or calculated fields.
Toggle button	A button that represents an on or off setting.
Unbound object frame	A container for displaying an object not tied to an underlying table.

TABLE 10-1   Access Design Controls

Each type of control also has an appropriate set of properties, such as name, caption, source, format, decimal places, color, filter, position, and size. All the properties relevant to the currently selected control are displayed in a window called a *property sheet*. You see how to examine and set these properties in the section "Using Property Sheets."

Working in the Design Window

Similarities also exist in the form and report Design windows. The toolbars and menus are nearly identical and the design surface looks the same. The only difference between them shows up at the beginning of a new design. The report Design window shows the page header and footer sections by default, but in the new form Design window, the form header and footer sections are optional, and only the detail section is shown at the outset. You can add the headers and footers to the form design, if needed.

Because the two Design windows are so similar, the following paragraphs focus on the form Design window, while pointing out any significant differences in the report Design window.

Touring the Form Design Window

To start a new form, choose Forms in the left pane of the Database window, and then do one of the following:

- Double-click the Create Form In Design View shortcut item on the Forms page. This opens a blank form design that isn't based on any existing table or query.

- Double-click the Create Form By Using Wizard shortcut item on the Forms page. This starts the Form Wizard.

- Click New on the Forms page.

- Choose Insert | Form.

 • Click New Object and choose Form.

NOTE   *The Reports page on the Database window has similar options for starting a new report design. Shortcut items on both pages enable you to start a new design from Design view or with a wizard. The New Report dialog box has some of the same options, but has only two AutoReport options—Columnar and Tabular—and the Label Wizard has replaced the PivotTable Wizard.*

The last two methods both open the New Form dialog box where you can choose to use one of the Form Wizards, create one of five different AutoForm designs, or create the design directly in the Design view.

In addition to choosing the method of creating the new form, you have the option of selecting a table or query as the basis for the form. This isn't required for either a form or a report unless you plan to add fields to the design. A *switchboard* is an example of a form without any data and a cover sheet for a report needn't contain any field data.

After choosing Design view and selecting a table as the basis, choose OK to open the empty form design. Access arms you with tools to help create the form, including a design toolbar and a formatting toolbar, some new menu items, a control toolbox, a field list, and a group of property sheets. The design surface also has a grid and rulers that help you align and space the controls in the design. Figure 10-1 shows the form Design window with all the tools visible, including the field list from the Workorders table. All these dialog boxes can be displayed by clicking a toolbar button or by choosing from the menu bar. The next section explains what these tools are used for and how to reach them.

FIGURE 10-1   The Design window and its tools

To show either of the toolbars or the toolbox, right-click in the menu bar or in a toolbar, and then choose from the displayed list. To hide the toolbar or the toolbox, clear the check mark from the list.

You can also choose from the View menu to show or hide them. Use the Toolbox button on the Form Design toolbar to display or hide the toolbox.

TIP   Toolbars are usually "docked" at the top of the window. You can quickly convert the toolbars into floating windows by dragging the move handle (the vertical lines of dots at the left end of the bar when it's docked) away from the docked position. You can also click a line between two buttons and drag the bar away from the dock, but it's easier to use the move handle. That way, you won't accidentally start something by clicking a button. To return a toolbar to the top of the window, drag it by the title bar until the frame stretches out to the width of the window and loses its title bar, and then release the mouse button.

The Form Design Toolbar

The Design window also displays the special Form Design toolbar and, optionally, the Formatting (Form/Report Design) toolbar.

Many of these commands are available on the View, Insert, or Format menus. The Report Design toolbar has most of the same buttons with only two exceptions:

- The Print Preview button shows instead of the Form View button.

- An additional button, Sorting and Grouping, appears between the Toolbox and the AutoFormat buttons.

The Formatting Toolbar

Forms and reports use the same toolbar for customizing the appearance of the elements in the design. The buttons on the Formatting toolbar become available when one or more controls are selected in Design view. More about selecting form sections and controls in "Selecting Controls and Other Objects." These toolbar buttons have no menu equivalents.

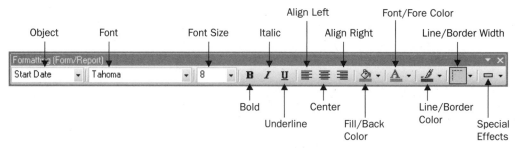

The Toolbox

You have three ways to open the toolbox:

- Click the Toolbox button.
- Choose Toolbox from the View menu.
- Right-click in a toolbar and select Toolbox from the list of available toolbars.

Most of the buttons on the toolbox represent the controls you can add to the design. To add a control, click the desired button and click the design where you want the control. For some controls, you can draw an outline to specify the size of the control.

The first two buttons are special, however. When the first button, Select Objects, is pressed in, you can click one of the control object buttons to add a control to the design.

NOTE   *You can't actually turn off the Select Objects button, but when you want to add several controls of the same type, you can lock down that control button by double-clicking it. This deactivates the Select Objects button until you click it again or press* ESC *to unlock the control button.*

The second button is the Control Wizards button, which automatically invokes one of the Control Wizards when you add its control to the design. Wizards are available for adding List boxes, Combo boxes, option groups, command buttons, subforms, and subreports. If the button is deactivated, a wizard won't be forthcoming when you add one of those controls.

NOTE   *The Option Group Wizard and the Subform/Subreport Wizards are part of the Additional Wizards group. If they don't start when you add one of these controls, you need to run the Access Setup program again and check Additional Wizards.*

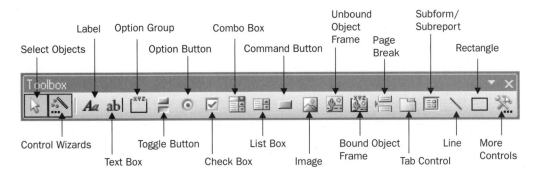

The toolbox is usually a floating window, which means you can resize it or drag it by the title bar to any location on the screen to get it out of the way. You can also dock the toolbox on one side, the top, or the bottom of the Design window. When docked, the title bar disappears, so when you want to drag it back into the window, drag it away from the edge by the move handle. You can also drag the toolbox borders to change the dimensions of the floating window. To remove the toolbox from the screen, click the Close button.

The Property Sheets

Property sheets list all the properties that pertain to the form or the selected form section or control. The properties are grouped by category into four tabs, with a fifth tab showing the entire list. The categories are Format, Data, Event, and Other. As usual, Access gives you more than one way to open a property sheet for the selected object. Simply click the Properties toolbar button, double-click the selected object, or right-click on it and choose Properties from the Shortcut menu.

You use the property sheets to view the properties set for the controls and make any necessary changes. Some properties have drop-down lists of valid settings, others include the Build option.

NOTE   *If you selected more than one control, the property sheet shows only those properties the group has in common. If the selected controls have no properties in common, the sheet is blank.*

The Field List

The field list resembles the lists you saw in the Relationships window and in a query design, but without the asterisk. To display the field list, click the Field List toolbar button or choose Field List from the View menu. You use the field list to add fields to a design by dragging the name to the design grid. A text box control in the design displays the field value and an attached label shows the field caption, which might be different than the field name.

The Alignment Tools

The horizontal and vertical *rulers* help you place controls accurately in the design. The rulers are optional; you can show or hide them by selecting View | Ruler while you're in Design view. The single command, Ruler, applies to both the vertical and horizontal rulers. You can also right-click an empty area of the form design and choose Ruler from the Shortcut menu.

TIP   You can also use the rulers when you want to select more than one control in the design, as you see in "Selecting Controls and Other Objects."

The *grid* shows as faint dots and lines in the design background. To show or hide the grid, choose View | Grid. One of the settings you can choose from the Format menu is Snap To Grid. With this setting selected, Access automatically aligns the controls to the nearest grid mark.

TIP   You can also change the grid granularity to increase or decrease the precision of the control placements. The grid fineness is a property of the form or report design itself, and is set in the Format tab of the property sheet. The grid is preset to 24 increments per inch horizontally and vertically. You can change either of these settings to any value from 1 to 64 by entering the value in the GridX (horizontal) or GridY (vertical) form property.

Starting a New Design

To illustrate creating a new form design, let's build a data entry form for Home Tech Repair to enter new workorder data. To start the new form, click Tables in the Objects bar in the Database window, and then do the following:

1. Select the Workorders table.

2. Click the arrow next to New Objects on the toolbar, and then choose Form from the list. The New Form dialog box opens.

3. Choose Design View.

4. Click the drop-down arrow in the lower box and choose Workorders from the list of existing tables and queries, and then click OK. The blank form shows in Design view.

5. Click the Field List and Toolbox buttons or choose both from the View menu. You can also right-click the empty design and choose Toolbox from the Shortcut menu.

6. Keep the form design open for adding fields and titles.

By default, the form design doesn't fill the window, but you can resize the design grid by dragging the form borders.

A new form consists only of the detail section where most of the information is to be displayed, one record at a time. If you want some text or other information displayed in a form header or footer, add the section by choosing View | Form Header/Footer. You can also right-click the form design and choose Form Header/Footer from the Shortcut menu. Both sections are added to the design, and they appear at the top and bottom of the form with all the record data between. If you want one and not the other, you can shrink the unwanted section to nothing. Report designs automatically include page headers and footers in addition to the detail section. You can add report headers and footers by choosing View | Report Header/Footer.

You can also add page headers and footers to forms. In a form, the information placed in the page header and footer appears only when the form is previewed or printed, not when it's open in Form view. Choose Page Header/Footer from the View menu or the Shortcut menu to add a form page header and footer.

Adding Controls

You can add all types of controls to the design with the toolbox, but it's easier to use the field list to add text box controls for the table fields. In the following paragraphs, you see how to add fields from the Workorders table, a form title and subtitle, and some calculated fields.

From the Field List

The Field List contains the names of all the fields in the record source. When you drag a field from the list to the design, Access creates a new control that shows field values in the Form view. You can add fields from the list to the design in three ways:

- Drag a field name from the list to the design. Dragging the field name to the design looks much like dragging a field name to the query grid. When you drop the button, the control appears in the form with its attached label.

- To add all the fields to the design at once, double-click the field list title bar to select all the names, and then drag the group to the design. The text boxes and attached labels appear in a tight column in the form design.

- Use the standard SHIFT-click or CTRL-click to select contiguous or dispersed field names, and then drag the group to the design.

The field list remains open until you click the Close button, or click the Field List button again, or choose View | Field List.

To get back to the Home Tech Repair data entry form and add fields from the Workorders table, do the following:

1. Click the Workorder Number field in the field list and drag the button to the design at about the 1-inch mark on the horizontal ruler.

2. Drag the other fields from the field list to positions in the design resembling Figure 10-2. You need to expand the form both horizontally and vertically to place the fields as shown.

Once you have all the fields you want in the design, you can close the field list to make more room on the screen. Next, add a form header, and use the toolbox to add a title and subtitle to the header.

FIGURE 10-2   Adding the other Workorder fields

From the Toolbox

To add a control, click the appropriate button and draw the control outline in the design. What happens next depends on the type of control you're adding. If it's a Label control, the insertion point appears inside the outline ready to enter the label text. If you want to add several controls of the same type, you can double-click the button to lock it down and not have to click it for every control.

To add a title in the Workorders form header, do the following:

1. Choose View | Form Header/Footer. The new sections are added to the form design. You can also right-click an empty area of the design and choose Form Header/Footer from the Shortcut menu.

2. Move the mouse pointer to the dividing line between the Form Header and Detail sections and, when it changes shape to a double vertical arrow, click-and-drag the line down ½ inch on the vertical ruler.

3. Click the Label toolbox button and draw an outline in the Form Header across the form. The outline appears with the insertion point at the left, ready to type text.

4. Type **Home Tech Repair** and click outside the label box or press ENTER, and then click it again to select the label control.

5. Use the Formatting toolbar to change the font size to 18, italic, and centered. Figure 10-3 shows the form design with the new header.

6. Widen the form header section some more to add a subtitle.

7. Click the Label toolbox button and draw a box beneath the title, and then type **Data Entry Form—Workorders** in the label control.

FIGURE 10-3   Adding a title to the form header

8. Use the Formatting toolbar to customize this text, so it's bold and font size 10.

9. Click the View toolbar button to switch to Form view to see how the design looks now.

Adding a Calculated Control

A *calculated control* contains values from multiple text, number, currency, or date fields in the record source. For example, in an earlier chapter, you saw how to combine text values from first and last name fields into a single whole name field. Another example is to create a single field address from separate address, city, state, and ZIP code fields with the expression:

[Address]&", "&[City]&", "&[State]&" "[ZIPcode]

The quotation marks enclose embedded spaces and a comma that separate the values. You can also combine currency or date fields, for example:

- **[Birthday]-Date()** displays the number of days until your next birthday.
- **[Price]*1.07+[Shipping&Handling]** computes and displays the sales price, plus 7 percent tax, and adds the shipping and handling charges.

TIP *You can often save processing time by performing the calculations at the query level, instead of in the form or report design. Then use the query as the basis for the form or report.*

Now add two calculated fields to the Workorders data entry form that will display the total cost of the job and the number of days estimated to complete the work by doing the following:

1. Click the Text Box control button in the toolbox and click the area to the right of the Material Cost field. Access adds an unbound text box control.

2. Double-click the new control or click the Properties button to open the property sheet for the new unbound text box. You can also right-click a control and choose Properties from the Shortcut menu.

3. Click the Data tab and enter the following expression in the Control Source property box: **=[Material Cost]+[Labor Cost]**. Notice you must start the expression with an equal sign (=) or Access assumes the expression is a field name.

4. Double-click the attached label that shows Text*n* and type **Total Cost**.

5. Repeat Steps 1 through 4 to add another calculated field to show estimated work time with the expression **=[Completion Date]-[Start Date]** and label it **Work Time (days)**.

6. Switch to Form view to see the design with the new calculated fields.

Completion Date:	3/10/2003	Work Time (days)	13
Material Cost:	$1,182.43	Total Cost:	1813.6125
Labor Cost:	$631.18		

You can see that while the two cost fields retain the currency format with the dollar sign and two decimal places, the Total Cost field did not. You have to set the format and other properties separately for calculated fields. The section "Selecting Controls and Other Objects" discusses selecting controls and changing their properties.

TIP *A simple calculated control is the current date. In the Control Source property, type the expression: =Date().*

Copying a Control

If you want more than one copy of the same control, you have two ways to do that: copy-and-paste or duplicate. You can make as many duplicates as you want. Then you can modify them to create a group of similar controls.

To duplicate a control, click the control to select it, and then choose Edit | Duplicate. A copy of the control appears just below the first. You can repeat this technique to build a column of evenly spaced duplicate controls, which you can move around the design after duplicating them.

TIP *If the control has a label, click the control, not the label.*

If you don't care if the copies are evenly spaced, use the standard copy-and-paste routine. Select the control and click Copy, or right-click and choose Copy from the Shortcut menu. If no other control is selected when you click Paste, the copy appears in the upper-left corner of the design. Then you can drag it to the desired location in the design. If you select a control near where you want the copy, the copy is pasted just below the selected control.

When you copy a control, Access includes any associated properties. A copy of a text box control includes a copy of the attached label.

NOTE *If you only want to copy the format of a control to other controls, rather than add more controls, use the Format Painter.*

Looking at More Controls

The last button in the toolbox is labeled More Controls. When you click this, a long list of additional controls is displayed, including ActiveX and OLE controls. Move the mouse pointer to the arrow at the bottom of the list to see even more controls.

To add one of these to the form design, click the control name, click in the form design, and then draw the outline in the design where you want to see the control. If you select an OLE control, you must have the OLE server registered. The Calendar Control that you add in Chapter 12, for example, is one of the options when installing Microsoft Office 2003.

NOTE *You can also add these ActiveX controls to a form design by choosing Insert | ActiveX Control and selecting the control you want from the Insert ActiveX Control dialog box.*

Dressing Up with Lines and Rectangles

While they aren't essential, lines are useful in forms and reports to create a visual separation between parts of the design. A heavy line can help focus attention on a specific area. You can draw a line anywhere in a form or report section.

To draw a line, click the Line toolbox button and click where you want the line or drag the pointer to draw the line. If you only click within the design, Access draws a solid horizontal line, 1-inch long and 1-point thick. When you drag to draw the line, you can drag it in any direction and any length. To make sure the line is horizontal or vertical when you draw it, hold down SHIFT while you draw.

Rectangles come in handy as boxes that group related data or as a means to emphasize another control. For example, in a form, you can draw a box around a set of command buttons to set them off from the rest of the design.

To draw a rectangle, click the Rectangle toolbox button and draw the box in the design. After drawing the line or rectangle, you can use the Formatting toolbar buttons to change the line or border thickness, choose colors, and add a special effect. You can also use the property sheet to change the line or rectangle border style to a dashed or dotted line, for example.

TIP   *If you draw a rectangle around other controls and add a background color, you might obscure the other controls. To cure this, select the rectangle and choose Format | Send To Back to place it behind the others.*

Modifying Controls

You can customize the controls you add to a form or report design to present information in just the right way. Controls can be moved about in the design, resized, and any of their properties can be changed to create the appropriate effect. To change any control, you must first select the control to focus Access on the object you want to work with.

Selecting Controls and Other Objects

You have many ways of selecting the form or report design, one of the design sections, or one or more controls. The Object button on the Formatting toolbar displays a complete list of every element of the design from the form (or report) itself to each of its sections and all the controls in the design, including any added lines and text. The list is in alphabetical order. To select one of these, choose from the list. You might need to scroll down the list to find the element you want to select.

Selecting the Form or a Form Section

You can select the form itself in the following ways:

- If the rulers are displayed, click the form selector, the small square in the upper-left corner where the horizontal and vertical rulers meet.

Form selector

- Choose Edit | Select Form (or Report) or press CTRL-R.

- Click anywhere in the plain gray background outside the form design.

When the form is selected, the form selector shows a small black square. After selecting the form, you can view and change any of its properties, including the record source, in the form property sheet.

In addition to choosing from the Object list, you can do one of the following to select a form or report section:

- Click the section selector, the small box in the vertical ruler opposite the section bar.

Section selector ⸺⸺⸺⸺⸺⸺⸺⸺⸺⸺⸺ Section bar

- Click the section bar.
- Click anywhere in the gray background of the section.

When a section is selected, the section bar, the horizontal divider that contains the section title, appears shaded.

Selecting Controls

That leaves the controls themselves. To select one control, you can simply click the control or choose the control name from the Object list on the Formatting toolbar. When you select a control, a set of small dark squares called *handles* appear around the control. You use these handles to move and resize the controls. The larger squares are the *move handles* and the smaller ones are the *sizing handles.* More about moving and resizing in the section "Moving and Resizing Controls."

Move handles   Sizing handles

If you want to make the same change to several controls at once, you can select more than one of them in one of the following ways:

- Hold down SHIFT as you click each control.
- To select a column of controls, click the selection arrow in the horizontal ruler above the controls.
- To select a row of controls, click the selection arrow in the vertical ruler to the left of the controls.
- To select a block of controls, click the selection arrow in one of the rulers and drag to draw a rectangle around the controls. This selects all the controls inside or partially within the rectangle.
- To select a block of controls within the design, but not a complete column or row, click the design outside of any control and draw a rectangle around the controls.
- To select all the controls in the design, choose Edit | Select All or Press CTRL-A.

TIP *When you click one of the rulers and draw a rectangle to select a row or column of controls, you can choose to include controls completely or only partially enclosed within the rectangle. Choose Tools | Options and click the Forms/Reports tab. The Selection Behavior options include Partially Enclosed (the default) and Fully Enclosed.*

To remove the selection, click anywhere outside the selected objects. To remove only a few controls from a group of selected controls, hold down SHIFT and click each of the controls you want to exclude.

A text box control is a special case because it contains two parts that can be treated together or separately. The attached label is usually the field name and the edit region displays the field value. If you click the edit region to select a text box control, you can change the text box properties. If you click the attached label, only the label is selected and you can change its properties. Either way, you can move them together or separately.

You can tell which element you selected by the size and number of handles that appear around the control. The following shows two text box controls: the edit region of the Labor Cost control is selected, while the label of the Material Cost control is selected.

Once you select the controls you want to work with, you can move, resize, align, or space them equally or change any of their properties.

Grouping Controls

If you have several controls you want to look and behave alike, you can define them as a single group and format them all at the same time. To create the control group, select all the controls you want to include and choose Format | Group, including the labels belonging to the text box controls. A frame appears around the set of controls, which doesn't show up in Form view. The new form, shown next, contains the cost fields in a single group.

To remove the group designation, choose Format | Ungroup.

Moving and Resizing Controls

One reason to select a control is to change its size or move it to a different position in the design. As mentioned earlier, when you select a control, handles appear around the control. These handles are used to move and resize a control or a selected group of controls.

Moving Controls

To move a control in the design, move the mouse pointer to the move handle—the larger square in the upper-left corner of a selected control. When the pointer changes shape to an open hand, click-and-drag the control to the desired position. You can drag it over other controls to place it where you want it.

Again the text box control is a special case because it has two move handles. If the pointer shows as an open hand, the control and its label move together. If the mouse pointer changes to a pointing hand, instead of an open hand, you can move the edit region by itself. When you move the mouse pointer to the move handle of the attached label, it always changes to a pointing hand, so you can move the label by itself. You can't move both parts with the move handle in the label unless you have selected the label.

TIP *Dragging a control by its move handle can be inaccurate, so if you want to move a control a smaller or more precise distance, select the control and hold down* CTRL *while you press the appropriate arrow key. Each key press moves the control one fourth of a grid unit in the direction of the arrow. Holding down* CTRL *while you drag a control temporarily turns off the Snap To Grid feature.*

If you selected more than one control, you can drag any one of them and they'll all move together.

Resizing Controls

A selected control has seven sizing handles, one on each side and one at each corner, except the corner with the move handle. Dragging one of the side handles changes the width or height, while dragging a corner sizing handle can change both height and width at once.

If you selected several controls, they all change to the same size when you drag the sizing handle of one of them.

TIP *Again, if you need to make more precise adjustments in the size of the selected control, hold down* SHIFT *this time while you click the appropriate arrow key. Each key press increases or decreases the size of the control by one grid unit.*

The Format menu and the Shortcut menu also have options that help you size one control or a group of controls, so they match in length or width. First select the controls you want to resize, and then choose Format | Size, or right-click and point to Size in the Shortcut menu.

The first command, *To Fit*, resizes a control to fit its contents. For example, if you've drawn a long label control and entered short text, choose the To Fit command to reduce the size of the control to fit the entered text. The second command, *To Grid*, automatically adjusts the size of the control, so all four corners fall on the nearest grid points.

Tip   *Double-clicking one of the sizing handles automatically resizes the control to fit the contents.*

The remaining four commands adjust the size of each control in a group of controls relative to the tallest, the shortest, the widest, or the narrowest of the group.

Tip   *The* Snap To Grid *command, when checked, automatically adjusts the control size when you drag the size handles, so their boundaries are on gridlines.*

Aligning and Spacing Controls

Having the controls in a form evenly lined up helps give the form a professional look. To align a group of controls, select them first, and then choose Format | Align, or right-click and point to Align in the Shortcut menu. You have several choices for alignment relative to the members of the group. All members of the group align with the top or left-most member of the group.

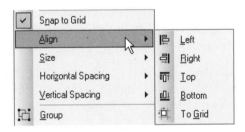

The last command in the Align menu, To Grid, places the upper-left corner of all the selected controls on a grid mark. If you have Snap To Grid checked, this is automatically done.

Tip   *When aligning controls, be sure to select only those in the same row or the same column. If you have controls in the group from a different area of the form, they will be aligned with the rest, creating a confused appearance.*

When you have a row or column of controls that you want uniformly spaced across or down the form or report, you can use the Horizontal Spacing or Vertical Spacing commands in the Format menu. These commands are also used to increase or decrease the spaces evenly between the controls.

The Horizontal and Vertical Spacing options are as follows:

- **Make Equal**   Controls at the left and right, or the top and bottom of the group remain fixed, while the controls between are moved to equalize the intervening spaces.

- **Increase**   The leftmost or top control remains fixed and the space between the remaining controls is increased by one grid interval.

- **Decrease**   Similar to Increase, except the space between the controls is decreased by one grid interval.

Using Property Sheets

Properties establish the characteristics of form and report design elements. Everything in a form or report design has properties: controls, sections, and even the form or report itself. Control properties set the structure, appearance, and behavior of the controls. Properties can also determine the characteristics of the text and data contained in a control.

Property sheets contain lists of all the properties that pertain to the selected control or group of controls. To open a property sheet for a control, do one of the following:

- Double-click the control.

- Select the control and choose View | Properties.

- Select the control and click Properties on the toolbar.

- Right-click the control and choose Properties from the Shortcut menu, or select the control and press ALT-ENTER.

The list of properties depends on the current selection. The All tab of the property sheet for the Workorder Number text box control shows all the control's property settings. As you can tell by the scroll bar, more properties are in the list.

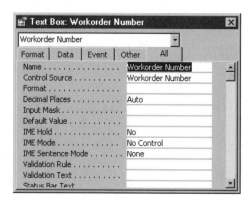

The properties are grouped in the sheet by type: Format, Data, Event, Other, and All. Click the tab that will show the properties you want to change or stay with All to see the entire list.

To change a property, click the property in the list, and then do one of the following:

- Type the desired setting in the property box.
- If an arrow appears in the property box, select the desired setting from the list.
- If a Build button (...) appears, click it to display a builder or a dialog box with a choice of builders, depending on the type of control.

TIP   *When you click a property in the property sheet, you can see a description of the property in the status bar. If you need more information about the property or how to use it, press F1.*

The calculated field, Total Cost, which we added to the Workorders data entry form earlier, needs to show currency symbols. To set the format property, do the following:

1. In the form Design window, double-click the edit region of the Total Cost text box control. The property sheet opens.
2. Click the arrow in the Format property box and choose Currency from the list.

Other items of interest are in the property sheet for the Total Cost text box. For example:

- Look in the status bar for a description of the Format property.
- The Name property isn't Total Cost, but Text13. Recall that Total Cost isn't a real field name, but is only the label attached to the unbound text box control. Access automatically assigns a name to a new control when it's added to the design. This name is an identifier that Access uses in expressions, macros, and procedures.
- You can see the expression that defines the calculated field. If it's a long expression, right-click the Control Source property line and choose Zoom from the Shortcut menu to see the entire expression. You can also click the property box and press SHIFT-F2 to open the Zoom box.

To apply the same property settings to a group of controls of the same type, first select them all, and then open the property sheet. Only those properties common to all members of the group are visible in the sheet.

Once you open a property sheet, it remains on the screen until you close it. To set properties of a different object in the design, either select the object from the drop-down list at the top of the property sheet or select the control in the design.

Assigning a Default Value

When you assign a default value to a bound control in a form or report design, the value you enter overrides any default value set in the underlying table design. Unless you enter a different default value, the one you assign is stored in the field when a new record is entered in the form. For example, if you're entering new bid data and one of the fields in the form is the date, you can assign the current date as the default value. This automatically stores the current system date in the new record.

To assign the current date as the default value, type **=Date()** in the control's Default Value property box.

NOTE   *Another way to include the current date in a form or report is to choose Insert | Date and Time to open the Date and Time dialog box. Then click Include Date and choose a date format. To include the time, check Include Time and choose a time format. If a header section is in the form or report, Access places the Date/Time text box there; otherwise, it goes in the Detail section. Date and time values added this way are part of the design and aren't stored in the underlying table.*

Specifying a Validation Rule

To apply a validation rule to a control in the form or report, enter the expression in the Validation Rule property box. You can also click the Build button to use the Expression Builder to construct the rule. The validation rule you enter as a control property is enforced, in addition to any that were set in the table design.

If your expression is long, you can press SHIFT-F2 to open the Zoom box, where you can see the whole thing.

Type the message you want displayed when a violation occurs into the Validation Text property box.

Changing Default Control Properties

Access has provided a default set of properties for each type of control. The set specifies the general appearance and behavior of that type of control. For example, the default properties for a text box control determine the font size and alignment of text within the attached label. Another default text box property automatically includes the field name as an attached label. This set of properties is called the *default control style* for that control type.

If you find you're making the same changes to most of the controls of a certain type, you can change the default property setting. For example, if you usually want a larger font size in your text boxes, change the Font Size from the default size of 8 to a larger size. Or, if you don't want the attached labels for every text box, change the Auto Label property on the Format tab to No. If you're starting a new form, you can save time by setting the default styles before adding the controls.

TIP   *When you change a default setting to the one you use most, it saves space. Access doesn't have to store both the default and custom settings.*

To change a default property setting, do the following:

1. Click the tool in the toolbox for the desired control type.

2. Click Properties on the toolbar. The property sheet for that control type opens, but the title bar indicates these are the default settings, instead of the settings for a particular control in the design.

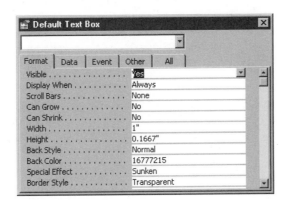

3. Change the setting in the default property sheet.

The changes you make affect only the new controls you add to the design; the existing controls aren't changed. The changes remain in effect for the current design until you change them again.

NOTE   *Some of the text box control properties can be set only in the Default Text Box property sheet. For example, Auto Label and Auto Colon (on the Format tab) work together. When both are set to Yes, Access automatically adds the field name as an attached label followed by a colon. Label X, Label Y, and Label Align, which position the attached label with respect to the text box, also appear only in the default property sheet. See the Quick Reference on the CD for a complete description of text box and other control default properties.*

If you already made changes to a control and you like what you see, you can copy the changes quickly to the control type's default style. Any new controls then would use the properties from the existing control as a default control style. Select the control with the characteristics you want as defaults for subsequent controls, and then choose Format | Set Control Defaults.

Using the Formatting Toolbar

The *Formatting toolbar* is a quick way to change the appearance of the text in selected controls. The toolbar is optional when you're designing a form or report. To see the Formatting toolbar, choose View | Toolbars and check Formatting (Form/Report). You can also right-click any menu bar or toolbar and choose Formatting (Form/Report) from the Shortcut menu.

The Formatting toolbar has, in addition to the Object button already discussed, eight buttons for formatting text in the design. These eight buttons change the font name, size, and style, and align the text within the control boundaries. The last five buttons give you a quick way to change the color and style of many elements in the design.

The three color buttons display a color palette you can use to change the color of the background, the font, or the border of a control. The fourth button changes the thickness of the selected control's border and the last button adds special effects to a control or an entire section, such as raised, sunken, shadowed, etched, chiseled, and flat effects. If you want to keep one or more palettes on the screen to make several changes at once, drag the palette away from its toolbar button. Click the Close button on the palette to close it.

TIP   *If you want to apply the same formatting property changes to a group of similar controls, select them all, and then change the common property.*

Formatting Conditionally

Conditional formatting was introduced in Access 2000. You can use it with text boxes and combo boxes. With *conditional formatting,* you can specify a default format for the control and up to three additional formats that are applied under special conditions: the current value of the field, when the field gets focus, or when an expression evaluates to True. The expression can refer to the values in other fields in the same record. For example, if the date in a field is more than 30 days ago, display the value in this field underlined and in red on a light green background.

To activate conditional formatting, select the control you want to apply it to and choose Format | Conditional Formatting. The Conditional Formatting dialog box shows two areas: one for setting the default format and one for specifying a conditional format to be applied under specific conditions.

The formatting choices include bold, italic, and underline, as well as text and background colors. The button on the right end of the condition box enables or disables the control if the condition is met. When a control is enabled, you can reach it by pressing TAB. If a control is disabled, it's skipped in the tab order. The box in the middle displays an example of how the chosen formatting will look.

To set conditional formatting, first set or keep the existing default format, and then move to Condition 1. In the first box, you have a choice of conditions:

- **Field Value Is**   Defines the value or range of values for which to apply the format settings.

- **Expression Is** Applies the formatting if the expression you enter evaluates to True.
- **Field Has Focus** Applies the formatting to the field as soon as it gets focus.

Depending on which selection you make in the first condition box, other specifications can be made in the other boxes. If you choose Field Value Is in the first box, you have a choice of several comparison operators.

If you choose Expression Is, you have only one box in which to enter the expression. Field Has Focus requires no additional criteria.

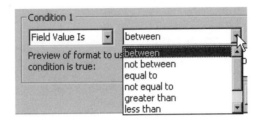

After defining the condition, use the formatting buttons to set the format to apply if the condition is met.

Choose Add to add another condition. You can specify up to three conditional formatting scenarios for each text box or combo box control. The conditions are ranked with the first one taking precedence. If the first condition isn't met, the second is evaluated, and so on. Figure 10-4

FIGURE 10-4 Conditionally formatting a text box control

shows the Conditional Formatting dialog box with settings for the Total Cost text box control. The three conditions are the following:

- If the Total Cost exceeds $5,000
- If the Total Cost is less than $1,000
- If the Labor Cost is greater than the Material Cost

If you want to remove a condition, choose Format | Conditional Formatting again and click Delete in the dialog box. The Delete Conditional Format dialog box opens, where you can check the conditions you want to delete, and then click OK.

Changing a Control Type

When you change your mind about what type of control you want in the form or report, Access lets you change the control type dynamically. Not all types can be converted and you're limited to the types you can convert to, depending on the original control type.

To change a control type, click the control you want to change and choose Format | Change To. You can also right-click the control and point to Change To in the Shortcut menu. A list appears displaying the list of controls to which the selected control can be changed. Click the new type of control. If a control type is dimmed in the list, you cannot change the selected control to that type. Table 10-2 describes the types of conversions permitted by Access.

When you change to another type of control, the applicable properties are copied from the original control to the new control. If the original control has property settings that don't exist for the new control, they're ignored. If the new control has properties that weren't used in the original control, Access assigns the default settings for the new control.

TABLE 10-2
Permitted Control
Conversions

Original Control	Permitted Conversions
Label	Text box
Text box	Label, list box, combo box
List box	Text box, combo box
Combo box	Text box, list box
Check box	Toggle button, option button
Toggle button	Check box, option button
Option button	Check box, toggle button

Deleting Controls

To delete a control, select the control and press DEL or choose Delete from the Edit menu. If you change your mind, you can restore the control by clicking Undo on the toolbar (or choosing Edit | Undo). With the stacked Undo/Redo, you needn't act immediately. You can select the action to undo from the Undo drop-down list next to the Undo button on the Form Design toolbar. You can delete more than one control by selecting them all, and then pressing DEL.

Adding Other Objects and Special Effects

One of the important aspects of Access is you can add objects created by other applications to a form or report. For example, you can add a chart you created in Excel, a picture from Paint, an image from Photo Editor, or a document from Word, to name only a few.

You can add a picture, a sound clip, or another object either as a bound or unbound object, depending on the purpose of the object. A *bound object* is stored in the underlying record source and changes as you move from record to record. For example, a picture of an employee is stored in each record in the Employees table.

An *unbound object* is part of the design instead of the record source and is stored with the design. It remains the same when you move to a new record in the form. A picture of a company logo in a form header or a letterhead is an example of an unbound object.

Linking vs. Inserting Objects

You have two ways to add an object to your design: inserting or linking. When you *insert* a picture or other object in your form or report design, Access stores a copy of the object in your database where it's always available. You can make changes to an inserted object from Access.

When you *link* to a picture or other object, it remains in its original file and isn't stored in your database. You can make changes to the object file separately and the changes will show in your form or report.

TIP   *One advantage to linking over inserting is you don't increase the size of your database with large picture files. If the linked object file is moved or renamed, however, you lose the link and must restore it.*

Here are a few examples of using bound and unbound objects and images:

- For an image that doesn't need updating, such as the company logo, insert an image control.
- If you need an Excel chart or a Word document that will change often, use an unbound object frame and link it to the foreign file.
- If you need to see a different image for each record, such as an employee picture, insert a bound object frame.

The advantage of linking objects is that they're updated automatically. Linked objects in reports are updated when the report is previewed or printed. Linked bound objects in forms are updated when the object gets focus in Form view. Linked unbound objects in forms are updated when the form is opened.

NOTE *When you link an object to a form or report, Access creates an automatic link by default. You can change the links to bound and unbound object frames to manual updating. Remember, if the control is a bound object, you must change the link for every record. Background pictures and pictures in image controls are always updated automatically.*

Adding Bound Objects

When you have an OLE Object field in your table, you can add it as a bound object to your form or report. To add the object to the design, drag the field name from the field list to the design. Access creates a bound object frame to contain the field. The frame is part of the design, while the bound object is still part of the underlying record source.

NOTE *You can add a bound object frame control to the design first using the toolbox, and then bind it to the field by setting the frame's Control Source property to the name of the OLE Object field.*

To edit a bound object in a specific record, open the form in Form view and locate the record you want to change. Then go to the Edit menu, point to the corresponding Object command, and click Edit. You can also right-click the object frame, choose the corresponding command, and then click Edit.

The source application launches where you can make the desired changes to the object.

Adding an Unbound Object

You can add an existing object to a form or report design, or you can create a new one using the source program from within the Access Design window. To add an unbound object to the design, begin by doing the following:

1. Click the Unbound Object Frame toolbox button and draw an outline of the object in the design. You can also choose Insert | Object after clicking the design. The dialog box opens. (Your list might be different.)

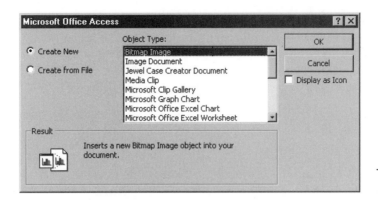

2. Choose Create New to build a new object or choose Create From File to choose an existing object.

3. If you chose to create a new object, select the type of object and click OK. The source program in which you can create the object launches. When you finish creating the new object, close the program and you return to Access.

4. If you chose to get the object from a file, you can enter the filename, including the complete path in the text box, or click the Browse button to look for the file. Other options in the box include Link, which you check if you want to link to the file instead of embedding a copy. After entering the filename, click OK.

TIP   *Another option available to both new and existing objects is Display as Icon, which shows the object as an icon in the form or report, instead of displaying the whole object. The user can click the icon to see the object.*

When you finish in the dialog box, the object appears in the form or report design. If you want to modify the object later or play the sound in Form view, open the property sheet for the new object and change its Enable property to Yes.

To edit an object in Design view, double-click the object, or right-click and choose *name of source program* Object | Edit from the Shortcut menu. You can also select the object and choose Edit | *name of source program* Object | Edit. All these methods launch the source program where you can edit the object.

If you're working in the source program, you can use the standard copy-and-paste procedure to insert the object into the Access form or report. Select the object you want to add and copy it to the clipboard. Then switch to Access, click the design where you want the object, and choose Edit | Paste or click Paste.

Adding a Picture

Image controls are used to display pictures or other images. To add a picture to the form or report design, click the Image toolbox button and draw the outline of the picture in the design. You can also choose Insert | Picture. The Insert Picture dialog box opens where you can locate and select the picture you want. If you click the arrow next to the View button in the Insert Picture dialog box and choose Preview, you can see a display of the picture (see Figure 10-5). Once you select the picture, click OK to insert it in the design.

If you use the Insert menu to add the picture, the form or report design expands to fit the picture. If you created an image control, the picture is limited to the outline you drew and you probably need to enlarge the frame or change the object's Size Mode property.

The *Size Mode* property sets the size of the image with respect to the frame that contains it. The options are Clip, Stretch, and Zoom. The *Clip* option crops the image to fit the frame, leaving the center portion of the picture in the frame. The *Stretch* setting sizes the image to fit both dimensions of the frame. If the proportions of the image aren't the same as the frame, the image might appear distorted. The *Zoom* setting sizes the image to fit either the width or the height of the frame, whichever is the more restrictive, and keeps the original relative height and width. The Zoom setting can leave spaces either on both sides, or on the top and bottom of the frame.

FIGURE 10-5
The Insert Picture dialog box with a preview

TIP   *Image controls can also be used to display unbound objects. Image controls load much faster than unbound object frames, so unless you want to update the object, insert it as an image control.*

Changing Pictures

If you change your mind about the picture and want to see a different one, you can delete the control and add another one, or you can simply change the Picture property on the control's property sheet. The Picture property shows the complete path and filename of the picture in the image control. Click the Picture property box, and then click the Build button to open the Insert Picture dialog box. Then choose another picture to replace the first one and click OK.

Changing Form and Report Properties

Forms and reports have many properties in common, such as Record Source, Filter, Order By, Width, and several event properties. Each of these can be changed in the object's property sheet and some can also be changed in Design view.

Changing the Record Source

To change a form or report record source, do the following:

1. Click the form or report selector, and then click Properties.

2. Click the Data tab and click the down arrow in the Record Source property box.

3. Choose the new record source from the drop-down list of all tables and queries in the current database.

You can also click the Build button to the right of the Record Source property box to start the Query Builder where you can create a new query to use as the record source.

When you change the record source, some of the text boxes no longer represent fields in the underlying record source. You immediately see a marker in the upper-left corner and a tag next to it because no field exists in the new record source with that name.

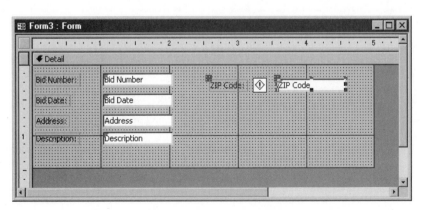

When you rest the mouse pointer on the tag, you can see the reason for the marker. To see how to fix it, click the tag and choose from the drop-down list. This is a big improvement over earlier versions of Access that simply displayed #Name? or #Error? with no clue as to what was wrong.

Applying Filters and Sort Orders

When you create a form or report based on a table or query with a filter or a specified sort order, both are included in the object's properties. The sort order is automatically applied, but the filter could or could not be, depending on how you created the form or report:

- If you created the form or report from a table that wasn't open in datasheet view, the filter is inherited, but not applied. You must apply it when you need it.

- If you created the form or report from a table that was open in datasheet view and it contained filtered data, the filter is applied every time you open the report. But the filter is applied only the first time you switch to view the form. After you save and close the form, the Filter property is inherited, but you must apply the filter yourself by clicking Apply Filter.

NOTE *If you change the filter in the underlying table or query after the form or report was created, it has no effect on the records in the form or report.*

Resizing a Form or Report

You have two ways to change the width of a form or report design: Drag the right border or, for a more precise setting, change the Width property in the Format tab of the property sheet. The height of a report is usually determined by the page setup and the height of a form is usually limited by the screen size.

To change the height of a section in a form or report, drag the section bar below the section you want to change up or down. You can also open the section's property sheet and set the Height property to a more precise measure.

NOTE *If you created a form that doesn't fill the window, you can resize the Form view window to fit the form. With the Form window less than maximized, choose Window | Size to Fit Form, and then save the form. If the Default View property is set to Single form, the window is cropped to fit one record in the form. If the property is set to Continuous Forms, the form is cropped to remove a partial record at the bottom of the form. If only one record is displayed partially, the window is expanded to show as much of the record as possible. See Chapters 11 and 12 for more information about customizing form properties.*

Using AutoFormat

Access has provided several attractive formats for forms and reports that add style to the design. To apply the style to a form or report under construction or already completed, do the following:

1. Open the object in Design view and click the form or report selector.

2. Click the AutoFormat button or choose Format | AutoFormat.

3. Click Options to see how you can apply the font, color, and border attributes selectively.

If you click Customize, you open another dialog box where you can do the following: create a new AutoFormat based on the form design you're working on, modify the selected AutoFormat in the AutoFormat dialog box with attributes in the current form design, or delete the selected AutoFormat completely. This last option is handy if you create a custom AutoFormat, and then decide it's no longer useful.

NOTE *If you want to apply AutoFormat to only one section in the form or report design, click the section selector before you open the AutoFormat dialog box. You can also use AutoFormat for a single control.*

Adding a Background Picture

Adding a picture in the background of a form or report is a little different than adding one as a control. A *background picture* is a property of the form or report, and is found on the Format tab of the form or report property sheet. To add a background picture, do the following:

1. Select the form or report with one of the following methods:

   - Click the form selector.
   - Choose Edit | Select Form (or Report).
   - Choose Form or Report from the Object list on the Formatting toolbar.

2. Open the property sheet and click in the Picture property box on the Format tab.

3. Click the Build button, select the picture you want from the Insert Picture dialog box, and then click OK.

Figure 10-6 shows the title page of a report with a picture of Home Tech Repair equipment in the background.

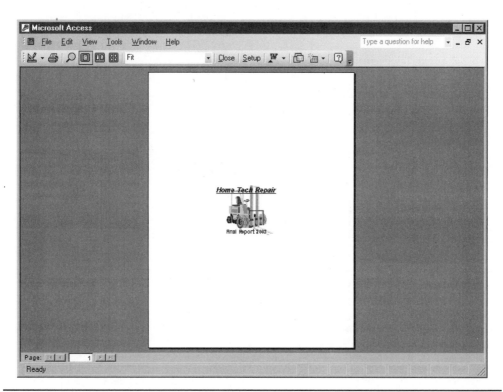

FIGURE 10-6   Previewing the first page of the annual report with a background picture

---

Note   *In some designs, you might want to overlap controls with one in the foreground and the other behind. The Bring To Front and Send To Back commands on the Format menu determine which of the controls is in the foreground.*

Adding a New Object to a Group

If your database is accessed by several people who have different uses for the information, you can group the database objects based on their area of interest. You can use the standard Favorites group that Access provides or create a new group. For example, one group might apply to Workorders and another to Employees.

To add an object to a group, right-click an object name in the Database window and choose Add to Group from the Shortcut menu. Choose the group from the list of existing groups.

If you want to create a new group, choose New Group instead of the name of an existing group, enter the group name in the New Group dialog box, and then click OK. The object is added to the new group. As you add groups, their names appear under Groups in the Database window.

Summary

With the information in this chapter, you're equipped with all the building blocks you need to create substantial forms and reports. This chapter included instructions for applying the tools Access provides to help with the efforts.

The next chapter discusses the Form Wizard and the way to use it to create impressive forms. This wizard lets you choose the form layout and style. After the wizard is finished, you can make changes in the design to get exactly the effect you want. The following chapter continues with form customization.

Using the Form Wizard

Armed with the basic information about creating Access forms and reports, now it's time to put the Form Wizard to work. With this wizard, you can create many types of forms for data entry and viewing. Special forms you can build with the wizard include hierarchical forms showing data from two or more related tables, PivotTables and PivotCharts for summarizing data, and a wide variety of other charts that graphically represent table data.

In this chapter, you can see how to use the Form Wizard to create a data entry form based on an existing query. Then you modify the Form Wizard's finished product in a number of ways.

Creating a New Form Design

Access forms are used for viewing and entering data. Designing a form that presents the data so the information is easily understood and data entry is as foolproof as possible is important. While the Access Form Wizard can do all—or most—of the work for you, this wizard only does what you ask. So, it pays to plan ahead and design the form on paper before invoking the wizard.

TIP *If you have data collection forms already in use, you might want to create a replica of the form on the screen to make computerized data entry look familiar to the user.*

Designing the Form

The Home Tech Repair production manager wants a form that shows the current work orders with the following information: work order and bid numbers, address, customer's name, supervisor's name, job description, plus all the cost information, including the extended cost that adds the overhead expenses. Although she hasn't specified the arrangement of the data in the form, you should sketch it out and show it to her for approval before starting to create the Access form. Figure 11-1 shows a rough sketch of the new Current Workorders form.

After reviewing and incorporating the comments returned by the prospective users of the form, you must search for the data you need in the form design.

In Chapter 8, you designed a query that linked the Bid Data and Workorders tables. The query has most of the fields needed in the Current Workorders form and also has two

Carla: Please review this form design and add your comments:

Current Workorders

Date:

Supervisor   Bid Number

Address   City   State

Bid Date

Principal

Material Cost
Labor Cost
Total Cost
Cost + Overhead

Description

Thanks, G. Prior, ext 583

FIGURE 11-1 Planning a new form for collecting data

calculated fields: Total Cost and an additional expression, Extended Cost, that adds 15 percent overhead expenses to the Total Cost value. This query would be a good basis for the new form. If you need to add more fields to the form, you can add them to the query first or add them to the form design after the wizard is finished. If the query is used for other purposes, modifying the form, rather than changing the query design, is better. The Current Workorders query included the calculated fields.

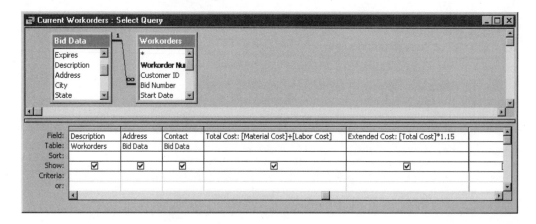

When you use the Form Wizard, you choose one or more tables or queries as the basis, and then select the fields in the order they are to appear in the form.

Starting a New Form

As discussed in Chapter 10, you can start a new form from a number of places and in a number of ways, many of which lead to the New Form dialog box (see Figure 11-2) where you choose the type of form you want to create. To open the New Form dialog box, do one of the following:

- If you want to base the form on a single table, select the table or query name in the Tables or Queries page of the Database window, click the New Object toolbar button, and then choose Form from the list.

- To start a new form with a table or query open in Datasheet or Design view, click New Object, and then choose Form.

FIGURE 11-2   Choosing a form style in the New Form dialog box

---

NOTE   *If you create a new form while the table or query is open in Design view, you won't be able to see the form in Form view until you close the underlying table or query.*

- Click the Forms button in the Objects bar of the Database window and choose New.
- Click anywhere in the Database window and choose Insert | Form.

If you selected a table or query name before opening the dialog box, that name is displayed in the box. If not, you can choose one from the drop-down list in the New Form dialog box or wait and choose one in the wizard's first dialog box. Choose the type of form you want to create or choose one of the wizards to help you out and click OK.

TIP   *If you choose one of the AutoForm designs or the Chart Wizard, you must choose a table or query to use as the basis before proceeding.*

You can also start a new form by double-clicking one of the shortcut items in the Forms page:

- Create form in Design view
- Create form by using the wizard

The Form Wizard creates forms using one or more tables or queries and displays data from the record source. The Chart Wizard, the PivotTable Wizard, and the PivotChart Wizard build special purpose forms. These are discussed briefly in the section "Looking at the Other Wizards."

Choosing an AutoForm

In the New Form dialog box, you have a choice of AutoForm styles or wizards, in addition to starting with a blank form design. The *AutoForm* choices include the Columnar style, which is the same as the form you see when you click the New Object: AutoForm button. Other AutoForm options in the New Form dialog box include Tabular and Datasheet. Figure 11-3 shows examples of the three most commonly used styles. PivotTable and PivotChart styles are discussed in more detail in Chapter 15.

- The *Columnar* style arranges all the fields on the screen in one or more columns, depending on the number and size of the fields.
- The *Tabular* style places all the data for one record in a line across the form. If the record has many fields, you must scroll to the right to see them all.
- The *Datasheet* style is similar to the table Datasheet view. This style is often used for subforms that show data from multiple records related to the record displayed in the main form—for example, details of the workorders (subform) run by a specific supervisor (main form).
- The *PivotTable* style summarizes and analyzes data in a table, query, or form. You can apply different levels of detail and organize data dynamically by dragging fields and items in the PivotTable.

FIGURE 11-3 Examples of three common AutoForm styles

- The *PivotChart* style is similar to the PivotTable, except it shows a graphical analysis of the data in a table, query, or form. You use the same means of dragging fields and items in the design.

Choose the AutoForm style you want and click OK, or simply double-click the choice.

All the AutoForms arrange the fields in the same order as in the table structure or the query grid. The table or query name appears in the form title bar and the form adopts the most recently used style.

Selecting the Form Data

When you choose Form Wizard from the New Form dialog box or double-click the shortcut item, the first wizard dialog box opens where you choose the table or query to use as the basis for the new form.

To start a new form design based on the Current Workorders query, do the following:

1. Select the Current Workorders query in the Queries page of the Database window, click the New Object button, and then choose Form (not AutoForm).

2. Double-click Form Wizard in the New Form dialog box or select Form Wizard and click OK. The first Form Wizard dialog box opens (see Figure 11-4).

NOTE   *If you haven't selected a table or a query either before opening the New Form dialog box or from the list in it, the Form Wizard automatically selects the first table in the alphabetic list of tables and queries. You can change the record source in the first dialog box, if necessary.*

The Current Workorders query name shows in the Tables/Queries box and the Available Fields list shows all the fields in the query, including the calculated fields. The fields appear in the same order as in the query design grid. To place the desired fields in the Selected Fields list, do any of the following:

- To add all the fields in the Available Fields list, click the double right chevrons.
- To add a single field, double-click the field name or select the field name and click the single right chevron.
- To remove a field, double-click the field in the Selected Fields list or select the field and click the single left chevron.
- To remove them all, click the double left chevrons.

To continue with the Current Workorders form, do the following:

1. Click the double right chevrons to add all the fields from the Current Workorders query to the Selected Fields list.

2. Click Next. The Form Wizard's second dialog box opens.

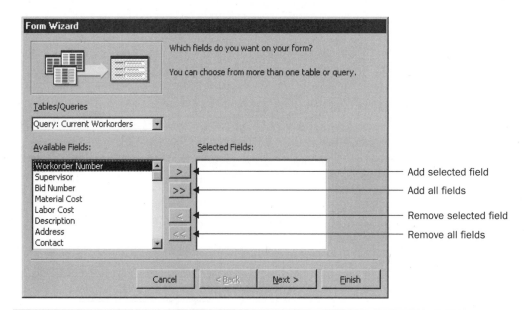

FIGURE 11-4   Choosing fields for the form design

TIP   *If the fields in the Available Fields list aren't in the order you want to see in the form, choose the fields, one at a time, in the order you want them to appear. You can also insert a field name in the Selected Fields list by selecting the field name above where you want the new one, and then selecting the field from the Available Fields list and clicking the right chevron. Selecting them in the right order in the Form Wizard dialog box saves having to move the controls around in the form design.*

If you select fields from more than one table, the Form Wizard creates a main form with one or more subforms. Creating hierarchical forms is discussed in the section "Creating a Hierarchical Form from Related Tables."

Choosing the Form Layout and Style

The second Form Wizard dialog box offers a choice of six form layouts: Columnar, Tabular, Datasheet, Justified, PivotTable, and PivotChart (see Figure 11-5). When you select a layout, a sample appears in the left pane. The first three are the same as the AutoForm layouts shown earlier. The Justified layout resembles the Tabular layout, except all the fields appear on the screen without having to scroll. The row of fields is wrapped to multiple lines, as necessary. The last two arrange the fields as a PivotTable or PivotChart. Select each layout option and look at the preview pane.

For the Current Workorders form, select the Columnar layout, and then click Next.

NOTE   *When working with any of the Access Wizards, you can always click Back and return to the previous dialog box to change a setting. After you click Finish, you cannot return to the wizard to change that design; you must work in the Design window.*

FIGURE 11-5   Choosing a form layout

The next dialog box shows a list of ten styles from which to choose. These are the same styles you see when you click the AutoFormat toolbar button, as shown in the previous chapter. Choose a style and click Next to reach the final Form Wizard dialog box.

In this last dialog box, you name the form and decide whether to view the data in the new form or to go directly to the Design view to modify the design. After entering the form name, click Finish to save and open the form. Once the wizard is finished, you can go about customizing the Current Workorders form for your special needs.

What If the Form Is Blank?

When you finish with the Form Wizard, the form opens in Form view unless you checked Modify the form's design in the final dialog box. If all you see is the style background with no data or field names, one of the following could be to blame:

- You might have based the form on a table that doesn't contain any data. Open the table and see if it has records.

- You might have based the form on a query that doesn't return any data. For example, the criteria could be so strict that they exclude all the records. To see if the query returns data, do the following:

1. Switch to Design view and double-click the form selector.

2. Click the Build button to the right of the Record Source property to open the Query Builder with the query design displayed.

3. Click View to run the query.

Modifying the Form Design

While the Form Wizard does a good job of creating a form, you can do a lot to improve the result. For example, you can do the following:

- Add a form header with a title.
- Resize the form to fit the window.
- Resize the window to fit the form.
- Add special controls, such as the current date.
- Move, resize, and reformat the controls.
- Change the text of attached labels.
- Add lines and rectangles for emphasis.
- Change the progression of the cursor through the controls when the TAB key is pressed (the tab order).

Before starting to modify the new Current Workorders form, look at the form properties to see how they influence the appearance and behavior of the form.

Looking at Some of the Form Properties

To examine the form properties, double-click the form selector to open the property sheet. These properties affect the entire form. Other properties can be set to apply to form sections and individual controls on the form.

- The *Format* properties control all aspects of the form appearance from the caption in the title bar to the palette source that controls the colors.

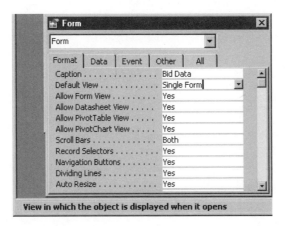

- The *Data* properties determine what data is displayed and affect how the form handles the data, including the filter and sort order, and whether to use the form only for data entry.

- The *Event* properties are used to specify what is to happen when the form opens or closes, or when the user does something such as update a record, press a key, or click a command button. Forms have over 30 event properties to which you can attach actions when creating an application. Chapter 18 discusses events and event procedures.

- The *Other* tab includes miscellaneous properties such as Pop Up and Modal, which determine the form's behavior with respect to the rest of the work space. Other properties also specify custom menus and toolbars, and they add links to custom help topics.

- The *All* tab of the property sheet contains the complete list of form properties.

To see a description of a property, click in the property box and read the text displayed in the status bar. You can see the default setting for the property when you're starting a new form, before you begin to make changes to the properties.

NOTE   *For a complete discussion of form and control properties, consult the Quick Reference on the CD that accompanies this book.*

Changing Form Sections

Access forms can contain several sections:

- The *detail section* contains the record data. You can show data from one record in the detail section or as many records as can fit on the screen.

- The *form header section* contains information to show at the top of the screen for every record—for example, a title, instructions, or command buttons that open another form or print the current form. The information is printed at the top of the first page.

- The *form footer section* contains information to show at the bottom of the screen for every record and at the bottom of the last page of the printed form.

- The *page header section* contains information such as a title, graphics, or column headings that appear at the top of each page when the form is printed or previewed. This section isn't visible in Form view.

- The *page footer section* contains information that appears at the bottom of each page when the form is printed or previewed. This section isn't visible in Form view.

Adding Form Header and Footer Sections

By default, a form created by the wizard from a single table or query has a detail section and form header and footer sections. The form header and footer sections contain information that appears at the top and bottom of the form. This information remains on the screen as you scroll through records in the detail section.

The thin form header section appears above the detail section. If you scroll down the form design, you also see the footer section. To increase the size of the form header section, move the mouse pointer to the detail section bar. When the pointer changes to a black plus sign (+) with up and down arrows, click-and-drag the bar down.

To add a title to the form header, do the following:

1. Open the toolbox, click the Label control button, and then draw a frame in the form header section.

2. Type **Current Workorders** in the new label.

3. Click outside the label control, and then click it again to select it.

4. Using the Formatting toolbar, change the font size to 18, and make it bold and centered.

5. Right-click the label and choose Size | To Fit from the shortcut menu, or choose Format | Size | To Fit. The label box frame shrinks to the size of the text in it.

Figure 11-6 shows the Current Workorders form design with a title in the new header section.

***

TIP   *When you check Form Header/Footer in the View menu, both sections are added to the form design. If you don't have information to put in the footer and you don't want the section to take up room in the form, you can drag the bottom form border up to reduce the footer section space to zero.*

Changing Section Properties

All the sections in a form have the same properties. Double-click one of the section selectors to open the property sheet for the section. The sheet shows fewer properties than the form itself. Most of the section properties apply to formatting. There are no Data properties and only five Event properties for form sections.

Four of the important section properties are Visible, Can Shrink, Can Grow, and Force New Page. The Visible property (default is Yes) shows or hides the form section. This is useful when you want to keep information confidential. The Can Grow and Can Shrink properties allow a section automatically to expand or reduce vertically to accommodate all the data in the section. The default settings for these two is No. The Force New Page property

FIGURE 11-6   Adding a title to the form header section

can start printing the form section on a new page rather than on the current page, before or after printing the current section.

Page header and footer sections have fewer properties because the information in them doesn't appear in Form view; it only appears when the form is printed. You can set the height, color, and any special effect for the page sections.

NOTE *The header and footer sections needn't have the same properties.*

Moving and Adding Controls

The wizard places controls in the form in a straightforward way according to the layout you choose in the dialog box, not always in the most logical arrangement. When the wizard is through, you almost always need to move some controls around and resize some that display short values to reduce empty space and add more controls. If the query didn't have all the fields you want in the form, now is the time to add them to the record source.

In the next few paragraphs, you see how to modify the form by changing and adding controls, including the current date. Refer to Chapter 10 if you need to review how to select controls, and how to use the moving and sizing handles.

Moving and Resizing Controls

With the Current Workorders form in Design view, rearrange the text boxes so the Address and Contact fields are below the Supervisor field, leaving some space below the Contact text box. Then drag the Description text box to the right side of the form next to Labor Cost. Resize the Description text box, so it's more square and fits in the space. Then select Bid Number in the field list and drag it to the four-inch mark on the horizontal ruler in line with the Supervisor field.

NOTE *When you're moving a control past other controls, you can drag it right over the other controls without interfering with them.*

Modifying a Label

When you add a calculated field to a query design, the field is often named Expr1. This is what shows up as the label if you didn't rename the field in the query design grid. Use one of the following ways to change the label Extended Cost to With Overhead:

- Double-click the label and edit the text.
- Select the label and enter the new text in the Caption property in the Format tab.

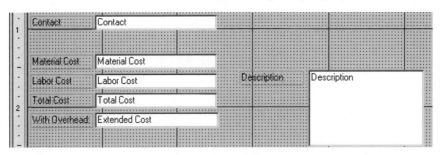

Adding New Controls

The Current Workorders query doesn't have all the fields you want to see in the Current Workorders form. To add more bound text box controls, change the query that's the form's Record Source property and include the additional fields. If you're using a table as the record source, you might need to create a query that includes the fields from the original table, plus the additional fields from related tables.

CAUTION   *If you're planning to use a form for data entry, be sure the design includes all the required fields and that you set the same validation rules in the form as in the tables.*

To add more fields from the related tables used in the query, open the form in Design view and do the following:

1. If the property sheet is already visible, click the form selector or select Form from the drop-down list. If not, select the form and click Properties.

2. Click in the Record Source property box on the Data tab, and then click the Build button. This starts the Query Builder, which looks much like the query design grid except for the words "Query Builder" in the title bar.

3. Hold down CTRL while you select the City and State fields in the Bid Data field list, and then drag the group to the grid. The position in the grid is unimportant right now.

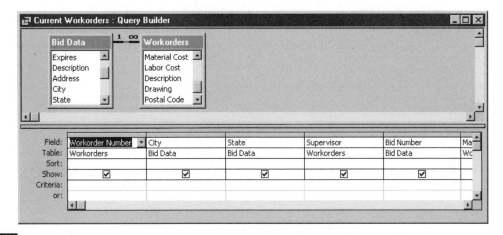

4. Click Save, and then click the Close button to return to the form design.

The additional fields are now available to the form and the field list is displayed. You can add fields to the form in two ways:

- The quickest way is to drag the fields from the field list to the form design.

- You can also add a new bound text box control for each of the fields and set the control source to the field you want to add.

Follow the next steps to complete the addition of the City and State fields:

1. Select the City field in the field list and drag it to a position in the design below the Bid Number field, and then drag the State field next to the City field.

2. Resize the City and State labels to fit the text, and then resize the State text box because it will contain only two characters. Move the State text box next to its attached label.

3. To make the three address fields all the same height, click the vertical ruler level with the row of text boxes to select all three and choose Format | Size | To Tallest.

4. Now align them by choosing Format | Align | Top while they're still selected.

You can also add a line to separate the material and labor cost from the calculated fields that show the total and extended costs. First, move the two calculated fields down a little to make room for the line. Then click the Line control button and draw a line across under the Labor Cost text box. You can change the line thickness, style, and color by selecting from the Border properties lists.

TIP   *Don't use the vertical ruler to select the two calculated fields. You'll also select the Description text box.*

The last control to add to the Current Workorders form is the current date, which appears in the form header section. To add the date, do the following:

1. Choose Insert | Date and Time. The Date and Time dialog box appears (see Figure 11-7). The Date and Time command can be included in the expanded Insert menu.

2. Check Include Date (if it isn't already checked) and select the middle date format (Medium Date), which displays dates as dd-mmm-yy.

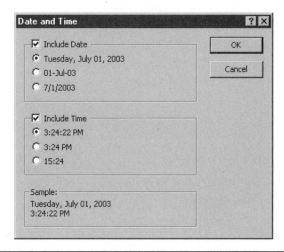

FIGURE 11-7   Setting the date and time properties

3. Clear the Include Time check box and click OK. The expression = *Date()* appears in the upper-left corner of the form header section.

4. Drag the date control down to just above the detail section bar.

Figure 11-8 shows the completed Current Workorders in Form view.

TIP   *When you switch to Form view, choose Window | Size to Fit Form to resize the window. This works only if the form Design view wasn't maximized.*

Sorting and Filtering Data in a Form

Once you're viewing data in the form, you can filter the records just as in a datasheet: use Filter By Selection, Filter By Form, Filter For Input, or Advanced Filter/Sort to limit the records. To sort records in the form, place the cursor in the field you want to sort on and click one of the Sort buttons. You can also enter filter and sort expressions in the form's property sheet.

If the form is based on a table or query that already has a sort order or filter saved with it, the form inherits both properties. A sort order is automatically applied to the records in the form. Whether the filter is automatically applied to the records in the form depends on the status of the table or query when you created the form.

- If the table or query was open and the filter applied when you created the form, the filter is automatically applied to the records in the form. The word "(Filtered)" appears to the right of the navigation buttons at the bottom of the form and "FLTR" appears in the status bar to remind you of the filter. To remove the filter, click the Remove Filter button, which appears pressed in when a filter is applied, or choose Records | Remove Filter/Sort.

FIGURE 11-8   The completed Current Workorders form in Form view

NOTE   *The filter isn't saved with the form, so if you close and reopen it, you see all the records.*

- If the table or query was closed and saved with the filter, the filter is inherited by the form, but isn't automatically applied. Click the Apply Filter button or choose Records | Apply Filter/Sort.

If you construct and apply a different filter or sort order, the new property replaces the one inherited from the underlying table or query.

NOTE   *To disable all filtering of records in the form, set the Allow Filters property to No. This disables the Filter By Selection, Filter By Form, Filter For Input, and Advanced Filter/Sort.*

Using the Form for Data Entry

Forms are the principal user interface with the database information. You can view all the data, search for specific records, enter new records, and edit existing records. To accomplish these tasks efficiently, you must know how to get around in the form and how to move through the records in Form view.

To open a form in Form view where you can view and edit data, double-click the form name in the Forms page of the Database window or select the form name and click Open. In Form view, you can add a new record by clicking the New Record button to show a blank form. You can also edit existing records using the navigation tools or the Edit menu.

To open a form in Design view where you can modify the design, select the form name and click Design.

You can also right-click the form name in the Database window and choose Open (to open in Form view) or Design view from the shortcut menu.

The Form view toolbar buttons are the same as in Datasheet view. The View button has five options: Design view, Form view, Datasheet view, PivotTable view, and PivotChart view. When you view the form that includes a subform in Datasheet view, you can see the related records from the subform by clicking the expansion symbol (+) next to the record row. The View menu has the same five commands.

Sizing the Form

If your form window isn't maximized to fill the Access window, you can adjust the form window to fit the form. In Design view, drag the form boundaries in to fit the contents of the form, and then switch to Form view and do the following:

1. If the form window is maximized, click the Resize button in the title bar to reduce it.
2. Choose Window | Size To Fit Form. Access adjusts the window around the form boundaries.
3. Click Save to save the new form size.

If the form's Default View property is set to Single Form, the window is cropped or expanded to fit the displayed record. If a single record is too large for the screen, Access expands the window to display as much of the record as possible.

If the Default View is set to Continuous Forms, Access crops any partial record showing at the bottom of the screen. If only one record fits in the window, Access expands the form window to display as much of the record as possible.

Navigating in the Form

As with datasheets, you can operate in two different modes in a form: navigation and editing. In *Navigation* mode, the cursor moves to other fields; in *Editing* mode, it moves among characters in a field. The keypresses have different consequences, depending on the current mode. For example, in Editing mode, pressing RIGHT ARROW moves the insertion point one character to the right. In Navigation mode, this moves the cursor to the next field to the right and usually selects the value.

To change modes, do the following:

- To switch from Editing mode to Navigation mode, press F2 or click in a field label. You can also press TAB or SHIFT-TAB to leave Editing mode and move to another field.
- To switch from Navigation mode to Editing mode, press F2 or click the text box.

Clicking the navigation buttons at the bottom of the form moves the cursor to the first, previous, next, or last record. You can enter a specific record number to move to that record. Choosing from the Edit | Go To menu also moves the cursor to other records. These methods move the cursor to the same field in another record.

Table 11-1 describes the keystrokes you can use to navigate through records and fields in a form.

Destination	Keystrokes
First field of the first record	CTRL-HOME
First field of the current record	HOME
Last field of current record or the first record in the current record's subform	END
Last field of last record or the first record of the last record's subform	CTRL-END
Current field in the next record	CTRL-PGDN
Current field in the previous record	CTRL-PGUP
Next field	TAB or RIGHT ARROW
Previous field	SHIFT-TAB or LEFT ARROW
Specific record	F5, enter record number, and press ENTER
Previous record or page	PGUP
Next record or page	PGDN

TABLE 11-1   Navigating with Keystrokes

NOTE   *You recall the options set in the Keyboard tab of the Options dialog box affect the behavior of the TAB, ENTER, and ARROW KEYS (choose Tools | Options). If you change their default settings, some of the keystrokes in these tables might behave differently.*

When you're in Editing mode, you need to move around in the field data and insert or delete characters. Many of the same keys are used, but with different results.

Changing the Tab Order

Each time you press TAB in Form view, the cursor moves to another field. The progression of the cursor through the fields in the form is called the *tab order.* Each text box control is assigned a tab index number indicating its position in the sequence. The first control in the order has 0 as the tab index number, the second has 1, and so on. Access sets the tab order to match the order in which the fields were added to the design.

If you open the Current Workorders form in Form view and press TAB a number of times, you see the order isn't logical. The tab order reflects the way the fields were originally positioned in the query grid. Some of the fields have been moved in the design and the tab order doesn't automatically change to match. The three fields added later are at the end of the tab order.

To change the tab order so the cursor moves more logically through the records, do the following:

1. Open the form in Design view and click the detail section.
2. Choose View | Tab Order. The Tab Order dialog box opens, showing a list of all the text box controls in the detail section.

3. To reposition a control, click the row selector, move the mouse pointer to the row selector, and then drag the row to a new position. You can also select a group of rows and reposition them as a group.

4. Repeat Step 3 until you have the order the way you want it, and then click OK.

TIP *Clicking the Auto Order button in the Tab Order dialog box rearranges the controls in order from left-to-right and top-to-bottom. If this is the way you want the cursor to move through the fields, click Auto Order instead of moving the controls by hand.*

When you change the tab order in the form design, Access rearranges the fields in the form's Datasheet view to match.

Text box controls have three properties that involve the tab order:

- *Tab Stop*, which you can set to No to keep the cursor from reaching the field by means of pressing TAB. You can still select the field for editing; it just isn't part of the tab order.

- *AutoTab*, which, when set to Yes, automatically moves the cursor to the next field in the tab order when the last character permitted by an input mask is entered.

- Tab Index, which indicates the control's position in the order, beginning with 0. For example, if you choose Auto Order in the Tab Order dialog box, the third control in the order, Address, has a tab index of 5.

Locating Records

Searching for specific records by examining the value in one or more fields is the same in a form as in a datasheet. You use the same Find and Replace dialog box to specify the search string and the scope of the match, part or all of the field.

To display a specific record in the form, place the insertion point in the field you want to look for and click Find, or choose Edit | Find. If you want to replace the current field value with another, choose Edit | Replace, or click the Replace tab in the Find and Replace dialog box. Refer to Chapter 6 for more information about using Find and Replace.

Viewing Multiple Records

If you want to see more than one record on the screen, you can switch to the form's Datasheet view or change the form's Default View property from Single Form to Continuous Forms. When you choose Form view from the View button or from the View menu, the form appears with as many records as can fit on the screen.

Home Tech Repair uses a form named Roster as a quick way to look up employees. When the Roster form is set to Single Form, only one record appears on the screen, as the following shows. The Form view window has been resized to fit the form by choosing Window | Size to Fit Form.

Figure 11-9 shows the same Roster form with the Default view set to Continuous Forms. You might have to drag the lower border of the form to view multiple records.

NOTE   *When you use the scroll bar to move through records in a continuous form view, Access always makes sure a complete record appears at the top of the screen, while only a partial record might appear at the bottom, depending on the size of a single record. Using* PGUP *and* PGDN *causes the previous or next set of whole records to appear onscreen. For example, in the Roster form, only four complete records are visible at once with a partial record at the bottom of the screen. When you press* PGDN, *the partial record moves to the top where it appears in its entirety with three more complete records below it and another partial record at the bottom.*

FIGURE 11-9   Showing the roster in a continuous form view

Printing the Form

Although forms are used mostly for data viewing, entering, and editing, you can also preview and print the form. Click the Print Preview button to see how the form will look when printed. See Chapter 13 for information about setting printing options and running the page setup for special print jobs.

Looking at the Other Wizards

Two other wizards are available from the New Form dialog box: the Chart Wizard and the PivotTable Wizard. The *Chart Wizard* converts data in your tables into a variety of charts, including bar charts, pie charts, and line graphs. If you want to illustrate trends over a period of time, you use a bar chart or a line graph. If you want to show relative frequencies or other proportions, use a pie chart. The following pie chart is based on the Home Tech Repair Workorders table and illustrates the percent of jobs started in each month.

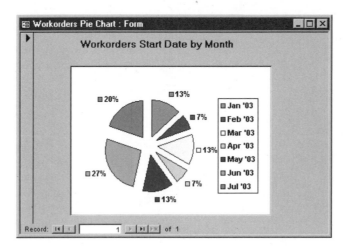

> **NOTE**   *You must have Microsoft Graph installed to use the Chart Wizard. You can install it from the Microsoft Office 2003 CD.*

The chart has been added to a blank form, as an OLE Unbound object frame, by the Chart Wizard. To make changes to the chart, such as exploding the pie shown here or adding captions to the pie wedges, use the Microsoft Graph applet. To launch it, switch the form to Design view and double-click the chart.

The *PivotTable Wizard* takes large amounts of data from your tables and summarizes it in rows and columns in a similar, but more flexible, way to crosstab queries. You need to have Excel installed to modify PivotTables created by the wizard.

Chapter 15 contains more information about creating visual form and report elements containing charts, graphs, PivotTables, and PivotCharts.

Creating a Hierarchical Form from Related Tables

A *hierarchical form* usually consists of a main form and one or more subforms. The main form shows data from records on the "one" side of a one-to-many relationship and the subforms show data from records on the "many" side.

If your main form has many controls and no room exists for a subform, you can link the forms instead. When you click a command button in one form, it opens the other form showing data that's synchronized with the record in the first, much like clicking the subdatasheet expansion button in Datasheet view.

You can create a form and a subform at the same time using the Form Wizard by choosing fields from related tables. For example, to create a hierarchical form showing the list of work orders currently under way for each customer, choose fields from both tables. The Form Wizard can determine how the tables are related and decide which data goes in the main form and which goes in the subform.

To create the Workorders By Customer hierarchical form, do the following:

1. Start the Form Wizard with the Customers table and, in the first dialog box, choose the Customer ID, First Name, Last Name, and Billing Address from the Customers table.

2. Choose the Workorders Table in the Tables/Queries list and add the Workorder Number, Bid Number, Start Date, Completion Date, Supervisor, Material Cost, and Labor Cost fields. Then click Next.

3. The second dialog box (see Figure 11-10) asks how you want to view the data—in other words, which records go in the main form and which go in the subform? Access assumed the Workorders data (on the "many" side of the relationship) goes in the subform. The other two options in the dialog box let you specify whether the data should be arranged as a form with a subform or as separate, linked forms.

4. Accept the default options, and then click Next. The next dialog box offers four layouts for the subform: Tabular, Datasheet, PivotTable, or PivotChart. Choose Datasheet and click Next.

5. Choose the style for the form in the next dialog box and go on to the final box, in which you name the form and the subform, and then choose to view the form or open the form in Design view.

6. Enter the name Workorders by Customer Form for the main form and leave the default name for the subform. Then click Finish.

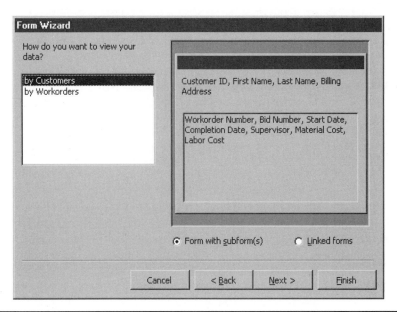

FIGURE 11-10   Creating a form with a subform

Main form   Subform

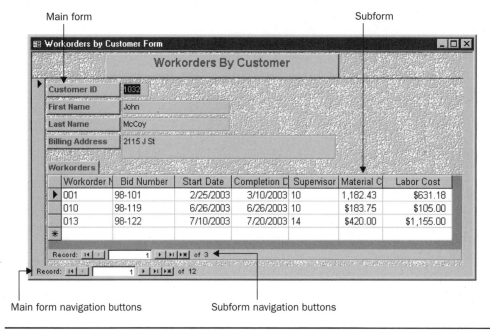

Main form navigation buttons   Subform navigation buttons

FIGURE 11-11   The completed hierarchical form

Figure 11-11 shows the completed hierarchical form with a few modifications, such as a title in the form header. The columns in the subform have also been resized to fit the screen. You can modify the subform in place. To modify the subform design, open the main form in Design view and click the subform selector or any of the controls in the subform. Modify the subform and its controls the same as in the main form.

You can also add a new or an existing form as a subform within another form by using the Subform/Subreport Control Wizard or simply drag the form you want as a subform into the Design view window of the main form. If an existing relationship exists between the record sources of the two forms, Access determines which are the linking fields.

See the next chapter for more information about creating subforms and linking forms to see related information.

Summary

This chapter has shown you how helpful the Form Wizard can be when you want to create a form. More wizards can help construct the perfect form. Control Wizards can help when you want to add combo boxes, list boxes, option groups, and command buttons. In the next chapter, you see how to use these tools in new forms.

When you use Access, you see pop-up forms that prompt for user action, such as dialog boxes, where you make choices about what to do next. In the next chapter, you see how to create your own custom dialog boxes and other special types of forms, such as switchboards, for user interaction.

Customizing Forms

With all the building blocks at your disposal, including the help of the Form Wizard, you're ready to explore some of the ways you can make forms more flexible and practical. This chapter offers constructive ideas for creating custom forms. You can add special controls to a form that help with data entry, print records, or open another related form to see additional information. Access provides tools that help you add command buttons to perform specific actions, as well as improve data entry accuracy and validity.

This chapter continues with examples from the Home Tech Repair database and also introduces you to a real-life, operational database-management system in use by local law enforcement personnel. The Police database discussed in the section "Introducing the Police Department Database" is primarily user interactive and demonstrates some of the special applications of Access forms.

Starting a New Custom Form

When you start a new custom form without the help of the Form Wizard or one of the AutoForm templates, you begin with an empty Design view window. If you chose a table or query in the New Form dialog box to use as the basis for the form, you can display the field list and drag the fields into the form design. If you haven't already chosen the basis for the form, you can define it in Design view by selecting the table or query from the form's Record Source property list.

No law says you have to base a form on data. You can create a form that displays courses of action from which to choose or one that simply displays a welcoming screen, which times out after a few seconds. The first sections of this chapter dwell on forms that contain data, while later sections discuss special-purpose forms.

Placing and Customizing Data-Related Controls

In the last chapter, you saw how to add bound text-box controls to a form design by dragging the field names from the field list. In addition to the text box controls in which you enter and edit data, list and combo boxes enable you to choose from a list of values. List boxes limit your choice to values in the list, but combo boxes usually let you type entries, as well as choose from the list. Either of these can be bound or unbound. If *bound*, the selected or entered value is stored in the field to which it's bound. If *unbound,* the value isn't stored in a table, but can be used by another control or as a search criterion.

Creating List and Combo Boxes

Selecting a value from a list is often quicker and safer than trying to remember the correct value to type. Because list and combo boxes are similar, how do you decide which type of control to use in the form?

- The values in a list box are always visible and you're limited to the values in the list. To choose from the list, click the entry and press ENTER or TAB. You can also choose one of the values by typing the first letter of the value and pressing ENTER or TAB. (If you have more than one value starting with the same letter, the first one is selected.) You cannot enter a value that isn't on the list. List boxes are best when you're limited to only a few values because, otherwise, the list box takes up valuable viewing space.

- The values in a combo box aren't displayed until you click the arrow to open it, so these values take up less room on the screen than a list box. Like the list box, you can select one of the values by clicking it or by typing the first few characters of the value into the text box area of the combo box. If the Auto Expand property is set to Yes, the default setting, Access automatically fills in the rest of the value. In addition, you can type in values that aren't in the list unless you set the combo box Limit To List property to Yes.

NOTE *When the characters you type match the first few characters in one of the values, the combo box Auto Expand property specifies whether Access automatically fills in the text box portion of the combo box with a value from the underlying list. As you type, Access displays the first value in the list that matches the characters. If you set the Limit to List property to Yes and the combo box list is dropped down, Access automatically fills in the matching value as you type in the text box, even if the Auto Expand property is set to No.*

List boxes and combo boxes both consist of rows of data with one or more columns, which can appear with or without headings. One of the columns contains the values you want to store in the field (bound control) or use for other purposes (unbound control); the other columns contain explanatory information.

Figure 12-1 compares examples of list and combo boxes that contain lists of the employee last names from the Home Tech Repair database. The figure also shows a text box for comparison. The list box is always open, but is limited to the size you draw in the form design. If the list is wider or longer than the space allowed, Access adds scroll bars. The combo box list is, by default, the same width as the control in the design, but you can change the width to fit the list. Scroll bars are also added to combo boxes, when necessary.

To add a list box or a combo box to a form design based on the Employees table, open a blank form in Design view and do the following:

1. Make sure the Control Wizard button is pressed, and then click the List Box or Combo Box tool in the toolbox.

2. Click the form design or draw an outline where you want the control to appear. The wizard's first dialog box opens (see Figure 12-2). For both the List Box Wizard and the Combo Box Wizard, the first dialog boxes are nearly identical.

FIGURE 12-1
Comparing a list box with a combo box

3. Choose one of the options (both wizards offer the same options):

- **I want the box to look up the values in a table or query.**   If you choose this option, the box displays field values from the table or query you choose.

- **I will type in the values that I want.**   If you choose this option, the list contains values you type into the next dialog box.

- **Find a record on my form based on the value I selected in my combo box.**   This option is used to create a combo box that acts as a search string to find a specific record and display it in the form. This option creates an unbound control.

4. After making a choice in the first dialog box, click Next. Depending on your choice in Step 3, do one of the following:

- If you chose the first option, select the table or query that contains the values the box will display. Then click Next, select the fields you want to see in the list, and click Next again.

FIGURE 12-2
Starting a new combo box with the wizard

- If you chose to type in the values, enter the number of columns you want to see and the values to display. Choosing this option skips the next dialog box.

TIP   *Press* TAB *to move to the next row in the list of values. If you press* ENTER, *you advance to the next wizard dialog box. In that case, click Back to return to the value list dialog box.*

- If you chose the third option, choose the field whose values you want to see. The value you choose in Form view acts as a search value. Then click Next.

5. In the next dialog box, adjust the column widths to show the values and decide to show or hide the primary key field. Then click Next.

6. The next dialog box asks what you want Access to do with the value you select in the list box or combo box:

    - **Remember the value for later use.**   Saves the value for use by a macro or procedure. When you close the form, the value is erased.

    - **Store that value in this field.**   With this option, you select the field in which you want to store the selected value.

7. If you want a label attached to the box, type it in the last dialog box, and then click Finish.

Changing the Control Type to Combo Box or List Box   If you want a list or combo box in place of a text box already in a form, changing the control type is easy. To change the control type, do the following:

1. Select the control, and then choose Format | Change To. Change To might be one of the shaded commands on the Format menu.

2. The list that appears shows a list of all the control types; the only types you can change are the selected control types to appear in bold. For example, you can change the selected text box control only to a Label, a List Box, or a Combo Box. You can also right-click the control and point to Change To in the shortcut menu to see the same list.

3. Choose the kind of control you want. The control is changed in the design.

4. Open the combo box or the list box control's property sheet and click the Row Source property, and then click the Build (…) button to start the Query Builder.

5. Select the Employees table in the Show Table dialog box, click Add, and then click Close.

6. Drag the Last Name field to the query grid and close the query window.

7. Respond Yes to the message about saving the changes. The Query Builder places the following SQL query statement in the Row Source property box:

```
SELECT Employees.[Employee ID], Employees.[Last Name] FROM Employees;
```

8. Change other properties as necessary.

NOTE *Refer to Chapter 10 for a list of which controls can be changed to which other types.*

Creating Unbound List and Combo Boxes

An *unbound list* or a *combo box* can display either a set of fixed values you enter when you create the box or specific values from a table or query. The value chosen from the control list isn't stored in a field in the underlying table. You can use the value for other purposes, such as looking up a record with that value in a field.

To add a combo box to an Employee form that displays the record for a selected employee, do the following:

1. Start a new form based on the Employee table and add the desired fields to the form.

2. Start the Combo Box (or List Box) Wizard as before and, in the first dialog box, choose the third option: Find a record in my form based on the value I selected in my combo box. Then click Next.

3. Choose Last Name as the field value to show in the list, and then click Next.

4. Choose Hide key column (recommended) and click Next.

5. In the final dialog box, enter **Show record for:** as the control label and click Finish.

When you use the combo box in Form view, you select a value from the list and Access moves to the first record with that value in the corresponding field. This option gives you a quick way to move to a specific record in Form view.

TIP   *If you click Back to return to the dialog box where you selected Last Name, you see Access added the primary key field, Employee ID, to the list when you weren't looking. You chose to hide it in the next box, so it won't appear in the list.*

Setting List and Combo Box Properties

If your form contains a bound list box or a combo box, the control inherits most of its properties from the field properties you set in the table design. When you use a wizard to create one, Access sets certain other properties for you. You can modify these properties by changing the settings in the property sheet to make them work the way you want. To see a description of a property, select the property and read the text in the status bar. For example, the List Rows property sets the maximum number of items to display in the list.

Combo Box: Combo32	
Combo32	
Format	Data	Event	Other	All
Format	
Decimal Places	Auto
Column Count	2
Column Heads	No
Column Widths	0";1"
List Rows	8
List Width	1"
Visible	Yes
Display When	Always
Left	4.3333"
Top	1.3333"

Adding Yes/No Controls

Three different types of controls can be used to view or enter a Yes/No value in the underlying table or query: check boxes, option buttons, and toggle buttons. When you have a limited number of alternative choices in one field, you can also group the controls together in an option group. The grouped options work as a single control and only one of them can be selected. The *option group* can display the list of choices as any of the three types of Yes/No controls.

When you select or clear a check box, option button, or toggle button, Access displays the value in the table or query according to the format property set in the table design (Yes/No, True/False, or On/Off). Figure 12-3 shows how the various Yes/No controls appear when the values are Yes and No.

Check Boxes and Option Buttons

A check box displays a check mark in a small box if the value in the underlying field is Yes. The box is empty if the value is No. An option button displays a black dot in a circle if the value in the underlying field is Yes. The circle is empty if the value is No.

FIGURE 12-3
Examples of
Yes/No controls

Toggle Buttons

When the toggle button appears pressed in, the value in the underlying field is Yes. If the button appears raised, the value is No. You can enter a caption for the button by entering text in the control's Caption property box.

NOTE *An attractive thing about toggle buttons is you can use a picture on the button instead of text, creating a more interesting appearance.*

Option Groups

An option group offers a limited set of mutually exclusive alternatives, usually four or fewer. The *option group control* consists of a frame around a set of check boxes, option buttons, or toggle buttons. If the option group is bound to a field, the frame itself is the bound object, not the individual controls in the group. Option groups are used only with number fields, but you can apply them to Yes/No fields by using the numeric values for Yes (-1) and No (0).

When you create an option group, you specify the values of the options in terms of meaningful numbers to the underlying field. When you select an option in the group, that numeric value is stored in the field.

If Access isn't bound to a field, it uses the value of the option you choose to carry out one of a list of actions, such as print the report you chose or open another form.

Although you can create an option group without the help of the wizard, taking advantage of the wizard is much easier. To create an option group, make sure the Control Wizard button is pressed in on the toolbox, and then do the following:

1. Click the Option Group tool and click the form design where you want the upper-left corner of the group to appear. The wizard draws a one-inch square box. Then click Next.

2. In the first wizard dialog box, enter the text you want to see as choices in the group. Press TAB to enter the next choice. After entering all the values, click Next.

3. In the second dialog box, set the default option, if desired, and then click Next.

4. Specify the Option Value property for each of the options in the group. This property must always be a number. This is the value passed to the field when the option is selected. By default, the values are consecutive integers: option 1 has the value 1, option 2 has the value 2, and so on. For a Yes/No field, set the Yes option to -1 and the No option to 0. Then click Next.

5. The next dialog box asks you which field you want to store the value in (bound) or if you want Access to save the value for later (unbound). If the form doesn't have a record source, the wizard skips this dialog box.

6. Next, choose the type of control and the style you want to see in the option group, and then click Next.

7. In the final wizard dialog box, enter the name you want as the label for the group. This text then appears in the group frame. Then click Finish.

Note   *If you have a set of options that relate to the same type of information, but apply to different fields, you can still keep them together in the form. Arrange the independent options in a group and draw a rectangle around them to resemble an option group. The options won't be automatically set as mutually exclusive, however.*

Adding User-Interactive Controls

Because a form is often used to enter data, the user is constantly interacting with the form and the controls it contains. Some of the controls are directly associated with table data, such as text boxes, list boxes, combo boxes, and the button types, such as toggle, option, and check boxes with which you can set a Yes/No value. The most common control unrelated to data is the command button, used in Form view to perform an action. When the user clicks a command button, Access recognizes this event, and then carries out the response you specified for the event.

Introducing Events and Event Properties

Access is an object-oriented, event-driven application. Nothing happens until the user tells it what to do by pressing a key or clicking the mouse button. An *event* is an occurrence recognized by an Access object. You can define a response to events by setting the event property of the object or the control.

Examples of events include the following:

- Pressing or releasing a key.
- Opening or closing a form.
- Moving the cursor to or away from a control.
- Applying a filter to records in a form.
- Changing or deleting the value in a control.

Every time you press a key or click a button, you're initiating an event to which Access will respond. The action Access takes depends on the event property specified. For example, clicking the Open command button (the event) in the Database window opens the selected object (the response). When you move to another record after entering or editing data, the event causes Access to check any validation rules automatically and, if no violation exists, to save the record. These actions are triggered by the system, based on the built-in event properties.

You can set event properties for any of the controls in your form or report design to carry out the appropriate action. When you set an event property, you attach a set of commands to the event. These commands can be in the form of a macro or an event procedure containing Visual Basic statements. Then, when you click that command button or press that key, Access knows what to do.

The Access wizards also provide a number of predefined procedures you can attach to standard events, such as clicking a command button. The Click event occurs when you quickly press and release the left mouse button on a control. The On Click event property specifies what is to happen when you click the left mouse button on that control.

Another important term when discussing events is *focus*; a control is said to get focus when it's selected or the cursor is in it. For example, when you press TAB to move through the controls on a form, focus is shifted from one control to another according to the tab order.

Adding Command Buttons

The Command Button Wizard is on hand to help create over 30 different types of command buttons, ranging from moving to the next record to closing the form. The wizard guides you through the selection of the category of action you want and the specific procedure to execute. It also lets you identify the button with text or a picture.

To add a command button to a form, do the following:

1. Make sure the Control Wizard button is pressed in, click the Command Button tool, and then click in the form design. The first Command Button Wizard dialog box appears (see Figure 12-4). The list at the left shows the available action categories. The list at the right shows specific actions that fall into the selected category. Each category has a different set of actions. As you highlight an action in the list, a sample appears in the left pane.

2. Select the category you want, select the specific action, and then click Next. Depending on your choice of action, the wizard displays additional dialog boxes requesting information, such as the name of the form to open or the report to preview.

3. After choosing the options required by the action you selected, the next wizard dialog box lets you choose between text and a picture for the button. You can accept the default text or enter your own. If you don't like the default picture, click Show All Pictures and choose another one, or click Browse and look in another folder. After making your choice, click Next. As you select a picture from the Show All Pictures list, you can see how it looks in the left Sample panel.

4. Enter a name for the button or accept the default name. Then click Finish.

You can modify the properties of the command button later to change between a picture and text. Of course, you can always move and resize a command button, just like any other control in the form design. Command buttons are included in the tab order of the form design. That is, as you press TAB to move around in Form view, a command button gets focus when its turn comes. Then pressing ENTER is the same as clicking the command button.

FIGURE 12-4
Choosing the type of command button

TIP *If you use a picture on a button, creating a control tip, which explains what happens when the button is clicked, is a good idea. A control tip automatically displays below the button when you move the mouse pointer over the command button. You can customize the tip the wizard provides by entering the tip in the ControlTip Text property. If you created a status bar message using the StatusBar Text property, it appears in the status bar when you select the control to which it applies. You can create your own custom help, as you see in the section "Adding Custom Help."*

When the Command Button Wizard builds the button for you, it writes an event procedure containing Visual Basic code to store with the form. For example, you can use the wizard to add a command button to print the current record in the Current Workorders form. To add this button, start the wizard, choose the Record Operations category and the Print Record action in the first dialog box, and then click Finish to accept the remaining default options.

CAUTION *If you choose Form Operations and Print Form as the action to take, Access prints all the records as one continuous form on multiple pages. If you want to print only the current record, choose Record Operations and Print Record in the Command Button Wizard dialog box.*

Adding Hyperlinks

In Chapter 6, you saw how to add a hyperlink field to a table and how to insert a hyperlink address in the field. A hyperlink in a table can jump to a different address for each record. For example, the hyperlink field Drawing in the Home Tech Repair Workorders table contained addresses of files containing scanned engineering drawings.

The hyperlink address you enter in the field in a record appears in Form view, like other fields. To add the field to the form design, drag the hyperlink field name from the field list to the form design.

FIGURE 12-5   Working in the Insert Hyperlink dialog box

If you don't need to tie the hyperlink address to a record, you can add it to the form in Design view as an unbound control. You can add a hyperlink to a form design either as a label or an image. Both jump to the target address when you click the control in Form view.

To add a hyperlink as a label to the Home Tech Repair Roster form that will jump to the Employees table, do the following:

1. With the form open in Design view, click the Insert Hyperlink toolbar button or choose Insert | Hyperlink. The Insert Hyperlink dialog box opens (see Figure 12-5).

2. Enter the file name for the hyperlink in the Address text box, as follows:

   • Select the file from the list.

   • If the file you want to jump to is in the folder, type the file name preceded by two periods and a backslash, for example: **..\HomeTech Repair.mdb**.

   • If the file isn't in the current path, type the entire path and file name.

   • Click the Browse for File button (the open folder icon).

3. Next, click Bookmark to open the Select Place in Document dialog box where you can specify the object to jump to.

4. Click the plus sign (+) next to Tables and select Employees from the list of tables in the database (see Figure 12-6). Then click OK.

5. Enter **Lookup Employees** in the Text to display box to see it in the hyperlink instead of the address.

6. Click ScreenTip and enter **Display Employees table** in the Set Hyperlink ScreenTip dialog box, and then click OK. The default is the complete hyperlink address.

7. Click OK to close the Insert Hyperlink dialog box.

8. Drag the hyperlink control to the position you want in the form design.

You can test the new hyperlink in the form design by right-clicking and choosing Hyperlink | Open Hyperlink from the shortcut menu.

When you switch to Form view, the hyperlink appears as an underlined label. Rest the mouse pointer on the hyperlink to see the ScreenTip. Click it to open the Employees table in Datasheet view.

NOTE *If you select a control in the form before inserting the hyperlink, the new hyperlink appears just below the label of the selected control. If no control is selected, the hyperlink appears in the upper-left corner of the form. From there, you can drag the hyperlink to any position in the form design.*

FIGURE 12-6
Selecting the target of the hyperlink

To add a picture that follows a hyperlink, add an image control to the design and change its Hyperlink Address and Hyperlink Subaddress properties to specify the target file.

TIP   *To add a hyperlink in the form of a command button or an image, turn off the Control Wizard before adding the button or image control to the form design. After placing it in the design, select the button, and then enter the Hyperlink Address and Hyperlink Subaddress properties. Also, set the Caption property to the text you want to display on the button.*

In Chapter 11, you saw what might cause a blank form created by the Form Wizard. If the form you create yourself is empty, one of the following reasons could be the cause:

- The form might not be bound to any record source. Check the Record Source property.
- The form might be in Data Entry mode, in which case a blank record is displayed when you open the form.
- If you added a form header or footer section, they might be so big, the detail section doesn't appear on the screen.

Creating a Multiple-Page Form

Access gives you two ways to create a multiple-page form: by inserting a page break control or using the tab control. A *page break* separates the form horizontally into two or more pages, which are separate controls. To move sequentially among the pages, press PGUP or PGDN. Tab controls produce multiple-page forms that combine all the pages into a single control. To move between pages in a tab control, click the desired tab.

Using the Page Break Control

To insert a page break, click the Page Break Control tool in the toolbox, and then click in the form where you want the split. Access shows a short dotted line at the left border where the break occurs.

TIP *Be sure you place a page break between controls. If the page break lines up horizontally within part of a control, the data in the control is then split between the pages.*

Pages aren't necessarily full-screen height. If you want every page to be the same size and show only one page at a time, design the form with evenly spaced page breaks. Use the vertical ruler to help place the page breaks.

After placing the page break, change some of the form properties, as follows:

- Change the Cycle property on the Other tab from the current default All Records to Current Page, which keeps you from moving to the next page when you press TAB at the last control in the tab order on one page.

- Change the Scroll Bars property on the Format tab from Both to Horizontal Only to remove the vertical scroll bar. This prevents scrolling to a different page. If the form isn't wider than the screen, you can set the property to Neither and remove both scroll bars.

Switch to Form view, and then press PGDN and PGUP to see if the page breaks are properly placed.

NOTE *Each page is treated as a separate section. If you plan to print the form and want each form page printed on a separate page, change the section's Force New Page property to Yes.*

Adding a Tab Control

Tab controls are easier and more efficient than page breaks because all the pages in the form belong to a single control. They are useful for presenting groups of information that can be assembled by category. Tab controls are also widely used as dialog boxes. For example, the Options dialog box (Tools | Options) has a tab for each of 11 categories of options, such as Keyboard and Tables/Queries.

To create a tab control, do the following:

1. In Design view, click the Tab Control tool in the toolbox, and then click in the design where you want the tab. Access places a tab control with two pages.

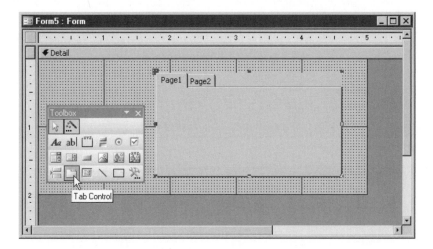

2. Add controls to each page, just as with a single-page form, clicking the tab to change pages. The only exception when adding controls is, while you can copy-and-paste controls from one page to another or from another part of the form, you can't drag them.

3. Next, do any of the following:

   - Change the default tab name by double-clicking the page and entering the new name in the Caption property on the Format tab.

   - Add another tab or delete a tab by right-clicking the tab control border and choosing Insert Page or Delete Page from the shortcut menu. When you delete a page, the last page to be inserted is removed. If you right-click in a page instead of the tab control border, that page is deleted.

   - Change the order of the tabs by right-clicking the tab border and choosing Page Order from the Shortcut menu. Select the page and click Move Up or Move Down to reorder the pages by selecting and dragging the control names in the list.

   - Change the tab order of controls on a page by right-clicking in the page and choosing Tab Order. Rearrange the list of controls in the Tab Order dialog box. Choose Auto Order to set the tab order relative to the control locations in the design.

4. After placing the controls on the pages, check each one to make sure it fits. You can resize the tab by dragging the borders. All pages of the tab control will be the same size.

5. Switch to Form view and test the new tab control.

TIP   *If you try unsuccessfully to make the tab control smaller, the controls on one of the pages could prevent the reduction. Access doesn't crop any controls to fit the tab control. You might need to move or reduce a control on one of the pages first.*

Figure 12-7 shows two copies of the Roster form, so you can see both pages of the tab control.

To create this form, do the following:

1. Open the Roster form in Design view and maximize the window.

2. Click the Tab Control tool in the toolbox and draw a tab control frame in the lower half of the form design across the width.

FIGURE 12-7   Creating a two-page tab control

3. Use the vertical ruler to select all the controls in the upper half and click Copy on the toolbar.

4. Right-click in the tab control and choose Paste from the shortcut menu. The controls from the Roster form appear in the first page of the tab control.

5. Click the second page tab and drag the other fields from the field list.

6. Double-click in a page to open the property sheet and change the Caption property. Then click in the other page and also change its caption.

7. Delete the controls from the upper half of the form and reduce the form height to show only the tab control, and then switch to Form view.

Customizing a Tab Control

Two property sheets are used to customize a tab control: the tab control property sheet and the page property sheet. To customize the tab control, double-click the control border outside of a page to open the property sheet. For example, you can change the style to show tabs or buttons, specify multiple rows of tabs, or set the height and width of the tabs.

To set individual page properties, double-click in the page area. You can enter the text you want to show on the page's tab or even add a graphic to it.

Adding Special Controls

In addition to images, unbound option groups, lines, and rectangles, you can add other special controls to a form design to enhance its appearance or provide additional information.

Calculated controls can combine data from more than one field into processed or summary information. Remember, one of the rules of relational databases is you don't include a field in a table that could be derived from fields already in the table.

Other special controls fall into the category of *ActiveX controls,* which were called *OLE Custom Controls* in earlier versions of Access. The More Controls toolbox button mentioned in Chapter 10 opens the list of all the custom controls available in your system, including the ActiveX controls.

Adding Calculated Controls

Including a calculated field in a form or report is often helpful. For example, in the last chapter, a query was used to add two calculated fields to the Current Workorders form. One field totaled the labor and material costs, and the other added a 15 percent overhead cost. You can also add a calculated field to a form directly without using a query. An unbound text box control is usually used for a calculated field, but you can use any control that has a Control Source property, which tells Access where to get the information to display. Combo boxes, list boxes, bound and unbound object frames, toggle buttons, option buttons, and check boxes all have a Control Source property.

The calculation is based on an expression you enter in the Control Source property box. An *expression* always begins with an equal sign (=). The expression contains operators and functions, in addition to the names of the fields or controls involved in the calculation.

Three types of operators are available for use in expressions:

- *Arithmetic operators,* such as +, -, *, ^, /, \, and Mod, which are used to compute results.

- *Comparison operators,* such as = <, >, <, >=, <>, and Between, which are used to create criteria expressions.

- *Logical operators,* such as And, Eqv, Imp, Not, Or, and Xor, which produce a Yes or No value.

NOTE   *See the Quick Reference on the CD for a compete list of operators used in Access expressions and many examples of useful expressions.*

Access provides nearly 200 built-in functions to help create the expression you want for the calculated control. All functions are followed by parentheses, which enclose the arguments of the function. *Arguments* identify the values the function uses to come up with a value.

Brackets around an identifier in an expression indicate the name of an Access object, such as a table, query, field, form, report, or control. If you type in the expression, you must include the brackets if the name includes a space or special character, such as an underscore. Otherwise, Access automatically adds the brackets.

NOTE   *When you create a calculated field, Access gives it a default name, such as Textnn, where nn is a sequential number created as Access adds the controls. If you change the Name property to another name, be sure you don't use the name of any of the controls in the expression.*

Here are some examples of expressions you can use as the Control Source property for a calculated field:

- **=[Labor Cost]/[Total Hours]**   Computes the average hourly cost.

- **=Format(Now(),"ww")**   Displays the week number in the current year.

- **=IIF([Award Date]="Lost","Review bid","Create workorder")**   Tests the value in the Award Date field. If the field contains the word "Lost," the value of the calculated field is "Review Bid"; otherwise, it displays "Create workorder."

- **=Count([Bid Number])**   Displays the number of records with a value in the Bid Number field.

- **=Sum([Qty]*[Price])**   Displays the total of the values obtained by multiplying the Qty and Price values in each record.

TIP   You can use the name of a calculated control in another expression if the expression doesn't use an aggregate function, such as Avg or Sum. You can use only field names from a table, query, or SQL statement in aggregate functions.

To add a calculated field to a form design, do the following:

1. In Design view, click the Text Box control tool, and then click in the form design to place the control.

2. Enter the expression using one of the following methods:

   - Type the expression directly into the calculated control box. Be sure to precede the expression with an equal sign (=).

   - Type the expression, again preceded by an equal sign, in the Control Source property box in the property sheet.

   - For more complex expressions, click Build next to the Control Source property to open the Expression Builder.

3. Switch to Form view to test the new calculated field.

TIP   If you created an expression in a query that you can use in a calculated field in a form, copy-and-paste it in the Control Source property of the calculated control. Then place an equal sign in front of the expression.

Using the Expression Builder

The *Expression Builder* is a dialog box, also known as a *modal form*, which means you can't do anything else until you close the form by clicking either OK or Cancel. The dialog box is divided into two parts: the upper part contains the expression under construction; the lower part contains all the elements you can add to the expression. Between the two is a row of buttons you can use to add operators to the expression.

The lower half of the form contains three columns, the leftmost of which lists all the different groupings of elements, such as database objects, functions, constants, operators, and common expressions. The illustration shows the Expression Builder as it appears when you click Build (…) in the Control Source property of a new calculated field in the Current Workorders form. Notice the Current Workorders folder appears open in the left column and the center column displays all the elements of the form design. The objects and functions available in the Expression Builder depend on where you were when you launched it.

Double-click any item in the list that shows a plus sign to expand it to show all the elements in the group. When you select an item in the left column, the elements in the item are listed in the center column. The right column lists elements from the selected item in the center column. If you select a field or control name in the center column, the right column shows <value>, plus an alphabetical list of related properties. To add the item to the expression, double-click it in the right column or select it and click Paste.

TIP   *You can always edit the expression you're building by clicking in the Expression Builder upper pane.*

TIP   *A shortcut to adding a field or control value to the expression is to double-click it in the center column.*

To add the expression [Total Cost]*1.15 in the Expression Builder, do the following:

1. With the Current Workorders folder open in the left column, scroll down the center column and double-click the Total Cost control name. Notice Access automatically encloses the control name in brackets.

2. Click the asterisk (*) operator button to add it to the expression.

3. Type **1.15** to finish the expression and click OK. The Expression Builder dialog box closes and you return to the form design.

NOTE   *If you look at the Control Source property for the calculated control, you see Access has added the equal sign at the beginning of the expression.*

If you want to add a function to an expression, double-click Functions to open the folder, and then choose Built-In Functions. Next, choose the function category from the center column and the function itself from the right column. Each function has a set of arguments of various data types—some required and others optional. The message at the bottom of the Expression Builder dialog box shows the function syntax. See the Access Help topic about an individual function for information about the proper use and the exact requirements.

Adding Common Expressions

One of the folders in the left column of the Expression Builder dialog box is labeled Common Expressions. When you click the folder to open it, you see a list of six common expressions dealing with page numbers, date/time values, and current user.

ActiveX Controls

ActiveX controls extend your reach to products supplied by third-party developers. Each one is a separate file with the .ocx file extension. The file contains all the code, methods, events, and properties necessary to function in an Access environment.

Some ActiveX controls come with Access 2003 and others can be installed later. After you install the control according to its installation program, all you need to do is register it, so Access knows the program exists in your system and where to find it. Some ActiveX controls are automatically registered during installation, while others must be registered manually.

After adding an ActiveX control to a form design, you can open the property sheet for the control and change its properties as necessary.

Registering ActiveX Controls

To see which ActiveX controls are already registered in Access, choose Tools | ActiveX Controls. The ActiveX Controls dialog box lists all the controls currently registered. Your list might be different. If you don't see the control you want, click Register to open the Add ActiveX Control dialog box. Locate the folder and file where the control was installed, select it, and click OK. The control is added to the list.

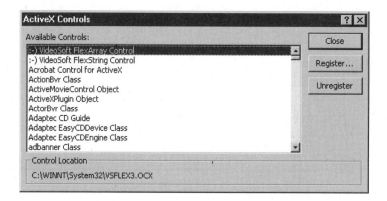

NOTE   *If you're sure you won't be using the ActiveX control any more, you can take it out of the registry by selecting it in the ActiveX Controls dialog box and clicking Unregister.*

Adding a Calendar Control

The *Calendar control,* one of the most popular ActiveX controls, displays dates graphically on a calendar. The custom control has properties that enable you to set and retrieve dates in a table. For example, Figure 12-8 shows the Workorders Form with a Calendar control that displays the Start Dates of the workorders in Workorders table.

As you navigate among the records, the month changes to show the value in the Start Date as a pressed-in date in the calendar.

To add a Calendar control to a form, do the following:

1. Start a new form based on the Workorders table and add the fields to the design.

2. With the form open in Design view, do one of the following:

   • Click the More Controls tool in the toolbox, and then select Calendar Control 11.0 from the displayed list. Now draw a frame in the form design where and in the size you want the calendar to appear.

- Choose Insert | ActiveX Control and select Calendar Control 11.0 in the Insert ActiveX Control dialog box, and then click OK. The calendar is automatically placed in the form design in the upper-left corner and showing the default size.

3. Open the property sheet for the Calendar control, click the arrow next to the Control Source property, and choose Start Date from the list.

The Calendar control has many properties you can set to create a custom appearance. In addition to the individual properties in the property sheet, you can open the Calendar Properties dialog box to make changes. To open the dialog box, click Build (…) next to the Custom property on the Other tab of the property sheet.

FIGURE 12-8   Adding a Calendar control

Adding an AutoDial Control

You can use the Command Button Wizard to create a command button you can click to dial a selected phone number automatically. You need a dial-up modem connected to your computer and a regular telephone connected to the same line for this to work.

To add this special control, do the following:

1. Open the form in Design view.

2. Make sure the Control Wizards button in the toolbox is pressed in, and then click the Command Button tool.

3. Click in the form where you want the button. The Command Button Wizard starts.

4. In the first dialog box, click Miscellaneous in the Category box, and then click Auto Dialer in the Actions box. Click Next.

5. Choose one of the pictures of a telephone and click Finish.

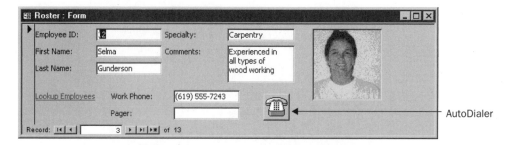

When you click the button in Form view, the AutoDialer dialog box opens. If you moved the cursor to a telephone number field before clicking the button, the number appears in the box. If not, you can enter a number in the empty Number box. Choose OK to dial the number.

The Setup button in the AutoDialer dialog box opens a dialog box where you can set the modem properties.

Introducing the Police Department Database

The Police database is used 24 hours a day by a local police department in support of law enforcement and on behalf of citizens. This is a mostly user-interactive data management system that tracks incidents and maintains records of all people who report, or who are involved in, activities that require police attention—for example, crimes such as burglaries, auto theft, vandalism, and spousal abuse; traffic collisions, with or without injuries; and even people who come in to be fingerprinted as a requirement for employment.

The people who use the database include the following:

- Police officers in the field who call the station to find out if the person they stopped for speeding has a previous violation. The dispatcher at the station looks in the database for prior contacts.

- Victims of traffic accidents who need case information to send to their insurance companies.

- Parents of missing children who want to know if the child has been located.

The database consists of four tables: two main tables and two collateral tables used mainly for lookup.

The *Alpha Card table* lists all people who have filed a report or called in an incident, or who might be a suspect in some sort of incident, for example:

- A rental car agency reports a stolen vehicle.

- A home owner reports a burglary.

- A police officer responds to a two-car injury accident and identifies both drivers and one passenger. This report results in three separate records in the Alpha Card table, one for each civilian involved in the accident.

The *Alpha Entry table* contains details of the report and is related to the Alpha Card table with a one-to-many relationship. The Alpha Card table is on the one side and the Alpha Entry table is on the many side. The Index primary key field, an AutoNumber, in the Alpha Card table links to the Index field, the foreign key, in the Alpha Entry table. Here are the relationships between the four tables in the Police database.

The third table, *Entry Explanation,* contains more understandable explanation of the police shorthand descriptions in the Entry field on the Alpha Entry table. This table is related one-to-one with the Alpha Entry table with a left outer join. Referential Integrity has also been enforced, so Cascade Delete could be enabled. This has been found to be convenient because when the Alpha Entry record is deleted the corresponding Explanation record is also deleted and the user doesn't have to look for the Explanation record to delete it.

The last table, *Penal Codes,* is a list of penal code numbers and their descriptions used as a lookup list.

The principal user interface is the Alpha Card form (see Figure 12-9), which shows all the entries linked to that individual. The main form in the upper half shows the data from the Alpha Card table. The lower half is a subform that shows all the related entries from the Alpha Entry table. Both the main form and the subform have record navigation buttons. The printer command button prints the current record and the Explanation button opens a pop-up form displaying an explanation of the entry. These special controls are discussed in subsequent sections in this chapter.

Another major form in the Police database is the Alpha Entry form, which is a tabular form showing all the records in the table. The Alpha Entry form also includes a command button that opens the Alpha Card form with the same index number, so the officer can see the identity of the person involved, as well as any prior entries for that person.

NOTE   *If you're unable to open the Alpha Card form, you might not have imported the custom menus and toolbars with the database. See Appendix B for instructions about importing the database from the CD.*

Adding a Subform

The main form and subform in a hierarchical form are synchronized so the subform displays only the records related to the record currently displayed in the main form. You

FIGURE 12-9   The Police Alpha Card form

can enter new records in either the main form or the subform. A main form can have as many subforms as you need and you can even nest subforms up to two levels, which means you can have a subform within a subform.

You saw in the last chapter how to create a main form and a subform at the same time using the Form Wizard. Simply create a new form with fields from two or more related tables. If the relationship is one-to-many, the wizard shows fields from the "one" side in the main form and fields from the "many" side in the subform. If you already have a main form and want to add a subform to it, you can use the Subform/Subreport Wizard available in the control toolbox.

With the Subform Wizard

You can use the *Subform Wizard* to create and insert a new subform or to insert an existing subform into a main form. To use the wizard to add the Alpha Entry Subform to a copy of the Alpha Card form, do the following:

1. Open the Copy of Alpha Card form in Design view.

2. Make sure the Control Wizards button is pressed in and click the Subform/ Subreport tool in the toolbox.

3. Click in the form design and draw an outline where you want the subform. You usually want the subform to span the width of the detail section in the form below the information in the main form. After the wizard starts, do one of the following:

   - If creating a new subform, click Using existing Tables and Queries, and then click Next. Now choose from the Tables/Queries list and fields lists, just as when you create a regular form with the Form Wizard. Then click Next.

   - If you already created and saved the form you want to insert, choose Use an existing form and select Alpha Entry Subform from the drop-down list (see Figure 12-10), and then click Next.

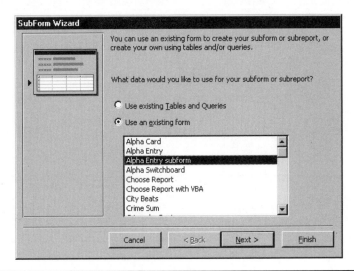

FIGURE 12-10   Choosing an existing form as the subform

4. In the next dialog box, you can choose from a list of links assumed by Access or choose to define your own. If you choose to define you own, the dialog box includes boxes where you can choose the fields that link the main form to the subform (see Figure 12-11). Choose the Index field in both forms, and then click Next.

5. Enter a name for the subform or accept Alpha Entry Subform, and then click Finish.

6. Open the property sheet and click the subform border (not the label).

7. Click the Data tab and make sure the Link Child Fields property refers to the foreign key in the subform and the Link Master Fields property refers to the linking field in the main form.

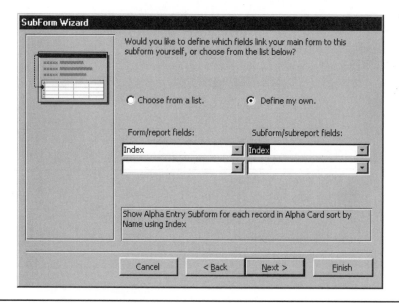

FIGURE 12-11   Setting the linking fields

Without the Subform Wizard

If you already created and saved the form you want to insert into the main form as a subform, the easiest way is to drag it to the form design from the Database window. To accomplish this, do the following:

1. Open the main form in Design view, and then press F11 or click Database Window.

2. Choose Window | Tile Vertically, so you can see both windows at once.

3. Click the Forms tab in the Database window and drag the Subform icon from the Database window to the form design, usually into the Detail section (see Figure 12-12).

4. Open the property sheet and click the Data tab.

5. Click the subform border, and check that the Source Object is Alpha Entry Subform.

6. Click in the Link Child Fields property, then click the Build button to open the Subform Linker to check the linking fields

7. Click OK and close the properties sheet.

Using the Hierarchical Form

To move from the main form to the subform, click in the subform, usually in a record selector or an editable area. To return to the main form, click an editable control or its label. When you work in Navigation mode, some special key combinations move the cursor from the subform back to the main form, for example:

- Pressing CTRL-TAB moves the cursor through the sequence of editable controls in the main form, and then moves to the first record in the subform. Pressing the combination again moves to the first control of the next record in the main form.

- Pressing CTRL-SHIFT-TAB moves the cursor to the previous control in the main form or, if the cursor is anywhere in the subform, it moves the cursor to the last control in the tab order of the main form.

- Pressing CTRL-SHIFT-HOME moves the cursor to the first editable field in the main form, even if it was pressed while the cursor was in the subform.

Each form has its own set of navigation buttons that you can use to move among the records. The subform also has a vertical scroll bar to move other records into view. You can add new records, or edit or delete existing records in either the main form or the subform using the standard data entry techniques.

FIGURE 12-12   Dragging the subform to the form design

CAUTION   *Make sure the cursor is in the right place—in the main form or the subform—before you try to add or delete records.*

You can also sort records and set filters to limit records in either the main form or the subform using standard sorting and filtering methods.

Modifying a Subform

The complete subform design is included with the main form design. You can make changes to it in place. Select the control in the subform you want to change, and then change it as usual. If you want to work on the subform in its own window, right-click the subform and choose Subform in New Window from the shortcut menu. You can also choose View | Subform in New Window.

Tip   *The subform control in the main form is a separate control and has different properties than the subform object. To select the subform control, click one of the subform boundaries. To select the subform for making changes in the subform itself, click the form selector for the subform.*

Linking and Synchronizing Forms

Each month, the Los Padres Police Department purges entries that were kept the required period of time. To do this, the user opens the Alpha Entry form. This is a tabular form showing all the entries in Daily Report (DR) number order. One of the fields is Purge, which contains the date when the record should be removed from the file. If this entry is the last one connected to the individual, the Alpha Card should also be removed. To view the related record in the Alpha Card file, use the Command Button Wizard to add a command button at the right end of the Alpha Entry record that opens the Alpha Card form for the same Index number.

Index	DR	Entry	Code	Date	Purge	Remarks	
1	95-0648	V/BATTERY	242	6/14/2001	6/14/2004		
3	94-1659	V/GRAND THEFT BIKE	487	4/25/2000	4/25/2007		Open Alpha Card Form
3	96-1390	TURNED IN FOUND PROPERTY		0/21/2002			
3	96-0013	DRIVER #1/NONINJ TC		1/8/2002			
3	96-0837	V/BURGLARY	459	7/11/2002			
4	91-5358	V/BURGLARY	459	0/15/1999	10/15/2006		

Record: |◄| ◄| 1 |►| ►I|►*| of 131

When you click the command button in Form view, the Alpha Card form opens showing only that single record. The word "(Filtered)" in the navigation button area indicates that only the one record has been extracted. Figure 12-13 shows the Alpha Entry form and the resulting Alpha Card record with the windows tiled vertically. The record for Index 4 is the current record in the Alpha Entry form and the Alpha Card form shows the related record. The status bar displays the text set in the Status Bar Text property.

The Police database includes one other form that's linked to the Alpha Entry subform. The *Explanation form* is a pop-up form displaying an explanation of the entry that appears in the Alpha Entry subform. To add this feature, first create the pop-up form. A *pop-up form* is a special-purpose form, like the toolbox or property sheet, which can be kept on the screen while you're doing other things. The pop-up form remains on the screen until you close it.

FIGURE 12-13 Viewing the Alpha Card record for a specific entry

In contrast, a dialog box doesn't let you do anything else until you respond to the options presented in the box and click OK, Close, Cancel, or another button in the box. In Chapter 21, you see how to create custom forms that can be used as dialog boxes.

To create a pop-up form that displays an explanation of the entry selected in the Alpha Entry subform, start a new form based on the Entry Explanation table. Add both fields to the design and resize the form to the smallest possible height and width.

Then open the property sheet for the form and change the following properties:

- Set Scroll Bars to Neither.
- Set Record Selectors, Navigation Buttons, Dividing Lines, Auto Resize, and Auto Center all to No.
- Set Border Style to Thin.
- Set Min Max Buttons to None.
- On the Other tab, set Pop Up to Yes.

Now add a command button to the form footer of the Alpha Entry subform that opens the Explanation form for the selected entry by doing the following:

1. Open the Alpha Entry subform in Design view by one of these methods:
   - In Alpha Card form Design view, click the subform form selector.
   - Choose Alpha Entry subform in the Forms tab of the Database window, and then choose Design.

2. The form already has a header and footer section. Drag the lower border of the form down to make room for a command button, if necessary.

3. Make sure the Control Wizards button is pressed and click the Command Button tool. Then click in the left end of the form footer section.

4. Choose Form from the Categories list, Open Form from the Actions list, and click Next.

5. Choose Explanation as the form to open, and then click Next.

6. In the next dialog box, choose Open the Form and Find Specific Data to Display, and then click Next.

7. Select EntryNo and the linking fields in both tables. Then click Next.

8. Choose Text instead of Picture for the button, enter Explanation in the box, and click Next.

9. Enter Explanation as the name for the command button and click Finish.

Figure 12-14 shows the explanation of the entry selected in the Alpha Entry subform. The pop-up form remains onscreen until you close it.

NOTE   *The way the form is designed, when you move to another entry, you must click the Explanation button again to see the explanation for that entry. If you want to synchronize the two forms so the Explanation form follows the subform selection, you need to add a macro or an event procedure to one of the event properties. Chapter 19 discusses creating and using macros.*

Adding Custom Help

You've already seen some of the ways you can get help from Access. When you move the mouse pointer over a toolbar button, a tool tip pops up, displaying the name of the button. The status bar displays messages related to the current activity or object, including the description you entered for the fields in your table design.

FIGURE 12-14   Explaining the current entry

Then, in nearly every window, you can click the Help button to get an explanation of virtually any object on the screen. Pressing F1 also brings you context-sensitive Help messages. If all else fails, type a question in the Type a Question for Help box and press ENTER to look for help on a certain subject.

When you design your own application, times might occur when a quick reminder can help with entering data, creating a filter, or printing a report. Access lets you create your own custom tips and status bar messages as properties of a form or report. You can also create custom tips that pop up when you click a What's This button (the one with a question mark) on your form, and then click one of the controls.

Custom Control Tips

The *ControlTip Text property* specifies the message that appears when you move the mouse pointer over a control in the form. Short tips are best, but you can enter up to 255 characters, if you want. To create a Control Tip, select the control and type the message in the ControlTip Text property box on the Other tab.

Status Bar Messages

A *status bar message* is a good way to display instructions for entering data in a control or explaining the options in an option group. *Status Bar Text* is a control property available for any control on a form you can select. The message displays when the control gets focus.

To specify a message to display in the status bar, type the text in the Status Bar Text property box on the Other tab. You can enter up to 255 characters, but the amount of text displayed is limited by the physical space across the status bar. This depends on the size of the window and the font you use for the message.

TIP   *Try to keep the status bar messages brief. A lengthy message can be truncated and could cause some confusion on the part of the user.*

Validating or Restricting Data in Forms

Access gives you several ways to validate or restrict data entered in forms. You can create controls, such as check boxes, that limit the data to Yes/No values or a list box that requires a value be picked from the list. You can also set certain form and control properties that limit or restrict data entry.

Validating with Properties

When you designed your tables, you set field properties to help ensure valid data. You created input masks, entered validation rules, and specified default values for some of the fields. This is the preferred way to validate data because you only have to do it once. Any bound control you add to a form inherits the properties you set in the table design. If you wait and add the validations and restrictions to a form, you need to do it for every form that refers to that data.

Times could occur, however, when you want to superimpose more validation in the form. For example, you might want to display different error messages when the data is invalid or prevent entering data in a field altogether. If you want to validate unbound controls, you must do it in the form design. The validation rules for controls in a form are created the same as for a field in table design. You can ask for help from the Expression Builder if you need it.

The Default Value, Validation Rule, Validation Text, and Input Mask properties are the same as for table fields.

Three form properties determine the liberties the user can take with data in the form: Allow Edit, Allow Additions, or Allow Deletions. Set these to Yes or No. You can also set the Data Entry property to Yes so the user only sees an empty form with no existing data.

Each control has two additional properties: Enabled and Locked. If the control is enabled, it can receive focus. If the control is locked, the control becomes read-only.

If you set one of these properties in the table design and set the same property to a different value in the form design, the bound control property overrides the field property. For example, if you want to set the default value for a date field to today's date in the form instead of the value set as the field property in the table design, type **=Date()** in the control's Default Value property box. This takes precedence over the setting in the field property.

The order in which validation rules are applied is as follows:

1. Rule specified by a macro or event procedure that responds to the Before Update event.

2. Rule specified as control Validation Rule property.

3. Rule specified as the field Validation Rule property.

4. Rule specified as the table Record Validation Rule.

CAUTION   *If you change any of the validation rules in table Design view, these changes are enforced on controls based on those fields, even if you added the controls to the form before making the changes.*

Enabled Setting	Locked Setting	Results
Yes	Yes	Control can receive focus. The data is displayed normally and can be copied, but can't be edited.
Yes	No	Control can receive focus. Use this combination to allow editing of objects in unbound object frames. The data is displayed normally and can be copied or edited.
No	Yes	Control cannot receive focus. Data is displayed normally, but can't be copied or edited.
No	No	Control cannot receive focus. Control and data both appear dimmed and are disabled.

TABLE 12-1   Combining Enabled and Locked Properties

You can combine property settings to accomplish specific purposes. For example, if you want the form to be read-only, set Allow Edits, Allow Additions, and Allow Deletions all to No.

Combining the Enabled and Locked property settings for a control can create custom results as shown in Table 12-1.

You can also combine the Enabled and Tab Stop properties. If you set Enabled to Yes and Tab Stop to No, the control can't be selected by pressing TAB, but it can still be selected by clicking the control or its label.

Validating with Events

Attaching macros or event procedures to form and control event properties can give you additional flexibility and power over data entry. For example, you can require that at least two of three fields must be filled in before you can save the record. You would also use an event procedure if the validation refers to controls on other forms or if the control contains a function.

If you want to validate the data before the whole record is updated, add the procedure to a form event. To validate the data before moving to the next control, add the procedure to a control event. Table 12-2 shows a few of the form and control events that you can use for data validation.

See Chapter 18 for more information about events and their sequence of occurrence, and how to make the macros that will carry out the actual validation.

Event	Description
Before Update (form)	Rule enforced before saving new or changed data in a record.
On Delete (form)	Rule enforced before deleting a record.
Before Update (control)	Rule enforced before saving new or changed data in a control.
On Exit (control)	Rule enforced before leaving control.

TABLE 12-2   Data Validation Events

Summary

You might never want to add hyperlinks or a calendar to a form but, if you do, this chapter contains all the information you need to add these and other special controls. The most important aspect of form design isn't "What new and exotic things can I add to it?" but, rather, "What does the user need to see and know to do his or her job?"

One of the most flexible features of form design is the capability to link subforms to a main form to show related data from more than one table. You saw examples of using subforms in this and the preceding chapter where records from a table on the "many" side of a one-to-many relationship were displayed in a subform with the data from the "one" side in the main form.

Starting with the next chapter, you learn how to create reports for distributing information to outside users. You also make further use of the Police database introduced in this chapter, as well as continue to see examples using the Home Tech Repair database. You create reports first with the help of the Report Wizard, and then from scratch in report Design view. Chapter 14 also discusses special reports that group and summarize data, or print envelopes and mailing labels.

PART II

Using the Report Wizard

The Access Report Wizards help you prepare many types of reports—from simple ones that contain complete information from one or more tables to reports that calculate and summarize information, and present it in a variety of visual representations. You can also create multiple column reports to be used for printing mailing labels of all kinds and use Access tables for mail merge applications.

In this chapter, you see examples of reports using different databases: the Access Northwind sample database, as well as the Home Tech Repair and Police databases introduced in earlier chapters. No single database has all the elements necessary to display the versatility of Access report writing.

The Report Wizard, described in this chapter, guides you through creating a simple report based on one table, a more complex report based on two tables, and, finally, a summary report that groups records and calculates summary values. After using the Report Wizard, you can then modify the design to add special features and set report properties. Chapter 14 continues the discussion of reports by addressing customization, subreports, and mailing labels.

Creating a New Report Design

Although you create Access reports using the same techniques as for creating forms, major differences exist between forms and reports with respect to the design concepts. *Forms* deal with data and the processes of data management, such as data entry, validation, and retrieval. *Reports*, on the other hand, deal with information derived from the data. For example, the numbers 999900000 are simply data and mean nothing to you until you turn the sequence into information: 999-90-0000, which turns into a Social Security number.

Forms are used primarily by people who are acquainted with computers and database management systems, so forms can be somewhat abbreviated, assuming the user understands the process at hand. Reports are much more widely distributed and need to be designed for the needs and understanding of their intended audience.

What Is the Purpose of the Report?

The differences between forms and reports necessitate a much wider range of report design features, which, in turn, creates a more complex design problem. As with form design, you start the process by defining what you want from the report. Concentrate first on the intended recipients and the level of detail they want to see. Management wants to see information to help it make strategic decisions, such as trends in sales and summary economic data. Operational personnel want more detailed information relating to ongoing business, such as stock levels and employee performance.

Figure 13-1 shows examples of three types of reports. You can see all these reports in the Northwind database in the Program Files\Microsoft Office\Office\Samples folder.

NOTE   *If you installed Office 2003 in a folder other than the default, the path to Northwind will be different.*

The top report shows a summary of sales by product category, complete with a chart illustrating the information. This type of report is suitable for a manager who makes decisions based on product popularity. The second report shows a detailed list of all products in the store in alphabetic order. This kind of report is used by operational personnel to look up an item when a customer calls to ask if the product is in stock. If you want to carry this kind of report into the stock room to check current inventory levels, you might want to add the storage location field, and then sort or group the records by that value.

The lower report is an example of a special purpose report used for printing invoices. The report is based on a query that extracts information from several related tables containing shipper, customer, order, product, and salesperson data.

TIP   *A report can be designed to print on a preprinted form, which can be scanned and saved as a report template. See Chapter 14 for information on printing reports on preprinted forms.*

Consulting the future users of the report is essential to the design process and drawing a sketch of the proposed report for review by the intended users is helpful. Unfortunately, even experienced business people don't always predict everything they want in a report until they see the finished product; then they identify other things they need in the report. For this reason, you should plan on the design process being an iterative one that continuously improves the product.

Selecting, Sorting, and Grouping the Data

Once you collect the requirements for the report content and appearance, you can begin to locate the required data in the database. It might be stored in a single table or distributed among several related tables. If the data is stored in several tables in the database, make sure the tables can be linked, if they aren't already related.

Sorting Records

Next define the sort order for the records in the report. For example, do you want the records in chronological order or by some identifier, such as the primary key? If a sort order is saved with the table, you can apply it automatically in the report. For example, if you have a mailing list for sending promotional material to your customers, you might want to sort the outgoing mail by ZIP code to save on postal costs.

Sales by Category

Wednesday, February 28, 2003

Beverages

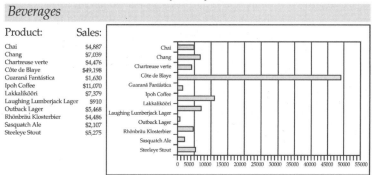

Product:	Sales:
Chai	$4,887
Chang	$7,039
Chartreuse verte	$4,476
Côte de Blaye	$49,198
Guaraná Fantástica	$1,630
Ipoh Coffee	$11,070
Lakkalikööri	$7,379
Laughing Lumberjack Lager	$910
Outback Lager	$5,468
Rhönbräu Klosterbier	$4,486
Sasquatch Ale	$2,107
Steeleye Stout	$5,275

Alphabetical List of Products

A

Product Name:	Category Name:	Quantity Per Unit:	Units In Stock:
Aniseed Syrup	Condiments	12 - 550 ml bottles	13

B

Product Name:	Category Name:	Quantity Per Unit:	Units In Stock:
Boston Crab Meat	Seafood	24 - 4 oz tins	123

C

Product Name:	Category Name:	Quantity Per Unit:	Units In Stock:
Camembert Pierrot	Dairy Products	15 - 300 g rounds	19
Carnarvon Tigers	Seafood	16 kg pkg.	42
Chai	Beverages	10 boxes x 20 bags	39
Chang	Beverages	24 - 12 oz bottles	17
Chartreuse verte	Beverages	750 cc per bottle	69
Chef Anton's Cajun Seasoning	Condiments	48 - 6 oz jars	53
Chocolade	Confections	10 pkgs.	15
Côte de Blaye	Beverages	12 - 75 cl bottles	17

E

Product Name:	Category Name:	Quantity Per Unit:	Units In Stock:
Escargots de Bourgogne	Seafood	24 pieces	62

F

Product Name:	Category Name:	Quantity Per Unit:	Units In Stock:
Filo Mix	Grains/Cereals	16 - 2 kg boxes	38
Fløtemysost	Dairy Products	10 - 500 g pkgs.	26

NORTHWIND TRADERS   **INVOICE**

One Portals Way, Twin Points WA 98156
Phone: 1-206-555-1417 Fax: 1-206-555-5938

Date: 28-Feb-2003

Ship To: Ernst Handel
Kirchgasse 6
Graz 8010
Austria

Bill To: Ernst Handel
Kirchgasse 6
Graz 8010
Austria

Order ID:	Customer ID:	Salesperson.	Order Date.	Required Date.	Shipped Date.	Ship Via.
11072	ERNSH	Margaret Peacock	05-May-1998	02-Jun-1998		United Package.

Product ID:	Product Name:	Quantity:	Unit Price:	Discount:	Extended Price:
2	Chang	8	$19.00	0%	$152.00
41	Jack's New England Clam	40	$9.65	0%	$386.00
50	Valkoinen suklaa	22	$16.25	0%	$357.50
64	Wimmers gute Semmelknödel	130	$33.25	0%	$4,322.50

Subtotal:	$5,218.00
Freight:	$258.64
Total:	$5,476.64

FIGURE 13-1   Some typical useful reports

Filtering Records

At times, you might want to limit the records in a report based on a certain filter criterion. For example, you might want to prepare a report for the ordering clerk to use in placing orders. The report would include only those products that have fewer items in stock than the minimum number recommended. You can base the report on a query that extracts only the data you want or apply a filter to the report later. To complete the report, you could also include the name and telephone number of the supplier of each product.

Grouping Records

Records are often grouped in a report. This is a good way to relate data from several records and convert it into meaningful information. For example, you could group sales by quarter in an attempt to predict future inventory requirements. You can even include charts and graphs in your report that illustrate the information even more clearly.

Specifying Summary and Calculated Fields

Once the records are grouped, summaries and calculated fields can add an important element to reports. They can save the reader's time by doing much of the data evaluation work for them. For example, the first report shown in Figure 13-1 is intended to compare the sales of various beverage products. The manager is considering eliminating some of these product lines and needs information to decide which ones are no longer popular. If the report summarizes sales data over a period of time and presents it in a report, the manager then has all the required numeric information already summarized.

Starting a Report

You can create a report in three basic ways:

- Use the Access AutoReport feature.
- Use one of the Report Wizards.
- Create your own design in the report Design view.

Like most Access activities, you have several ways to start a new report design. Once you try them, you can decide which is your favorite method. You can begin from anywhere in the Database window. Use one of the following methods to open the New Report dialog box.

Click Reports under Objects in the Database window, and then click New in the Database window.

- Choose Insert | Report from any object page.
- Click the New Object button and choose Report from the list.
- Click Tables or Queries under Objects and select a table or query name. Then choose Insert | Report, or click the New Object button and choose Report from the list.

The New Report dialog box offers six ways to create a report, including three wizards and two AutoReport layouts. If you select or open a table or query before starting the new report, the name also appears in the dialog box.

The next step is to choose from the New Report dialog box list and select a table or query as the basis for the report, if desired. You must select a table or query if you want to choose one of the AutoReports. If you choose one of the wizards without first selecting a table or query as the basis, you can do so in the first wizard dialog box. If you choose Design view without naming a table or query, you don't have access to any field names unless you enter a table or query in the Record Source property, but you can add other controls to the design.

Click OK after making the selections in the New Report dialog box to move on to the report building process.

Choosing an AutoReport

AutoReport creates a quick report of all the data in a table or query. The report isn't fancy, but it's useful for checking and verifying the data in your table. When you print the records from Datasheet view, the data appears in a tabular layout resembling the datasheet itself. The default AutoReport created by choosing Insert | AutoReport or by choosing AutoReport from the New Object button list is columnar with the field names down the left column and the field values in the right column.

NOTE *AutoReport places all fields in the same order as they appear in the table or query, and uses the table or query name as the report title. The name also appears in the Report window title bar, even though the report isn't yet saved. When you try to close the report preview, Access asks if you want to save the report.*

You have more flexibility when you create an AutoReport by selecting from the New Report dialog box. You have a choice of Columnar or Tabular styles. Again, you must select a table or query as the basis before Access creates an AutoReport.

AutoReports created by choosing from the New Report dialog box use one of the predefined report styles, including a title, formatted field names, page numbers, and the current date.

After creating the AutoReport, you can print it as it appears or switch to Design view and make changes. An AutoReport is so quick and easy, unless you plan to use it quite often, don't bother to name and save it. To close the report without saving the design, click the Close button or choose Close from the File menu and respond No when asked if you want to save the changes.

Using the Report Wizard

The *Report Wizard* is similar to the Form Wizard, and it presents a series of dialog boxes that guide you through the design process. Most of the dialog boxes present the same kinds of options, but the Report Wizard includes a couple of new ones that let you choose the sorting, grouping, and summarizing specifications. The examples in the remainder of this chapter use the Home Tech Repair database, as well as the Police database introduced in the previous chapter. The Police database is used on a 24-hour basis and maintains a log of incidents reported to the department. It provides a central source of information in support of the officers in the field, as well as the citizens in the community.

Creating a Single-Table Report with the Report Wizard

In the first example, the Report Wizard creates a report based on the Alpha Entry by Code Query that limits the data in the Alpha Entry table of the Police database to only those with a numeric incident code. This screens out the employment fingerprint and traffic collision reports that don't involve a crime.

Field:	EntryNo	Index	Entry	DR	Code	Date
Table:	Alpha Entry	Alpha Entry	Alpha Entry	Alpha Entry	Alpha Entry	Alpha Ent
Sort:						
Show:	☑	☑	☑	☑	☑	
Criteria:					<>0	
or:						

To create this new report with the help of the Report Wizard, do the following:

1. With the Police database open, click Reports under Objects and double-click the Create Report by Using Wizard option. You can also open the New Report dialog box and choose Report Wizard.

2. Click the down arrow in the Tables/Queries box and choose the Alpha Entry by Code Query as the basis for the report, and then click OK.

3. The first dialog box is the same as in the Form Wizard in which you choose the fields you want to include in the report from the tables and queries in the database. Select all the fields in the Alpha Entry by Code Query, and then click Next.

4. In the second dialog box, the wizard asks if you want to group the records by any of the field values. Select Code as the name of the field you want to group by and click the right arrow (>), as shown in Figure 13-2.

   • If you change your mind, select the field name and click the left arrow (<) to remove the group designation. The up and down arrows near Priority change the grouping order level.

Add grouping field

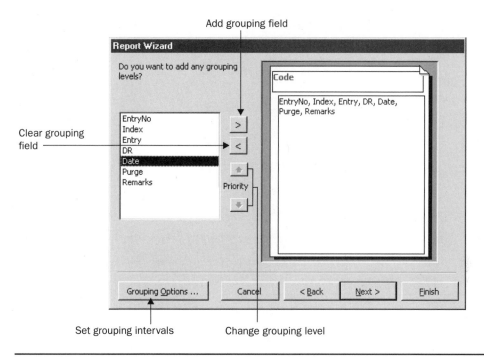

Clear grouping
field

Set grouping intervals   Change grouping level

FIGURE 13-2   Choosing the grouping levels

- If you're grouping on a field with numeric values, you can group by an interval such as 50 or 100. Click Grouping options and choose from the drop-down list in the Grouping intervals dialog box.

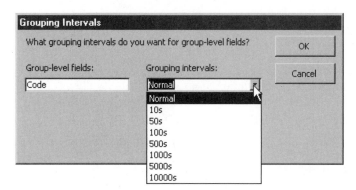

- If one of the fields you're grouping on is a number or currency field, the Summary Options button becomes available. More about adding summaries in the section "Creating a Summary Report with the Report Wizard" and in Chapter 14.

FIGURE 13-3   Specifying the sort order

5. Click Next to move to the next dialog box, which is another one unique to the Report Wizard, which asks if you want to sort your records within the groups in other than primary key order. The groups are automatically sorted in ascending order by the group field value. Figure 13-3 shows a sort specified by Date in ascending order. You can sort on up to four fields by clicking the arrow next to the sort box and choosing the field from the list. If you want the sort in descending order, click the Ascending button to the right of the sort box. When you are done, click Next.

TIP   *The fields needn't all be sorted in the same order. You can sort by one field in ascending order and the next in descending order.*

6. In the next dialog box (see Figure 13-4), you select the layout you want for the report and the print orientation. If you select a lot of fields, you might want to change the orientation to landscape. Select a format and look at the sample in the left pane. For this report, select Align Left 1 and click Next.

TIP   *An option also asks the wizard to adjust the width of the fields, so they can all fit on the page. This might result in losing characters in the column headings or currency symbols in the field data, but you can adjust the column widths later in Design view.*

7. The next wizard dialog box offers six different styles from which to choose. The styles apply to the font size and style, the line spacing, and color—much like with the Form Wizard—but are more suited to printed output. As you select each style, an example is displayed in the sample pane on the left. Select the desired style and click Next.

FIGURE 13-4   Choosing the report layout and orientation

8. The final dialog box is the same as with the Form Wizard: You give the report a name and choose whether to view the report or go directly to Design view. Enter **Alpha Entry by Code Report** as the report name and click Finish.

Figure 13-5 shows a Print Preview of the Alpha Entry by Code Report generated by the Report Wizard. If you also want an interpretation of the code to appear with the code number in the group header, add the Description field from the Penal Codes table to the query.

Creating a Three-Table Report with the Report Wizard

When you use the Report Wizard to create a report based on two or more tables or queries, you can specify which table contains the main data and which contains the subordinate data. In the example in this section, the Alpha Card table is specified as the parent table and the Alpha Entry table as the related child table. The Entry Explanation table, which is related one-to-one to the Alpha Entry table, is also included. The resulting report shows multiple Alpha Entry records for a single Alpha Card record.

TIP   *When you choose fields from one or more tables, the Report Wizard automatically creates a query, which is run every time to open the report. The query is a SELECT statement that appears as the report Control Source property. If the query is complex, you can save processing time by creating the query yourself and using it as the basis for the report.*

To create the three-table report, do the following:

1. Double-click the Create Report by Using Wizard item on the Reports page, or open the New Report dialog box, choose Report Wizard, and then click OK.

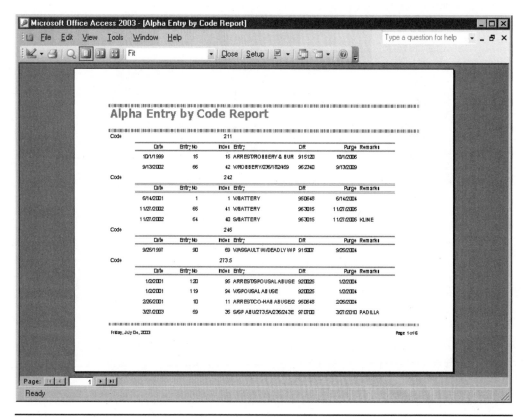

FIGURE 13-5   The Alpha Entry by Code Report in Print Preview

2. In the first dialog box, choose the Index and Name fields from the Alpha Card table. Then select the Alpha Entry table in the Tables/Queries box and choose the EntryNo, Entry, Code, and Date fields. Finally, select the Entry Explanation table and choose the Explanation field. Then click Next.

NOTE   *If you select fields from two or more tables that aren't related, Access displays a message box asking if you want to quit the Report Wizard and edit the relationships. Click OK to open the Relationships window and the Show Table dialog box. After relating the tables, you must restart the Report Wizard. If you don't want to relate the tables, click Cancel and you return to the first dialog box where you can remove the unrelated fields.*

3. In the second dialog box (see Figure 13-6), the wizard asks how you want to view the data. This dialog box appears only if you chose fields from more than one table or query. Access assumes the parent table of the relationship is to appear as the main data. Accept the choice and click Next.

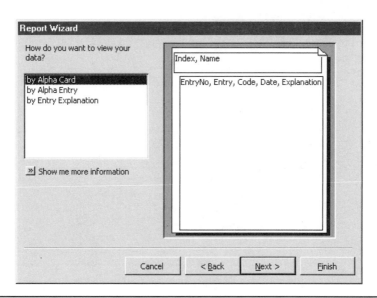

FIGURE 13-6   Choosing the table containing the main data

TIP   *The Show me more information button opens the Report Wizard Tips window where you can ask to see several examples of how the wizard can group your data in the report. Click Close to return to the Report Wizard.*

4. The next dialog box, similar to the one shown earlier in Figure 13-2, shows the Alpha Card fields in the upper box, and the Alpha Entry and Entry Explanation fields in a list below. Select any grouping levels you want in this dialog box. Click Next twice to skip this and the Sort Options dialog box to reach the Layout dialog box in which you select a layout.

5. Choose Outline 1, keep the Portrait orientation, and click Next twice.

6. In the last dialog box, name the report **Alpha Card with Entries** and click Finish.

TIP   *Don't use any special characters, such as an ampersand (&), in the title you give the wizard. Although the file is named using the character, when the title appears on the first page of the report, the character is converted to an underline.*

Figure 13-7 shows the printed first page of the new Alpha Card with Entries report. As you navigate through the pages, you see that several improvements should be made. For example, the column headers might appear on one page and the corresponding Alpha Entry data is carried over to the next. To correct this, you can group on the Index field and specify the group not be broken between pages. In addition, the Date fields need to be widened to see the full date values. The next chapter discusses this and other modifications you can make to improve the report design. You might also like to see a group divider between the index lists. The report title text is again incomplete.

Alpha Card with Entries

Index		1		
Name		ALLEN, FRANK ROGER		

EntryNo	Date	Entry	Explanation	Code
1	6 /14/95	V/BATTERY	Victim of battery	242

Index		3		
Name		AIYER, ROBERT L		

EntryNo	Date	Entry	Explanation	Code
134	7 /11/96	V/BURGLARY	Victim of house burglary	459
133	1 /8 /96	DRIVER #1/NONINJ TC	Driver #1 in a non-injury traffic collision.	
132	10/21/96	TURNED IN FOUND	Turned in jewelry found in store parking lot.	
2	4 /25/94	V/GRAND THEFT BIKE	Victim of grand theft. Bicycle was stolen.	487

Index		4		
Name		AILLEM, PAUL CALVIN		

EntryNo	Date	Entry	Explanation	Code
3	10/15/93	V/BURGLARY	Victim of burglary	459
135	12/3 /96	R/O STOL/RCVD	Registered owner of recovered stolen vehicle.	10851

Index		5		
Name		AIZENBAUM, ESTELA		

EntryNo	Date	Entry	Explanation	Code
4	8 /6 /94	V/ATTEMPT AUTO THEFT	Victim of an attempted auto theft.	10852

Index		6		
Name		AKEN, HAILESILASSIE B		

EntryNo	Date	Entry	Explanation	Code
5	3 /31/96	DRIVER #1/NONINJ TC	Driver #1 in non-injury traffic collision	

Wednesday, February 28, 2001

FIGURE 13-7   Printed Alpha Card with Entries report

Troubleshooting the Report

If the relationships among the three tables used in this report aren't set properly, the report might not contain complete information. For example, the default relationship uses an inner join. An *inner join* includes only records where both parent and child have the same value in the linking field. So, if an Alpha Entry record is related to the Entry Explanation table with an inner join, you won't see any Alpha Entry records that have no corresponding Entry Explanation record.

To solve this problem, edit the relationship and change it to the second option in the Edit Relationship dialog box, a left outer join. This will include all the records from the Alpha Entry table and only those from the Entry Explanation table that match.

Another useful feature of this relationship is to enforce referential integrity and choose Cascade Delete. This automatically cleans up the database by deleting the explanation records when the entry record itself is deleted.

Creating a Summary Report with the Report Wizard

The Report Wizard's summarizing capabilities are useful when you create reports involving numeric or monetary information. When you choose to group records, the wizard makes summarizing options available with which you can compute the total value; determine the average, minimum, and maximum of the group of values; compute a grand total; and calculate the percent of the grand total represented by each of the groups. The wizard might not create exactly the report you want to see, but it can save you a lot of time with the arithmetic. You can always modify the report appearance later.

For this example, turn back to the Home Tech Repair database. This database has some currency fields that can demonstrate the summary options by creating a report that summarizes the workorders grouped by supervisor. When you choose to group the records by Supervisor, the next dialog box in which you set the sort order now has the Summary Options button available. Clicking this button opens the Summary Options dialog box, which shows the names of all the fields in the report that contain number or currency data. Both the Material Cost and Labor Cost fields are from the Workorders table.

Click the check boxes for all the summary values you want the wizard to calculate for you. In the Show option group, you can choose to include the detail records with the summaries or show only the summary values. The other option, Calculate percent of total for sums, includes the relative size of each group sum compared to the grand total, which is calculated and printed at the end of the report.

Figure 13-8 shows the printed first page of a report that groups the Home Tech Repair workorders by supervisor and computes the sum, average, minimum, and maximum of the Material Costs and Labor Costs for each group of workorders. The Report Wizard also automatically counts the number of detail records in each group and displays it at the top of the summary section. A two-point dash-dot line has been added to the group footer as a visual way to separate one supervisor's workorders from the next.

Workorder Summary

Supervisor	10			
	Start Date	**Workorder Number**	**Material Cost**	**Labor Cost**
	2/25/01	001	$472.50	$472.50
	6/25/01	009	$1,100.00	$450.00
	7/10/01	013	$400.00	$1,100.00
	7/23/01	016	$250.00	$125.00

Summary for 'Supervisor' = 10 (4 detail records)

Sum		$2,222.50	$2,147.50
Avg		$555.63	$536.88
Min		$250.00	$125.00
Max		$1,100.00	$1,100.00
Percent		23.38%	14.60%

Supervisor	12			
	Start Date	**Workorder Number**	**Material Cost**	**Labor Cost**
	3/15/01	002	$1,155.00	$840.00
	4/15/01	004	$115.50	$315.00
	6/15/01	008	$400.00	$750.00
	7/12/01	014	$75.00	$300.00
	7/15/01	015	$420.00	$100.00

Summary for 'Supervisor' = 12 (5 detail records)

Sum		$2,165.50	$2,305.00
Avg		$433.10	$461.00
Min		$75.00	$100.00
Max		$1,155.00	$840.00
Percent		22.78%	15.67%

Supervisor	13			
	Start Date	**Workorder Number**	**Material Cost**	**Labor Cost**
	6/15/01	007	$2,500.00	$7,200.00

Wednesday, February 28, 2001

FIGURE 13-8 Summarizing workorder costs by supervisor

TIP *The group containing workorders headed by Supervisor 13 is split between pages 1 and 2 in the report. One of the group section properties is Keep Together, which can be set to No, Whole Group, or With First Detail. Set this property to Whole Group if you want to keep the group header, the detail section, and the group footer together on the page. Chapter 14 contains more information on grouping records in a custom report and setting group properties.*

Previewing the Report

When the Report Wizard finishes creating the report design, you have a choice of going directly to the report Design view or previewing the report as it will be printed. If you haven't used the Report Wizard or you want to preview an existing report, select the desired report name in the Reports page of the Database window, and then do one of the following:

- Click the Preview button in the Database window, and then choose File | Print Preview, or press ALT-P.
- Click the Print Preview toolbar button.
- Right-click the report name in the Reports tab, and then choose Print Preview from the shortcut menu.

The Layout Preview is another way you can check the report design. The window looks like the Print Preview window, but it doesn't include all the records in the report. The layout shows all the design elements and just enough records to verify the design is correct. Layout Preview is available from the View button only when the report is open in Design view.

Working in the Print Preview Window

The Access Print Preview window gives you many ways to view the report, including moving around a single page and among pages, looking at several pages at once, and changing the magnification, so you can see the details more clearly. Returning to the Police database, Figure 13-9 shows the Alpha Card with Entries report in Print Preview.

To close the Print Preview window, do one of the following:

- Click the Close toolbar button.
- Press ALT-C or ESC.
- Choose File | Close.

NOTE   *If you open a report in Design view, and then switch to Print Preview, clicking the Close button or pressing C or ESC returns to Design view. However, choosing File | Close or clicking the Close button in the upper-right corner of the Print Preview window also closes the Design view window. You could be asked if you want to save the report before it closes.*

Navigating in the Preview

The horizontal and vertical scroll bars enable you to move about on the current page. The navigation buttons at the bottom of the Print Preview window let you move among pages in the report. Click one of the buttons to move to the first, previous, next, or last page of the report. You can also enter the page number in the page number box and press ENTER to move to a specific page.

You can use many shortcut keys to navigate in a report preview, as well. See the Access Help topic, "Keyboard Shortcuts," for a list of all the combinations you can use in Print Preview.

Viewing Multiple Pages

Using the Print Preview toolbar buttons, you can view up to five pages adjusted to fit the screen or up to 20 pages arranged in four rows of five pages each.

FIGURE 13-9 Viewing the new report in the Print Preview window

To view one complete page at a time, do one of the following:

- Click the One Page toolbar button.
- Right-click and choose One Page from the shortcut menu.
- Choose View | Pages and choose One Page from the list.

To view two or more complete pages adjusted to fit the screen, choose Fit in the Zoom box, and then use one of the following methods:

- Click the Two Pages toolbar button.

- Click the Multiple Pages toolbar button and drag the mouse pointer over the grid to select the number of pages and the arrangement you want.

Choose View | Pages and choose the number of pages from the list. You have a choice of one, two, four, eight, or twelve pages.

Right-click and choose Multiple Pages from the shortcut menu. Then drag the mouse pointer over the grid to select the number of pages and the arrangement you want to see.

To return to previewing a single page, click the One Page toolbar button.

Changing the Magnification

When you first open the Print Preview window, the report is automatically displayed with the Fit option, which sizes the page in the window vertically. You can increase or decrease the degree of magnification to almost any value or ask Access to adjust the report to fit on the screen.

Click the Zoom toolbar button to toggle between Fit and the last magnification you set.

To change the magnification more precisely, click the arrow next to the Zoom combo box on the toolbar and choose a percentage between 10 percent and 1,000 percent from the list, or enter a value, and then press ENTER. The number of pages you chose to preview at once determines the degree of magnification when you choose Fit.

You can also right-click anywhere in the report preview window and click Zoom in the shortcut menu, where you have the same choices as with the toolbar Zoom button.

When the mouse pointer passes over the report preview, it changes to a magnifying glass, which you can click to zoom in and out in the report. This alternates the preview between Fit and the last percentage you chose. When the glass shows a minus sign (-), clicking zooms out, making the preview less magnified. Clicking the magnifying glass with a plus sign (+) zooms in on the area where the pointer was when you clicked it. This provides a quick way to zoom in on a specific part of the report, for example, a group summary field.

Using the Layout Preview

You have another way to preview a report, called *Layout Preview*, which shows just enough data to demonstrate every section of the report. If your report contains many detail records, it's helpful to see several components on the screen at once, instead of having to navigate through it page by page. You must be in Design view to switch to the Layout Preview.

To see the Alpha Card with Entries report in Layout view, do the following:

1. Click View and choose Design view, or choose View | Design view. If you opened the Print Preview window from the Design view, click Close to return to the Design view.

2. Click View and choose Layout Preview, or choose View | Layout Preview.

The Layout Preview of the report shows an abbreviated version of the Print Preview. For example, the Layout Preview of the Alpha Card with Entries report is reduced from 15 pages in Print Preview to 2 pages. To return to Print Preview, close the Layout Preview, and then switch from Design view to Print Preview.

Printing the Report

You can print the report from either preview window, the Design view, or from the Database window without opening the report. Printing from the Layout Preview only prints the layout pages, not the complete report. Some print commands send the report directly to the printer without opening the Print dialog box; others open the dialog box where you can select other print options.

To print the report from the Layout or Print Preview window, do one of the following:

- Click the Print toolbar button. This sends the report directly to the default printer.
- Right-click the report and choose Print from the shortcut menu,
- Choose File | Print, or press CTRL-P to open the Print dialog box.

NOTE: *If you're viewing the report in Layout Preview, only the elements that appear in the layout are printed, not the entire report.*

To print a report from the Database window, select the report name, and then perform one of the preceding steps.

You can also print the report from Design view by clicking the Print toolbar button and sending the report directly to the printer, or by choosing File | Print, which opens the Print dialog box. This prints the report itself, not the report design.

If you want to change any of the page options, such as the margins, the page layout, the printer selection, the number of columns on the page, or the page size, you need to run Page Setup. After setting the page specifications, you can choose the print options, such as number of copies and the range of pages to print.

Running Page Setup

You can open the Page Setup dialog box from any view of a report or from the Database window without opening the report by starting File | Page Setup. If you're in the Database window, select the report name before choosing Page Setup. If you're previewing the report in either the Layout or Print Preview, you can also right-click the report and choose Page Setup from the shortcut menu.

The page settings are stored with the report, so you need to set them only once and they'll be in effect every time you print the report. The Page Setup dialog box has three tabs: Margins, Page, and Columns.

- Click the Margins tab to set the width of each of the four page margins and also choose whether to print the data only, without any of the labels or other unbound objects.

TIP   *If you want to change the default page margins, so you don't have to change them for each report separately, choose Tools | Options and click the General tab. Specify the margins in the Print margins group and click Apply or OK. This affects only new forms and reports, not existing ones. See Chapter 16 for more information about customizing the Access workplace.*

- Click the Page tab to set the orientation of the print on the page, and the paper size and source, as well as to select a different printer if you have more than one in your system. The choice of paper sources depends on the printer you're using.

If you want to print using a printer other than the default printer, click Use Specific Printer, and then click the Printer button. This opens a dialog box that displays a list of the printers currently installed in the system. Select a different printer and click OK to return to the Page Setup dialog box.

NOTE *Use the Column tab to choose the number of items across the page, their row and column spacing, their size, and the layout on the page. This is used mostly for printing mailing labels that come in predesigned sheets. Access offers ready-made layouts for most of the commercially available label sheets. Chapter 14 describes using the Columns tab when printing mailing labels.*

After you make all the desired changes to the page setup, click OK to return to the previous view of the report or the Database window.

Modifying the Report Design

The method you use to open a report in Design view depends on where you start:

- From the Database window, select the report name and click Design, or right-click the report name and choose Design View from the shortcut menu.
- From the Print Preview or the Layout Preview window, click Close if you previewed the report from Design View, or click the View button and choose Design view if you previewed from the Database window.

Working in the report Design view is almost identical to working in the form Design view. The controls are the same, although you include fewer types of controls in reports. The ways you select sections and controls, and the way you change their properties are the same as with form designs. Placing, positioning, and sizing controls in the report design also use the same techniques.

Touring the Report Design Window

The report Design window is similar to the form Design window. The menu bar is the same, and the only new toolbar button is the Grouping and Sorting button, which you learn about in Chapter 14. The View button shows Print Preview in the report Design window, instead of the Form View icon shown in the form Design view. The Formatting toolbar is exactly the same and the report control toolbox is identical to the one you saw when working with forms. To switch between views of the report, click the View button. When working in report Design view, the View button list includes Design view, Print Preview, and Layout Preview.

Examining Report Sections

If the report design looks more cluttered than the form designs you worked with in the last chapter, it's probably because of the extra sections—the Page Header and Footer sections. The wizard automatically adds these sections when it creates a report. The *Page Header section* contains information to be printed at the top of each page, such as the field names used as column headings. The *Page Footer section* contains information to be printed at the bottom of each page, such as the current date and the page number.

The *Report Header and Footer sections* contain information to be printed only once, at the beginning or the end of the report. The *Detail section* contains the bulk of the data in the report.

Two optional sections, the *Group Header and Footer sections*, contain information to be printed at the top and bottom of each group of records. These sections are used when you group the records by the values in a specific field, such as by Code as in the Alpha Entry by Code Report shown earlier.

You select a section in a report design the same way as in a form design by using one of the following methods:

- Click the Object toolbar button and choose the desired section from the list.
- Click the section selector at the left of the section label line.
- Click anywhere in the section label line.
- Click anywhere in the section, outside of any control.

To change the size of a report section, select the section and drag the lower boundary up or down. The report and page sections come in pairs, so if you want to remove one, reduce its height to zero. The section must be empty before you can do that. When you add a group, you needn't use both the header and footer. You can choose whether you want a group header or footer, or both, by setting the group properties.

Setting Report and Section Properties

You open and use the property sheets in a report design the same as in a form design, and many of the properties are the same. Three report Format properties apply to the report header and footer sections, as well as the grouping of records in the report. Two Data properties relate to sorting and filtering the records. Two Other properties specify whether records are locked while the report is being previewed or printed and how you want to group dates in the report. Click in the property and read the descriptive text in the status bar.

When you create a report with a special title page and you don't want to print the page header or footer information on the same page, set the Page Header and Page Footer report properties to Not With Rpt Hdr. Then set the report header Force New Page property to After Section to continue printing on a new page.

If you want the report footer information also printed on a separate page at the end of the report, set both the Page Header and Page Footer properties to Not With Rpt Hdr/Ftr, and then set the report footer Force New Page property to Before Section.

When you create a report based on a table or query saved with a sort order or a filter, the report inherits both properties. If you look at the report properties, you can see the Filter and Order By expressions saved with the table. The Order By On property is set to Yes and the records are sorted by the inherited sort order. The inherited filter isn't applied. To apply the filter, set the Filter On property to Yes. To remove them both, change the settings to No. If you want to change the filter or sort order, type a new expression in the Filter or Order By property box.

Each of the report sections also has a list of properties you can set to get exactly the appearance and behavior you want. For example, the section name, whether the section is visible or not, the height, back color, and special effect, and a tag that stores extra information about the section.

Page headers and footers have no additional properties, but the remaining sections—report header and footer, group header and footer, and detail sections—share several other properties, for example:

- *Force New Page* specifies whether report sections are printed on a separate page, rather than on the current page.

- *New Row Or Col* specifies whether a section is printed in a new row or column within a multiple-column report.

- *Keep Together* specifies whether to print a section all on one page or to print across two pages.

- *Can Grow* and *Can Shrink* allow the section to grow or shrink vertically, depending on the data in the section.

The Group Header section has one more property unique to that section: *Repeat Section*, which is used to specify whether a group header is repeated on the next page or column when a group spans more than one page or column. The default setting is No. If the group header contains column headings and other relevant information, you might want to print it at the top of each page or column.

Placing and Adjusting Controls

You place controls in a report design using the control tools in the toolbox, just the same as with a form design. To resize and move controls, you can drag the handles and use the options in the Format menu. All the methods are the same as with form design.

Changing the Report Style

One of the Report Wizard dialog boxes showed you a list of styles from which to choose. If you don't like the style you selected there, you can change to one of the other styles in the list by clicking the report selector (the small square at the intersection of the report rulers), and then clicking the AutoFormat toolbar button in Design view. You can also choose Format | AutoFormat to open the same dialog box. If you want to reformat a report section rather than the entire report, select that section first.

Customizing a Report AutoFormat

Using the Customize button in the AutoFormat dialog box, you can create a custom format and add it to the list of AutoFormats available to your reports. You have three options:

- Create a new AutoFormat based on the one used in an open report.
- Modify an existing AutoFormat with the changes you made to the format of the open report.
- Delete an AutoFormat from the list.

Before starting to customize a format, click the Options button, check the attributes you want modified, and then click Customize.

As you select an option, an explanation is displayed in the lower panel. Select one of the three Customize Options, and then click OK, or click Cancel to return to the AutoFormat dialog box. If you choose to create a new AutoFormat, Access asks you to enter a name for it. Once you save the new AutoFormat, it's available to any new reports.

You can use the options to apply the font, color, and border formatting selectively. By default, all three options are checked. If you clear them one at a time, you can see the difference in the displayed sample.

Adding Page Numbers and Date/Times

The Report Wizard automatically added page numbers and the current date/time to the Page Footer section of the Alpha Card with Entries report. A *page number* is an unbound text box control that you can add to a report design and format in several ways. A *date/time field* is also an unbound control and is based on your current system date/time settings.

Adding a Page Number

If you haven't used the Report Wizard and you want to add a page number to your report, choose Insert | Page Numbers to open the Page Numbers dialog box. You have several options in the Page Numbers dialog box regarding the page number format, position, and alignment. You can also suppress printing the page number on the first page of the report.

The dialog box offers two page number formats: Page *N* and Page *N* of *M*, where *N* is the page number and *M* is the total number of pages.

NOTE   *You can see the Report Wizard used the Page N of M option in specifying the page numbers in the Alpha Card with Entries report. The expression that appears in the page number text box control is ="Page "&[Page]&" of "&[Pages]. This expression concatenates alphabetic characters with the Page (current page number) and Pages (total number of pages) field values. The characters enclosed in quotation marks appear in the page number field. Notice spaces follow the word "Page" and are on both sides of the word "of" to separate the words from the numbers. The ampersand signs (&) are the concatenation operators. The result is, for example, Page 12 of 25 pages.*

You can position the page number either in the page header or footer by selecting from the Position options.

The page number alignment options include the following:

- *Left*, which places the text box at the left margin.
- *Center*, which places the text box centered between the right and left margins.
- *Right*, which places the text box at the right margin.
- *Inside*, which places the text box at the left margin on odd pages and at the right margin on even pages.
- *Outside*, which places the text box at the right margin on odd pages and at the left margin on even pages.

If you don't want to print the page number on the first page of the report, clear the check in the Show Number on First Page box.

Changing the Page Numbers Format

The Page Numbers dialog box gave you a choice of two formats for the page number text box. You can also enter a custom expression in the Control Source property of the page number text box, which includes characters with the values. Some other expressions you might want to use for page numbers are

Expression	Displays
=[Page]	1, 2, 3
="Entry Report: Page "&[Page]	Entry Report: Page 1, Entry Report: Page 2, Entry Report: Page 3
=[Page]&"/"&[Pages]&"Pages"	1/3 Pages, 2/3 Pages, 3/3 Pages

Adding a Date/Time Control

To add the current date and time to the report, choose Insert | Date and Time. The Date/Time dialog box lets you include the date and/or the time and gives you a choice of formats for each.

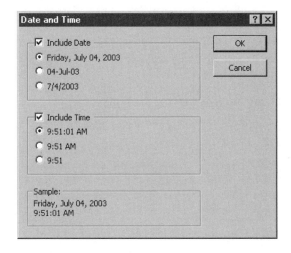

If the report design has a Report Header section, the date/time control is automatically placed there. If not, it goes in the Detail section. You can drag it to any place you want in the design.

NOTE   *The Report Wizard added the expression =Now( ) to the Page Footer section of the Alpha Card with Entries report. This prints the current system date at the bottom of each page. You could also use the expression =Date( ) to insert the current system date. Many other built-in Date/Time functions are available from the Expression Builder, which return the date and time components (day, month, year, hour, week, and so on) in a variety of ways.*

If you look at the properties of the date/time control in the report, you can see the Control Source property is the expression =*Now()* and the Format is Long Date. This displays the date with the day of the week, as well as the date, for example, Monday, January 1, 2004. You can change the Format property in the property sheet to one of the other Date/Time formats.

Adding Page Breaks

If left to its own devices, when a page fills up, Access starts a new page. You can add a page break control within a section to tell Access where you want a new page to begin. For example, you have a report title and an abstract of the report's contents all in the Report Header section, but you want them printed on separate pages. To accomplish this, click the Page Break button in the toolbox and place the control in the Report Header section between the controls you want on the first page and those you want on the second page. Access displays the position of the page break as a short dotted line at the left edge in the report design.

Saving the Report Design

When you create a report with the help of the Report Wizard, the report is saved for you using the name you entered in the final wizard dialog box. If you don't use the wizard, save the report design frequently as you refine it. This guards against catastrophe and gives you a recent starting point if something goes wrong. Choose File | Save, press CTRL-S, or click the Save toolbar button to save the report without closing the Design window. To close the report, choose File | Close.

You have two other options when saving a report design:

- File | Save As, which opens the Save As dialog box where you can choose to save the report design to the current database with the same or a new name.

- File | Export, which opens the Export Report To dialog box, where you locate the folder in which you want to save the report and enter a report name. See Chapter 22 for more information about exporting Access reports and other objects.

Using Report Snapshots

Access 2002 began offering a new type of report called a *report snapshot*, which is a separate file with the .snp extension that contains a copy of every page of an Access report. The copy includes high-fidelity graphics, charts, and pictures, and it preserves the colors and the two-dimensional layout of the report.

The advantage of a report snapshot is you can save time and money by distributing the report electronically, rather than photocopying and mailing the printed version. The recipients can then preview online and print only the pages they want.

To view, print, or mail a report snapshot, you need the Snapshot Viewer program installed. The *Snapshot Viewer* is a standalone executable program that comes with its own control, help file, and related files. By default, the Snapshot Viewer is installed by Access the first time you create a report snapshot. You can use the Snapshot Viewer to view a snapshot from the Internet Explorer version 3.0 and later or from any application that supports ActiveX controls.

NOTE   *While you need Access 2003 to create a report snapshot, the recipients don't need it to view the snapshot. They need only a combination of the Snapshot Viewer and another program, such as Windows Explorer, a web browser, or an e-mail program, such as Microsoft Exchange or Microsoft Outlook.*

Creating a Report Snapshot

To create a report snapshot from an existing report, do the following:

1. Select the name of the report in the database window and choose File | Export.

2. The Export Report As dialog box opens (see Figure 13-10) where you choose Snapshot Format in the Save as type box.

3. If you don't want to use the same name as the Access report, choose the drive and folder to export to in the Save in box and enter the file name in the File name box.

4. Check Autostart and click Export.

The Snapshot Viewer automatically starts and displays a preview of the report snapshot. The new report snapshot inherits any current sort order and filter settings in the underlying recordset.

FIGURE 13-10   Exporting a report as a report snapshot

Viewing the Report Snapshot

The Snapshot Viewer window (see Figure 13-11) has a standard menu bar with commonly used File, View, Window, and Help menus. It also shows a navigation bar at the bottom of the window you can use to move among the pages in the report snapshot. The Print button opens the Print dialog box.

The Snapshot Viewer works much like the Print Preview window in Access. You can change the magnification by clicking in the page. If the whole page shows on the screen, clicking it increases the magnification. If already magnified, clicking reduces the preview to its former magnification.

You can right-click in the report and choose from the same options as the Navigation bar in addition to the Zoom command. You can zoom to a magnification from 10 percent to 200 percent or choose Fit to show one complete page in the window. The Fill command widens the page to fill the width of the window.

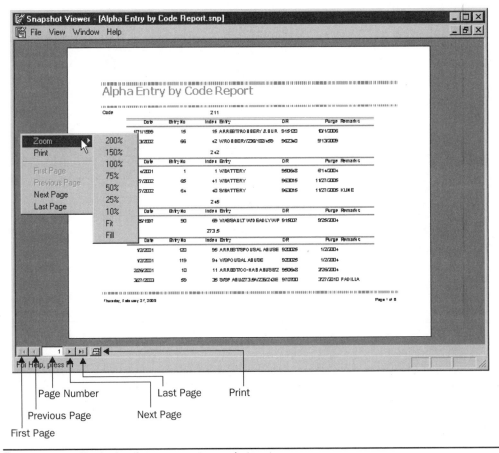

FIGURE 13-11   Previewing the new report snapshot

> *TIP*   *If you saved the report snapshot and want to view it again, you can open the Snapshot Viewer from the Windows Explorer. Start the Windows Explorer and locate the .snp file. Double-click the file name and the Snapshot Viewer launches and displays the report snapshot.*

Sending the Report Snapshot

You can send the report snapshot to others in electronic mail by using the Send command in the Snapshot Viewer. With the report snapshot open in the Snapshot Viewer, choose File | Send.

Summary

This chapter has only begun the discussion of the variety of printed material Access and the Report Wizards can produce. So far, you learned the fundamentals of report construction and how to use the Report Wizard for creating standard detail and summary reports. You also had a glimpse of the advantages of using report snapshots for electronic distribution of Access reports.

The Report Wizard can create reports from several related tables and arrange the information in almost any way you choose. You have the opportunity to summarize any numeric or currency field values in several ways to include more useful, analytic information.

The next chapter delves deeper into customizing reports and creating special purpose reports, such as a report based on a parameter query that requests information from the user. You see how to create a report from scratch and add special types of controls, including a subreport that contains the detail data related to the data in the main report. The chapter also describes how to create columnar reports for such purposes as printing mailing labels.

Chapter 15, the final chapter in this trio of chapters dealing with printed Access products, looks at the analytical tools provided by the Chart, PivotTable, and Pivot Chart Wizards.

Customizing Reports

W hen you create reports with Access, you're limited only by your imagination. Access offers so many tools and features for creating custom reports, you can design and print information any way you like.

In addition to printing table or query data grouped and arranged in special orders, you can create reports that print data in columns on the page. A special type of columnar report can be used to print mailing labels or labels for other purposes, such as book plates or floppy disk labels.

This chapter discusses creating custom reports from the Design view, as well as printing labels with the help of the Label Wizard. Most of the examples deal with data in the Police database introduced in Chapter 12. You might want to keep the Police database open as you work through this chapter.

Creating a New Report Design

Creating a new report with the help of the Report Wizard is by far the easiest way to start a custom report, but you can also start from an empty report design. All you need to do is double-click the Create report in Design view shortcut on the Reports page of the Database window. Then specify the underlying table or query in the Record Source property.

You can also open the New Report dialog box, choose Design View, and then click OK. If you want to base the report on a table or query, do one of the following:

- Select the table or query name in the Database window before opening the New Report dialog box.

- Select the table or query name in the New Report dialog box before clicking OK.

If the report isn't based on table or query data, you can insert only unbound controls, such as labels, lines and rectangles, and unbound objects. You can also include hyperlinks to other objects.

Figure 14-1 shows the new Design view for a report based on the Alpha Card table in the Police database. All three report design tools appear in Figure 14-1: the toolbox, the property sheet, and the field list. Notice the page header and footer sections are automatically added to the design with the detail section. A new form design contains only the detail section by default.

FIGURE 14-1   Starting the new Alpha Card report in Design view

After opening the report Design view, use the field list to drag the fields to the design. Use the toolbox to place other controls and the property sheet to create the appearance you want.

Adding Headers and Footers

A report design can include pairs of header and footer sections: report header and footer for printing information at the beginning and end of the report, and page header and footer for printing information at the top and bottom of each page. To add a header/footer pair, choose View | Page Header/Footer or View | Report Header/Footer.

To delete the header/footer pair, choose View and remove the check mark before the Page Header/Footer or Report Header/Footer option. If any controls are in the section you try to delete, Access displays a message asking if you want to delete all the controls in the sections. Click Yes to delete them or No to abandon the deletion.

CAUTION   *All deletions are permanent. Always save the report design before you delete controls or sections so you have a copy to fall back on. Then, if you change your mind, you don't have to start over. You can also close the design without saving the changes and open it later in its original condition, before the deletions.*

To change the height of a section, drag the lower section boundary up or down. If the section contains controls, you can't shrink it beyond the control borders. To keep from having too much blank space when you print a report with no information in the header or footer, do this: shrink the height by dragging the lower boundary up or by setting the Height property to 0. You needn't select the section first to drag the boundary.

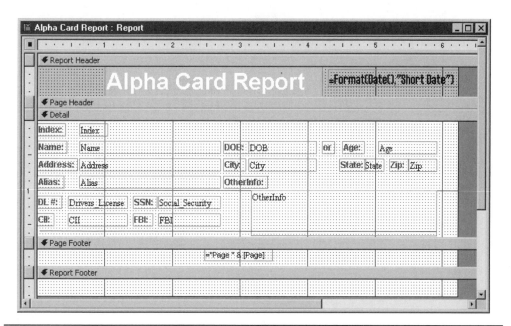

FIGURE 14-2   The Alpha Card Report in Design view

TIP   *If you selected the section and the property sheet is open when you resize the section, you can see the Height property value change as you drag the boundary.*

To suppress the printing of a section that contains information, set the section's Visible property to No. The section still appears in Design view; it just doesn't print.

The Page Header and Page Footer report properties on the Format tab of the property sheet specify whether to print the information on the first page with the report header or on the last page with the report footer. The settings for both properties are the following:

- *All Pages* prints the information on every page.
- *Not with Rpt Hdr* prints on all but the first page.
- *Not with Rpt Ftr* prints on all but the last page.
- *Not with Rpt Hdr/Ftr* prints on all pages except the first and last.

Figure 14-2 shows the Alpha Card Report in Design view. The report header section contains a title and the current date. The page header has been reduced to a zero height and the page number has been added in the center of the page footer. If you need to review how to insert dates and page numbers, refer to Chapter 13. A line control was added to the bottom of the detail section to separate the detail information of each record. Finally, the Soft Gray style was chosen from the AutoFormat dialog box.

Figure 14-3 shows the report in Print Preview.

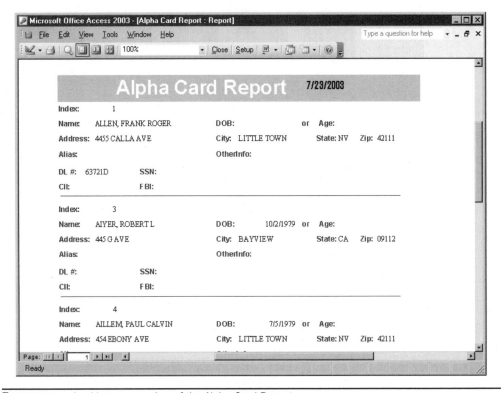

FIGURE 14-3   Looking at a preview of the Alpha Card Report

Customizing with Special Controls

Reports aren't user interactive, so they can contain fewer types of special controls. Command buttons and option groups, for example, have no place in reports. You can add calculated fields, graphics, and images to a custom report, either bound or unbound. You can also add hyperlinks, although they aren't "live" within the report.

Adding Calculated Fields

Reports often include calculated fields contained in an underlying query. You can also add calculated controls, as described in Chapter 10. A *calculated control* is a text box whose Control Source property is set to an expression that produces the desired value. The expression can contain combinations of text, number, currency, or date/time fields from the record source.

Calculated controls are often used to show summary information in reports with grouped records. The section "Sorting and Grouping Records in a Report" discusses grouping records and summarizing data with expressions and aggregate functions.

Adding Graphics and Images

As discussed in Chapter 10, you have two ways to insert a graphic or image in a report: as an image control or as an OLE object in an unbound object frame. The advantage of using an image control is it loads quicker than the OLE object in a frame. If you think you might need to edit the OLE object, embed it in an unbound object frame where you can double-click to open the application that created the object.

To add an image control to a report, do the following:

1. Click the Image control tool and click in the report design where you want to place the upper-left corner of the image. Access draws a square frame for the image and opens the Insert Picture dialog box.

2. Locate and select the image you want and click OK. The frame expands to accommodate the full size of the image.

3. Resize the image frame by dragging the sizing handles.

4. Change the image control Size Mode property to Stretch or Zoom.

To insert the image in an unbound object frame, click the Unbound Object Frame tool and draw the frame in the report design. A dialog box opens in which you can choose Create New or Create from File. Then you can locate and select the image you want in the report.

If the object you want to insert in the frame is an existing Office document or other file originated by an application that supports OLE, check Create from File and type in the path of the file you want to insert.

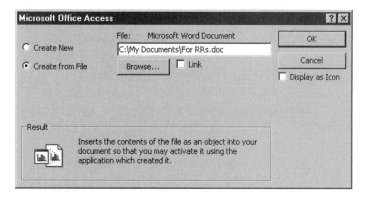

Figure 14-4 shows a report design with a photograph of two roses embedded as an image and a Word document embedded as an OLE Object in an unbound object frame. If you want to edit the Word document, double-click the object in Design view and edit it in place. The photograph in the image control isn't editable.

***

NOTE   *You can also link an OLE Object to a report design, instead of embedding it by choosing Link in the dialog box. Linking leaves the object in the host application and provides a path to the object in the report. This saves disk space and ensures the latest version of the object, but it can cause problems if the path to the linked object is changed.*

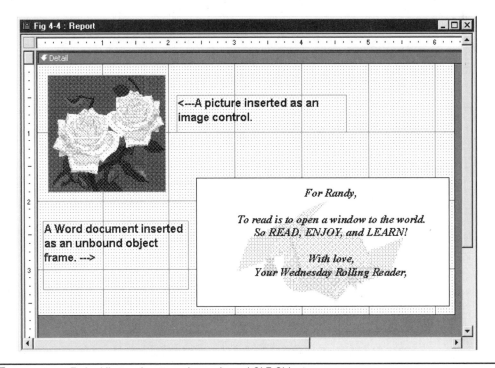

FIGURE 14-4 Embedding an image and an unbound OLE Object

Adding a Bound OLE Object

Bound OLE Objects are OLE Object data type fields from the underlying table or query. To add a bound object to the report design, simply drag the field name from the field list to the design. Access automatically draws the bound object frame for the object.

NOTE *An OLE Object data type is only a pointer to the object. Such a field cannot be used to sort or index records.*

You can also draw the bound object frame first using the control tool, and then bind it to the field in the underlying record source by setting its Control Source property to the name of the field.

Adding a Hyperlink

You can add a hyperlink to a report design the same way as to a form design by clicking the Insert Hyperlink button or choosing Insert | Hyperlink. After you specify the target of the hyperlink, you can test it in the report Design view by right-clicking the hyperlink and choosing Hyperlink | Open Hyperlink from the shortcut menu.

The hyperlink isn't live in the report in Access Print Preview, but it does become active when you export the report to another Office application, such as Word or Excel. From the receiving application, you can open the document and click the hyperlink to jump to the address.

When you add a hyperlink to a report design, Access places it in the upper-left corner of the detail section. From there, you can move it to any position in the report design.

Adding a Background Picture

Pictures can serve a special purpose in a report other than as an illustration—for example, as a company logo watermark that shows behind the printing. When you add a background picture to a report, it applies to the whole page and is a report property. To add a watermark to the Alpha Card Report design, enter the path and file name of the picture you want to use in the report's Picture property, and then set other report properties as follows:

- The Picture Type property specifies whether the picture is embedded or linked.

- The Picture Size Mode property can be set to one of the three size modes: Clip, Stretch, or Zoom. Refer to Chapter 10 for a description of the effects of setting size modes.

- The Picture Alignment property determines the position of the picture in the report. The available settings are Top Left, Top Right, Center, Bottom Left, and Bottom Right.

- When the Picture Tiling property is set to Yes, the picture is repeated across and down the page, beginning at the position specified by the Picture Alignment property, and it spreads in four directions. For example, if you set the alignment to Center, a complete picture appears in the center of the page, perhaps, with incomplete versions fanning out from it. If you choose to tile the picture, use the Clip size mode setting.

- The Picture Pages property specifies on which pages to print the background picture: All Pages, First Page, or No Pages.

Basing a Report on a Parameter Query

Basing a report on a parameter query enables the user to set the criteria for the report at run time. For example, the police department would like to see a list of incidents reported during a specific time period. When you try to preview the report based on the parameter query, you're prompted to enter the parameters, the same as when you try to run the query itself.

Access also gives you the tools to print the entered parameters in the report, usually in the report header section.

Creating the Parameter Query

To create a parameter query that extracts Alpha Entry records having a date within an arbitrary time period, do the following:

1. Select the Alpha Entry table in the Database window and choose Insert | Query, or click the New Object button and choose Query.

2. Choose Design view in the New Query dialog box and click OK.

3. Double-click the asterisk in the Alpha Entry field list to add all the fields to the query.

4. Double-click the Date field to add it to an empty column in the grid and clear the check mark in the Show row, so the value won't appear twice in the report.

5. Type the following in the Criteria row of the Date field:

Between [Type beginning date] And [Type ending date]

Field:	Alpha Entry.*	Date
Table:	Alpha Entry	Alpha Entry
Sort:		
Show:	☑	☐
Criteria:		Between [Type beginning date] And [Type ending date]
or:		

6. Save the query as Entries by Date.

If you run the query, Access displays two parameter prompts: one requesting Type beginning date and the other, Type ending date. Enter the desired dates and click OK to see the list of Alpha Entries reported within that time period. See Chapter 9 for more information about parameter queries.

Creating the Report

A report based on the parameter query also prompts for the parameter values when you open the report in Print Preview. To create a simple report based on the parameter query, do the following:

1. Select the Entries by Date query in the Database window and choose Insert |
   Report, or click the New Object button and select Report.

2. Choose AutoReport: Tabular in the New Report dialog box and click OK.

3. Because Access immediately opens the new report for preview, it prompts for
   the parameters.

4. Enter the desired beginning date in any valid date format and press ENTER or click OK.

5. Repeat Step 4 to enter the ending date. When you click OK, the report opens in
   Print Preview.

6. Click Close to switch to Design view where you can modify the report design as
   required.

Printing the Parameters in the Report Header

Access treats the prompt expression as a valid control source for a text box. The selection parameters can be printed with the report by adding text box controls to the design. You can add two text boxes: one for each parameter or combine the parameters in an expression in a single text box. To print the parameters in the report header as one text box, do the following:

1. Click the Text Box control tool and place the control in the report header section.

2. Click outside the new control, and then select the attached label and press DEL to remove the attached label.

3. Double-click the new text box control to open the property sheet and enter the following expression in the Control Source property box:

   =**"Between "&[Type beginning date]&" and "&[Type ending date]**

   (More about combining text and field values in report designs in the section "Manipulating Text Data.")

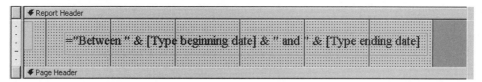

4. Resize the control to fit the expression.

5. After making the final touch-ups, save the report and switch to Print Preview. Figure 14-5 shows a preview of the report displaying Alpha Entries reported between January 1, 2003 and March 31, 2003.

FIGURE 14-5 Viewing the Entries by Date report

Troubleshooting Custom Reports

When you design a report, several problems can occur. For example, when you print the report, you might see too much white space. To solve this problem, reduce the size of the controls to fit the values they contain and move them closer together.

If every other page is blank when you preview or print the report, the width of the report exceeds the available width of the paper and spill-over pages result. The total width of the report plus the right and left margin settings must not exceed the width of the paper. To correct this problem, either reduce the width of the report or change the margin settings with Page Setup. You could also change the page orientation to landscape.

If the report prints a blank page at the end, you might need to reduce the size of the report footer. If no controls are in the report footer, reduce its height to zero by dragging the lower boundary or by setting the Height property to 0.

If data spills over to the next page, reduce the overall height of the report or decrease the top and bottom margins.

If you choose to add the parameters as two text box controls, you can edit the attached labels to read "Between" and "and." This method requires more alignment and size adjustments than putting both parameters in one text box.

TIP *If you're unexpectedly prompted for parameters when you try to print or preview a report, you might have misspelled a field name in the report design. The name in the design doesn't match any in the underlying table or query. If you created an expression using field names, one of them could also be misspelled. Another possibility is you used a control name, instead of a field name in an aggregate function, such as Sum or Count. Aggregate functions must use field names, not control names.*

Sorting and Grouping Records in a Report

As you saw in the previous chapter, one of the most useful features of Access reports is the capability to sort and group records based on the value in one or more of the fields. After doing so, you can summarize the information in many ways to illustrate trends and draw conclusions. Such summaries are critical to the decision-making process and Access can do most of the arithmetic for you.

You can change the sort order the report has inherited from the underlying record source. Records can be grouped on Text, Number, Date/Time, Currency, or AutoNumber field types or expressions containing those field values. Access nests up to ten group levels, each group subordinate to the previous group.

Depending on the data type of the group-on field, you have different options about how to group the records. For example, if the field is a Text field, you can group on the entire value or the first few characters of the value. Date/Time values can be grouped by each value or any time increment of the value—year, day, hour, minute, and so on.

Changing the Sort Order

You can remove or reapply the sort order inherited from the record source by setting the report's Order By On property. Choose No to remove the sort order or Yes to reapply it. If you want to use the inherited sort order, you must also set the Filter On property to No.

To sort the records in the report in a different order than the underlying table or query, set the report's Order By On property to Yes and its Order By property as follows:

- To sort the records by values in one field in ascending order, type the field name enclosed in brackets followed by ASC—for example, **[Code] ASC**.

- To sort the records by values in one field in descending order, type the field name enclosed in brackets followed by DESC—for example, **[Last Name] DESC**.

- To sort the records by values in more than one field in ascending or descending order, type each field name enclosed in brackets, followed by ASC or DESC, and separated by commas. For example, the setting **[Code] ASC, [Last Name] DESC** sorts first by the Code field in ascending order, and then by the Last Name field in descending order.

If you don't specify ASC or DESC, Access automatically sorts in ascending order. The new setting overrides the inherited sort order without affecting the data source. Be sure to set the Order By On property to Yes to effect the new sort order.

NOTE   *If you create the report with the Report Wizard and specify a sort order, it overrides the inherited sort order. You can still change the order in the Design view if you change your mind.*

Adding Group Sections

To illustrate grouping records in a report, create a new report based on a query that extracts only those records with a value in the Code field. This eliminates Alpha Entry records not related to a potentially criminal offense. The Alpha Entry by Code query contains the expression <>0 in the Criteria row of the Code column in the grid. After dragging the field names from the list to the detail section of the new Entries by Year Report, you can proceed to group the records by the year the incident was reported.

   To add a group section to an existing report, switch to Design view and click the Sorting and Grouping toolbar button or choose View | Sorting and Grouping. This opens the Sorting and Grouping dialog box in which you set the sort order and choose the field or expression on which you want to group. To group the records, do the following:

1. Select the field to group on from the drop-down Field/Expression list or enter an expression.

2. Select the order in which you want the groups arranged. (The detail records within each group appear ordered by the value in the primary key field of the parent table or query unless you change the report Order By property.)

3. Set the group properties in the lower pane of the Sorting and Grouping dialog box.

4. Set one or both group sections' properties to Yes to add a group header or footer.

The Sorting and Grouping dialog box settings group the records by the year value in the Date field. The Date groups appear in ascending order from the earliest year to the latest, and the report has both a group header and a group footer section. You can see the new Date group header and footer sections in the design behind the dialog box.

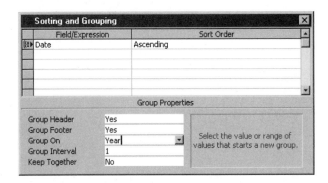

The properties in the lower pane of the Sorting and Grouping dialog box apply to the way the groups are formed and displayed. The Group Header and Group Footer properties add the group sections when set to Yes.

NOTE   *You must choose a group header or footer for Access to group the records. If you don't select Yes in either the Group Header or Footer property, the records aren't grouped. Instead, the records are only sorted by the field or expression.*

The options available in the Group On property list vary with the data type of the field or expression entered in the Field/Expression column. Each Value is the default setting for all data types, which groups by the same value in the field or expression. Other grouping options for data types include the following:

- **Text**   Prefix Characters groups by beginning characters. Enter the number of characters in the Group Interval property.

- **Date**   Year, Qtr, Month, Week, Day, Hour, and Minute group by dates or times in the same interval.

- **AutoNumber, Currency or Number**   Interval groups values that fall within the interval specified in the Group Interval property.

The Group Interval property specifies the interval or the number of characters on which to group. For example, you might want to group records by values in a currency field in $50 increments. Set the Group Interval property to 50 and the first group then includes values from $0 to $49, the second from $50 to $99, and so on.

The Keep Together property can prevent a group that occupies less than a page from being split over two pages. If the group is larger than one page, this property is ignored. The options are as follows:

- *No* (the default), which allows the group to be split.
- *Whole Group*, which keeps the entire group together on one page.
- *With First Detail*, which keeps the group header and the first record in the detail section together on the same page.

NOTE   *The group header and footer sections also have a Keep Together property, which is a little different from the group property set in the Sorting and Grouping dialog box. The group property refers to the entire group, while the section properties refer only to that section. However, if you want the group Keep Together property to take effect, the group section Keep Together properties must be set to Yes.*

Customizing Group Headers and Footers

You must include one of the group sections to group records in a report, but you needn't print any information in it. For example, you want to group records by Code, but you don't need to summarize by totals or averages. Changing the section's Visible property to No suppresses previewing and printing the section. If no information is in the group section, you can reduce its height to 0, exactly as any other section in the report.

To remove a group header or footer, open the Sorting and Grouping dialog box, and then change the corresponding property to No. If you placed information in the section you try to delete, Access warns you will delete the information with the section.

TIP   *You can set the Repeat Section property of the group header section to Yes to have the information printed on the next page when the group spans more than one page or column.*

If you switch the Entries by Year Report to Print Preview, you can see the Alpha Entry records are, indeed, grouped by year, but it's not obvious. The grouping would stand out more if the year value appeared in the group header section. Moving the field labels to the group header would also allow more room for the field data in the detail section. Unfortunately, attached labels can't be dragged to a different section, so cut-and-paste them into the group header above the text box controls. You might need to move them a bit to line up with the data in the detail section.

Next, to add a new text box control to the group header that shows the year value for the group, do the following:

1. Click the Text Box control tool in the toolbox and place the control in the group header section.

2. Open the property sheet and enter the expression **=Year([Date])** in the Control Source property box. The Year() function extracts the year value from the Date field.

3. Select the attached label, click in it, and then replace Text*n* with **Year Reported:** as the label for the year control.

4. Switch to Print Preview to see the year value in the group header.

Adding Summaries and Running Totals

In Chapter 10, you saw how to add calculated controls to form and report designs by using expressions. You can also use calculated controls to summarize data in a report. In the last chapter, you saw how the Report Wizard offered to add summaries to a report that contained groupings. You were limited to arithmetic summaries involving number, currency, or AutoNumber fields. When you design your own report with groupings, you can use many more types of group summaries, including running totals that accumulate the value throughout the report.

Calculated text boxes are controls that rely on values in table or query fields for their values. You can use any expression with operators and functions to compute the summary value by setting the Control Source property of the control. You saw an example earlier when the year value was added to the Date group header in the Entries by Year Report.

Adding a Count Summary

Now, let's add a summary to the group footer to the Entries by Year Report that counts the number of Alpha Entry records in each group, and then adds another summary to the report footer that shows the total number of records in the report.

1. In the report Design view, click the Text Box control tool in the toolbox and click in the group footer at the left end of the section to place the new text box control.

2. Open the property sheet and type **=Count([Entry])** in the Control Source property box.

3. Change the Align property to Left, so the number appears closer to the label.

4. Change the label to **Total This Year:**. Then move and resize the text box and label controls to fit.

5. Increase the height of the report footer section to make room for the grand total summary field.

6. Select the calculated control in the group footer and click Copy. Next, click in the report footer near the left end, and then click Paste. A copy of the group summary control appears in the report footer.

7. Click in the label and change the caption to **Grand Total:**

```
        ◆ Date Footer
   ┊  Total This Year: ┊ =Count([Entry]) ┊
        ◆ Report Footer
   ┊  Grand Total: ┊ =Count([Entry]) ┊
```

TIP   *The expression you used in the group footer works just as well in the report footer. Access summarizes all the records in the report when you place the control in the report footer.*

Adding a Running Total

When you deal with financial data, being able to show running totals—within groups and overall—is often important. You can add a calculated control that sums up the values in a group, accumulates the values from group to group, and, finally, prints the overall total for the whole report.

When you create a calculated control using one of the aggregate functions, such as Sum, Avg, Count, and so on you can set the Running Sum property to Over Group or Over All. The Over Group setting accumulates the values in the group, and then resets the value to 0 at the beginning of the next group. The Over All setting accumulates the values to the end of the report, printing subtotals at intermediate points, as required.

Numbering Items in a Report

Sometimes having each of the items in a report numbered is handy, so you can reference it uniquely by number—for example, if you're taking part in a teleconference and need to be sure you all are talking about the same item. To number the items, do the following:

1. Add a calculated text box control to the detail section in a prominent position at the left of the record data.

2. Remove the new text box label.

3. Double-click the new control to open its property sheet and change the Control Source to the expression **=1**.

4. Set the Running Sum property to Over All, which increments the calculated text box value by 1 for each record in the detail section.

This works for grouped records as well. To number the records in each group separately, add the calculated control to the detail section, as shown previously, but set the Running Sum property to Over Group instead of Over All.

TIP   *If you're only interested in the summary data in a report, you can suppress printing the details by changing the detail section Visible property to No or set the section height to 0.*

Applying the Finishing Touches

To finish the Entries by Year report, add a title in the report header. Because the information in the report header prints only on the first page of the report, you can add a continuation title and the page number to the page header, which prints on every page except the first. To do this, choose View | Page Header/Footer and shrink the page footer section because nothing will be placed in it. Then change the report Page Header property to Not with Rpt Hdr.

Finally, draw some lines under the titles to separate the report header and page header from the rest of the report, and then draw another line at the bottom of the group footer to separate the groups.

Figure 14-6 shows the completed report in Design view and Figure 14-7 shows the printed first page of the report.

Modifying and Adding Groups

To change the sort order of the records in an ungrouped report or of the groups in a grouped report, open the Sorting and Grouping dialog box and choose from the Sort Order drop-down list.

If you want to change the grouping levels of existing groups, click the row selector of the group you want to move. Then click it again and drag the row to the desired position in the list of groupings. If the groups you move have headers or footers, Access moves

FIGURE 14-6   The Entries by Year report design

Alpha Entries Grouped by Date Reported

Year Reported: 1990

Date	Entry No.	Cod	Inde	Entry	Purge Date
6 /24/90	73	488	50	V/PETTY THEFT	6 /24/02

Total This Year: 1

Year Reported: 1993

Date	Entry No.	Cod	Inde	Entry	Purge Date
12/19/93	118	459	93	V/BURGLARY	12/19/00

Total This Year: 1

Year Reported: 1994

Date	Entry No.	Cod	Inde	Entry	Purge Date
10/26/94	19	20001	16	R/O VEH #1/H&R FELONY	10/26/01
11/5 /94	39	459	21	V/BURGLARY	11/5 /01
4 /16/94	76	459	52	V/BURGLARY	4 /16/01
3 /27/94	75	459	52	V/BURGLARY	3 /17/01
9 /25/94	90	245	69	V/ASSAULT W/DEADLY	9 /25/01
12/18/94	92	459	71	V/BURGLARY	12/18/04

Total This Year: 6

Year Reported: 1995

Date	Entry No.	Cod	Inde	Entry	Purge Date
4 /9 /95	41	459	23	ARREST/BURGLARY & 496.1	4 /9 /02
12/10/95	107	459	84	V/BURGLARY &	12/10/02

Total This Year: 2

Year Reported: 1996

Date	Entry No.	Cod	Inde	Entry	Purge Date
10/15/96	3	459	4	V/BURGLARY	10/15/03
8 /7 /96	7	487	8	V/GRAND THEFT	8 /7 /03
7 /5 /96	26	10851	16	R/O STOL VEH	7 /5 /03
7 /16/96	28	10851	16	R/O/STOL VEH	7 /16/03
7 /18/96	30	10851	16	R/O/STOL VEH	7 /18/03
12/20/96	48	10851	29	R/O STOL TRLR	12/20/03
1 /29/96	51	10851	30	R/O/RCVD VEH	1 /29/03
1 /27/96	50	10851	30	R/O/STOL VEH	1 /27/03
8 /6 /96	61	10851	37	R/O/STOL VEH	8 /6 /03

FIGURE 14-7   Printed first page of the Entries by Year report

them and all the controls they contain to the new positions in the report design. The controls might need some adjustment after repositioning.

To change the group-on field or expression, select it and choose another field from the drop-down list or enter a different expression. If you want to add an additional grouping level, click the next empty Field/Expression row and choose the field from the drop-down list or enter an expression. You can also insert a grouping level above an existing one by clicking the row selector where you want the new level and pressing INSERT.

To remove a grouping, click the row selector and press DEL.

Adding a Second Level Grouping

As an example of adding a second grouping level, group the Entries by Year Report by quarter within the year group by doing the following:

1. Open the Entries by Year Report in Design view, and then click the Sorting and Grouping button.

2. Click the Field/Expression column of the empty second row and choose Date from the drop-down list.

3. In the lower pane, set the Group Header property to Yes and leave the Group Footer property as No.

4. Change the Group On property to Qtr and leave the Group Interval at 1.

5. Close the Sorting and Grouping dialog box.

6. Add an unbound text box to the left end of the detail section and enter the expression **=DatePart("q",[Date])** in its Control Source property box.

7. Change the Hide Duplicates property to Yes.

8. Delete the new control's attached label and place a label in the top Date Header section reading **Qtr**.

9. Save the report as Entries by Quarter and switch to Print Preview to view the changed report.

Figure 14-8 shows a preview of the report that now groups the Alpha Entry records by the year the entry was reported, and then by quarter. You could also edit the report title accordingly.

FIGURE 14-8   Previewing the Entries by Quarter Report

TIP   *The DatePart function extracts a specific part of an existing date value. See "Custom Formatting Symbols" in the Quick Reference on the CD for more details.*

Printing an Alphabetic Index

By combining the Group On and Group Interval settings, you can create an alphabetic list of items grouped by the leading character. For example, to create a list such as the one shown in Figure 14-9, do the following:

1. Select the Member List table in the Database window and choose Insert | Report.

2. Select Design view in the New Report dialog box and click OK.

3. Place the LastName field in the detail section and delete the attached label.

4. Click the Sorting and Grouping button, choose LastName as the field to group on, and set the following group properties:

   - Set Group Header to Yes.

   - Set Group Footer to No.

   - Set Group On to Prefix Characters.

   - Set Group Interval to 1.

FIGURE 14-9
Printing an
alphabetic
Member List

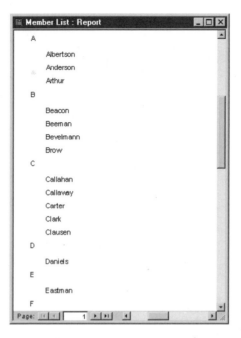

5. To place the initial character in the group header, add a text box control to the group header and delete the attached label.

6. Set the new text box control Control Source property to **=Left([LastName],1)**. Figure 14-10 shows the completed report design, as well as the Sorting and Grouping dialog box.

CAUTION *Be careful not to use the word "Name" as a field name. Access reserves that word as the name of the current object. If you use the expression Left([Name],1) in the group header, you will see M (the first letter of the report name) in every group header. Many more reserved words are in the Access language.*

Hiding Duplicates and Other Tips

Duplicate values appearing in the detail section can clutter up a report. For example, a report grouping the Alpha Entry records by code would show multiple records with the same code value. You have two ways to alleviate the problem: move the Code field to the group header section where it will be printed only once or leave it in the detail section and change the control's Hide Duplicates property to Yes.

Two other properties are useful when printing reports containing memo fields that might contain a varying amount of data or, possibly, none at all. Changing the Can Shrink property to Yes prevents blank lines when no value is in the field. Changing the Can Grow property to Yes lets the field value expand, if necessary.

PART II

FIGURE 14-10
Reviewing the
Member List
report design

Adding a Subreport

A *subreport*, a complete report in its own right, is inserted into another report, called the *main report*. A main report can be either bound or unbound. A *bound main report* is based on a table or query and its subreports contain related information. For example, the main report could contain details about the year's business, while the subreport could show charts and graphs summarizing and illustrating the numbers in the main report. A bound main report might also have two or more subreports that provide parallel information, but only relate to the main report and not to each other.

An *unbound main report* isn't based on a table or query, but can serve as a container for one or more subreports—for example, an annual report in which the main report is a title page with some introductory information, and the subreports contain parallel information unrelated to each other about the business during the previous year.

A main report can include as many subreports and subforms as necessary. You can also add up to two levels of subreports. A first-level subreport can contain another subreport or a subform. If the first level is a subform, it can contain only another subform, not a subreport, as the second level.

Creating a Subreport Control

You use the Subform/Subreport control tool in the toolbox to create a new subreport in the current report design. The Subform/Subreport Wizard creates the subreport based on your selections in the series of dialog boxes. It also saves the finished subreport as a separate report whose name appears in the Reports tab of the Database window.

As an example of creating a new subreport, let's add the Alpha Entry information to the Alpha Card Report, relating the two reports by the Index field. To be safe, save the Alpha Card Report with a different name before adding the subreport as follows:

1. Right-click the Alpha Card Report name in the Database window and choose Save As from the shortcut menu.

2. Enter the new name, **Alpha Card with Subreport**, in the Save As dialog box and click OK.

To create the subreport containing related Alpha Entry information, do the following:

1. Open the Alpha Card with Subreport report in Design view and open the toolbox. Make sure you've pressed in the Control Wizard button on the toolbox.

2. Increase the height of the detail section and move the line to the bottom to make room for the subreport in between.

3. Click the Subform/Subreport tool and click in the report design between the last row of controls and the line at the bottom of the detail section. Access draws a square frame in the report design and opens the first dialog box, where you can select an existing report or form as the subreport or create a new one.

NOTE   *You can also draw a custom subreport frame to the desired size before releasing the mouse button and starting the wizard.*

4. Choose Use existing Tables and Queries to create the new subreport, and then click Next.

5. In the next dialog box, select Alpha Entry from the Tables/Queries drop-down list, click >> to select all the fields, and then click Next.

6. Accept the link the wizard suggests, which links the report and subreport by the Index field, and then click Next.

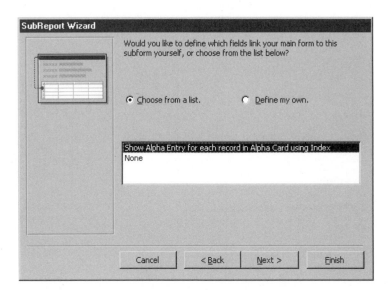

7. Accept Alpha Entry subreport as the report name or enter a different name, such as **Alpha Entries**, and then click Finish to return to the main report Design view.

8. Delete the subreport label, if necessary, and then move and resize the subreport control as appropriate.

Figure 14-11 shows a preview of the report with the new subreport. The style adopted for the subreport depends on the style most recently accessed. Your subreport's style could be different. As you can see in the preview, you can make several refinements in the subreport to improve its appearance. For example, you could hide the Index field and spread out the remaining controls to make room for the Entry information. In addition, the Code field doesn't need so much room.

TIP   *Access doesn't print the page header and footer sections in a subreport. If you put the column labels for your subreport in the page header, they won't appear when you print the report. If the subreport doesn't exceed the page length, you can place the column headings in the subreport report header section, which is printed. The wizard placed the column headings in the report header section in the previous Alpha Entry subreport. If the subreport is likely to span two or more pages, place the column headings in the subreport group header and set the Repeat Section property to Yes.*

Inserting an Existing Subreport

To use an existing report as a subreport, make sure the underlying tables or queries are properly related to the main report, and then open the Subform/Subreport Wizard, as previously shown. Instead of choosing Table/Query in the first wizard dialog box, choose

FIGURE 14-11   Previewing the new subreport

Reports or Forms, and then select the desired report or form from the drop-down list of all the reports and forms in the current database. Follow the instructions in the remaining wizard dialog boxes.

> **TIP**   *A quick way to insert an existing report into another report as a subreport is to drag it from the Database window. Open the main report in Design view, and then press F11 to switch to the Database window. Drag the name of the report you want as the subreport to the section where you want the subreport to appear in the main report. Access adds the subreport control to the design. You can also drag a datasheet from the Tables page of the Database window to the report, in which case the Subreport Wizard starts with the dialog box suggesting the linking field. You must have the Control Wizard button on the toolbox pressed in for this to work.*

Linking the Report and Subreport

If you insert the subreport in a bound report, the underlying tables must be linked, so both reports contain corresponding data. You need to set the links in the Relationships window before trying to insert the subreport.

When you use the wizard to create a subreport or drag an existing report or datasheet from the Database window, if one of the following conditions is met, Access automatically links the main report and subreport:

- The reports are based on related tables.

- The main report has a primary key and the table in the subreport contains a field with the same name and the same or compatible data type.

- Both reports are based on queries whose underlying tables meet either of those same conditions.

The linking fields must be included in the underlying record source, but you don't have to show them in either report. The wizard automatically includes linking fields, even if you don't select them with the field picker.

If, for some reason, the wizard hasn't linked the tables properly, you can set the properties yourself by doing the following:

1. Open the main report in Design view.

2. Select the subreport control and open the property sheet.

3. Enter the name of the linking field in the subreport in the Link Child Fields property box.

4. Enter the name of the linking field in the main report in the Link Master Fields property box.

TIP   You must use the field name, not the name of the control. If you aren't sure of the field names, click the build button (...) next to one of the linking properties to open the Subreport Field Linker dialog box. Click Suggest to see the same link suggestions presented by the SubReport Wizard.

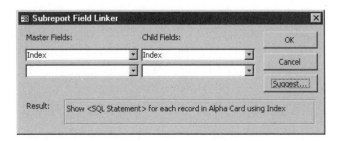

You can link on more than one field by entering the field names in the property sheet, separated by semicolons, or by selecting them in the Subreport Field Linker dialog box.

Modifying a Subreport Control

The first thing you might want to do with a new subreport control is to edit or delete the attached control label. Do this in the main report Design view. Then make changes in the subreport design to match the style and arrangement of the controls in the main report.

You make modifications to a subreport design just like any other report. You can work on it in the main report Design window or choose View | Subreport in New Window to work on it alone.

Subreport controls share many of the properties with other types of controls, for example, the position and size properties, as well as the Special Effect and border properties. By default, the Can Grow property is set to Yes and the Can Shrink property is set to No. In addition to the link field properties, the subreport has a Name property, set to the name you saved the file with, or the name you entered in the Subform/Subreport Wizard dialog box.

The Source Object property is unique to subforms and subreports, and contains the type and name of the object, for example, the Source Object property of the subreport in the Alpha Card with Subreport is Report.Alpha Entry subreport.

Designing a Multiple-Column Report

Another way to arrange information in a report is in columns. When information is arranged in a tabular layout, it's easy to scan down a column of data and compare values in different records. Arranging the information in columns makes focusing on individual records easy because all the data for one record is grouped together.

The Report Wizard gives you a choice of tabular or columnar layout in one of the dialog boxes. Choosing Columnar creates a report with the fields arranged in a single column on the page. Using Page Setup, you can change the layout to include as many columns as can fit across the page. For example, if you rearrange and resize the controls in the report design, you can reduce the width of a column to two inches, and then specify three columns on the page. Figure 14-12 compares the columnar report created by the Report Wizard with the same data in a newspaper column report.

FIGURE 14-12 Comparing columnar reports

You can place controls anywhere in the page or in the report header and footer sections because they span the entire width of the page when you print the report. If you grouped the records, the group header and footer, as well as the detail section, span only the width of the column. So, place the controls you want in the group sections within the width you allow for the column.

When designing a multiple-column report, use the following formula as a guide to the page layout:

```
(Column width * Number of columns) + (Column spacing * (Number of columns -1)) +
Right margin + Left margin <= Paper width
```

To create this three-column report, do the following:

1. Select the Name List table in the Database window and choose Insert | Report.

2. Choose AutoReport: Columnar from the New Report dialog box.

3. In Design view or Print Preview, choose Page Setup from the File menu. The three-tab Page Setup dialog box opens.

4. Click the Columns tab and change the Number of Columns to **3**.

5. Leave the Column Spacing at the default **.25"**. If you left some space between the bottom control in the detail section and the lower boundary of the section, you can also leave the Row Spacing at **0**.

6. In the Column Size group, set the Width to **2"**. You can also set the Height here or use the height drawn in Design view.

7. Choose OK. If you were in Print Preview, the report shows the new layout. If not, switch to Print Preview to see how the report looks.

TIP   *If the report design exceeds the page width, Access displays a warning when you try to switch to Print Preview. Then you can either enter a smaller column width, reduce the column spacing, or reduce the size of the side margins. If you reduce the column width, be sure to change the controls in the group and detail sections to fit.*

Another setting in the Columns dialog box is the Column Layout option group. This option determines the order in which the records are laid out on the page. The default is Down, then Across, which places records down the page in the first column to the bottom of the page, and then moves to the second column, and so on. The alternative choice is Across, then Down, which places the records across the first row to the right margin of the page, and then moves to the second row, and so on.

Grouping Records in a Multiple-Column Report

When you create a multiple-column report with grouping levels, you can specify to keep the groups together in a row or column, depending on the Column Layout setting, when printing the report. You can also have a group start in a new row or column by setting combinations of group and report properties.

Starting a Group in a New Row or Column

If you grouped the records in the report and want to set each group apart when the report is printed, you can ask Access to start a new column or row with each new group by setting the group section (header or footer) New Row Or Col property. Your choices are as follows:

- *None,* which lets the setting in the Page Setup dialog box and the available space on the page determine the row or column breaks.

- *Before Section,* which starts printing the group section (usually the header) in a new row or column, and then prints the next section (usually the detail) in the same row or column.

- *After Section,* which starts printing the group section in the current row or column, and then prints the next section in a new row or column. This option can be used to print the group headers alone in the first row or column, and then the detail section in the second row or column.

- *Before & After,* which starts printing the group section in a new row or column, and then prints the next section in a new row or column. This option can be used to cause the information in the group header section to stand apart from the information in the detail section.

You might have to play around with combinations of the Column Layout options in the Columns tab of the Page Setup dialog box and the New Row Or Col group section property settings to get the effect you want in the report.

Keeping Groups Together in Rows or Columns

Earlier in this chapter, you saw how to keep data together on a page by setting group properties in the Sorting and Grouping dialog box, and by setting report properties in the property sheet. If you arranged the records in columns and you want to keep the group together, do the following:

1. In Design view, click the Sorting and Grouping button to open the dialog box.

2. Click the group level you want to keep together and set the Keep Together property in the lower pane to Whole Group or With First Detail.

3. Display the report property sheet and change the Grp Keep Together property to Per Column.

NOTE   *If you set the Column Layout in the Columns dialog box to Across, and then Down, the group is kept together in a row. The Down, and then Across setting keeps the group together in a column.*

Printing Mailing Labels and Envelopes

Labels are used for many purposes: mailing addresses, name tags, disk labels, and book-plates (From the library of . . .). Because labels are usually smaller than a sheet of paper, you can print many of them on one page. This leads to a multiple column per page report layout like the one in the previous section. Label printing is so common that Access provides a special Label Wizard to help with the layout.

After you create the label design, you can use it to print addresses on envelopes as well, with a few changes to the page layout. Through the Label Wizard, you can create your own custom label size and layout, and then save it to use again.

Using the Label Wizard

In one of the Label Wizard's series of dialog boxes, you can select from a long list of predefined label layouts that match commercially available label stock. You can prepare labels for printing on continuous-feed or sheet-feed printers. The Label Wizard helps with every stage of the label design, including choosing the layout, changing the text appearance, adding field data to a prototype label, and even offering to sort the labels for you before printing.

As an example of printing mailing labels, the local police department keeps the names and addresses of the Retired Senior Volunteer Program (RSVP) members in the Name List table in their Access database, so monthly notices can be mailed to the members.

To create mailing labels for the volunteers, do the following:

1. Open the New Report dialog box and choose Label Wizard. If you haven't already selected the table or query that contains the label data, select Name List from the drop-down list and click OK.

2. In the first dialog box, you can set the following options:

   - Select the desired Unit of Measure: English or Metric.

   - Select the Label Type: Sheet feed or Continuous.

   - Choose the brand of label from the Filter by manufacturer drop-down list.

   - Choose the desired label from the Product Number list. The dimensions are specified as height × width.

   - If you want to create a custom label size, click the Customize button.

   - If you already created some custom label sizes, you can choose Show custom label sizes to see that list.

3. Click Next to open the second dialog box where you can select the font name, size, and weight, and text colors. Italics and underlining are also options here.

NOTE   *These settings apply to all the text in the label. You can change individual lines of text later in the Design view. For example, you might want the addressee's name to be in bold text, but not the address.*

4. Click Next to continue. The next Label Wizard dialog box displays a blank label prototype where you arrange the data.

   - To move a field to the prototype label, double-click the field name in the Available Fields list or select it and click >.

   - To remove a field from the prototype label, select the field and press DEL.

   - To move to the next line, press ENTER.

   - Enter spaces, punctuation, and other characters as necessary as you place the fields.

   Access automatically concatenates the values in the fields and trims the spaces from the names and addresses. Notice the spaces entered between the field names and the comma entered between the City and State fields.

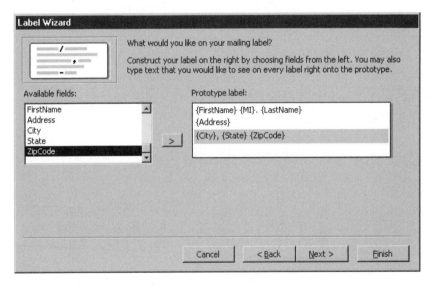

5. Click Next to move to the next dialog box where you can choose to sort the records before printing the labels. Then click Next to move to the last Label Wizard dialog box where you enter a name for the label design.

NOTE   *If you don't specify a sort order, the labels are arranged in the same order as the source table, ascending based on the first field in the table. If the label report is based on a query, the labels are arranged in ascending order based on the leftmost field in the grid.*

Figure 14-13 shows a preview of the new labels for the Name List, using the Avery 5160 label size. The labels are sorted by Last Name.

TIP   *A good idea is to print one page of the new labels on plain paper and compare it with your label stock before committing to print many pages of labels on expensive label sheets.*

Manipulating Text Data

Click View and choose Design View to see the new Name List label in Design view.

Now you can see how the Label Wizard created the calculated text box controls. The Label Wizard combined the text values in special expressions using the concatenation operator (&) and the Trim function. The *concatenation operator* serves to combine the values

FIGURE 14-13   Previewing the new labels

in the field with any other characters you want, enclosed in quotation marks. The *Trim function* displays the field value without leading or trailing spaces.

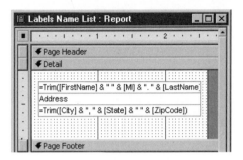

Other text functions are also useful when combining text values. In addition to the Trim function, the *LTrim function* removes only the leading spaces, while the *RTrim function* removes only the trailing spaces. Be sure to add a space between the field names and literal characters in the same line in the prototype label or all the characters will run together.

The Left function used earlier when creating the alphabetic list report lets you display only the first few characters of the text value. The number of characters to display is specified as the second argument in the function statement. The Right function displays the last few characters.

You can create your own calculated control expressions to combine text values by using these tools and functions. Type the expression in the Control Source property box of the calculated text box or directly into the control in the design. Always begin the expression with the equals sign (=). Here are some examples of expressions you can use in calculated controls placed in forms and reports:

- **="None"**   Displays None
- **="Mr/Mrs " & [First Name] & " " & [Last Name]**   Displays the first and last names preceded by Mr/Mrs and separated by a space.
- **=Trim([City])**   Displays the City field with no leading or trailing spaces.
- **=Left([Last Name],3)**   Displays the first three characters in the Last Name field.
- **=IIf(IsNull([MI]),[FirstName]&" " &[LastName],[FirstName] & " " & [MI] & " " & [LastName])**   Uses the IIf function to test the MI field for a null value. If the field is null, only the first and last names are displayed. If the field is not null, all three field values are displayed. All values are separated by spaces.

Printing Addresses on Envelopes

You can use the same report design you created for printing the labels to print the addresses on envelopes. All you need to do is change the Page Setup options to reflect the different size and arrangement of the controls. First, save the report you created for printing labels with a different name, and then open the report in Design view and make any changes to the text in the report.

Summary

This chapter covered designing custom reports for many purposes, but an almost unlimited number of features and tools are still in the Access repertoire. As you work with report designs and begin to realize how versatile Access can be in presenting information in a variety of ways, you'll gain even greater understanding.

The last remaining piece of information retrieval and presentation involves graphically presenting information in such a way that the viewer can perform analyses and detect trends in the underlying data. The next chapter discusses three tools for doing this: the Chart Wizard, the PivotTable Wizard, and the PivotChart Wizard. The *Chart Wizard* helps create charts and graphs from Access table data, which you can edit using the Microsoft Graph applet. The *PivotTable Wizard* helps create spreadsheet-like tables from Access table data that you can edit using Excel. The *PivotChart Wizard* presents a graphical analysis of data in a table, query, or form.

PART II

Creating Charts and Graphs

Charts and graphs enhance data presented in forms and reports by summarizing the information and illustrating it in easily understood ways. With these tools, the reader can analyze trends and make comparisons. Access offers a wide variety of chart types including column, bar, line, pie, XY scatter, area, and many others. Many of the types can also be shown in three dimensions. If you want the chart to reflect the values in the currently displayed record, you can also link the chart to a field in the underlying table or query.

Creating a New Chart

When you decide to add a chart to a form or report, you must first understand the purpose of the chart. Do you want to point out trends over a period of time or compare the relative values summarized by groups? The local police department, for example, is interested in the increase or decrease of violent crimes over the last four years. This type of chart would involve tabulating the number of crimes reported during each year and displaying the results as a column chart or a line chart.

The police are also concerned with the crime rates in different areas of the city. Such a comparison can be illustrated with a bar or column chart, as well as a pie chart in which each area is represented by a slice of the pie.

Other decisions that must be made during the planning stage are whether to embed the chart in the form or report, or to create a freestanding chart that can be available to more than one form or report. If you embed the chart in the form or report, you can link the chart to data in the underlying table or query and the chart then changes for each record. If you want the chart to remain the same as you move through records, leave the embedded chart unlinked.

If you create a chart in another application, such as Excel, you can import the chart to your form or report. Choose Insert | Chart and choose the chart. You can also click the Unbound Object Frame button on the toolbox and copy the chart to that.

TIP   *The fundamental rule when you design a chart or any other user-oriented object is to keep it simple. Just because Access and the other Office applications offer all kinds of bells and whistles, this doesn't mean you need to clutter your products with a lot of touches that may obscure the point you're trying to make. Keep the purpose of the chart in mind as you look at the tools Access and Microsoft Graph offer.*

The Anatomy of a Chart

A chart is composed of *elements*, some of which relate to the data, while others relate to the structure of the chart itself. Figure 15-1 shows a typical chart based on data taken from the Northwind sample database that came with Access. This chart compares the sales of eight categories of products during the year 1997.

Many other types of charts can show comparisons among data groups. For example, Figure 15-2 shows the same data displayed in an exploding pie chart. Many of the same elements appear in this chart, in addition to a few new ones: a legend, a slice, and data labels. Data labels can be displayed with the percentage of the whole the group represents, as the figure shows or with the data name or both.

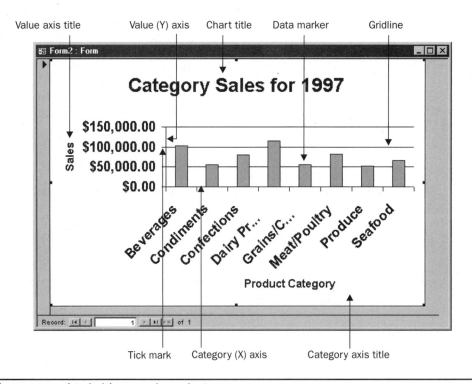

FIGURE 15-1   A typical Access column chart

FIGURE 15-2   A pie chart with data labels

Another reason to include charts in a form or report is to show trends over a period of time. Figure 15-3, which uses data from the Police database, shows a line chart that tracks the number of crimes reported over a four-year period. The crimes are grouped as violent or nonviolent and a legend is included that identifies the lines. This chart includes the data labels, which show the number of crimes at each data point on the lines. The legend that appears at the right of the chart identifies the individual categories of information.

NOTE   *The lines appear in different colors when displayed on the screen or printed with a color printer, but when they're printed in black and white, you must rely on the shape of the data points to identify the data series.*

The line chart has been embedded in a simple report with a title and subtitle added to the page header. The report could be much more comprehensive in real life.

Before I move on, understanding each of the main elements in a standard chart is important (refer to Figure 15-1).

- The *Category (X) axis* is the horizontal line at the bottom of the chart that usually identifies the data in the chart. For example, when you plot sales by product, the product name appears on the Category axis.

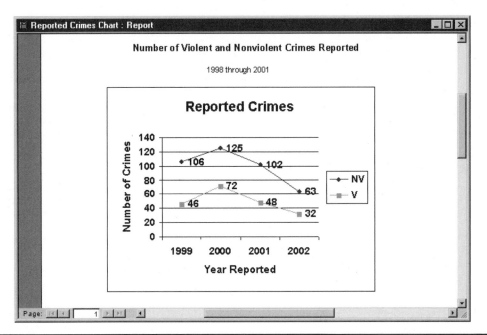

FIGURE 15-3   A line chart showing a trend

- The *Value (Y) axis* is the vertical line that measures the values in the chart data—for example, the sales in dollars or other currency.

- The optional *Z axis* appears in 3-D charts and also measures values. The Z axis appears to project outward from the chart.

- A *series* is a group of related data values from one field in the underlying record source. For example, in a sales by product chart, each year's sales total would represent one of a series of values. The values are grouped together in one category: the product type. A series is a further partitioning of grouped field data, which adds more detail to the chart.

- *Titles* help explain the purpose and scope of the chart. Titles are optional and can appear at the top of the chart and by each axis.

- *Gridlines* are horizontal or vertical lines that appear across or up and down the chart at the tick marks.

- *Tick marks* are short lines that appear on the axes to mark evenly spaced segments. They help to read the values and determine the scale of the chart.

- *Scale* defines the range of values in the chart and the increments marked by tick marks on the axes. This is usually determined by the Chart Wizard, but you can change the scale and spacing of the tick marks.

- A *slice* is a wedge of a single-field pie chart, which represents the relative value of one data point with respect to the whole.

- *Data markers* are the elements that show the value of the data—for example, bars, columns, slices of a pie chart, small icons on a line chart, and so on.

- *Data labels* are the actual values that can be displayed above or near the data markers. Figure 15-2 shows percentage data labels with each slice of the pie.

- The *legend* is the list that identifies the members of a series of data values. For example, in Figure 15-3, the legend next to the chart indicates which line represents which type of crime.

Selecting the Data for the Chart

Once you decide on what you want the chart to accomplish, you can begin locating the data the chart will require. If the data is all contained in one table, you can use the table as the basis for the chart. If not, you can create a select or cross tab query that groups and summarizes the data for the chart. With a select query, you can combine data and add calculated fields such as an extended price, as well as add totals that summarize field values.

You can use up to six fields of any data type, except OLE and Memo. Only two requirements exist:

- You must include at least one field for categorizing data, such as the year the crime was reported or the area of the city where it occurred.

- You must also include a field or a calculated field that you can add up, average, or count, such as the number of violent crimes or the sales during the third quarter of 2002.

TIP   *If you include a date/time field in the chart, you can group the values with the wizard instead of creating a query to do the job.*

A simple chart might contain only two fields—one as the category and the other as the data or value that corresponds to the category. For example, in Figure 15-1, only two fields exist: Product Category used as the category and Sales, which was summed to form the value.

Using the Access Chart Wizard

The way you begin to create a new chart depends on the type of chart you want. Do you want a standalone chart in its own form or report design, or a chart embedded in an existing form or report? In either case, you eventually use the Chart Wizard to create the chart. The chart is built in a chart control in the form or report.

To create a new chart, start the Chart Wizard by doing one of the following:

- If you're creating a freestanding chart, start a new form or report, and then choose Chart Wizard in the New Form (or Report) dialog box. Then select the table or query you want to use as the basis for the chart and click OK.

TIP   *You can also use one of the other methods you learned in the previous chapters to open the New Form or New Report dialog box.*

- If you want to insert a new chart in an existing form or report, open the form or report in Design view and choose Insert | Chart. Then click in the design where you want to place the chart. The Chart Wizard opens and, in the first dialog box, asks you to select the table or query to use as the basis for the chart.

Once you specify the underlying record source, follow the instructions in the wizard dialog boxes as follows (this example uses the Crimes by Beat Number table in the Police database):

1. Choose the fields you want to use in the chart—for example, Year, Crime Type, and Number of Crimes. You need at least one field as the category and one as the data. You can choose up to six fields. Then click Next.

2. In the next dialog box, select the type of chart you want to create (see Figure 15-4), and then click Next. You can click each type of chart and read a description in the right pane.

3. The next dialog box (see Figure 15-5) shows you the Chart Wizard's interpretation of the arrangement of the fields in the layout of the sample 3-D column chart.

4. Access has guessed which field to use as the category, but this isn't always what you had in mind. Click the Preview Chart to see how this arrangement would look.

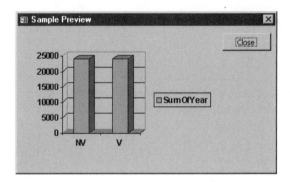

The preview doesn't show what the chart is meant to present—the number of crimes by type reported in each year. It shows the number of years in which violent and nonviolent crimes were reported. To change this layout, close the Preview window and do the following:

1. Drag the SumOfYear label to the area below the chart to replace Crime Type. The label changes to Year because it represents a category on the X axis, rather than a numeric value on the Y axis.

2. Drag the Number of Crimes field button to the Data area below the Preview Chart. The label changes to SumOfNumber of Crimes.

3. Drag the Crime Type field button to the Series area.

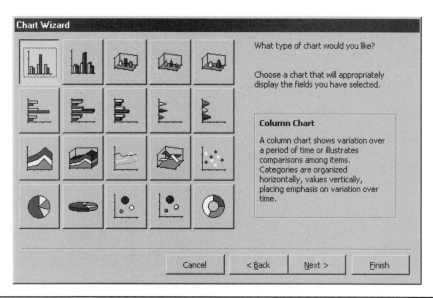

FIGURE 15-4   Select the type of chart with the Chart Wizard

4. To remove a field from the Preview Chart, drag it off the chart. The field name is replaced by Series, Data, or Axis, depending on the chart area. Figure 15-6 shows the new layout.

FIGURE 15-5   Working in the Chart Wizard's layout dialog box

FIGURE 15-6   Modified chart layout

5. Click the Preview Chart button again to see the effects of the changes.

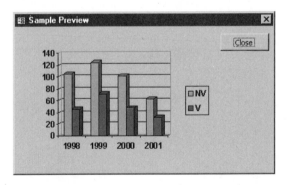

6. Close the Preview window and click Next.

7. In the final Chart Wizard dialog box, you can enter a name for the chart, such as "Crimes by Year Chart," or accept the name of the table or query you used as the basis. You also have the option of displaying a legend explaining the series data. When you close the dialog box, you can open the form or report and display the chart, or you can go directly to Design view to edit the form or report.

8. Click Finish and see the chart in the new form. You may have to resize the form or the chart control to get the appearance you want.

A *3-D chart* has a third dimension, depth that creates a back wall, an end wall on the left, side walls, and a floor. The back wall and end wall meet at the corner. You can set the pattern and color properties of each of these features to get the appearance you want in the chart.

It is important to realize you don't have to go to the trouble of creating a query to summarize the data for the chart. Create the chart and let the Chart Wizard do that for you. When you drag a field to the Value area in the sample chart, the Chart Wizard assumes you want to use the Sum aggregate function to create the value, but you can change to another function by double-clicking a number field, choosing from the Summarize dialog box, and then clicking OK.

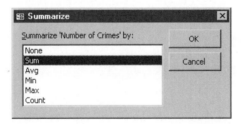

NOTE   *When you first create a chart, it shows sample data rather than the data you asked it to process. Don't worry, the chart will show the real data the first time you view the form in Form view or the report in Print Preview.*

Printing and Saving the Chart

In the final Chart Wizard dialog box, you assigned a title to the new chart, but you haven't yet named the host form or report, as you can see from the Form1: Form name still in the title bar. To name and save the form or report containing the chart, choose File | Save and enter the desired filename. The new name is added to the Database window.

When you reopen the form or report containing the chart, it contains the current data from the underlying record source.

When you preview the chart in Form view or Print Preview, you can print it or switch to Design view to make changes.

TIP *If you're producing reports and find you need to create a lot of charts, you can save time by adding the Chart button to the form and report control toolbox. See Chapter 20 for information about customizing menus and toolbars.*

Linking to Record Data

When you start a new chart from within a form or report design, Access assumes you want to link the chart to one of the fields in the underlying record source, so that different data appears in the chart with each record. To do this, you first create the host form or report, and then insert the new or existing chart.

For example, create a columnar form based on the City Beats table, which contains only two fields: the beat number and a brief description of the territory. Then switch to Design view and create a new chart by doing the following:

1. Choose Insert | Chart and click in the design just below the text box controls in the form. (Or, use the Chart button in the toolbox if you added it.) Be sure you have made room in the section for the embedded chart.

2. In the first Chart Wizard dialog box, choose the Crimes by Beat Number table as the basis for the chart and click Next.

3. In the second dialog box, select the fields you want in the chart. For this chart, choose Year, BeatNo, Crime Type, and Number of Crimes from the field list, and then click Next.

4. In the next dialog box, choose a simple column chart and click Next.

5. In the layout dialog box, drag the Year field to the Axis area, the Number of Crimes to the Data area, and the Crime Type to the Series area. Then click Next.

6. In the next dialog box (see Figure 15-7) the wizard suggests BeatNo as the linking fields in both the form and chart because they have the same name. If no matching names are between the tables, the wizard makes no suggestion. You can change the linking field names or choose not to link the chart to the form at all by choosing <No Field>. Click Next to move to the final dialog box, which is the same as before, and name the form "City Beats Crimes."

NOTE *The linking fields needn't have the same names, but they must have the same kind of data and be of the same or compatible data types.*

Figure 15-8 shows the finished form with the linked chart. As you move through the records, the heights of the data column markers change to reflect the number of crimes reported in that beat area.

TIP *Reconstructing the chart when you move to the next record may take a few seconds, so be patient.*

FIGURE 15-7   The Chart Wizard offers to link the chart to records in the form

If you open the form in Design view and look at the properties of the chart control, you will see that the Link Child Fields and Link Master Fields are both set to the BeatNo field.

NOTE   *If you already created the chart and want to embed and link it in a form, you can set the Link Child Fields and Link Master Fields properties yourself in the chart control property sheet.*

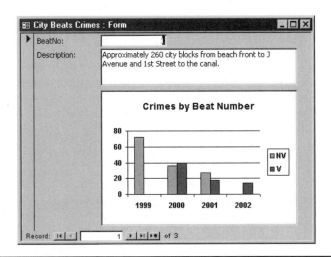

FIGURE 15-8   The new form with a linked chart

Adding an Existing Chart

You can insert an existing chart created within the current database or in another Access database into a form or report. To add a chart created in the same or another Access database, you can drag or copy the chart from one form or report to the other. To use drag-and-drop to insert the chart from another database, you must have two instances of Access running.

To insert a new chart created with Microsoft Chart, another Office program, open the form or report in Design view and do the following:

1. Click the Unbound Object Frame toolbox button and click where you want the chart. You can also draw the frame in the design.
2. In the Insert Object dialog box, click Create From File and enter the path to the file, or click Browse to locate the file if you don't know the path.
3. If you want to link the chart to the form or report, select Link. If you want the chart to appear as an icon instead of the full chart, select Display As Icon. Then click OK.

Modifying the Chart

The tools you use to modify a chart depend on what kind of changes you want to make. If you want to change any of the properties or the position of the control, do so in Access. If you want to change the underlying data, you can create a new query and change the Row Source property of the chart within Access. You can also edit the SQL statement in the Row Source property rather than create a new query.

However, if you want to change any of the chart's elements, such as the axis titles or the chart type, or change the appearance of the chart, you must activate Microsoft Graph for in-place editing.

Modifying with Access

To modify the chart with Access, open the host form or report in Design view and select the chart control frame. With the frame selected, you can do the following:

- Drag the frame to a different position in the form or report.
- Drag the sizing handles to change the frame size. This resizes only the frame. Double-click the chart object to activate Microsoft Graph and change the size of the chart itself. By default, the chart frame's Size Mode property is set to Clip. Change this to Stretch or Zoom if you need to resize the frame.
- Use the Formatting (Form/Report) toolbar to change the frame's fill color, border color and width, and special effect.
- Open the property sheet and change any of the control properties including the Row Source, Link Master Fields, and Link Child Fields.

For example, to unlink the Crimes by Beat Number chart from the form, do the following:

1. Open the City Beats Crimes form in Design view.

2. Select the chart control and open the property sheet.

3. Delete the BeatNo field names from the Link Master Fields and Link Child Fields properties.

When you return to Form view and move through the records, you can see the chart no longer changes with each record. Instead, it shows the total crimes for all beats with each record.

TIP   *If disk space is a concern, you can save space by converting the unbound object control to an image control. Select the chart in form or report Design view and choose Format | Change To. Then select Image, the only option available to an unbound OLE object control. The data shown in the chart won't be updated with changes in the underlying record source. Use caution with the transformation because it can't be undone.*

Editing the Row Source Property

If you created the chart in Access with the Chart Wizard, it creates a query whose SQL statement becomes the row source for the chart. You can modify the row source using the query grid or by editing the SQL statement itself.

To change the row source, do the following:

1. Open the Sum Crimes report in Design view and open the property sheet for the chart control.

2. Click the Build button (...) next to the Row Source property to open the SQL Statement: Query Builder dialog box to see the Sum Crimes Chart created from the Sum Crimes query, together with the Query Builder dialog box.

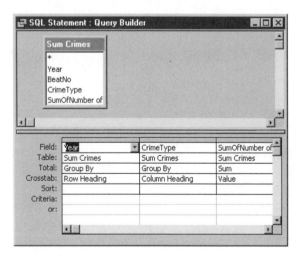

3. To limit the chart to crimes occurring in specific years, enter **Between 2000 And 2002** in the Criteria row of the Year column.

4. Close the Query Builder dialog box and respond Yes to save the changes. Then switch to Print Preview.

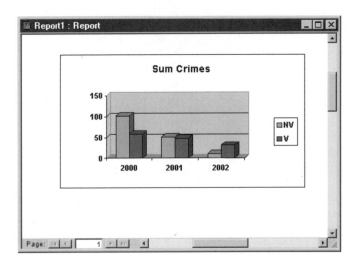

NOTE   *If you plan to limit the time interval before finishing with the wizard, you could also set the chart interval in the Chart Wizard dialog box.*

Editing the Chart Legend

When you add a series to the chart layout that summarizes data within the category, as shown in Figure 15-9, the legend isn't always as informative as possible. The two charts illustrate the same data and are based on tables that contain the same data, but use different table structures.

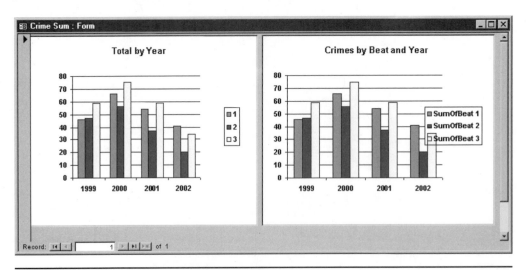

FIGURE 15-9   Two charts illustrating the same data

The chart on the left is based on the Crimes by Beat Number table:

Crimes by Beat Number : Table				
SumLine	Year	BeatNo	CrimeType	Number of Crim
1	1999	1	V	16
2	1999	1	NV	30
3	1999	2	V	12
4	1999	2	NV	35
5	1999	3	V	18
6	1999	3	NV	41
7	2000	1	V	24
8	2000	1	NV	42

Record: 1 of 24

The Chart Wizard created a crosstab query that totals the number of both types of crimes reported for each beat.

The chart legend in the chart on the left takes its values from the value of the field whose Cross tab row shows Column Heading, which is BeatNo (1, 2, and 3). The legend would be more informative if you edited it to read Beat 1, Beat 2, and Beat 3.

Field:	Year	BeatNo	Number of Crimes
Table:	Crimes by Beat Number	Crimes by Beat Number	Crimes by Beat Number
Total:	Group By	Group By	Sum
Crosstab:	Row Heading	Column Heading	Value
Sort:			
Criteria:			
or:			

You have two ways to do this after opening the Query Builder for the Row Source property:

- Open the Query Builder and change the BeatNo field in the query grid to the expression **"Beat "&[BeatNo]**. Be sure to include a space after **Beat** within the quotation marks to separate it from the number. Then close the Query Builder and save the change.

Field:	Year	Expr1: "Beat " & BeatNo	Number of Crimes
Table:	Crimes by Beat Numl		Crimes by Beat Numl
Total:	Group By	Group By	Sum
Crosstab:	Row Heading	Column Heading	Value
Sort:			
Criteria:			
or:			

- Choose View | SQL View (or click the View button and choose SQL View) and change the PIVOT clause from:

```
PIVOT [BeatNo];
```

to:

```
PIVOT "Beat "&[BeatNo];
```

TIP   *If you make the change in the grid, the SQL statement changes to match and vice versa.*

The legend in this chart now reads Beat 1, Beat 2, and Beat 3.

The chart on the right in Figure 15-9 is based on the more compact Crimes by Beat and Year table.

LineNo	Year	Type	Beat 1	Beat 2	Beat 3
1	1999	V	16	12	18
2	1999	NV	30	35	41
3	2000	V	24	18	30
4	2000	NV	42	38	45
5	2001	V	18	10	20
6	2001	NV	36	27	39
7	2002	V	14	8	10
8	2002	NV	27	12	24
(AutoNumber)					

Record: 1 of 8

For this chart, the Chart Wizard created a select query that sums the value in each of the Beat*n* fields by year. The legend shows SumOfBeat 1, SumOfBeat2, and SumOfBeat3. You can use the same two methods to change the legend text, add expressions to the Field row of the query grid, or edit the SQL statement.

Field:	Year	Beat 1	Beat 2	Beat 3	
Table:	Crimes by Beat and Year	Crimes by Beat and Year	Crimes by Beat and Year	Crimes by Beat and Year	
Total:	Group By	Sum	Sum	Sum	
Sort:					
Show:	☑	☑	☑	☑	
Criteria:					
or:					

Open the form in Design view and start the Query Builder as before. Then do one of the following:

- Type **Beat 1:** before the Beat 1 field name. Repeat for Beat 2 and Beat 3 field names.
- Switch to SQL view and edit the AS clauses by deleting "SumOf" from each clause.

CAUTION   *Be sure to leave the brackets around the field names in the SQL statement because they contain spaces.*

```
SQL Statement : Query Builder                                    _ □ ×
SELECT [Crimes by Beat and Year].Year, Sum([Crimes by Beat and Year].[Beat 1]) AS
[SumOfBeat 1], Sum([Crimes by Beat and Year].[Beat 2]) AS [SumOfBeat 2],
Sum([Crimes by Beat and Year].[Beat 3]) AS [SumOfBeat 3]
FROM [Crimes by Beat and Year]
GROUP BY [Crimes by Beat and Year].Year;
```

Save the changes and switch to Form view. Figure 15-10 shows the two charts with their new legends.

Editing with Microsoft Graph

Microsoft Graph is an applet you can use from within Access to edit the charts you created with the Chart Wizard. When you activate Microsoft Graph, special toolbars appear in the Access window you use to edit the chart in place.

Microsoft Graph serves many programs and not all its features apply to Access charts. In this chapter, I cover the main features that help you modify charts you included in Access forms and reports, and leave you to experiment with others.

To activate Microsoft Graph, double-click the chart control in the form or report Design view. Figure 15-11 shows the Entries by Quarter form in the Access window when Microsoft Graph is active. In addition to the form window containing the chart, a Datasheet window appears containing unrelated sample data. Notice the crosshatched border around the chart that indicates Microsoft Graph is currently running.

The title you entered in the Chart Wizard dialog box appears as the chart title in Microsoft Graph, but the data shown in the datasheet is all sample data used for illustration only.

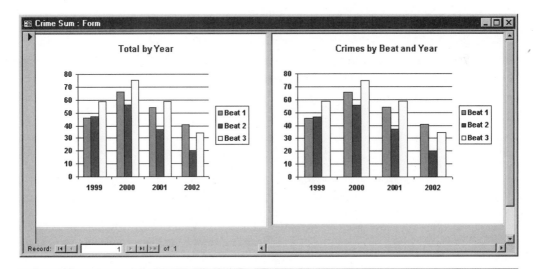

FIGURE 15-10   Charts with legends edited in Access

FIGURE 15-11   A typical Microsoft Graph window

To show or hide the datasheet, do one of the following:

- Choose View | Datasheet, which toggles the Datasheet window in focus and out.
- Right-click the Chart window and choose Datasheet from the shortcut menu.
- Click the Close button to close the Datasheet.

To leave the Microsoft Graph window and return to the Access form or report Design view, click anywhere outside the chart object. The changes you made to the chart in Microsoft Graph appear in the Access chart. You must save the form or report design to save the changes.

Looking at the Microsoft Graph Toolbars

The Microsoft Graph window normally has two toolbars: Standard and Formatting. Three other toolbars are available on demand: Drawing, Picture, and WordArt, which you can use to add special objects to the chart. To display a toolbar, right-click in any toolbar and select the one you want to use. You can also choose from the View | Toolbars menu.

The first combo box on the Standard toolbar is used to select a chart object. The By Row and By Column buttons change the display of the series. Click Chart Type to change to a different type of chart. The Gridlines buttons display or hide the horizontal or vertical gridlines.

The *Graph Formatting* toolbar has many of the common font name, size, weight, and alignment buttons, in addition to a few unique to Microsoft Graph. All these formatting activities are available by selecting the chart element and choosing Format | Selected chart element.

The Increase Decimal button adds one decimal place to the right of the decimal point. The Decrease Decimal removes the right-most one. The three Style buttons add a currency symbol, a percent sign or a comma thousands separator to numeric values.

Changing the Chart Appearance

To change the size of the chart, select the chart area and drag the sizing handles until it reaches the proper size.

Formatting Text Elements   You have the same options when formatting most of the text elements in the chart. Select the element and choose Format | Selected object to open the

Format dialog box. You can also press CTRL-1 to open the Format dialog box for the selected element. The Format Chart Title dialog box has three tabs: Patterns, Font, and Alignment.

NOTE   *Select Fill Effects in the Format dialog box to open another dialog box where you can choose gradients, fill textures, or patterns, and even select a picture to use as a background.*

The Font tab contains the standard font name, size, weight, colors, and effects, such as underline, strikethrough, superscript, and subscript. When you select the chart title or one of the axis titles and choose Format | Selected, the Alignment tab appears in which you can choose the text alignment, plus the orientation. You can have the text displayed vertically or at a specific angle by clicking the arc in the Orientation area.

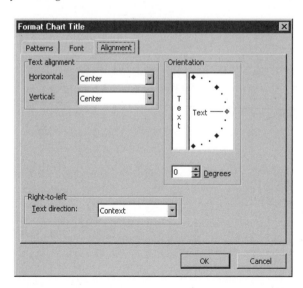

If you select the legend and choose Format | Selected Legend, the Alignment tab is replaced by the Placement tab, in which you can choose to display the legend at the bottom, corner, top, right, or left of the plot area.

Formatting Other Chart Elements   When you select one of the axes and choose Format | Selected, the Format Axis dialog box shows five tabs: Patterns, Scale, Font, Number, and Alignment. The Patterns, Font, and Alignment tabs are the same as for text elements. The other tabs offer the following options:

- The options in the Scale tab depend on which axis you select. If you select the Value (Y) axis, you can choose to set the minimum and maximum values manually for the axis, as well as the major and minor units for the gridlines and tick marks. The alternative is to let Microsoft Graph set these values automatically. You can also specify where the Category (X) axis is to cross the Value axis and whether to arrange the values in reverse order.

- The Number tab gives you a selection of number categories and specific formats for the values on the Value (Y) axis. Also, a check box links the values to the source data. Clear this to create a snapshot chart that doesn't update with changes in the underlying data.
- When you select the Category (X) axis, the formatting options are slightly different. The Scale tab contains options that relate to data categories instead of values.

When you format the data series by clicking one of the columns, bars, or other representation of the data, the Format dialog box contains four or five tabs, depending on the type of data series. For example the column and line series Format dialog box shows five tabs: Patterns, Axis, Y Error Bars, Data Labels, and Options. The 3-D column Format dialog box shows four tabs: Patterns, Shape, Data and Options. The pie series Format dialog box also shows four tabs: Patterns, Axis, Data Labels and Options.

The Patterns tab offers the same color, border, and fill options as before. The other tabs offer the following options:

- The Axis tab specifies whether to plot the series on the primary or secondary axis. The secondary series is plotted against values placed in a Value axis on the right side of the plot area. A sample chart illustrates the choice.

- The Y Error Bars tab gives you the option of displaying the statistical error estimation or the standard deviation in the values either as values or percentages. You can choose to display plus errors, minus errors, or both. This option is handy for presenting the results of statistical survey for which you need to express the level of confidence.

- In the Data Labels tab, you can choose to display the data values and labels with the data series. You can display the values as percentages or in the unit of the value itself.

- In the Options tab for a column data series, you can choose to have the series overlap and set the amount of overlap, as well as specify the amount of space between the sets of data series. Options vary with the different types of data series.

The Shape tab in the 3-D column chart Format dialog box includes other 3-D figures such as pyramids, cylinders and cones.

Tip   *You can add graphics, such as lines, arrows, and shapes, to the chart in Microsoft Graph by displaying the Drawing toolbar and clicking the appropriate button. You may need to use the Format | Placement menu to move the shape in front or in back of the chart elements.*

When you choose to format the data table you added below the chart, you see only two tabs in the Format dialog box: Patterns and Font. To format the plot area or the walls of a chart, you have only the Patterns options.

Changing Chart Type   You have two means of changing the chart type:

- Click the Chart Type toolbar button and choose from the palette containing 18 chart types.

- Choose Chart | Chart Type and choose from the Chart Type dialog box. The Standard Types include 14 types with many sub-types for each. In the Standard Types tab, press and hold the button below the Chart subtype pane to see a sample of the selected chart. The Custom Types tab shows an additional 20 chart types from the built-in list of charts and, if you created any custom chart types, they're displayed when you choose Select from User-Defined.

After making your selection, click OK to apply it to the current chart. You can also specify a chart type as the default chart.

Setting Chart Options   When you choose Chart | Chart Options, the Chart Options dialog box opens with six tabs: Titles, Axes, Gridlines, Legend, Data Labels, and Data Table.

The tabs offer the following options:

- In the Titles tab, you enter the text you want to display as the chart title and the axes titles. You can specify a primary and secondary title for each axis, but only one for the chart itself.

- In the Axes tab, you specify whether to display the axes and choose the method by which to display the Category (X) axis.

- In the Gridlines tab, you specify whether to display the gridlines on one or both of the axes. You can choose to display both major and minor gridlines on each axis.

- In the Legend tab, you choose whether to display the legend with the chart. The Legend tab also gives you the same options as the Placement tab of the Format dialog box for placing the legend: Bottom, Corner, Top, Right, or Left.

- The Data Labels tab includes the same options as the Data Labels tab in the Format Data Series dialog box.

- In the Data Table tab, you can choose to display the data in the underlying data source in a grid attached to the bottom of the chart. When you choose to display the data table, you can also display the legend keys with it. Figure 15-12 shows the Total by Year chart with the corresponding data table. If you choose not to display the legend keys, then the colored squares at the left of the data table row headings don't appear. The Data Table option isn't available for several of the chart types, such as pie, XY scatter, and surface.

NOTE *If you need a statistical analysis of the data over time, you can add a trendline. The Add Trendline option in the Chart menu draws a line in the chart, which can be used in regression analysis of a large sample of recorded data. Once a trend is established, the line can be extended to predict future performance. Trendlines are also used to create a moving average, which smoothes out fluctuations in data and shows the pattern or trend more clearly.*

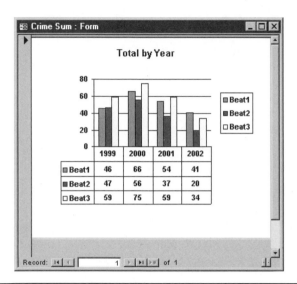

FIGURE 15-12 Adding the data table to the chart

Troubleshooting Charts

Sometimes the changes you make in Microsoft Graph fail to show up in the chart when you switch to Form view or Print Preview in Access, even though they appeared in Design view. For example, you can change the column headings in the Microsoft Graph datasheet to display the text you want in the legend. When you return to Access, the new labels appear in the design, but not in Form view or Print Preview.

The reason for this seeming inconsistency is you have several places in which to specify the chart information and Access must set an order of precedence to decide which values to use. The order is:

- First, the data in the underlying table or query—for example, the field names or the expressions in the Field row of the query grid.
- Second, the contents of the Row Source property.
- Last, the data entered in Microsoft Graph.

So, if you set the legend text in Microsoft Graph, but the underlying query column headings are different, they override the Microsoft Graph settings.

If the columns don't appear in the order you want in the chart, open the Query Builder and rearrange the fields, left to right, in the order you want them sorted. Then choose the Sort order for each.

Summary

This chapter concludes the discussion of customized output from Access and brings to a close the part of the book devoted to retrieving and presenting information. Trying to anticipate what every reader needs in the area of information storage and retrieval is impossible, but I did attempt to give you a wide view of the capabilities within Access. The many Help topics can expand on the information presented in these nine chapters.

The next chapter begins the discussion of improving the Access workplace. The topics covered include changing the workplace options, setting startup options, and adding commands to the startup sequence. Later, in the next part of the book, you learn about creating and using macros to further automate the database application.

PART

Improving the Workplace

Customizing the Workplace

Many of the features discussed in this chapter were briefly mentioned in previous chapters and some are covered later. The purpose of this chapter is to capture all the workplace options in one place for easy reference. Using the many Access and Windows options, you can change the default appearance and behavior of a database application, keyboard actions, hyperlinks, search and filter routines, and form and report design windows, among many other aspects of your workplace.

In addition to the changes you can make that affect the current Access database, you can change many startup options, such as displaying a startup form, opening a specific database, and displaying custom menus and toolbars.

This chapter also discusses changes you can make to set the appearance and behavior of the helpful Office Assistant.

Personalizing the Workplace

You needn't accommodate yourself to the layout and behavior of the Access environment the way it is when first installed. The Access developers attempted to design a workplace that would be appropriate for most users, but if you want to change some aspects, this is easy. For example, if you have a large screen, you might want to see a larger font size. You can, of course, change each of these factors every time you work with Access, but changing the default settings saves time.

Rearranging Icons

In the Database window, each page displays icons representing objects of that type in the current database. You can change the icon size and amount of detail shown with the icons, as well as arrange them in a specific order.

The buttons at the top of the Database window and the commands in the View menu contain the means for displaying the object icons as follows:

- *Large Icons* shows expanded object icons in rows with the name below each one.

- *Small Icons* shows smaller object icons in rows, but with the name beside each one.

- *List* shows the object icons in columns with the name beside each one.

- *Details* shows each object icon in a single row with its name and four additional columns containing other information about the object: the description you entered in the object property sheet, the time/date the object was last modified, the time/date the object was created, and the type of object.

NOTE   *To add a description that will appear when you choose Details, right-click the object icon in the Database window and choose Properties from the shortcut menu. Enter the description in the Description box in the General tab, and then click OK.*

When you show the object icons with the details, you can make other adjustments to the display:

- Resize the column width by dragging the vertical column separator in the column heading.

- Resize the column width to fit the widest information in it by double-clicking the column separator.

- Sort the icons by one of the detail categories by clicking once in the column heading to sort in ascending order. Click the column heading again to change the order to descending.

The View | Arrange Icons commands sort the icons in ascending order by name, type, date/time created, or date/time modified. These commands accomplish the same arrangements as clicking once in the column headings of the details. The Auto Arrange command, which is available only if you selected Large Icons or Small Icons, moves the icons back into the specified arrangement.

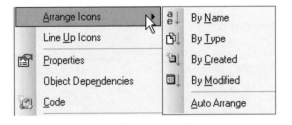

You can drag the icons to another position in the Database window, and then use the View | Line Up Icons command to straighten up the rows and columns. The Line Up Icons command moves the icons slightly to the nearest row/column intersection. Line Up Icons is only available if you're showing large or small icons.

Creating a Shortcut

If you use an Access object regularly, you can create a shortcut that launches Access and opens the database object directly from the Windows desktop. The easiest way is to drag the object from the Access Database window to the Windows desktop. You must first resize the Access window so you can see the area where you want to place the shortcut icon. When you double-click the shortcut, Access opens the database that stores the object and displays the object.

NOTE *To delete a shortcut, click it and press DEL. This doesn't delete the object itself, only the shortcut.*

Another way to create a shortcut is to use the Create Shortcut command on the object shortcut menu. With this method, you can create a shortcut in a location other than the desktop by entering a path in the Create Shortcut dialog box. Type a new path in the *Location* box or click *Browse* to search for the desired location and have Access fill in the path for you. If the database is on a network, Access automatically selects *This Database is on the Network* and fills in the path in the *Full Network Path* box.

NOTE *If you moved the database that's the destination of a shortcut, remove the shortcut and create a new one with the new path.*

Setting Workplace Options

Access is installed with certain characteristics set as defaults. For example, the width of the print margins, the default database folder, the color of hyperlinks, the gridlines, and the font styles in a datasheet are all set by default. If you change specific default values when you work with a database, you can reset the default value to the one you use the most. All default values can be overridden later, if necessary.

NOTE *Access stores most option settings in the workgroup information file, instead of in your database file. Changes you make to those settings in the Options dialog box apply to any database opened or created by a colleague who uses the same workgroup information file. See Chapter 24 for more about the workgroup information file.*

To change default values, choose Tools | Options and click the tab that contains the values you want to change. To change values on more than one tab, click another tab. When you finish setting the default values, click OK to close the dialog box.

The Options dialog box has 12 tabs, as shown in Figure 16-1. The following sections describe the commonly applied options.

NOTE   *When you open the Options dialog box, the visible tab is the one you last accessed.*

View Options

The options on the View tab (refer to Figure 16-1) all relate to what you see at startup, while working in the Database window, or when creating a macro.

TIP   *If the underlined shortcut keys don't show in the options, press* ALT *to display them.*

In the *Show* group, you can choose to show or hide the following items:

- *Status bar* displays the status bar at the bottom of the screen.
- *Startup Task Pane* displays the opening Access side pane that enables you to select an existing database or to create a new one.
- *New object shortcuts* displays the two or three items in the Database window you can double-click to start a new database object. For example, Create a form by using the wizard.
- *Hidden objects* displays any object in the Database window that's been specified as hidden by setting the Hidden property to Yes. The object appears as a dimmed icon.
- *System objects* displays system tables created by Access or the user as dimmed icons. The names of system objects created by Access all begin with MSys and aren't

FIGURE 16-1
Setting default
View options in the
Options dialog box

normally displayed. A user can also create a system object by giving it a name with USys as the first four characters.

- *Windows in Taskbar* places a button on the Windows taskbar for every open database object or window.

In the *Show in Macro Design* group, you have only two options, both of which relate to creating and editing macros.

- The *Names column* setting displays the Macro Name column by default in the macro design grid where you enter an optional macro name.

- The *Conditions column* setting displays the Condition column by default in the macro design grid where you enter the conditions under which the macro action is to take place.

See Chapter 19 for more information about creating macros.

The *Click options in database window* setting offers you the choice between clicking once or double-clicking to open an object in the Database window. The default is Double-click open, but if you want to click only once to open an object, change to Single-click open.

NOTE   *If you already changed to single-click in the Windows Control Panel, you also have to change it in Access.*

General Options

The General tab (see Figure 16-2) shows options that don't fit into any of the other categories of settings.

- You can enter any number in the *Print margins* group that's compatible with your printer and paper size, ranging from 0 to the height or width of the printed page. Override the default settings established here by running Page Setup before printing a form or report.

- The *Recently used file list* setting determines the number of file names to display when you choose File in the menu bar or when the Getting Started task pane appears. Enter the desired number or choose from the drop-down list.

- If you select the *Provide feedback with sound* option, you activate sounds to accompany such tasks as a print job completion or an alert notification. You can customize sounds for this option through the Sounds dialog box in the Windows Control Panel. If you installed a sound card after you installed Office 2003, you must reinstall the .wav files from Office Setup.

CAUTION   *The sound option affects all Office programs.*

- Checking *Compact on Close* automatically compacts and repairs the database when you close it, if the size will be reduced by at least 256K.

FIGURE 16-2
Setting General
default options

- Checking *Remove personal information from file properties on save* automatically deletes your name, the name of your company, and any other personal information you entered in the Database Properties dialog box.

- The *Default database folder* specifies the default folder in which you want to save new databases. Enter the complete path to the folder.

- The *Web Options* button opens a dialog box in which you can specify the default appearance of new hyperlinks. You can choose the text colors for hyperlinks, one color before you have clicked it to jump to the target and a different color after you have jumped to it. You can also include underlining with the address.

Sharing on the Web

SharePoint Team Services is new with Office 2003 and provides a means to collaborate among multiple users over the Web. From Access, you can use the SharePoint Team to link tables to, import tables from, and export tables to web site lists. The SharePoint Services web site uses Windows .NET Server 2003 with Internet Information Services (IIS) as the web server. All user data, web data, and application information is stored in Microsoft SQL Server databases.

- The *Service Options* button opens a dialog box where you can choose to participate in customer feedback, look for material on Office Online, or join a Shared Workspace.

- The *Use four-digit year formatting* applies the format to the current database or to all databases, even if the Format property of the field or control is set to show a two-digit year.

- The *Name AutoCorrect* group helps Access propagate name changes to objects that refer to the renamed object. The group offers three options that help fix common side effects that occur when you make changes in an object via a user interface. Access stores an identifier for each object and tracks naming information. When Access notices an object has been changed since the last Name AutoCorrect, it runs it again for all items in that object. For example, if you added a text box to a form that's bound to the Alpha Card table and you change the Alpha Card table name to Alpha Card Plus, Access can track down all the items from the original Alpha Card and change their names to match the new table name.

The three options you can check for Name AutoCorrect are as follows:

- *Track name AutoCorrect info* stores information it needs to correct naming errors, but doesn't immediately correct them. You can also look at object dependencies, so you're aware of potential renaming problems. Keeping this option checked is a good idea.

- *Perform name AutoCorrect* tries to update references to objects that you renamed. This doesn't cover references in macros and Visual Basic modules.

- *Log name AutoCorrect changes* creates a log named AutoCorrect Log that contains the changes it makes to the database each time it runs Name AutoCorrect.

- In the *New database sort order* setting, you can choose from a list of 33 language settings that change the default alphabetic sort order for new databases. The General setting applies to English, French, German, Italian, Portuguese, and modern Spanish. To change the sort order for an existing database, select the language, and then compact the database.

Edit/Find Options

The Edit/Find tab (see Figure 16-3) shows settings that all relate to finding, replacing, and filtering records in the current database.

FIGURE 16-3
Setting Edit/Find
default options

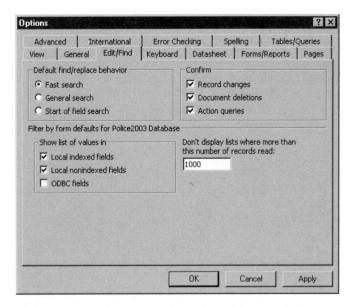

The *Default find/replace behavior* setting determines the extent of the search. These options are also available on an immediate basis in the Find and Replace dialog box.

- *Fast search* searches the current field only and matches the entire field.
- *General search* searches all the fields and matches any part of the field.
- *Start of field search* searches the current field and matches only the beginning characters in the field.

The *Confirm* group requires Access to display a message requiring a confirmation of the current operation under specific conditions, such as when a record changes (*Record changes*), when you delete a database object (*Document deletions*), or when you run an action query (*Action queries*).

The *Filter by form defaults for…* group contains options that limit or extend the size of the value list displayed in the Filter By Form window and sets the maximum number of records to read to build a value list for a given field. The more fields you include in the filter operation, the longer it takes. These settings apply only to the current database.

- *Local indexed fields* limits the value list to the indexed fields in the current database.
- *Local nonindexed fields* includes the fields in the current database that aren't indexed.
- *ODBC fields* includes fields in a linked table in an external source.
- Enter a number in the *Don't display lists where more than this number of records read* box to set the maximum number of records you want to read to build the list of unique values for the field. If the number of records exceeds this amount, no values at all are displayed for the field in the Filter By Form window.

Keyboard Options
The settings in the Keyboard tab (see Figure 16-4) determine the consequences of pressing certain keys, such as ENTER, TAB, RIGHT ARROW, and LEFT ARROW.

FIGURE 16-4
Setting Keyboard
default options

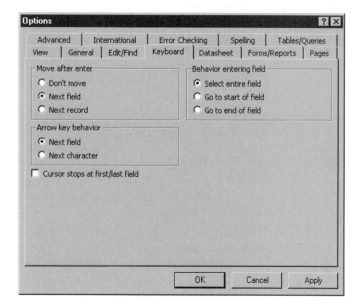

The *Move after enter* option refers to the behavior of the insertion point (cursor) after pressing ENTER.

- *Don't move* keeps the insertion point in the current field.
- *Next field* moves the insertion point to the next field. This setting works with the *Behavior entering field* settings to complete the behavior.
- *Next record* moves the insertion point to the next record in the table or form.

The *Arrow key behavior* settings specify what occurs when you press RIGHT ARROW and LEFT ARROW.

- *Next field* moves the insertion point to the next or previous field when you press RIGHT ARROW or LEFT ARROW. To move the insertion point within the field, press F2 to enter Edit mode, and then use the arrow keys.
- *Next character* moves the insertion point to the next or previous character in the current field when you press RIGHT ARROW or LEFT ARROW.

The *Behavior entering field* group determines what happens when the insertion point enters a field.

- *Select entire field* selects all the characters in the field.
- *Go to start of field* places the insertion point in front of the first character in the field without selecting any characters.
- *Go to end of field* places the insertion point at the end of the field after the last character without selecting any characters.

The *Cursor stops at first/last field* setting locks the insertion point within the current record and prevents the RIGHT ARROW and LEFT ARROW keys from moving the insertion point to the next or previous record.

Datasheet Options

The Datasheet tab (see Figure 16-5) includes the following default value settings:

- *Default colors* enables you to specify the default font, background, and gridline colors for the datasheet. When you click the drop-down arrow, a list of 16 colors with samples appears. Click the desired color.

- *Default font* enables you to select the font name from the list of fonts installed on your system. You can also choose from nine font weights ranging from Thin to Heavy; the default setting is Normal. Choose the font size from the drop-down list that contains font sizes ranging from 8 to 72 points or enter a number in the box. Check *Italic* and/or *Underline* to set that style as default.

- *Default gridlines showing* determines whether to show or hide the horizontal and vertical gridlines in the datasheet.

- *Default column width* specifies the width of the columns in a new datasheet. You can change the width easily in the datasheet by dragging the column dividers. Type a new default width in the box. The default width uses the system unit of measure.

- *Default cell effect* is normally set to *Flat*, but you can change this to *Raised* or *Sunken* to create a special effect in the datasheet.

- *Show animations,* when checked, shows movement in the datasheet. For example, when you insert or delete a column, the other columns can be seen to slide over.

- The *Show Smart Tags on Datasheets* setting, when checked, displays the Smart Tag Action button when you move to a field that has a Smart Tag attached.

Form and Report Options

The settings in the Forms/Reports tab of the Options dialog box (see Figure 16-6) all relate to designing a form or report.

FIGURE 16-5
Setting Datasheet default options

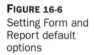

FIGURE 16-6
Setting Form and
Report default
options

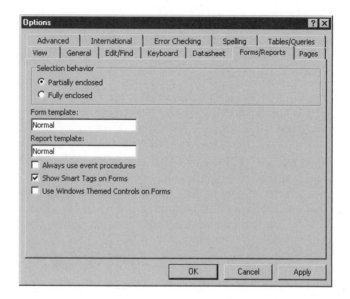

- The *Selection behavior* group relates to the results of drawing a rectangle in the design to select controls. *Partially enclosed* selects all controls with any part within the drawn rectangle, while *Fully enclosed* selects only those controls totally within the drawn rectangle.

- The *Form template* and *Report template* settings enable you to specify an existing form or report as the template for new designs. Type the name of the form or report you want to use as the default template.

- The *Always use event procedures* setting, when selected, takes you directly to the VB Editor window when you click the Build button in a property sheet, bypassing the Choose Builder dialog box. With the setting cleared, the Choose Builder dialog box appears, offering the choice of Expression Builder, Macro Builder, or Code Builder.

- The *Show Smart Tags on Forms* setting, when checked, displays the Smart Tag Action button when you move to a control that has a Smart Tag attached.

- The *Use Windows Themed Controls on Forms,* when checked, applies the Windows theme (or scheme, depending on your version of Windows) set in the Display Properties dialog box to Access forms.

Page Options

The Pages tab contains two groups of options. The *Default Designer Properties* specify design features, such as colors, style, and section indent size. You can use the *Default Database/ Project Properties* section to enter the default page folder or enter an ODC or Microsoft Data Link to use as the default connection file.

PART III

Advanced Options

The Advanced tab (see Figure 16-7) contains five groups of options and a list of timing settings. Many of the settings in this tab relate to a multiple-user environment and interfacing with external applications.

- Use the *DDE operations* options to set the behavior of the database when dealing with other applications. *Ignore DDE requests* does just that—it ignores Dynamic Data Exchange (DDE) requests from external sources. *Enable DDE refresh* allows updating DDE links at an interval specified in the Refresh Interval setting. See Chapter 23 for more information about interacting with external applications.

- Enter the name of the one or more values you want the Command function to return in the *Command-line arguments* text box. The command-line arguments customize the way Access starts up. For example, open a database automatically, run a macro, supply a user account name or password, or open a database for exclusive access or as read-only.

The next group of selections in the Advanced tab deals with shared databases and interactions with external sources.

- *OLE/DDE timeout (sec)* sets the period of time after which Access reattempts to perform an OLE or DDE operation that failed. Enter a number between 0 and 300 seconds.

- The *Refresh interval (sec)* option relates to the *Enable DDE refresh* option and specifies the time after which Access automatically updates records in a Datasheet or Form view. Enter a number between 1 and 32,766.

- The *Number of update retries* refers to the number of times Access tries to save a changed record locked by another user. Enter a number between 0 and 10.

FIGURE 16-7
Setting the
Advanced default
options

- Set the *ODBC refresh interval (sec)* to a number between 1 and 32,766 to specify the interval after which Access automatically refreshes records you're accessing through ODBC. This is only used if the database is shared on a network.

- The *Update retry interval (msec)* option sets the time (in milliseconds) after which Access automatically tries to save a changed record locked by another user. Enter a number between 0 and 1,000.

In the *Default File Format* option, you can choose between Access 2000 and Access 2002-2003 as the default format for new databases.

In the *Default open mode* group, you have a choice between *Shared,* which allows others to open the database at the same time you have it open, and *Exclusive,* which gives you sole access to the database. See Chapter 24 for more information about running Access in a shared environment.

You can set the *Default record locking* option to *No locks,* which doesn't lock records while they're being edited; *All records,* which locks all the records in a form or datasheet (and the underlying tables) as long as the form or datasheet is open; or *Edited record,* which locks only the record currently being edited.

The last option in the Advanced tab is *Open databases using record-level locking,* which minimizes the page size required by the Unicode format representation. When you check this option, instead of locking an entire page that might include several records, only one row or record is locked at a time.

International Options

The International tab (see Figure 16-8) contains options that deal with the direction and alignment of text, and the movement of the cursor through data. These have been added to accommodate Middle Eastern language users.

FIGURE 16-8
Setting
International
default options

The *Default direction* group offers the choice between Left-to-right and Right-to-left.

- The *Left-to-right* selection starts entering data in the left-most column and places the next data in the column to the right, and so on.
- *Right-to-left* places the first field in the right-most column and places the next in the column to the left, and so on. To apply this option, you must have Right-To-Left language enabled by Microsoft Office Language Settings.

In the *General alignment,* you have a choice between Interface mode and Text mode.

- The *Interface mode* sets General alignment consistent with the user interface language. For example, if the direction is left-to-right, the text is aligned left.
- The *Text mode* sets General alignment according to the direction of the first language-specific characters it encounters.
  - Check *Use Hijri Calendar* to change to the Middle Eastern calendar.
  - In the *Cursor movement* group, you have a choice between Logical and Visual.
- If you choose *Logical,* the cursor moves within bidirectional text, according to the direction of the language it's encountering. For example, if you have English and Arabic words in the same sentence, the insertion point moves left-to-right in the English text, and then starts at the rightmost character of the Arabic word and continues to move in a right-to-left direction.
- If you choose *Visual,* the cursor moves within bidirectional text by moving to the next adjacent character. For example, if you have English and Arabic text in the same sentence, the insertion point moves left-to-right through the English text, and then continues at the leftmost character of the Arabic word and continues in the left-to-right direction.

Error Checking Options

Automatic error checking is new with Access 2003 and most welcome. It identifies errors in form and report designs, and offers suggestions for correcting them. You can choose to apply automatic error checking to five general types of errors. You set these rules in the Error Checking tab of the Options dialog box. See Chapter 10 for examples of how error checking can help with form and report design.

To request error checking, check the *Enable error-checking* box. Then choose a color for the error indicator, the small triangle that appears in the upper-left corner of the control that caused the error.

The categories of rules you can specify include the following:

- *Unassociated label and control* that occurs when you select a label and a control not associated with each other.
- *New unassociated labels* that occurs when you add a label to a form or report not associated with another control.

FIGURE 16-9
Setting Error
Checking default
options

- *Keyboard shortcut errors* that occur when you select a control on a form that shows an invalid shortcut key (the underlined character you can use with ALT to move focus to the control), for example, an unassociated label, a duplicate shortcut key, or a space used as the shortcut key.

- *Invalid control properties* that occur when you select a control with invalid values in one or more properties.

- *Common report errors* that occur when the report has an invalid sorting and grouping definition. Also occurs when the report width exceeds the paper width.

Spelling Options

The Spelling options tab contains options for adjusting the AutoCorrect feature, changing the dictionary, and setting exceptions to correcting apparent misspellings. The spelling options are shared with other Office users.

Table and Query Options

The Tables/Queries tab of the Options dialog box is divided into two major sections: one for table design and the other for query design (see Figure 16-10).

The Table design group includes field size and type choices, as well as specifying prefixes to use for automatically indexing fields. The Table design default settings include the following:

- The *Default field sizes* group includes the default size for text and number data type fields. You can enter any number in the *Text* box and choose from the drop-down

FIGURE 16-10
Setting Table and
Query default
options

list in the *Number* box. The number choices are Byte, Integer, Long Integer, Single, Double, Decimal, and Replication ID.

- *Default field type* setting is usually Text, but you can select any of the nine field types as the default, including OLE Object, Hyperlink, or Memo.

- The *AutoIndex on Import/Create* setting is used when you import a table from an external source or create a new table in Design view. This setting tells Access to index on all fields automatically that begin or end with the characters you type in the box. Multiple entries are separated by semicolons. For example, the entries in the AutoIndex box instruct Access to create an index on all fields whose names begin or end with the characters ID, key, code, or num.

The *Show Property Update Options buttons,* when checked, gives you the option of propagating property changes you made in a table or query to controls bound to that field. The *Query design* default settings include the following:

- Checking *Show table names* displays the table names in the Table row of the query grid. This helps to keep track of the field source when multiple tables are used in a query.

- Checking *Output all fields* displays all the fields in a query's underlying tables and queries when you run the query. The fields aren't added to the query grid. When you select this option, only the new queries are affected.

- The *Enable AutoJoin* option automatically creates an inner join between two tables in the query grid. If you want to define the relationships yourself, clear the option. For two tables to be autojoined, they must have fields with the same name and of the same data type, and one of the fields must be the primary key field for that table.

- The *Query design font* options set the default font and size for the query results.

- The *Run permissions* setting determines whether others are permitted to view data retrieved by queries or to run action queries. The *User's* setting applies the permissions defined for that classification of user. If you change it to *Owner's*, all users have the owner's permission to view or run the query, but only the owner can save changes to the query or change the ownership of the query. Changing the default setting affects only new queries.

- Choose the *SQL Server Compatible Syntax (ANSI 92)* option if you want Access to format queries for the current or all new databases exclusively in ANSI 92 standard syntax. This setting ensures SQL server compatibility.

Setting Some Command Bar Default Options

Access provides the opportunity to change some of the command bar default options, such as whether to show ScreenTips and, if you do, also to show the shortcut key combinations that accomplish the same thing. You can change the size of the buttons on the default toolbars and add animation to the menu bar as well.

To change default command bar settings, choose View | Toolbars | Customize or right-click anywhere in a toolbar or the menu bar and choose Customize from the shortcut menu. In the Customize dialog box, click the Options tab (see Figure 16-11).

FIGURE 16-11
Changing default menu and toolbar settings

In the *Other* group of options in the Options tab, check *Large Icons* to enlarge the toolbar buttons. To return the buttons to their original size, check the option again.

When you click the drop-down arrow next to Font in one of the Formatting toolbars, you see the names of the available fonts, each displayed in its respective font. If you want to view the font names in the default font (usually Arial), clear the *List font names in their font* option.

Although the ScreenTips that pop up when you rest the mouse pointer on a toolbar button can be helpful, you can suppress them by clearing the *Show ScreenTips on toolbars* setting. To restore the ScreenTips, repeat the process and check the option. If you check *Show ScreenTips on toolbars*, the *Show shortcut keys in ScreenTips* option becomes available, displaying the corresponding shortcut key combination—for example, Cut (CTRL-X).

CAUTION   *These settings affect all the Office programs, so make sure you want these settings in effect when you're working in Word or Excel.*

Choose from the *Menu animations* drop-down list to change the way menus display when you choose a command. You have the choice of (System default), Random, Unfold, Slide, and Fade.

See Chapter 20 for more information about customizing menus and toolbars, and how to make use of the other two tabs in the Customize dialog box.

Creating Custom Groups

Groups help you organize different database objects by placing shortcuts to the objects in custom group. For example, you can group all the pieces you use to create and print your company's annual report. You can always place an object in the Favorites group, but if you want to begin grouping objects from your Access database in a group other than that, you can create a new custom group. You can also add objects from other applications to the group.

To create a new group, right-click one of the objects you want to add to the group and choose Add to Group | New Group from the shortcut menu. A New Group dialog box opens where you enter the name for the new group. Then click OK.

You can also create a new group without adding an object to it immediately by right-clicking an existing group button, such as Favorites, and choosing New Group from the shortcut menu. Then name the group and click OK.

The new group name is added to the Groups list in the left pane of the Database window.

To add another object to the group, right-click the object in the Database window, and then point to Add to Group in the shortcut menu and select the name of the group where you want to place the object.

TIP   *You can also drag the object icon to the group name in the left pane of the Database window and drop it there.*

The object always remains in its original location. Only a shortcut is added to the group.

To rename or delete a group, right-click the group button and choose Rename Group or Delete Group from the shortcut menu. If you choose to delete a group that contains shortcuts, Access warns you all the shortcuts will also be permanently deleted. The original object is unaffected by deleting the shortcut from the group.

If you choose to rename the group, a Rename Group dialog box opens where you can type a new name, and then click OK.

Changing the Way Access Starts

Access receives information from several sources that tell it how to start and what to show when it does start. Some startup settings affect only the current Access database, while others affect the way Access itself appears and behaves. The easiest way to control Access at startup is by setting options in the Startup dialog box.

The startup options you set in the Startup dialog box apply only to the current database, so you can choose different options for each of your databases or applications. When you set a startup option, such as a title bar with a custom name and icon, Access automatically sets the corresponding database property for you. To set startup options, choose Tools | Startup to open the Startup dialog box.

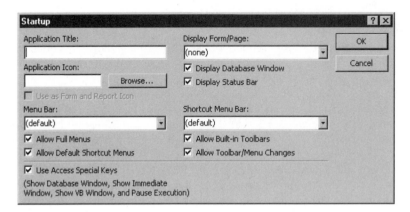

Most of the changes in the startup options take effect the next time you open the database. Only the Application Title and Application Icon options take effect as soon as you close the dialog box.

TIP   *After you set startup options, you can bypass them by pressing* SHIFT *when you open the database.*

- *Application Title*   To display a custom title in the Database window title bar, enter the text you want to display in the Application Title box.
- *Application Icon*   To add a custom icon to the title bar in place of the default Access icon in the Windows title bar, type the name of the bitmap (.bmp) or icon (.ico) file in the Application Icon box. If you don't know the name of the file you want to use, click the Browse button next to the box and use the Icon Browser to locate the file.

TIP   *If you're creating an application to be distributed to multiple users, you should place the icon file in the same folder as the host application.*

- *Menu Bar*   When you create your own custom global menu bar that offers limited commands, you can control what your users can do with the database. Use this option to replace the default menu bar with your custom menu bar by choosing the name of the menu from the drop-down list. This choice has no effect on the custom menu bars you created for a form or report. See Chapter 20 for information about creating custom startup menu bars.
- *Allow Full Menus*   When this option is checked, the user can have access to all the built-in menus. If you clear this option, Access hides certain menus, such as View and Insert, which give the user the power to open an object in Design view and make changes.

- *Allow Default Shortcut Menus* Leave this option checked to allow access to the built-in shortcut menus that appear when right-clicking an object, a toolbar, or a menu bar. Clear the option to disable all shortcut menus. If you want the user to use the shortcut menus, but not to customize toolbars and menu bars, leave the option checked, but clear the *Allow Toolbar/Menu Changes* check box.

- *Display Form/Page* Many applications display a special form or data access page when opening—either as a welcoming screen or as a switchboard with a list of choices of actions to take next, such as enter/edit data or preview a report. After you create the special form and save it in the current database, you can use it as the startup form. To choose a form for display at startup, click the drop-down arrow in the Display Form Page box and choose the form from the list of forms in the current database.

- *Display Database Window* If you don't want the user to see the Database window behind the opening form, clear the Display Database Window check mark. The Database window might still be accessible by pressing F11. If you hide the Database window, the startup form must be a switchboard with navigation tools for using the database. See Chapter 21 for more information about creating and using switchboard forms.

- *Display Status Bar* Clear this option to prevent displaying the status bar at the bottom of the window.

NOTE *This option applies only to the current database, but you can keep from displaying the status bar in all databases by clearing the* Status Bar *option in the View tab of the Options dialog box.*

- *Shortcut Menu Bar* Select the name of a custom shortcut menu to replace the built-in shortcut menus for forms and reports in the current database. Choose Default to use the built-in shortcut menus.

- *Allow Built-in Toolbars* Check this option to give the user access to all the built-in toolbars in the current database or to clear the option to prevent user access. If you want the user to use, but not to modify, the built-in toolbars, select this option and clear the Allow Toolbar/Menu Changes option. If you want the user to use and modify the toolbars, select both options.

- *Allow Toolbar/Menu Changes* Check this option to permit the user to modify any of the built-in or custom toolbars and menu bars in the database. Clear the option to lock the toolbars, which disables the right mouse button click on a toolbar and the Tools | Customize command.

TIP *If this option is cleared, the user can still move, size, and lock toolbars and menu bars, unless specifically denied in the Customize dialog box for the toolbar or menu bar.*

- *Use Access Special Keys* When selected, you can use the special key combinations that display the Database or Immediate window, menu bars, or modules in the

Module window. If you cleared this option and specified a custom menu bar, the built-in menu bar isn't accessible. The special keys are as follows:

- F11, which brings the Database window to the front if you're in the Access window
- CTRL-G, which displays the Immediate window
- CTRL-BREAK, which, in a project, stops retrieving records from the server
- ALT-F11, which starts the Visual Basic Editor

CAUTION   *You can use the selections in the Startup dialog box instead of, or in conjunction with, the actions contained in the AutoExec macro. An AutoExec macro is a series of actions that take place when you open the database, but after the Startup options have taken effect. In view of the sequence of events, avoiding conflicts between the two is important. For example, the AutoExec macro could undo the options you set in the Startup dialog box. See Chapter 19 for more information about AutoExec macros and how they are used.*

Modifying the Office Assistant

If you decide you want to use the *Office Assistant*, it can offer help and tips, as well as answer questions relating to the Office program you're currently using. Just like the list you see when you type a question in the question box, the Assistant can display the list, plus specific tips about using the features or keyboard shortcuts more effectively and a variety of messages.

The Office Assistant is an animated character with sound, which you can change to any one of the six characters that come with Office. You can drag the Assistant anywhere on the screen to be less obtrusive. You can also set many options to customize the Office Assistant to match your needs.

Showing and Hiding

To open the Office Assistant, choose Help | Show the Office Assistant. If the Office Assistant hasn't been installed, Access asks if you want to install it now. Click Yes. You could be prompted to insert the Microsoft Office CD. To hide the Office Assistant, right-click the character and choose Hide from the Shortcut menu. You can also choose Help | Hide the Office Assistant to close the assistant. To close the Office Assistant balloon, click the character.

Setting Office Assistant Options

To customize the help offered by the Assistant, you can change some of the options. If the Assistant balloon is visible, click Options to display the Options dialog box (see Figure 16-12). If the balloon isn't visible, right-click the character and choose Options from the shortcut menu.

To prevent the Office Assistant from appearing at all, clear the *Use the Office Assistant* option. The other options, except for the *Reset my tips* button, become unavailable.

FIGURE 16-12
Setting Office
Assistant options

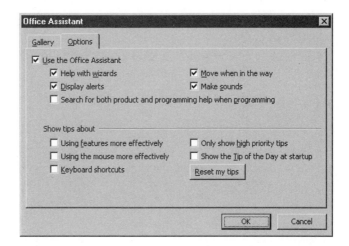

The remaining options in the upper group specify the Assistant's behavior:

- *Help with wizards* makes the Office Assistant available to help when you're running an Access wizard. An option at the bottom of the final wizard dialog box offers this choice.

- *Display alerts* displays messages from Access in the Assistant window instead of a message box, if the Assistant is open.

- Select the *Search for both product and programming help when programming* option if you want both Access and programming help when generating VBA code.

- *Move when in the way* moves the Office Assistant out of the way of other screen elements, such as dialog boxes.

- If you have a sound card and speakers installed, *Make sounds* turns on the sound effects for the Assistant. The sounds vary with the character.

The selections in the *Show tips about* group tell the Office Assistant what types of tips to display.

- *Using features more effectively* displays tips about getting the most from Access features.

- *Using the mouse more effectively* displays tips about speeding up your work with the mouse.

- *Keyboard shortcuts* shows you shortcut key combinations that can also speed up your work.

- Selecting *Only show high priority tips* displays only important tips, such as those that save time.

PART III

- *Show the Tip of the Day at startup* displays a randomly selected tip each time you start an Office program.
- Click the *Reset my tips* button to allow the Office Assistant to repeat tips already shown.

Choosing a Different Assistant

To change the character used by the Office Assistant, click Options in the Assistant balloon, and then click the Gallery tab (see Figure 16-13). Use the Next and Back buttons to preview each of the alternative characters, watch their actions, and hear the accompanying sounds.

When you find the one you want, click OK. Access asks if you want to install the new Assistant. Click Yes to install it. After the change of character, the Office Assistant dialog box closes and the new Assistant appears on the screen.

Summary

This chapter has given you an overall view of the changes you can make to your Access environment using several different tools. Most of the customization deals with the appearance and behavior of Access and its objects, such as rearranging the desktop and creating shortcuts to commonly used objects.

The many options available in the Options dialog box are discussed and the valid settings are listed. You can also change the way Access starts by specifying a startup form and a custom title bar and icon.

The Office Assistant is a helpful tool when you're first learning how to use Access. You can even customize the Assistant by changing the options or installing a new animated character. Once you become familiar with the basics, you can eliminate the busy Office Assistant.

The next chapter concentrates on improving Access performance, especially with large databases. It discusses using the Access Analyzer Wizards and the Database Utilities to streamline your database and ensure reliability.

FIGURE 16-13
Choosing a different Office Assistant character

Improving Database Performance

In this hectic information age, we're always looking for ways to speed up operations and improve the accuracy and consistency of the results. Optimization is the ultimate goal and stacking up performance improvements is a way to get close. Access includes many ways you can help yourself create an efficient database, including the *Analyzer tools,* which can examine the organization of your database and suggest ways you can improve the distribution of information among the tables and speed overall database performance.

One of the most important goals of a database is to maintain accurate and complete information. A new tool in Access 2003 helps you to prevent errors by publishing the interdependencies among your database objects. So, if you rename or delete an object, you can find out what else is affected.

For the purpose of security and reliability, you also have tools to back up and restore databases in case of emergency. Other tools compact the database to take less disk space and repair damaged databases.

Optimizing a Database

Access provides two analytical tools that can save you a lot of time and help you optimize a new database. You can also help to optimize the performance of a database, without using the Analyzers, by focusing on each of the elements that comprise the database—for example, the user's access to the database, the features of the database, including the filters and indexes, as well as the objects themselves.

Using the Analyzer Wizards

The *Table Analyzer* examines the distribution of data among the tables, and presents suggestions and ideas for further improvements. Another tool, the *Performance Analyzer,* looks at any or all of the objects in the database and makes suggestions for improving their performance. The Performance Analyzer can also examine the relationships you've established in the database and the set of all Visual Basic code modules in the database, including class and standard modules.

Both of these tools are available by choosing Tools | Analyze and selecting from the submenu.

Table Analyzer

When you design a new database, you do the best you can to reduce the redundancy of data by creating a set of related tables. If you notice your database has a table showing repeated values in a field, you can use the Table Analyzer to help you split the table. The Access Table Analyzer can look at the data distribution and, perhaps, make suggestions for additional optimization, including adding more indexes and further normalization.

To start the Table Analyzer, choose Tools | Analyze | Table. The first two dialog boxes give you a good description of the process of table optimization by first describing the problem, and then showing possible solutions to the problem. Each dialog box also offers a look at examples of the problems and the solutions. Figure 17-1 shows the first of the two introductory dialog boxes.

The second Table Analyzer dialog box shows how it plans to solve the problem by splitting tables, so each piece of data is stored only once.

The third Table Analyzer dialog box shows a list of tables in the current database (see Figure 17-2). Select the table that contains repeated data and click Next. In the next dialog box, you can choose to let the wizard decide how to split the data or do it yourself. If you let the wizard decide, the next dialog box presents a diagram of the suggested redistribution of information.

TIP   *If you expect to use the Table Analyzer often and don't want to see the two introductory dialog boxes each time, clear the check mark next to Show introductory pages? in the dialog box showing the list of tables.*

FIGURE 17-1
Starting the
Table Analyzer

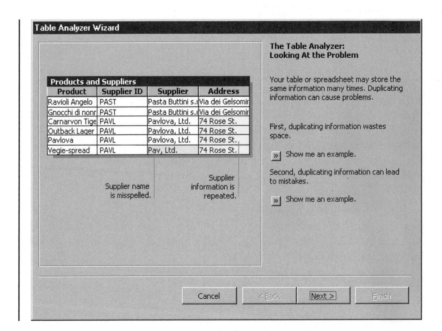

PART III

FIGURE 17-2
Selecting the
table to analyze

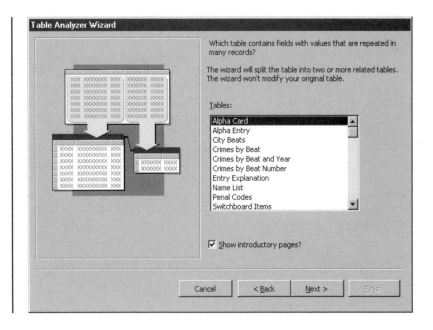

In Figure 17-3, the Table Analyzer found that the values in the ZIP code and City fields are repeated many times in the Police database Name List table. It suggests you create a lookup table for each field with a link from the new Table2 to the original Name List table and an additional link from the new Table3 back to Table2. Notice the wizard hasn't changed any table names: changing the table names is only a suggestion.

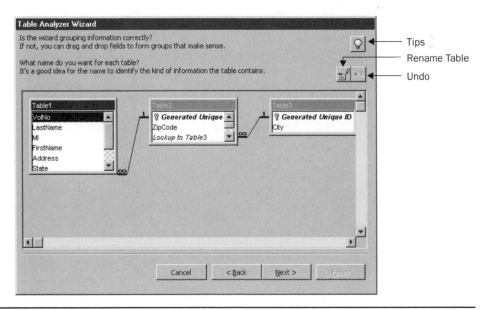

FIGURE 17-3   The Table Analyzer has suggestions.

TIP   *Click the Tips button (the light bulb icon) to get instructions about how to handle the wizard's suggestions.*

To change a table name, select the table, click the Rename Table button in the upper-right corner of the dialog box, and enter a new name. When you change the name of the related table, the wizard changes the table name in the linked field in the primary table to match. If you change your mind about the new name you entered for a table, click the Undo button next to the Rename Table button, and then enter a different name.

If the way the fields are grouped doesn't make sense to you, drag the field names from one table to the other to change them. Click Next to move to the dialog box in which you verify the primary key fields are correct (see Figure 17-4). The wizard has, by default, added a unique field to each new table and corresponding linking fields.

Each of the new tables has a designated primary key field, but Table1 (VolunteerStaff) has no primary key field. You can specify a primary key for Table1 in two ways:

- Select an existing field that you know has unique values and click the Primary Key button. The key symbol appears next to the field name.

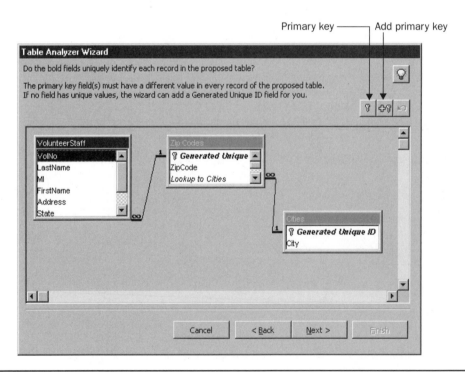

FIGURE 17-4   Verifying the primary key fields

- Select the table and click the Add Primary Key button. A new Generated Unique ID field is added to Table1.

After adding key fields, click Next. In the final dialog box (see Figure 17-5), the wizard offers to create a query for you that uses the same name as the original table and looks like the original table. Allowing the wizard to do this lets you work with the data all in one place and guarantees all the forms and reports you created using the original table as a basis will continue to work properly. You can also choose to create this query yourself, if you prefer.

If you chose to decide which fields to place in which tables (refer to Figure 17-3), the next dialog box shows only the original table without the new Table2. You can create the new table by dragging a field name from the list in Table1. You can also rename the tables and define the primary key field for the new table using buttons in the dialog box. After you click Next, the wizard offers to create a query for you as before.

Performance Analyzer

The *Performance Analyzer* looks at any or all of the objects in the database and suggests ways you can improve the application's performance. When you finish with the Performance Analyzer, many of the suggestions can be implemented automatically. To start the Performance Analyzer, choose Tools | Analyze | Performance. The first dialog box includes a tab for each type of database object. Each tab contains the names of all those objects in the current database. The

FIGURE 17-5
The final
Table Analyzer
dialog box

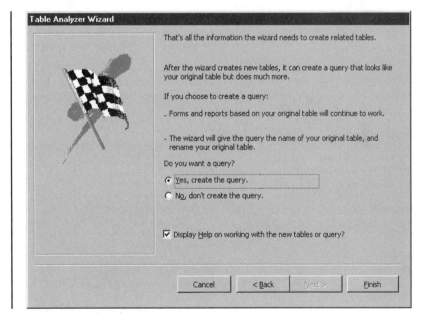

PART III

Current Database tab contains the Relationships and VBA Project options. The All Object Types tab contains all the names in one place. You can tell by the leading icon what kind of object it is.

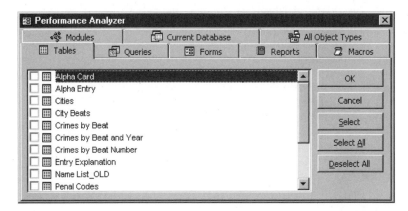

To choose which objects to examine, select the appropriate tab and select the object names. Click Select All on a tab to choose all the objects. To analyze the entire database, click the All Object Types tab, choose Select All, and then click OK. A message box keeps you informed about the progress of the analysis and, when all the objects are inspected, the wizard displays a dialog box with a list of recommendations, suggestions, and ideas (see Figure 17-6). Any problems that were fixed are also denoted. The Analysis Notes pane describes the general overall findings. When you select one of the items in the list, additional explanations are displayed in the Analysis Notes pane.

FIGURE 17-6
The findings of the Performance Analyzer

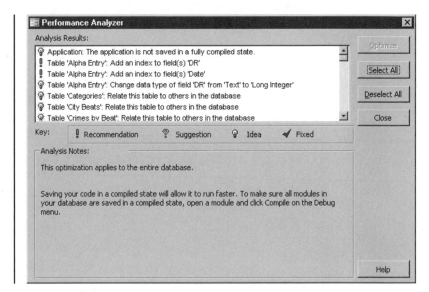

TIP   *If you include queries in the objects to analyze, be sure to have enough data in the tables to give the query a good workout.*

The Analyzer has recommended you add an index to the DR and the Date fields of the Alpha Entry table. When you select one of these recommendations, the Analysis Notes pane shows that, if you index on this field, it benefits the Alpha Entry table and your queries run faster. To implement a recommendation, select it, and then click Optimize. After considering all the items in the list, click Close to close the Performance Analyzer.

CAUTION   *The Performance Analyzer doesn't always have the whole picture. Accept its recommendations and suggestions carefully. For example, adding indexes might improve query performance, but they also increase the disk space needed for the database and could slow entering and editing data.*

Optimizing Tables and Queries

After you do all you can to normalize the database and distribute data efficiently among the tables, you can do a few other things to speed data processing. Some examples are the following:

- Choose the appropriate data type for each field to save space and improve join operations. In addition, if you know the range of values to be stored in the field, choose the smallest field size the data type will accept. You have no choice with Date/Time fields, but you can reduce the default 50-character field size for Text fields if the data is, for example, a ZIP code.

- Make sure the fields on either side of a relationship are of the same or a compatible data type.

Optimizing with Indexes

In addition to the primary key, which is automatically indexed, you can create indexes on one or more fields to find and sort records faster. Indexes can speed queries if the fields on both sides of the join are indexed. In a one-to-many relationship, the primary table is already indexed on the primary key field, but creating an index for the field in the related table helps when the query is run. In addition, indexing any field used in a criteria rule in the query reduces processing time for the query.

Multiple-field indexes help distinguish between records that might have more than one record with the same value in the first field. If you're creating a multiple-field index, use only as many fields as necessary.

NOTE   *While indexes can speed searches, sorts, and queries of related tables, they can also add to the database size. Each index represents a condensed lookup table. Additional problems can occur in a multiple-user environment because indexes can reduce the concurrency of the database, thereby limiting the ability of more than one user to modify data at the same time.*

Optimizing Queries

Among the guidelines for optimizing queries are the following:

- Include only the fields you need in the query. If a field isn't needed in the result set, but you're using it as a criterion, clear the Show check box in the query grid.

- Avoid calculated fields in a query as much as possible. If you nest the query in another query as a subquery, you slow the operation considerably. If you need an expression in the result of the query, instead, add a control to the form or report and use the expression as the control source. If necessary, prompt the user to enter a value required by the expression in a parameter query.

- Use Between...And... in a criteria expression rather than the > and < operators.

- If you want to count all the records in the recordset, use Count(*) instead of Count([<_fieldname_>]).

- Don't use domain aggregate functions, such as DSum, in a query. Access must retrieve all the data in the linked table before running the query, even if the data isn't included in the query.

- When grouping records by values in one of the joined fields, be sure to place the Group By aggregate function in the field that's on the side of the join containing the values you want to summarize. If you place Group By in the joined field, Access must join all the records, and then calculate the aggregate using only the necessary fields.

- Use as few Group By aggregates as possible. You might, instead, be able to use the First function in some cases.

- Try not to use restrictive criteria on nonindexed or calculated fields.

- If you need to place criteria on one of the fields used to join two tables in a one-to-many relationship, you can place it on either field in the grid. Run some tests to see which placement results in a faster query.

- If you're working with fairly static data, consider running a make-table query and using the resulting table instead of the query as the basis for forms and reports. You can always run the make-table query again if the data changes. Be sure to add indexes to the resulting table.

- When you create a Crosstab query, try to use fixed column headings to avoid the time it takes to update them.

TIP *To save even more time running queries, always save the query in a compiled state. When you simply save the query after making modifications in Design view, you're saving the query file. A query isn't compiled until it's run. To save the compiled query, run it by opening it in Datasheet view, and then save it. The query is optimized if it's compiled with the same amount of data as your application will have.*

Working with Linked Tables

Although linked tables look just like your own tables when you use them in forms and reports, they're stored in another database file. Every time you access the linked table, Access must retrieve the records from that file, which takes time. If the linked table is on a network or in a SQL database, this might take even more time because of the network traffic.

You can reduce the time it takes to retrieve the records from a network or an SQL database in these ways:

- If you don't need to see all the records from the linked table, use filters or queries to limit the number of records and reduce transfer time.

- Paging up and down among records causes Access to load the records into memory, which takes time. If you want to add new records to the linked table, choose Records | Data Entry. This avoids loading all the records into memory, and then having to page through them to the end of the recordset to add new records when the table first opens in Datasheet or Form view.

- If you usually add new records to the linked table, create a data entry form and set the form's Data Entry property to Yes. This also avoids loading and displaying all the records from the linked table.

- When you need to query a linked table, don't use functions in the criteria. And, especially, don't use domain functions, which require Access to load all the data in the linked table before executing the query.

- You can also create problems for the other users on the network who want to use the same data. Lock the records no longer than necessary.

Optimizing Filter By Form

The Filter By Form defaults for database name settings in the Edit/Find tab of the Options dialog box can improve the performance of all tables and queries, as well as all text box controls that use the Database Default setting in the Filter Lookup property. As discussed in Chapter 16, the Filter By Form Defaults group of options can limit the displayed list of values to indexed fields only or include local indexed and nonindexed fields. You can also set a limit on the number of values to display in the list in the displayed filter form.

If the list of field values takes too long to display, you can optimize the Filter By Form for a single text box control on a form by setting the control's Filter Lookup property (on the Data tab) to Never. This suppresses displaying the field values on the drop-down list in the Filter By Form window.

Optimizing Forms and Reports

Most of the optimization strategies can be used on both forms and reports, as well as on subforms and subreports. You can also apply techniques to individual text box and combo box controls to improve their performance in forms and reports.

The following tips apply to both forms and reports:

- Base the subform or subreport on a saved query that includes only the required fields and with a filter that results in only the required set of records.

- If the record order isn't important, you can save time by not sorting records in an underlying query, especially if the query uses fields from multiple tables.

- Try not to sort or group on expressions.

- Make sure the underlying query is itself optimized before loading the form or report.

- Index on the fields you use for sorting or grouping.

- Don't overdo the design with bitmaps and graphic objects. But, when you need to add graphics, convert the unbound object frame controls to image controls, which take less time to load.

- You can save a lot of disk space by using black-and-white bitmaps rather than color.

- Don't overlap controls unless absolutely necessary. Access must draw the controls in the form or report window twice to place overlapping controls.

- Use subforms and subreports sparingly; they occupy as much space as the main form or report. Base all subforms and subreports on queries instead of tables. Include only the necessary fields because more fields decrease performance.

- Index all fields in a subform or subreport linked to the main form or report. In addition, index all fields used in criteria.

- When you need to include data from an external table, you can save time by importing the table, rather than linking. This does take more space, however.

- If the form or report has no event procedures associated with it, make sure the form or report Has Module property is set to No. The form or report can load faster and take less disk space without the reserved class module space.

Specially for Reports

When you're opening a report from a procedure, you can test the Has Data property to see if the underlying recordset is empty. If it has no records, you save time if you branch to the next operation and avoid opening the useless report.

Before printing a report, set the Fast Laser Printing property (on the Other tab) to Yes if you're using a laser printer. If you're using a nonlaser printer, printing in landscape orientation can take more time because of the mechanical motion across the page.

Specially for Forms

A few more strategies apply only to forms:

- Don't leave a form open if you aren't using it. Access still must refresh the window whether or not you're working in it.

- Design a form with as few controls as possible. More controls reduce the efficiency of the form. If you need a lot of controls, consider adding a tab control to create a multiple-page form with controls grouped logically on the pages.

- If the underlying record source contains many records and you're planning to use the form primarily for data entry, change the form's Data Entry property to Yes. When the form opens, it automatically moves to the end of the recordset and displays a blank record in the form. If you open the form with records showing, Access must read every record before it can display a blank new record.

- If you don't expect to edit the records in a subform, you can save time by setting the subform's Allow Edits, Allow Additions, and Allow Deletions properties all to No. An alternative is to set the Recordset Type to Snapshot, instead of the default Dynaset. These are properties of the subform object itself, not the subform control on the main form.

- Use a hyperlink instead of a command button to open a form. Command buttons added with the help of the Command Button Wizard result in an event procedure written in VB code. Without VB code, you can eliminate the class module and save space and time.

Optimizing Controls

List box and combo box controls all show field values from which you can choose. They're bound to a field in the underlying record source. When you use a wizard to create the list box or combo box control, it automatically constructs an SQL statement and assigns it to the control's Record Source property. You can save time by basing the control on a saved query instead of the SQL statement, which must be evaluated each time you activate the control.

To convert the wizard's SQL statement to a saved query, do the following:

1. Open the control's property sheet and click the Build button next to the Row Source property. The SQL statement appears in the Query Builder window.
2. Choose File | Save and enter a name for the query.
3. When you close the Query Builder window, Access asks if you want to save the query with that name and update the property with the query name. Respond Yes.

You can optimize the behavior of these controls in several more ways:

- Include only the necessary fields in the query that you specify as the Row Source property for the control. Adding extra fields slows the display of the list.

- If they are different fields, be sure to index on both the first field displayed in the combo box or the list box, as well as on the bound field in the underlying table.

- Set the AutoExpand property of the combo box control to No if you don't require the fill-in-as-you-type feature.

- If you do use the fill-in-as-you-type feature by setting the AutoExpand property to Yes, be sure the first field in the displayed list is a Text data type, rather than a Number data type. Access converts the numeric value to text to find a match for completing the entry. Using text in the first field eliminates the need for this conversion.

- You usually include the bound field in a lookup combo box list but, if you don't, don't use expressions for the bound field or the displayed field. Also, use single-table (or query) row sources and don't add restrictions to the row source.

- If you don't expect the data to change, base the control on imported, rather than linked, data.

- Use the default format and property settings for the controls. Access saves only the exceptions to the default settings with the form. If you find you're changing the same property frequently, you can change the default setting for the control.

Avoiding Errors

A new tool in Access 2003 can help you avoid those pesky #Error# messages where you wanted to see data. These errors occur when you rename a table, query, or one of the fields. The *Name AutoCorrect* feature creates name maps that store interdependency information between database objects. The name maps apply to tables, queries, forms, and reports in an Access database.

TIP   *You must have Track Name AutoCorrect Info checked to view dependency information. Choose Tools | Options, and then click the General tab.*

The *Object Dependencies* feature works both ways: you can look at all the objects that depend on the object you're working on, as well as look at all the objects your current object depends on. Being able to look at these lists helps to maintain the database and keeps it free of errors caused by a missing or renamed object. The Object Dependencies pane appears in the pane at the right of the screen.

NOTE   *You must have permissions to open an object in the database in Design view to look at the dependency information.*

Before you can view the current dependencies, you must close the table, query, form, or report you're working with. This ensures the most accurate and current information. To view the dependencies, do the following:

1. Select the object name in the Database window.

2. Choose View | Object Dependencies or right-click and choose Object Dependencies from the shortcut menu.

3. The Dependencies pane lists the objects that rely on the object you selected (see Figure 17-7). You might see a dialog box warning you that Dependency information needs to be updated before you can view object dependencies. This could take several minutes. Click OK.

4. If you want to see the list of objects that use the one you selected, click Objects that I depend on.

5. Click an expand icon (+) to see the elements of that object (see Figure 17-8).

To find the types of objects and how they depend on one another, see the Help topic About object dependencies (MDB) for a complete list of objects and their dependencies.

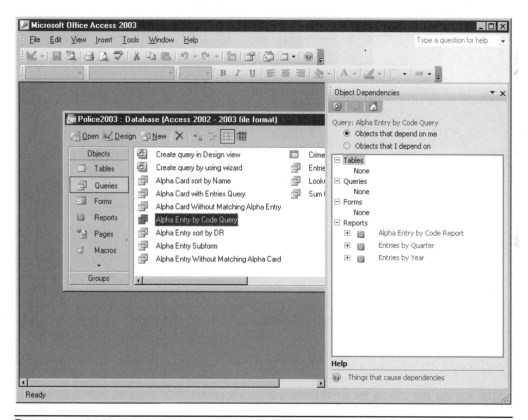

FIGURE 17-7   Looking at what depends on me

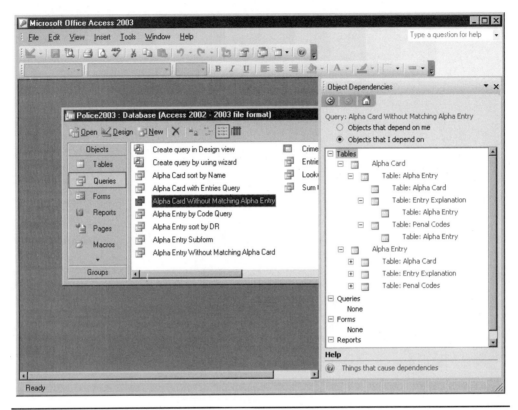

FIGURE 17-8   Looking at what I depend on

Backing Up and Restoring a Database

To reduce the risk of losing data, a good idea is to have a backup copy of your database. The database must be closed before you can back it up. If you're working in a multiple-user environment, make sure all the users have closed the database before you start the backup process. You can make a backup copy in several ways:

- Double-click the My Computer shortcut and open successive folders until you locate the folder that contains your database. Drag the file name in the Windows Explorer list from the hard disk to another disk drive.

- Right-click the file name or database shortcut in Windows Explorer and point to Send To in the shortcut menu, and then click the drive to which you want to copy.

- Use Microsoft Windows 2000 or later Backup and Recovery Tools, the MS-DOS Copy command, or other third-party backup software. Some programs also offer the option of compressing the files.

You can also use Access to create a backup database. This creates a regular copy of the database with no compression or other reformatting. To restore the database, simply copy it back to where you want to use it. To back up the database with Access, do the following:

1. Choose File | Back Up Database.

2. In the Save Backup As dialog box, enter the name and location for the backup copy.

3. Click Save.

If you're working in a multiple-user environment with user-level security, also be sure to make a backup copy of the workgroup information file. You won't be able to start Access if the file is damaged or missing. See Chapter 24 for more information about workgroups and shared databases.

You can also back up individual objects of your database without copying the entire file. To do this, create a new, blank database and import the objects into it from the original database. See Chapter 22 for information about importing database objects.

To restore the database from a copy, use the recover feature of the same method you used to make the backup copy. If you used Windows Explorer, drag the file name from the floppy disk list to the database folder on the hard drive.

CAUTION   *If the backup copy and the existing database in the database folder have the same name, you can replace the existing database when you restore the backup copy. If you want to save the original database, rename it before restoring from the backup copy.*

Compacting and Repairing a Database

Access provides some useful tools for managing databases. One of these tools converts databases to or from previous versions of Access. Another creates an MDE file from the current database. An MDE file contains compiled versions of all the code in the database with none of the source code. MDE databases run faster, but the user cannot access the source code for viewing or editing.

NOTE   *See Appendix A for information about converting databases to and from Access 2003.*

Another utility repairs and compacts a database to use disk space more efficiently. As you delete tables and queries, your database can become scattered about on the disk with useless small blocks of space between. Compacting the database makes a copy of the database and rearranges the file to make better use of the disk space.

If a database becomes damaged in some way, Access usually detects this when you try to open the database or if you try to compact, encrypt, or decrypt it. When damage is found, Access offers the option to repair the database at once. If, however, your database begins to act strangely, and Access hasn't noticed any damage, you can use the Compact and Repair Database utility manually.

You can compact an open database in place by choosing Tools | Database Utilities | Compact and Repair Database. Access takes only a few moments to compact the database, showing progress in the status bar.

If the database isn't open, you can compact it to the same file name or to a different name, drive, or folder. To compact and repair a closed database, do the following:

1. Close all databases and, from the empty Access window, choose Tools | Database Utilities | Compact and Repair Database.

FIGURE 17-9 Selecting the database to compact

2. In the Database to Compact From dialog box (see Figure 17-9), select the name of the database you want to compact and click Compact.

3. In the Compact Database Into dialog box, specify the drive and folder for the compacted database and enter a name for the copy or choose a name from the list.

4. Click Save. If you choose the same name as the original database, Access asks for confirmation before replacing the file.

TIP *You can stop the process at any time by pressing* ESC *or* CTRL-BREAK.

If the compaction was successful, and you chose to use the same name and path for the compacted file, Access replaces the original database file with the compacted version. If Access isn't successful with compacting a database, one of the following reasons might be to blame:

- Another user could have the database open.

- Your disk didn't have enough free space for both the original copy and the compacted copy of the database. To remedy this, delete as many unnecessary files as possible and try compacting the database again.

- You might not have permission to copy all the tables in the database. You need both Open/Run and Open Exclusive permissions to make copies of the data. If you aren't the owner of this database, find the owner and try to obtain permission. If you are the owner, update the permissions for all the tables.

- Some earlier versions of Access allowed the back quote character in a database object name. This is no longer permitted. Open the database in the previous version and change the object name and all references to the object in queries, forms, reports, macros, and code.

- The database might be on a read-only network or the file attribute could be set to Read Only.

NOTE *If the file size would be reduced by more than 256K, you can save time by specifying that the database is automatically compacted when you close it. Check the Compact on Close option on the General tab of the Options dialog box. If another user has the database open, Access won't compact it until the last user closes it.*

Documenting a Database

One of the most important tasks in a database management system is documentation, especially if many people are involved with its development and use. One of the Access analysis tools is the *Documenter,* which analyzes the current database and prints a report of the details of the entire database or only specified parts.

To run the Documenter, do the following:

1. Choose Tools | Analyze | Documenter. The Documenter dialog box opens, showing nearly the same eight tabs as the Performance Analyzer. Each tab displays a list of objects in the database.

2. Select the items on each tab you want to document or choose Select All on the All Object Types tab to select everything in the database, including the relationships and the database properties.

3. If you want to limit the amount of information to print in the table definitions, click Options, and then check the desired options in the Print Table Definition dialog box (see Figure 17-10).

4. To limit the information in another object type, select one of them and click Options. Each object has a list of details from which to select.

5. After making all your selections, click OK twice to start the Documenter.

TIP *You can stop the Documenter any time by pressing CTRL-BREAK or ESC.*

FIGURE 17-10
Choosing the
features to print

The status bar shows the progress of the analysis with messages and odometers. When the Documenter is finished, the report is opened in Print Preview. Figure 17-11 shows the first printed page of the Documenter's analysis of the Products table in the Northwind database.

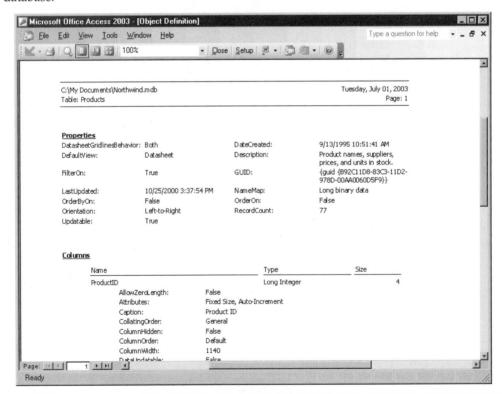

FIGURE 17-11   Printing the Northwind Products table definition

---

TIP   *You might want to look at how many pages the definition report contains before you start to print it. Some definitions, even with small databases, are quite lengthy. If you want to save the report, you can output the definitions to one of several file formats: HTML format, an Excel worksheet, a Rich Text Format file, a DOS text file, or as a file in report snapshot format. Choose File | Export to open the Export Report To dialog box and select the desired file format from the Save as type box, enter a name for the report, and then click Export.*

Summary

While this chapter might seem to contain a lot of unrelated and detailed information, all the suggestions are relevant to producing an efficient database. Both time and space have visible effects on efficiency and whatever you can do to optimize both factors can help.

Access provides many tools for optimization in its own workplace. Each of the Access database objects can be optimized by following the rules and guidelines presented in this chapter.

Access provides the means to compact and repair a database to improve disk storage efficiency. This chapter has also addressed the issue of backing up a database to ensure the retention of important information.

The next chapter begins to explore the world of creating an application that can be controlled by the user. In an event-driven program—such as Access—understanding the concept of events and learning when and in what sequence events occur is important. After you become familiar with events, you can proceed to create macros and event procedures that carry out specified actions when events occur.

Understanding Events and the Event Model

Although you can manage a database adequately using the Access wizards and other tools without knowing anything about events, when you begin to build a customized application that the user can control, you need to understand events and know when and in what sequence they occur. Then, you can create macros to carry out appropriate responses to all the user's actions. When you decide to work with Visual Basic for Applications to create VBA procedures, this information will be useful.

This chapter contains most of the details about events necessary to create a basis for subsequent chapters that discuss writing macros to automate an Access application. Skim through this chapter to get enough of an understanding of events, and then refer to it from later chapters to find specific information.

What Are Events?

Access is an *event-driven program,* which means it responds to a variety of events as they occur. In fact, if no event occurs, nothing happens at all. An *event* is something that happens to a certain object, a recognized action that occurs and triggers some type of response. For example, when you click a command button, the *Click event* occurs and the command button's event property specifies a response.

Events are usually caused by the user, but Access also responds to events resulting from system changes or external influences. For example, a specified timer interval expires, data in the table changes, linked data is updated, or a filter finds no records that match the criteria. When an event occurs, you can have Access respond with a specific action by running a macro or executing a VBA procedure.

The macro or VBA procedure is attached to an event property of the object to which the event occurs. For example, when the user clicks a command button, you want the Alpha Entry form to open. You would create a macro or VBA procedure that opens the form and specifies it as the On Click event property for the command button.

> **Tip** *When you create a command button using the Command Button Wizard, the wizard automatically creates a VBA procedure and adds it to the button's On Click property.*

The next chapter discusses creating macros that respond to events. First, let's take a close look at events, what they are, and when they occur.

Types of Events

Events are grouped into eight categories, depending on the effects of the event. For example, some events relate to the data, others to filters, and still others to keyboard actions. The following sections describe each type of event and list the commonly used events that fall into each classification.

Each event corresponds to a property of the object to which it applies. The property usually has the same name or a name similar to the event (but with spaces and sometimes beginning with "On"). For example, the Change event corresponds to the On Change property of several controls. You can set the property to respond to the event in a specified way.

Data Events

A *Data event* occurs when data is entered, edited, or deleted in a datasheet or a form. For example, when the user enters data into a text box control in a form or selects a value from a combo box, a Data event occurs. In addition, when the entry focus moves from one record to another, this is classified as a Data event. A control has focus when it can receive user input by means of the mouse or keyboard action. Table 18-1 describes some of the more common Data events and the Access objects to which each applies.

Event	Applies To	When It Occurs
AfterInsert	Forms	After a record is added to the database.
AfterUpdate	Forms, controls	After a control or record is updated with modified data. Also occurs when the control or record loses focus or you choose Records | Save Record to update the current record without moving to another. Occurs for both new and existing records.
BeforeInsert	Forms	When you begin to type the new data in a new record, but before you add the record to the database.
BeforeUpdate	Forms, controls	Before a control or record is updated with modified data. Occurs when the control or record loses focus or you choose Records | Save Record. Occurs for both new and existing records.
Change	Controls	When the contents of a text box control or the text box portion of a combo box control changes. When you type a character in the control or change its Text property with a macro or procedure.

TABLE 18-1   Some Common Data Events

Event	Applies To	When It Occurs
Current	Forms	When focus moves to a record and it becomes the current record. Occurs when the form is first opened and when focus moves from one record to another in the form. Also occurs when you requery the form's record source by choosing Records I Remove Filter\Sort or with a macro action.
NotInList	Controls	When you enter a value in a combo box that isn't in the combo box list.

TABLE 18-1   Some Common Data Events *(continued)*

Here's some additional information about the Data events and what they can be used for:

- The BeforeUpdate and AfterUpdate events don't occur when the value in a calculated field changes.

- You can use the BeforeUpdate record event to validate data, especially with complex validation rules that involve more than one value. You can display different error messages for different data, giving the user the opportunity to override the rule violation, if desired. Use the Validation Rule property for controls in a form, as well as the Validation Rule and Required properties specified in the table design for fields and records in forms.

- The BeforeUpdate event can also be used to cancel updating the record before moving to another record in case of an error. It can also check to see if a value was already entered in the control.

- You can use the AfterInsert event to requery the underlying recordset (the datasheet result of running the query) to incorporate new data when a record is added to the form.

- The Change event can be used to coordinate data among several controls in the form.

A problem can occur when you use the NotInList event to enable the user to add a value to the combo box list. If you set the AutoExpand property for the combo box control to Yes, Access selects matching values from the list as you enter characters in the text box part of the control. So, if you want to add the name John to the list, but Johnston is already on the list, the AutoExpand property fills out the complete Johnston value and the NotInList event doesn't occur. The cure for this is to enter a space after you enter the new value, so it no longer matches a value in the list. Then the NotInList event occurs when you move to the next control.

CAUTION   *The Change event can result in cascading events—a never-ending loop. If the Change event procedure alters the contents of the control, the Change event occurs again, which triggers the Change event procedure again, and so on. If you plan to use the Change event, don't create two or more controls that affect the contents of each other.*

Error and Timer Events

One error event, *Error,* is important in an application for handling errors during operation. The Error event is often used to intercept Access error messages and replace them with more helpful messages that relate to the application.

The other error event, *Timer,* is used for synchronizing data on forms and reports by refreshing the data at regular intervals. This event occurs when the interval specified in the form's Timer Interval property has elapsed.

Filter Events

Filter events apply only to forms and occur when you apply an existing filter or create a new filter for the form. The *ApplyFilter event* occurs when you apply or remove a filter using any of the filter commands. The ApplyFilter event can be used to change a form display, so it hides or disables controls, depending on the filter criteria.

The Filter event occurs when you choose one of the filter methods to create a new filter. You can use the Filter event to remove an earlier filter, so extraneous criteria aren't carried over to the next filter. To do this, set the form's Filter property to a zero-length string using a macro or an event procedure that completely clears the filter criteria.

Focus Events

Focus events (see Table 18-2) occur when a form or control gets or loses focus. Two Focus events apply to both forms and reports, and they occur when the object becomes active or inactive. Some other Focus events apply only to forms or controls in forms.

Event	Applies To	When It Occurs
Activate	Forms, reports	When a form or report becomes the active window by opening it, by clicking it, or by clicking a control on a form.
Deactivate	Forms, reports	When a different Access window replaces the form or report as the active window, but before it becomes the active window. Doesn't occur when focus moves to a window in another application, a dialog box, or a pop-up form.
Enter	Controls	Before a control receives focus from another control or as the first control in a newly opened form. Occurs before the GotFocus event.
GotFocus	Forms, controls	When a control receives focus or a form with no active or enabled controls receives focus.
LostFocus	Forms, controls	When a form or control loses focus.

TABLE 18-2   Some Common Focus Events

The Enter event occurs before focus moves to a control, so you can use the event to display instructions for entering data in the control or other information.

You can use the GotFocus and LostFocus events to set the control's Visible and Enabled properties. These events are also used to display a message in the status bar when a control, such as an Option button, has focus. The message clears when the control loses focus.

Keyboard Events

All *keyboard events* apply to forms and controls that have focus. A form can receive focus only if it contains no controls or if all visible controls are disabled and cannot get focus. The object with focus receives all the keystrokes. When the Key Preview form event property is set to Yes, the keyboard events are invoked for the form before they're invoked for the controls on the form. The default setting is No.

- The *KeyDown event* occurs when you press any key on the keyboard while the form or control has focus.

- The *KeyPress event* occurs when you press and release a key or any key combination that produces a standard ANSI character while the form or control has focus.

- The *KeyUp event* occurs when you release a pressed key while a form or control has focus. The object that has focus receives the keystrokes

Holding the key down causes repeated KeyDown or Key Press events. If you're using the KeyUp event, holding the key down causes the KeyUp to occur after all the KeyDown and KeyPress events have occurred. All these key events occur when you send a keystroke to a form or control using a macro with the SendKey action. KeyUp and KeyDown are often used to recognize function keys, navigation keys, key combinations that use CTRL, SHIFT, or ALT with another key, and number keys from the keyboard or the number keypad. KeyUp and KeyDown don't occur when you press ENTER if the form has a command button whose Default property is Yes. Pressing ENTER is the same as clicking the command button. They also don't occur when you press ESC if the Cancel property is set to Yes.

The KeyPress event doesn't indicate the physical state of the keyboard; it only indicates the character pressed. The event accepts any printable character, CTRL combined with a character, ENTER, or BACKSPACE.

TIP *Pressing* BACKSPACE *results in an ANSI character and triggers the KeyPress event, but pressing* DEL *does not.*

Mouse Events

All the mouse events (see Table 18-3) apply to both forms and controls. Again, a form can receive focus only if it contains no controls or if all visible controls have been disabled and cannot get focus.

The Click event, one of the most common events, occurs when you press the left mouse button. Click and DblClick only apply to the left mouse button. The other mouse buttons don't trigger the Click or DblClick event. You can use the MouseUp or MouseDown event to differentiate between the mouse buttons.

Event	When It Occurs
Click	When you press and release the left mouse button on a control or its label.
	When you click a record selector or an area outside a section or control in a form.
	When you select a combo box or list box by pressing TAB or an arrow key, and then press ENTER.
	When you press SPACEBAR while a command button, check box, option button, or toggle button has focus.
	When you pass the mouse pointer over a hyperlink and click the left mouse button when the pointer changes to a pointer hand.
DblClick	When you press and release the left mouse button twice on a control or its label.
	When you double-click a record selector or a blank area in a form.
MouseDown	When you press a mouse button while the mouse pointer is on a form or control. It also happens when the SHIFT, ALT or CTRL key is down while the mouse button is pressed.
MouseMove	When you move the mouse pointer over a form, form section, or control.
MouseUp	When you release the mouse button while the pointer is on a form or control.

TABLE 18-3   Some Common Mouse Events

NOTE   *The mouse events don't apply to attached labels; they apply only to freestanding labels. Clicking or double-clicking an attached label triggers the event for the associated control.*

The result of the DblClick event depends on the type of control you clicked:

- If the control is a text box, double-clicking selects the entire word.
- If the control is an OLE object, the source application starts where you can edit the object.

If you don't double-click quickly enough, the action is treated as repeated Click events.

CAUTION   *The MouseMove event can occur when a form moves under the mouse pointer, even if the pointer doesn't move. If you run a macro or event procedure that moves the form, you can generate unexpected MouseMove events.*

Print Events

Print events apply only to reports and they occur for each section of the report when the report is either being printed or formatted for printing.

The *Format event* occurs when Access determines what data goes in each report section, but before the section is formatted for previewing or printing. You can use the data in the current record to change the page layout by creating a macro or VBA procedure for this event. Depending on the section of the report, the Format event applies to a different set of data:

- In the detail section, Format occurs for every record.
- In the group header, Format applies to all the data in the header section, plus the first record in the detail section.
- In the group footer, Format applies to all the data in the footer section, plus the last record in the detail section.

The *NoData event* occurs when a report has an empty recordset. If the report isn't bound to a table or query, it doesn't occur and it doesn't occur for empty subreports either. If you want to hide an empty subreport, you can attach a macro or event procedure that suppresses previewing or printing to the subreport's Has Data property.

The *Page event* occurs after the page is formatted, but before it's printed. You can use it to draw a border around a page or add a graphic to the report. This can save disk space that would otherwise be used for storing the graphic with the report design.

The *Print event* occurs after formatting, but before printing the report. A macro or event procedure attached to it can be used to perform calculations, such as running page totals after the data is prepared for printing on a page.

Window Events

Window events occur when you open, close, or resize a form or report window.

The *Load event* occurs when the form is opened and records appear on the screen. You can use the Load event to specify default control settings or to display calculated data in the form.

The *Open event* occurs when you open a form, but before the first record is displayed. You can use the Open event to display a message asking if the user wants to add new records. If the response is Yes, the form can go quickly to a blank record at the end of the recordset. If not, it continues to display the first record. With a report, the Open event occurs when the report opens, but before it begins printing.

Forms and reports behave differently when based on an underlying query. When you open a form, the query runs before the form is displayed. When you open a report, the Open event occurs before the query is run, giving you the opportunity to enter query parameters or other criteria.

The *Resize event* occurs when you change the size of a form or when the form is first displayed and expanded to its previously saved size. You can use the Resize event to cause certain controls on the form to be repositioned or resized to accommodate the change in the form size.

Understanding the Sequence of Events

Many types of events can happen to an object in a short period of time. When you begin to create macros that will govern how an application operates, understanding not only when events occur, but also the sequence in which they occur is important. This is especially important if you intend to have two or more macros executing in response to events and want them executed in a specific order. You must know to which events to attach the actions.

Form Control Events

Two types of events occur when you're moving about the controls in a form. When focus moves from one control to another, *Focus events* occur. When you add or change data in a control, *Data events* occur.

Moving Among Controls

When you move to another control on the same form, the Enter and *GotFocus* events occur in that order.

NOTE　*An exception to this rule is this: the Enter event doesn't occur for the items grouped in an option group, it occurs only to the option group control. The Exit event also applies only to the option group control. The toggle buttons, check boxes, or option buttons in the option group experience only the GotFocus and* LostFocus *events.*

If you're opening a form that has one or more active controls, certain other events occur before those two:

```
Open(form)→Activate(form)→Current(form)→Enter(control)→GotFocus(control)
```

Conversely, when you move to another control, the control loses focus, and the Exit and LostFocus events occur in that order.

If you're closing a form that has one or more active controls, other *Form events* occur as well:

```
Exit(control)→LostFocus(control)→Unload(form)→Deactivate(form)→Close(form)
```

Working with Data in a Form

When you enter new data or change existing data, and then move focus to a different control, the BeforeUpdate and AfterUpdate events occur in that order. Then the Exit and LostFocus events for the changed control follow immediately after.

Whenever the contents of a text box or combo box control changes, the Change event occurs before either the BeforeUpdate and AfterUpdate events occur. In fact, the Change event occurs in conjunction with keyboard events every time you press a key to enter or edit data. The sequence for each time you press a key while in the text box or the text box portion of a combo box is:

```
Key→DownKeyPress→Dirty→Change→KeyUp
```

In the special case, when you enter a value in the text box portion of a combo box control that isn't in the displayed list of values, the NotInList event occurs after the Change event, but before any other Control or Form events. If the Limit To List property for the combo box control is set to Yes, this also triggers an Error event. The sequence is as follows:

```
KeyDown→KeyPress→Dirty→Change→KeyUp→NotInList→Error
```

NOTE   *This sequence of events is often used to display a message box asking if you want to add the value to the list, even though the property specifies limiting the values to those in the list.*

Form Record Events

Events occur for records in forms on several occasions:

- When the record gets focus
- When you update the data in a record by moving to the next or previous record
- When you delete one or more records
- When you add a new record

When you move from one record to another in a form or save the current record by choosing Records | Save Record, the update events apply to the current record in the form. By contrast, when you move from one control to another within the same record in a form, the update events apply to the individual controls in the form. Only when you move to another record do the form update events occur.

Moving Focus and Updating Data

At the top level are the Form events that occur when you move focus to a record on the form, enter or edit the data in the record, and, finally, move to another record. The Form events that occur are:

```
Current(form)→BeforeUpdate(form)→AfterUpdate(form)→Current(form)
```

If you changed the data in a record and leave the record, the Exit and LostFocus events occur for the last control that got focus in that record, before you enter the next record. The form itself becomes current when you are moving to the next record. The events occur after the AfterUpdate event for the form and before the Current event for the form as follows:

```
AfterUpdate(form)→Exit(control)→LostFocus(control)→RecordExit(form)→Current(form)
```

As you move among the controls within the same record on a form, several events occur for each control that gets focus. When you open a form and change the data in a control, the following events occur:

```
Current(form)→Enter(control)→GotFocus(control)→BeforeUpdate(control)
→AfterUpdate(control)→Exit(control)
```

Then, if you move focus to another control, the events reflect the shift in focus:

```
Exit(control1)→LostFocus(control1)→Enter(control2)→GotFocus(control2)
```

When you finish working in one record and move to the next, the following events occur in which the record is updated and the form itself becomes current until another control gets focus with the Enter event:

```
BeforeUpdate(form)→AfterUpdate(form)→Exit(control2)→LostFocus(control2→
RecordExit(form)→Current(form)
```

PART III

Note *When moving between records, the BeforeUpdate and AfterUpdate events apply to the form. When moving between controls in the same record in the form, they apply to the controls.*

Creating New Records

To add a new record, you move to the blank record on the form and type data in a control. Creating a new record triggers the following sequence of events:

```
Current(form)?Enter(control)→GotFocus(control)→BeforeInsert(form)
→(control update events)→AfterInsert(form)
```

The BeforeUpdate and AfterUpdate events for the controls and for the new record occur between the BeforeInsert and AfterInsert form events.

Deleting Existing Records

When you delete a record from the form, Access displays a dialog box asking for confirmation of the deletion and the following events occur:

```
Delete→BeforeDelConfirm→AfterDelConfirm
```

The confirmation dialog box is displayed after the BeforeDelConfirm event. If you cancel the deletion with a macro or event procedure with the Delete event, the dialog box isn't displayed at all, and the BeforeDelConfirm and AfterDelConfirm don't occur.

Form and Subform Events

Events occur when you work with forms whenever you open or close a form, move between two forms, move between a main form and a subform, or work with the data displayed in the form.

Opening or Closing a Form

When you open a form, the sequence of events depends on whether the form has any enabled controls. If it does, the sequence of Form events is:

```
Open→Load→Resize→Activate→Current
```

These events are followed by the Control events. If no active controls are on the form you open, the GotFocus event occurs for the form between Activate and Current.

When you close a form, the following events occur for the form:

```
Unload→Deactivate→Close
```

If no active controls are on the form, the LostFocus event occurs for the form between Unload and Deactivate.

Note *Open occurs before Load, so you can cancel Open, but you can't cancel Load. Conversely, Close occurs after Unload, so Unload can be canceled, but Close cannot.*

Moving to Another Form

More than one form can be open at a time, but only one form can be the active form. When you switch between two open forms, the Open, Load, and Resize events occur for the second form while the first is still active. Then the Deactivate event occurs for the form you're leaving and the Activate event occurs for the form you're switching to and it becomes current.

Deactivate also occurs for the form when you switch to another open window unless the window is one of the following:

- A dialog box
- A form whose Popup property is set to Yes
- A window in another application

When you move to a form that's already open, the Open event doesn't recur for the form.

Changing Data in a Form

When you work with data in a form, the Form and Control events occur in a sequence as you move between records and edit the data in them. The Form events occur first as you open the form and move to the first control, and then the Control events take over. The following events occur when you first open the form:

```
Open(form)→Load(form)→Resize(form)→Activate(form)→Current(form)→
Enter(control)→GotFocus(control)
```

When you finish entering data in the last control in the form and close the form, the following sequence of events occurs:

```
Exit(control)→LostFocus(control)→Unload(form)→Deactivate(form)→Close(form)
```

If any of the data in a control in the form is changed, the BeforeUpdate and AfterUpdate events for both the form and the control occur before the Exit event for the control takes place and starts the form-closing sequence.

Using Subforms

All the events that occur for a form also occur for a subform. The subform and its data are loaded before the main form, using the same sequence of events. The exception is the *Activate event*, which occurs only for the main form.

When you close a form that contains a subform, a similar sequence of events occurs, but in reverse order: the form and its records are unloaded before the subform and its records. Also, the *Deactivate event* occurs only for the main form. To summarize, the closing events for the main form, the subform, and the controls occur in the following order:

1. The events for the controls on the subform, including Exit and LostFocus
2. The events for the controls on the main form, including the subform control
3. The events for the form, including Deactivate and Close
4. The events for the subform

PART III

Keystrokes and Mouse Click Events

Keyboard and mouse events are initiated by the user while working in a form or with controls in the form. *Keyboard events* occur when you press a key or a key combination while the form or control has focus. A keyboard event also occurs if you use a SendKey macro action or a procedure to send the ANSI character keystroke equivalent to the control.

Mouse events occur for forms, form sections, and controls on the form when you manipulate the mouse or press one of its buttons. Releasing a mouse button also triggers an event.

Using the Keyboard

The following events occur when you press a key on the keyboard while a control has focus:

```
KeyDown→KeyPress→KeyUp
```

If you press the key and hold it down, the KeyDown and KeyPress events alternate repeatedly until you release the key. Then the KeyUp event occurs.

If the key you press isn't an ANSI character, the KeyDown and KeyUp events occur, but not the KeyPress event. Pressing and holding down a non-ANSI key causes the KeyDown and KeyUp events to alternate repeatedly.

If the key you press changes the data in a text box control, the Change event occurs between the KeyPress and KeyUp events.

If the keystroke moves focus from one control to another, the KeyDown event occurs for the first control, while the KeyPress and KeyUp events occur for the second control. For example, if you edit the data in a text box control, and then press TAB to move to the next control, the following sequence of events occurs.

```
KeyDown(control1)→BeforeUpdate(control1)→AfterUpdate(control1)
→Exit(control1)→LostFocus(control1)→Enter(control2)→GotFocus(control2)
→KeyPress(control2)→KeyUp(control2)
```

Using the Mouse

When you place the mouse pointer on a control in a form and click the mouse button, the following events occur.

```
MouseDown→MouseUp→Click
```

TIP   *Notice the Click event doesn't occur until after the MouseUp event.*

If you use the mouse to move focus from one control to another, the sequence of events is as follows:

```
Exit(control1)→LostFocus(control1)→Enter(control2)→GotFocus(control2)
→MouseDown(control2)→MouseUp(control2)→Click
```

If you move to another control by other means, such as pressing TAB, and then clicking the mouse button, the Current event for the form occurs between the LostFocus event for the first control and the Enter event for the second.

When you double-click a mouse button on a control other than a command button, both the Click and DblClick events occur, each with a corresponding MouseUp event, as follows:

```
MouseDown→MouseUp→Click→DblClick→MouseUp
```

If the control is a command button, a second Click event follows the second MouseUp event.

The *MouseMove event* is independent of the other mouse events and occurs when you pass the mouse pointer over the form, a form section, or control. The MouseMove event is often used to display ScreenTips and other comments explaining parts of a form.

Report and Report Section Events

Report and *Report section events* occur when you open or close a report. Opening a report for previewing and printing both trigger the same sequence of events. Some of the Report section events occur during or after section formatting and before printing the section.

The following events occur if you open a report for previewing or printing, and then close the report or switch to a different Access window:

```
Open→Activate→Close→Deactivate
```

If you have two reports open and you switch between them, the Deactivate event occurs for the first report, followed by the Activate event for the second. The Deactivate event doesn't occur for the report if you switch to a dialog box, a pop-up form, or a window in a different application.

When the report you open is based on a query, the Open event occurs before the query is run. This is useful for entering the criteria for the query in a procedure that responds to the Open report event. The procedure could open a dialog box in which the user is prompted to enter a value to be used in the parameter query.

When you preview or print the report, each section is formatted individually and prepared for printing after the Activate report event and before the Close report event. When all the sections are formatted for printing, the report is closed and deactivated. The sequence is as follows:

```
Open(report)→Activate(report)→Format(section)→Print(section)→Close(report)
→Deactivate(report)
```

Some special events can occur while a section is being formatted or after formatting is complete, but before printing. These events are the following:

- *Retreat,* which occurs when Access returns to a previous section to make changes during formatting. For example, if you set a group's Keep Together property to Whole Group or With First Detail, Access must return to the previous report section to determine if the controls can all fit on the page. The Retreat event is also useful for maintaining the positioning of report items on a page.

- *NoData,* which occurs if no records are in the report.

- *Page,* which occurs after formatting, but before printing. If you want to add special formatting to customize the report's appearance, you can attach a procedure to this event.

Setting Event Properties

Event properties are used to run a macro or a VBA procedure each time the associated event occurs. The tables in an earlier section of this chapter describe the events and indicate to which objects each applies. When an event applies to a form, control, or report, that object has an event property that corresponds to the event. This is the property you set to create the appropriate response to the event.

For example, enter the name of a macro in the On Click property of a command button and it will run when you click the button.

To set an event property, open the property sheet for the object, and then click the Event tab. Figure 18-1 shows the Event property sheet for a form.

Depending on how you intend to create a response to the event, do one of the following:

- To set the property to an existing macro, choose the macro name from the drop-down list in the event property.

- To set the property to a macro in a macro group, choose the name from the drop-down list. The name then appears in the list as *macrogroupname.macroname.*

- To set the property to an existing VBA procedure, choose [Event Procedure] from the drop-down list. Only one event procedure can exist for each event property, named with the name of the property.

- To set the property to an existing user-defined function, enter an equal sign (=) followed by the function name, and then empty parentheses: *=functionname().*

FIGURE 18-1
Setting an event property for a form

NOTE *The status bar displays a brief description of the event property when the insertion pointer is in the property box. Press F1 to open the Help topic for that event property.*

If you want to create a new macro, VBA procedure, or function for the event property, click Build (...) to the right of the property box or right-click the property and choose Build from the shortcut menu. In the Choose Builder dialog box, do one of the following:

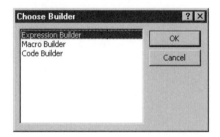

- Select Macro Builder to create a new macro for the property or to edit the already specified macro. See Chapter 19 for information about creating and editing macros and macro groups.

- Select Code Builder to open the Module window where you can create a new VBA procedure or edit one already specified for this property.

- Select Expression Builder to choose a built-in function or create a user-defined function for this property.

Summary

This chapter presents an overview of events and how they can be harnessed to customize an application. In addition, it lists many of the common types of events and the objects to which they apply, as well as the sequence in which they occur. Once you understand events, you're ready to proceed to creating your own macros, so the application responds properly to each user action and system event.

As you're building macros in the next chapter, you can refer to the event details in this chapter. Attaching the macro action to the proper event for it to execute at the intended time and operate on the intended object is important.

The next chapter launches into automation with macros and gives many useful examples of macros that display message boxes, filter records, and even change the flow of operations.

Automating with Macros

Macros provide a quick and easy way to program your Access application to do just what you want. With macros, you can specify customized responses to user actions, such as clicking a button, opening a form, or selecting an option in an options group. Macros can also respond to system conditions, such as an empty recordset.

Although the Access Control Wizards offer an easy way to add user interaction to a form or report, they don't always have exactly the right response. Creating a macro as a response to an event is an alternative to using a Control Wizard. Writing event procedures in Visual Basic is another alternative, but it requires some skill in programming with precisely constructed commands written in established syntax. VBA procedures are either stored with the form or report that activates them or they're stored as modules that are available from the Modules page of the Database window. Macros are easier because you select the actions and their arguments from predefined lists, which virtually precludes any errors in construction. You might as well start with a macro and you can always convert the macro to a VBA procedure later, if necessary.

This chapter discusses macros, how to create them, and how to attach them to events to get the desired response. In subsequent chapters, you see how to use macros to customize menus and toolbars, as well as how to create opening switchboards for an application. The Police database introduced earlier is used as the sample database in this chapter.

How Do Macros Work?

A *macro* is a list of one or more actions that work together to carry out a particular task in response to an event. Each *action* carries out one particular operation. You create the list of actions in the order in which you want them to execute. In addition to selecting the action to be taken, you specify other details of the action called *arguments*, which provide additional information, such as which form to open or how to filter the records to be displayed.

You can also set conditions under which the macro action is to be performed, such as to display a message box if a field contains a certain value or is blank. The macro runs only if the condition evaluates to True. If the condition is False, the action is skipped. Then, if another action is in the macro, it's executed. If not, the macro stops.

To run a macro, you assign it to the event property of a form, report, report section, or control. Once an event occurs, the macro assigned to it automatically executes, beginning with the first action in the list. For example, a macro that opens a form and moves to a blank record for data entry can be assigned to the On Click event property of a command button on a switchboard or other form. When you click the button, the macro executes.

The process of using macros to automate an application is a simple one, composed of these steps:

1. Create and save the macro.

2. Open the form or report to which the macro applies and select the specific control.

3. Open the property sheet for the control and click the Event tab.

4. Click the desired event property and choose the macro name from the drop-down list.

5. Save the form or report and switch to Form view or Print Preview to try it.

Macros are individual Access objects listed in the Macros tab in the Database window. Once you create and save a macro, it's available for attaching to an event property of any object in your database. Not all macro actions are appropriate for all objects, however, just as not all events occur to all objects. For example, if you create a macro that opens a form, you would probably attach it to the On Click event property of a command button or an option group, but not to a control in a report.

The section "Choosing Actions" describes categories of macro actions and how they're used.

NOTE   Access macros are quite different from the recorded macros you might have used in other programs. Access doesn't record keystrokes in a macro. Macros in Access are more like a programming language in which the actions are the commands. You select specific actions from a list of more than 50 predefined actions and add the action arguments.

Creating a Macro

The first step in creating a macro is to design the macro carefully by listing the actions you want performed when the event occurs. Each action might require specific arguments or need to be performed only under certain conditions.

Next, verify you're choosing the right event for the macro to respond to. Refer to Chapter 18 for information about events and when they occur.

When you complete the planning and design of the macro action list, you're ready to open the Macro window.

Touring the Macro Window

To start a new macro, click New in the Macros tab of the Database window. The Macro window opens, showing a blank macro. The drop-down list in the Action column (see Figure 19-1) contains a list of actions from which to choose. Entries in the Comment column are optional, but highly recommended as a reminder of what the macro is meant to accomplish.

TIP   Comments are especially useful because macros are stored as separate objects, not linked with a particular form or report. The comments can explain how the macro is used and to which events it's attached. This can be important if you rename the macro. You need to find all the references to the macro and change the name there, as well.

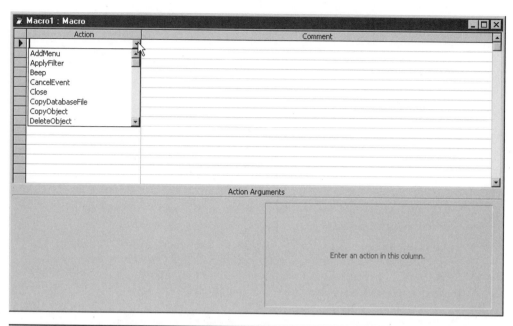

FIGURE 19-1   Working in the Macro Design window

Once you select an action from the list, the lower pane displays the associated arguments. Some are required, while others are optional, depending on the action.

The Macro window toolbar has some new buttons and new menu commands:

- The Macro Names button adds the Macro Name column to the macro sheet. Also use View | Macro Names.

- The Conditions button adds the Condition column to the macro sheet. Also use View | Conditions.

- The Insert Rows button inserts one or more blank rows in the grid above the selected row. If you select more than one row, that number of rows is inserted. Also use Insert | Rows.

- The Delete Rows button deletes the selected row or rows. Also use Edit | Delete Rows.

- The Run button runs the macro. Also use Run | Run.

- The Single Step button runs the macro one action at a time and displays intermediate information. Also use Run | Single Step.

The lower pane is called the Action Arguments pane and it displays information about the current row of the macro. The lower-right pane in the Macro window displays information about the currently active part of the macro sheet. For example, in Figure 19-1, the first row is selected and the message Enter an action in this column is displayed in the information pane. As you work in the macro sheet, the pane shows other information and comments.

Creating a Simple Macro

As an example, create a macro in the Police database that opens the Alpha Card form in read-only mode by doing the following:

1. Click New in the Macros tab of the Database window to open the blank macro sheet.

2. In the first row of the macro, click the Action drop-down arrow and choose OpenForm from the list.

3. The Action Arguments pane now contains the arguments for the OpenForm action and the information pane describes the selected OpenForm action. The Form Name argument is required. Other required arguments show default selections. The optional arguments are blank in the pane.

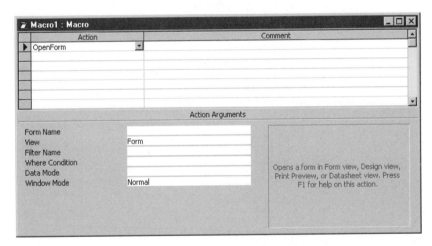

4. Click the Form Name box in the Action Arguments pane and select a form from the drop-down list of all the forms in the current database.

5. Set the other arguments as follows:

- View (required): Choose from the list of options including Form (default), Design, Print Preview, Datasheet, PivotTable, or PivotChart. Leave the default Form view.

- Filter Name (optional): Enter the name of the filter to limit or sort the records in the form. This can be a query or a filter saved as a query. Leave this blank because you want all the records.

- Where Condition (optional): Enter a SQL WHERE clause that limits the records in the form. You can click the Build button next to the argument box to start the Expression Builder if you need help. Again, you want all the records, so don't add a Where Condition.

NOTE *See "Introducing Structured Query Language" in Chapter 9 for information about the SQL WHERE clause.*

- Data Mode (optional): Choose from the list of data entry modes: Add, to allow adding new records; Edit, to allow editing of existing records; or Read Only, to prevent any additions or editing. Choose Read Only from the list.

- Window Mode (required): Choose from the list of window modes, including Normal (default); Hidden, which hides the form; Icon, which displays the form minimized; or Dialog, which sets the form Popup and Modal properties both to Yes. Leave the Window Mode with the default Normal setting.

6. Close the Macro window, enter a name for the macro in the Save As dialog box, and then click OK. If you return to the Macros tab of the Database window, you can see the name of the new macro.

Choosing Actions

Access offers actions that cover data management activities, such as opening forms and reports, printing reports, filtering data, validating data, moving among records in a form, playing sounds, displaying message boxes, and even exchanging data with other programs.

To add an action to a macro, you can either choose from the drop-down list or type the name yourself. As with many lists offered by Access for choosing an item, if you begin to type the name of the action, Access automatically fills in the remaining characters for you.

- To navigate between controls or records, use the FindNext, FindRecord, GoToControl, or GoToRecord action.

- To modify an Access window, use Maximize, Minimize, MoveSize, or Restore action.

- To open an object, use OpenForm, OpenModule, OpenQuery, OpenReport, or OpenTable action.

- To set the value of a field or control, or a property of a form, control, or report, use SetValue action.

- To print a report, use OpenReport action and set the View argument to Print Preview. If you want to print the report without previewing, set the View argument to Print.

- To run a query, use the OpenQuery action and set the View argument to Datasheet.

PART III

> **NOTE** *See "Programming with Macros and SQL" in the Quick Reference on the CD for a complete description of all the macro actions and their arguments.*

Setting Action Arguments

Most macro actions have a list of associated arguments that give Access more information about how you want to carry out the action. Some arguments are required and others are optional. When you add an action to a macro, the argument list appears in the lower pane.

You can usually type the value you want in the argument box, but many offer drop-down lists. If you enter a value, some require it to be included in the list. A description of the current argument is displayed in a pane to the right of the argument list. If you need more help, press F1 with the insertion point in the argument box.

> **TIP** *In some cases, choices for one argument can determine which choices are available for an argument further down in the list. For this reason, setting the arguments in the order they're listed in the Action Arguments pane is best.*

If the argument requires an object name, you can enter the name or drag the object from the Database window to the argument box. When you drag an object from the Database window, Access automatically sets the appropriate arguments for that action.

Instead of selecting from a list or entering a value, you can enter an expression that evaluates to the argument value you want to use. Always precede the expression with an equal sign so Access recognizes it as an expression instead of an identifier. For example, the expression *=[EntryNo]* sets the argument to the value in the EntryNo control.

> **TIP** *The equal sign rule has two exceptions: the Expression argument of the SetValue action and the RepeatExpression argument of the RunMacro action give unexpected results if you use an equal sign. They evaluate the expression twice.*

If you want help from the Expression Builder, click the Build button, which appears at the right of the argument box when you click an argument that accepts an expression.

Not all arguments accept expressions. For example, you must select from the list for the ObjectType argument. If you use an expression where one isn't permitted, you get an error message.

> **NOTE** *If you want to refer to a control on another form, you must use the full object identifier syntax: [Forms]![formname]![controlname]. The ! symbol indicates what follows is an object named by the user. If the object was named by Access, you would use a period (.) to separate the object names. In addition, both forms must be open.*

Testing and Debugging a Macro

After you complete the macro, you can run it to see if it behaves as planned. You have a choice of running the complete macro at once or stepping through each action one at a time.

If an error occurs in the macro or you don't get the results you expect, use the step-through method of running the macro.

Starting the Macro

After you finish adding the actions and setting the arguments, you can run a macro in several ways. While still in the Macro window, click the Run button or choose Run | Run.

After you name and save the macro, you can run it from the Database window by one of the following methods:

- Select the macro name and click Run.
- Double-click the macro name.
- Right-click the macro name and choose Run from the shortcut menu.
- Choose Tools | Macro | Run Macro, and then enter the macro name in the Run Macro dialog box.

TIP   *If your macro depends on a particular form or report being open before it can run, open the form or report first.*

If an error occurs during the operation, Access displays an error message. Read the message, and then click OK to open the Action Failed dialog box. This tells you which action in the macro failed and the arguments being used at the time. The following Arguments box shows the second argument is missing from the GoToRecord action. You can tell by the two commas with no argument between them. It also shows any conditions that were in effect. Your only option in this dialog box is to click Halt to stop the macro. Before closing the dialog box, note the action name and other data about where the fault occurred. Then, it's up to you to switch to the Macro window to correct the problem.

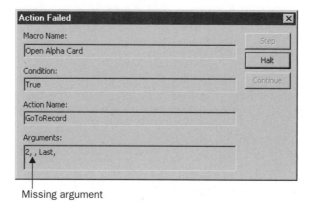

Missing argument

PART III

Stepping Through a Macro

If you create a macro with many actions and it contains an error, you can use the Single Step method to move through the macro, one action at a time. You must be in the Macro window to step through the macro actions. To start stepping through the macro, click Single Step or choose Run | Single Step, and then click Run or choose Run | Run to carry out the first action. A Macro Single Step dialog box opens showing the details of the first step in your macro.

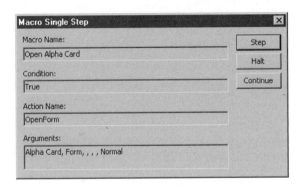

> **NOTE** *The Single Step mode remains in effect until you turn it off. Click the Single Step button again, or choose Run and clear the Single Step command.*

Your options in this dialog box are as follows:

- Step (default), which moves to the next action.
- Halt, which stops macro execution.
- Continue, which stops Single Step mode and runs the rest of the macro without stopping. If another error occurs, the macro stops and an Action Failed dialog box appears.

> **NOTE** *Your macro might cause other macros to run. For example, an OpenForm action in a macro might open a form that has other macros assigned to the OnOpen, OnLoad, or other event properties. If other macros run as a result of the macro you're testing, their steps are also displayed in the MacroSingleStep dialog box. You can tell it's a different macro by the name in the MacroName box.*

Modifying a Macro

After you see how a macro runs, you might decide to make some changes to it, such as adding another action, changing the order of the actions, adding a condition to the action, adding a Where Condition argument to limit the records, or creating additional macros to include in a macro group.

To open a macro for modification, select the macro name in the Database window and click Design. Use the Insert Rows and Delete Rows toolbar buttons or the Insert and Edit menu commands to add or delete actions. You can also use the standard Cut, Copy, and Paste operations to edit a macro. The Undo button is available to reverse the recent changes, as well.

TIP *If the macro operates on important data, make a temporary copy of the data to work with during the modification process. This way, if anything goes wrong, you haven't destroyed valuable information.*

After making the changes to the macro, save it again. If you save it with a different name, be sure to change all references to the macro accordingly.

Adding Conditions to a Macro

When you want a macro to run only under specific circumstances, you can add a condition to one or more of the macro actions. The macro condition states this effectively: If this condition is true, run this action. If it is not true, go to the next action, if any. This is a highly useful tool when programming an application. You can use conditions to set values of controls or control properties and even run additional macros. Such test comparisons aren't case sensitive.

Some examples of using conditions are the following:

- If the balance of an account is negative, change the color of the number to red.
- If a student's grades are exemplary, print a congratulatory message.
- If the inventory level of an item is low, display a message to remind you to reorder.
- If the order exceeds a specific total, calculate the amount due with a volume discount.

NOTE *Don't confuse the macro condition that determines whether the action takes place with the Where Condition that limits the records in the form or report. The macro condition is entered in the Condition column of the macro sheet and the Where Condition is an argument of many macro actions.*

Normally, a condition applies only to the action on the same row in the macro sheet. If the condition isn't met, the next action is executed. To continue the condition to the next action, enter an ellipsis (…) in the Condition column of the next row. You can apply the condition to several sequential actions.

TIP *When you're debugging a macro, you can temporarily disable an action by entering False in the Condition column. This can help to isolate the problem.*

You can also use conditions to create an If…Then…Else structure in a macro. This conditional logic runs one or more actions if the condition is met and a different set if the condition evaluates to False.

To add the Condition column to the macro sheet, click the Conditions button or choose View | Conditions. Type the logical expression for the condition in the row with the action you want to carry out if the condition is True. If you want to use the Expression Builder to help with the expression, right-click in the Condition column and choose Build from the shortcut menu.

NOTE *You cannot use a SQL expression as a condition in a macro. SQL expressions are used only in Where Condition arguments.*

Running a Macro with a Condition

When you run the macro, Access evaluates the condition and does the following:

- If the condition is True, Access runs the action on that row, and all actions directly following it, that have an ellipsis (…) in the Condition column. Then Access runs any additional actions that have blank conditions until it encounters another condition, a macro name in the Macro Name column, or the end of the macro.

- If the condition is False, the action is ignored as are any additional actions with an ellipsis (…) in the Condition column. Then Access moves to the next action, if any.

Table 19-1 shows some examples of expressions you can use as conditions with macro actions. All the fields in the expressions are in the form from which the macro originates, unless otherwise specified.

NOTE *Notice the use of identifiers to specify a control in a form other than the one from which the macro was launched. The referenced form must be open at the time the macro runs.*

Choosing Between Two Actions

How about the case where you want one thing to happen if a condition is true and something else to happen if it's false? You can use a macro to do that by using two versions of the same

Expression	Evaluates to True if:
[State]="CA"	CA is the value in the State control.
Forms![Alpha Entry]![Purge]<Date()	The Purge field on the Alpha Entry form is earlier than the current date.
[State] In ("CA","AZ","NV","NM") And Len([ZipCode])<5	The State value is one of those in the list and the value in the ZipCode field contains fewer than five characters. Combines two conditions into a single expression.
DCount("*","Alpha Entry", "[Index]=Forms![Alpha Card]![Index]")>5	More than five records are in the Alpha Entry table whose Index value matches an Index value in the Alpha Card table. Uses the DCount aggregate function.

TABLE 19-1 Examples of Conditional Expressions

condition. If you follow the conditional action with another action without using the opposite condition, the second action is always carried out.

For example, you want to do one thing if the Start Date is empty and carry out a different action if it shows a date. You could use the IsNull function in both conditions as follows:

IsNull("Start Date") Carry out the action when the Start Date is empty.

Not IsNull("Start Date") Carry out the action for a Start Date value.

Assigning a Macro to an Event Property

Once you create the macro to carry out the action you want, you need to decide when you want it to happen. Access responds to all kinds of events that occur when you're working with a form or report, including mouse clicks, changes in data, changes in focus, and opening or closing a form or report.

Chapter 18 contains a description of commonly used events, including when they happen and in what sequence. Assigning the macro to the right event in a sequence is important.

After you decide when you want the macro to run, you set the corresponding event property of the form, report, or control to the name of the macro. For example, if you want to run a macro that sounds a beep when a form opens, assign the macro to the On Open property of the form.

To attach a macro to an event property, do the following:

1. Open the form or report in Design view, and then select the form, report, section, or control.

2. Open the property sheet and click the Event tab to see a list of events that can occur for the selected object.

3. Click the property whose event you want to run the macro and choose the macro name from the drop-down list.

4. Save and close the form or report design.

NOTE   *If you select a macro name, and then click Build (...) next to the property box, you open the macro Design window where you can view and edit the selected macro.*

When the event occurs, the built-in response, if any, occurs first, and then the macro runs. For example, when you click a button, the built-in response occurs and the button appears pressed. If you attach a macro to the On Click event property, the macro runs next.

TIP   *If you want the macro to occur when you click either the control or its label, select them both before opening the property sheet. Then choose the macro name in the On Click event property for the multiple selection.*

Deciding Which Event to Use

Although the property sheet shows quite a long list of event properties for forms and controls, you'll use a few of them more often. Here are some of the commonly used form and control event properties:

- *On Open* occurs when the form opens, but before the first record is displayed. Use this property to open, close, or minimize other forms or to maximize this form.

- *On Current* occurs when the form is opened and focus moves to a record or the form is refreshed or requeried. Use this to synchronize data among forms or to move focus to a specific control.

- *Before Update* occurs after focus leaves a record, but before the data is saved in the database (also after a control loses focus, but before the control is changed). Use to display a message to confirm the change before it's completed.

- *After Update* occurs after the record changes are saved in the database (also after a control loses focus and after the control is changed). Use to update the data in other controls, forms, or reports or move focus to a different page, control, or record in the form.

- *On Click* occurs when you press and release the left mouse button over a control.

- *On Enter* occurs when you move to a control, but before it gets focus. Use to display information about data to enter in the control or a request for user password.

Reports have fewer event properties because little user interaction occurs with a report. Some of the more common event properties used to attach macros and event procedures to reports are as follows:

- *On No Data* runs a macro when the report has an empty underlying recordset. Use to cancel the print event.

- *On Open* runs a macro when the report opens, but before printing begins. Use to prompt for a filter for the records to be included in the report.

- *On Page* runs a macro after the page is formatted, but before printing begins. Use to add a graphic or border design to the report.

Report sections also have a few event properties to which you can attach a macro or event procedure.

NOTE   *Most of the macros used in an application are attached to the default events for the object. A* default event *is the event most often associated with a particular object, not one that occurs automatically. For example, the Click event is the most common event associated with command buttons and check boxes, while Open is the most common event for forms. When you use the Macro Builder to create a macro for an object, the macro is automatically attached to the default event.*

Some Common Uses for Macros

When you work with a database, Access causes many things to happen in response to your actions. You might be unaware that you can customize the database with macros to accomplish many similar operations according to your designs. Here are some of the more common applications for macros.

Displaying a Message Box

The *MsgBox action* is one of the most useful macro actions when interacting with the user. You can use it to display warnings, alerts, and other information. The MsgBox action has four arguments: Message, Beep, Type, and Title. Table 19-2 describes the values you enter in each of the arguments.

TIP   *Don't enclose the message in quotation marks unless you also want the marks displayed with the message.*

If you like the format of the built-in Access error messages, you can create the same effect with your own messages. The Message action argument can contain three sections separated by the @ character. The first section is text displayed as a bold heading and can be used as an alert. The second section appears in plain text below the heading and is used for an explanation

TABLE 19-2 MsgBox Action Arguments	Argument	Description
	Message	Enter the text of the message you want displayed when the macro runs. You can enter up to 255 characters; the box expands accordingly. You can also enter an expression preceded by an equal sign (=) that evaluates to a text message.
	Beep	Specifies whether to sound a beep signal when the message box opens. Set to Yes (default) or No.
	Type	Sets the type of message box, each of which displays a different icon. Choices are None (default), Critical (a red circle with an *X*), Warning? (a bubble with a question mark), Warning! (a yellow triangle with an exclamation mark), or Information (a bubble with a lowercase *i*).
	Title	Text that displays in the message box title bar. If left blank, the box is titled Microsoft Office Access.

of the error. The third section appears below the text of the second section, also in plain text, with a blank line between.

Validating Data

Usually, you ensure valid data is entered in a form by specifying a validation rule for the control in the form or by setting record and field validation rules in the underlying table design. For more complex data validation, use a macro or an event procedure to specify the rule.

The recommendation is that you use a macro or an event procedure if any of the following situations are present:

- You want to display different error messages for differing errors in the same field. For example, if the value is above the valid range, display one message; if the value is below the valid range, display another.

- You want the user to be able to override the rule. In this case, you can display a warning message and accept the user's confirmation or cancellation.

- The validation refers to controls in other forms or contains a function.

- The validation rule involves conditions based on more than one value. For example, if the user checks Credit Card as the method of payment, be sure the number and expiration date are also entered in the form.

- You have a generic validation rule that can be used for more than one form. When you want to apply it to a control on a form, run the SetValue macro action that sets the Validation Rule property for the control.

One example of using a macro to validate data is checking to make sure certain reports of serious criminal activity in the Police Alpha Entry table are never purged from the database. The macro is based on a condition that compares the Code value, which identifies the crime, with the value in the Purge field. The Purge field contains the date when the record could be erased from the file. The report of certain crimes is never to be erased. If the Code is in a certain range, no date should be entered in the Purge field. Figure 19-2 shows a macro that accomplishes this data validation. A date value was entered in the record that has a code between 11000 and 19999. Attach the macro to the Before Update event property of the text box control that contains the data in question.

FIGURE 19-2   Creating a macro for data validation

Filtering Records

The Northwind sample database that comes with Access contains a clever example of using a macro to filter records. The macro is associated with the Customer Phone List form (see Figure 19-3), which contains an alphabetic list of all the current customers. When you click one of the buttons at the bottom of the form, the list is filtered to show only those customers whose company name begins with the selected letter. The All button at the right of the row of buttons shows as pressed in, indicating all the names appear in the list.

NOTE   *If it's installed, the easiest way to find the Northwind sample database, is to choose Help | Sample Databases. If it isn't installed, run Setup again and change the Access options to include the Sample Databases.*

The Alpha Buttons macro applies a filter to the list, depending on which button is pressed. The row of buttons is an option group control, which returns a value representing the option selected. By default, the first item returns 1, the second returns 2, and so on. The macro (see Figure 19-4) uses the returned value in a condition for the ApplyFilter action. The Where Condition argument for each ApplyFilter action specifies the appropriate filter.

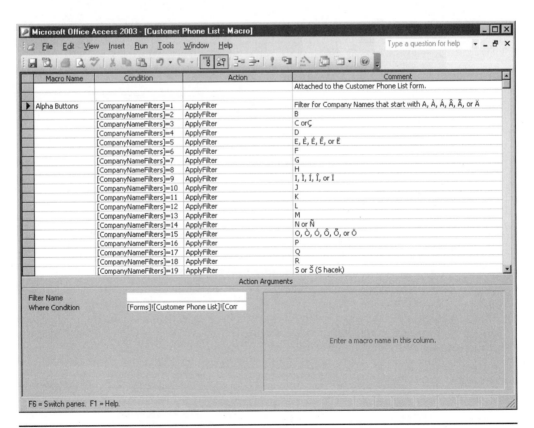

FIGURE 19-3   The Northwind Customer Phone List form

FIGURE 19-4   The macro behind the Customer Phone List

NOTE *Because Northwind Traders deals with customers worldwide, the filter must accommodate alphabet symbols from other languages, as well as English.*

The resulting recordset includes all records whose CompanyName field begins with any of the letters enclosed in brackets in the Where Condition argument.

When no records match the filter, you see an empty datasheet if no provisions are made for that case. If you scroll down the macro actions to the final rows (see Figure 19-5), you can see that if the record count is greater than 0, the records are displayed and the macro stops. The ellipsis (...) in the StopMacro row carries over the condition from the previous row.

If no records are returned by the filter, a message is displayed. When the user clicks OK to clear the message, all the records return to the screen because of the ShowAllRecords action. Then the SetValue action changes the value of the option group to 27, the number of the All button, so it appears pressed. The condition is carried over three actions in this sequence.

To see how the macro is attached to the form, switch to Form view and look at the event property sheet for the option group. The After Update event property is set to the Customer

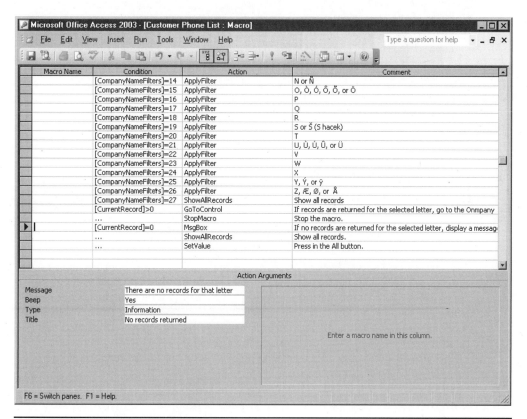

FIGURE 19-5 The closing macro actions

Phone List.Alpha Buttons macro, which causes the macro to run when the user clicks one of the buttons in the option group.

NOTE   *The Alpha Buttons macro is part of a macro group named Customer Phone List. When referring to a macro that's one of a group of macros, you must use the full name: macrogroupname.macroname. The names needn't be enclosed in brackets or quotation marks, even if they include spaces. More about macro groups in the section "Create a Macro Group."*

Setting Values and Properties

SetValue is a useful macro action that sets the value of a field, control, or property of a form, a form datasheet, or a report. You can set a value for almost any control, form, and report property in any view with the SetValue action.

The action has two arguments, both required: Item and Expression.

- The *Item* argument contains the name of the field, control, or property whose value you want to set. When you enter the name in the Item argument box, you use the control name if the control is on the form or report from which the macro is called. If the control is on another form or report, you must use the full identifier including the form or report name: Forms!*formname*!*controlname*. If you're setting the value of a property, add the property name to the identifier preceded by a period: Forms!*formname*!*controlname*.*property*. If it's a form or report property, omit the control name and the preceding "!".

- The *Expression* argument contains the value you want to set for the item. Again, use full syntax when referring to any Access objects in the expression. Use the Expression Builder if you need help. Don't precede the expression with an equal sign.

Setting Control Values

In addition to entering the value itself, you can set the value of a control based on the value of another control in the same or a different form or report. You can also use the result of a calculation or the value returned by an option group to set the value of a control.

For example, when you're adding new records to the Alpha Entry recordset in the subform of the Alpha Card form, you can compute the value of the Purge field. Depending on the Code value, the entry might be purged from the person's file after a certain length of time, usually three or seven years. To save data entry time, you can write a macro that examines the Code value and uses the DateAdd function to set the Purge date by adding a specified number of years to the Date field value.

NOTE   *The first argument in the DateAdd function, yyyy, indicates that the interval you want to increment is the year part of the date value. The second argument is the number to add and the third names the control that contains the original date.*

Setting Control Properties

Many of the properties of forms, reports, and controls can be set by running a macro. For example, you can hide a control from view on the form or disable it so the user can't enter data in it. You can also change colors, fonts, and other appearance properties.

As an example of setting a property with a macro, disable the Drivers License control if the subject of the Alpha Card report is younger than 16. To do this, set the Enabled property to No. When a control is disabled, it still appears on the screen, but it's dimmed and you can't reach it by pressing TAB or by clicking it.

To make sure you enter the correct identifier, you can use the Expression Builder. After adding the SetValue action to the macro, click Build (...) next to the Item argument to open the Expression Builder, and then do the following:

1. Double-click the Forms folder, and then double-click the All Forms folder in the left panel to open the list of forms in the current database.

2. Choose the Alpha Card form. A list of all controls and labels in the form appears in the center panel.

3. Choose Drivers_License. A list of all the properties that apply to the Drivers License text box control appears in the right panel.

4. Choose Enabled and click Paste. When you click OK, the expression is placed in the Item argument box.

To complete the macro, enter No in the Expression argument and add a condition to the action row that runs the macro only if the Age value is less than 16. Then attach the macro to the Age control's After Update event property. You probably want to add another macro to reenable Drivers_License when you move to the next record.

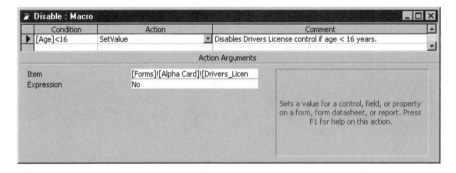

If you want to hide a control, set its Visible property to No.

If the property value is a string expression, enclose it in quotation marks in the Expression argument box.

To set report section properties, refer to the section by its number.

Changing the Flow of Operations

Adding conditions that determine whether a macro action is carried out is one way to control the flow of operations. If the condition evaluates to True, the corresponding action takes place. You can add the MsgBox function to a macro condition to let the user decide which action to carry out.

The MsgBox function is similar to the MsgBox action with the exception that the function returns one of seven different values, depending on which button the user clicks in the message box. The MsgBox function displays a dialog box containing the message and waits for the user to click a button indicating the user's choice. Several arrangements of buttons are available in the dialog box.

The MsgBox function has three main arguments; only the first is required:

- *Prompt* is a string expression displayed in the dialog box. You can display up to 1,024 characters, depending on the font size.

- *Button* is a number equal to the sum of three values that specify the visual characteristics of the message box, such as the number and type of buttons, the default button, the icon style, and the modality of the message box.

- *Title* is a string expression displayed in the dialog box title bar.

Two additional optional arguments can specify a Help file and context number in the file where you can find context-sensitive help.

You can display seven different buttons in various arrangements, as well as a choice of four icons. You can also specify which of the buttons is the default. Table 19-3 lists these button arrangements and dialog box features with their numeric values. The buttons are placed in the message box in the order—from left to right—they're listed in the table.

PART III

TABLE 19-3
MsgBox Function Button Argument Settings

Value	Buttons To Display:
0	Display only the OK button.
1	Display the OK and Cancel buttons.
2	Display the Abort, Retry, and Ignore buttons.
3	Display the Yes, No, and Cancel buttons.
4	Display the Yes and No buttons.
5	Display the Retry and Cancel buttons.
	Icons To Display:
0	Display no icon.
16	Display the Critical Message icon.
32	Display the Warning Query icon.
48	Display the Warning Message icon.
64	Display the Information Message icon.
	Specify The Default Button:
0	Set the first button as default.
256	Set the second button as default.
512	Set the third button as default.
768	Set the fourth button as default.

For example, if you want the message box to display the Yes, No, and Cancel set of buttons (3) with the Warning Query icon (32) and set the Yes button as the default (0), enter the sum 3 + 32 + 0 = **35** as the second argument in the MsgBox function.

NOTE   *The message box normally opens as application modal, which requires the user to respond to the message box before continuing. Additional argument settings can be used to change that. For example, if you want to make it system modal, which suspends all applications in the system until the user responds, add 4096 to the other values in the second argument.*

When the user clicks a button in the message box, the corresponding value is returned, which the macro condition can use to determine the next action to take. Table 19-4 lists the values returned by each type of button.

When you use the MsgBox function in a macro condition, you can compare the returned value to a specific number and carry out the action if the comparison is True. For example, you can use the MsgBox function to display a confirmation message before deleting a record. The box contains three buttons: Yes, No, and Cancel. If the user clicks the Yes button, the function returns 6, so if any other value is returned, the user didn't click Yes. Figure 19-6 shows a macro using the MsgBox function in a condition that evaluates to True if the function returned any value except 6 (Yes). If the value isn't 6, the deletion event is canceled. You could add other conditions that carry out actions as a result of the other button selections.

NOTE   *The Button argument in the MsgBox function in Figure 19-6 is 291, the sum of the Yes, No, Cancel button arrangement (3), the Warning Query icon (32), and setting the second button (No) as the default (256).*

After you save the Verify Deletion macro, attach it to the form's Before Del Confirm event property. The message box displays when you select a record and press DEL. In Figure 19-6, the Alpha Entry record for Index 24 was selected before pressing DEL. You can see it's been deleted from the Form view, but isn't confirmed yet. If you respond by clicking Yes, Access displays another confirmation message if the deletion can result in cascade deletions of other records or interfere in some other way with the relationships in the database.

TABLE 19-4
Values Returned by
MsgBox Function

Button	Returned Value
OK	1
Cancel	2
Abort	3
Retry	4
Ignore	5
Yes	6
No	7

FIGURE 19-6   Using the MsgBox function in a macro condition

Nesting Macros

If you want to run one macro from another, use the RunMacro action and set the Macro Name argument to the name of the macro you want to run. The RunMacro action is similar to choosing Tools | Macro | Run Macro, and then selecting the macro name. The only difference is the Tools command runs the macro only once. With the RunMacro action, you can repeat the macro many times.

The RunMacro action has two arguments in addition to the Macro Name:

- Repeat Count, which specifies the maximum number of times the macro is to run.

- Repeat Expression, which contains an expression that evaluates to True (-1) or False (0). The expression is evaluated each time the RunMacro action occurs. When it evaluates to False, the called macro stops.

The Repeat Count and Repeat Expression arguments work together to specify how many times the macro runs.

- If both are blank, the macro runs only once.

- If Repeat Count contains a number, but the Repeat Expression is blank, the macro runs the specified number of times.

- If the Repeat Count is blank, but the Repeat Expression contains an expression, the macro runs until the expression evaluates to False

- If both arguments contain entries, the macro runs the specified number of times or until the expression evaluates to False, whichever occurs first.

When the called macro is finished, Access returns to the calling macro and runs the next action after RunMacro.

NOTE *You can call a macro in the same macro group, as well as a macro in another group. If you enter a macro group name as the Macro Name argument, the first macro in the group runs.*

You can nest macros to more than one level. The called macro can, in turn, call another macro, and so on. As each macro finishes, it returns control back to the macro that called it.

Create a Macro Group

If you create several macros that apply to controls on the same form or report, you can group them together as one file. Using macro groups offers two advantages:

- It reduces the number of macro names in the Database window.
- You can find all the macros for a single form or report in one place where they're easy to edit, if necessary.

To create a macro group, open the macro sheet as usual and display the Macro Name column by clicking the Macro Names button or choosing View | Macro Names. Add a macro to the sheet and enter a name for it in the Macro Name column of the first row of the macro. Add the rest of the actions to the macro.

To add another macro, enter the name in the Macro Name column and add the actions you want to occur.

When Access runs a macro in a group, it begins with the action in the row that contains the macro name and continues until it finds no more actions or encounters another macro name. After adding all the macros to the group, close and save it as usual with the group name.

TIP *The macros in a group are much easier to read if you leave at least one blank row between the macros. You can also leave several rows blank at the top of the macro and add information in the Comment column that explains the purpose of the macro and where it's called from. Then the macro starts on the next row, where the Name and first Action appear.*

When you assign macros from a group to an event property, you need to use the group name, as well as the macro name. In the property sheet for a control, the drop-down list in an event property shows compound names for all the macros in a group, as well as the names of all the single macros. The group name and the macro name both appear separated by a period: *macrogroupname.macroname*. Figure 19-7 shows the macro group, Choose Report, which you meet in Chapter 21 when you see the Choose Report dialog box.

Assigning AutoKeys

Access offers a special macro group named *AutoKeys,* in which you can assign an action or set of actions to a specific key or key combination. These act like the shortcut key combinations you can use to carry out a menu command. Pressing the key or combination of keys carries out the action you specify. You can add as many individual macros to the group as you need, each one named with the key or key combination that runs it.

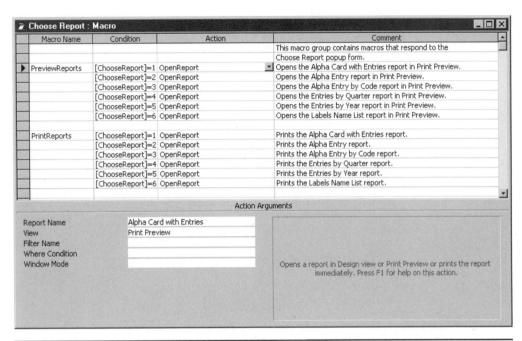

FIGURE 19-7 The Choose Report macro group

For example, the following macro opens the Alpha Card form when the user presses CTRL-F.

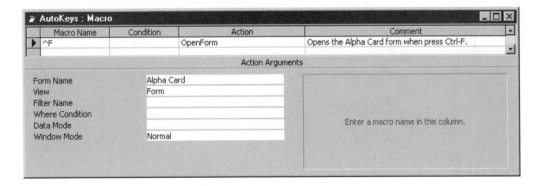

CAUTION *If you use a key combination Access already uses, such as CTRL-C for Copy, your actions replace the Access key assignment. Be warned, also, that resetting to default assignments will remove all custom assignments.*

Table 19-5 shows a list of valid AutoKeys key combinations. These combinations are part of the set that can be used by the Visual Basic SendKeys statement. The SendKey syntax

TABLE 19-5
AutoKeys Key
Combinations

Key Combination	Macro Name
CTRL+Any letter or number key	^A, ^4
Any function key	{F1}
CTRL+Any function key	^{F1}
SHIFT+Any function key	+{F1}
INS	{INSERT}
CTRL+INS	^{INSERT}
SHIFT+INS	+{INSERT}
DEL	{DELETE} or {DEL}
CTRL+DEL	^{DELETE} or ^{DEL}
SHIFT+DEL	+{DELETE} or +{DEL}

form is used as the macro name. The carat symbol (^) represents CTRL and the plus sign (+) represents SHIFT. Function keys and other key names are enclosed in curly brackets ({}).

Documenting Macros

Because macros are database objects, they're listed in the database Properties dialog box on the Contents tab. To view the list, choose File | Database Properties and click the Contents tab. Then scroll down the list until you reach the macro section.

If you want to keep documentation for the macros and macro groups in your database, you can print the macro description. With the macro name selected in the Database window, choose File | Print or click Print. In the Print Macro Definition dialog box, check the categories of information you want to print:

- *Properties* includes the container, date created, date of last update, owner, and user.
- *Actions and Arguments* lists all the actions with their conditions, if any, and the values of all the arguments.

- *Permissions by User and Group* lists user permissions, such as admin, and group permissions, such as Admins and Users.

NOTE   *If you only want to view the definition on the screen, choose File | Print Preview instead of File | Print, and then make the same selections in the Print Macro Definition dialog box.*

Creating an AutoExec Macro

You can create a special macro that runs when you first open a database. The AutoExec macro can carry out such actions as open a form for data entry, display a message box prompting the user to enter his or her name, or play a sound greeting.

All you need to do is create the macro with the actions you want carried out at startup and save it with the name AutoExec. A database can have only one macro named AutoExec.

When you open a database, all the startup options you set in the Startup dialog box take place first. You can see these by choosing Tools | Startup. Then Access looks for a macro named AutoExec, if one exists, and executes the actions in it.

You can bypass both the startup options and the AutoExec macro by pressing SHIFT when you open the database.

CAUTION   *Many of the same options can be set in the AutoExec macro as in the Startup dialog box. Be careful not to include conflicting settings in the macro. See Chapter 16 for information about the startup settings.*

Summary

Properly constructed macros carry out actions when you want them to and in the way you want. They're useful for responding to user input and manipulating data. As you work with macros, you can begin to see their potential.

In the next two chapters, macros are used to customize command bars and to create switchboard forms that open when you start an application. The switchboards give the user a list of activities from which to choose, such as enter or edit data, preview a report, or go to another list of activities.

PART III

Customizing Menus and Toolbars

In Access 97, Microsoft began blending the three types of user interaction tools into a single global concept: the command bar. While the terms toolbars, menu bars, and shortcut menus are still valid in Access 2003, and they do describe differing implementations, the methods used to create and modify custom command bars are the same for all types. The purpose is to make them more consistent, as well as easier to use and customize.

Many of the command bar elements are interchangeable among the three types. For example, you can add toolbar button images to menu bars and shortcut menus or you can add menus, submenus, and menu commands to toolbars.

You've worked with all these interaction tools extensively during the previous chapters in this book and when running other Office programs. In this chapter, you see how to work with and customize built-in command bars, as well as create custom command bars for an application.

Using Access Command Bars

The basic element of toolbars, menu bars, and shortcut menus is the command the user chooses to cause an action to take place, such as to print a report or run a query. You reach a command by the single act of clicking a toolbar button or by making choices from a hierarchy of menus and submenus.

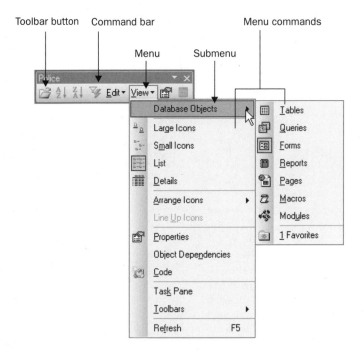

The command can appear as a button with an image or a menu command showing text. Menu commands with equivalent toolbar buttons often also display the icon that appears on the button. You can set options, so both menu commands and buttons can show text and images.

The commands can be grouped as a set of items in several ways:

- In a menu, such as the New, Open, Get External Data, and Close commands on the File menu.

- On a toolbar, such as the Print, Print Preview, and Spelling buttons on the Form View toolbar.

- In a shortcut menu, such as Cut, Copy, and Paste commands.

- In a submenu, such as the Import and Link Tables commands on the File | Get External Data submenu.

In any of these groupings, the individual commands can be represented by images, text, or both.

Some command bars are classified as *global* and are available to any database or application. *Built-in* command bars are predefined and are automatically displayed in specific views in any database. *Custom* command bars are user-defined and are limited to the database in which they were created. Custom command bars can also be attached to specific forms or reports.

Showing/Hiding Built-in Toolbars

The built-in Access toolbars appear automatically in certain contexts. For example, when you're in Form Design view, the default toolbars are Form Design and Formatting (Form/Report). If you right-click one of the toolbars, you see that you can also display several other toolbars.

To add toolbars not in the list to the window, open the Customize dialog box using one of the following methods:

- Choose Customize at the bottom of the toolbar shortcut menu.
- Choose View | Toolbars | Customize.
- Choose Tools | Customize.

The Toolbars tab of the Customize dialog box contains a list of all three types of available toolbars. Click the check box of any toolbar you want to add to the display, and then click Close.

As you can see, the two default toolbars for the Form Design view are already checked, as well as Menu Bar, the global menu. To remove a toolbar from the display, clear the check mark and click Close. Toolbars are immediately added to or removed from the screen behind the dialog box when you click a check box in the Customize dialog box. You cannot remove the global Menu Bar this way.

You can also remove a toolbar from the display by right-clicking any toolbar and removing the check mark from the name in the drop-down list. If the toolbar isn't the default for this view, the name will also be removed from the drop-down list. Default toolbar names remain on that list even though they aren't showing.

NOTE   *If you open a toolbar in a view it doesn't normally appear in, that toolbar stays on the screen until you close it, even if you close and reopen the database. Similarly, if you close a toolbar in a context where it normally appears, the toolbar remains closed until you reopen it. To reopen the toolbar, check it in the Customize dialog box's list of toolbars or right-click in a toolbar and check the toolbar in the drop-down list.*

The drop-down list of available toolbars includes Web and Task Pane in any Access view. Choosing Task Pane displays the Getting Started Task Pane or the last Task Pane you worked with. Choosing Web displays a web toolbar that looks like the Internet Explorer toolbar. When you click a button or enter a URL in the Address box, Internet Explorer carries out the action you selected.

Other toolbars are optionally available in many views. Right-click in one of the toolbars to see which toolbars are available. For example,

- In form Design view, the Form Design, Formatting (Form/Report), and Toolbox bars are available.

- In table Datasheet view, the Table Datasheet and Formatting (Datasheet) toolbars are available.

- In query Design view, the Query Datasheet and Formatting (Datasheet) toolbars are available.

Three additional toolbars aren't defaults for any view, but they appear in the Toolbars list in the Customize dialog box:

- The Source Code Control toolbar displays buttons you can use to control changes while creating Visual Basic code in a multiple-developer environment.

- The Utility 1 and Utility 2 toolbars are empty, built-in toolbars you can use to create custom global toolbars, as described in the section "Creating a Global Toolbar."

Two other items on the Toolbars list that aren't really toolbars are Menu Bar and Shortcut Menus. *Menu Bar* displays the default menu bar for the current view. The names of any new custom command bars you create appear in alphabetical order at the end of the list.

When you check Shortcut Menus in the Toolbars list, a menu bar is displayed, which contains all the built-in shortcut menus. As shown in Figure 20-1, clicking Report on the Shortcut Menus menu bar displays a list of shortcut menus associated with various elements of a report object, such as Design View Title Bar or Design View Control. When you click one of the elements in the list, you see the shortcut menu that displays when you right-click that part of the report in either the Design view or Print Preview.

If you create custom shortcut menus, the names aren't displayed separately in the Toolbars list. Instead, they're listed as menu items in the Custom category on the Shortcut Menus menu bar.

Showing/Hiding Toolbar Buttons

You needn't display all the default toolbar buttons on a toolbar. Using the Toolbar Options button, you have a choice of which buttons to display. Click the Toolbar Options button (a

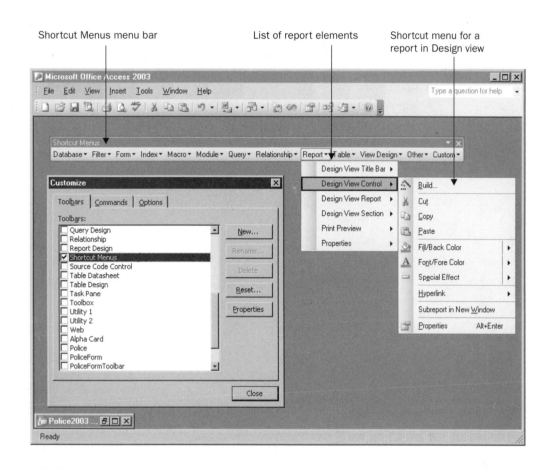

Shortcut Menus menu bar   List of report elements   Shortcut menu for a
report in Design view

FIGURE 20-1   Viewing the list of built-in shortcut menus

gray area rather than a conventional button) on the right end of the toolbar (or at the right
end of the title bar next to the Close button if the toolbar is floating) to display the list of
buttons available to that toolbar. Then click the Add or Remove Buttons drop-down arrow
and point to the toolbar name in the list of toolbar buttons currently showing. Figure 20-2
shows the list of buttons normally displayed on the Table Datasheet toolbar. The arrow at
the end of the list indicates additional buttons aren't in view.

To hide a button, clear the check mark next to the button name. To restore the button to
the toolbar, check it in the list again.

NOTE   *When you remove a button from the toolbar, the equivalent menu command isn't removed
from the menu.*

FIGURE 20-2   The available buttons in the Toolbars Options list

Moving/Resizing Command Bars

A command bar is *docked* if it's fixed to one edge of the window. Menu bars and toolbars normally appear docked at the top of the window. You can drag them away from the edge and turn them into *floating* command bars, which can be moved about on the screen. A docked command bar has no title bar, while a floating command bar has an identifying title bar. The toolbox that you use when you're working in a form or report Design View is an example of a toolbar that is, by default, a floating toolbar, which can be docked if you want.

To move a toolbar or menu bar from its docked position, click-and-drag its moving handle (the stack of small dots at the left end of the bar). You can also click an empty space or any separator bar in the menu bar or a toolbar to drag it away from the dock. After moving the command bar away from the edge of the window, you can drag the toolbar borders to change the height and width of the bar.

To dock the command bar to an edge of the window, drag it to the side until it spreads to the full height or width of the window.

You can also change the arrangement of the menu bar and the toolbars when they're docked. For example, if you want the toolbar to appear above the menu bar, click the toolbar's moving handle and drag it over the menu bar.

Changing Menu and Toolbar Options

In addition to repositioning and resizing a built-in menu or toolbar, you can use the Options tab of the Customize dialog box to set other features. The upper pane sets options for the menus and toolbars as personalized by Access. The lower pane contains options that change the way command bars look and behave. Table 20-1 describes the effects of each option.

Option	Description
Show Standard and Formatting toolbars on two rows	Displays the two default chart toolbars that appear in separate rows when you're editing a chart in Access.
Always show full menus	Shows all commands on menus. Clear the check mark for this option to show only the basic or frequently used commands on personalized versions of the menus. Affects all Office programs.
Show full menus after a short delay	Expands the menu when you open the menu and rest the mouse pointer on it. Always checked unless the previous option is cleared, and then it can also be cleared.

TABLE 20-1   Menu and Toolbar Options

Option	Description
Reset menu and toolbar usage data	Clears the menu and toolbar settings that were automatically saved as you chose menu commands and toolbar buttons.
Large icons	Displays larger button images. Affects all Office programs.
List font names in their font	Displays the drop-down list of fonts in the Formatting toolbars as a sample of the font.
Show ScreenTips on toolbars	Displays the name of the button when the mouse pointer rests on it. Affects all Office programs.
Show shortcut keys in ScreenTips	Includes the shortcut key combination to the button name in the ScreenTip. Affects all Office programs except Excel.
Menu animations	Determines the way menus react when displayed. Choices are (System default), Random, Unfold, Slide, and Fade.

TABLE 20-1   Menu and Toolbar Options *(continued)*

The following toolbar has large icons and displays both ScreenTips and shortcut keys. Notice the double arrows at the right end of the toolbar, indicating additional buttons are out of view offscreen.

These option settings all remain in effect until you change them.

Customizing Command Bars

Access provides so many useful menu bars and toolbars, why would anyone want to create custom command bars? One reason could be you don't want the user to make changes in a form or report design. You can remove the View button from the toolbar to keep the user from switching to Design view.

Other possible customizations are:

- Adding a Save Record button to the toolbar, so the user can quickly test the validity of the data just entered without leaving the record.
- Removing the New Object button from the toolbar to keep the user from designing new forms, reports, or other Access objects.

- Tailoring the commands and button options to match the terminology and practice of a specific application.

You use the Customize dialog box to create and customize all three types of command bars. Modifying built-in command bars and creating new custom command bars use the same techniques and tools. The difference between a modified built-in command bar and a new customized command bar is this: the modified command bar is available to all databases, while the custom bar is available only to the database where it was created.

After adding menu commands and buttons to a new or modified command bar, you can set many of its properties to achieve the appearance and behavior you want. For example, you can control whether the command bar can be docked, moved, or resized, and even specify the type of animation to show when commands are selected. You can change button icons and also create your own images.

The Customize dialog box also contains the option to restore a modified built-in command bar to its original state.

Creating a Global Toolbar

You have two ways to create a custom toolbar that's available to all your databases: modify a built-in toolbar or create a new global toolbar. The list of available toolbars in the Customize dialog box includes the blank Utility 1 and Utility 2 built-in toolbars. When you add buttons and menu commands to them, they become custom global toolbars and are available to all the databases and Access client projects. They're treated as modified built-in toolbars, not as custom toolbars.

NOTE *You cannot rename the global toolbars created in Utility 1 and Utility 2. You can modify them later if you need to place different buttons and menu commands on them or you can modify a different built-in toolbar to use as a global toolbar.*

Creating Custom Toolbars and Menu Bars

Whether you're creating a new custom toolbar, a menu bar, or a shortcut menu, it all begins the same way:

1. Open the Customize dialog box using one of the methods described earlier.

2. Click the Toolbars tab, click New, and then type a name for the new toolbar in the New Toolbar dialog box.

3. Click OK. A tiny, empty toolbar appears in front of the Customize dialog box and the toolbar name, Alpha Card, appears in the Toolbars box.

4. On the Toolbars tab, click Properties. The Toolbar Properties dialog box opens.

Toolbar Properties	? ☒

Selected Toolbar: `Alpha Card`

Toolbar Properties

Toolbar Name: `Alpha Card`

Type: `Toolbar`

Docking: `Allow Any`

☑ Show on Toolbars Menu   ☑ Allow Moving
☑ Allow Customizing   ☑ Allow Showing/Hiding
☑ Allow Resizing

[Restore Defaults]   [Close]

5. Here's where the processes diverge. Do one of the following:

- To continue with a custom toolbar, set the toolbar properties, as described next.
- If you want to create a new menu bar, choose Menu Bar from the Type list and then set the properties.
- If you want to create a new shortcut menu, choose Popup from the Type list and set the properties.

6. Choose Close when you finish setting the properties.

The Selected Toolbar box in the Toolbar Properties dialog box shows the name of the toolbar. Click the down arrow to see the list of all toolbars, menu bars, and shortcut menus in the current database. Table 20-2 describes each of the properties you can set for custom toolbars and menu bars. Although the properties are called Toolbar Properties, they apply equally to menu bars. Shortcut menus have fewer properties available.

> **NOTE** *You cannot change many of these properties as they apply to built-in command bars, only custom command bars.*

> **NOTE** *If you change the toolbar type to Popup to create a shortcut menu, the only property available is Allow Customizing. All others are dimmed. Access displays a warning if you try to change a toolbar or menu to a popup.*

Property	Description
Toolbar Name	Shows the name entered in the New Toolbar dialog box or the name of the selected built-in toolbar. Edit the name here, if desired.
Type	Shows the type of the selected toolbar. Toolbar is the default setting. Click the arrow to see a list of command bar types: Menu Bar, Toolbar, and Popup (shortcut menu). To change the type of a selected command bar, choose a different type.

TABLE 20-2   Setting Custom Toolbar Properties

Property	Description
Docking	Specifies the type of docking you want to permit for this toolbar: Allow Any (default), Can't Change, No Vertical (limits docking to the top and bottom of the screen), or No Horizontal (limits the docking to the sides of the screen). If you choose any setting but Can't Change, be sure to select Allow Moving, too.
Show on Toolbars Menu	Displays the toolbar name in the list when you right-click a toolbar or choose View I Toolbars.
Allow Customizing	Permits changes to the appearance and behavior through the Customize dialog box.
Allow Resizing	Permits resizing of the floating toolbar. Docked toolbars can't be resized.
Allow Moving	Permits moving the toolbar between the docked position and floating. When not docked, you can drag the toolbar to other locations on the screen.
Allow Showing/Hiding	Permits showing or hiding the toolbar.

TABLE 20-2   Setting Custom Toolbar Properties *(continued)*

After setting the desired properties for the new toolbar, menu bar, or shortcut menu, you can proceed to add buttons and menus.

If you're modifying a built-in toolbar, some of the properties aren't available. For example, the Toolbar Name and Type properties are dimmed because you can't rename a built-in toolbar or change its type. Also, the Show on Toolbars Menu option is dimmed because the built-in toolbars in context with the current view are always shown on the list when you right-click the toolbar or choose View I Toolbars. The Restore Defaults button, which you can click to restore a built-in toolbar to its original condition, does become available, however.

Adding/Deleting Toolbar Buttons

Once you begin creating a new toolbar, you can add buttons to it in two ways:

- Copy or move a built-in or a previously created custom button from another toolbar.
- Select the button from the list of commands in the Commands tab of the Customize dialog box.

Figure 20-3 shows the commands in the Query Design toolbar. The commands in the list that show an ellipsis (...) after the text, such as Show Table, open a dialog box. Ones with a vertical bar and a black triangle, such as Query Type, open a submenu.

Many types of commands are available in the Commands box, including the built-in buttons that appear in built-in toolbars. The commands are grouped into categories. Click the desired category to see the commands available in that category. You might have to examine more than one category to find the button you want—some are stored in unusual categories.

FIGURE 20-3
Categories and
Commands in
the Customize
dialog box

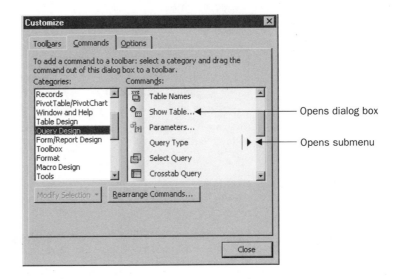

Some other categories have useful controls you can add to a command bar. For example, the All Tables category shows a list of all tables in the current database in the Commands pane. These commands open the table in Datasheet view.

Similarly, the All Queries category offers commands that open queries in Datasheet view. The All Forms commands open forms in Form view, while the All Reports commands open reports in Print Preview. Commands from the All Macros category run the selected macro.

To add a button from the Customize dialog box:

1. Choose the type of command you want in the Categories list. The Commands list shows images and text of commands in that category.

2. When you find the button you want, drag it to the toolbar. When you see a dark I-beam, drop the button on the toolbar.

3. Continue to add other buttons to the toolbar. You can drop a button between two buttons already in the toolbar. The bar expands as you add buttons. To move a button already in place, drag it to the desired position.

If another toolbar has a button you can use, you can move or copy it to the new toolbar. Using an existing button is easier than starting from scratch. An additional advantage is, when you copy or move a command from a built-in toolbar, the command keeps all the pointers to Access Help topics.

CAUTION   *Moving a button from one toolbar to another removes it from the source toolbar.*

You must have both toolbars showing to do this. The Customize dialog box can be open or closed. To copy a button from another toolbar:

• If the Customize dialog box is open, hold down CTRL while you drag the button.

• If the Customize dialog box isn't open, hold down CTRL-ALT while you drag the button.

CAUTION *If you copy a built-in button, the copy isn't independent of the original button. If you make changes to the copy of the button, the same changes also affect the built-in button. If you intend to make changes to the button, creating a new custom toolbar and dragging the buttons from the Commands box is better.*

To move a button from another toolbar:

- If the Customize dialog box is open, drag the button to the new toolbar.
- If the Customize dialog box isn't open, hold down ALT while you drag the button.

TIP *If you want to add a button that opens a database object in its default view, you can simply drag the object from the Database window to the toolbar. The Customize dialog box must be closed to do this. The button ScreenTip displays the name of the object it opens.*

To remove a button with the Customize dialog box open, drag it off the toolbar or right-click the button and choose Delete from the shortcut menu. When you delete a built-in button, it's still available from the Commands box, but deleting a custom button removes it permanently. If the Customize dialog box isn't open, hold down ALT while you drag the button off the toolbar.

TIP *If you want to keep custom buttons for later use instead of deleting them completely, create a new toolbar for storing them until you need them. Move the buttons from one toolbar to the other, and then hide the new toolbar by clearing the check mark in the Toolbars box of the Customize dialog box.*

You can customize toolbar buttons in many ways, including adding text and shortcut keys. Buttons on a toolbar can be grouped by category or special purpose with vertical separator bars. See the section "Modifying Command Bars" for information about customizing toolbar buttons and menu commands.

Adding Built-in Menus

You can add built-in menus to a toolbar or a menu bar by the same two methods: drag from the Commands box of the Customize dialog box, or move or copy from an existing toolbar or menu bar. The only difference between adding toolbar buttons and menus is that the menus, by default, show only text, while the buttons show only an image. These properties can be changed and customized.

With the new menu bar or toolbar showing, open the Customize dialog box and click the Commands tab. Scroll down the Categories list and select Built-in Menus. Figure 20-4 shows some of the available built-in menus.

Drag the menu from the Commands box to the menu bar or toolbar, and then drop the menu when you see the dark I-beam.

FIGURE 20-4
Selecting a
built-in menu

Moving and copying menus is the same as moving and copying buttons. Deleting built-in menus is also the same as deleting buttons.

Most of the commands in the built-in menu are carried over, depending on the context of the new menu bar or toolbar.

Adding Custom Menus

If you want to add a custom menu to a toolbar or menu bar, you create it in place on the bar. To add a new custom menu, do the following:

1. With the toolbar or menu bar showing, open the Customize dialog box and click the Commands tab.

2. Scroll down the list of Categories and click New Menu.

3. Drag New Menu from the Commands box to the menu bar or toolbar.

4. Right-click the New Menu, enter a name in the Name box of the shortcut menu, and then press ENTER, as shown in Figure 20-5.

FIGURE 20-5
Adding a new menu to a toolbar

5. Add commands to the new menu by choosing from the Commands dialog box or moving or copying from other menus, as described in the next section.

Adding Menu Commands to a Toolbar or a Menu Bar

Menu commands can be added to both toolbars and menu bars using the same procedure. The menu commands are placed in a column under the menu name.

To add a menu command, do the following:

1. With the menu bar, toolbar, or shortcut menu showing, open the Customize dialog box and click the Commands tab.

2. Click the appropriate menu or view category in the Categories box.

3. Drag the command from the Commands box and rest it on the menu in the menu bar or the toolbar. When you see the list of commands already in the menu (or, if the menu is new, an empty box) and drag the command to the position where you want it to appear, a horizontal bar appears in the drop-down menu just above the position where the command is to be inserted. When the bar is in the right place, release the mouse. If the menu is new, release the mouse button over the empty box.

In the following example, the Print Preview command is added as the first command in the new custom menu, named Forms/Reports.

NOTE   *If you add a menu command to a built-in menu, such as the File menu that appears in more than one view, that command appears in all views of the menu.*

You can also move or copy a menu command from another menu bar, toolbar, or shortcut menu. If you're moving or copying a menu command to a menu in a different menu bar or toolbar, both the source and destination bars must be showing. The Customize dialog box must also be open to move or copy a menu command.

- To move the command, drag it over the menu where you want it to appear and, when you see the list of the commands in the menu, release the mouse at the desired position.

- To copy the command, press CTRL while you drag the command to the new menu or toolbar.

To delete a menu command from a menu or toolbar, do the following:

1. Open the Customize dialog box and show the menu bar or toolbar that contains the command you want to delete.

2. Click the menu on the menu bar or toolbar that contains the command you want to remove.

3. Drag the command off the menu and away from the other menu bars or toolbars.

CAUTION   *If you remove a command from a built-in menu, the command is removed from that menu in every menu bar in which it appears.*

Adding a Submenu

A *submenu* is a menu within a menu and it's created the same way as a menu. To add a custom submenu to an existing menu, do the following:

1. Drag the New Menu command from the Commands box to the menu you want to contain the submenu. When you see the horizontal line, release the mouse and the New Menu control is placed with the other menu commands. The only difference is that the new menu shows a pointer indicating it opens another list of menu commands.

NOTE   *You can also add one of the built-in menus or toolbar buttons that opens a submenu, and then customize its commands.*

2. Right-click New Menu and type a name for the submenu, such as **Run Queries**, and then press ENTER.

3. Slowly click the new submenu to display a small empty box to the right of the submenu where the menu commands are to be placed. If you click too fast, the box doesn't appear.

4. Select and drag a command, such as a query name from the All Queries category, to the empty box and, when the I-beam appears, release the mouse. The Forms/ Reports menu has two submenus: the built-in View menu and a custom submenu for running queries.

5. Drag the names of the other queries you want in the submenu from the All Queries list to the submenu.

Adding Commands to a Shortcut Menu

When you close the Toolbar Properties dialog box after choosing Popup as the toolbar type, the new shortcut menu is added to the Custom category on the *Shortcut Menus* toolbar. The Shortcut Menus toolbar is the group designation for all shortcut menus in the application. When you're ready to complete the shortcut menu, do the following:

1. Open the Customize dialog box and click Shortcut Menus in the Toolbars box on the Toolbars tab. The Shortcut Menus toolbar appears at the top of the screen.

2. Click the Custom category on the Shortcut Menus toolbar.

3. Add menu commands from the Customize dialog box the same way as for menu bars and toolbars. You can also move or copy commands from other menus.

NOTE   *A shortcut menu can be global or context-sensitive. To specify a shortcut menu as global, set the option in the Startup dialog box as described in the section "Specifying Global Command Bars." A context-sensitive shortcut menu contains commands that relate to the object to which it's attached.*

Attaching a Custom Command Bar to an Object

Reports, forms, and controls have properties that specify which, if any, command bar is to be displayed when the object is in view.

- The *Menu Bar property* specifies the menu bar to display when a form or report has focus. If the property is left blank, Access displays the built-in menu bar for the form or report or the global menu bar as defined in the Startup dialog box.

- The *Toolbar property* specifies the toolbar to use with a form or report when it's opened. If the property is left blank, Access displays the default toolbar for the form or report.

- The *Shortcut Menu Bar property* specifies the shortcut menu to display when you right-click a form, report, or a control on a form (but not a control on a report). If the property is left blank, Access displays the default shortcut menu or the global shortcut menu as defined in the Startup dialog box.

To set one of these properties, open the object's property sheet and click the Other tab. Select the name of the command bar from the drop-down list next to the appropriate property box. Repeat the process for each form, report, or control to which you want to attach a command.

NOTE *Forms and controls have an additional command bar property, the Shortcut Menu property, which is set to Yes or No, depending on whether you want the user to be able to open the shortcut menu. You can set this property to No in the property sheet or with a macro to protect the form from unauthorized changes, which could be made with commands that appear in the default shortcut menu.*

When you attach a custom command bar to a form, the bar appears only when the form is in Form view. Similarly, a custom command bar attached to a report appears only in Print Preview.

Specifying Global Command Bars

A global menu bar replaces the built-in menu bar in all the windows in an application, except where you specify a custom menu bar for a form or report. A global shortcut menu replaces the shortcut menus for datasheets, forms, form controls, and reports.

To specify a custom menu bar or a custom shortcut menu as the default for the entire database or application, you need to change the settings in the Startup dialog box. To set global command bars to replace the defaults, do the following:

1. Choose Tools | Startup to open the Startup dialog box.

2. Click the arrow next to the Menu Bar box and select the name of the custom menu bar to use instead of the default. The list includes only custom menu bars.

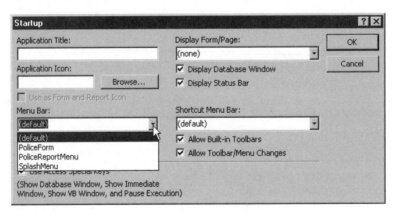

3. Click the arrow next to the Shortcut Menu Bar box and select the shortcut menu to use instead of the default.

4. Click OK to close the dialog box.

Other settings can restrict the user's access to full menus, default shortcut menus, and built-in toolbars. See Chapter 16 for more information about setting startup options.

The changes take effect the next time you open the database. To bypass the startup options, press SHIFT while the database is opening.

TIP   *If all the built-in toolbars or some of the built-in menus no longer appear on the screen when they're supposed to, you could have changed some settings in the Startup dialog box. Be sure to check Allow Built-in Toolbars and Allow Full Menus to bring them back to their default views. If you still don't see all the menus, they might have been removed from the menu bar. The menus are still available from the Customize dialog box, so you can easily return them to the built-in menu bar.*

Deleting a Custom Command Bar

To delete a custom toolbar, menu bar, or shortcut menu, open the Customize dialog box as usual, and then click the Toolbars tab. Select the item you want to delete and click Delete. If the toolbar or menu bar is a built-in one you modified, the Delete button isn't available. Instead, click Reset to remove the custom features and restore the built-in command bar to its original default state.

Deleting a shortcut menu is a little different. You must convert it to a toolbar before you can delete it. Perform the following steps to delete a custom shortcut menu:

1. Open the Customize dialog box and click the Toolbars tab, and then select any toolbar. Shortcut menus don't appear in the list, so you need to select any toolbar to get started.

2. Click Properties to open the Toolbar Properties dialog box.

3. In the Selected Toolbar box, choose the name of the shortcut menu you want to delete.

4. Choose Toolbar in the Type list to change it to a toolbar, and then click Close to return to the Customize dialog box. The shortcut menu name is added to the list of toolbars.

5. Select the name of the shortcut menu (now a toolbar) in the list of toolbars and click Delete. Click OK to confirm the deletion.

Modifying Command Bars

Most changes to command bars are made with the Customize dialog box open. You can add more buttons, menus, and menu commands, and then rearrange them on the bar. The Rearrange Commands feature on the Commands tab is new with Access 2003 and it provides a single platform for modifying command bars. The Rearrange Commands dialog box also gives you access to a shortcut menu where you can specify other settings and properties for individual commands.

To make changes in a command bar, it must be visible when the Customize dialog box is displayed. Open the Customize dialog box and select all the toolbars you want to work on. Then select the Commands tab and click the Rearrange Commands button. The Menu Bar box in the Rearrange Commands dialog box contains a complete list of all the menus and submenus in the Menu Bar. In Figure 20-6, the File menu from the built-in Menu Bar is selected in the Menu Bar box, and the menu items and submenus are displayed in the Controls box below it.

You can select any of the menus in the Menu Bar, and work with the menu commands
and submenus contained in the menu. Figure 20-7 shows the Tools menu selected in the
Menu Bar box with the list of commands and submenus it contains. If you want to work
with the menu commands in one of the submenus, select it in the Menu Bar box. Then you
can see the menu commands from that submenu in the Controls box.

To work with toolbars, click the Toolbar radio button. The Toolbar box displays a list of all the currently visible toolbars. To select the one you want to work with, scroll down the list.

Moving Controls

To rearrange the controls in a toolbar, select the toolbar from the list of toolbars, and then select the control you want to move. Clicking the Move Up button moves the control up one position. Clicking the Move Down moves it down one position.

You can move individual commands in the Menu Bar from the Menu Bar box this way, but you can't move the menus themselves. For example, you want to see the View menu first in the bar instead of the File menu. To move a menu in the Menu Bar, you need to select Menu Bar from the list of toolbars. Then you see the list of the menus in the Controls pane. Select one and click Move Up or Move Down as before.

Adding and Deleting Controls

To add a new control to the Menu Bar or one of the toolbars, first select the control in the Controls list where you want to place the new control. It'll be added before the selected control. Then click the Add button. The Add Command dialog box opens with the same collection of categories and commands you can see in the Commands tab of the Customize dialog box. Pick the category and select the command you want, and then click the OK button.

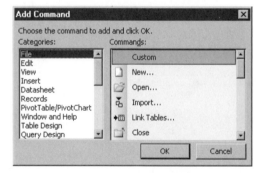

To delete a command from a toolbar, select the command in the Controls box and click the Delete button. You aren't asked to confirm the deletion.

Modifying a Selected Control

If you want to make changes to an individual control's appearance or behavior, you can select the control and click the Modify Selection button. This opens the same shortcut menu that you might remember from previous versions of Access (see Figure 20-8). Table 20-3 describes the settings in the list. If the control is a button, additional commands are available.

FIGURE 20-8   Editing buttons and menu commands

Selection	Description
Reset	Restores the default properties of a built-in button, menu, or menu command. Not available for custom buttons, menus, or menu commands.
Delete	Removes the button, menu, or menu command from the toolbar. Built-in objects are still available in the Commands box, but custom objects are deleted permanently.
Name	Enter a new name in the Name box and press ENTER. You can rename both built-in and custom buttons, menus, and menu commands.
Default Style	Displays a button with only an image and a menu command with text and an image, if one exists.

TABLE 20-3   Editing Buttons and Menu Commands

Selection	Description
Text Only (Always)	Displays text only with no image on both buttons and menu commands.
Text Only (in Menus)	Displays text only with no image on menu commands and only an image with no text on buttons.
Image and Text	Displays both an image, if one exists, and text on buttons and menu commands.
Begin a Group	Adds a dividing line before or above the button, menu, or menu command.
Assign Hyperlink	Assigns a hyperlink to the command or removes an existing link.
Properties	Opens the Control Properties dialog box for the selected toolbar, menu bar, or shortcut menu.

TABLE 20-3   Editing Buttons and Menu Commands *(continued)*

NOTE   *If you selected a button, the list includes several image properties: Copy Button Image, Paste Button Image, Reset Button Image, Edit Button Image, and Change Button Image.*

Grouping Controls

When you have a set of buttons, commands, or menus that relate to similar operations, you can group them in a command bar by adding separator bars between controls. For example, the Print, Print Preview, and Spelling buttons appear in a group on the Database toolbar with a bar before Print and another after Spelling.

Use the Move Up or Move Down buttons to place the controls together. Then add a bar at the left of a button or menu, or above a menu command, by selecting the control and clicking the Modify Selection button. Choose Begin a Group from the menu. The Begin a Group option isn't available for a leftmost or top control in the command bar.

To remove the separator bar, repeat the process and clear the Begin a Group check mark.

Adding an Access Key

Characters that appear underlined in the text of a menu or menu command represent *access keys,* or *hot keys,* as they're sometimes called. Pressing ALT plus the access key character selects that menu or menu command. When you customize toolbars and menu bars, you can specify access keys.

To designate a character in the name as the access key, precede the character by an ampersand (&). When the command is displayed, the character appears underlined. For example, to add an access key to the City Beats form name in the menu command, enter "&City Beats" as the command Name. If another menu command already uses C as the access key, use another character, for example, "City &Beats."

TIP   *When you specify access keys for multiple menu commands in a single menu, be sure to assign a different character to each command. If two commands have the same access key, only the first in the list is activated when you press ALT plus the key character.*

Adding and Editing Images

Built-in toolbar buttons and many of the built-in menu commands show icon images, which you can customize for your application. You can copy images from one button or command to another, copy a graphics image from another program, choose from a palette of existing images, or even design your own image with the Image Editor.

To copy from one toolbar or menu bar to another, you must have the Customize dialog box open, as well as both bars showing. Click the Rearrange Commands button, and then do the following:

1. Select the button or command that contains the image you want to copy and click the Modify Selection button.

2. Choose Copy Button Image from the shortcut menu.

3. Back in the Rearrange Commands dialog box, select the button or command you want to show the image and click Modify Selection again. Then choose Paste Button Image.

NOTE   *If you change the image for a command on a built-in menu or toolbar, all views showing that command bar will reflect the changed image.*

To copy an image from a graphics program, copy the image to the clipboard, right-click the button or command you want the image to appear on, and then choose Paste Button Image from the shortcut menu.

TIP   *You get the best results if you choose a graphics image the same size as the built-in image, which is 16 × 16 pixels. Resizing the imported image can blur the resolution.*

To change a button icon to one of the predefined images, select the image you want to change and click the Modify Selection button. Then choose Change Button Image from the shortcut menu. Click an image in the palette to copy it to the button or command.

Assigning a Hyperlink

You can add a custom button or menu command to a command bar that jumps to a specified hyperlink in the current database, to another location on your hard drive or local network, or to a web page. To add a hyperlink command, open the Customize dialog box and do the following:

1. On the Commands tab, drag the Custom command from the Commands list to the command bar. Custom is the first command in the File category.

2. Select the new Custom button and click the Modify Selection button.

3. Choose Assign Hyperlink | Open.

4. In the Assign Hyperlink dialog box scroll down the list of files in the Current Folder and select the hyperlink address to which you want to jump. See Chapter 12 for information about browsing for hyperlink addresses.

Changing Control Properties

The last command on the Modify Selection shortcut menu opens the Control Properties dialog box, where you can make further modifications to the buttons, menus, and menu commands on a menu bar or toolbar. For example, set the Control Properties dialog box for the Filter By Selection button.

All the properties can be set for buttons and menu commands. Some are also available for menus. The control properties you can set are as follows:

- **Caption**   Enter or edit the name of the control. The ampersand (&) before *S* indicates it as the access key for this button. Available for menus.

- **Shortcut Text**   Enter the text you want displayed next to the menu command to indicate the shortcut key or key combination, such as CTRL-C. The shortcut key is defined in the AutoKeys macro. With a menu command, the shortcut key text appears to the right of the command. With a toolbar button, the shortcut key text is displayed in the ScreenTip (if you checked the Show Shortcut Keys in ScreenTips box for the button on the Options tab of the Customize dialog box).

- **ScreenTip**   Enter the text to be displayed in the ScreenTip when the mouse pointer rests on the control. If you leave this blank, the control name is displayed as a ScreenTip. Available for menus.

- **On Action**   Enter the name of the macro or the Visual Basic function procedure you want to run when the control is selected. Select from the list, which displays the names of all the macros in the current database, or type a function name. A function name must be preceded by an equal sign (=). The On Action property works like an event property for other objects. Available for menus.

- **Style**   Choose from the same four style options that appeared in the shortcut menu: Default Style, Text Only (Always), Text Only (in Menus), or Image and Text.

- **Help File**   Enter the path and file name of the compiled Help file that contains the Help text. Built-in commands have Help files in the Office folder. Available for menus.

- **Help ContextID**   Enter the context ID number of the Help text in the Help file indicated in the Help File box. The Filter By Selection tip text is number 3893 in the file. Available for menus.

- **Parameter**   Enter the name of any parameter to be passed to the event procedure specified in the On Action property.

- **Tag**   A string that can be used to refer to the control in an event procedure. You can use a tag to assign an identification string to an object without affecting any of its other property settings or causing other side effects.

TIP   To change the properties of other controls on the current toolbar or menu bar without closing the dialog box, click the drop-down arrow next to the Selected Control box and choose from the list of controls.

Click Close when you finish making all the desired changes.

Changing the Width of a Combo Box Button

Some of the buttons on built-in toolbars are combo boxes that display a list of options when you click the drop-down arrow next to the button—for example, the Object button on the Formatting (Form/Report) toolbar, which displays a list of the sections and controls in the current form or report. If the items in the list are longer than the box is wide, you might want to widen it. If the button takes up more room on the toolbar than is necessary, you can decrease the width.

To change the width of a combo box button, do the following:

1. Open the Customize dialog box and click the combo button. A blank rectangle appears around the combo box button.

2. Move the mouse pointer to the right or left edge and, when it changes to a double-pointed arrow, drag the edge of the box. You get the same result by dragging either edge.

Restoring Built-in Command Bars

You can restore all or any part of a modified built-in command bar to the original default settings. You can restore the entire toolbar or menu bar to show the original buttons and menus with or without restoring the original default properties. Or, you can choose to restore only certain individual menus, buttons, or commands.

When you restore an entire built-in toolbar or menu bar, Access displays all the buttons and commands in their original appearance and arrangement. The property settings for the toolbar or menu bar are also restored, including the screen location and size, as well as showing or hiding the bar, whichever was its original state.

To restore a toolbar or menu bar, do the following:

1. Open the Customize dialog box and click the Toolbars tab.

2. Click Properties to open the Properties dialog box and, in the Selected Toolbar box, select the name of the toolbar or menu bar you want to restore. Notice the Toolbar Name and Type property boxes are dimmed because it's a built-in toolbar.

3. Click Restore Defaults and click Close.

If you want to reset only the buttons and menus on a built-in toolbar, menu bar, or shortcut menu, you can do so from the Customize dialog box. On the Toolbars tab, choose the name of the toolbar or menu bar you want to restore, and then click Reset. If you want to reset a shortcut menu, select Shortcut Menus in the list of toolbars and click Reset. This resets all the built-in shortcut menus you modified.

You can restore the original settings of a single toolbar button or menu command in a toolbar, menu bar, or shortcut menu. To restore the settings, open the Customize dialog box and click the menu bar or toolbar that contains the settings you want to restore. The menu bar or toolbar appears on the screen behind the dialog box. Then right-click the object and choose Reset in the shortcut menu.

NOTE   *If you restore a menu that appears in more than one menu bar, such as File or Edit, you also restore the menu in the menu bars for all other views that use this menu.*

If the button you want to restore opens a list of options, you cannot use the Reset command to change back to the default image. Instead, if you changed the image on the built-in button or menu command and you want to restore it to the original image, right-click and choose Reset Button Image in the shortcut menu.

Summary

Creating and using customized command bars gives you many opportunities to build exactly the application you want. You can include only those menus and commands that apply to the job. You can exclude irrelevant menus and commands, as well as those that could even jeopardize the integrity of the database as a whole.

The next step in creating a unique operating environment for your application is to add dialog boxes that serve as decision points for the user. In these switchboards, the user can choose the next action to take and can even make further choices from pop-up dialog boxes that offer alternatives. Creating switchboards and other user-interactive tools is covered in the next chapter.

Creating Custom Switchboards and Dialog Boxes

When creating an application for a user who wants to concentrate on its purpose and the special tasks it requires, you can add custom user interfaces. Two special-purpose forms can be added to an application, which can be used as switchboards for choosing activities and as dialog boxes for acquiring user input. In this chapter, you work with the Bayview Police Department database, introduced in Chapter 12.

A switchboard can offer the user a single point of entry into the application with a list of custom activities. With a mere click on a switchboard item, the user branches to the operation. With Access, you have two ways to build a switchboard: use the built-in Switchboard Manager or create your own unbound form with selections that branch to the activities you want. Each approach has its advantages, as you learn in this chapter.

Working with Windows applications, you're no doubt familiar with dialog boxes and their many uses. A dialog box offers a set of options from which to choose, such as which form or report to open, which filter to apply, or what action to take next. Custom dialog boxes can also prompt the user for data. You can create forms that work like custom dialog boxes and contain options relevant to the application in easily understood text.

Creating Switchboards

Switchboard is a term borrowed from the telephone industry that's used to indicate a single point of entry into an application with a list of connections to activate next. When the Access Database Wizard creates a new database, it always adds at least one switchboard as the user interface. Figure 21-1 shows the main switchboard for the Order Entry database.

In addition to the main switchboard, two other switchboard pages are included in the user interface in the Order Entry database:

- The Forms Switchboard, reached by clicking Enter/View Other Information item.
- The Reports Switchboard, reached by clicking Preview Reports.

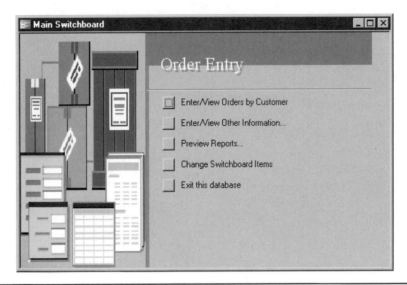

FIGURE 21-1 The Order Entry database main switchboard

The ellipsis (...) following each of those items tells users they open secondary switchboard pages.

You can make changes to any of the switchboards the wizard creates for you. For example, you can add an item to the Main Switchboard to access the Internet or add other reports to the list in the Reports Switchboard. Access includes the Switchboard Manager to help make changes to wizard-built switchboards, as well as to help create your own from scratch. Notice that one of the items on the Main Switchboard in Figure 21-1 is Change Switchboard Items, which launches the Switchboard Manager. Editing a switchboard created by the Database Wizard is the same as editing one you created with the Manager. The section "Modifying the Switchboard" discusses modifying switchboards.

Using the Switchboard Manager to Create Switchboards

The switchboard system is the last piece of an application that's designed and created after all the forms, reports, and queries are completed. The switchboard system for a database consists of a hierarchical arrangement of switchboard *pages,* beginning with the main switchboard, usually branching out to two or more subordinate pages. Each page contains a set of *items* with commands that carry out a specified activity. Most items also include an *argument* that specifies which form to open, which report to preview, which macro or procedure to run, and so on.

NOTE *If you already have a switchboard system and only need to make some changes, refer to the section "Modifying the Switchboard" for help in making the changes.*

To start the Switchboard Manager, choose Tools | Database Utilities | Switchboard Manager. If your database already has a switchboard system, all the switchboard pages are listed in the Switchboard Manager window. If your database doesn't already have a valid switchboard, the Manager displays a message asking if you want to create a new one. Click Yes.

The first Switchboard Manager dialog box (see Figure 21-2) starts with the mandatory default main switchboard page.

In addition to Close, the options in the dialog box are as follows:

- *New,* which opens a dialog box where you can build a new page.
- *Edit,* which enables you to edit the selected page in this dialog box.
- *Delete,* which removes the selected page from the switchboard system.
- *Make Default,* which assigns the selected switchboard page as the default that can be set to display at startup.

Adding Items to the Page

If you're creating a new switchboard system, the first step is to add items to the main switchboard by selecting the page in the Switchboard Manager dialog box and clicking Edit. This opens the Edit Switchboard Page dialog box (see Figure 21-3), which has only one available option at this time: New.

No items are in the main switchboard for the Police database yet. Before adding them to the switchboard, enter **Bayview City Police** as the switchboard name in place of Main Switchboard. Then begin adding the list of items you decided should appear when the

FIGURE 21-2   Starting a new main switchboard

FIGURE 21-3 The Edit Switchboard Page dialog box

database starts up. To start placing the choices on the switchboard, click New to open the Edit Switchboard Item dialog box.

TIP *To return to the main switchboard, always add an item at the end of the list on all switchboard pages, except the opening switchboard. The item moves control back up the switchboard tree to the main switchboard. The opening switchboard should have an item that closes the database.*

Three entries define a switchboard item:

- Enter the text you want to appear in the list of items in the Text box.
- Choose the command you want from the drop-down list next to the Command box.
- Depending on which command you choose, enter the command argument in the third box. The title of the box and the arguments vary with the command chosen.

When creating a switchboard system, you place the most commonly performed tasks as options on the main switchboard page. Then place less often used or subordinate choices on secondary pages that can be reached from the main switchboard.

The activity most often carried out in the Police application is to look up or enter Alpha Card information in the Alpha Card form. This form also displays the Alpha Entry information in a subform. To begin the Police switchboard system, do the following:

1. Type **Enter/Edit Alpha Card Data** in the Text box in the Edit Switchboard Item dialog box.

2. Click the drop-down arrow next to Command and choose Open Form in Edit Mode.

TIP *You can use the ampersand (&) character in the item's Text box to specify access keys for the items in the switchboard. Type the & just before the letter you want to use with* ALT *for selecting the item. For example, Enter/Edit &Alpha Card Data. Then the user has a choice of clicking the item or pressing* ALT-A *to choose the item.*

The Switchboard Manager offers eight different commands, which cover most of the actions you'd want to initiate from a switchboard. Table 21-1 describes the commands and the arguments they require, if any.

Command	Description	Argument
Go to Switchboard	Opens another switchboard and closes this one.	Name of destination switchboard
Open Form in Add Mode	Opens a form for data entry with a blank record showing.	Form name
Open Form in Edit Mode	Opens a form for viewing and editing data.	Form name
Open Report	Opens a report in Preview mode.	Report name
Design Application	Opens Switchboard Manager to make changes to the current switchboard.	None
Exit Application	Closes active database.	None
Run Macro	Runs a macro.	Macro name
Run Code	Runs a Visual Basic procedure.	Procedure name

TABLE 21-1   Commands Offered by the Switchboard Manager

After you choose the command, the third line changes to the appropriate argument name, in this case, Form.

When you click the drop-down arrow next to the Form box, the Manager displays a list of all the forms in the Police database.

Choose Alpha Card from the list, and then click OK. You return to the Edit Switchboard Page dialog box where you now see the new item in the Items on this Switchboard list.

Repeat the same steps to add the following two items to the main switchboard:

- Enter/Edit Alpha Entry Data, which opens the Alpha Entry form in Edit mode.
- Preview Alpha Card with Entries, which opens the Alpha Card with Entries report.

Adding a New Switchboard Page

The Police database user might want to open several more forms and reports, but not as often as the ones already added as items to the main switchboard. The less frequently used forms and reports can be grouped on secondary switchboard pages. To add a new page to the switchboard system, do the following:

1. Click Close to close the Edit Switchboard Page and return to the Switchboard Manager dialog box.

2. Click New to start a new page.

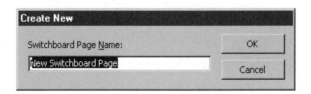

3. Type **Enter/Edit Other Data** in the Switchboard Page Name box and click OK. Include an ampersand if you want to specify an access key for this item.

4. The new page name is added to the list in the Switchboard Manager dialog box. Select the Enter/Edit Other Data switchboard page and click Edit to open the Edit Switchboard Page dialog box as before.

5. Click New to open the Edit Switchboard Item dialog box and type **Enter/Edit City Beats**. Then choose Open Form in Edit Mode from the Command list and City Beats from the Form list.

6. Repeat step 5 to add the following items to the list:

   • Enter/Edit Name List, which opens the Name List form in Edit mode.

   • Enter/Edit Entry Description, which opens the Explanation form in Edit mode.

7. Finally, add the item that returns to the main switchboard. Type **Return to Main Switchboard**, choose Go To Switchboard from the Command list, and choose Bayview City Police from the Switchboard list.

Figure 21-4 shows the completed Enter/Edit Other Data page.

NOTE   *As you add pages to the switchboard tree, remember to add items to the main switchboard to branch to the page, as well as adding the item to the page that moves back up the tree. Otherwise, the user doesn't have a way to move from page to page within the switchboard system.*

The items are added to the page in the order you define them. If you need to rearrange them, select an item in the Edit Switchboard Page dialog box, and then click Move Up or Move Down to change its position in the list. Each click moves the item up or down one position.

To complete the Police switchboard system, create another page titled Preview Other Reports, and add the items to it that will open other reports, as specified in the item text:

   • Alpha Entry

   • Entries by Code

   • Entries by Qtr

   • Entries by Year

   • Print Labels

   • Return to Main Switchboard

NOTE   *When you create a subordinate switchboard page, you needn't add items to it right away. You do need to create the page, however, before you can place an item on the main switchboard that will open it. One development strategy is to create all the pages first, and then add the items.*

When all the pages are completed for the switchboard system, close the Switchboard Manager. The Switchboard form now appears in the Forms page of the Database window. Double-click the form name (Switchboard) to open the main switchboard form in Form view. Figure 21-5 shows the completed Main Switchboard for the Police database.

FIGURE 21-4
Items added to the
Enter/Edit Other
Data switchboard

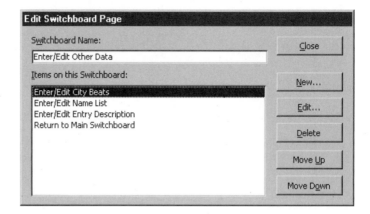

NOTE   *A new table has also been added to the Tables page named Switchboard Items, which you examine in the section "Viewing the Switchboard Items Table."*

The Switchboard Manager has used the same colors and arrangement for your switchboard as the Database Wizard used for the Order Entry database. All it lacks is a picture to make it complete.

Adding a Picture

The blank area at the left of the switchboard items in the Access template is intended for a company logo or other image. You can add a picture to the switchboard form just as with any other form. When you add a picture to one switchboard page, the same picture appears on all the pages. In fact, any changes you make to the switchboard design affect all your switchboards.

FIGURE 21-5
The new Police
Main Switchboard

Bayview City Police

Bayview City Police

- Enter/Edit Alpha Card Data
- Enter/Edit Alpha Entry Data
- Enter/Edit Other Data
- Preview Alpha Card with Entries
- Preview Other Reports
- Exit This Database

When you open the switchboard form in Design view, you don't see any of the switchboard items you added to it. What you see is more of a template of how all switchboards look with blank command buttons and text boxes. The actual items are stored in a separate table—Switchboard Items—discussed in the section "Viewing the Switchboard Items Table."

To add a picture to the switchboard, open the Switchboard form in Design view and do the following:

1. Choose Insert | Picture.

2. In the Insert Picture dialog box, locate the picture you want to use, and then click OK. Access places the picture in the upper-left corner of the form. This probably covers some of the switchboard.

3. Resize the picture to fit within the solid background.

4. Click the Properties toolbar button to open the property sheet for the picture and change the Size Mode property to Stretch. If the image is distorted, change the property to Zoom and resize the frame to fit the picture dimensions.

5. Switch to Form view and click the Preview Other Reports item. Figure 21-6 shows the Preview Other Reports page of the completed switchboard.

> **NOTE**   *The picture used here is the contacts.gif file found in the Dbwiz subfolder in the Office\ Bitmaps folder. This is one of the pictures used by the Database Wizard.*

Displaying the Switchboard at Startup

When you select a switchboard in the Switchboard Manager dialog box and click Make Default, you designate that page as the one to display when the Switchboard form opens. You still have to tell Access to display the default switchboard by setting the Display Form/ Page option in the Startup dialog box to the Switchboard form.

FIGURE 21-6
The completed Preview Other Reports switchboard page

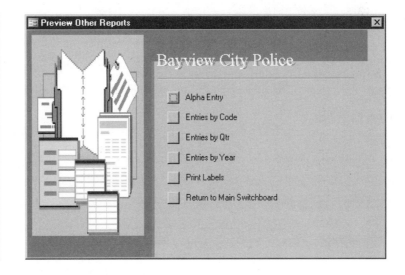

Choose Tools | Startup, click the arrow next to the Display Form/Page box, and then choose Switchboard from the list. The change takes effect the next time you start the database. To bypass the switchboard display after setting it as the default startup form, hold down SHIFT while the database opens.

TIP   *Even though you designate the switchboard as the startup form, the Database window appears on the screen behind a switchboard that isn't maximized. To prevent the user from having access to the Database window, clear the Display Database Window option in the Startup dialog box. After the database is open, you can still bring the Database window to the front by pressing F11.*

Modifying the Switchboard

To edit any item on a switchboard page, open the Switchboard Manager and use the Edit buttons. If the Database Wizard created the switchboard, open the Switchboard Manager by clicking Change Switchboard Items in the opening switchboard. If you used the Switchboard Manager directly to create the switchboards, start the Manager by choosing Tools | Database Utilities | Switchboard Manager. Then do the following:

1. Choose the switchboard you want to change and click Edit.

2. To add an item, click New and enter the text. Then choose a command and an argument.

3. To change an item, select it and do one of the following:

   - To change the displayed text, the command, or the argument, click Edit.

   - To delete the item, click Delete.

   - To move the item in the list, click Move Up or Move Down.

4. Close the Switchboard Manager.

You can also delete an entire switchboard by selecting it in the Switchboard Pages dialog box and clicking Delete. The page and all its items are deleted.

To change the switchboard that displays when you start the database, select the switchboard you want to display instead and click Make Default. The startup option is still set to display the Switchboard form, but the Switchboard Manager has designated a different page as the default switchboard. This takes effect the next time you open the database.

Changing the Picture

Whether the Database Wizard added a picture to the switchboard or you inserted it in the one you created with the Switchboard Manager, you can swap it for another picture. The pictures the wizard uses are specially designed and sized for use in switchboards.

To change the picture to another special switchboard bitmap, do the following:

1. Open the Switchboard form in Design view.

2. Double-click the picture control to open its property sheet.

3. Click the Format tab, and then click the Build (...) button next to the Picture property.

Image: Image22

| Image22 | |

Format | Data | Event | Other | All

Picture	C:\Program Files\Microsoft Office11\OFFICE11\BITMAPS\DBWIZ\CONTACTS.GIF
Picture Type	Embedded
Size Mode	Stretch
Picture Alignment	Center
Picture Tiling	No

4. The Insert Picture dialog box opens where you can locate the image you want (see Figure 21-7). The special images used by the Database Wizard are located in the Bitmaps\Dbwiz folder where you installed Office. The picture shown in the Asset Tracking switchboard is the assets.gif file in that folder.

Viewing the Switchboard Items Table

When you use the Switchboard Manager to create a switchboard, Access creates a new table named Switchboard Items. Each record in the table represents an item in one of the switchboard pages and each field in the record describes what command the button carries out and the argument it uses. Figure 21-8 shows the table created for the Police database switchboards.

Table 21-2 describes the contents of the Switchboard Items table. You can widen the columns in the table, but don't make any other changes in the table design.

NOTE *The first row of each switchboard contains 0 in both the ItemNumber and the Command field, indicating the ItemText is the switchboard caption and is to be displayed in the title bar.*

FIGURE 21-7   Inserting a different switchboard picture

FIGURE 21-8   The Switchboard Items table

The Argument field needs a little explanation. The first row contains Default in the Argument field, indicating the Main Switchboard has been specified as the default switchboard to be displayed at startup if the Display Form/Page option is set to Switchboard.

Field	Contents
SwitchboardID	A sequential number assigned to the switchboard page.
ItemNumber	A sequential number assigned to each item on a page, beginning with number 1. Together with the SwitchboardID, this forms the primary key that uniquely identifies the item and the switchboard page. Switchboards have ItemNumber 0.
ItemText	The text entered in the Text box of the Edit Switchboard Item dialog box.
Command	The number representing the command selected from the Commands list in the Edit Switchboard Item dialog box. Commands are numbered sequentially in the order they appear in the list. For the Switchboard page itself, the Command is 0.
Argument	The number of the switchboard, the name of a form, report, macro, or procedure to be used by the command in the Commands list in the Edit Switchboard Item dialog box.

TABLE 21-2   The Switchboard Items Table

A number in the Argument field represents the ID number of the switchboard as the goal of the command, Go To Switchboard. For example, the fourth row shows 2 in the Argument field, indicating the command is to display switchboard number 2, Enter/Edit Other Data.

You can make changes in the switchboards by editing the information in the table, but using the Switchboard Manager is easier and safer. When you make changes with the Switchboard Manager, the changes are also made to the Switchboard Items table. If you make changes to the form in Design view, they aren't necessarily translated to the table and, if you do a lot of customizing to the form, it might not work the way you want. You could be better off creating a form from scratch with all the customization, and then designating it as the startup form. The next section shows you how to make your own switchboards.

Creating a Switchboard from Scratch

The purpose behind creating a switchboard from scratch is so you can build a customized form without being subjected to the limitations imposed by the Switchboard Manager. The form should be designed to help the user run all the tasks required of the application, such as entering data and printing reports. The switchboard form is usually the last piece of the application to be created, after all the tables, queries, forms, and reports are designed and saved in the database.

To create a switchboard from scratch, start with a blank form that isn't bound to an underlying table or query, and then add command buttons that trigger macros or event procedures to carry out the actions you want. The form isn't a real switchboard with the Switchboard items table and a Switchboard Manager, it simply works like a switchboard by giving visual entry into choices of actions. The properties of a switchboard form are quite different from the normal data entry form that shows record navigation buttons and scroll bars. You can also add unbound text boxes and combo boxes to give the user more options with macros and queries.

To begin a new switchboard form, do the following:

1. Open the Forms page in the Database window and click New.

2. In the New Form dialog box, choose Design view, leave the lower box blank, and then click OK. A new blank form appears in the window.

Before you begin placing command buttons on the form, change some of the form properties, so it appears more like a switchboard.

Setting the Form Properties

Open the form property sheet by double-clicking the form selector or choosing Edit | Select Form, and then clicking the Properties toolbar button. You can also choose Form in the Object toolbar button and click Properties. On the property sheet, set the form properties on the Format tab as follows:

- Enter the text you want to see in the switchboard title bar in the Caption property box.

- Make sure the Default view is Single Form.

- Leave the Allow Form View property as Yes and change the other three Allow... properties to No.

- Change Scroll Bars to Neither to remove both the horizontal and vertical scroll bars.

- Change Record Selectors to No because there won't be any data on the form.
- Change Navigation Buttons to No because the user won't be moving among records.
- Change Dividing Lines to No because the form won't display records.
- Set Auto Resize to Yes, so the form always appears as the same size in Form view.
- Set Auto Center to Yes to ensure the form opens in the middle of the window where it's easier to view and use.

If you want the switchboard form to display a different color, click the detail section selector to change to the section property sheet. Then click the Build button next to the Back Color property box and choose from the color palette. You can also click the Fill/Back Color button on the Formatting (Form/Report) toolbar and choose a color from the drop-down palette.

After setting all the desired properties, save and name the form. When you open the form in Form view, it appears totally blank, but colorful.

Adding Command Buttons with the Wizard

The next step is to begin adding controls to the form that will carry out the desired actions. You can add command buttons to carry out specific actions or hyperlinks to jump to a different form or other location. The type of control you use for a switchboard depends on what it's intended to do.

- If the switchboard item is designed to carry out a single action, such as open a form in Form view, you can use the Command Button Wizard to add a command button.
- If the item must carry out two or more actions, you need to add the button without the Command Button Wizard and create a macro or Visual Basic event procedure to attach to the button's OnClick event property.
- Hyperlinks can also be used to open another form or preview a special part of a report.

NOTE   *See Chapter 10 for more information about Control Wizards and how to use them.*

Before you begin to add command buttons and labels to the switchboard, you might want to draw a rectangle in which to place them. This helps to group the items and give your switchboard a special flavor. You can also add pictures and titles outside the rectangle.

TIP   *If you place buttons on the form, and then draw the rectangle, the box will be in front of the buttons and their labels. To fix this, select the rectangle and choose Format | Send to Back.*

Add the first item, Enter/Edit Alpha Card Data, to the main switchboard with the Command Button Wizard as follows:

1. Open the blank form in Design view and click the Toolbox button.

2. Click the Control Wizards button on the Toolbox, and then click the Command Button control tool.

3. Click on the form where you want the command button to appear. The Command Button Wizard appears.

4. Choose Form Operations in the Categories list and Open Form in the Action list, and then click Next.

5. Choose Alpha Card from the list in the next dialog box and click Next.

6. Choose the option Open the form and show all the records, which opens the form in Edit mode, and then click Next.

7. Choose Text and delete the caption so the button is blank like a standard switchboard item, and then click Next.

8. Enter **Alpha Card Data** as the name for the button and click Finish.

9. In the Design window, resize the button to a small square, and then add a Label control next to the button and enter the text **Enter/Edit &Alpha Card Data**.

10. Select the button and look at the OnClick event property in the property sheet. The [Event Procedure] entry refers to the code the wizard created to carry out the choices you made in the dialog boxes.

TIP   *The ampersand (&) creates an access key (ALT-A in this example) for the label that carries out the action attached to it. So far, no action is associated with the label—only the button—but you can attach the same event procedure the wizard created for the button with a few slight changes.*

Copying the Button Event Procedure

In a real Switchboard form, you can click either the command button or the label text to its right to perform the button's action. If you want to make your homemade switchboard form work the same way, you need to configure the label's properties, so that clicking the label runs the same procedure as clicking the command button. To make this work, copy the procedure from the command button's On Click property to the label's On Click property, as described in this section.

   You're about to be introduced to some Visual Basic code and given a chance to modify it for your button label. To see the procedure, click the On Click event property box and click Build (...) next to [Event Procedure], or click the Code button on the Form Design toolbar. The Visual Basic Editor window opens, showing the following procedure. Alpha_Card_Data is the name of the button and Click is the event. (Text following the apostrophes are newly added comments and would be ignored by the program.)

```
Private Sub Alpha_Card_Data_Click()
On Error GoTo Err_Alpha_Card_Data_Click

    Dim stDocName As String         'These two statements declare
    Dim stLinkCriteria As String    'variables as strings.

    stDocName = "Alpha Card"        'This statement names the form
                                    'to open. The next statement opens
                                    'the form and sets the filter.
    DoCmd.OpenForm stDocName, , , stLinkCriteria


Exit_Alpha_Card_Data_Click:        'Quits the procedure.
    Exit Sub

Err_Alpha_Card_Data_Click:         'Traps any run time errors.
    MsgBox Err.Description              'Displays an error message.
    Resume Exit_Alpha_Card_Data_Click  'Goes to the Exit above.


End Sub
```

To add this procedure to the label's On Click property, do the following:

1. In the Visual Basic Editor window, select all the statements of the procedure except the first (Private Sub...) and the last (End Sub), and then click Copy to place it on the clipboard.
2. Click the View Microsoft Access button to return to the form Design view.
3. Select the button label and open the Event tab on the button's property sheet.
4. Click Build next to the On Click property and select Code Builder to open the Visual Basic Editor window for this event property.
5. Place the insertion point in the line below the Private Sub line, and then click Paste.

The procedure you just pasted into the label's On Click property refers to the command button: the command button's name appears in the procedure four times. Because you want the label to carry out the same action as the button when you click it, all you need to do is change the button name to the label name wherever it appears. The easiest way to do this is to copy the label's name from the Sub statement—**Label2** in this case—to the clipboard and paste it in place of the button name (Alpha_Card_Data) in four places. After copying the label name to the clipboard, select the complete button name, Alpha_Card_Data, and click Paste. Be careful to retain the underline characters that replace spaces in the names in their proper places. You have now edited the procedure so it works with the label, as well as with the command button.

Adding Command Buttons and Attaching Macros

Unfortunately, the Command Button Wizard can create only a limited number of procedures. You might need a command button that does something the wizard can't write. When you add command buttons or other controls to the form without the help of the Control Wizard, you must create your own macros or Visual Basic code to carry out the desired action. To avoid cluttering the Database window with a lot of little macros, build all the macros for the switchboard in one group, and then specify the individual macros in the On Click event properties for the buttons and their labels.

If the switchboard opens other switchboard pages, create the blank forms for the secondary pages, and then save and name them. Then you have all the form names and you can create all the macros at once. The macro group for the Alpha Card main switchboard might look like the following. (The first item in the Police main switchboard was added earlier by the Command Button Wizard and it doesn't require a macro.)

Macro Name	Action	Comment
Alpha Entry	OpenForm	Switchboard item to open Alpha Entry form.
Other Data	OpenForm	Switchboard item to open Other Data page.
Card Report	OpenReport	Switchboard item to preview Alpha Card report.
Other Reports	OpenForm	Switchboard item to open Other Reports page.
Exit	Close	Closes the main switchboard.

SwitchMacro : Macro

By attaching a macro or procedure to the label, as well as to the button, and including access keys in the switchboard item labels, you have four ways to trigger the action. Click the button, click the label, press ALT with the access key, or press TAB to move focus to the button, and then press ENTER.

To add a command button without the wizard, do the following with the form open in Design view:

1. On the Toolbox, be sure the Control Wizard button isn't pressed in, click the Command Button tool, and then click the form design where you want the button.

2. Select the button name, Command*n*, in the command button and press DELETE. You can also open the property sheet and delete the Caption property.

3. Resize the button to a small square that matches the first button.

4. Click the Label tool and draw a label next to the new button, and then type **Enter/ Edit Alpha &Entry Data** in the new label. The label identifies *E* as the access key for the control.

5. Use the Format | Align and Format | Size commands to make the buttons the same size and line up the new controls.

6. Click outside the label control and hold down SHIFT while you select the command button and its label. By selecting both controls, you can attach a macro to them both at once.

7. Open the property sheet for the multiple selection and click the Event tab.

8. Click the arrow next to the On Click property and select SwitchMacro.Alpha Entry from the drop-down list of macros (see Figure 21-9).

9. Switch to Form view and test the new button and label.

Continue to add the rest of the items to the main switchboard, and then proceed to the other secondary switchboard pages using the same methods.

TIP   *Another way to create a command button that runs a macro is to create the macro, and then drag it from the Database window to the form design. The following DBWindow button runs the DBWindow macro, which contains only two actions: SendKeys, which sends the F11 keystroke to the application to open the Database window, followed by Close, which closes the switchboard form.*

Adding a Hyperlink Command Button

You might want to jump either to your web site or another location on the hard drive. For this, you can add a command button that follows a hyperlink. To add a hyperlink command button, do the following:

1. Turn off the Control Wizard and click the Command Button tool. Then click the switchboard form where you want the button.

2. Resize as necessary and open the new button's property sheet.

3. Enter the text you want to see on the button (if any) in the Caption property box on the Format tab.

4. Click the Hyperlink Address property and enter the path to a file on the hard drive, a UNC path, or a URL. If you need help, click Build next to the Hyperlink Address property and use the Insert Hyperlink dialog box to help compose the correct address.

In the following illustration, the command button opens the Alpha Card Report in Print Preview. The caption is underlined because it's a hyperlink. The Hyperlink Address property is blank because the report is an object in the active database. The Hyperlink SubAddress shows the object type, Report, followed by the report name.

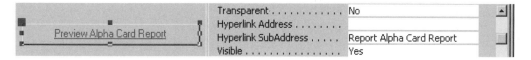

When you switch to Form view and click the hyperlink command button, the report opens for preview.

See Chapter 12 for details about adding hyperlinks to form designs.

Creating a Custom Dialog Box

A *dialog box* is a special type of window that pops up and stays on the screen until you make a selection, even if this selection is only to cancel the box. Creating custom dialog boxes for an application is much like creating switchboards. You start with a blank, unbound form and add controls that you can select to carry out specific actions. After completing the form, you create macros or event procedures, and then attach them to the corresponding controls on the form.

FIGURE 21-9   Attaching a macro to two controls

In this section, you create a dialog box that offers a choice of Police reports when the user clicks the Print button on the Alpha Card form. You create this custom dialog box in four major steps:

- Create the form and add an option group control with a list of available reports from which to choose and three command buttons. One button shows the selected report in Print Preview, the second prints the report, and the third closes the dialog box.

- Create a macro group with a macro for each of the options in the group.

- Attach the macros to the event property of the option group.

- Set the form properties to look and act like a dialog box.

Designing the Form

To create the Choose Report dialog box for the Police database, do the following:

1. Start a new form without choosing a table or query as a basis.

2. In form Design view, click the Toolbox button if the toolbox isn't showing and make sure the Controls Wizard button is pressed.

3. Click the Option Group control tool and draw a frame in the empty form design to start the Option Group Wizard.

4. In the first wizard dialog box, enter the label names for the options in the group. After entering a name, press DOWN ARROW or TAB to move to the next line. If you press ENTER, you move to the next dialog box. After entering all the option labels, click Next.

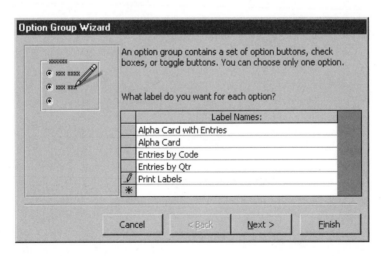

5. In the next wizard dialog box, you can choose one of the options you just entered as the default or choose not to have a default option. Accept the first option as the default and click Next.

6. When the user selects an option from the group, a value is returned. In this dialog box, you can change the default sequential integer values. Unless you have a special

reason to change the returned values, it's better to leave them alone, accept the default, and then click Next.

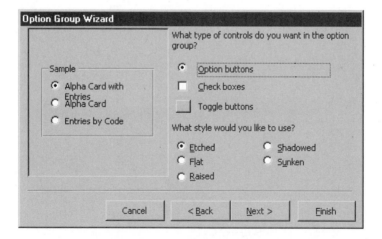

7. The next wizard dialog box shows a variety of styles for the option group and the options in it. Choose Option buttons as the type of control and Raised as the style, and then click Next.

8. In the final wizard dialog box, enter **Choose Report** as the caption for the group to be displayed at the top of the group frame, and then click Finish.

9. Select the option group frame and open the property sheet. Choose the Name property on the Other tab and enter **Choose Report** as the name for the option group. Click Finish.

10. Save and name the new form.

The new form in Form view shows the options group with the choice of reports. The next step is to add the command buttons to display the selected report in Print Preview, print the selected report, and close the form. Do this without the help of the Command Button Wizard because you want to attach macros to the buttons instead of using the default operations offered by the wizard.

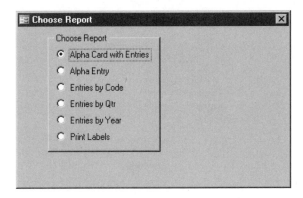

To add the three command buttons, make sure the Controls Wizard button on the toolbox is *not* pressed, and then do the following:

1. Click the Command Button tool and click in the form design. Repeat twice more, spacing the buttons as desired. They show the default captions: Command*n*.

2. Select the first button, click it, and then type **Preview**. Press ENTER to save the new caption.

3. Repeat step 2 to change the default captions on the other two buttons to **Print** and **Cancel**.

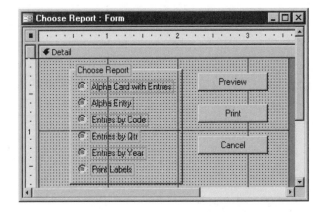

4. If the buttons aren't evenly spaced or accurately aligned, select all three and use the Format | Align or Format | Vertical Spacing command to adjust the buttons.

5. If the buttons vary in size, choose Format | Size and make them the same size.

So far, the controls on the Choose Report form don't carry out an action. You need to create the macros that run when the control is clicked and do what's intended.

Creating and Attaching the Macros

You need a macro for each of the command buttons in the form. In addition, you must convey to the Print and Preview macros which report to open. The macros you attach to the Preview and Print buttons must distinguish among the reports and open the one chosen in the option group.

The option group returns a value, depending on which item in the group was selected. As you saw, the Option Group Wizard set default return values so, if you click the first item, the group value is 1, if you click the second item, the value is 2, and so on. You can use this value in the macro condition to choose the specific report to preview or print.

Creating the Macro Group

To build a macro for the Preview button, do the following:

1. Click New in the Macros tab of the Database window, and then click the Macro Names and Conditions toolbar buttons to show the two optional columns.

2. Type **PreviewReports** as the name of the first macro and choose OpenReport as the Action.

3. In the Action Arguments pane, choose Alpha Card with Entries from the drop-down list of Report Names and choose Print Preview as the View argument.

4. Next enter the condition under which to preview the report: **[ChooseReport]=1**. ChooseReport is the name of the option group and 1 is the value of the group when you select the first item in the group.

TIP   *If you're in doubt about the name of the control, look at the Name property on the Other tab of the control's property sheet.*

5. Move to the next row and repeat steps 3 and 4 to open the Alpha Entry report in print preview with the condition that the ChooseReport group value is 2.

6. Continue to define macro actions to open the remaining reports in print preview. You should have six actions in the PreviewReports macro, each opening a different report in print preview.

7. You could add a final action in the macro to close the Choose Report form, so you can see the Print Preview window. Set the following arguments for the Close action:

   • Object Type—Form

   • Object Name—Choose Report

   • Save—No

8. Leave an empty row and create a new macro named **PrintReports** to print each of the reports using the same conditions. Don't include the Close action with the second macro, so the pop-up dialog box remains on the screen for further selections.

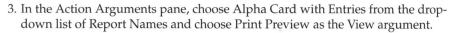

TIP *An easy way to add the conditions to the **PrintReports** macro is to copy the [**ChooseReport**]=*
part of the condition and paste it in subsequent lines, and then add the values.

The macro command for the Cancel button can be simply Close with the Choose Report
form name as the argument. Figure 21-10 shows the completed macro group from the
Choose Report form.

Attaching the Macros to Form Controls

To attach the macros to the command buttons, do the following:

1. Double-click the Preview command button to open the property sheet.

2. Click the Events tab and choose the macro name from the drop-down list next to the
   On Click event property. Figure 21-11 shows attaching the PreviewReports macro in
   the Choose Report macro group as the action to carry out when the button is clicked.

3. Repeat steps 1 and 2 to attach the PrintReports macro to the Print button and the
   Cancel macro to the Cancel button.

Setting Form Properties and Style

The last phase of creating a custom dialog box is to change some of the form properties to
make it look and act more like a dialog box than a data entry form. A dialog box is a pop-up

Macro Name	Condition	Action	Comment
			This macro group contains macros that respond to the
			Choose Report popup form.
PreviewReports	[ChooseReport]=1	OpenReport	Opens the Alpha Card with Entries report in Print Preview.
	[ChooseReport]=2	OpenReport	Opens the Alpha Entry report in Print Preview.
	[ChooseReport]=3	OpenReport	Opens the Alpha Entry by Code report in Print Preview.
	[ChooseReport]=4	OpenReport	Opens the Entries by Quarter report in Print Preview.
	[ChooseReport]=5	OpenReport	Opens the Entries by Year report in Print Preview.
	[ChooseReport]=6	OpenReport	Opens the Labels Name List report in Print Preview.
PrintReports	[ChooseReport]=1	OpenReport	Prints the Alpha Card with Entries report.
	[ChooseReport]=2	OpenReport	Prints the Alpha Entry report.
	[ChooseReport]=3	OpenReport	Prints the Alpha Entry by Code report.
	[ChooseReport]=4	OpenReport	Prints the Entries by Quarter report.
	[ChooseReport]=5	OpenReport	Prints the Entries by Year report.
	[ChooseReport]=6	OpenReport	Prints the Labels Name List report.
Cancel		Close	Closes popup form.

Action Arguments

Report Name	Alpha Card with Entries
View	Print Preview
Filter Name	
Where Condition	
Window Mode	

Opens a report in Design view or Print Preview or prints the
report immediately. Press F1 for help on this action.

FIGURE 21-10   The macro group for the Choose Report form

FIGURE 21-11   Attaching a macro to the Preview command button

modal form. *Pop-up* means it opens and stays on top of other windows, even when it's no longer the active window. *Modal* means you must hide or close the form before you can work in any other object or menu command.

To set these and some other properties, open the form in Design view and double-click the form selector to open the form property sheet. Then set the form properties as described in Table 21-3. All the properties are on the Format tab, except PopUp and Modal, which are on the Other tab.

Property	Setting	Purpose
PopUp	Yes	Form remains on top of other windows.
Modal	Yes	Form retains focus until it's closed.
Caption	Choose Report	Displays text in title bar in Form view instead of form name.

TABLE 21-3   Property Settings for a Custom Dialog Box

Property	Setting	Purpose
Allow Form View	Yes	Permits the form in Form view.
Allow Datasheet View	No	Prevents switching to Datasheet view.
Allow PivotTable View	No	Prevents switching to PivotTable view.
Allow PivotChart View	No	Prevents switching to PivotChart view.
Scroll Bars	Neither	Removes scroll bars from the form.
Record Selectors	No	Removes record selectors from the form.
Navigation Buttons	No	Removes navigation buttons from the form.
Dividing Lines	No	Removes horizontal lines from the form.
Auto Center	Yes	Centers the form automatically when it opens. If you want the form to appear in a special place, set to No.
Border Style	Dialog	Form has a thick border and includes only a title bar with a control menu box.
Control Box	Yes	Displays the control menu box in the title bar in Form view, so the user can close the form.
MinMax Buttons	None	Prevents the user from resizing the form in Form view.

TABLE 21-3 Property Settings for a Custom Dialog Box *(continued)*

CAUTION   Always leave a way for the user to close the form, such as the control menu box, the Close button, or a button that runs a Close macro action. If you accidentally create and display a modal form without a means to close it, you can use the ALT-F4 key combination to close the form. Then return to the Design view and add a visible means to close it.

Two additional features that help turn a form into a dialog box are the default button for the form and the Cancel button:

- The command button specified as the default button is pushed automatically when the user presses ENTER. The default button shows with a darker border than the rest of the buttons on the form.

- The command button specified as the Cancel button is pushed automatically when the user presses ESC.

You can assign any one button in the form as the default button and another button as the Cancel button by setting the Default or Cancel control property to Yes.

Preview	Name . . . . Preview
	Default . . . . Yes
	Cancel . . . . No

FIGURE 21-12
The completed
Choose Report
dialog box

While you're working with the command button properties, you can add ScreenTips that appear when you rest the mouse pointer over the button. To add ScreenTips, type the text in the button's ControlTip Text property box on the Other tab of the property sheet.

If the form shows too much blank space in Form view, return to Design view and drag the right border in until it nearly touches the controls.

TIP   *You can't use the Window | Size to Fit Form command with this form because it's modal. This means you can't do anything outside the form while it's open, not even clicking a toolbar button.*

Figure 21-12 shows the finished Choose Report dialog box.

Creating a Dialog Box for User Input

In Chapter 9, you saw how to create a parameter query that prompts the user to enter the criteria for the query. You can use a custom dialog box to accomplish the same thing. For example, the following dialog box prompts the user to enter the DR value of the Alpha Entry records he wants to see. It includes instructions to ensure a valid input value.

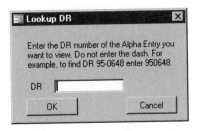

After entering the DR value and clicking OK, a query runs, using the value as the criteria for the DR field. For this example, make a copy of the Alpha DR Query and name it Lookup DR. Then you can change the criteria of the DR column to get the value from the dialog box instead of a parameter prompt.

Setting the Input Form Properties

The Lookup DR form has several special features, in addition to the properties that make it a dialog box, as described in the previous section. These include the following:

- The DR box is an unbound text box named FindDR.
- The FindDR text box is first in the tab order with a Tab Index property of 0.
- The OK command button Default property is set to Yes, so the user can simply press ENTER after typing the DR value to run the query.
- The Cancel command button Cancel property is set to Yes, so the user can press ESC to close the dialog box.

Creating the Macros

The LookUpDR macro group contains two macros, one for each command button:

- The Run Query macro, which is attached to the OK button, contains two actions: OpenQuery, which runs the Lookup DR query in Datasheet view in read-only mode, and Close, which closes the Lookup DR form.
- The CloseForm macro closes the Lookup DR form without running the query.

Modifying the Query

To pass the DR value from the form to the query, the Criteria must be set to the unbound text box control in the form. To do this, type **[Forms]![Lookup DR]![FindDR]** in the Criteria row of the DR column in the Lookup DR query grid.

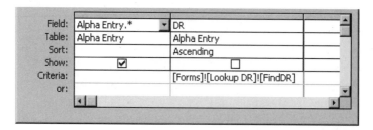

Each of the three parts of the statement is enclosed in square brackets to indicate each is an identifier that refers to objects and controls. The first element defines the object type,

Forms. The exclamation point (!) indicates the element that follows was named by the user. The second element identifies the specific form, Lookup DR, and the third identifies the unbound text box control, FindDR, in the form.

TIP   *Be sure to clear the check box in the Show row of the DR column or you'll have two copies of the DR values in the query results.*

Summary

The switchboards and custom dialog boxes discussed in this chapter can add significantly to the efficiency of an end-user application by presenting interfaces tuned to the goal of the application and to the level of the intended user. A switchboard system can help the user perform the tasks required of the application by offering a list of activities from which to choose. A main entry point into the application can be set to appear when the database first starts.

Custom dialog boxes can be used for many purposes, each of which can get information from the user before continuing to carry out an action. Such dialog boxes can be designed to look and perform like the built-in Access dialog boxes.

PART III

IV
PART

Sharing Data with Others

Exchanging Database Objects and Text

Your application developments can proceed more rapidly when database objects are reused or modified, rather than being developed from scratch. Access provides a number of useful functions and tools to enable you to exchange database objects between Access databases. Functions also exist that support the exchange of Access objects with other types of databases, such as dBase, Paradox, or SQL tables and databases that support the ODBC protocol. You can also exchange Access data in the form of text files.

This chapter, together with the next one, covers the exchange of information between Access and the outside world. This chapter concentrates on exchanging information between Access databases and other database programs. The next chapter expands the discussion of data exchange by including other programs, such as word processors and spreadsheets, as well as covering mailing the data to another destination.

Access database objects include tables, queries, reports, forms, pages, macros, and modules. This chapter describes techniques for exchanging many of these database objects by:

- Copying objects among Access databases
- Importing or linking Access data
- Importing or linking other database formats
- Using linked or imported tables
- Exporting to Access databases
- Exporting objects to other database formats
- Importing and exporting text files

Copying Objects Among Access Databases

Modifying existing objects is generally easier than developing tables, forms, and reports from scratch. A first step in the modification of existing Access database objects is to copy the objects you want to edit or modify.

Efficient and simple techniques exist for copying objects among Access databases. Standard copy-and-paste operations, as well as drag-and-drop techniques, can be used to copy objects from one Access database to another.

Copy-and-Paste

To copy and, subsequently, to paste an Access database object, you must select the object to be copied from the Database window. Objects in this window are selected by first clicking the appropriate button under Objects, and then selecting an object on that page. With the new Office 2003 clipboard, you can copy as many as 24 objects before you need to paste them into their ultimate destination and clear space for more copied objects.

To copy the Alpha Card table from the Police database:

1. Click Tables under Objects in the Database window.

2. Select the Alpha Card table from the list of tables.

3. Use one of the following to copy the table to the clipboard:

   • Click the Copy toolbar button.

   • Choose File | Copy.

   • Right-click the table name and choose Copy from the shortcut menu
     or press CTRL-C.

If your objective at this point is to copy the table to the same database, you have three ways to paste the table:

   • Click the Paste toolbar button.

   • Select Edit | Paste.

   • Right-click the Tables page outside any table name and choose Paste from the
     shortcut menu or press CTRL-V.

When tables are copied, options are presented in a Paste Table As dialog box, which asks for a name for the table, as well as presents the following options:

   • Pasting the structure of the table (without its data)

   • Pasting the structure of the table and its data

   • Appending the data to an existing table

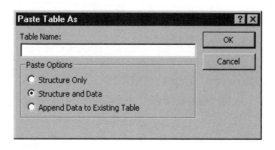

TIP   If you choose to paste the data to an existing table, you might have problems with duplicate primary key fields or unique index values. You also need to consider different table structures. See Chapter 9 for information dealing with append queries and how to solve their problems.

If you're copying an object to another database (rather than within its own database with a different name), you can start a second instance of Access and open the destination database. Then tile the two Access windows in a split-screen format. Next, copy the object from the source database, select the object category in the destination Database window, and paste into the destination database. If you don't want to use two instances of Access, close the source database after you copy the object, open the corresponding page in the destination database, and then click Paste.

NOTE   Copying an object generates a copy of all the properties of that object. For example, when a form is copied, the format, source data, event specifications, filters, and all other properties are copied with the form.

Drag-and-Drop

A drag-and-drop technique can also be used to copy objects between databases. To use drag-and-drop, two instances of Access must be active at the same time. The source database must be open in one Access window and the destination database must be open in another Access window.

To drag an object from one window to another:

1. Make sure both Database windows are open to the same object page, and then select the object to be copied in the first database.

2. While holding the left mouse button down, drag the item to the destination database.

3. Release the mouse button and the new object appears in the destination database.

TIP   When drag-and-drop techniques are used to copy tables, the Paste Table As window doesn't appear. As a result, when tables are copied this way, the table structure and its data are both pasted into the destination database, while the original object remains in the source database. If you want only the structure, open the copied table and delete all the records.

Importing or Linking Access Data

Two other important techniques for adding Access data to an Access database or project are importing and linking. *Importing* is used to copy Access data or other objects into an Access database from other Access databases. Importing is also used to bring data into an Access database from dissimilar sources, such as a dBASE or Paradox application; this is discussed later in this chapter (see "Importing or Linking to Other Data Sources"). *Linking* is a way of connecting to and using data in an Access database without copying the data from the other database. You can import or link data from Access versions 2.0, 7.0/95, 8.0/97, 9.0/2000, and 10.0/2002 to Access 2003 databases or projects.

> **Import vs. Link**
> You should choose to import data into an Access database if you expect to use the data only in Access and not depend on another program to maintain the data. Access is more efficient when working with its own tables and you can modify the data just the same as native-grown data.
>
> You should choose to link with data in another program if you rely on the source program to update the information. Linking is also useful in a multiuser environment, where you split an existing database and place the data on a network server. Users can then share the database and create their own forms, reports, and other objects.

NOTE *If you're importing or linking a database that requires a password, you must enter the password before you can proceed.*

Importing Objects

The first case to look at is the importing of all objects from one Access database to another. To start importing an object, do the following:

1. Choose File | Get External Data. You have a choice of Import or Link Tables.

2. Choose Import. The Import dialog box opens (see Figure 22-1) where you locate and select the database file that contains the objects you want to import. You can also right-click in the Database window and choose Import from the Shortcut menu.

FIGURE 22-1 Selecting a file from the Import dialog box

3. When you locate the database file from which you want to import objects, select it and click Import. The Import Objects dialog box opens where you can choose which objects to import. In this example, the Northwind database is selected from sample Access applications, and the Products and Categories tables are imported.

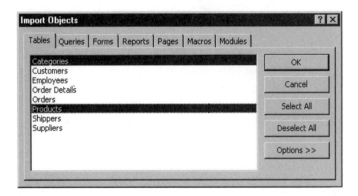

4. To choose which objects to import, click the desired Object tab and do one of the following:

   - Select each object name individually.
   - Click Select All.
   - To remove an object from the import list, select it again, or click Deselect All to remove all selected objects.

5. Repeat step 4 for all the desired object types.

6. After selecting all the objects you want to import, click OK to close the Import Objects dialog box and return to the Database window where you can see the imported objects.

Figure 22-2 shows the Police Database window with the newly imported Categories and Products tables. The imported tables are now part of the Police database and don't appear different from the native tables.

NOTE *Unlike copied data, you can't append imported data to existing tables directly except for spreadsheets or text files, which are discussed in Chapter 23. You must import the table first, and then run an append query to add the data to the other table. See Chapter 9 for information about append queries and how to use them.*

If you import a table that includes Lookup fields, remember to import the tables or queries the fields refer to and get their values from. Otherwise, every time you open the table in Datasheet view, you get an error message for each missing table or query. If you don't want to or can't import the supporting value tables or queries, you can change the imported table design by changing the field Display Control property on the Lookup tab to Text Box for each Lookup field.

FIGURE 22-2
Tables imported
to the Access
database

If you try to import a table that's already linked to another table, you link to the source table data instead of importing it.

Setting Import Options

When you click Options in the Import Objects dialog box, the box expands to show a lower pane with three sets of import options.

The first set of options supports the importing of other table features, such as the relationships, custom menus and toolbars, as well as some database specifications.

- The *Relationships* option is selected by default, and it includes the relationships you defined for the tables and queries you import.

- The *Menus and Toolbars* option includes all the custom menus and toolbars in the database from which you're importing. However, Access won't import any menu or toolbar that has the same name as one in the destination database.

- The *Import/Export Specs* option includes all the import and export specifications set for the source database. See the section "Importing and Linking Text Files" for information about setting import specifications.

The second set of options, *Import Tables,* applies to the imported tables and determines whether to import both the table definition and the data (default) or only the definition. This is useful for creating a copy of the table structures for a new database without including any existing data.

The third set of options, *Import Queries,* applies to any queries you select to import, and specifies whether to import queries as queries (default) or run the query and import the resulting recordset as a table.

Once opened, as you click other object tabs, the Options pane remains open.

CAUTION   *Reasons for importing some objects or combinations of objects must be examined carefully. For example, importing a form without importing its underlying tables or queries can result in problems that might be difficult to resolve. An attempt to invoke the form generates an error message indicating the underlying record source is missing. Logical, useful groupings of objects should be imported and, in most cases, this means tables should be imported to provide the field definitions and data for all the forms, queries, reports, pages, macros, and modules you choose to import. Relationships should also be included whenever importing more than one table.*

Linking Access Tables

Linking to tables in another Access database makes them available without copying them into the active database. Linking saves space and reduces the need to maintain redundant data. And linking ensures you always have access to current information. However, linking also means you're dependent on an object that resides in another environment where it might be renamed, moved, or deleted. Linked objects can be moved from one folder or from one disk to another, which could break the link.

CAUTION   *If you're linking to a table in a database that's password-protected, you must enter the correct password to continue. When you enter the password, it's stored in an unencrypted form with the link information and any user who can open your database can also open the linked, password-protected database. See Chapters 24 and 25 for more information about multiple users and security.*

To link to a table in another Access database, do the following:

1. Open the destination database, in this example, Police.

2. Start the linking process by choosing File | Get External Data | Link Tables from any page in the Database window. You can also right-click in the Database window and choose Link Tables from the Shortcut menu. The Link dialog box appears, which is similar in appearance to the Import dialog box.

3. In the Link dialog box, select the Microsoft Office Access file type, and then select the database you want to link to your active database. Next, click Link. In this

example, the sample Northwind database is selected as the source of the linked table. The Link Tables dialog box opens, showing only a Tables tab because tables are the only Access objects that contain data.

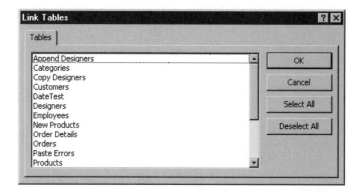

4. Select one or more of the available tables, and then click the OK button. In this example, the Suppliers table is linked to the Police database. The table is marked in the list of tables with an arrow indicating the table is a linked table (see Figure 22-3).

NOTE   *If you link two related tables from the same database, the relationship is retained.*

Importing or Linking to Other Data Sources

Access can import data or link to existing tables in a number of the most prevalent database management systems, as well as from other sources, such as word processors or HTML files. Access provides specific recognition of some database table formats. The process of importing or linking to foreign databases that aren't Access databases is similar to the

FIGURE 22-3   Showing a linked table in the Database window

import or link functions for Access databases. This section discusses importing from or linking to dBase and Paradox databases, as well as techniques for importing data from other sources supported by Access.

You can both import and link dBASE III, IV, 5, and 7 files, as well as Paradox 3.*x*, 4.*x*, 5.0, and 8.0 files. For version dBASE 7 and Paradox 8.0, you need the updated ISAM drivers available from Microsoft Technical Support.

You can also import and link data from ODBC data sources, such as the Microsoft SQL Server and Visual FoxPro. You need a connection to the appropriate ODBC data source and the data source defined.

Data types are generally compatible among these database management systems, although they aren't labeled consistently. For example, dBASE Character and Paradox Alphanumeric data types both become Text fields in Access. dBASE Float and Paradox Currency types become Number fields in Access with Field Size property set to Double. dBASE calls Yes/No fields Logical.

Using Data from dBASE or Paradox

Importing a dBASE table or a Paradox file into an Access database is similar to importing a table from an Access database. Other database programs, such as FileMaker Pro, can export DBF-formatted files, which you can import into Access the same as an original dBASE file. The example shown here imports a dBASE table into the Access database. To import the foreign table, do the following:

1. Choose File | Get External Data | Import or right-click in the Database window and choose Import from the Shortcut menu. This brings up the Import dialog box as before.

2. In the Files of type area, select the database file types. Then locate and select the file you want to import.

3. In the case illustrated here, select the Employee.dbf file, and then click Import.

4. After a few seconds, you should see a message indicating EMPLOYEE has been successfully imported into the open Access database. Click OK.

5. Locate and import other files as necessary or click Close to close the dialog box and return to the Police database window.

Once the table is imported, it looks and behaves just like an Access table. Importing Paradox files uses the same procedures.

Another approach to making use of data from a dBASE or Paradox database is to use the Link Tables operation by choosing File | Get External Data | Link Tables. You can also right-click the Database window and choose Link Tables from the Shortcut menu. The Link dialog box appears, in which you select the appropriate file type and the specific file to be linked.

When you import a dBASE file, Access creates a table with the same name as the .dbf file and imports the data. When you link to a dBASE file, Access also requires the associated dBASE index files be linked. If you choose to link to a dBASE file, the Select Index Files dialog box appears where you can choose the indexes (.ndx and .mdx files) associated with the .dbf file.

- If there are none, click Cancel and proceed with the link operation.
- If you select one or more index files, the Select Unique Record Identifier dialog box prompts you to select the corresponding index field. Your index must have a unique value for each record or difficulties could occur when you try to update records.

After importing or linking a dBASE file, you can set field properties for the table. If you import a file with no primary index, you can set one in Access. When you update the file with Access, the index is automatically updated as well. If you use dBASE to update the file, you must also update the corresponding index in dBASE before trying to open the file in Access.

Figure 22-4 shows a linked dBASE file in the Database window by displaying the arrow (indicating a linked file) and a dB icon indicating NewCats is a linked dBASE file.

If you select a Paradox table to link to, you need the index (.px) file and the memo (.mb) file, if the table has any. Without these files, you won't be able to open the linked table in Access. If the Paradox table doesn't have a primary index, you must create one in Paradox to update the table in Access.

Importing and Linking Text Files

Text files are useful when importing or linking the data to Access tables. If no other common data format exists between the source of the data and Access, you can create a text file with the source program and import that into Access. Most relational, hierarchical, or

FIGURE 22-4   Showing a linked dBASE table

network-oriented database management systems can generate a text version of the data using some kind of record selection function. Once text files have been generated, they're either *fixed-width* text files (files consisting of rows of data of the same length) or *delimited* text files (files containing records that use special characters—typically commas—to indicate the separation between data fields). Most delimited text files also use a text qualifier—usually double quotation marks—to delimit strings. Fixed-width or delimited text files can be imported or linked to an Access database using the same external data importing and linking functions used for data from any source.

Using Delimited Text Files

Importing or linking a delimited text file begins with the same sequence as other importing and linking operations. Prior to starting the importing/linking process, however, you must specify a table ready to receive the data—either a new table definition with the appropriate field definitions or an existing table to which this new data can be appended.

NOTE *Creating a table definition to receive the data from delimited text files can be accomplished using basic table definition techniques (see Chapter 4) or by copying the table definition from an existing table. Care must be taken to account for the proper number of fields, field length, and data type selection to import text data correctly.*

To import a text file, open the Import dialog box as before, and then do the following:

1. In the Import window, select Text Files in the Files of type box.

2. Locate the text file you want to import and double-click its name, or select it and click Import.

3. The Import Text Wizard dialog box appears, displaying sample data from the selected text file. The Import Text Wizard analyzes the selected file and determines whether it's a fixed-width text file or a delimited file. Figure 22-5 shows the text file we're importing—SENIORS.TXT—has been determined to be a delimited text file.

4. Click Next to see how the file is formatted. In the case illustrated here (see Figure 22-6), the wizard determined the fields in this file are delimited by commas, the text fields are bound by quotation marks, and the first row doesn't contain field names.

5. Next, do one of the following:

   • If you agree with the results of the Import Text Wizard's processing, click Next.

   • If you disagree, adjust the selections (for the delimiting character, the text qualifier, and whether the first row contains field names) until you're satisfied they're accurate, and then click Next.

6. At this point, you must decide whether to import the data to a new table or append to an existing table. If you select In an Existing Table, select a table name from the drop-down list, and then click Finish. Figure 22-7 illustrates an example of selecting an existing table to receive the data.

PART IV

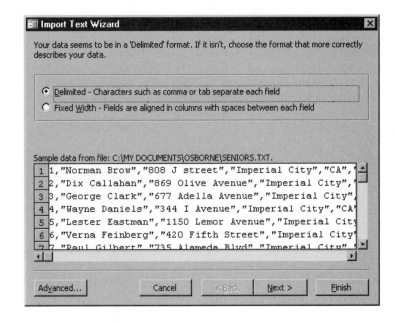

NOTE *You can append text files to an existing table if the first row of the text file matches the table's field names.*

7. Because the field names aren't in the first row of the text table, choose to import the data to a new table, and then click Next. The Import Text Wizard asks you to specify

PART IV

FIGURE 22-7
Selecting a table
to receive the data

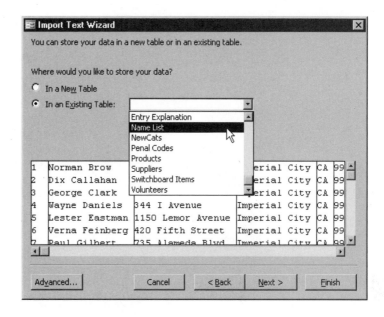

information about each field in the file (see Figure 22-8). The wizard names the fields,
Field1, Field2, and so forth until you rename them. Enter or verify the field name,
data type, if the field is indexed, and whether you want to import or skip that field.

8. After completing the field information, click Next and the wizard suggests specifying
a primary key field, by letting the wizard add one, specifying an existing field, or
choosing not to have a primary key (see Figure 22-9). Click Next.

FIGURE 22-8
Setting imported
field information

FIGURE 22-9
Adding a
primary key

9. The final step in importing the data is to enter a name for the new table and click Finish.

TIP   *If the import process seems to take a long time, errors might be occurring. Press* CTRL-BREAK *to cancel any time during the process.*

Import Errors

Improperly defined data or data of an improper length could cause errors that are recorded in an import-processing error table. If this occurs, Access creates an Import Errors table containing descriptions of the errors that occurred when importing the text file or spreadsheet to an Access database. The table shows the field names and row numbers of the data that caused the error.

Some of the possible import errors are the following:

- **Field Truncation**, which occurs when the text value is longer than the Field Size property setting for the destination field.

- **Type Conversion Failure**, which occurs when a value is the wrong data type for the destination field.

- **Key Violation**, which occurs when a duplicate primary key value appears.

- **Validation Rule Failure**, which occurs when a field value breaks the rule defined in the Validation Rule property for the destination field.

> - **Null in Required Field**, which occurs when the Required property of the destination field is set to Yes and a null value occurs.
>
> - **Unparsable Record**, which occurs when a text value contains a character specified as the text delimiter character.
>
> If the problem is with the data, edit the file. If you're trying to append data to an existing table, you might need to change the table definition. After correcting the problems, import the file again. When a value contains the delimiter character, edit each field to repeat the character twice. When you finish, check the destination files to make sure no duplicate copies exist of some of the records.

Linking delimited text files with the Link Text Wizard involves the same process as importing with two exceptions: you aren't asked if you want to link to an existing table or create a new one and you're also not prompted for a primary index because you're not creating a new table.

Using Fixed-Width Text Files

The Import Text Wizard reacts a little differently once fixed-width text files are detected. The second Wizard dialog box (see Figure 22-10) shows the fixed-length data with vertical lines between fields and a ruler at the top. The wizard asks you to confirm whether the lines seem to indicate the proper separation point between fields and provides guidance as to how to move or reposition the lines:

- To create a line, click the position where a field separation is desired.

FIGURE 22-10
Adjusting the field widths with the Import Text Wizard

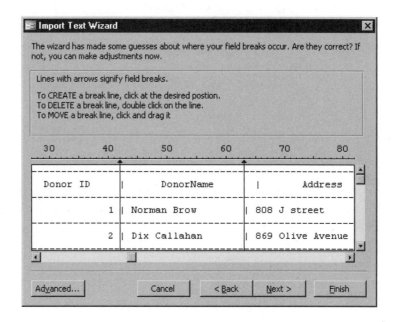

- To delete a line, double-click the line to remove the field separation.
- To move a line, click-and-drag the line to the proper position.

Once adjustments are completed, the process of identifying the destination table and completing the import or link is the same as with delimited files.

Changing Import Specifications

The import specifications for a text file can be changed using the Advanced features of the Import Text Wizard. When the Advanced button is clicked, an Import Specification dialog box appears (see Figure 22-11), which enables you to specify a number of table characteristics including the following:

- The file format (delimited or fixed-width)
- If delimited, the field delimiter and text qualifier characters
- The language and code page in which you can choose a different language and set the logical text layout to one of the right-to-left reading codes. As a step toward compatibility with Asian markets, you can set the code for importing or exporting text files in a right-to-left reading direction. Click the Code Page drop-down arrow in the Import Specification box to see the list of code page conversion options

- The specifications for dates, times, and numbers
- Information for each incoming field, such as name, starting and ending position in the record, data type, whether the field is to be indexed, and whether to omit the field from the import

Once the text file characteristics are satisfactorily specified, the OK button returns you to the Import Text Wizard dialog box, where clicking the Finish button completes the text import action and places the table in your Access database.

Using Linked or Imported Tables

Linked or imported tables are used just as any other Access table with some precautions. Imported tables have essentially become new tables within your Access database. Linked

FIGURE 22-11
Setting specifications in the Import Specifications dialog box

tables, however, still reside within the environments in which they were created. Thus, issues such as renaming the table or changing its characteristics, have implications for relating the linked table to its original source environment.

Renaming a Linked Table in Access

The linked table might have a name that isn't meaningful in your Access database. You can give it a more relevant name without disturbing the link. Renaming a linked table is the same as renaming a native table.

1. Select the table in the Database window.
2. Select Edit | Rename or right-click and choose Rename from the Shortcut menu, and then edit the old name or enter a new name.

NOTE *When a linked table is renamed in Access, the name of the linked table isn't changed in its original environment. Renaming the linked table in an Access database simply changes the name used within that particular database. The longer table names in Access (up to 64 characters) can support more descriptive naming conventions than other applications offer, some of which still limit table names to eight characters and don't allow spaces.*

Changing Linked Table Properties

Table properties of linked tables are usually set by the database that owns the table. The field properties and the validation rules are also set by the source database. Data entered in Access must conform to most of the properties set for the originating database fields, such as default values, minimum or maximum values, field format, text options, and any other validation requirements.

Field properties you can change in a linked table include Format, Decimal Places, Input Mask, and Caption. If you want to change other field properties in a form, set them for the controls bound to the fields.

Changing the basic properties or validation rules of a linked table requires access to the table through its original database application. If the table is in a database environment other than Access, that database management system must be available to support efforts to change table properties.

Updating Links with the Linked Table Manager

When the location of a linked table is changed, using the Linked Table Manager database utility within Access is a recommended method of reestablishing the proper path or linkage to the table. The Linked Table Manager doesn't physically move files, it only updates the path leading to the file location. The Linked Table Manager can be consulted in two cases:

- To examine or refresh links
- To change the path or location of linked tables

NOTE   *The Linked Table Manager doesn't move database or table files; it only updates the path to the object. If you want to move the file to a new location, use Windows Explorer, My Computer, or the MS-DOS Move or Copy commands. After you move the file, you can use the Linked Table Manager to refresh the link.*

To refresh links, do the following:

1. To start the Linked Table Manager, select Tools | Database Utilities | Linked Table Manager. The Linked Table Manager dialog box displays a list of all tables linked to the current database with the table name and the current path (see Figure 22-12).

2. Click Select All or check only the table links you want to refresh, and then click OK.

3. If the Manager is successful in locating the file, it displays a message to that effect. If not, it prompts for the location of the table by displaying a Select New Location Of *Tablename* dialog box where you can locate the file and change the path.

NOTE   *The Linked Table Manager has no way of refreshing links to tables whose names were changed in the source database after linking. Delete the current link and start over.*

To change the path to a linked table, open the Linked Table Manager, as previously discussed, and do the following:

1. Select the Always prompt for new location option in the Linked Table Manager dialog box.

2. Check the tables whose paths you want to change, and then click OK.

FIGURE 22-12   Selecting linked tables in Linked Table Manager dialog box

3. Designate their new location in the Select New Location of *Tablename* dialog box and click Open. If you need to, you can use the Search feature (choose Tools | Search) in the Select New Location dialog box to locate elusive files.

4. Click OK to close the message box, and then click Close.

TIP   *If more than one of the tables you selected were moved to the new location, all the links are updated at once.*

Unlinking Tables

Unlinking a table removes the linkage to a table in another (source) database. The procedure for unlinking a table is identical to that for deleting a table, however, the Delete function doesn't delete the linked table. It only deletes the link to the database.

CAUTION   *If your intention is to delete a link to a table in another database and not to delete a complete table and its data, be sure to select a table name with the arrow indicating it's a linked table. If you inadvertently select a regular table—as opposed to a linked table—and perform a Delete, the table and its data will be lost.*

PART IV

To unlink a table, do one of the following:

- Select the linked table to be unlinked and press DELETE or choose Edit | Delete.
- Right-click the table name and choose Delete from the Shortcut menu.

Respond Yes when Access asks for confirmation of the deletion.

Exporting to an Existing Access Database

Exporting data or database objects to another Access database is a straightforward process. Exporting has the same functionality as copying-and-pasting. The same data formats are supported as with importing.

1. To export a table, select the table name in the Database window and choose File | Export, or right-click the table name and choose Export from the Shortcut menu.

2. An Export Table To dialog box appears in which to locate and select the destination database and select the export file type in the Save as type box (see Figure 22-13).

3. Click Export.

4. Accept the existing name or enter a new name for the destination table in the Export dialog box.

5. Select to export both the table definition and data, or only the definition.

6. Click OK.

When you're exporting database objects other than tables, the basic steps are the same. The exception is the final step isn't required because you're exporting only an object design without any data.

Tip   *Exporting database objects operates as a one-at-a-time function. When multiple objects are to be exported to an Access database, it might be more expedient to open the destination database and use the File | Get External Data | Import command, which can be used to import multiple objects at once.*

FIGURE 22-13   Choosing a destination for the exported table

Exporting to Another Database Format

Access supports exporting data to the same database and text formats as are acceptable for importing and linking. Access can also export data in the proper formats for other applications, such as spreadsheets (Excel and Lotus 1-2-3), text files, HTML, or XML files, as discussed in the next chapter.

CAUTION   When you export data to older database programs—such as dBASE or Paradox, which limit table names to eight characters, not including the file extension—the longer table names are truncated to comply with the limitation. This can result in duplicate names. To prevent this, make a copy of your table with a shorter name before exporting the copy.

To export data to these formats, follow these steps:

1. Select the table in your active database and select File | Export, or right-click the table name and choose Export from the Shortcut menu.
2. In the Export Table To dialog box, choose the dBASE or Paradox file format in the Save as Type box.
3. Click the arrow next to Save in and select the drive and folder to export to.
4. Enter the destination file name in the File name box and click Export.

Exporting to Text Files

When you want to export data from an Access database to a text file, you call on the Export Text Wizard, which works much like the Import Text Wizard described earlier. The wizard helps you specify the format of the exported Access file and determine where the output is to be stored. The following steps describe how to export data to a text file using the Export Text Wizard.

1. In the Tables page of the Database window, select the table containing the data you want to export to a text file.

2. Choose File | Export or right-click and choose Export from the Shortcut menu.

3. In the Export Table ... To dialog box, select Text Files in the Save as type box.

4. In the Save in box, select the folder to receive the exported text data.

5. In the File name box, enter the name of the text file you want to assign to the exported data or select an existing file to receive the data. Click Export.

6. The Export Text Wizard dialog box (see Figure 22-14) appears, displaying data from the selected table. You have the choice between saving a fixed-width text file or a delimited file.

7. Click Next.

8. If you chose Delimited, the next dialog box (see Figure 22-15) contains the specifics of the delimiters, text qualifiers, and other features of each field.

   • If you agree with the results of the Export Text Wizard's processing, click Next.

   • If you disagree, adjust the selections (for the delimiting character, the text indicator, and whether the first row contains field names) until you're satisfied they're accurate. Then click Next.

FIGURE 22-14
Selecting the text file type with the Export Text Wizard

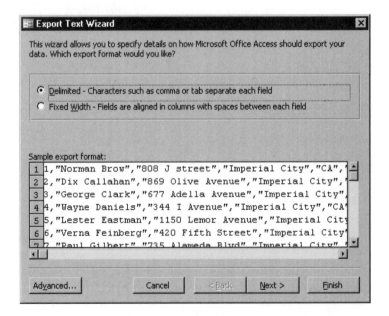

FIGURE 22-15
The Export Text
Wizard lets you
choose how to
format the text file

9. If you chose Fixed Width, the next dialog box asks for verification of the field lengths. You can drag the divider lines left or right to change the fixed-length of the fields. Figure 22-16 shows the same table being exported as fixed width.

10. Click Finish to complete the export.

FIGURE 22-16
Exporting the text
file as fixed width

You can also use the Export Text Wizard to customize the export specifications for a text file the same way you set the import specifications with the Import Text Wizard. When you click the Advanced button in the Export Text Wizard, an Export Specification dialog box appears, enabling you to specify the file format (fixed-width or delimited), the language and code page settings, the specifications for dates, times, and numbers, and field information. The options are the same as for importing, including encoding for a right-to-left language.

Summary

Importing, linking, and exporting data are important ways of sharing data between Access databases, as well as with other applications. These data exchange functions are essential tools in sharing data with other Microsoft Office 2003 applications, as well as Paradox, dBASE, and other database management systems. The functions that support these data exchange operations, such as Get External Data, Export, and the Import and Export Text Wizards, have a number of options and should be the subject of considerable experimentation to ensure the results are useful and reliable. In the next chapter, you learn about the issues of exchanging data with outside sources and sharing data with multiple users.

Exchanging Data with Outside Sources

The last chapter focused on exchanging data within the Access management realm, with other database management systems, and with text files. In this chapter, you learn how to exchange information between an Access database and an outside source—data from a word processor, a spreadsheet or an HTML document. A successful exchange of data with these outside sources involves a sequence of steps that are intended to ensure the end result is useful. For example, records moved into Access from a word processor or a spreadsheet need to be evaluated and, in some cases, edited to be compatible with the table's data structure.

This chapter describes the procedures you can use for data exchange operations with outside data sources. Procedures are described for:

- Copying or moving records from word processors and spreadsheets
- Saving Access objects as external files
- Working with Microsoft Word
- Working with Microsoft Excel
- Working with HTML
- Mailing Access database objects

Copying or Moving Records

To copy or move records from other applications to Access, make sure the data is arranged in an appropriate format, and then use the selection, copy, and paste functions in Access to move the records you want. The following sections describe specific approaches for moving data among word processors and spreadsheets.

Copying or Moving Data from a Word Processor

You can use two approaches to copy or move records from a table created with a word processor. The first approach is to save the desired records to a text file with fixed length or delimited records, and then import them into the target table. Procedures for importing these text files to an Access table are described in the previous chapter.

The second approach to moving records from a word processor to Access is to perform a copy-and-paste operation. For this copy/paste approach to work properly, be aware of these two major points:

- The records in the word processing file must already be in a table or properly separated by tab characters.

- The columns in the word processor table should be in the same order as the fields in the Access table you're targeting.

When you copy data, you place a copy of that data in the destination file and leave the original data alone in the source file. When you move data, you delete it from the source and place it in the target file.

When performing copy or move operations, the Access database must be open to receive the new data. You can add new records to either a datasheet or a form. If you're adding records to a datasheet, the columns aren't required to have the same names as the fields, but the data being copied or moved should be the same data type.

If you're adding records to a form, the data is copied or moved to text box controls, which are bound to table fields and have the same names as the incoming data columns. If the column names don't match the control names or the columns have no names, the data is moved or copied to the form in the tab order.

On the receiving end, you can replace existing records or add to the records already in the datasheet or form. When you replace records in a datasheet, you select the same number of records to eliminate as you selected to bring in from the word processor. In a form, you can replace only the current record.

To move or copy word processing data, do the following:

1. In the word processor application, select the records you want to move or copy using the selection method provided by the application. In Microsoft Word, this can be as simple as clicking the left mouse button on the first record you want, and then holding the left mouse button down as you drag the cursor down the file until the last desired record is highlighted (see Figure 23-1).

2. Then, do one of the following, both of which place the selected records on the clipboard:

   - If you want to move the records from the word processing file to the Access database, choose Edit | Cut, click the Cut toolbar button, or press CTRL-X.

   - If you want to copy the records, as opposed to moving them, choose Edit | Copy, click the Copy toolbar button, or press CTRL-C.

3. Open the datasheet or form you want to paste the records into, and then do one of the following:

   - If you're replacing records in Datasheet view, select the records you want to replace, and then choose Edit | Paste, click the Paste toolbar button, or press CTRL-V. If you select fewer records in the target than in the source table, the selected records are replaced and the excess records from the source table are ignored. If you select more records in the target table, they're replaced with the

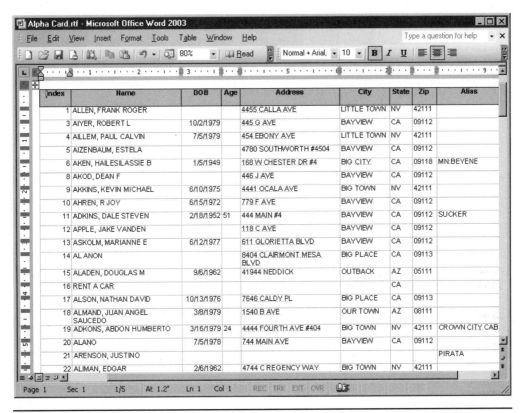

Index	Name	DOB	Age	Address	City	State	Zip	Alias
1	ALLEN, FRANK ROGER			4455 CALLA AVE	LITTLE TOWN	NV	42111	
3	AIYER, ROBERT L	10/2/1979		445 G AVE	BAYVIEW	CA	09112	
4	AILLEM, PAUL CALVIN	7/5/1979		454 EBONY AVE	LITTLE TOWN	NV	42111	
5	AIZENBAUM, ESTELA			4780 SOUTHWORTH #4504	BAYVIEW	CA	09112	
6	AKEN, HAILESILASSIE B	1/5/1949		168 W CHESTER DR #4	BIG CITY	CA	09118	MN:BEYENE
8	AKOD, DEAN F			446 J AVE	BAYVIEW	CA	09112	
9	AKKINS, KEVIN MICHAEL	6/10/1975		4441 OCALA AVE	BIG TOWN	NV	42111	
10	AHREN, R JOY	6/15/1972		779 F AVE	BAYVIEW	CA	09112	
11	ADKINS, DALE STEVEN	2/18/1952	51	444 MAIN #4	BAYVIEW	CA	09112	SUCKER
12	APPLE, JAKE VANDEN			118 C AVE	BAYVIEW	CA	09112	
13	ASKOLM, MARIANNE E	6/12/1977		611 GLORIETTA BLVD	BAYVIEW	CA	09112	
14	AL ANON			8404 CLAIRMONT MESA BLVD	BIG PLACE	CA	09113	
15	ALADEN, DOUGLAS M	9/6/1962		41944 NEDDICK	OUTBACK	AZ	05111	
16	RENT A CAR					CA		
17	ALSON, NATHAN DAVID	10/13/1976		7646 CALDY PL	BIG PLACE	CA	09113	
18	ALMAND, JUAN ANGEL SAUCEDO	3/8/1979		1540 B AVE	OUR TOWN	AZ	08111	
19	ADKONS, ABDON HUMBERTO	3/16/1979	24	4444 FOURTH AVE #404	BIG TOWN	NV	42111	CROWN CITY CAB
20	ALANO	7/5/1978		744 MAIN AVE	BAYVIEW	CA	09112	
21	ARENSON, JUSTINO							PIRATA
22	ALIMAN, EDGAR	2/6/1962		4744 C REGENCY WAY	BIG TOWN	NV	42111	

FIGURE 23-2   An Access table saved as an RTF file

Publishing with Word

You can use an Office Link to save the output of a datasheet, form, or report automatically as an RTF file and load the file into Word. For example, suppose you created a custom form or report that you want to include in your company's annual report being created in Word. After creating the form or report design, simply load the output into the Word document. The file is saved in the folder you specified as your Default database folder in the General tab of the Options dialog box. When you launch Word, you can open the Access file from Word. Access refers to this as "publishing" the data in Word.

NOTE   *One of the differences between this process and the process of saving a datasheet as a mail merge data source is this: forms and reports can be published, as can tables and queries. For mail merge, tables and queries are the only accepted Access objects.*

To publish an Access object into Word, do the following:

1. Select the name of the table, query, form, or report you want to save and load into Word. If you want to load only part of a datasheet, open the datasheet first, and then select the records you want to load.

2. Choose Tools | Office Links or click the Office Links toolbar button, and then click Publish It with Microsoft Word.

This saves the selected object or data in a file in the Access folder, opens Word automatically, and opens the file for review and editing. The file is saved in a table in RTF. Figure 23-3 shows the result of publishing the Alpha Entry by Code query datasheet in Word.

Using Merge It with Microsoft Word

An Access database is often an ideal place to store addresses and names of customers, business associates, or friends. Being able to use these names and addresses in correspondence is a

EntryNo	Index	Entry	DR	Code	Date	Purge	Remarks
1	1	V/BATTERY	950648	242	6/14/2001	6/14/2004	
2	3	V/GRAND THEFT BIKE	941659	487	4/25/2000	4/25/2007	
3	4	V/BURGLARY	915358	459	10/15/1999	10/15/2006	
4	5	V/ATTEMPT AUTO THEFT 664/	943060	10852	8/6/2000	8/5/2007	
7	8	V/GRAND THEFT	933113	487	8/7/1999	8/7/2006	
8	9	CITE/POSS <OZ MARIJ	971875	11357	7/18/2003	7/18/2005	
9	10	V/PETTY THEFT	962101	488	8/20/2002	8/20/2005	STARK
10	11	ARREST/CO-HAB ABUSE/245A1	950648	273.5	2/26/2001	2/26/2004	
12	12	V/BURGLARY	944755	459	12/9/2000	12/9/2015	
13	13	V/PETTY THEFT/BIKE	944790	488	12/8/2001	12/8/2004	
14	14	L/O STOL/RECD VEH	944538	10851	11/21/2000	11/21/2007	
15	15	ARREST/ROBBERY & BURGLARY	915120	211	10/1/1999	10/1/2006	
16	16	R/O STOL VEH	941499	10851	4/13/2000	4/13/2010	
18	16	R/O STOL/REC VEH	951265	10851	4/19/2001	4/19/2008	
19	16	R/O VEH #1/H&R FELONY	915564	20001	10/26/2000	10/26/2004	
20	16	R/O STOL VEH	941503	10851	4/14/2000	4/14/2010	
21	16	R/O STOL VEH	971145	10851	5/18/2003	5/18/2010	STARK
24	16	R/O RECD VEH	971145	10851	5/19/2003	5/18/2010	STARK
26	16	R/O STOL VEH	932593	10851	7/5/2000	7/5/2007	
28	16	R/O/STOL VEH	932756	10851	7/16/1999	7/16/2007	
30	16	R/O/STOL VEH	932779	10851	7/18/2000	7/18/2006	

FIGURE 23-3 The results of publishing a query to Word

valuable capability. Once the link between Access and Word is established, you can open Word at any time to print form letters, envelopes, or labels using the current data from Access.

A query might be the ideal way to simplify Access data structures for this mail merge function. Your table for customer names and addresses might have a number of other fields, such as a telephone number or date of last order, which you needn't pass on. A query that selects only those fields relevant to addressing correspondence can be designed to support mail merge actions (that is, Name, Title, Company, Street Address, City, State, and ZIP code). The Word mail merge feature can do this after receiving the table data as well, but you might as well not clutter the exchange of data with unnecessary fields.

To merge data from an Access table or query using the Microsoft Word mail merge functions, follow these steps:

1. In the Database window, select the table or query containing the data.

2. Choose Tools | Office Links or click the Office Links toolbar button, and then select Merge It with Microsoft Word.

3. The Microsoft Word Mail Merge Wizard dialog box appears, giving you a choice of linking your data to an existing Microsoft Word document or creating a new one. Once you select one of these options and click OK, Word starts up and opens either a new document or the specific document you selected.

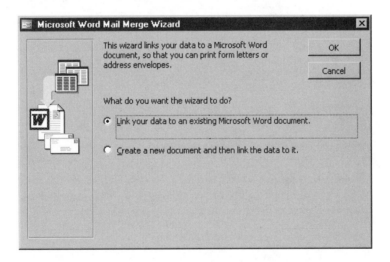

4. In Word, a toolbar appears with a button called Insert Merge Fields. When you click this button, the list of fields from the Access table is displayed. Select the specific fields you want to insert in your document, and then place them in the document. Figure 23-4 shows a new Word document with a dialog box listing the fields from the NameList Access table as the data source. For further information about how mail merge works, consult your Microsoft Word documentation.

FIGURE 23-4   Using an Access table as the mail merge data source

Working with Excel

The association between Excel and Access can be a two-way street. You can make use of Excel data in Access by importing or linking. You have three ways to make use of Access data in Excel or another spreadsheet program:

- Export the Access datasheet as unformatted data.
- Save the output of a datasheet, form, or report as an Excel file or worksheet.
- Load the output of a datasheet, form, or report directly into Excel.

When you use either one of the last two methods, most of the formatting is preserved. A form is saved as a table of data. If you're saving a report that includes grouped data, the group levels are saved as outline levels in Excel.

Importing from and Linking to Excel Spreadsheets

Before you try to import or link to data from an Excel or other spreadsheet, make sure the data is arranged in a tabular format. The spreadsheet must also have the same type of data in each column as the target Access datasheet and the rows must contain the same field in each position.

You can choose to import or link an entire spreadsheet, or only the data from a named range of cells within the spreadsheet. Usually, you create a new table from the imported or linked spreadsheet data, but you can also append the data to an existing datasheet if the spreadsheet column headings are the same as the table field names.

TIP   *Access tries to assign appropriate data types to the imported data fields, but it doesn't always make the correct assumption. Before you do any work on the new table, be sure the field data types are what you want. You should also check the assumed field properties and set additional properties, such as formatting, to fit the intended table use in Access. Number field formatting might differ between Excel and Access.*

If you're importing from Excel version 5.0 or later, you can select one or more of the worksheets in the workbook. You can't import multiple spreadsheet files from Excel 4.0 or from Lotus 1-2-3. If you want one of these spreadsheets, you must open the program and save each spreadsheet as a separate file before importing.

To import or link an Excel spreadsheet, invoke the Import Spreadsheet Wizard by doing the following:

1. Choose File | Get External Data, and then click Import or Link Tables. You can also right-click the Database window and choose Import or Link Tables from the Shortcut menu.

2. In the Import (or Link) dialog box, select Microsoft Excel in the Files of Type box.

3. In the Look In box, select the drive and folder where the spreadsheet file you want is located, and then select the file name and click Import or Link.

4. In the first Import (or Link) Spreadsheet Wizard dialog box, you can choose to import a specific worksheet or a named range of cells, and then click Next.

PART IV

5. In the next wizard dialog box, check First Row Contains Column Headings, and then click Next. Clear the check box if the first row contains field data instead of column headings.

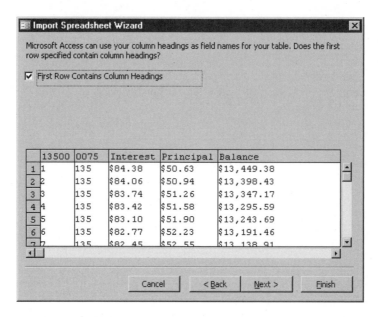

NOTE *If you indicate the first row contains the column headings and some headings contain data that can't be used for valid Access field names (if, for instance, the heading is blank), Access displays a message to that effect and automatically assigns valid field names.*

6. In the third wizard dialog box, choose to store the data in a new table or in an existing one. If you want to store the data in an existing table, select the table name from the list of tables in the current database. Click Next.

7. In the next wizard dialog box, you can set the field options for each field in the worksheet:

   • Click in the Field Name box and enter a new name for the field.

   • Choose Yes in the Indexed box to create an index on that field.

   • Change the data type, if applicable, in the Data Type box.

   • Choose to skip the field when importing the spreadsheet.

8. Click the next field header and make other changes. After making the desired changes to each field, click Next.

9. In the next dialog box, choose Pmt No as the primary key. You can also let Access add a field as the primary key or choose not to have a primary key at all. Then click Next.

10. In the final wizard dialog box, you can accept the same name as the Excel range or enter a new name for the Access table, and then click Finish. An option in this dialog box lets you run the Table Analyzer with the new table to see if it can be made more efficient.

The new Payment Table in Access contains the data located in the Excel range of cells (see Figure 23-5).

Figure 23-6 shows the table design created by the Import Spreadsheet Wizard. Notice the Pmt No is specified as the primary key field. You can now change the Pmt Amt data type to Currency to improve the appearance of the table data.

Exporting a Table or Query to Excel

Exporting all or part of a datasheet to an Excel spreadsheet is similar to exporting to other file types. In the Export...As dialog box, select the desired Microsoft Excel version or other spreadsheet file type from the Save as Type list. Then locate the folder where you want to store the exported data. If you're adding the data to an existing spreadsheet, select the name; otherwise, enter a new file name in the File name box.

Check the Save Formatted option in the Export...To dialog box if you want to keep the same fonts and field width, as well as preserve the data that displays in the Lookup fields. The export process takes a little longer with this option, but you won't have to restore the formatting in the spreadsheet. The spreadsheet file created by Access contains the field names in the first row and data in the subsequent rows.

When you choose the Save Formatted option, the Autostart option becomes available, which automatically launches Excel with the data on the screen when you click Export.

Pmt No	Pmt Amt	Interest	Principal	Balance
1	135	$84.38	$50.63	$13,449.38
2	135	$84.06	$50.94	$13,398.43
3	135	$83.74	$51.26	$13,347.17
4	135	$83.42	$51.58	$13,295.59
5	135	$83.10	$51.90	$13,243.69
6	135	$82.77	$52.23	$13,191.46
7	135	$82.45	$52.55	$13,138.91
8	135	$82.12	$52.88	$13,086.03
9	135	$81.79	$53.21	$13,032.82
10	135	$81.46	$53.54	$12,979.27
11	135	$81.12	$53.88	$12,925.39
12	135	$80.78	$54.22	$12,871.18
13	135	$80.44	$54.56	$12,816.62
14	135	$80.78	$54.22	$12,762.40

Record: 1 of 14

FIGURE 23-5 The Payment Table imported from Excel

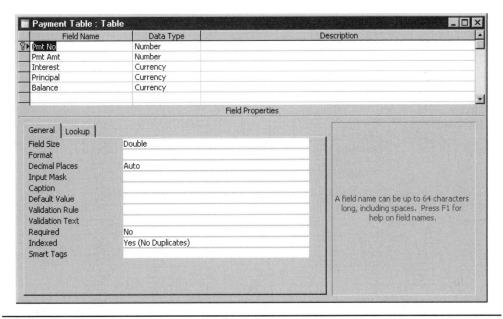

FIGURE 23-6   The imported Payment Table table design

Using Analyze It with Microsoft Excel

The Analyze It with Microsoft Excel Office Link is useful for sending data to Excel for data analysis and charting. Although Access has some charting capabilities, you have more resources when you let Excel do it for you. Once you construct charts in Excel, you can include them in your Access form or report by placing them into unbound object controls.

Loading database information into Microsoft Excel is done using the Analyze It with Microsoft Excel command in the Office Links menu. All the formatting done in Access, such as font styles, field size, and colors, can be transferred to the Excel spreadsheet. Report groups are saved in the worksheet as outline levels and forms are saved as simple data tables.

To load Access data into an Excel worksheet, do the following:

1. In the Database window, select the name of the datasheet, form, or report you want to load into Excel. If you want to send only part of a table, open the datasheet first and select the records you want to load.

2. Choose Tools | Office Links or click the Office Links toolbar button and click Analyze It with Microsoft Excel.

After a moment, Excel opens, showing a new worksheet with the data from the Access object (see Figure 23-7). The selected records are saved as an Excel file (.xls) in the same folder as the Access database.

NOTE   *Because some of the number formatting might be different in Excel, when you choose Save Formatted, you could see a warning that some of the formatting might be lost.*

	A	B	C	D	E	F
1	Product ID	Product Name	Supplier	Category	Quantity Per Unit	Unit Pri
2	1	Chai	Exotic Liquids	Beverages	10 boxes x 20 bags	$18
3	2	Chang	Exotic Liquids	Beverages	24 - 12 oz bottles	$19
4	3	Aniseed Syrup	Exotic Liquids	Condiments	12 - 550 ml bottles	$10
5	4	Chef Anton's Cajun Seasoning	New Orleans Cajun Delights	Condiments	48 - 6 oz jars	$22
6	5	Chef Anton's Gumbo Mix	New Orleans Cajun Delights	Condiments	36 boxes	$21
7	6	Grandma's Boysenberry Spread	Grandma Kelly's Homestead	Condiments	12 - 8 oz jars	$25
8	7	Uncle Bob's Organic Dried Pears	Grandma Kelly's Homestead	Produce	12 - 1 lb pkgs.	$30
9	8	Northwoods Cranberry Sauce	Grandma Kelly's Homestead	Condiments	12 - 12 oz jars	$40
10	9	Mishi Kobe Niku	Tokyo Traders	Meat/Poultry	18 - 500 g pkgs.	$97
11	10	Ikura	Tokyo Traders	Seafood	12 - 200 ml jars	$31
12	11	Queso Cabrales	Cooperativa de Quesos 'Las Cabras'	Dairy Products	1 kg pkg.	$21
13	12	Queso Manchego La Pastora	Cooperativa de Quesos 'Las Cabras'	Dairy Products	10 - 500 g pkgs.	$38
14	13	Konbu	Mayumi's	Seafood	2 kg box	$6
15	14	Tofu	Mayumi's	Produce	40 - 100 g pkgs.	$23
16	15	Genen Shouyu	Mayumi's	Condiments	24 - 250 ml bottles	$15
17	16	Pavlova	Pavlova, Ltd.	Confections	32 - 500 g boxes	$17
18	17	Alice Mutton	Pavlova, Ltd.	Meat/Poultry	20 - 1 kg tins	$39
19	18	Carnarvon Tigers	Pavlova, Ltd.	Seafood	16 kg pkg.	$62
20	19	Teatime Chocolate Biscuits	Specialty Biscuits, Ltd.	Confections	10 boxes x 12 pieces	$9
21	20	Sir Rodney's Marmalade	Specialty Biscuits, Ltd.	Confections	30 gift boxes	$81
22	21	Sir Rodney's Scones	Specialty Biscuits, Ltd.	Confections	24 pkgs. x 4 pieces	$10
23	22	Gustaf's Knäckebröd	PB Knäckebröd AB	Grains/Cereals	24 - 500 g pkgs.	$21
24	23	Tunnbröd	PB Knäckebröd AB	Grains/Cereals	12 - 250 g pkgs.	$9
25	24	Guaraná Fantástica	Refrescos Americanas LTDA	Beverages	12 - 355 ml cans	$4
26	25	NuNuCa Nuß-Nougat-Creme	Heli Süßwaren GmbH & Co. KG	Confections	20 - 450 g glasses	$14
27	26	Gumbär Gummibärchen	Heli Süßwaren GmbH & Co. KG	Confections	100 - 250 g bags	$31
28	27	Schoggi Schokolade	Heli Süßwaren GmbH & Co. KG	Confections	100 - 100 g pieces	$43
29	28	Rössle Sauerkraut	Plutzer Lebensmittelgroßmärkte AG	Produce	25 - 825 g cans	$45

FIGURE 23-7   Access data in an Excel worksheet

Working with HTML Documents

The Hypertext Markup Language (HTML) is the standard markup language you can use to create documents on the Web, better known as *web pages*. HTML uses tags, which the web browser interprets to display page elements, such as text and graphics, and how to respond to user actions. While HTML dictates how the document should look, it falls short of defining the data and the data structure.

Importing Data from HTML Documents

You use the same Get External Data routine to import HTML lists and tables:

1. Choose HTML Documents in the Files of Type box.

2. Locate and select the file you want to import, and then click Import.

The Import HTML Wizard dialog boxes are the same as those of the Import Spreadsheet Wizard, except for the first box where you choose between a worksheet and a named range in Excel.

A few exceptions to watch for when importing or linking to an HTML document are the following:

- Access doesn't import any .gif or .jpg image files embedded in the HTML document.
- If a table is embedded within a table cell in the HTML file, Access creates a separate table for it.
- If data spans rows or columns in an HTML table, Access duplicates the data in each cell.

Exporting Data to HTML Documents

To begin exporting an Access datasheet or form to an HTML document, select the table, query, or form in the Database window, and then choose File | Export as usual. In the Save as type box, choose HTML Documents.

The Save Formatted and AutoStart options work as before. If you checked Save formatted, the HTML Output Options dialog box appears when you click Export. In this dialog box, you can enter the location of an HTML template or click Browse and look for the one you want.

NOTE   *An HTML template includes the tags and tokens unique to Access. These markers indicate where to put output and other information in the HTML files. If you don't specify a template, Access provides a default scheme.*

When you want to export a report to an HTML document, Access exports the report as multiple HTML files—one for each printed page. The first file is named with the report name and subsequent files use the report name followed by Page1, Page2, and so on.

All the controls and features of the report, including any subreports, are exported correctly except for lines, rectangles, and OLE objects. You can still use an HTML template file to include images in the report header or footer.

Mailing Access Objects

You can send Access tables, queries, forms, reports, report snapshots, and even modules attached to an e-mail message. When you attach objects or data to an e-mail message, the attachments can be converted to Excel, RTF, MS-DOS text, HTML, or report snapshot formats as part of the Send To operation.

When you select an object and choose File | Send To, you have two options:

- *Mail Recipient,* which can be used to e-mail a data access page as the body of the message.
- *Mail Recipient (as Attachment),* which attaches the selected database object to an e-mail message.

NOTE *To e-mail an Access database object, you must install an electronic mail application that supports Messaging Application Programming Interface (MAPI), such as Microsoft Outlook, Microsoft Exchange, or Eudora.*

To attach an Access object to an e-mail message, do the following:

1. Select the object you want to send in the Database window. If you want to send only some of the records from a table or query, open the table or query in Datasheet view, and then select the records you want to send.

2. Choose File | Send To or right-click the object and point to Send To in the Shortcut menu, and then click Mail Recipient (as Attachment).

3. The Send dialog box opens. Choose the file format you want to use for your e-mail attachment, and then click OK. If you selected only part of the datasheet in Step 1, two options become available in the Output group: All, which attaches the entire datasheet to the e-mail message, and Selection, which attaches only the selected data.

4. If you choose HTML, the next dialog box gives you the opportunity to attach an HTML template. You can accept the file name displayed in the HTML Output Options dialog box, enter a different name, and then choose Browse to locate another file. Or, you can clear the template box and not use a template. Click OK.

Your e-mail client program opens an e-mail message form where you can address your message, add text to the message, and send it out. The object you selected to send is automatically attached to the message.

Splitting a large database might take a while. The wizard is deleting the tables from the current database, creating a new database with the tables, and then linking the current database to the new back-end tables.

When you open the Tables tab of the current database after splitting, you can see the tables listed are all links to another database (see Figure 24-5) by the link icons next to the names in the list. If you open the new back-end database, you can see all the tables listed on the Tables tab, but the other tabs are all empty.

To customize the distributed database environment further, you can reduce network traffic even more by moving relatively static tables, such as lookup tables containing data that doesn't change often, to the front-end databases. If the data in the lookup table changes, you can make the changes in the back-end version and alert the users to copy the data to their own lookup tables. Temporary tables should also be stored locally to prevent conflicts, as well as to reduce network traffic.

If you need to change the link to any of the back-end tables, choose Tools | Database Utilities | Linked Table Manager. In the Linked Table Manager dialog box, choose the affected tables and check the Always Prompt For New Location check box (see Figure 24-6). Then, when you refresh the link to the table, you have the opportunity of changing the location of the linked table in the standard file location dialog box.

CAUTION *When you link tables, you can leave a security hole, unless you secure both the front-end and the back-end tables.*

Preventing Exclusive Access

When multiple users are sharing a database, competition for data access can occur. If one user opens the database with exclusive access, no other user can work with it. To prevent, or at least discourage, this from happening, set the Default Open Mode to Shared in the Advanced tab of the Options dialog box. Then instruct all the users not to open the database in Exclusive mode. See Chapter 25 for information about including security in a multiple-user environment.

FIGURE 24-5   Tables are linked to the back-end database

FIGURE 24-6   Setting to prompt for a new table location

You can also set up a security system that prevents Exclusive mode opening by certain users and permits it for others. The database administrator must be able to open the database in Exclusive mode to perform duties, such as compacting and backing up the database.

Replicating a Database

Replication is the process of making copies of the table data in a database for use in different locations, but in which the data can be totally synchronized. Only the data is synchronized—not the other database objects. Each user can have a separate copy of the database with the master file centrally located where it can be updated with the data changes made in the remote replicas.

Replication isn't a good idea if you expect a lot of data entry and editing in the individual replicas. Conflicts can arise when the same data is updated by two users and conflicts take time to resolve. Replication also isn't recommended if your data must be real-time and completely current at all times. Even if the master database is updated at frequent intervals, it isn't 100 percent current between updates.

The master database where all the changes are implemented is called the *Design Master* and the copies are called *replicas*. The Design Master and the replicas might contain both replicated objects and unique objects. Each replica can be tailored to a location or a specific type of data, while the common data can be synchronized and shared with the other users. Design changes in shared database objects can be made only in the Design Master.

Caution   *Once a database is replicated, Access makes so many changes to it there's no turning back. So, before you even think about creating a replica or performing any other act on an entire database, make a backup copy of the database.*

Before you make a backup copy, be sure everyone who was using the database has closed it, so you save the latest and most consistent information. Use the Windows Explorer or another program to copy the database to the disk or other medium.

Consequences of Replication

Before you decide to replicate your database, understanding the changes that are going to occur is important. These changes will significantly increase the size of the database while decreasing its flexibility. For example, several new system tables and system fields might be added to the database. If you want to see these system tables and fields, choose Options | View and check the System Objects option.

AutoNumber fields behave differently when you replicate a database. The *AutoNumber fields* set to incremental numbering change to random numbering. Existing records retain their values, but new records are assigned AutoNumbers randomly. If any applications depend on autonumbering, you can add a Date/Time field to provide sequential ordering of new records.

Certain size limitations are also the result of the addition of the three system fields. Each record might contain a maximum of 2,048 bytes. The system fields use a minimum of 54 bytes to store the identifiers, indexes, and information about changes in the record. This reduces the amount of space left for record data. In addition, a table might contain up to 255 fields, 4 of which are taken up by the replication system fields. Each Memo and OLE Object field adds a system field.

The size of the database increases because of the addition of the system tables, which can grow significantly, depending on the frequency of synchronization. Some of the tables are emptied after synchronization.

When you replicate a database, Access offers to make a backup copy for you. If you respond Yes, the copy is added to the same folder as the original. You can copy it from there to another medium later.

If some of the users need only parts of the database, you can also create a partial replica that contains only those objects they need. For example, a manufacturing company might have several factories in different states. The main headquarters would maintain the master database, while each local factory would have a *partial replica*, containing only the information relating to its location and activities. Partial replicas can reduce network traffic and costs, while offering greater security and smaller local databases.

The *Briefcase* method of creating a database replica was invented for the user who wants to work on the database with a laptop. Once the Briefcase replica is created, it can be synchronized with the Design Master like any other replica.

Database Administration in a Multiuser Environment

As soon as more than one user can open a database at the same time, someone should be assigned as the database administrator (DBA), who is responsible for ensuring the integrity and security of the database. Among the issues that must be addressed by the DBA are the following:

- Controlling read/write access to the data
- Setting up the user groups with the appropriate levels of access and security
- Adding new users to a group and removing users from a group

- Ensuring accurate, current record data and minimizing data-locking conflicts
- Editing database objects as necessary and ensuring all users have current versions
- Backing up and compacting the database

Controlling Data Editing

If two users attempt to edit a record at the same time, the results can be unpredictable. Some form of data locking is necessary to ensure the integrity of the database. Allowing one user exclusive access to a record is called *record locking*. When a data page (a unit of data storage), recordset object (a table or query), or a database object is locked, it's read-only to all users, except the one who's currently entering or editing the data in it.

Access provides three levels of record locking, ranging from no locks at all to locking all the records in the recordset. You can set the default record-locking scheme in the Advanced tab of the Options dialog box (see Figure 24-7). Choose Tools | Options and click the Advanced tab where the choices are the following:

- No locks (optimistic record locking)
- Edited record (pessimistic record locking)
- All records

The Default record-locking setting in the Options dialog box applies only to datasheet views of tables and queries. If you want to set the record locking for forms or reports, set the Record Locks property on the Data tab of the object's property sheet. The choices are the same as in the Options dialog box. Setting record locks for a report prevents changes in

FIGURE 24-7   Setting record locking on the Advanced tab of the Options dialog box records in the underlying table or query while the report is previewed or printed. You can also set the Record Locks property for a query and override the default setting.

A new record-locking option that became available with Access 2000 is *record-level locking*. In support of the new Unicode format used for storing characters, the size of a page of data has doubled, from 2K bytes to 4K bytes. This can decrease performance by locking too many records if the records contain only a few bytes. For example, the Penal Codes table in the Police database contains only 54 bytes, so locking a page of Penal Codes records would lock over 70 records.

NOTE   *Access stores data in blocks called* pages. *These pages aren't related to data access pages. Each page contains from 2K to 4K bytes of data, many records from the database. Accessing the disk takes precious time so, when Access reads data, it can read a whole page from the disk, rather than accessing the disk to read one record at a time.*

With the default record-level locking in effect, Access locks only a single record. This applies to accessing data only through a form. If you want to disable this option, clear the check box in the Advanced tab of the Options dialog box. The setting takes effect the next time you open the database with File | Open. It doesn't take effect if you open the database by selecting the file name from the list of recently used files at the end of the File menu. The record-locking scheme set in the Default Record Locking option group is unaffected by the record-level locking setting.

The No Locks Strategy

No Locks, the default setting when you start a new database, is called *optimistic record locking* because it's used where few record write conflicts are expected. Access doesn't lock the record during editing. The edited record is locked only at the exact moment it's being saved. The assumption here is that one user probably will have completed saving the record before another user tries to edit it. Using No Locks ensures all records can be edited at any time, but it also can cause editing conflicts among the users.

When you try to save changes to a record another user has changed since you began editing it, a Write Conflict dialog box appears with the following options:

- Save Record, which saves the record with your changes, overwriting the other user's changes

- Copy to Clipboard, which copies your version of the record to the clipboard for further analysis

- Drop Changes, which discards your changes in favor of the previous changes

Edited Record Strategy

The *Edited Record* record-locking strategy is called *pessimistic locking* because it's assumed much competition will occur for access to records for editing. If it's important for all editing of a record to be completed before another user has access to it, the Edited Record strategy is required. As soon as one user begins to edit a record, no other user can make any changes to it until the first user saves the changes. Other users can view the record, but they cannot change it.

The only difference in the display of the record is that the universal symbol for No—the circle with a diagonal line through it—appears in the record selector instead of a pencil, which appears with the No Locks method.

All Records Strategy

This restrictive record-locking strategy locks all records in the form or datasheet, as well as the underlying tables, for the entire time it's open. No one else can edit the records. One case in which this strategy would be useful is when you're running an update query that applies to several different records and you want to make sure all the affected records are locked until the query is completed.

Choosing a Locking Strategy

The strategy you choose depends on your data, how many users share the application, and how they use the data. For most multiuser environments, the No Locks strategy can be the most effective, even though some brief write conflict errors can occur. The overall performance of the system is more efficient than with the other record-locking strategies.

If more imperative reasons exist for locking records during editing, use one of the other locking strategies.

If the data in a form, report, or query is acquired from an Open Database Connectivity (ODBC) database, Access treats it as though the No Locks setting were selected and disregards the Record Locks property setting.

Minimizing Conflicts

One way to reduce the number of locking conflicts is to arrange the workload, so each user attends to different parts of the database. For example, one user updates records for sales in the western states, another for the southern area, and so on.

When two users try to update the same record and cause a conflict, Access tries several times to save the record, hoping it'll be freed from the lock, before displaying the Write Conflict message. The period of time that elapses between tries is specified in the Update

Retry Interval setting. The Number of Update Retries setting determines how many times Access should try to save the record before giving up.

You can try different combinations of these two settings. For example, set the Number of Update Retries to 0 to have Access display the Write Conflict message at once. Set both to higher values to reduce the number of write conflicts by letting Access try to save the record more times, with a longer interval between attempts. However, with this arrangement, users might complain the system appears slow. Experiment with these settings to settle on the right combination for your application.

Table 26-1 describes these and other settings that help avoid data-locking conflicts. The settings are found on the Advanced tab of the Options dialog box.

Updating Records with Refresh and Requery

If the data in your shared database changes frequently and it's important for the user to have up-to-date data, you can use two methods to keep the data current:

- *Refresh* offers a periodic quick update of the data currently on the screen.
- *Requery* completely rebuilds the underlying recordset by running the query or applying the filter again.

Refresh updates only those records already appearing in Datasheet or Form view. When you refresh the datasheet or form, records aren't reordered or deleted, and those that no longer meet the filter criteria also aren't removed. To update the recordset to reflect these actions, you must requery the records.

Option	Settings	Description
Refresh interval	0 through 32,766 seconds. Default is 60 seconds.	Sets the number of seconds between automatic updating of records in Datasheet or Form view. Setting to 0 results in no automatic updating.
Number of update retries	0 through 10. Default is two tries.	Sets the number of times Access tries to save a record locked by another user before displaying a Write Conflict message.
ODBC refresh interval	0 through 32,766 seconds. Default is 1,500 seconds.	Sets the number of seconds between automatic refreshing of records accessed using ODBC. Setting to 0 results in no automatic updating.
Update retry interval	0 through 1,000 milliseconds. Default is 250 milliseconds.	Sets the number of milliseconds between automatic attempts to save a record locked by another user.

TABLE 24-1   Advanced Options for the Multiuser Environment

PART IV

The default interval for refreshing records is 60 seconds, which might be too long in critical situations. You can reset the interval to 10 or 15 seconds. If you set the interval too low, Access creates a lot of network traffic. To refresh a table, query, or form manually, open the table or query in Datasheet view or the form in Form view, and then choose Records | Refresh.

Requerying completely rebuilds the underlying recordset. The easiest way to requery is to press SHIFT-F9.

TIP Requerying is somewhat of a nuisance to the user because the form or datasheet returns to the first record in the recordset. If you were working with a record deep in the recordset, you must manually return to it after requerying. Remembering the record number doesn't help much because the record order might have changed with the requery.

Editing Shared Database Objects

Even though you do your best to have all the database object designs completed before setting up the database for shared access, changes are bound to be necessary later. Any local objects can be modified at any time, but the shared objects require special consideration.

Before you begin to make significant design changes to a shared database, be sure you open it in Exclusive mode by selecting Open Exclusive from the Open button in the Open Database dialog box. Pick a time to do this when other users don't require access to the database, such as the middle of the night.

If the required design changes are less invasive, you can safely modify the objects while the database is open in Shared mode. To make changes to a table design, the table must not be in use by another user. If the table or any query, form, or report based on the table is open, the table design cannot be changed. In this case, you can still view the table design, but Access informs you the table is read-only.

The converse is also true—if you're modifying a table design, the table and any query, form, or report based on it is unavailable to another user. A good idea is to have the changes well-thought-out and specific before opening the table design. Then keep the table design open as briefly as possible.

NOTE The Name AutoCorrect feature keeps track of object and field name changes, and tracks down locations where they're referenced. The changes are effected in all the references. This feature isn't available for replicated databases.

Other helpful tips when you need to edit shared database objects are the following:

- When you edit a query, form, or report design already in use by another user, that user won't see the new version until the object is closed and reopened.

- If the objects you want to change are dependent on each other, be sure to edit them all at the same time, so they'll be consistent.

- Make sure no one is using the macro you want to edit by opening the database in Exclusive mode. If you change a macro someone's using, you can cause problems.

Summary

When multiple users need access to the same database, it's essential to ensure all users have the same data. This chapter discusses a few of the ways this can be accomplished. Sharing a single file stored on a server with multiple users is one way. Another way is to split the database into a front-end database that contains the database objects and links to the data tables on the back-end database. The concept of a set of replicated databases is mentioned as a more complex arrangement.

As multiple users make changes to the data at the same time on a LAN, provisions must be made to prevent conflicts from occurring. Various record-locking schemes are available in Access, some of which are quite lenient, while others are more strict.

Securing a Database

So far, we've discussed limiting user access to a database to maintain data accuracy and integrity. Record locking helps prevent inadvertent data corruption. Now, we look at avoiding intentional interference with a database. The main purpose of database security is to prevent unauthorized access to the information, either for viewing or editing. A second, no less important, goal of database security is to prevent design modifications by unqualified individuals. Even the slightest change in a form design or a data validation rule can cause problems, which can be difficult to locate and correct.

Access provides two levels of security for databases:

- Global protection through the use of database passwords
- User-level security based on the Access security model

You can protect an entire database or single objects in the database, as well as distinguish between users and offer different levels of access to each.

NOTE *The subject of database security is complex and this chapter only begins to open the discussion. Consult other resources, including the Access Help topics, for more complete information about security procedures and techniques.*

Securing a Database with a Password

Protecting a database with a database password is more appropriate for the single-user database than for a networked, multiple-user database, but it's the simplest way to keep the information from prying eyes. You must have exclusive use of the database to assign a password. Anyone who knows the password can open the database and, once the database is open, the user can do anything with it. You can also assign passwords to a security account.

While this method is secure, it applies only to opening the database. Once open, the data and all the database objects are available to the user for viewing or editing unless other types of security have already been defined, as described in the section "What Is Needed to Secure a Database?" In addition, Access stores the password in an unencoded form, which might compromise your database security. To be safe, always make a back-up copy of the database before adding the password and store the copy in a secure location.

CAUTION   *Don't use a password for a database you plan to replicate. You can't synchronize replicated databases if they have assigned passwords.*

To add password protection to a database, make sure all other users have closed the database, and then do the following:

1. Open the database in Exclusive mode by clicking the down arrow next to the Open button in the Open dialog box, and then choosing Open Exclusive from the menu.

2. Choose Tools | Security | Set Database Password. The Set Database Password dialog box appears. This menu command isn't available if the current database is a member of a replica set.

3. Enter the password you want to use in the Password box, repeat it in the Verify box, and then click OK. If the two entries aren't the same, Access asks you to reenter the password in the Verify box.

Here are some guidelines for creating your password:

- Create a strong password by combining uppercase and lowercase letters with numbers and symbols, up to 20 characters. For example, aZ!24hQ6 is a strong password, while AtHome is a weak password.

- Don't include leading spaces, ASCII characters 10 through 31, or any of the following characters: " \ [ ] : | < > + = ; , . ? *.

- Never use a word that appears in the dictionary.

CAUTION   *Don't forget your password! You won't be able to open the database and there's no means by which to bypass the requirement for a password. Always select a word you can remember easily, such as the name of your favorite cat. As a backup, write it down in a safe place, just in case.*

The next time you try to open the database, Access requires you to enter the password.

To remove the password, open the database again in Exclusive mode and choose Tools |
Security | Unset Database Password. Then enter the password in the Unset Database Password
dialog box and click OK.

NOTE *Some security problems might occur if one of the tables in a password-protected database is
linked to a second database that doesn't require a password. The password for the first database
is stored with the linking information in the second database. Then, any user who can open the
second database can also open the linked table in the protected database. The password is also
stored in an unencoded form in the unprotected database, making it readable to any user.*

Securing a Multiple-User Database

When multiple users of a database exist, security becomes more complicated. Not all users
require access to all parts of the database, yet someone must be responsible for every object
in the database. Organizing users in groups helps simplify the security problem. You can
allow each group to carry out specific actions on specific objects in the database. All the
information about the workgroup is stored in a separate file called the workgroup
information file (WIF) with the file extension .mdw. The default WIF is System.mdw.

Understanding the User-Level Security Model

The user-level security scheme has two advantages: no user can inadvertently break the
application by making design changes and sensitive data is protected. The Access user-level
security model is based on the concept of workgroups consisting of a group of users who
share data in a multiuser environment. The members of the workgroups are listed in user
and group accounts. A *group account* is a collection of *user accounts.*

Each member of the workgroup is allowed a specific amount of freedom with respect to
the database and its objects. For example, members of one group account might be permitted
to enter and edit data, but not to modify a form design. Another group might be allowed to
view only specific data and be denied access to sensitive information.

The four elements of the Access user-level security model are users, groups, permissions,
and objects.

- A *user* is a person who uses the database. In a secured database, the user must sign
  on with his or her name and password to use the database.

NOTE *Access user accounts aren't related to Windows user accounts.*

- A *group* is a set of users who have the same security level and need access to the
  same areas of the database. You grant the same permissions to the users in the
  group. Individual users can belong to more than one group and have additional
  access to the database.
- A *permission* grants a user or group the right to perform a specific act on a database
  object. For example, the Open/Run permission gives the user the right to open a
  database, form, or report, or to run a macro.

- An *object* refers to any of the Access tables, queries, forms, reports, macros, or modules in addition to the database itself.

User accounts are usually organized by groups, each with a specific set of permissions. User accounts consist of a single user who might own objects and have permissions for those and other objects in the database. User accounts are stored in the WIF the users will join when they access the database.

Group accounts are made up of users and can also own database objects. Group accounts are used to assign a common set of permissions to multiple users. A user can belong to more than one group, in which case the user has the sum of all the group permissions.

The administrator users are members of the Admins group and have full permissions for the secure database and its objects. The database administrator or the object owner can grant permissions to users and groups to carry out specific actions on database objects. Two types of permissions exist, as in the following:

- Explicit permissions granted directly to an individual user.
- Implicit permissions granted to a user who's a member of the group that enjoys that permission. If the user is removed from the group, the permissions are revoked.

The user's set of permissions is the intersection of the two types of permissions.

Table 25-1 describes the permissions that can be granted to any user or group for specific types of objects. Permissions can be further limited to individual objects.

You can assign these permissions to users and groups in the WIF, as described in the section "Assigning and Removing Permissions."

Another concept in the security model is that of *ownership*. All database objects must be "owned" by some user. The owner is responsible for the object and has the ultimate

Permission	Allowed Actions
Open/Run	Open a database, form, or report, or run a macro
Open Exclusive	Open a database for exclusive use
Read Design	Open any object in Design view, but not make changes
Modify Design	Open any object in Design view and make modifications or deletions
Administer	Have full access to all objects and the security system, including the right to assign permissions to other users
Read Data	Open tables and queries for viewing, but not for editing or entering data
Update Data	Open tables and queries for viewing and editing existing data, but not inserting or deleting data
Insert Data	Open tables and queries for viewing and adding new data, but not for modifying or deleting existing data
Delete Data	Open tables and queries for viewing and deleting data, but not for modifying or adding data

TABLE 25-1   User-Level Security Permissions

FIGURE 25-5
Adding users to
the workgroup
information file

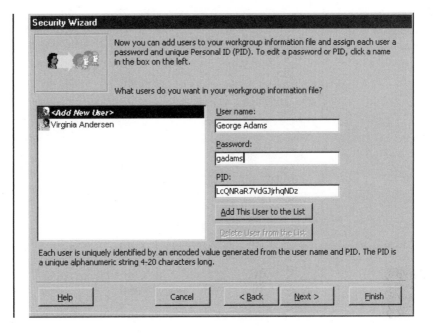

or PID by selecting the name from the list on the left. The names, PIDs, and any passwords you created with the wizard are printed in the report the wizard creates. Click Next to move to the next dialog box.

9. In the next to last Security Wizard dialog box (see Figure 25-6), you assign the users added in the previous dialog box to a group. You can work either way in this dialog box:

- If you choose Select a User and Assign the User to Groups, the drop-down list contains the list of users and the group names appear below. Check the group name and choose user names to add from the drop-down list.

- If you choose Select a Group and Assign Users to the Group, the drop-down list contains the group names and the user names appear in the box below. Select a group name from the drop-down list, and then check all the user names you want assigned to the group.

10. Click Next to move to the final dialog box, where you're prompted for a name for the unsecured backup copy of the database. Click Finish to complete creating the new WIF. The backup copy has a .bak file extension.

After creating the new WIF, the Security Wizard displays a report of the setting used in the file. You can save the report as a report snapshot, or you can print and store the hard copy in a safe place. If you ever need to rebuild the WIF, you'll need all this information.

Only members of the Admins group and the Admin user have access to objects in the new database. No permissions have been granted to the Users group, so you need to add them to control the security of the database and its objects.

FIGURE 25-6
Assigning users
to groups

Creating a Workgroup Without the Wizard

The default workgroup is defined in a workgroup file, System.mdw, created by the Access Setup program and stored in the folder where you installed Access. When you want to define user-level security, you create a new WIF to contain the user and group accounts for all the members of the workgroup. The new WIF also contains the passwords used by the users. The security accounts in the WIF can be assigned permissions for databases and objects. The permissions are stored in the secure database, rather than in the WIF.

NOTE   *You can modify the default WIF, but that will affect all the databases you open except for those with their own custom WIFs.*

Before creating a new workgroup, decide where you want to store the WIF. You can modify the default WIF, use an existing file, or create a new one. For a secure WIF that can't be duplicated, don't use the default System.mdw file. If you want to use an existing file, be sure it was created with a unique workgroup ID (WID). The location of the WIF is stored in the Windows Registry.

To create a new WIF, use the Workgroup Administrator, as follows:

1. Close any open database and choose Tools | Security | Workgroup Administrator.

2. The Workgroup Administrator dialog box shows the name and location of the WIF and explains the purpose of a WIF. It also offers three buttons: Create, Join, and OK. Click Create to start a new WIF.

Organizing User Accounts

Maintaining database security is much easier if the users are organized by department or function, and they're assigned to group accounts. The group is assigned permissions on the basis of its activities and needs. Users are assigned to the group that permits the activities they require. When users log on to a secured database, they log on with their user account, not the group account. After logging on, the users inherit all the permissions of the group, plus any permissions assigned specifically to the individual user accounts.

To create any type of security account, you must log on as a member of the Admins group. Then you can use the User and Group Accounts dialog box (see Figure 25-9) to do the following:

- Create and delete user and group accounts
- Add a user to a group
- Remove a user from a group
- Change or clear a user password

Every account must have a personal ID (PID) that's saved with the account name. This isn't the same as a password, which each user creates later.

Creating and Deleting User Accounts

To create a new user account, do the following:

1. Start Access with the workgroup in which you want to include the new user account, and then open a database.
2. Choose Tools | Security | User and Group Accounts.

3. In the User and Group Accounts dialog box, click the Users tab, and then click New. The New User/Group dialog box opens.

Type a unique name for the new user account and a PID. Follow the same guidelines as for creating a password.

Figure 25-9
Setting user and
group accounts

FIGURE 25-9
Setting user and
group accounts

TIP   For security reasons, the PID should be a unique combination of alphanumeric characters that have no actual meaning and don't form a word.

4. Click OK when you finish.

CAUTION   Be sure to keep a copy of the exact name and PID you enter for the new account. You'll need them if you have to re-create the account. The PIDs are case sensitive, but the names aren't.

To delete a user account, open the Users tab of the User and Group Accounts dialog box and select the name of the account you want to delete from the Name drop-down list. Then click Delete and respond Yes when asked for confirmation or respond No to cancel the deletion. After you make all the necessary deletions, click OK to close the dialog box.

NOTE   You can't delete any of the built-in users from the Users group and you must leave at least one user in the Admins group. You also can't delete the Admin user account.

Creating and Deleting Group Accounts

Creating a new group account is much the same as creating a new user account, except you do it in the Groups tab (see Figure 25-10) in the User and Group Accounts dialog box, instead of the Users tab.

When you click New, the same New User/Group dialog box opens where you enter the name and PID for the new group. The group name follows the same rules as the user name.

To delete a group, on the Groups tab, select the group name from the Name drop-down list, and then click Delete. Respond Yes to the confirmation request to delete the group or respond No to cancel the deletion, and then click OK.

NOTE   The built-in Admins and Users group accounts can't be deleted.

FIGURE 25-10
Adding a new
group account

Adding and Removing Users from Groups

As with all activities involving database security, you must log on as a member of
the Admins group to add a user to a group or to remove one from a group. To add a
user to an existing group, do the following:

1. Start Access in the workgroup containing the security accounts. If you don't know
   whether you're starting in the right workgroup, use the Workgroup Administrator
   to see which workgroup is current and, if necessary, change the WIF.

2. Open a database and choose Tools | Security | User and Group Accounts, and
   then click the Users tab.

3. Select the name of the user you want to add to the group from the Name
   drop-down list.

4. In the Available Groups box, select the group you want the user added to, and then
   click Add. The group name is added to the Member Of list.

5. If you want to add this user to other groups, repeat step 4. If you want to add other
   users to groups, repeat steps 3 and 4.

6. Click OK when you finish adding users to the groups.

NOTE   *To create a security administrator account, create a new user account and add it to the
Admins group.*

To delete a user from a security group, open the Users tab of the User and Group Accounts
dialog box as before and select the name of the user you want to remove in the Name box.
Then select the group name in the Member Of box and click Remove. Repeat these steps for
all the users you want to remove and click OK when you're finished.

The default Users group is an exception. Because Access automatically adds all users to the group, the only way you can remove a user account from the Users group is to delete the account altogether.

TIP   *To document the arrangement of users and the groups they belong to, click the Print Users and Groups button on the Users tab of the User and Group Accounts dialog box. You have the option of printing only the users, only the groups, or both. The list of users includes the user names and the groups each user belongs to. The list of groups includes the group names and the users who belong to that group.*

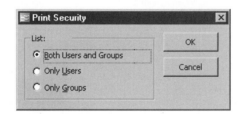

Creating or Changing Account Passwords

By default, when you add a new user account to a workgroup, Access assigns a blank password to it. The Admin account also is assigned a blank password. To make sure no one can log on using an existing user name, you should have all users enter unique passwords for their accounts.

To create or change a security account password, do the following:

1. Start Access using the workgroup the account is in and log on with the user account name.

2. Open a database and choose Tools | Security | User and Group Accounts.

3. Click the Change Logon Password tab (see Figure 25-11) and enter the current password in the Old Password box. If no password has been defined for the account, leave the box blank.

4. Enter the new password in the New Password box. The password is case sensitive and can contain up to 20 characters, including any except the ASCII 0 (null) character.

5. Enter the same characters in the Verify box, and then click OK.

CAUTION   *Be sure to copy the password you entered and save it in a secure place. If you forget it, an Admins user must clear the password before you can log on to the database and create a new password.*

To clear a password, you must log on as a member of the Admins group, and then do the following:

1. Open the User and Group Accounts dialog box, and then click the Users tab.

2. Select the user account name from the Name drop-down list and click Clear Password.

3. Repeat step 2 to clear other user account passwords, and then click OK when finished.

Requiring Logon

All users of a database are automatically logged on as Admin users until you add a password to the Admin user account. Then, when users try to start Access, they must enter their user account names and passwords. To activate the logon procedure, do the following:

1. Start Access using the workgroup to which you want to add the logon password.
2. Choose Tools | Security | User and Group Accounts, and then click the Users tab.
3. With the Admin user account selected in the Name box, click the Change Logon Password tab. (Refer to Figure 25-11.)
4. Leave the Old Password box blank because no password exists yet, and then type the new password in the New Password box, up to 20 characters. Passwords are case sensitive.
5. Type the password in the Verify box, and then click OK.

The next time you or another member of the workgroup starts Access, the Logon dialog box appears. Enter the user account name in the Name box and the account password in the Password box. If your password is blank, leave the password box blank. Then click OK.

To turn off the Logon dialog box, start Access using the workgroup whose logon you want to deactivate, and then return to the Users tab of the User and Group Accounts dialog box. Select Admin in the Name box and click Clear Password. Deactivating the Logon procedure doesn't remove any user-level security you defined for the database; it only lets you start Access without logging on.

Assigning or Changing Permissions and Ownerships

Permissions are granted to a user, either explicitly to the individual user account or implicitly to the group account of which the user is a member. The owner of an object is the user who

FIGURE 25-11
Changing the
logon password

created it. To assign default permissions or to change permissions or ownerships for a database object, you must be one of the following:

- A member of the Admins group of the WIF in use when the database was created.
- The owner of the database object
- A user who has Administratar permission on the object

To view or change the permissions and ownerships, choose Tools | Security | User and Group Permissions. Figure 25-12 shows the User and Group Permissions dialog box with one tab for working with permissions and another for changing object ownership.

NOTE   *In addition to the list of all existing objects in the database, you can select <New Tables/ Queries> to include any future tables or queries in the permissions. If you selected a different Object Type from the list, the <New...> option in the Object Name list shows that object type.*

Assigning and Removing Permissions

To work with permissions, open the database that contains the objects using the WIF that contains the user or group accounts to which you want to assign permissions. Then open the Permissions tab of the User and Group Permissions dialog box. In the Permissions tab, you can do any of the following:

- To see what permissions a user already enjoys with respect to a specific object, click the Users option button, and then select the user account name in the User/Group Name box. Select the type of object from the Object Type drop-down list, and then select the specific object from the Object Name box. The check boxes in the Permission area show which permissions have been explicitly granted to the user. Implicitly granted permissions show in the group permissions list.

FIGURE 25-12
Changing user and
group permissions

- To see what permissions a group has on an object, click the Groups option button and select the group account name from the User/Group Name box. Then select the object type and name the same as for user account permissions. The Permission area shows the permissions currently granted to the group account.

- To change permissions, select the user or group account first, and then select the object type. Select one or more objects from the Object Name list and check or clear the permissions.

TIP *To select multiple contiguous objects in the list, drag the mouse pointer over the names. To select multiple scattered objects, hold down* CTRL *and click the objects you want.*

After you finish with each object or set of objects, click Apply to keep the dialog box open for more changes. When finished, click OK.

Some tips to remember when changing permissions are the following:

- Some permissions are related and, when granted, automatically grant other permissions. For example, if you click the Update Data permission for a table, the Read Data and Read Design permissions are automatically checked because they're needed to modify data. Similarly, if you clear the Update Data or Read Data permission for a table, the Modify Design permission is also automatically cleared.

- If you modify an object and save it with the same name, the permissions are unchanged. If you copy it or save it with a different name, you must reassign the permissions.

- When you change permissions on objects containing Visual Basic code, such as forms, reports, or modules, the permissions don't take effect until you close and reopen the database.

Transferring Object Ownership

To transfer ownership of an object to a different user or group, click the Change Owner tab of the User and Group Permissions dialog box (see Figure 25-13). The list in the upper box displays the objects of the type selected in the Object Type box, together with their current owners.

To change ownership of an object, do the following:

1. Select the object type in the Object Type box.

2. Select one or more objects in the list. You can select them by dragging over the names or holding CTRL as you click the names.

3. Click Groups to see a list of group accounts in the New Owner drop-down list or click Users to see the user accounts.

4. Select the group or user name from the New Owner list and click Change Owner. Ownership is transferred to the group or user selected in the New Owner list.

5. Make any other changes in ownership, and then click OK when you finish.

TIP *When you transfer ownership of an object to a group account, all members of the group are automatically granted ownership permissions on the object.*

FIGURE 25-13
Changing
ownership of
Access objects

You can also transfer ownership of a complete database to another administrator. Start Access using the new administrator's workgroup ID and create a new blank database. Then import all the objects from the original database to the new one.

***

NOTE   *Query objects have default permission options that control viewing data returned from the query or after running an action query. The Run Permissions option on the Tables/Queries tab of the Options dialog box can be set to Owner's or User's. If you choose Owner's, all users have the owner's permission to view or run the query. However, only the owner can change the query design or transfer ownership of the query to another user. If you choose User's, the permissions for that class of users apply and any user can change the query or transfer its ownership to another user. The change in setting applies only to new queries. Existing queries are unaffected.*

Securing a Replicated Database

Because you cannot secure a replicated database with a password, the best way is to set user permissions on each of the replicated database objects. The permissions you set don't get in the way of synchronization.

Removing User-Level Security

Removing the user-level security created for a database involves returning ownership to the database and all the objects in it to the default Admin user. To do this, you need to log on as the workgroup administrator who's a member of the Admins group. After logging on to the database, give the default Users group full permissions on all objects. Then exit Access and log on again as Admin, and then create a blank database in which to import all the objects from the original database.

CAUTION   *The result of this process is a completely unsecured database. Be aware that any workgroup or user can open the new database. The workgroup information file in effect when you import the objects from the original database is the one used for the Admin group with the new database. All imported objects are owned by the user who imported them.*

To remove the established user-level security, do the following:

1. Launch Access, log on as the workgroup administrator, and open the secured database.
2. Choose Tools | Security | User and Group Permissions and click the Permissions tab.
3. Click Groups and select Users in the User/Group Name box.
4. Select Table from the Object Type drop-down list and select all the tables in the database by dragging the mouse pointer down through the whole list.
5. Select all the available permissions for that type of object and click Apply.
6. Repeat steps 4 and 5 for each of the other types of objects, and then click OK.
7. Exit Access and restart, logging on as Admin.
8. Create a new blank database and import all the objects from the original database into it.

NOTE   *If the users are still using the current workgroup information file, clear the password for Admin to avoid the Logon dialog box. If you reverted to the default workgroup information file, this step isn't necessary.*

Other Security Measures

While creating secure workgroups can ensure complete security of a database, other, less rigorous methods exist for maintaining database safety. Encoding a database renders it unreadable with a program other than Access, for example, with a debugger or a text editor. Hiding specific objects from user view can prevent sensitive data from leaking to unauthorized users. When you deliver an end-user application, you want to make sure no user can modify any of the Visual Basic code behind forms or reports or in the database modules. If you compile the code in it, the code cannot be read or changed.

Repairing a Damaged Workgroup Information File

Everyone hopes it won't happen but, sometimes, the workgroup information file becomes damaged and you won't be able to open the database that relies on that WIF. The way you can solve this problem depends on whether you used the Workgroup Administrator to create the WIF in the first place and whether you saved a backup copy of the file.

- No matter how you created the WIF, if you saved a backup copy, use Windows Explorer or other program to copy the most recent copy of the file to the folder where Access is installed or to the original path.

- If you used the default WIF and you didn't make a backup copy, you must reinstall Access to re-create the default WIF.

- If you used the Workgroup Administrator to create the file and you didn't save a backup copy, you must use the Administrator to re-create the file. Start the Administrator by typing in the same case-sensitive name, organization, and workgroup ID you used before. ·

- If you used the Workgroup Administrator to join a file on a path other than the folder where Access is installed, and you didn't save a backup copy, create a new copy using the same method you used to create the original file and type the same case-sensitive name, organization, and workgroup ID entries as before.

The security account information is stored in the WIF so, if you have to create a new file, you need to re-create the security accounts with the same names and personal ID entries. The permissions and object ownership are stored in the secure database and needn't be redefined, but they must be connected with the same accounts as in the original database.

Encoding and Decoding a Database

When you encode a database, it's compacted and rendered completely unreadable by a word processor or any utility program. Encoding a database doesn't restrict access to database objects. Decoding the database reverses the process and restores its original form.

You must be the owner of the WIF and you must be able to open the database in exclusive mode. The database must also be closed before you can encode it and you must have enough storage space for both the original and the encoded versions of the database file. To encode a database:

1. In an empty Access window, choose Tools | Security | Encode/Decode Database.

2. In the Encode/Decode Database dialog box, select the database you want to encode and click OK.

3. In the Encode Database As dialog box, specify the drive and folder where you want to store the encoded database, and then click OK. You can even save the encoded database in a web folder by choosing Web Folders from the Save In drop-down list.

If you choose to store the encoded database with the same name and in the same folder as the original database, Access asks for confirmation before replacing the original file. If you confirm this, Access automatically replaces the original file with the successfully encoded version. If the encode operation fails, the original database isn't deleted. Once the database is encoded, you use it as you normally would.

NOTE *If the database is protected by user-level security, you must be a member of the Admins group with Open Exclusive permission for all the tables to encode or decode the database.*

To decode an encoded database, repeat the same steps as for encoding and specify the drive and folder for storing the decoded file from the Decode Database As dialog box.

Hiding Database Objects

If you have objects in your database that you want to keep from view, you can prevent them from appearing in the Database window. Hiding the objects doesn't provide more security than simply removing them from view. To hide an object, do the following:

1. Select the object in the Database window and click the Properties toolbar button, or right-click the object name and choose Properties from the Shortcut menu.

2. Click the Hidden option at the bottom of the General tab of the Properties dialog box (see Figure 25-14), and then click OK.

When you return to the Database window, the object no longer appears. To see the names of objects that have been hidden, choose Tools | Options and click the View tab. Click the Hidden Objects option in the Show group, and then click OK. The hidden objects appear dimmed in the Database window, but they can still be opened.

To remove the Hidden property, open the General tab of the Properties dialog box and clear the Hidden option.

TIP   *Another way to hide an object from view is to use a system file prefix with the object name. For example, name a new form or rename an existing form with the USys prefix and it won't appear in the Forms tab of the Database window, unless you selected the System Objects option in the Show group of the View Options dialog box. You can also use the MSys prefix to hide objects.*

FIGURE 25-14
Hiding individual
database objects

Summary

This chapter briefly introduces you to the highly complex problem of securing an Access database against both inadvertent and intentional intrusion. The techniques you can use to protect data and the database design from unauthorized users range from requiring a password to log on to the database to the multidimensional user-level security strategy.

Converting to Access 2003

When Access 2003 arrives, you'll probably want to convert your databases to the new version immediately. If you're already using Access 2002, no conversion is necessary because versions 2002 and 2003 use the same file format. You can open an Access 2000 or later database in Access 2003 without having to convert it. Then, once in Access 2003, you can change the design of objects in the database to take advantage of new features in 2003. When you open it in Access 2000, the new 2002–2003 features you added are simply ignored.

You can convert from any earlier version of Access with the information presented in this appendix. You might, instead, want to keep the database in the earlier version and run it with Access 2003. This is important if your database is used by more than one user and all the users haven't upgraded to Access 2003 yet. You can convert an Access database created in Access 2.0 or later to either Access 2000 or 2002–2003 format.

You can also convert an Access 2002–2003 formatted database back to an earlier version.

Secured databases present a special problem during conversion because they're associated with a user-level security workgroup information file.

Deciding on a Conversion Strategy

Before setting out to convert the database, you need to examine the way the database is used currently. Most likely, you'll want to convert it to take advantage of the new design features of Access 2003. However, you can enable the database to run in Access 2003 without conversion. *Enabling* a database lets you view and edit data, but you won't be able to save changes in the design of any of the objects. If you want to modify an object, you must open the database in the original version or convert it to Access 2003.

If your database is shared among several users, not all of whom can convert to Access 2000 or 2002–2003 format, you can split the database and convert part of it and keep other parts unchanged. This way, the database can be shared by users on different versions of Access.

Once the database is converted to 2000 or 2002–2003 format, you're no longer able to open it with the original version of Access. If you convert an Access 2000 database to 2002–2003, you can't open it in 2000, but you can convert it back. You can also convert an Access 2000 or 2002–2003 database back to Access 97, but not to version 2.0 or 95.

If you're using an Access 2000 database, you needn't convert it to 2002–2003 unless you want to save it as an MDE file, which must be in the 2002–2003 file format.

Converting a Database

Before you start to convert the database, be sure to make a backup copy. Keep this copy until you're satisfied the database has converted correctly and you've mastered Access 2003. You can convert the database to a different name in the same folder or use the same name in a different folder.

To convert the database to Access 2002–2003 file format, do the following:

1. Close the database you want to convert. If you're operating in a multiple-user environment, make sure all other users have also closed the database.

2. In an empty Access 2003 window, choose Tools | Database Utilities | Convert Database | To Access 2002–2003 File Format.

3. The Database to Convert From dialog box opens where you select the database you want to convert, and then click Convert.

4. In the Convert Database Into dialog box, which looks similar to the Database to Convert From dialog box, enter a new name for the converted database, or choose a different location and either use the same name or enter a new one. Then click Save.

Access converts the database to the file format you chose. You might see messages about compile errors during the conversion because some of the Visual Basic commands might no longer be valid. You can correct the code after conversion.

If the database you're converting has linked tables, make sure the tables remain in the original folder, so the converted database can find them. If Access can't find them, the converted database won't work properly. After you convert the database, you can move the linked tables to another location and use the Linked Table Manager to restore the links. The linked tables aren't converted, so you must convert them separately.

NOTE   *Enabling or converting a secured database requires some extra steps and considerations. Converting a secured database is covered in the section "Converting a Secured Database."*

When you convert a version 2.0 or 95 database to Access 2000 or 2002–2003, the built-in toolbars and custom toolbars are automatically converted to the new toolbar style. Custom menu bars created in Access 95 with the Menu Builder or with macros using the AddMenu action are interpreted as the new style menu bars, but they aren't automatically converted. Therefore, they can't be modified with the Customize dialog box until you convert them. You can use the Tools | Macro command to create new style menus, toolbars, and shortcut menus from the macros created in the earlier version. Then you can modify them with the Customize dialog box.

Converting a Workgroup Information File

If you want to take advantage of the new security and performance improvements with Access 2000 or 2002–2003, re-create the workgroup information file (WIF) after the database has been converted. Don't create the WIF if some of the users are still using pre-2000 versions of Access. Create the new WIF by entering the exact, case-sensitive name, company, and workgroup ID you used in the previous version. If you don't get them exactly right, the Admins group will be invalid.

If you're upgrading from version 2.0, you need to convert the WIF, which is stored as an .mda file, to the new .mdw file type. If you're upgrading from Access 95 or 97, you needn't convert the WIF, but you should compact it after converting the database. Then tell the users to join the compacted WIF before opening the database.

Next, re-create the group and user accounts in the new WIF, again making sure to enter the exact group or user name and personal ID for each group. When the new WIF is complete, instruct the users to use the Workgroup Administrator to join the new WIF. See Chapter 25 for more information about multiple-user environment and workgroups.

Converting a Secured Database

To convert or even enable a secured database, you must meet specific requirements and log on with certain permissions. Access 2003 creates a new workgroup information file and makes it the current file when first installed. You must join this new workgroup information file that defines the users of the database before you can convert it. If a different file was in use when the database was secured, join that workgroup information file instead of the default Access workgroup information file.

When you log on to convert the database, you must have the following permissions:

- Open/Run and Open Exclusive permissions for the database
- Administer permissions for the MSysACEs and MSysObjects system tables
- Modify Design permissions for all the tables in the database or you must be the owner of them
- Read Design permissions for all objects in the database

NOTE   *If you log on as Admin or as a member of the Admins group, you'll automatically be granted these permissions.*

The conversion process is the same as for unsecured databases once you log on with sufficient permissions.

If all the users of the database have converted to Access 2000 or later, you can convert the entire database to 2000 file format. If all the users have upgraded to 2002 or later, convert the database to the 2002–2003 file format. You can still use the workgroup information file without converting, but the recommendation is it should also be re-created in 2002 or later.

If they aren't all upgrading, however, you can share the database and the workgroup information file across the different versions, using methods described in the section "Sharing a Database Across Several Access Versions."

Converting a Replicated Database

When all users of the replicated database have upgraded to Access 2003, you can convert the replica set. The process involves making a complete test set, including a Design Master and several replicas for use in Access 2003. The test set must be kept completely isolated from the original set to be entirely safe, preferably on a separate computer. Be sure to synchronize all replicas before converting, so you have a complete set of data.

After creating several replicas from the new test Design Master, choose Tools | Database Utilities | Convert Database to convert the test Design Master and the test replicas to Access 2003. Synchronize the converted Design Master with the newly converted replicas and operate the database as it's intended. After you're satisfied the test set works as planned with Access 2003, delete all the members of the test set and convert the original replica set.

Once the replica set is converted to Access 2003, you can no longer open it with Access 97, 2000, or 2002-2003.

Enabling a Database

As mentioned earlier, if you aren't converting the database because all users haven't yet upgraded to Access 2003, you can still use the database created in an earlier version with your version 2003. By enabling a database, you can view database objects and add, delete, or modify records, but you cannot modify any existing object design or add new objects to an enabled database from Access 2003. You must open the database using the version it was created with to modify object designs or add new objects.

The first time you open an Access 97 or earlier database with Access 2003, the Convert/ Open Database dialog box asks if you want to convert it to Access 2002–2003 or simply open it in the original format.

When you choose Open Database and click OK, a message appears explaining the database was created by an earlier version and you can edit the data, but you won't be able to make any changes to the database objects. This message also gives you instructions for converting the database to Access 2003, if you want. You see the same message each subsequent time you open the earlier version database.

You can't link or import an Access 2003 table into an enabled database, but you can go the other way and open the version 2002–2003 database and export tables to the previous-version database. You can also cut, copy, and paste data from version 2002–2003 tables to previous-version tables.

When you enable a previous-version database in Access 2003, any custom toolbars are converted to the new style for consistency of viewing, but the conversion isn't saved when you close the database. Custom menu bars are also interpreted as the new version 2002–2003 style. Menu bar macros aren't converted, but they're still supported.

If you're enabling a secured database, re-create the workgroup information file in Access 2003 to make sure it retains its security. If this isn't possible, use the Workgroup

Administrator to join the previous-version secure WIF. Using the previous-version WIF keeps all the security, except the protection for the Visual Basic code.

Sharing a Database Across Several Access Versions

To use a database with several versions of Access, you can create a front-end/back-end database out of it. Leave the data in the oldest version as the back end and convert the other objects to the later version front end. To build the single-file Access database, do the following:

1. Convert the entire database to 2002–2003 format.

2. Open the converted database and choose Tools | Database Utilities | Database Splitter.

3. Split the database into a front end and back end, and then delete the back-end database created by the Database Splitter Wizard.

4. Then choose Tools | Database Utilities | Linked Table Manager to link the new Access 2003 front end to the tables in the previous-version database.

Now you have the best of both worlds: users of previous versions of Access can continue to use the previous version, while users who've upgraded to Access 2003 can add new features to their front-end databases. If the original database was created in Access 2.0, users of several different versions of Access can work with the database:

- Access 2.0 users with the original database

- Access 95 and 97 users with either the enabled original database or a converted front end

- Access 2000 and later users with a converted front-end database linked to the previous-version back-end database

---

NOTE   *If the database is already a front-end/back-end application, you only need to convert the front end and leave the back end alone. Then run the Linked Table Manager to link the converted front end to the original back-end database.*

Converting from Access 2002–2003 to Access 97

If you need to use an Access 2002–2003 database on an Access 97 system, you can convert it if it isn't a member of a replica set. You'll lose any features and functionality unique to Access 2002–2003 in the conversion, including the following changes:

- Any of the table data that relied on the new Unicode compression might not convert correctly. Some of the characters used in the newer format database might not have equivalent characters in the Access 97 256-character set.

- If the database includes a field with the new Number FieldSize property Decimal setting, the database can't be converted. You must change the FieldSize property to another setting such as Single or Double, or change the field's data type to Currency before converting the database.

Some special conditions need to be considered when converting an Access 2002–2003 database to Access 97:

- If the database is protected by user-level security, remove it before trying to convert. After it's converted, you can secure the database in Access 97.
- If the database is protected with a password, you needn't remove the password before converting the database.
- You must log on with Open/Run and Open Exclusive permissions for the database and Read Design permissions for all the objects in the database.

To convert an Access 2002–2003 database to Access 97, open the database, make sure no other user has it open, and then do the following:

1. If you protected the code with a password, open the Visual Basic Editor window, choose Tools | Properties, and then enter the password in the Password box on the Protection tab of the Project Properties dialog box.
2. Return to the Access window and choose Tools | Database Utilities | Convert Databases | To Access 97 File Format.
3. In the Convert Database Into dialog box, enter a name for the previous-version database you want to create from the Access 2002–2003 version, and then click Save.

Converting from Access 2002–2003 to Access 2000

An Access 2002–2003 file can be easily converted to Access 2000 file format. Some features only available in 2002–2003 aren't available in the converted database. For example, Visual Basic procedures that use objects, functions, or other elements new to Access 2003 can cause compile errors when you open the file in Access 2000.

NOTE *For more information about converting Access files, see the Help topics "About converting an Access file" and "Troubleshooting converting an Access file."*

PART IV

What's on the CD

Instructions for Using the Access Quick Reference on the CD-ROM

On the CD that accompanies this book is a reference resource you can use to look up specific details of properties, specifications, formats, and other items that apply to designing and creating Access databases. To use the Quick Reference, you must have Adobe Acrobat 4.0 or higher installed on your computer. If you don't already have Adobe Acrobat, a copy is included on this book's CD. To view the Quick Reference material, double-click the PDF file. When it opens, you'll see a listing of contents in the left pane and the space where the pages will be displayed on the right-hand side. If you select any topic on the left-hand side, the pages associated with the topic will automatically display on the right-hand side. You can use the magnification tools under the View menu to make the text more readable and to enlarge any detail on a given page.

The following shows an outline of the information in the Quick Reference, which you can readily reach on the CD.

Storing Information
Database Specifications
Database Templates
Database Objects
Database Properties
Relationships and Joins
Table Specifications
Table and Index Properties
Table Fields
Data Types
Field Properties
Display Formats
Custom Formatting Symbols
Custom Format Strings
Input Masks

User Interaction and Object Design
Built-in Toolbars
Form and Report Design
Form and Report Specifications
Form and Report Format Properties
Form and Report Data Properties
Form and Report Event Properties
Form and Report Other Properties
Form and Report Section Properties
Dialog Box and Pop-Up Form Property Settings
Controls and Control Properties

Retrieving and Distributing Information
Filtering Records
Entering Filter Criteria
Creating Expressions
Arithmetic Operators
Comparison Operators
Logical Operators
Queries
Query Specifications
Query Properties
Aggregate Functions
Producing Reports
Page Setup and Options
Controlling the Print Process

Information Exchange
Text and Graphics Converters and Filters
Compatible File Formats
Import and Export Options and Specifications

Changing the Access Environment
Access Wizards, Builders, and Add-Ins
Setting Default Options
Changing Startup Options

Programming with Macros and SQL
Macro Specifications
Macro Actions
SQL Syntax

Instructions for Using the Access Database Files on the CD-ROM

The CD-ROM accompanying this book contains all the material you need to reproduce the Access database objects described in the text. You have a choice of developing the database designs from scratch using the table data or viewing and working with the completed databases. All the files are contained in the Access Database Files folder on the CD. To reach the database files, do the following:

1. Insert the CD-ROM in your CD drive. If you set AutoPlay, the CD will open and you can skip to step 4.

2. Otherwise, click Start in the Windows desktop and select Run from the list.

3. Type your CD drive letter followed by a colon (:) in the Run dialog box and click OK.

4. Double-click the eula.pdf file to review the End User License Agreement that governs your use of the sample Access database files.

5. Double-click the Access Database Files folder icon to display a dialog box containing icons for all the files in the folder. You can tell the type of file by the accompanying icon.

You can now copy or import any of the files to your hard drive.

To use a complete sample database, you must import, rather than copy, the files to your system. To import the files, do the following:

1. Create a new empty database in a folder on your hard drive.

2. Choose File | Get External Data | Import.

3. Click Options in the Import dialog box, and then check Menus and Toolbars in the Import group of options. If you don't include the custom menus and toolbars, you'll get errors when you try to open the Police forms and reports that reference custom command bars.

4. Click each object tab and choose Select All to import all the objects from the database.

5. The image files are embedded in the Home Tech Repair database, so you needn't copy them unless you want to work with them separately.

To use only the tables, you can copy the HTR Tables and Police Tables databases directly to your hard disk.

The Access Database Files folder on the CD-ROM contains the following files:

Filename	File Type	Contents
Home Tech Repair.mdb	Access database	Complete Home Tech Repair database
HTR Tables.mdb	Access database	Home Tech Repair tables only
Police2003.mdb	Access database	Complete Bayview City Police database
Police Tables.mdb	Access database	Police tables only
Barb.gif	GIF image	Home Tech Repair Employee picture
Charlie.gif	GIF image	Home Tech Repair Employee picture
CopdRick.gif	GIF image	Home Tech Repair Employee picture
DickS.gif	GIF image	Home Tech Repair Employee picture
Doug.gif	GIF image	Home Tech Repair Employee picture

PART IV

Filename	File Type	Contents
John.gif	GIF image	Home Tech Repair Employee picture
Rick.gif	GIF image	Home Tech Repair Employee picture
Tony.gif	GIF image	Home Tech Repair Employee picture
Bay2.gif	GIF image	Scanned drawing for Home Tech Repair Workorders table
Bay window.gif	GIF image	Scanned drawing for Home Tech Repair Workorders table
Fireplace.gif	GIF image	Scanned drawing for Home Tech Repair Workorders table

The HTR Tables and Police Tables databases contain only the data from the tables in the complete databases. Each table has a primary key field identified, but no relationships have been established between tables. The Switchboard Items table that appears in the complete Police database isn't included among the tables in the Police Tables database.

The Home Tech Repair sample database forms include hyperlinks to other locations. You need to edit the hyperlink addresses to match their location in your system. See Chapter 6 for information about editing hyperlinks.

The Badge Picture images are embedded in the Employees table in the Home Tech Repair database. If they aren't, you can insert the images individually, using the technique discussed in Chapter 6.

Index

INTERNATIONAL CONTACT INFORMATION

AUSTRALIA
McGraw-Hill Book Company
Australia Pty. Ltd.
TEL +61-2-9900-1800
FAX +61-2-9878-8881
http://www.mcgraw-hill.com.au
books-it_sydney@mcgraw-hill.com

CANADA
McGraw-Hill Ryerson Ltd.
TEL +905-430-5000
FAX +905-430-5020
http://www.mcgraw-hill.ca

**GREECE, MIDDLE EAST, & AFRICA
(Excluding South Africa)**
McGraw-Hill Hellas
TEL +30-210-6560-990
TEL +30-210-6560-993
TEL +30-210-6560-994
FAX +30-210-6545-525

MEXICO (Also serving Latin America)
McGraw-Hill Interamericana Editores
S.A. de C.V.
TEL +525-1500-5108
FAX +525-117-1589
http://www.mcgraw-hill.com.mx
carlos_ruiz@mcgraw-hill.com

SINGAPORE (Serving Asia)
McGraw-Hill Book Company
TEL +65-6863-1580
FAX +65-6862-3354
http://www.mcgraw-hill.com.sg
mghasia@mcgraw-hill.com

SOUTH AFRICA
McGraw-Hill South Africa
TEL +27-11-622-7512
FAX +27-11-622-9045
robyn_swanepoel@mcgraw-hill.com

SPAIN
McGraw-Hill/
Interamericana de España, S.A.U.
TEL +34-91-180-3000
FAX +34-91-372-8513
http://www.mcgraw-hill.es
professional@mcgraw-hill.es

**UNITED KINGDOM, NORTHERN,
EASTERN, & CENTRAL EUROPE**
McGraw-Hill Education Europe
TEL +44-1-628-502500
FAX +44-1-628-770224
http://www.mcgraw-hill.co.uk
emea_queries@mcgraw-hill.com

ALL OTHER INQUIRIES Contact:
McGraw-Hill/Osborne
TEL +1-510-420-7700
FAX +1-510-420-7703
http://www.osborne.com
omg_international@mcgraw-hill.com